Crime and Justice

Crime and Justice
A Review of Research
Edited by Michael Tonry

VOLUME 27

The University of Chicago Press, Chicago and London

This volume was prepared under Grant Number 92-IJ-CX-K044 awarded to the Castine Research Corporation by the National Institute of Justice, U.S. Department of Justice, under the Omnibus Crime Control and Safe Streets Act of 1968 as amended. Points of view or opinions expressed in this volume are those of the editors or authors and do not necessarily represent the official position or policies of the U.S. Department of Justice.

The University of Chicago Press, Chicago 60637
The University of Chicago Press, Ltd., London

© 2000 by The University of Chicago
All rights reserved. Published 2000
Printed in the United States of America

ISSN: 0192-3234

ISBN: 0-226-80851-3

LCN: 80-642217

Contents

Preface

Turning the other cheek has lacked popular acceptance, so that at all times and all places, when human beings have violated the core interests of others, those others have felt it necessary or prudent and proper to respond in punitive ways. Premodern peoples conceptualized serious wrongful acts as insults to God or ancestors, breaches of taboos or traditions, rather than as crimes against the state, but serious wrongs have usually elicited reactions, and the reactions have generally hurt. The biblical injunction "an eye for an eye, a tooth for a tooth" was intended to limit condign punishment, not to encourage severity (only an eye for an eye, not a crucifixion for stealing). In our time, governments have sought to influence crime rates and patterns through changes in punishment practices. In other places and times, blood feuds and healing rituals have sought to restore equilibriums, and in some, punishments have been imposed because that was seen as the right or morally obligatory thing to do, regardless of any effects they might have.

These truisms are prompted by the publication of this, the twenty-seventh, volume of *Crime and Justice*. It will soon be a quarter century since the organizational meeting in 1977 and the two of us, having been the series' launching editors, have surely paid closer attention than anyone else to the ebbs and flows of its contents. While crime and punishment may be human constants, how societies conceptualize, react, and adapt to them changes, and with those changes the interests, preoccupations, and activities of research workers and research funders also change. The volumes of *Crime and Justice* have marched alongside.

The contents of this volume, while in no way a representative sample of the full range of contemporary research interests in criminology, provide clues to what is new and what endures. Over the past quarter-

century, crime and punishment have been fixtures in American political life, and efforts to affect crime rates through punishment policies
have been unremitting. In recent years, those efforts have increasingly
been augmented by exploration of other developmental, situational,
and community-focused techniques. Over the same quarter-century,
sophistication in use of research methods, measures, and data-analytic
techniques has steadily advanced. What one might expect to see, and
what we do see, is that crime policy preoccupations and marked advances in research methods and learning have shaped research and the
state-of-the-art reviews of research in which this series specializes.

The contents of this volume fall into three overlapping categories.
Essays on public opinion about crime and punishment, the experiences
of juveniles prosecuted in adult courts, and the effects of imprisonment
policies on crime rates address persisting issues. Whether public opinion leads or follows crime control policies, whether juveniles should be
removed from the partial shelter of the juvenile system and exposed to
the harsher glare of the adult, and whether "prison works" were no
less topical in 1977 than they are in 2000.

Essays on crime and public transport, restorative and community
justice, and cost-benefit analyses of crime prevention programs, however, address more recently salient subjects. It would be an overclaim
to urge that they represent the beginnings of a paradigm shift away
from the moralistic and emotional crime policies of recent times, but
it is not an exaggeration to say that they represent a growing recogni-
tion that more managerial and rationalistic approaches can at least usefully supplement contemporary crime control policies. While there is
no doubt that managers worried about crime on mass transit systems
in the 1970s and before, a body of sophisticated research began to
emerge only after Ron Clarke and others began in the 1980s systematically to explore situational approaches to crime prevention. While proponents of community and restorative justice urge that their ideas have
shaped human societies for millennia, systematic theoretical and empirical literatures appeared in bulk only in the 1990s. While there is
nothing per se new about cost-benefit analyses, their application to
non-criminal-justice-system anticrime policies became possible only
when quality literatures on situational, community, and developmental
prevention began to accumulate from the 1980s onward.

The third set of essays addresses subjects covered before in *Crime
and Justice* and documents changing interests and steady accumulations
of knowledge. An essay on guns and crime builds on earlier writings

by Phil Cook in volumes 4 and 14 but draws on new, more sophisticated research and addresses new issues. An essay on public opinion
about crime and punishment builds on Julian Roberts's work in volume
16 but is able to draw on a much larger and more diverse literature
than was earlier available. An essay on crime prevention cost-benefit
analyses could not have been written had people in the 1990s not begun to conceive of such programs as serious supplements to criminal
justice approaches, developed the knowledge summarized in volume
19, a thematic volume entirely devoted to crime prevention research,
and begun to document their costs and consequences.

So much for the menu. What precisely writers have to say on these
subjects, and whether the essays tell interesting and persuasive stories,
readers may find out for themselves.

It remains for us to say that we suffer and celebrate the ending of
our professional relationship with Mary Graham, long the National Institute of Justice's *Crime and Justice* overseer, and long our good friend
and kind-hearted tender. We suffer because we will miss her. We celebrate because we know she has moved on to other things she wants to
do. She has left us in the capable hands of Judy Reardon, for whose
help and advice we are grateful, and, somewhat more distantly, of Jeremy Travis, NIJ's director. Without Judy's aid, this volume would be
less than it is, and without Mary's and Jeremy's support, this series
would not exist. To them all, but especially to Mary, we give our
thanks.

Michael Tonry
Norval Morris

Francis T. Cullen, Bonnie S. Fisher,
and Brandon K. Applegate

Public Opinion about Punishment and Corrections

ABSTRACT

"Get tough" control policies in the United States are often portrayed as the reflection of the public's will: Americans are punitive and want offenders locked up. Research from the past decade both reinforces and challenges this assessment. The public clearly accepts, if not prefers, a range of punitive policies (e.g., capital punishment, three-strikes-and-you're-out laws, imprisonment). But support for get-tough policies is "mushy." Thus citizens may be willing to substitute a sentence of life imprisonment without parole for the death penalty. Especially when nonviolent offenders are involved, there is substantial support for intermediate sanctions and for restorative justice. Despite three decades of criticism, rehabilitation—particularly for the young—remains an integral part of Americans' correctional philosophy. There is also widespread support for early intervention programs. In the end, the public shows a tendency to be punitive and progressive, wishing the correctional system to achieve the diverse missions of doing justice, protecting public safety, and reforming the wayward.

In the not-too-distant past, rates of imprisonment were stable and showed no hint of escalating (Blumstein and Cohen 1973), experiments in decarcerating offenders were taking place (Scull 1977; Miller 1991), and talk of the "end of imprisonment" did not seem foolhardy (Mitford 1971; Sommer 1976). Commentators wrote of the "crime of punishment" (Menninger 1968), and criminologists characterized punishment as a "vestigial carryover of a barbaric past" that would "disap-

Francis T. Cullen is Distinguished Research Professor of Criminal Justice, and Bonnie S. Fisher is associate professor of criminal justice, both at the University of Cincinnati. Brandon K. Applegate is assistant professor of criminal justice at the University of Central Florida.

pear as humanitarianism and rationality spread" (Toby 1964, p. 332). Today, however, much has changed—so much so that the policy and ideological landscape of that previous era is unrecognizable. "Get tough" thinking and policies have replaced calls for more humanistic correctional practices, and their dominance appears unassailable. Virtually all contemporary commentaries on correctional policy begin, almost ritualistically, by chronicling—and most often decrying—the seemingly endless roster of policies designed in recent years to inflict increasing amounts of pain on offenders (Clear 1994): prison populations rising sixfold in a quarter century from 200,000 to over 1.2 million; the spread of mandatory prison sentences; the implementation of draconian drug laws that snare big and little "fishes" alike; the passage of three-strikes-and-you're-out statutes; the renewed use of the death penalty; attempts to reduce inmates' amenities, from weight lifting and television to support for college education; the return of chain gangs; and the invention of "scared straight" programs and boot camps.

We have moved, in short, from a time in which punishment and prison were unfashionable to a time in which punishment dominates policy discussions and the prison is embraced as the linchpin of the nation's response to crime. But why has this striking shift occurred? The sources of this transformation in thinking and policy are complex (Beckett 1997), but a commonsense, parsimonious explanation for harsher penalties is frequently offered: punitive policies simply reflect what the public wants. Fed up with intractable crime rates—fed up with coddled offenders victimizing them, people they know, and people they hear about—citizens collectively have made the rational assessment that more offenders should be locked up for longer periods (cf. Beckett 1997; DiIulio 1997). In this scenario, then, the movement to get tough on crime is an instance of "democracy at work"—of politicians implementing the harsh sanctions demanded by their constituents (Scheingold 1984; Cullen, Clark, and Wozniak 1985; Beckett 1997). This view rests on the assumption that citizens do, in fact, desire a correctional system that does little else than inflict as much punishment as possible. It is noteworthy that commentators make this precise claim; after all, do not public opinion polls demonstrate convincingly that Americans wish to get tough with crime?

Thus, in an opinion editorial in the *Wall Street Journal*, the noted, if controversial, historian Paul Johnson (1994, p. A10) asserts that "public opinion, in its attitude toward crime, is overwhelmingly repressive." As crime increases, says Johnson, "ordinary people not surprisingly become more and more hostile toward criminals." They lose their interest in "reforming" offenders and instead "want them punished, as severely and cheaply as possible. . . . They favor punishment that is deterrent and retributive." Echoing these sentiments, DiIulio (1997) contends that "with respect to crime control, all that Americans have ever demanded from government, and all that they have been demanding since the mid-1960s, are commonsense policies that result in the detection, arrest, conviction, and punishment of violent and repeat criminals." In particular, citizens want "policies that do not return persons who assault, rape, rob, burglarize, deal drugs, and murder to the streets without regard to public safety" (p. 2). It is noteworthy that the portrayal of harsh sentencing and correctional policies as the mere reflection of "what the public wants" is not unique to the United States but also is found, for example, in Great Britain and Canada (Hough and Roberts 1999; Roberts, Nuffield, and Hann 1999).

One immediate concern is whether public opinion should be the arbiter of sentencing and correctional policies. Public sentiments on policy issues must be accorded some weight in a democratic society, but justifying policies on the basis of what citizens want confronts a dismaying reality: much of the public—in the United States and elsewhere—is ignorant about many aspects of crime and its control. Pockets of insight occasionally surface. Thus research by Warr (1980, 1982) suggests that the public is generally aware of variations in the extent of different types of crimes (cf. Roberts and Stalans 1997). But in most other areas—including knowledge of trends in crime rates, of the prevalence of violent crimes, of recidivism rates, of specific criminal laws, of legal reforms, of legal rights in the criminal justice process, and of the extent to which the insanity plea is used successfully—the lack of knowledge is widespread (for a summary of research, see Roberts 1992; Roberts and Stalans 1997).

Most salient for our purposes, people's understanding of sentencing severity and options is restricted and often distorted. For example, it is not clear that citizens comprehend what sanctions, apart from imprisonment, can be given to offenders and, if alternatives to incarceration are handed out (e.g., probation, intensive supervision community service), what these community-based penalties actually entail (Roberts and Stalans 1997; Hough and Roberts 1999; Roberts, Nuffield, and Hann 1999). It also appears that in the United States and in other Western nations, the public underestimates the harshness of the sentences that are imposed on offenders (Roberts and Stalans 1997). Thus questions included in the 1996 British Crime Survey asked respondents to estimate the percentage of male offenders aged twenty-one and over who receive a prison term for rape, mugging, and burglary. For these three offenses, 83 percent, 82 percent, and 70 percent of the respondents, respectively, underestimated the actual rate at which imprisonment is used in England and Wales (Hough and Roberts 1998, 1999; in relation to Canada, see Doob et al. 1998).

The public's lack of knowledge about crime is not an isolated domain of ignorance. Citizens have large gaps in their knowledge about the political process and about most policy issues; they are "awash in ignorance" (Kinder 1998, p. 784) and have "fundamental public ignorance of the central facts of political life" (Neuman 1986, p. 14). When polled about fictitious policy issues, for example, substantial minorities express their views—obviously without any knowledge about these matters (Bishop, Tuchfarber, and Oldendick 1986). An analysis of almost any list of political issues, moreover, will reveal a "depth of ignorance" that is "breathtaking" (Kinder 1998, p. 785). To name but a few examples, large majorities of the American public in surveys did not know the name of their representative to the U.S. House, did not know the length of term served by U.S. Senators, did not know—despite enormous publicity in 1994—that the U.S. House "passed a plan to balance the federal budget," and did not know in 1987—despite "seven years of debate" on the issue of "giving aid to the Contras"—where Nicaragua was located (Kinder 1998, p. 785; see also Delli Carpini and Keeter 1996). Further, much of the information citizens are able to convey is "surface" rather than "deep" knowledge. When probed to relay more detailed, substantive information on political issues, the proportion of the public able to do so plummets to low levels (Delli Carpini and Keeter 1996, pp. 91–92).

Findings such as these often do, but perhaps should not, prompt excessive lamentation about the quality of political socialization and civics education in the United States. A lack of knowledge is not to be celebrated, but opinion researchers have long argued that public ignorance about political and policy issues is "rational" (Kinder 1998). Given the exigencies of everyday life and the endless array of issues to learn about—from crime to health care to welfare to the environment, to name but a few—these commentators suggest that the opportunity costs of being a "political junky" are unacceptably high for most citizens. Being knowledgeable about public policy issues, including crime and its control, simply is not cost-effective.

Yet, how can democracy, which depends on the will of an informed citizenry to make good policies, be effective when the public's political ignorance is rational? The solution, notes Kinder (1998, p. 797), is the "miracle of aggregation." Although individual citizens lack knowledge, when aggregated or taken as a whole, public opinion appears to "get things right." Thus support for the U.S. president declines when the country falls on hard or tumultuous times, and people favor shifts in social policies when the nation tilts excessively in one ideological direction or the other. As Page and Shapiro (1992, p. 388) observe in *The Rational Public*, the "public generally reacts to new situations and new information in sensible, reasonable ways."

The implications of the "miracle of aggregation" for crime-related policies are clear: even if individual citizens are not exquisitely knowledgeable about the punitiveness of current sentencing practices, their support for "getting tough" is a collectively rational assessment of the government's need to use stricter sanctions to afford greater societal protection (Page and Shapiro 1992, pp. 90–94; DiIulio 1997). Particulars aside, they have gotten the basic point right that the weakness of the criminal justice system has imperiled their well-being. As Bennett, DiIulio, and Walters (1996, pp. 34–37) put it, "the people know best."

This reasoning will not seem miraculous to all students of public opinion about crime. Levels of knowledge aside, public punitiveness does not seem to fluctuate—as one might expect of a rational public—as crime rates have risen, steadied, and fallen over the past two decades (cf. Page and Shapiro 1992). Instead, preferences for harsher penalties have remained entrenched at high levels. Critics will also note that the Pollyannaish view that the "people know best" ignores the role of politicians in manipulating public opinion and in ushering in a mean season in crime control. They have used rhetoric, too often racially tinged, to incite concern about public safety and have portrayed the crime problem as solvable only through measures that get tough with predators who otherwise would be allowed to roam free on the streets (Scheingold 1984; Beckett 1997).

A more fundamental problem, however, confronts those who claim that punitive policies reflect the wishes of a punitive public, whether in the United States or elsewhere: the empirical accuracy of this portrayal of the public as exclusively and unyieldingly punitive. Is it really true that citizens want only to heap more punishment on offenders and preferably to do so through imprisonment? Or is public opinion about sanctioning offenders complex and judicious—more balanced and moderate than authoritarian and harsh (Thomson and Ragona 1987)? The chief purpose of this essay is to assess what the public thinks about punishing offenders and about the use of varying correctional options. Based on a growing body of research, we propose that public opinion, while clearly punitive in important ways, nonetheless is progressive in equally important ways.

Adequately addressing the empirical question of what the public thinks quickly leads to the methodological issue of how public opinion is to be measured (for a summary of methodological issues in the measurement of crime-related opinions, see Roberts 1992; Roberts and Stalans 1997; more generally, see Schuman and Presser 1981; Biemer et al. 1991; Muircheartaigh 1997). Public views on crime have frequently been investigated through telephone surveys that measure opinions by asking respondents a limited number of questions—as few as one or two—about a major policy issue (e.g., support for capital punishment; what should be the main purpose of imprisonment). The best of these opinion polls use nationally representative samples and are conducted by reputable polling organizations (e.g., Louis Harris, Gallup). These surveys are especially influential because they often are reported in, if not commissioned and publicized by, the local and national news media.

These polls comprise an invaluable repository of data. Because polling organizations have asked a limited number of questions repeatedly over the years (e.g., whether the courts are harsh enough), the surveys are the main source of information on trends in public opinion about punishing offenders. When a "hot" policy issue bursts on the political scene (e.g., three-strikes-and-you're-out laws), they also are flexible enough to be used, with little notice, to question people on their views (i.e., quickly draw a sample and by telephone ask respondents one or two questions about the initiative). And perhaps most important, due to the representativeness of the samples employed in these surveys, their results can be generalized to the nation's population as a whole. Even so, these polls face an important limitation: Can public opinion be adequately measured by asking one or two questions? The answer depends on what "opinion" is being assessed.

If the interest is in a general or "global" view of an issue, then broadly worded polls may provide considerable insight (e.g., whether, in general, a person supports the practice of capital punishment). But opinions can be complex, with support for a policy, such as capital punishment, varying under different conditions (e.g., depending on what sentencing options respondents are given to choose from). Capturing this attitudinal complexity, sometimes called "specific" opinions, requires the use on surveys of a series of carefully designed questions or scales of questions. These surveys can be conducted by telephone or by mail. Most often, they are carried out by university researchers with a substantive interest in crime and not by major polling organizations. Although exceptions exist (Flanagan and Longmire 1996; Rossi and Berk 1997; Hough and Roberts 1998; Jacoby and Cullen 1998), researchers generally do not give these highly detailed surveys to national samples but rely on representative, and at times nonrepresentative, samples drawn from individual states or local communities. The results most often are published in scholarly journals and are not highly publicized.

Importantly, the methodological approach used in a survey not only constrains the type of opinion that can be assessed but also influences, if not biases, the conclusions that are reached about what the public thinks should be done with lawbreakers. Those arguing that the public favors an increasingly punitive response to crime invariably cite the national telephone polls that ask respondents only one or two questions about policy issues. Used by themselves, these polling data can result in a distorted picture of public opinion about punishment and corrections, for two reasons.

First, as noted above, complex opinions cannot be measured if complex questions are not used in an opinion survey. In the area of crime-related attitudes, public opinions often change not only quantitatively but also qualitatively when multiple questions, as opposed to single questions, are used on a survey to assess citizens' views. In particular, respondents tend to express less punitive sentencing preferences when, on surveys, they are given detailed information about the nature of the offender and his or her criminal offense, are provided with a menu of potential sentencing options that include community sanctions as well as imprisonment, and are asked to assign concrete sanctions (e.g., a particular prison term) to concrete offenders (e.g., a burglar) as opposed to answering broadly worded policy questions about punishing unspecified criminals (e.g., using "harsher punishments against criminals"). Accordingly, the failure to attend to data drawn from these more specific, if not sophisticated, surveys leads commentators to overestimate the public's punitiveness.

Second, progressive opinions cannot be discovered if they are not measured by an opinion survey. Many of the single-question or two-question national polls ask only about punishment-oriented issues, such as support for capital punishment or for harsher penalties by the courts. Taken alone, responses to these questions prompt the conclusion that the public is punitive (i.e., people favor capital punishment and harsher courts). These polls, however, do not simultaneously question the respondents about their views on correctional policies that might be considered more progressive, such as support for rehabilitation or early intervention programs. When released to the media, these polls thus publicize what they have measured—the citizenry's punitiveness—but remain silent on what they have not measured—the public's progressive, nonpunitive policy preferences. Notably, surveys that include questions that assess diverse ideological views on correctional policies find that public opinion is complex, progressive under certain conditions, and not unyieldingly punitive.

In this essay, we attempt to draw on multiple data sources in presenting what we believe is a textured portrait of public opinion about punishment and corrections. In assessing these data, we revisit the methodological issues touched on above and shape our interpretations accordingly. Our review leads to seven primary conclusions.

First, consistent with the claims of commentators such as Johnson and DiIulio, the public is punitive toward crime. Get-tough attitudes are real and not simply a methodological artifact. Second, this punitiveness is not fixed on a single point but is "mushy." Even when expressing punitive opinions, people tend to be flexible enough to consider a range of sentencing options, including sanctions that are less harsh than those they may have favored either at first thought or when provided with only minimal information on which to base their views. Third, members of the public must be given a good reason not to be punitive. They moderate their punitiveness when less stringent interventions have utility for victims, the community, and offenders. Fourth, violent crime is the great divide between punitiveness and nonpunitiveness. Citizens are reluctant to take chances with physically dangerous offenders; they generally want them behind bars. For nonviolent offenders, however, a range of correctional options will be entertained. Fifth, despite the sustained attack leveled against the concept of offender treatment, the public continues to believe that rehabilitation should be an integral goal of the correctional system. Sixth, people strongly support "child saving," encouraging both the rehabilitation of youthful offenders and the use of early intervention programs that seek to direct children at risk for future criminality into a conventional life course. In fact, compared to imprisonment, early prevention is favored by a wide margin as a solution to crime. Seventh, the central tendency in public opinion is to be punitive and progressive—to endorse the use of a balanced response to lawbreakers, which includes an effort to do justice, protect society, and reform offenders. When the full body of survey data are taken into account, it thus appears that with regard to punishment and corrections, the public is more rational than irrational in the policy agenda it embraces.

Before initiating our review, we must note that this essay has a specific assignment: to update, admittedly in a limited way, Roberts's (1992) comprehensive and informative analysis of public opinion that appeared earlier in *Crime and Justice* (see also Roberts and Stalans 1997, 1998). Our specific focus is on public opinion about policy proposals that, as the 1990s progressed, either continued to earn attention or freshly emerged as salient correctional issues. We are interested in mapping how citizens, at the turn of century, answer the question, What should be done with those who have broken the law?

Our effort to address this question comes in five parts. Section I assesses the degree to which Americans support capital punishment. We consider trends over time in death penalty attitudes. Most important, we show how support for capital punishment varies by the survey methods employed, especially by whether respondents are presented with the option of sentencing offenders to life in prison without the possibility of parole. We also review research on the controversial topic of the juvenile death penalty and on the impact of religion on support for executing offenders. Section II examines survey research on citizens' support for punitive crime control policies, such as harsher sentences and the use of imprisonment as a sanction. We focus as well on the issue of public support for three-strikes-and-you're-out laws. In contrast, Section III explores the degree to which the public endorses the use of community-based alternatives to incarceration. Special attention is given to whether intermediate sanctions and restorative justice are viewed favorably. Section IV reviews people's sentiments toward rehabilitation as a correctional goal. Views about specific features of correctional treatment and about juveniles' rehabilitation also are assessed. Further, we present data on public attitudes toward early intervention, especially with regard to whether citizens prefer to fight crime through prevention or through imprisonment. Finally, Section V, the essay's conclusion, sketches a portrait of "American public opinion" about punishment and corrections as a way of demarcating the responses to crime that citizens will support. We also offer brief thoughts on where future research on public opinion in this area might proceed and on what broader policy implications might be suggested by the substantive conclusions we distill from the extant body of survey research.

I. Public Support for Capital Punishment

As the ultimate penalty imposed by the criminal justice system, it is perhaps unsurprising that, compared with other crime-related matters, Americans are most often polled on their attitudes on capital punishment (Bohm 1991). The stakes in the battle to characterize the public's views on this issue are high. After all, if most Americans are willing to execute fellow citizens—and the proportion is especially high when offenders have committed egregious crimes—then it would be difficult to dispute that the use of severe punishments reflects the will of the people.

The existing research, however, reaches complicated conclusions about people's sentiments regarding the death penalty. When asked if they support capital punishment for convicted murderers, approximately seven in ten respondents say they do. The public's endorsement of executing murderers has been at or near this level since the early 1970s. However, support for capital punishment declines markedly when respondents are asked not simply if they support the death penalty (favor or oppose), but whether they would choose the death penalty or life in prison without the possibility of parole. Similar results are found when the public is questioned about capital punishment for juveniles convicted of murder. Finally, we also explore recent research on religion and the death penalty, again finding complex effects. Although religious fundamentalism tends to be related to support for capital punishment, a belief in religious forgiveness diminishes the embrace of punitive attitudes.

A. Current Attitudes

We examined eight national-level polls conducted by various organizations between 1995 and 1998. The respondents were asked a single-item question that varied slightly from survey to survey but typically focused on whether they supported capital punishment "for persons convicted of murder." The response categories usually were "favor," "oppose," and some amalgam of "don't know/not sure/no opinion/it depends." Across the eight polls, the percentage of respondents favoring capital punishment did not fall below two-thirds. Support for the death penalty ranged from a low of 66 percent to a high of 79 percent; in six of the eight polls the level of support exceeded 70 percent. The average of those endorsing capital punishment for all eight polls was 72 percent.[1]

These results suggest, then, that public support for capital punishment is substantial; other polling data reinforce this view. Although Americans generally oppose executing those who do not murder, this opposition is not complete and is fairly strong for some kinds of noncapital offenders. Thus, in a national poll, support for the death penalty was only 17 percent for armed robbers and 8 percent for home burglars. Nonetheless, respondents were evenly split on using the death penalty for convicted rapists, and by more than a 2:1 margin supported its use for those who sexually molest a child (Time/CNN/Yankelovich Partners Poll 1997).

Further, in a report titled "Americans Firmly Support Death Penalty," Gallup polling data revealed that citizens may embrace capital punishment even when innocent people are executed (Moore 1995). To be sure, the prospect of the innocent being put to death gives the public reason to reflect on the wisdom of capital punishment. One poll showed that 73 percent of a national sample agreed that the possibility that "innocent people may be wrongly convicted and executed is among the best reasons to oppose the death penalty" (Princeton Survey Research Associates/Newsweek Poll 1997). Similarly, a 1995 survey found that among those who supported capital punishment, 77 percent stated that they would be "more likely to oppose the death penalty" if they "learned that innocent people receive the death penalty" (Longmire 1996). Nonetheless, the Gallup Poll found that 57 percent of respondents—including 74 percent of those who initially said that they favored the death penalty—continued to support capital punishment even under the condition that "one out of a hundred peo-

---

[1] For seven of the surveys, we obtained the polling data over the Internet from a site that provides access to POLL, the Roper Center for Public Opinion Research's database of public opinion questions and results (http://dialog.carl.org). Information on accessing POLL may be obtained from the Roper Center (http://ropercenter.ucom.edu/index.htm). The seven polls, including the year each was collected and the percent of each sample favoring the death penalty, were: Harris Poll, 1996, 75 percent; Gallup Poll, 1996, 79 percent; General Social Survey, 1996, 71 percent; CBS New Poll, 1997, 67 percent; Princeton Survey Research Associates/Newsweek Poll, 1997, 66 percent; Time/CNN/Yankelovich Partners Poll, 1997, 74 percent; Fox News/Opinion Dynamics Poll, 1998, 74 percent. The eighth poll was from Longmire (1996), which reported data on a 1995 national survey, with 71 percent favoring the death penalty.

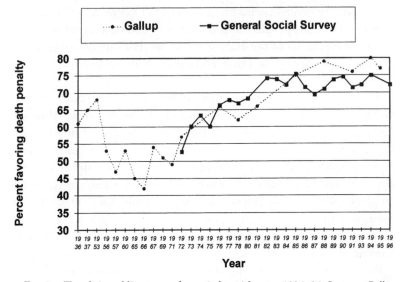

Fig. 1.—Trends in public support for capital punishment, 1936–96. Sources: Gallup Poll data for 1936 and 1937 from Zeisel and Gallup (1989, p. 286). Data for 1953–95 from Moore (1995, p. 25). Gallup Poll question: "Are you in favor of the death penalty for a person convicted of murder?" The 1936 and 1937 polls used slightly different wording, omitting the word "convicted" (Bohm 1991, p. 115). The General Social Survey data are from Smith (1998, p. 5). The question used in the 1972 and 1973 polls was: "Are you in favor of the death penalty for persons convicted of murder?" The 1974–96 polls used the question, "Do you favor or oppose the death penalty for persons convicted of murder?"

ple who have been sentenced to death were actually innocent" (Moore 1995, p. 24). Note should be taken that the 57 percent figure represents a 20 percentage-point decline from the 77 percent who initially favored executing convicted murderers. Moore (1995, p. 23) reminds us, however, that although support lessened when the condition of innocent people dying was introduced into the survey, the respondents still embraced capital punishment "by a two-to-one margin (57 percent to 28 percent)."

The public's support for the death penalty, moreover, has been stable for some time. Both the Gallup Poll and the General Social Survey have tracked capital punishment attitudes over lengthy periods. As figure 1 shows, since the mid-1970s, public support for the death penalty has been high and has fluctuated only marginally. In the Gallup Poll, between 1976 and 1995, the percentage favoring capital punishment ranged from 66 percent to 80 percent; the comparable 1976–96 figures for the General Social Survey were 66.4 percent to 75.4 percent (Moore 1995; Smith 1998). For two decades, therefore, a substantial majority of the American public has consistently endorsed the execution of convicted murderers.

In the two decades preceding the 1970s, however, support for capital punishment was markedly lower. The Gallup Poll has measured the public's views on the death penalty since 1936 (see fig. 1). The percentage of the poll's respondents favoring capital punishment was 61 in 1936 and 65 in 1937; by 1953, the figure reached 68 percent. Thereafter, however, a steady decline in support for murderers' execution transpired: 53 percent in 1956; 45 percent in 1965. In 1966, more Americans opposed the death penalty, 47 percent, than favored it, 42 percent (11 percent answered "no opinion" or "it depends"). By the next year, this trend reversed itself. Still, in the early 1970s, those favoring capital punishment held only a 9 percentage-point majority over opponents of this sanction (e.g., in 1971, 49 percent vs. 40 percent). This gap between supporters and opponents, however, has widened remarkably over time. By the mid-1970s, it had increased to 40 percentage points. In a 1995 Gallup Poll, the difference was 64 percentage points: 77 percent favoring and 13 percent opposing the execution of a convicted murderer (Zeisel and Gallup 1989; Moore 1995).

Why has the public ostensibly grown more punitive since the 1960s—so much so that support for capital punishment is now a normative or socially appropriate attitude to express? Various plausible explanations have been offered: the rising offense rates of the 1960s and the fear of crime it generated; the politicization of crime and the linkage of this issue to a broader concern for a breakdown of law and order; the emergence of racial conflict and the use of getting tough on crime as a means of appealing to people's underlying racism and antipathy toward minorities; the growing lack of confidence in the criminal justice system; and the movement away from social welfare explanations of crime, which stress social causes of offending and a lack of offender responsibility, to individualistic explanations of crime, which stress free choice and just deserts as a response to breaking the law (see, e.g., Rankin 1979; Scheingold 1984, 1991; Bohm 1987; Warr 1995a; Beckett 1997). However plausible these speculations are, they tend not to address the other half of the question: Why did support for the death penalty begin a steady decline by the mid-1950s and continue well into the next decade? It is possible that lower levels of support during this historical period were culturally anomalous—that they represented a departure from traditional American views toward capital punishment to which today's citizens have returned. If so, then the stability of support for the death penalty over the past three decades may not simply be a reaction to the turmoil and changes induced during the sixties but reflect core, deeply rooted cultural values that make Americans a punitive people.

B. Reconsidering Public Opinion Polls

Not all academic writings oppose capital punishment; in philosophy and economics, for example, occasional attempts are made to show its morality or utility (see, e.g., Ehrlich 1975; Berns 1979). However, although exceptions exist (Friedrichs 1989), the vast majority of scholarship published by other social scientists—especially by criminologists and sociologists—attacks capital punishment (for summaries, see Smith 1995; Hood 1998). Being against the death penalty is part of these scholars' professional or disciplinary ideology, and thus they are strongly motivated to produce knowledge that discredits its use. Toward this end, they have conducted studies showing that capital punishment does not deter and may actually increase crime (the "brutalization effect"), is administered in a racially biased way, is prone to mistake and to being wrongfully applied to innocent people, is imposed by juries who do not understand the sentencing instructions on aggravating and mitigating circumstances given by judges during the penalty phase of murder trials, is used against offenders who rarely recidivate, and is more costly to carry out than a sentence of life imprisonment.

Despite mounting evidence on the problematic nature of capital punishment, these scholars are confronted with a stubborn reality: the American public apparently wants to execute convicted murderers. Regardless of what knowledge they might produce, public opinion polls seem unaffected. These polls thus present a formidable barrier to abolishing capital punishment or decreasing its spread. With seven in ten adults supporting the execution of convicted murderers, how would the political will ever be summoned to restrict use of the death penalty?

Not surprisingly, then, these scholars have scrutinized public opinion research in hopes of discrediting it. If existing polling data or methods can be shown to misconstrue the "true" view of the public on capital punishment, then the seemingly sturdy foundation on which the American death penalty rests will be commensurately weakened.

Their attack on public opinion polls has been waged in two general ways (see Costanzo 1997).

First, in examining why people endorse the death penalty, these scholars have often linked support to a range of "unattractive" factors: racial prejudice, religious fundamentalism or biblical literalism, conservatism, antiabortion views, unwarranted fearfulness about crime, ignorance about the death penalty, and so on (see, e.g., Young 1991; Grasmick, Bursik, and Blackwell 1993; Barkan and Cohn 1994; Cook 1998; more generally, see Roberts and Stalans 1997). This strategy is subtle and, in this postmodern age, requires an exercise in deconstruction. To be sure, research of this genre is useful in uncovering empirical sources of death penalty attitudes, although the explained variation in these studies is generally low to modest (Grasmick, Bursik, and Blackwell 1993, p. 74). But note that support for capital punishment is virtually never traced to positive factors—or factors phrased in a positive way— such as a deep respect for the life of the victim, a genuine concern for the pain felt by the victim's family, and a reluctant but principled belief that an egregious breach of the moral order requires the taking of the offender's life. Instead, the underlying intellectual and ideological project is to delegitimate the public's embrace of capital punishment. Indeed, although the message is implicit, the research suggests that those who are secular humanists, progressive politically, advocates of racial justice, knowledgeable about crime, and supporters of a women's "right to choose" would not favor the death penalty. Of course, this account is a rough self-portrait of many of these scholars: if the public were like us, they would not support executing offenders!

Second and more noteworthy, these anti–death penalty social scientists have argued that the national polls, which measure capital punishment attitudes with a single question such as "Are you in favor the death penalty for a person convicted of murder?" make the mistake of attempting to assess a complex set of opinions in a simplistic fashion. These polls not only do not capture the nuances of people's views but, more disturbingly, are biased in the direction of artificially inflating support for capital punishment (Ellsworth and Ross 1983; Harris 1986). When surveys are more methodologically sophisticated, the public's seemingly firm support for executing murderers weakens.

One research strategy has been to differentiate between polls that ask about support for capital punishment in the abstract as opposed to a situation in which the decision to impose this lethal sanction is more personally salient or "real." In a 1984 survey of Texas residents, for example, Williams, Longmire, and Gulick (1988) found that support for the death penalty lessened when the respondents were asked if they would recommend imposing the death penalty as a juror in a murder trial as opposed to voting for a death penalty law or expressing general support for this policy. The slippage in support, however, was only 4–6 percentage points. Bohm, Clark, and Aveni (1991) used a similar approach to making the death penalty more concrete and personally salient: they asked whether people would actually perform the execution. They found that while 28 percent of their sample were opposed to capital punishment "for some people convicted of first degree murder," 47 percent of the respondents stated that they could not "pull the lever that would result in the death of an individual convicted of first-degree murder" (p. 368). More recently, Howells, Flanagan, and Hagan (1995) divided 291 California voters into two groups: those who watched a nature film and those who watched a film of two executions. In a pretest/posttest design, they discovered that among those viewing the executions videotape, 57 percent became less supportive of capital punishment, while 27 percent became more supportive. Although making executions more concrete tended to decrease endorsement of the death penalty, the degree to which the participants changed their views was small.

A second research strategy is to contrast the measurement of global and specific attitudes. Global attitudes are general or overall views that people possess about a policy issue; specific attitudes are the views they express when the policy is applied to a case that has a certain set of attributes. Specific attitudes are especially relevant to criminal justice policy because decisions are made about cases that involve offenders, victims, and acts, which may vary on many dimensions and interact in unique ways. It is possible, therefore, that a majority of the public might support capital punishment as a potential sanction but not support its application in most murder or death penalty–eligible cases.

Selected national surveys by the traditional polling organizations have addressed this issue. A 1996 poll by Princeton Survey Research Associates/Newsweek reported that 66 percent of the sample favored the death penalty. The respondents were then asked if they endorsed the death penalty "in each case of the following circumstances." When these circumstances were introduced, support for capital punishment declined markedly. Thus the pollsters found that those favoring the death penalty dropped to 56 percent "if the convicted person was led to violence because of political or ideological beliefs"; to 55 percent if the "convicted person was under the influence of drugs or alcohol at the time of the crime"; to 47 percent if the person "was severely abused as a child"; to 26 percent if the person "was provoked to violence by the victim"; and to 25 percent if the person "was only an accomplice to the person who actually did the killing" (poll obtained from http://dialog.carl.org).

Durham, Elrod, and Kinkade (1996) provide a judicious example of this approach (see also Ellsworth and Ross 1983). In a mail survey of 366 residents of Hillsborough County (Tampa), Florida, they presented respondents with seventeen vignettes describing a homicide. Two versions of the vignettes were used (thus making for thirty-four scenarios), although each respondent received only one version. The vignettes were constructed to vary aggravating and mitigating factors that are found in capital sentencing statutes. In this way, the researchers could assess the willingness to impose the death penalty when the respondents were judging cases that included specific information about factors such as the offender's record, the offender's intent, gang membership, victim characteristics and behavior, and the heinousness of the crime.

Across all vignettes rated, the respondents chose to impose the death penalty in 60.8 percent of the cases. This mean percentage, however, masks the substantial variation in support for capital punishment across the scenarios. Those supporting the offender's execution ranged from a low of 29.4 percent for one vignette to a high of 93.2 percent for another. In nine of the thirty-four vignettes, it is instructive that a majority of the respondents did not believe that the death penalty was "the appropriate punishment." As Durham, Elrod, and Kinkade (1996, p. 721) point out, the citizens were not indiscriminately vengeful or bloodthirsty but, rather, were "selective in their use of the death penalty." Only 13.1 percent of the respondents favored capital punishment in all cases.

These results counteract the more publicized single-item polls, which seem to suggest that two-thirds to three-fourths of the public support the execution of all convicted murderers. There may very well be a "hesitancy" among citizens to execute fellow Americans that these polls do not capture (Ellsworth and Ross 1983). Even so, Durham, Elrod, and Kinkade (1996) caution that their "data contain little evidence suggesting that capital punishment statutes do not reflect the public willingness to use the death penalty" (p. 728) and caution that "for some kinds of murders," death penalty polls "may *underrepresent* public enthusiasm for capital punishment" (p. 729).

Three findings bolster this conclusion. First, across the vignettes, only 5.2 percent of the respondents did not choose the death penalty for at least one case. Phrased differently, almost 95 percent of the sample's members were willing to support capital punishment for at least some murderers. Second, for vignettes that described a first-degree murder—as opposed to a felony murder or voluntary manslaughter— 74 percent of the respondents selected the death penalty as the appropriate punishment. Third, an experienced Tampa prosecutor was asked to assess which vignettes would normally be charged as death penalty cases; the prosecutor stated that in only 15 percent of the scenarios would the state seek the death penalty. Again, a majority of the respondents believed that the offender described in the vignette warranted capital punishment in 73.5 percent of the cases. Although this comparison is hardly definitive—after all, only one prosecutor was polled—it does suggest that a sizable proportion of citizens, even when rating specific cases, may be willing to endorse the death penalty's application more often than it is currently imposed by state officials.

C. Life in Prison without Parole

Durham, Elrod, and Kinkade's (1996) balanced interpretation of their data reveals that the public's judgments about the death penalty are selectively, but often strongly, punitive. A collateral question, however, is whether citizens are wed to capital punishment as the only way to inflict punishment on the offender. To a degree, this question may hinge on what the public wishes to accomplish through capital punishment. Previous research indicates that people have both retributive and utilitarian motives for embracing the death penalty (see, e.g., Warr and Stafford 1984; Zeisel and Gallup 1989). A 1997 Princeton Survey Research Associates/Newsweek Poll sheds further light on this issue (see http://dialog.carl.org). The respondents were asked what they believed "were among the best reasons to support the death penalty for persons convicted of murder." In this poll, 53 percent answered "yes" to the question of whether "one of the best reasons" was that "it is a deterrent, that is, fear of such punishment discourages potential murderers"; 48 percent said "yes" to "'a life for a life,' that is, anyone who takes another person's life deserves to be executed"; and 49 percent agreed that "it's not fair to make taxpayers pay to keep convicted murderers in prison for life." Note, however, that fully 74 percent chose as "among the best reasons" for supporting the death penalty that "it removes all possibility that the convicted person can kill again" (cf. Zeisel and Gallup 1989, p. 289).

This pervasive concern with preventing murderers from "killing again" raises the possibility that were this goal addressed in another fashion, the public's embrace of the death penalty might be loosened. Although not a fail-safe means of reaching this goal—inmates and correctional officers could still be victimized—the prevention of future homicides could indeed be substantially accomplished through a sentence of life in prison without the possibility of parole. It is noteworthy that perhaps the most important line of research on death penalty attitudes conducted by public opinion researchers in the 1990s is whether, instead of an offender's execution, citizens would support sentencing a convicted murderer to a life sentence without parole (see, e.g., Bohm, Flanagan, and Harris 1990; Bowers, Vandiver, and Dugan 1994; Sandys and McGarrell 1995; McGarrell and Sandys 1996; Moon et al. 1999; see also Whitehead 1998).

First, polling organizations have occasionally explored this issue. Based on a 1986 Gallup Poll, Zeisel and Gallup (1989, p. 290) analyzed how views toward the death penalty would be affected "if a life sentence without parole were available." They reported that the percent favoring capital punishment would decline by 19 percentage points, from 71 percent to 52 percent. In a 1998 Gallup/CNN/USA Today Poll, the respondents were asked, "What do you think should be the penalty for murder committed by a man?"; the same question was then asked with the murderer being a woman. Compared to polls taken at that time showing those favoring the death penalty averaging above 70 percent (see above), support for capital punishment in this survey was noticeably lower. For the male offender, 54 percent chose the death penalty while 36 percent chose "life imprisonment with absolutely no possibility of parole." For the female offender, the comparable numbers were, respectively, 50 percent and 38 percent (see http://dialog.carl.org).

Second, recognizing the policy potential in this pattern of results, scholarly opponents of the death penalty have systematically explored the impact on attitudes of providing the alternative option of life imprisonment. Theoretically, they have made the distinction between "acceptance" and "preference" (Bowers, Vandiver, and Dugan 1994; Sandys and McGarrell 1995). Although standard polling questions may reveal that the public accepts the use of the death penalty, the possibility remains that they may not prefer it instead of other sentencing options. This conceptual distinction thus requires a different methodological approach: people should be asked if they support the death penalty or other alternative sentences.

Analyzing survey data from twelve, geographically dispersed states, Bowers, Vandiver, and Dugan (1994) provide the most sophisticated analysis of this issue (see also Sandys and McGarrell 1995). Across these surveys, it is clear that the public "accepts" the death penalty for murderers: when asked a single-item standard polling question, those favoring capital punishment ranged from 64 percent to 86 percent, with a mean of 75.1 percent. Although not every option was asked in every survey, Bowers, Vandiver, and Dugan (1994) were able to compare whether this level of support changed when citizens were presented with four sentencing alternatives: life with parole possible after twenty-five years (LWPP25); life without parole (LWOP); life with parole after twenty-five years plus restitution (LWPP25 + R); and life without parole plus restitution (LWOP + R). The sentencing contingency of restitution usually involved having the convicted murderer being required to "work in prison industries for money that would go to the families of the victims."

The results of these survey data are striking. For the option of LWPP25, an average of 38.2 percent of the respondents preferred this option. Although 52.2 percent selected the death penalty, this support was substantially lower than that found in traditional polls where, again, support typically exceeds 70 percent of the respondents. When the option was life without parole, more people on average selected LWOP (47.7 percent) than the death penalty (43.1 percent). When the option included the possibility of parole but added in restitution, again more people selected LWWPP + 25 (49.9 percent) than the death penalty (42.8 percent). Most noteworthy, support for the noncapital punishment alternative was especially strong when the sentence was life without parole plus restitution. In this instance, LWOP + R was, on average, favored by 60.7 percent of the respondents compared to 31.6 percent who favored the death penalty—a decided gap in support of nearly 30 percent. Indeed, in all of the states studied, a majority of the citizens preferred LWOP + R. Further, in a more detailed analysis of data from New York and Nebraska, Bowers, Vandiver, and Dugan (1994) discovered that LWOP + R was chosen over the death penalty by a clear majority of those who initially had stated that they "strongly favored" capital punishment (55.7 percent to 32.5 percent in New York; 56.9 percent vs. 33.0 percent in Nebraska). A similar result has been reported by McGarrell and Sandys (1996; see also Brenner 1998).

Why are citizens so supportive of these sentencing alternatives in murder cases? As suggested above, one possibility is that these options effectively prevent murderers from killing again. Bowers, Vandiver, and Dugan (1994), however, provide additional insights. In the surveys conducted in New York and Nebraska, citizens were asked, "Which punishment do you think does the greatest good for all concerned?" In both surveys, a substantial majority selected the nondeath penalty option. In particular, they favored penalties that involved restitution to the families of murder victims. When asked, "Which punishment comes closest to your own personal ideal of justice?" a similar pattern of results emerged. These findings thus suggest that the public prefers a sentencing option that helps to restore victims. Accordingly, in their view, adding restitution to a lengthy or life sentence has more utility and, in the end, is more just than executing offenders.

The salient feature of this line of research is its direct and powerful policy implications. Studies that seek to show that support for the death penalty is somehow illegitimate because it is rooted in "unattractive" factors or that seek to specify when citizens might not endorse the death penalty suffer a decided disadvantage: other than suggesting that citizens should not or, under certain circumstances, do not support capital punishment, they offer no concrete advice on what should be done with convicted murderers. In contrast, the life in prison without parole studies have a concrete quality in that they tell us precisely what the public wants in place of executions. As Bowers, Vandiver, and Dugan (1994, p. 149) recognize, "people will accept the death penalty unless or until they have an alternative they want more."

At issue is whether legislators will endorse the life in prison without parole alternative. In their analysis of data from a 1991 survey of New York Legislators, Bowers, Vandiver, and Dugan (1994) provide unpromising results. Unlike citizens, few legislators expressed a willingness to shift their support from the death penalty to life in prison without parole (with or without restitution). Even when the option included restitution, 58 percent of the sample preferred the death penalty. Since 65 percent initially favored capital punishment, this decline of 7 percentage points is modest at best. Equally problematic, the legislators misperceived the public's views. They reported that among their constituents, 73 percent would support the death penalty over an option that included life imprisonment. Other studies have reported similar results. In a 1996 survey, 95 percent of Tennessee legislators stated that they favored the death penalty. Although 33 percent said that they preferred LWOP + R, a clear majority (53 percent) still endorsed capital punishment (Whitehead 1998). And in Indiana, McGarrell and Sandys (1996, pp. 507–8) found that legislators misperceived the public's support for LWOP alternatives: while only 26 percent of the citizens favored the death penalty over these alternatives, legislators assumed that 50 percent of their constituents would prefer capital punishment to an LWOP sentence.

Legislators, therefore, may prove to be a formidable barrier to substituting LWOP for the death penalty. It is plausible that a concerted educational campaign informing politicians of the public's true beliefs—especially their constituents' concern for offenders making restitution to the victims' family—could affect their personal views, the nature of legislative debate, and ultimately policy. But another caution should be added: there is a possibility that public opinion data could be used to justify "net widening." Scholarly opponents of capital punishment have constructed a persuasive reality: the public wishes to substitute LWOP sentences for the death penalty for convicted murderers. The risk, however, is that the public would feel comfortable using LWOP not only for offenders who are now receiving capital punishment but also for a range of murderers for whom the death penalty would not be pursued and who would not receive life imprisonment. That is, citizens' may prefer to execute fewer "convicted murderers" but also wish to lock up more of them for the rest of their lives (see Durham, Elrod, and Kinkade 1996).

D. Juvenile Capital Punishment

Almost half the states have laws that permit the execution of juveniles (Streib 1998). Although still used sparingly, as of April 1999 sixty-five offenders were on death row for capital crimes they committed under the age of eighteen (NAACP Legal Defense and Educational Fund 1999). The question remains, however, as to whether the public embraces the execution of youths and, if so, whether that support equals the level of support accorded adult capital punishment.

In a 1986 survey of six hundred residents in two Ohio cities, Skovron, Scott, and Cullen (1989) found that support for the execution of "juveniles over the age of fourteen convicted of murder" was only 25 percent in Cincinnati and 30 percent in Columbus. This survey was limited in the issues it probed, and the capital punishment question covered youths as young as fourteen. Further, much has changed in the intervening years: rising rates of juvenile violence (Sickmund, Snyder, and Poe-Yamagata 1997); the portrayal of youthful offenders as "superpredators" (DiIulio 1995); and persistent calls to abolish the juvenile court—a court based on the assumption that youths should be treated differently and more leniently (Feld 1997; see also Stalans and Henry 1994; Sprott 1998). In fact, more recent research shows greater support for the juvenile death penalty, although the data are sparse and complicated.

While less supportive of using the death penalty for youths than for adults, the public now appears to favor the execution of juvenile murderers—a finding that also appears to hold among legislators (Hamm 1989). In a 1991 Oklahoma City survey, Grasmick, Bursik, and Blackwell (1993, p. 66) found that 51.4 percent of the sample agreed that "sixteen-year-olds who are convicted of first degree murder generally deserve the death penalty." The comparable figure for adults, however, was 75.1 percent. Moore (1994) reports a similar pattern of findings based on a 1994 Gallup Poll. Although lower than the 80 percent figure for adults, 60 percent of the national sample of respondents favored the death penalty for a teenager convicted of murder (30 percent were opposed; 10 percent expressed no opinion).

Interpreting these results, however, is made more difficult because the few existing surveys have used different ages when referring to the youthful offenders being sentenced (e.g., a sixteen-year-old vs. an eighteen-year-old). Further, question wording might well affect the views expressed by the public (more generally, see Schuman and Presser 1981). For example, instead of asking people whether capital punishment should be imposed, Sandys and McGarrell (1995, p. 198) instructed their sample of Indiana residents to rate a statement expressing the view that this sanction should not be used. In response to the item, "The death penalty should not be imposed on a person who was younger than 18 at the time of the crime," over half the sample, 51 percent, agreed with this statement compared to 41 percent who disagreed.

Further, similar to research on adults, the public appears to prefer life imprisonment without parole to the execution of youthful offenders. In a 1998 statewide mail survey in Tennessee, Moon et al. (1999) found that 81.4 percent of the sample favored the death penalty for adults, while 53.5 percent did so for juveniles. Compared to the responses for adult offenders, fewer respondents "strongly favored" the capital punishment of juveniles while more respondents "strongly opposed" it. Over three-fifths of the sample also stated that capital punishment with youngsters should be used either not at all or in only a "few" cases. Most noteworthy, 64 percent preferred sentencing juvenile murderers to a life sentence with no possibility of parole. This figure climbed to 80 percent when the LWOP option included work and restitution to the families of the victims. Even among those who initially "strongly favored" the death penalty, a majority preferred the LWOP + R alternative to capital punishment.

E. Religion and the Death Penalty

One other recent development in the study of death penalty attitudes warrants consideration: the growing interest in the impact of religion on support for capital punishment. This research focus likely reflects two trends. First, in the 1990s, Christian conservatives came to play an increasingly prominent role on a range of cultural and, in turn, policy issues (Hunter 1991; Layman 1997). Second, it appears that scholars interested in crime-policy issues belatedly recognized the centrality of religion in the lives of Americans. Social scientists in general had tended to embrace "secularization theory," which proposed that modernization and economic development would lead inevitably to a decline in the cultural importance of religious beliefs. Yet, even as the nation ostensibly moves toward a postmodern and postindustrial phase, citizens continue to report extensive involvement in religion (see Hadden 1987; Wald 1992). Polls show, for example, that 96 percent of Americans say that they believe in God; 67 percent report that they are members of a church or synagogue; and 61 percent indicate that religion is a "very important" part of their lives (Newport and Saad 1997; Shorto 1997).

Most often, research has explored the influence of fundamentalist religious membership or beliefs, arguing that they increase support for capital punishment. Specifying this influence, however, has proven a daunting task. There is evidence that lends credence to the thesis that fundamentalism, especially a literal interpretation of the Bible, fosters endorsement of the death penalty (see, e.g., Young 1992; Grasmick, Bursik, and Blackwell 1993; Grasmick et al. 1993; Young and Thompson 1995; Borg 1997; Britt 1998). Even so, Britt (1998) finds that compared to nonfundamentalists, white fundamentalists are the most supportive of capital punishment but that African-American fundamentalists are less supportive. Some research, moreover, suggests that religious fundamentalism leads to supportive death penalty attitudes in the Bible Belt and southern states but not in other geographical areas, although the research findings on this point are inconsistent (Young 1992; Young and Thompson 1995; Borg 1997; Sandys and McGarrell 1997; Applegate et al., forthcoming). More generally, the research suggests that religious fundamentalism and biblical literalism are related to a range of punitive attitudes, such as support for stiff criminal legislation, for harsh sentencing, for treating juveniles more stringently, and for retribution as a penal philosophy (Grasmick et al. 1992; Grasmick, Cochran, et al. 1993; Grasmick and McGill 1994; Young and Thompson 1995; see also Leiber, Woodrick, and Roudebush 1995; Leiber and Woodrick 1997).

Applegate et al. (forthcoming), however, argue that much of the existing research is informed by a stereotypical view of religion: the tendency to see religion as a source of control and of politically conservative sentiments (for an exception, see Britt 1998). In embracing this limited conception of religion, researchers have not explored how religious messages of compassion and redemption might foster progressive criminal justice–related attitudes. Toward this end, in a 1996 statewide survey of Ohio residents, Applegate et al. (forthcoming) examined whether a belief in religious forgiveness was associated with a range of attitudinal outcomes, including the death penalty. Notably, controlling for other religious variables, forgiveness was negatively and strongly related to support for capital punishment, harsher courts, and general punitiveness and positively related to support for rehabilitation. This study reveals the importance in attitudinal research of being informed by a richer understanding of religion and of its potential role in shaping the worldviews people hold, including their judgments about the treatment of lawbreakers.

II. Public Support for Punishment

Because capital punishment is the ultimate penalty—a special issue that is the focus of interminable and heated debate—generalizing from studies of death penalty attitudes to what the public thinks about punishment in general is risky. Take, for example, the finding that the American public is apparently willing to support life in prison without parole over the death penalty. Does this result show that citizens are more judicious, and not nearly as punitive, as they are commonly portrayed? Or does it reveal only that people, while open to interchanging penalties, will only do so if these penalties are both quite harsh? Thus, although capital punishment has often occupied a central place in the study of public attitudes, a complete assessment of public opinion about corrections needs to move beyond this issue.

In this section, we report one body of research that is relevant to an assessment of the public's views on what should be done with law-breakers: studies that investigate support for punishment. The research reveals that the public harbors punitive attitudes toward offenders, favors the use of prison sentences as a response to crime, and is generally supportive of get-tough initiatives such as three-strikes-and-you're-out laws. This literature is important in showing that there is a large reservoir of punitive sentiments that are likely real and not easily dismissed as the mere artifact of the methodological approaches used to study public opinion. At the same time, citizens show a degree of flexibility in their willingness to support, or at least tolerate, sanctions other than imprisonment. Their support of three-strikes laws, moreover, diminishes substantially when specific, rather than global, opinions are measured. Finally, as we show in later sections, studies of punitiveness illuminate only one dimension of the public's thinking and, taken by themselves, can result in a distorted portrait of citizens' correctional ideology.

A. General Punitive Attitudes

To measure whether the public is punitive, one common strategy has been to present survey respondents with a statement—for example, "The best way to stop crime is to get tough with offenders"—and then to ask whether they endorse this view. The most commonly cited example of this type of research is the General Social Survey, which since 1972 has asked this question: "In general, do you think the courts in this area deal too harshly or not harshly enough with criminals?" The 1996 survey found that 78 percent answered "not harshly enough," while only 5 percent stated that the courts were too harsh (the remaining 11 percent answered "about right") (Maguire and Pastore 1998, pp. 134–35; Smith 1998). Figure 2 presents the trend data for the last quarter of the century. In 1972, 65.5 percent of the sample believed that the courts were "not harsh enough." Two years later, this percentage had jumped 13 points to 78.5 percent. In subsequent years, the percentage endorsing harsher courts fluctuated but remained above this figure; it reached a high of 87 percent in 1982 and was 85.1 percent in 1994. Although this figure dropped by 7 percentage points in

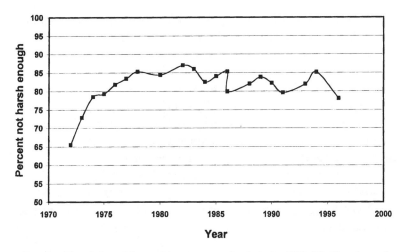

Fig. 2.—Trends in public punitiveness toward criminals, 1972–96. Data from the General Social Survey (Smith 1998, p. 5). Responses to the question: "In general, do you think the courts in this area deal too harshly or not harshly enough with criminals?"

1996, a stubborn reality remains: nearly four in five Americans believe that the courts in their communities are not sufficiently punitive.

Recent national polls suggest that the General Social Survey results are not idiosyncratic (all polls obtained from http://dialog.carl.org). A 1996 CBS News Poll, for example, asked whether respondents believed that "to solve the country's crime problem," it was more important for the "next administration" to "impose stricter sentences on criminals or increase the amount of police on the street." Notably, 54 percent selected "stricter sentences," more than twice the proportion of the sample choosing "increase police" (26 percent). In a 1998 survey conducted by Time/CNN/Yankelovich Partners, nearly three-fourths of the respondents stated that the U.S. Congress should give a "high priority" to "tougher crime enforcement legislation." Similarly, a 1997 survey by *U.S. News & World Report* and Bozell Worldwide reported that 72 percent of adults "strongly favored" and another 17 percent "favored" the policy of "tougher sentences for criminals." And a 1998 NBC News/Wall Street Journal Poll found that 78 percent of the respondents "strongly agreed" that "we should toughen and strengthen penalties for convicted criminals."

Although the public harbors punitive sentiments, the question remains as to what specific correctional policies they embrace. Because studies have not been designed to explore the full complexity of public opinion on the punishment of crime—in particular, how seemingly contradictory beliefs are interrelated (Innes 1993)—addressing this issue in a definitive way is not possible. Still, by weaving together various strands of information gathered from diverse studies, three general conclusions can be drawn (see Innes 1993). First, consistent with the research showing that the public is punitive, citizens are accepting of specific policies that inflict "penal harm" on offenders (Clear 1994). Second, for many Americans, punitive views exist side by side with progressive views, and thus they do not preclude support for policies aimed at improving the lives of offenders. Third, individuals tend not to hold punitive views rigidly; at least to a degree, they will moderate these views if given a compelling reason to do so. These themes are elaborated as this essay unfolds.

B. Support for Prisons

In light of the massive and seemingly unending growth in prison populations and in light of the dramatic way in which incarceration changes an offender's life, a key policy concern is whether citizens want lawbreakers incarcerated. One strategy for measuring the public's embrace of imprisonment is to present respondents with descriptions of a diverse set of crimes and then to ask that they use a response scale to select what sentence they would give the offender in each case. Depending on the study, the number of crimes rated, the amount of information used to describe the crimes, and the number and types of sentencing options provided can differ. These variations can potentially affect the results. Even so, this research generally shows widespread support for "locking up" offenders. "Simply put," observes Warr (1995b, p. 23), "Americans overwhelmingly regard imprisonment as the appropriate form of punishment for most crimes. Although the proportion who prefer prison increases with the seriousness of the crime, imprisonment is by far the most commonly chosen penalty across crimes."

Two national public attitude studies—the 1987 National Punishment Study reported in Jacoby and Cullen (1998; see also Jacoby and Dunn 1987) and a 1994 survey by Rossi, Berk, and Campbell (1997; see also Rossi and Berk 1997)—lend credence to Warr's assessment. Both studies used the factorial survey approach to construct vignettes that, in turn, respondents were asked to judge by assigning a sentence (see Rossi and Nock 1982). In this approach, a researcher first selects the information to be included in the vignettes, such as the types of crime, characteristics of the offender and victim, harm incurred by the victim, and so on. The computer then randomly combines these dimensions or variables to create a pool of unique vignettes (i.e., every vignette is different). In the survey, each respondent is given a unique or different set of vignettes to rate—much as individual judges in courtrooms across the nation impose sentences on a unique set of cases that come before them. A sample vignette from the National Punishment Study is as follows (Jacoby and Cullen 1998, p. 266): "The offender, a 22-year-old male, used a knife to intentionally injure a victim. The victim was treated by a doctor and was hospitalized. The victim was a 60-year-old female. The offender had a mental condition. The offender was drunk when he committed the crime. The offender was never convicted before for a violent offense. The offender was convicted once before for stealing money or property. The offender has served one previous sentence of one year in jail."

The factorial approach has the decided advantage of allowing respondents to rate fairly detailed scenarios that mirror, albeit imperfectly, the features of real-life criminal cases—a key reason its use is becoming common in scholarly research on public opinion. Previously, researchers wishing to have people rate realistic-sounding cases had to present all respondents with the same set of vignettes. The dimensions used in these vignettes—including the number of different crimes— had to be limited because of the permutations created by adding each new dimension (e.g., race of the offender, age of the victim). Fairly quickly, the number of vignettes feasible for respondents to rate would be surpassed (e.g., see Frank et al. 1989). The alternative and more frequently used approach was to present respondents with lengthy lists of offenses that contained little information beyond the nature of the crime itself (e.g., see Blumstein and Cohen 1980). A chief criticism of using this latter method is that it inflates punishment scores. Because the context or circumstances surrounding an offense are not presented, respondents may assume that the crime listed— for example, a murder—is the most egregious type (e.g., cold-blooded, not victim-precipitated) (Doob and Roberts 1984, 1988; Roberts 1992, pp. 126–27; Roberts and Stalans 1997, p. 208). Since the two national studies discussed here used the factorial survey approach, they are less susceptible to this potential methodological bias (cf. Durham 1993).

The National Punishment Survey included twenty-four offenses, which, in their various forms, were spread across 9,997 vignettes. The offenses were mainly traditional street crimes (e.g., arson, larceny, burglary, robbery, assault, forcible rape, drug offenses, drunk driving). It is noteworthy that the sample chose a prison or jail sentence as their preferred sanction for 71 percent of the vignettes. Other sentencing options included probation, fine, and/or restitution. With the exception of larceny of $10, a majority of the sample favored jail or prison for every offense. Even for relatively minor crimes, harsh penalties were preferred. For example, among respondents who selected imprisonment for offenders committing a larceny of $10, the median sentence given was one year while the mean exceeded two years. Similar findings were reported for burglary of a building for $10 and drunk driving with no accident. All other offenses were assigned more severe prison sentences. The mean prison or jail sentence for all offenses was over eleven years (135.7 months) (Jacoby and Dunn 1987; see also Zimmerman, Van Alstyne, and Dunn 1988).

The 1994 Rossi, Berk, and Campbell (1997) survey assessed the extent to which public opinion about sentencing matched the punishments outlined in the federal sentencing guidelines (for a discussion of these guidelines, see Tonry, pp. 72–79). Their survey covered seventy-three separate federal crimes that fell into twenty offense categories. Face-to-face interviews were conducted with 1,753 respondents age eighteen and over, with each person providing their sentencing preferences for a unique set of forty vignettes. In all, over seventy thousand different vignettes describing different crime scenarios were rated. The sentencing options included probation, a prison sentence of a length specified by the respondent, or the death penalty.

"Once convicted," conclude Rossi, Berk, and Campbell (1997, p. 277), "the public was quick to sentence the defendants to prison, but rarely for more than several years." Overall, the median sentence across all vignettes was 3.0 years; the mean sentence was 7.2 years, which reflected extremely long sentences being favored by a minority of the sample. Of the twenty crime types, only the category of "drug possession" had a median of less than two years in prison (median = 0.5 years). Of the seventy-three separate crimes, only six offenses had a median of less than one year in prison. Although incarceration was the preferred penalty, these scores seem less severe than the sentences in the National Punishment Survey. This finding, however, is likely the result of the crimes rated by the respondents. Because Rossi, Berk, and Campbell were examining crimes violating federal law, their list of offenses omitted many common street crimes (e.g., felony murder, rape, assault, residential burglary) and included many white-collar, fraud, civil rights, and drug crimes.

Four additional findings from this study warrant attention. First, with the assistance of the staff of the U.S. Sentencing Commission, Rossi, Berk, and Campbell (1997) used the federal sentencing guidelines to determine what the prescribed sentence would be for each vignette in their study. They then compared the sentences calculated based on the guidelines with the sentences given the vignettes by the public in their survey. The results were similar: a median sentence of 2.5 years computed from the guidelines versus 3.0-year median sentence assigned by the public. Previous research has tended to find that citizens assign harsher sentences than the time offenders actually serve in prison, although these results are not uniform across all studies (cf. Warr 1994, pp. 50–51; and Zimmerman, Van Alstyne, and Dunn 1988 with Robert and Stalans 1997, pp. 210–11). Relatedly, in a survey of Chicago area residents, Rich and Sampson (1990, p. 115) found, across offenses, a "sizable gap" in the number of years the public thought that an offender does and should spend in prison. For the crime of rape, for example, the respondents believed that offenders would be sentenced to less than nine years in prison, but that the sentence should be nearly thirty years.

Second, it should be realized that the Rossi, Berk, and Campbell (1997) results refer to the aggregated sentencing preferences or "central tendencies" of the public. Similar to past studies (see, e.g., Blumstein and Cohen 1980; Jacoby and Cullen 1998), individual respondents tend to agree on which crimes should be assigned relatively more or less punishment (e.g., robbery more than shoplifting), but they often disagree substantially on the absolute level of punishment (e.g., whether a robber should receive two years or four years). Further, individuals' opinions are not always stable, fluctuating even when given the same crime to rate in the same survey (a design feature incorporated for a subset of respondents in Rossi, Berk, and Campbell's study). These results suggest that people's opinions may not be fixed but "mushy" (Durham 1993) and that although sentencing guidelines may reflect the opinion of "the public," many individuals may have heated disagreements over particular sentences specified in the guidelines. Rossi, Berk, and Campbell (1997, p. 288) capture these issues: "There is apparently no clear view of an absolute scale of sentencing severity of punishment that corresponds directly to lengths of prison sentences. One person's 2-year sentence may be the equivalent of another's 4-year sentence. In addition, the differences between sentences are not distinct; respondents who gave a 4-year sentence on one occasion to a specific crime may give a different sentence on another occasion to the same crime. In other words, the punishment norms of our society are only dimly apprehended by respondents."

Third, citizens wished drug trafficking to be severely punished, with the median sentence being 10.0 years in prison. It is noteworthy, however, that the respondents gave virtually the same median and mean punishment regardless of whether an offender sold crack cocaine, cocaine, or heroin. The public's sentencing preferences were similar to the presumptive sentences for the federal guidelines for cocaine and heroin, but were less than half the guideline's severity for crack (ten years vs. twenty-two years). This finding is relevant to the major policy debate over whether crack and powder cocaine offenses should be differentially sanctioned, as is now the case on the federal level. As Tonry (1995, p. 188) notes, "the problem . . . is that crack tends to be used and sold by blacks and powder by whites, which means that the harshest penalties are mostly experienced by blacks." The public, it appears, does not embrace this distinction and, by implication, the racial disparity it produces.

Fourth, because Rossi, Berk, and Campbell (1997) examined federal crimes, a domain which includes many white-collar illegalities, their data set provides perhaps the best study of public views on the sentencing of upperworld offenders. Scholars from E. A. Ross (1907) to Edwin Sutherland (1940) to James Q. Wilson (1975) had argued that the public did not harbor punitive sentiments toward white-collar law-breaking. In the 1980s, however, a revisionist perspective emerged, which claimed the "social movement" against the "crimes of the rich and powerful" had changed public attitudes and increased public support for using the criminal law to sanction white-collar offenders (for a summary, see Evans, Cullen, and Dubeck 1993). Three surveys of communities in Illinois between 1979 and 1982, for example, found that more than eight in ten respondents agreed that "we should punish white-collar criminals just as severely as we punish people who steal money on the street" and that "white-collar criminals have gotten off too easily for too many years; they deserve to be sent to jail for crimes just like everyone else." Fewer than two in ten respondents agreed that "since white-collar criminals usually don't harm anyone, they shouldn't be punished as much as regular criminals" (Cullen, Mathers, Clark, and Cullen 1983). A 1981 survey in Illinois also showed that citizens were generally willing to assign criminal penalties—ranging from lengthy probation and fines to prison sentences—for a range of white-collar and corporate crimes. Prison sentences typically were favored by a clear majority of the respondents when physical harm occurred or was possible, such as knowingly selling contaminated food and manufacturing a defective automobile (Cullen, Clark, Link, et al. 1985; see also Frank et al. 1989).

Rossi and associates' national survey, which as noted was conducted in 1994, reinforces these findings (Rossi and Berk 1997, pp. 124–40; Rossi, Berk, and Campbell 1997). Consider the median sentences for these "violent" white-collar crimes: selling defective helicopter parts (ten years); marketing a drug after false testing (five years) or with side effects (four years); and a factory discharging toxic waste water (two years) or polluting the air (one year). Criminal sanctions, however, were not reserved for physically harmful offenses. Thus the median sentences for financial offenses were not inconsequential: fraudulently causing a savings and loan failure (five years); doctor filing fraudulent Medicare claims (five years); bank official embezzling bank funds (two years); insider stock fraud (two years); tax fraud (two years); antitrust bid rigging (four years) and price-fixing (one year); and illegal logging on federal land (one year). In general, sentences for traditional street crimes tended to be lengthier, but many exceptions to this rule occurred (see also Cullen, Clark, Link, et al. 1985). In any case, these results show that there is little public opposition to sending white-collar offenders to prison.

C. Firmness of Support for Prisons

Thus far, we have reviewed research suggesting that the public favors "harsher" sentences and prison terms, often lengthy ones, for most offenders. Is this support for "getting tough" unshakable? If so, it would present a formidable barrier to any attempt to implement progressive policies, such as community-based alternatives to prison.

One consideration suggesting that the public's punishment preferences are firm is that they rest, at least in part, on the normative consensus that "the punishment should fit the crime"—that is, on the embrace of the principle of retribution or just deserts. Previous research has found that measures of perceived crime seriousness are positively and clearly related to sentencing severity (see, e.g., Blumstein and Cohen 1980; Hamilton and Rytina 1980; Warr, Meier, and Erickson 1983; Jacoby and Cullen 1998). The nature of the crime, in short, is an important predictor of which offenders people believe should receive more or less punishment (although the relationship of seriousness to the absolute level of punishment is less strong). To the extent that sanctions violate this principle—such as when a violent offender is placed on probation or receives a short prison sentence—calls for tougher penalties are likely to occur. It is noteworthy that based on a Canadian study, Doob and Roberts (1988, p. 119) report that the main reason respondents gave for "why sentences should be made more severe" was that "offenders deserve more punishment" (76 percent rating this reason as "very important").

The connection between seriousness and severity ratings, however, does not mean that just deserts is the only principle guiding views about the use of imprisonment. Although norms of just deserts may place limits on how little punishment people will find acceptable, research indicates that the public also supports utilitarian goals for imprisonment and for punishment in general (see Sec. IV). In the National Punishment Survey, for example, offense seriousness scores explained the largest amount of variation in sentencing preferences (Jacoby and Cullen 1998). Still, when respondents were asked in a separate question what was the purpose of the sentence they assigned to the offender in the vignette, the goal of just deserts ranked fourth behind special deterrence, boundary setting, and rehabilitation as a "very important" reason for choosing the sentence (Jacoby and Dunn 1987; see also Warr and Stafford 1984). As Warr (1994, p. 52) notes, "There is no single dominant ideology of punishment among the U.S. public. When asked, individuals commonly invoke or support more than one theory of punishment, and no one theory appears to dominate public thinking about punishment."

Two considerations complicate matters further. First, survey research studies do not differentiate between what sentences people want imposed by the courts—and why—and then what they wish done with the offender while he or she is within the correctional system—and why (see Innes 1993). For example, a respondent may favor a prison sentence for reasons of just deserts but also believe that the offender should be given a chance to participate in a "boot camp" program or be given a chance to be released early by successfully completing a rehabilitation program. Studies of sentencing preferences, however, tend only to ask what sentence should be imposed and thus insufficiently measure the full correctional response citizens might endorse. Second and relatedly, rating what specific sentences should be assigned to individual defendants described in vignettes is not the same as making judgments about policies that affect the correctional system. Thus citizens may favor prison sentences for burglars but, in the face of system overcrowding and scarce tax revenues, also favor community alternatives for property offenders. In short, support for prisons and for harsh sentences may differ depending on which domain of attitudes is being measured.

Research also indicates that the public is ambivalent about the prison's effectiveness in preventing crime. This conclusion is supported by surveys conducted in various states during the nineties by Doble Research Associates (1994, 1995a, 1995b, 1995c, 1997, 1998). Most respondents opposed releasing violent offenders early from prison and favored longer prison sentences. Despite this fact, those surveyed generally agreed that "the vast majority of prison inmates sit around all day, playing cards and watching TV instead of working at a job that keeps them busy and helps them acquire skills to make them more employable when they get out." Citizens also do not believe that prisons are doing a good job punishing or rehabilitating offenders. Finally and most noteworthy, many Americans question whether prisons reduce crime. In an Iowa survey, for example, 60 percent of the sample stated that the "majority of inmates" would be "more dangerous" when they were released from prison; only 9 percent answered "less dangerous," while the remaining 31 percent answered "don't know" (Doble Research Associates 1997). Similarly, when asked if "jails and prisons are really schools for criminals that turn new inmates into hardened criminals," 48 percent of a New Hampshire sample agreed, 39 percent disagreed, and 14 percent did not choose an answer (Doble Research Associates 1998). And when asked about the potential impact of longer prison terms, 46 percent of Oregonians and 50 percent of Oklahomans answered "little or no effect on crime" (Doble Research Associates 1995b, 1995c).

Interpreting these research results is difficult. One possibility is that, regardless of what they believe prisons should accomplish, citizens are coming to see these facilities as having little utility beyond incapacitating offenders. In this scenario, prisons would be seen as offering a trade-off: they make offenders more criminogenic when released, but they prevent crime while these offenders are locked up. The trade-off becomes more worthwhile the longer offenders—especially those who inflict the most harm, violent criminals—stay behind bars. This calculus firms up support for incarcerating violent offenders but at the same time makes imprisoning nonviolent offenders less attractive. A bifurcated public opinion thus emerges: more insistent on prison sentences for violence and more open to alternatives for property, drug, and similar offenses (see the research cited in Sec. III). Ironically, critics of prisons—including criminologists and other social science scholars—may help to cement this way of thinking. To the extent that they have persuaded the public that prisons are so inhumane that they are incapable of inducing offenders to change, they may unwittingly provide a convincing rationale for not releasing "dangerous" offenders into society.

Another possibility is that because a significant portion of the public has doubts about the effectiveness of prisons, support for their use is widespread but not as deep as is commonly portrayed. Except for the most egregious offenses and intractable lawbreakers, citizens may presumptively favor prison terms but be open to alternatives, shorter sentences, and/or parole release if given a convincing reason to do so. In this scenario, the bulk of the public are rational decision makers who are not wed to a strict "lock 'em up" mentality. The challenge, of course, is to provide a justification for limiting the use of imprisonment that is coherent enough to maintain its persuasiveness across diverse sentencing situations.

Some backing for the view that support for prisons is somewhat "mushy" can be drawn from Turner et al.'s (1997) survey of 287 Cincinnati-area residents in 1995. They started with the assumption that punishment attitudes are not rigidly fixed at a single point but rather are best conceptualized as ranging from what sentence a respondent might prefer to what the person might be willing to "tolerate" or accept (Durham 1993; Bowers, Vandiver, and Dugan 1994). Using the factorial approach, vignettes were developed for two forms of robbery (with and without injury) and for two forms of burglary ($250 and $1,000 of stolen merchandise). In Ohio, these crimes carry a presumptive prison sentence of three to twenty-five years, depending on the characteristics of the offense and offender; one-third of Ohio's prison population is composed of people convicted of some form of robbery or burglary. The respondents were given a list of sanctions that included traditional probation, three intermediate sanctions, shock incarceration, and imprisonment. Each of these sanctions was described in detail. To measure "tolerance," the sample was first instructed to select the sanction that they would "most like" to give the offender; they then were asked what other sentences they would find "acceptable."

The analysis suggested four main conclusions. First, only a limited percentage of the sample selected "regular probation" as a preferred or acceptable sentence. Second, the preference for imposing a prison sentence or shock incarceration was fairly modest, ranging across the four offenses from 51.7 percent to 57.9 percent. In part, the lack of strong support for locking up offenders may be because the community-based sentencing options included intermediate penalties and were explained (e.g., "Strict Probation: John would live in the community, but must meet with a probation officer five times a week for two years"). Third, when "acceptable" sentences were analyzed, only 26.8–35.2 percent of the sample still insisted on the offender spending time incarcerated. Across all vignettes, about two-thirds of the respondents thus were willing to tolerate a community-based sanction. Fourth, even so, tolerance for sanctions was bidirectional, with many of those initially favoring community sanctions also finding imprisonment acceptable.

Taken together, these results reveal that for traditional "street criminals"—robbers and burglars—the public tends to prefer, and certainly is not strongly opposed to, assigning a prison term. Citizens also appear wary of "regular probation," a sanction that involves minimal contact with the offender. In contrast, they are willing to consider alternatives to incarceration if it appears that the community sanctions will involve some meaningful intervention (e.g., strict monitoring). We return to this point in Section III.

Finally, research on attitudes toward parole further illuminates the public's willingness to attenuate support for prison when furnished with a rationale for doing so. In a 1995 national survey, respondents were asked what measures they would favor or oppose as a means of reducing prison overcrowding. Only 8 percent favored shortening sentences and only 21 percent favored "giving the parole board more authority to release offenders early." In contrast, 64 percent endorsed the policy of "allowing prisoners to earn early release through good behavior and participation in educational and work programs" (Flanagan 1996b, pp. 88, 192). These results are similar to the findings of a survey conducted nearly a decade earlier in Ohio (Skovron, Scott, and Cullen 1988). This research suggests that while opposed to shortening prison terms in a sweeping and potentially arbitrary way, citizens will do so for offenders who have taken steps to improve themselves and whose prospects for community reintegration thus appear promising.

D. Support for Three-Strikes-and-You're-Out Laws

"Sentencing," argues Tonry (1996, p. 3), "matters in the 1990s more than ever before." Although battles over sentencing reform extend to the 1970s (Cullen and Gilbert 1982; Tonry 1992), the movement to constrain judicial discretion and to ensure that offenders would be "locked up" reached a feverish pitch in the nineties. From the mid-1980s into the early 1990s, the U.S. Congress and most states enacted a host of statutes mandating prison terms for a variety of offenses. By the end of the decade, virtually every state had a policy of mandatory minimum imprisonment (Tonry 1998). Truth-in-sentencing laws, which stipulate that offenders serve a high proportion (e.g., 85 percent) of the sentences imposed at trial, became commonplace (Ditton and Wilson 1999). Most salient, however, was the renewed enthusiasm for habitual-offender laws, which were repackaged under the label "three strikes and you're out." Between 1993 and 1995, twenty-four states and the federal government passed statutes that, with some variation, required life sentences—usually without the possibility of parole—for offenders convicted of three violent or serious crimes (Turner et al. 1995; Clark, Austin, and Henry 1997; see also Shichor and Sechrest 1996).

Does the public support three-strikes laws? At least as a general approach to punishing habitual violent offenders, the answer appears to be, yes. In a 1993 referendum, voters in Washington approved the first three-strikes statute by a 3:1 margin (Clark, Austin, and Henry 1997, p. 1); subsequently, the electorate in California ratified a three-strikes law passed by the state's legislature in 1994 by a margin of 72 percent for to 28 percent against (Shichor and Sechrest 1996, p. v). Opinion polls suggest that these results were not idiosyncratic. A 1994 Time/CNN Poll found that 81 percent of adults favored mandatory life imprisonment for anyone convicted of a third serious crime (cited in Applegate et al. 1996b, p. 518). In a 1994 Wall Street Journal/NBC News Poll, 76 percent stated that "life sentences without parole for criminals with three violent crimes" would make a "major" difference in reducing crime (Wall Street Journal 1994, p. A14). A study of Vermont residents in the same year reached similar results: 61 percent favored mandatory life sentences for three-time violent criminals, "even if this means the prisons will eventually be filled with lots of very old men who pose little danger to anyone" (Doble Research Associates 1994, p. 25).

It is questionable, however, whether citizens truly wish the three-strikes law applied to every offender who would qualify for a life sentence without parole (Finkel et al. 1996; Roberts 1996). Thus, in factorial survey studies in which concrete cases are rated, the impact of prior record on sentencing preferences varies across studies—although it tends to explain some variation—and its effects are outweighed by the seriousness of the current offense (see, e.g., Applegate et al. 1996*a*, 1996*b*; Rossi, Berk, and Campbell 1997; Jacoby and Cullen 1998).

Research by Applegate et al. (1996*b*) illuminates the gap between "global" and "specific" attitudes toward three-strikes laws. In a 1995 study of Cincinnati-area residents, the respondents showed extensive support for the general or global concept of "three strikes and you're out." Over 88 percent of the sample stated that they either "strongly" (52.1 percent) or "somewhat" (36.3 percent) supported passing a three-strikes law in Ohio that would give a life prison sentence to "anyone with two serious felony convictions on their record who is convicted of a third serious crime" (1996*b*, p. 522). In a second stage of the survey, however, Applegate and his associates had the respondents rate a specific vignette that included a mixture of crimes that would make the offender eligible for a mandatory life sentence. The offenses included in the factorial vignette were derived from a three-strikes statute then pending in the Ohio legislature. The respondents were asked to select a sentence from a list that ranged from "no punishment" and "probation" to "life in prison" with and without a chance of parole. Across the vignettes, only 16.9 percent assigned a life sentence. In various multivariate models, moreover, past record generally had little, if any, effect on the sentencing decisions. Finally, in another part of the survey, the respondents also were asked if there were any circumstances under which they would make exceptions to imposing a "three-strikes life sentence." These data showed at least a measure of flexibility in punishment attitudes. Thus a majority of the sample favored making exceptions when a third offense was relatively minor, when the offender was mentally ill, when the inmate is rehabilitated while in prison, and when incarcerating the offender would mean that a more dangerous inmate would have to be released.

These results suggest that members of the public can hold seemingly incompatible views: favoring the general principle of three strikes and you're out but not believing that this principle should be applied invariably to specific offenders under specific circumstances. Future research should be designed to probe respondents to explain why they voice discrepant views. Respondents may not be conscious of the gap between their global and specific attitudes, or perhaps their attitudes are a methodological artifact since distinct rating tasks are involved. The other possibility, however, is that different norms weigh more heavily in organizing public opinion in these two domains. Thus, in supporting three-strikes legislation, considerations of societal protection may be more salient: it seems like a good idea to take repeat, serious offenders off the street. In judging a vignette, though, the question of what is fair for the particular individual being sentenced becomes prominent (see Finkel et al. 1996). There may be consensus that dangerous people should be incarcerated for life but disagreement over who specifically qualifies for this designation and to what degree.

Although not addressing this question directly, Tyler and Boeckmann's (1997) survey of 166 residents of the East Bay area of San Francisco complicates our understanding of why the public might support three-strikes laws. Their analysis showed that support for California's three-strike initiative was not chiefly "instrumental": respondents concerned about crime and lacking faith in the courts were not more likely to endorse the initiative. Since the respondents were not asked directly why they supported the three-strikes proposal, this analysis cannot rule out that even those not gripped with concern about crime might have made the "rational" assessment that it was prudent to lock up repeat serious or violent offenders. Still, Tyler and Boeckmann's analysis also revealed that support for the three-strikes law was related to social values and concerns about the strength of social bonds in families. "Those citizens who feel that the moral and social consensus that holds society together is declining," they note, "are more supportive of punitive public policies" (1997, p. 256). In short, three-strikes laws may have struck a chord with the public not because they were a compelling crime control strategy but because they offered a symbolic means of affirming a shaky social order.

III. Public Support for Alternatives to Incarceration
In the 1990s, two issues—one occurring primarily at the front end of the decade, one primarily at the back end of the decade—dominated policy discussions about the nature of community-based corrections: intermediate sanctions and restorative justice. Although the effectiveness of these approaches in reducing offender recidivism is open to question, both enjoyed the support of liberals and conservatives (Cullen, Wright, and Applegate 1996; Levrant et al. 1999). "Intermediate sanctions"—penalties that exist "between prison and probation"

(Morris and Tonry 1990)—were favored by liberals as an alternative to prisons and by conservatives as a cost-effective means of punishing offenders. Restorative justice—the attempt to punish and reintegrate offenders into the community—was endorsed by liberals as another strategy for limiting the harm inflicted on offenders and by conservatives as a way of assisting victims.

Although not without important qualifications, public support for these initiatives appears to be fairly widespread. Thus research shows that citizens endorse the use of virtually all types of intermediate sanctions (e.g., community service, boot camps, intensive supervision programs). The public's backing of intermediate sanctions also appears to increase when its members are presented with information on the costs of prisons and on the nature of these community-based penalties. However, people support the use of intermediate sanctions primarily for nonviolent offenders as opposed to violent offenders and as an alternative not only for imprisonment but also for regular probation (i.e., they are not against net widening). Similarly, there is beginning to be evidence that restorative justice is favored by the public, in part, we suspect, because it promises to accrue benefits for—that is, to restore—victims, offenders, and the community. Once again, the public sees this type of sanction as mainly appropriate for nonviolent offenders.

A. Intermediate Sanctions

It is often stated that because traditional community correctional interventions—especially probation—are not viewed by Americans as punitive, a sentence other than imprisonment is seen as a sign of leniency (Flanagan 1996b). There is, in fact, evidence that the public views probation as a lenient punishment (Harlow, Darley, and Robinson 1995; see also Turner et al. 1997). In a 1996 national poll, 53.3 percent of the sample "agreed" that "community corrections programs are evidence of leniency in the criminal justice system." Only three in ten respondents disagreed, while the remainder (13.8 percent) were undecided (Flanagan 1996a, p. 6). In contrast, intermediate sanctions were intended to be sufficiently punitive to offer a "sensible" alternative to locking up offenders (Anderson 1998). Importantly, research indicates that in assessing the severity of punishments, the public views these sanctions "as intermediate in severity between the perceived harshness of prison and the perceived leniency of probation" (Harlow, Darley, and Robinson 1995, p. 86). Further, it would seem possible to structure intermediate sanctions in ways to have them match or outweigh the severity of incarceration (e.g., three years on intensive supervision as opposed to a six-month jail sentence), thus increasing the potential to interchange community-based punishments for a prison term. It is noteworthy that studies show that offenders also rate certain intermediate penalties as more severe than limited stays in prison (Petersilia and Deschenes 1994; Spelman 1995; see also Crouch 1993).

A fairly large body of research now shows that the U.S. public strongly supports the use of some intermediate sanctions, such as restitution programs, community service, boot camps, intensive probation supervision, and home confinement/electronic monitoring (see, e.g., Reichel and Gauthier 1990; Senese 1992; Brown and Elrod 1995; Elrod and Brown 1996; Flanagan 1996a; DiMascio et al. 1997, pp. 43–45). The chief qualification to this conclusion, however, is that support for intermediate sanctions is largely limited to nonviolent offenders (see, e.g., Doble Research Associates 1994, 1995a, 1995b, 1995c, 1997, 1998; Brown and Elrod 1995). In a 1995 North Carolina survey, for example, respondents were given a list of eight different intermediate sanctions and asked their "views about using the alternative sentences instead of prison for selected nonviolent offenders" (Doble Research Associates 1995a, p. 40). Those favoring each option ranged from 80 percent for house arrest to 98 percent for restitution. When asked to rate specific cases, they clearly favored prison over alternatives for violent offenders, drug traffickers, and recidivist burglars. They tended to embrace alternatives for those committing minor property offenses (e.g., shoplifting, joyride), drug addicts who sell minor amounts of cocaine, drunk drivers, and first offenders. Interestingly, when asked to assign alternatives, the respondents "individualized" their sentencing preferences (e.g., treatment centers for offenders with drinking or drug problems, boot camp for burglars) (Doble Research Associates 1995a, pp. 46–52).

These findings suggest that public support for incarcerating violent and repeat felony offenders is firm. Why the public favors locking up these offenders rather than using alternatives, however, remains to be systematically explored. If the constraint on using alternatives is "just deserts"—serious offenders simply deserve to serve a prison sentence—then it might be possible to "package" a group of intermediate sanctions to match the level of severity of imprisonment desired (e.g., one year of home confinement, restitution to victim, and two hundred hours of community service instead of a one-year prison sentence). If the concern is dangerousness and societal protection, then persuading the public that violent or repeat felony offenders should be "on the street" may prove more difficult. In local communities, public skepticism may have to be countered by showing that intermediate sanctions are effective in curtailing subsequent offending. As Petersilia (1997, p. 177) observes, studies have "shown that judges are more willing to place felons on probation when they perceive that the probation department can monitor the offender closely and that the community resources are sufficient to address some of the offender's underlying problems" (see also Gendreau, Cullen, and Bonta 1994).

The appeal of intermediate sanctions is complicated further by another consideration: citizens appear to be in favor of net widening. Although they may endorse employing intermediate sanctions as an alternative to prison for some offenders, they also wish these penalties to be used as an alternative to probation (Farkas 1993). In a 1995 survey, Oregonians were asked if the state should "make greater use of alternatives, like boot camp, community service, restitution, a work center, house arrest or strict probation even if they are more expensive than having an offender see a probation officer once a month." Despite the added cost, 65 percent of the sample "strongly favored" and 25 percent "somewhat favored" this proposal (Doble Research Associates 1995c).

There is some evidence, however, that support for prison terms will soften if respondents are presented with detailed information about the cost of prisons and about the nature of alternative sentences. Experimental studies conducted by the Public Agenda Foundation in Alabama (Doble and Klein 1989), Delaware (Doble, Immerwahr, and Richardson 1991), and Pennsylvania (Farkas 1993; Jacobs 1993) lend credence to this contention and show that exposure to knowledge may make intermediate sentences acceptable alternatives to imprisonment. Citizens in these states were asked to assign a sentence of either prison or probation to a list of "hypothetical cases" involving street crimes (e.g., burglary, robbery, rape, assault, petty theft, drug offenses). They were then shown a twenty-two-minute video "about prison overcrowding and five alternative sentences—strict probation, strict probation plus restitution, strict probation plus community service, house arrest, and boot camp—along with the main arguments for and against using the alternatives" (Farkas 1993, p. 13). They subsequently met for about ninety minutes in groups of fifteen citizens to discuss the issues "under the guidance of a neutral moderator" (Farkas 1993, p. 13). Finally, they completed a second questionnaire that retested their sentencing decisions—only this time they had the option of choosing one of the five intermediate sanctions.

The experiment's results were striking across all states. To take one example, in Pennsylvania, a majority of the respondents in the pretest favored prison in fifteen cases and probation in nine cases. In the posttest, however, a majority favored prison for only two crimes (forcible rape, fifth offense for a drug dealer/addict). The changes for several more serious crimes are especially revealing. Thus, for the offense of "armed robbery, first offense, pointed a loaded gun at the victim," the percentage of the participants favoring prison decreased from 76 percent to 36 percent when the alternative intermediate sanctions were available. A "burglary, second offense, armed, $5,000 stereo" stolen decreased 40 percentage points from 87 percent favoring imprisonment to only 47 percent endorsing this sentence (Farkas 1993, p. 14; Jacobs 1993).

These findings must be viewed with an appropriate measure of caution. The use of a different rating task in the pretest and posttest (where more choices were available) may have produced a response bias in favor of decreased support for prisons. Because the respondents were not provided intermediate sanctions as punishment options in the initial survey, the decline in the preference for prison sentences might have been an artifact of the increased choices in the posttest questionnaire. In an experiment patterned after those of the Public Agenda Foundation, however, Lane (1997) found that even with identical rating tasks, punitiveness among a sample of college students was reduced for every vignette they judged following systematic efforts to provide information about punishment. For example, when surveyed at the beginning of the course, 72 percent of the participants favored probation or an intermediate sanction for a second-offense car theft; a posttest at the end of the course showed that fully 88 percent chose a sentence that did not include incarceration. We should note that Lane's analysis did not show a strong relationship between the amount of knowledge students gained and their attitudinal change. The precise role of exposure to information in fostering less punitive views thus remained unclear.

The Public Agenda Foundation's findings should also be interpreted carefully in light of the particular information given to the respondents. Even though an effort was made to create a video that was evenhanded, the respondents' might have been less enamored with alternatives if they learned that intermediate sanctions have few, if any, effects on recidivism (Petersilia and Turner 1993; Cullen, Wright, and Applegate 1996; Gendreau, Clark, and Gray 1996), that some scholars believe that those under community supervision offend at high rates (Piehl and DiIulio 1995), and that almost a third of death row inmates committed their murders while under probation or parole supervision (Petersilia 1997, p. 183)—and so on. It certainly is conceivable that a different set of criminological "facts" might have resulted in increasing public punitiveness. In short, exposure to "knowledge" is more problematic than advocates of sentencing alternatives suggest, and an "informed public" is not necessarily a more lenient public.

Still, the results from the Public Agenda Foundation's studies are at least suggestive that citizens may be more flexible in their views on sentencing than other research indicates (see also Turner et al. 1997). In the foundation's studies, the participants functioned more as members of a town meeting than as survey respondents. They listened to information and discussed what they learned with fellow citizens. This process, replicated across three states, appeared to foster a willingness to consider the benefits of intermediate sanctions. Citizens are not necessarily opposed to imprisoning offenders—as we have noted—but ideological space for alternatives might be created by policy makers who take the time to provide their constituencies with a rationale for expanding the use of community sanctions.

B. Restorative Justice

Restorative justice has emerged as an influential development within corrections (Braithwaite 1998; Hahn 1998; Levrant et al. 1999). This approach rejects a strictly punitive, retributivist rationale for sentencing in which the state's main function is to inflict a just measure of pain on offenders. Instead, in the face of harm caused by criminal acts, its overriding goal is to restore—to make whole again—the victim, offender, and community. Although not inherently inconsistent with imprisonment, restorative justice attempts to have offenders repair the harm they have caused while keeping them in the community. In this paradigm, however, a nonincarcerative sentence is not an entitlement but earned. Offenders are expected to take responsibility and express remorse for their harmful acts; they also are obligated to apologize to and otherwise compensate their victims and the community (e.g., through restitution, community service). Ideally, the offender is forgiven by the victim and reintegrated into the community (Dickey

1998). From a religious perspective, this is a case of "hating the sin and loving the sinner" (Van Ness and Heetderks Strong 1997); criminologically, restorative justice is a manifestation of what Braithwaite (1989) calls "reintegrative shaming." This process is expected to make offenders less criminal.

Will the public support restorative justice as an alternative to imprisonment? Independent of its actual utility, which remains to be demonstrated more convincingly (Levrant et al. 1999), this approach is endowed with an attractive feature: it promises to "do justice" while at the same time having utility—of improving the lives of all involved. By contrast, a sentence of imprisonment—especially if it is purely punitive in content—fails to have the win-win quality of restorative justice; inmates might suffer but no one, in the end, is much the better for it. It is noteworthy, therefore, that research shows that sanctions with a restorative quality are strongly embraced by citizens. In a 1996 national poll, for example, respondents were asked what alternatives to prisons they thought would protect citizens against crime. Notably, 84 percent of the sample stated that restitution—"requiring probationers to work so that they can earn money to repay their victims"—would be "very effective" or "somewhat effective" in protecting public safety. The comparable figure for "requiring probationers to perform community service" was more than 77 percent (Flanagan 1996a, pp. 7–8). A 1998 New Hampshire poll revealed similar findings (Doble Research Associates 1998, pp. 29–30).

Even stronger evidence in favor of restorative justice can be drawn from a 1994 survey of Vermont citizens—a state that subsequently implemented a "reparative probation program" (Walther and Perry 1997). First, the respondents clearly supported the general concepts of offenders making restitution to victims, doing community service, and making apologies for wrongdoing. Second, when given a detailed explanation of "Community Reparation Boards where citizen volunteers would work with a judge to determine and oversee the sentence of selected nonviolent offenders," over nine in ten of the respondents favored the proposal. Third, the respondents opposed using this type of restorative justice for violent offenders (e.g., rapist, armed robber who shoots victim, armed burglar). Fourth, nonetheless, members of the sample did show a willingness to replace a prison sentence given to nonviolent offenders with a community-based restorative justice sanction. Thus a majority of the Vermont respondents favored using a restorative sanction even for repeat nonviolent offenders, such as an unarmed burglar, shoplifter, writer of bad checks, or drunk driver (Doble Research Associates 1994, pp. 29–41).

Research on public support for restorative justice is only in its beginning stages. Still, the existing data suggest that the principles underlying restorative justice are appealing to citizens. An important next step is to investigate under what conditions this approach might be extended to cover selected violent offenders. It also might be profitable to examine whether restorative justice might be used in conjunction with imprisonment and, potentially, to reduce the length of prison sentences. Again, a key advantage of this community alternative is that it gives people a persuasive reason to lessen their general punitiveness and inclination to support imprisonment: victims, offenders, and the community will be better off.

IV. Public Support for Correctional Rehabilitation

The rehabilitative ideal—the notion that the purpose of state sanctions should be to treat and cure offenders individually—emerged in the Progressive Era and served as the dominant correctional ideology into the beginning part of the 1970s (Rothman 1980). In 1968, for example, a Harris Poll revealed that over 70 percent of the American public believed that "rehabilitation should be the main goal of imprisonment" (Harris 1968). In the past quarter century, however, the paradigm of individualized treatment has been under sustained attack: by liberals for giving criminal justice officials the discretion to impose unequal and coercive punishments on harmless offenders; by conservatives for giving officials the discretion to impose lenient and community-based punishments on dangerous offenders; and by people of all political persuasions for being empirically bankrupt and ineffective in stopping recidivism (Cullen and Gilbert 1982). A revisionist movement, which is reaffirming rehabilitation and empirically challenging the doctrine that "nothing works" to change offenders, has emerged and is gaining vitality (see, e.g., Cullen and Applegate 1997; Currie 1998). Even so, the question remains whether, after years of delegitimation by both politicians and academic scholars, the American public still embraces rehabilitation as an integral goal of the correctional enterprise.

The research suggests four major conclusions. First, there is some evidence that since the 1960s, support for rehabilitation has declined. Second, even so, rehabilitation remains widely endorsed by citizens as an important function of the correctional system. This support largely holds regardless of the methodology (or question type) used in the opinion survey. Third, support for offender treatment is especially high for juveniles; "child saving" thus has not become unfashionable. Fourth and relatedly, early intervention programs, which target at-risk children and adolescents for help, are strongly advocated. In fact, when asked which option to fund with tax monies, a large majority of citizens favor early intervention programs over building more prisons.

A. Does the Public Still Support Rehabilitation?

There is now an extensive literature showing that the American public holds a "hybrid" (Tonry 1998, p. 206) theory of corrections, meshing together restributivist and utilitarian rationales for state legal intervention. Although those who are punitive tend not to favor offender treatment—and vice versa—a distinctive feature of corrections-related opinion is that citizens want offenders to be punished and rehabilitated. Scholars often discuss the philosophical and pragmatic conflicts between these approaches, but the public is reluctant to see the goals of punishment and treatment as mutually exclusive. While comfortable with the prospect of sending many lawbreakers to prison, the public also sees the wisdom of treatment programs that invest in offenders and reduce the threat they pose to the community. There is, in short, substantial evidence that the U.S. public does not endorse a purely punitive correctional system (see, e.g., Duffee and Ritti 1977; Gallup Report 1982; Flanagan and Caulfield 1984; Warr and Stafford 1984; Thomson and Ragona 1987; Cullen, Cullen, and Wozniak 1988; Cullen et al. 1990; Rich and Sampson 1990; McCorkle 1993; B. Johnson 1994; Flanagan 1996b; Applegate, Cullen, and Fisher 1997; Sundt et al. 1998).

Perhaps the most studied topic is the public's assessment of the "goals of imprisonment." This research suggests that there has been a decline in support for rehabilitation. As noted above, in 1968, the appeal of the rehabilitative ideal was extensive, with seven in ten Americans stating that offender treatment should be prison's chief purpose. Since that time, however, support for rehabilitation as the main goal of prisons has diminished (Pettinico 1994; Sundt et al. 1998). Table 1 shows the shifts in public opinion over a three-decade period. To an extent, the responses appear to be influenced by the number and wording of the response categories and by the wording of the questions asked (e.g., whether the offender is described as an "individual convicted of a crime," as a "man in prison," or as a "criminal who commits violence"). We can note, however, that five surveys reported in table

TABLE 1

Public Preferences for the Main Goal of Imprisonment, 1968–96, Percentage Agreeing with Each Goal Reported

Main Emphasis of Prison Should Be	Harris		Gallup 1982	Cincinnati		Ohio 1996	National	
	1968	1982		1986	1995		1995	1996
Rehabilitation	73.0	44.0	59.0	54.7	32.6	41.1	26.1	48.4
Punishment	7.0	19.0	30.0	5.7	27.2	20.3	…	14.6
Protect society	12.0	32.0	…	35.3	36.8	31.9	…	…
Punish and put away	…	…	…	…	…	…	58.2	…
Crime prevention/deterrence	…	…	…	…	…	…	…	33.1
Not sure/don't know/other	9.0	5.0	11.0	4.3	2.5	6.7	13.4	3.9

SOURCES.—1968 and 1982 Harris Polls reported in Flanagan and Caulfield (1984, p. 42); 1992 Gallup Poll reported in "Public Backs Wholesale Prison Reform" (1982, p. 16); 1986 and 1995 Cincinnati polls reported in Cullen et al. (1990, p. 9) and in Sundt et al. (1998, p. 435); 1996 Ohio poll reported in Applegate, Cullen, and Fisher (1997); 1995 and 1996 national polls reported in Maguire and Pastore (1997, pp. 154 and 155).

NOTE.—The Harris, Cincinnati, and Ohio polls asked: "What do you think should be the main emphasis in most prisons—punishing the individual convicted of a crime, trying to rehabilitate the individual so that he might become a productive citizen, or protecting society from future crimes he might commit?" The Gallup Poll asked whether it was "more important to punish [men in prison] for their crimes, or more important to get them started on the right road" (which was categorized as "rehabilitation"). The 1995 national poll asked whether the government needs to "make a greater effort" to "rehabilitate" or "punish and put away criminals who commit violent crimes." The 1996 national poll asked what should be the main goal "once people who commit crimes are in prison."

1 asked citizens virtually the same question and thus offer a basis for comparison that is potentially less influenced by methodological issues: the two Harris polls, the two Cincinnati polls, and the Ohio poll. Between 1968 and 1982, support for rehabilitation decreased in the Harris polls 29 percentage points to 44 percent. In the decade from 1986 to 1995, the decline in support for rehabilitation in the Cincinnati samples was 22.1 percentage points, with less than a third of Cincinnatians favoring the offender treatment option in the mid-nineties. The proportion of citizens endorsing rehabilitation was higher in a 1996 statewide Ohio sample—four in ten respondents chose treatment as their main goal of prisons—but this level of support still was substantially lower (31.9 percentage points) than the Harris poll conducted in 1968.

The data in table 1 suggest two related considerations. First, the 1995 national poll asked whether the government should place a greater emphasis on rehabilitating or "punishing and putting away" violent criminals. Note that only about a quarter of the sample endorsed treatment, although another 12.3 percent answered "both" (Maguire and Pastore 1997, p. 154; see also Gerber and Engelhardt-Greer 1996, p. 72). In contrast, the combined goal of punishment and incapacitation was favored by nearly six in ten respondents. With dangerous offenders, it appears that public protection trumps efforts to reform offenders.

Research by Sundt et al. (1998) reinforces this conclusion that citizens may be less supportive of treatment for violent as opposed to nonviolent offenders as the main goal of corrections (see also Cullen et al. 1990). In a 1995 survey of Cincinnati residents, Sundt et al. found that 66.1 percent of the respondents believed that rehabilitation would be "very helpful" or "helpful" for nonviolent offenders. The comparable figure for violent offenders was only 13.8 percent, although another 27.4 percent felt that treatment might be "slightly helpful" (1998, p. 437). A national study in the same year found that only 14.4 percent of the respondents believed that "most" violent criminals "can be rehabilitated given early intervention with the right program"; however, 44.8 percent did answer "some." The remainder of the sample answered either "only a few" (28.7 percent) or "none" (9.1 percent). Other research suggests that, in general, the public believes that only a minority of prison inmates will be "successfully rehabilitated" (see, e.g., Doble Research Associates 1995b, p. 40).

Second, it appears that once offenders are in prison, support for rehabilitating them is high. In the 1996 national study cited in table 1, almost half the sample members selected rehabilitation, rather than punishment or crime prevention/deterrence, as their preferred correctional goal "once people who commit crimes are in prison." There is clear support for offender treatment, it seems, so long as it does not place the public at risk (Flanagan 1996*b*). Scholars have argued that Americans have become increasingly less tolerant of all types of risks, including, presumably, of offenders who will potentially inflict physical harm (Friedman 1985). The interesting question that remains is under what conditions might citizens be willing, when dealing with violent offenders, to exchange prison terms for community-based programs that promise intensive rehabilitation and supervision. It seems likely that obtaining public support for such alternatives will involve addressing legitimate concerns about community safety and demonstrating the effectiveness of the interventions being undertaken (in this latter regard, see Andrews and Bonta 1998; Lipsey and Wilson 1998).

In examining table 1, however, it is possible to focus on the "glass being half empty" and to ignore the "glass being half full" (see, e.g., Pettinico 1994). Although Americans may place a priority on public protection and worry about whether violent offenders can be changed, it would be erroneous to conclude that they wish to eliminate rehabilitation from the correctional system. At the very least, it appears that a substantial minority of the public defines rehabilitation as their preferred goal of corrections. The precise figure is in dispute and depends on the methodology used, but it is likely that this proportion ranges between one-third and two-fifths of the citizenry. Perhaps the best current estimate we have is the 1996 survey in Ohio—a moderate state politically—which, like the original Harris poll, gives multiple response options and asks about "convicted criminals" in general. As table 1 shows, over 40 percent of this statewide sample chose rehabilitation as their main goal of imprisonment (see Applegate 1997; Applegate, Cullen, and Fisher 1997).

Three additional types of data lend additional credence to the view that rehabilitation retains support among the American public. First, the polls summarized in table 1 used forced-choice questions to make respondents select which correctional approach was their main goal. Selecting one option, however, does not necessarily mean that other goals are rejected. In fact, focusing on a single choice may distort the key feature of public opinion about corrections: citizens want the system to accomplish multiple goals (Warr 1994). In this regard,

Applegate, Cullen, and Fisher (1997, p. 246) showed this to be the case. When asked to rate the importance of various goals of imprisonment, over 90 percent of their Ohio sample rated protection and punishment as "important" or "very important." Although support was not as strong, more than eight in ten Ohioans defined rehabilitation as "very important" (45.1 percent) or as "important" (37.7 percent).

Second, surveys have asked people about their support for various correctional programs. Almost uniformly, the U.S. public has strongly endorsed such interventions. In a 1997 U.S. News and World Report and Bozell Worldwide Poll, more than three-fourths of the national sample favored "prisoner rehabilitation programs" (see http://dialog.carl.org).[2] The nationwide 1996 Survey of American Political Culture reported that 85 percent of those surveyed stated that "more treatment and education" was either "very important" or "important" to "solving" the crime problem (from http://dialog.carl.org). Similarly, a 1995 Oklahoma survey found that two-thirds of the sample favored "providing psychiatric treatment to every mentally ill inmate" and making "sure every inmate has a chance to get a high school diploma"—"even if this is more expensive than what we now do" (Doble Research Associates 1995*b*, p. 40; see also Flanagan 1996*b*, p. 84). And in Applegate, Cullen, and Fisher's (1997, p. 247) Ohio survey, more than eight in ten respondents agreed that "it is important to try to rehabilitate adults who have committed crimes and are now in the correctional system" (85.6 percent) and that "it is a good idea to provide treatment" both "for offenders who are in prison" (85.9 percent) and "for offenders who are supervised by the courts and live in the community" (85.9 percent). A majority of the sample even supported treatment for chronic offenders, with 54.2 percent agreeing that "rehabilitation programs should be available even for offenders who have been involved in a lot of crime in their lives."

Third, a limited amount of research has focused on whether citizens express support for rehabilitation after being asked to judge specific offenses or vignettes. In a 1992 survey of 397 residents in the Las Vegas, Nevada, area, McCorkle (1993) presented the respondents with brief scenarios of six street crimes: robbery, rape, molestation of several boys, burglary, selling drugs, and drug possession. They were then

---

[2] These public opinion data—and others in the text carrying the same reference—are drawn from an Internet site that provides access to POLL. Information on accessing POLL may be obtained from the Roper Center (http://ropercenter.ucom.edu/index.htm).

asked to agree or disagree with eight statements about what do to with the offender in each scenario; four statements assessed attitudes toward punishment while the other four gauged attitudes toward rehabilitation. There was clear support for dealing severely—including incapacitating—these street criminals. Nonetheless, across the six offenses, only a third of the sample agreed that "trying to rehabilitate this person would probably be a waste of time," while about 70 percent believed that "the offender would probably benefit from the psychological counseling programs offered in prison" and that "more effort needs to be made to expand and improve programs that would give this offender the chance to change his life." There was more ambivalence about whether "educational and vocational programs" would make an offender "not commit crimes in the future." Still, almost half the sample agreed with this statement (McCorkle 1993, p. 246).

Similar results were reached by Applegate, Cullen, and Fisher (1997; see also Applegate 1997), using a factorial vignette method and having the respondents evaluate whether they endorsed rehabilitating the offender described in the vignette. In addition to a variety of offender characteristics, each vignette focused on a street crime that was punishable by incarceration in the state of Ohio. The vignette also stated that the offender was sentenced to prison, intensive supervision probation, or regular probation and that the offender was involved in a psychological, educational, or vocational rehabilitation program (Applegate 1997). Again, over eight in ten respondents agreed, in reference to the offender portrayed in the vignette, that they supported "the use of rehabilitation," that "it was right to put people like [the offender] in programs that try to cure the particular problem that caused them to break the law," that "this type of rehabilitation program should be expanded," and that "trying to rehabilitate [the offender] will lessen the chances that he/she will go back into crime." Although less supportive, a clear majority—55.8 percent—also agreed that if the offender "successfully completes his/her rehabilitation program, he/she should have the opportunity to have his/her sentence reduced" (Applegate, Cullen, and Fisher 1997, p. 248).

In short, whether respondents rate goals of imprisonment, global statements about offender rehabilitation, or crime-specific vignettes, they show consistent support for rehabilitation as an integral function of corrections. The American people can be punitive and can be skeptical about any policy that does not incapacitate violent offenders, but they also believe that the state should make a concerted effort to help offenders change for the better. Future research might profit from exploring whether—despite three decades of attack—the rehabilitative ideal retains its appeal because of its potential utility, because of its moral message about the values that Americans, as a people, wish to embrace, or both (see Anderson 1998, pp. 16–17).

B. Support for Juvenile Rehabilitation

A century ago, the juvenile court was created with the special mission to "save" children from wayward behavior and a life in crime through individualized treatment (Platt 1969; Rothman 1980). Calls to transform, if not abolish, the juvenile court come from both sides of the political spectrum—from liberals skeptical about the efficacy of treatment and dismayed by the "arbitrary" nature of judicial discretion to conservatives who blame this overly "lenient" system for turning superpredators loose on an unsuspecting community. As Feld (1998, p. 189) notes, most legal reforms undertaken in the past decade have been targeted at "serious, persistent, and violent youth" and either have sought to increase the ease of transferring these offenders to adult court or have mandated that juvenile court judges sentence them to determinate, lengthier terms of incarceration.

To an extent, public opinion is consistent with this policy trend to "get tough" with youthful offenders (Triplett 1996; Roberts and Stalans 1997, pp. 270–75). A 1994 survey, for example, asked a national sample how "society should deal with juveniles under 18 who commit crimes." Over half, 52 percent, chose "give the same punishment as adults," while only 31 percent selected "less emphasis on punishment/ more on rehabilitation"; 13 percent volunteered that "it depends on circumstances" and 3 percent said "other" (Maguire and Pastore 1995, p. 178). A poll in the same year found that for "juveniles who commit a violent crime," over two-thirds of the sample preferred that they be "treated the same as adults" rather than "given more lenient treatment in a juvenile court" (13 percent) (Maguire and Pastore 1995, p. 179). And a 1995 national survey found that a high proportion of the respondents favored trying a juvenile as an adult for a serious property crime (62 percent), for selling illegal drugs (69 percent), and for a serious violent crime (87 percent) (Triplett 1996, p. 142; see also Schwartz 1992).

Interpreting these findings is difficult, however, because the questions used in the polls tend to focus on "serious" or "violent" offenders and ask about "treating juvenile criminals the same as adults." The public's responses may not be an unqualified endorsement either of efforts to abolish the juvenile court or of waivers to adult court but, rather, a reflection of the global view that serious youthful lawbreakers should not be treated leniently. Indeed, when queried about more specific policies, the public's views are more tempered. Based on a national survey, for example, Schwartz (1992) found that little more than a third of the sample agreed that a "juvenile convicted of a crime should receive the same sentence as an adult, no matter what the crime." The study also revealed that the respondents opposed to sending juveniles to "adult prisons" strongly favored community-based programs over training schools "for all but the most violent or serious juvenile offenders," and reserved transfer to adult court for youths who were seventeen and older (1992, see figs. 7, 9, 13, and 14; see also Schiraldi and Soler 1998). Similarly, other research shows that citizens reject giving prosecutors "total discretion . . . to try juveniles as adults for all felonies" (Schiraldi and Soler 1998, p. 598) and that people are reluctant to waive to adult court even juvenile murderers if they had been abused by their father (Stalans and Henry 1994). Further research is needed to untangle more carefully the factors that condition how harshly Americans wish juveniles to be punished.

Regardless, the existing research is clear in showing that the public not only embraces offender treatment as a core goal for juvenile corrections but also is more supportive of juvenile than adult rehabilitation (see, e.g., Cullen, Golden, and Cullen 1983; Steinhart 1988; Gerber and Engelhardt-Greer 1996, p. 69; Moon et al. 2000). In their 1995 Cincinnati survey, Sundt et al. (1998, p. 437) found that over eight in ten respondents felt that juvenile rehabilitation was either "very helpful" (40.3 percent) or "helpful" (45.3 percent); for adults, the combined figure was 60.3 percent. Applegate, Cullen, and Fisher's (1997, p. 247) Ohio survey discovered that over 95 percent agreed that "it is important to try to rehabilitate juveniles who have committed crimes and are now in the correctional system"; the figure for adults was 85.6 percent. Likewise, when asked where they would prefer to spend money on correction, 92 percent of Oregonians selected "rehabilitate juvenile offenders" versus "rehabilitate adult offenders" (73 percent) and "punish juvenile offenders" (77 percent) (Doble Research Associates 1995c, p. 65).

Research on the goals of corrections reinforces the conclusion that Americans retain a strong belief in "child saving." Thus Schwartz's (1992, see fig. 6) study found that when asked what should be the "main purpose of the juvenile court," 78 percent chose "treat and rehabilitate young offenders," while 11.9 percent chose "punish them" and 9.7 percent selected "both equally." In a 1995 national poll, people also were asked which correctional goal "should be the most important in sentencing juveniles." Half the sample answered "rehabilitation," far outstripping "retribution" (31 percent), "deterrence" (15 percent), and "incapacitation" (4 percent) (Gerber and Engelhardt-Greer 1996, p. 69). Finally, in a 1998 statewide survey in Tennessee, nearly two-thirds of the respondents stated that rehabilitation should be the "main emphasis of juvenile prisons." Only 18.7 percent selected punishment and 11.2 percent protecting society; the remaining members of the sample were "not sure." Further, more citizens were likely to choose rehabilitation as a "very important" goal than the other correctional approaches (Moon et al. 2000).

C. Support for Early Intervention Programs

Over the past decade, the emergence of "life-course" or "developmental" criminology has demonstrated that the roots of crime often can be traced to early childhood experiences and that early antisocial conduct is an important predictor for later criminality. These considerations suggest that interventions targeting high-risk children and adolescents might do much to prevent future offending (Farrington 1994). It is noteworthy, therefore, that a growing literature is emerging demonstrating the effectiveness of early intervention programs in reducing problem behavior and in increasing healthy, prosocial outcomes (see, e.g., Farrington 1994; Howell and Hawkins 1998). But will the American public support such efforts? Although the research is limited and further studies are warranted, the answer appears to be decidedly in the affirmative.

In a 1997 California survey of registered voters, over eight in ten respondents said that their "biggest priority is to invest in ways to prevent kids from taking wrong turns and ending up in gangs, violence or prison"; only 13 percent preferred "to build more prisons and youth facilities and enforce stricter sentences to guarantee that the most violent juvenile offenders are kept off the street" (Fairbank et al. 1997, p. 2). A 1998 poll replicated these results (78 percent) and also found that more than seven in ten Californians rated vocational training programs, youth center programs, afterschool programs, and full-service programs as "effective" for preventing "youth violence" (Resources for Youth 1998). A 1997 survey in Tennessee yielded similar results (Cullen et al. 1998). Thus "to stop crime," three-fourths of the sample favored spending tax dollars on the "early intervention option" as opposed to the "incarceration" option. Further, support was high—about eight in ten citizens or higher—for a range of early intervention programs, including preschool programs, treatment services for neglected or abused children, training in parenting skills, early identification by teachers and treatment of at-risk youths, after-school programs, drug education, school retention programs for delinquent youths, and treatment programs for families when youths are first convicted of a crime (1998, pp. 194–96).

V. Conclusions

In ending an essay it is customary to review what has been distilled from the research, to identify what might next be investigated, and to comment on what implications the findings might hold. We do not depart from this convention. Thus we begin this section by summarizing our main conclusions regarding the nature of public opinion about punishment and corrections. In doing so, we reiterate that people's attitudes are complex and more ideologically diverse than they are commonly represented. We then discuss six avenues for future research that might be profitably explored. We also make the point, however, that the basic contours of what we know about public opinion are unlikely to change even in the presence of additional studies. Finally, we draw one broad policy implication from the existing survey research: the lack of political will—not public opinion—is the main barrier to developing a more balanced approach to sentencing and correctional policy.

A. Mapping Public Opinion

In reviewing polling data and scholarly research from the past decade, it appears that public opinion about punishment and corrections is multifaceted and is easily misrepresented either by brief polls or by pithy phrases like "the public wants to get tough on crime." Capturing the complexity of citizens' views is challenging, although we close this essay by trying to do so. Like cartographers seeking to map uncharted territory, however, we are handicapped by incomplete information about the landscape we are crossing (much more research needs to be done) and by an incomplete idea of precisely where we should travel (we need better theories to direct our research and interpretations). In all, we offer seven central themes.

1. *The American Public Is Punitive toward Crime.* On a general or

"global" level, the public prefers or, at very least, accepts policies that "get tough" with offenders. Thus, when asked, they endorse capital punishment, harsher punishments, three-strikes-and-you're-out laws, prison terms for most offenders, and lengthy incarceration for violent criminals. These attitudes are not merely a methodological artifact but likely are a general propensity that underlies many people's thinking. The existence of these propensities does not mean that most Americans are mindlessly or uniformly punitive, only that their first impulse is often in this direction.

2. *Public Punitiveness toward Crime Is "Mushy," Not Rigid.* It is not clear that most citizens are highly committed to one fixed view toward the sanctioning of lawbreakers. This mushiness, as Durham (1993, p. 8) calls it, is significant because it suggests that, in contrast to how they may have answered simplistic polling questions, citizens may be willing to accept less punitive interventions. Most noteworthy, when given more information about offenders and more sentencing options—that is, when placed in a position comparable to that of a "real" judge or policy maker—people tend to modify their harshness. Attitudinal mushiness, however, does not extend in only one direction. Opinions about crime fluctuate and are likely to become more harsh if citizens are told disturbing stories about offenders and the nation's crime problem by the media or bully-pulpit politicians (see Beckett 1997).

3. *Utility Matters: People Must Be Given a Good Reason Not to Be Punitive.* The public appears to want the "punishment to fit the crime." Retribution or just deserts thus plays a role in how much punishment, more or less, people want individual offenders to receive. Even so, most Americans hold "hybrid" theories of corrections and believe that societal safety is a legitimate concern of state legal intervention. While inclined to give harsh punishments, they are potentially open to tempering their punitiveness if given a good reason for doing so. A good reason typically is rooted in notions of utility: it "makes sense." Thus people will favor correctional approaches that keep offenders in the community if they are persuaded that offenders will do service for the community, pay restitution, and improve themselves; they will support early release from prison or shorter sentences if inmates have been reformed and thus no longer need to reside behind bars at a cost of $25,000 a year; and they will relinquish support for the death penalty if persuaded that the offender will never kill again and will work to make the lives of the victim's family less burdensome. We offer this

simple thesis: the more a proposed sentence or correctional policy has utility for the community, victims, and offenders, the more Americans will support it. This thesis offers a lesson for progressives: less punitive interventions generally will not be endorsed—regardless of appeals to the values of justice and humanity—if they do not also have demonstrable utility.

4. *Violent Crime Is the Great Divide between Punitiveness and Nonpunitiveness.* The American public is risk averse. It sees no reason to "take chances" with offenders who have shown that they will physically hurt others. Although not enamored with the effectiveness of prisons—and sophisticated criminological debate aside (cf. Clear 1994 with Bennett, DiIulio, and Walters 1996)—it is "common sense" to people that offenders not on the street will not hurt them. Placing dangerous people in the community is not understandable. However, almost any option—except pro forma, unsupervised probation—is open for discussion when weighing what to do with the so-called nonviolent offender, even those who have been habitually criminal. Imprisonment is an acceptable option, but so, too, are intermediate sanctions. Deciding who does or does not qualify as a "violent" offender is a key issue in determining which lawbreakers fall on which side of this policy divide. Further, although an uphill struggle, all this does not mean that citizens will always reject community-based alternatives for violent offenders. The argument for doing so, however, will have to be awfully good.

5. *The Public Continues to Believe That Rehabilitation Should Be a Goal of the Correctional System.* The enormous criticism of correctional treatment, sustained now for three decades, has not succeeded in debunking rehabilitation in the public's eyes. Americans are perhaps less idealistic than they once were about the ability to change lawbreakers; they realize that treatment programs in prison may only succeed with a limited number of inmates. Still, they believe that corrections should, at least in part, involve the process of "correcting" offenders. Possibly, the belief that all but the most wicked can be saved is so deeply ingrained in the American cultural heritage that we, as a people, are not going to relinquish the correctional system to the darker philosophies of vengeance and warehousing. Rehabilitation offers the rare combination of morality and utility: it is possible to invest in and seek the betterment of offenders while simultaneously enhancing public safety ("I would rather have them come out better than they went in"). Progressives—especially those who have rejected offender treatment—may

wish to consider that the rehabilitative ideal remains one of the most viable and culturally sensible rationales for not inflicting unnecessary harm on lawbreakers.

6. *The Public Strongly Supports "Child Saving."* Support for "saving" children is not unconditional: for most citizens, youths who are violent or seriously criminal forfeit their status as "children" and require the kind of control typically reserved for adults. Otherwise, most Americans believe that "it is never too late" for wayward youngsters to change and that the correctional system should be involved in redirecting the lives of these offenders. Efforts at preventing at-risk children from ever "getting in trouble" are particularly appealing. Who, after all, can be against programs that save children from a life in crime and thereby make the community safer? Putting hardened criminals in prison may be necessary, but to much of the public it makes more sense to channel tax dollars into early intervention programs that derail the "hardening" process in the first place.

7. *The Central Tendency in Public Opinion Is to Be Punitive and Progressive.* When people break the law, most Americans want something sensible done. The public most rejects the idea that anyone can simply flaunt the law and then be given a meaningless penalty that is both lenient and ineffective. Citizens want some sign, some assurances, that an intervention of consequence follows a crime. In the end, they would like the correctional system to act responsibly: egregious crimes deserve egregiously harsh punishment, but less serious crimes can be assigned intermediate sanctions. Truly dangerous people need to be locked up, but if supervised correctly and made to repair the harm they have caused, perhaps many other offenders could be placed in the community. All the while, efforts should be made to rehabilitate lawbreakers, especially juveniles, while they are within the system. In short, do justice, protect society, and reform offenders. This admonition may contain conflicting philosophies and policy prescriptions, but it is the multifaceted or hybrid mission that most Americans believe the correctional system should work vigorously to realize.

B. Future Research

The study of public opinion about crime-related policies offers ample research opportunities. First, there is a desperate need for more sophisticated studies of correctional policies that use national samples. Take, for example, the philosophy of offender rehabilitation, which has long shaped policy and practice within corrections. Despite the centrality of the treatment ideal, to our knowledge there has never been a systematic study of public support for rehabilitation that has used a national sample. Instead, data from national samples are limited to occasional one-question polls or, even in the best studies, to several questions (e.g., Flanagan and Longmire 1996). More detailed local studies do furnish valuable information (e.g., Applegate 1997; Applegate, Cullen, and Fisher 1997); in fact, it is not clear that the results from community and state samples would differ dramatically from those drawn from surveys of national samples. Even so, the credibility of such research is diminished, since the generalizability of the findings to other contexts is open to question. In short, conveying persuasive conclusions on public opinion about rehabilitation or other correctional issues will require national data that cannot be dismissed by potential critics.

Second, we need to learn more about the relationship between "global" and "specific" attitudes. As discussed, research now reliably shows that when asked broad questions about sanctioning offenders, respondents are more punitive than when asked to use a detailed scale of penalties to punish specific offenders (see Roberts and Stalans 1997, pp. 218–22). We have hints as to why this is the case (e.g., broad questions elicit images of violent criminals—the very subset of offenders who people want most severely penalized). Even so, our understanding of why punitiveness tends to be people's initial response to questions measuring global attitudes remains in its beginning stages. We also know only a little about whether the sources of global and specific public opinion are the same or different, although some research suggests they may be fairly similar (Applegate et al. 1996*b*; see Applegate 1997). Similarly, few studies have explored how closely these two types of opinions are related to one another. Sprott's (1998) research, based on a 1997 survey of Ontario, Canada, respondents, reports that a global belief in the abolition of the juvenile court was related, but only in a complicated way (i.e., through other beliefs), to a preference for harsher sanctions in specific criminal cases. Perhaps more important, we have yet to learn which type of opinion—global or specific—is more salient to citizens. For example, when people enter the voting booth, do their global or specific attitudes play more of a role in shaping which lever they pull or box they punch?

Third, it is well documented that the public's knowledge of punishment and correctional issues is limited (Roberts and Stalans 1997). There is evidence that citizens underestimate the punitiveness of the sentencing process and, in turn, that this perception may foster their desire for the imposition of harsher sanctions (Hough and Roberts 1999). Findings such as these prompt the suggestion that efforts be made to "educate the public," presumably with the effect of making people less punitive, more open to progressive policies, and perhaps more confident in the performance of the correctional system (Roberts and Stalans 1997, pp. 291–93). Creating an informed citizenry, however, promises to be a daunting task. Even if knowledge is disseminated—likely a financially expensive proposition—it is possible that many people will simply dismiss the criminological "facts" being presented as mere rhetoric and, given the "rationality of ignorance," choose not to invest the time and energy to gain access to this knowledge (Kinder 1998). For these and other reasons, political scientists have long struggled with the question of whether "an informed public is possible" (Delli Carpini and Keeter 1996, p. 288). In this context, research is needed that explores how it is possible effectively to impart knowledge about crime policies.

These considerations lead to the broader issue of whether it matters that many individual citizens are ignorant about correctional policies. Recall the concept of the "miracle of aggregation"—the idea that when the ill-informed views of individual citizens are combined, the public's collective opinion is "rational" (Page and Shapiro 1992; Kinder 1998). In the area of crime, researchers might explore more fully whether a case can be made for a "rational public" (Page and Shapiro 1992). To a degree, this has been an implicit theme of this essay: overall and despite how citizens are often characterized, the public is fairly rational in its support of a crime-policy agenda that is balanced ideologically and committed to sensible correctional interventions.

These observations suggest a fourth area for future research. Is the public sufficiently rational that public opinion fluctuates, at least broadly, in response to real events in the wider environment? Page and Shapiro (1992) embrace this position, presenting data from the 1960s and 1970s linking urban turmoil and escalating crime rates to jumps in the public's punitiveness and to drops in the public's support for rehabilitation. Although "the trend toward punitiveness was not mechanical or inexorable," argue Page and Shapiro (1992, p. 92), "opinions reacted to information and events, moving in different directions at different times and distinguishing among different types of criminal justice policies." The alternative view is that public opinion reflects not the events of the day but manipulation by politicians and the media. Thus Beckett (1997) tests this possibility by investigating the timing of shifts in public opinion vis-à-vis the timing of when politicians undertake "initiatives" (e.g., give speeches and call for a "war" on a "problem," introduce legislation) and when media attention coalesces around an issue. Her data are favorable to the manipulation thesis, showing that changes in public concern about crime and drugs most often follow not rises in the incidence of the conduct in question but increases in political initiatives and media coverage focused on these issues (see also Scheingold 1984). "Popular attitudes about crime and drugs have been shaped to an important extent by the definitional activities of political elites," concludes Beckett (1997, p. 27). "These actors have drawn attention to crime and drug use and framed them as the consequence of insufficient punishment and control." Although valuable contributions, these studies should be extended with more diverse measures and, when feasible, tested in state and local contexts (see also Scheingold 1984).

Fifth, within the field of criminology, there has been increasing attention paid to studying crime across the life course (see, e.g., Sampson and Laub 1993). In contrast, to the best of our understanding, there is no comparable agenda under way to use a life-course perspective to organize knowledge and research on public opinion about crime-related issues. Nearly all public opinion polls on punishment and corrections are "snapshots" of adult respondents at one particular moment in time. These respondents are not followed over time—from childhood, into adolescence, and through the various stages of adulthood. As a result, we do not have much knowledge about how, and to what extent, beliefs about punishing offenders are formulated early in life. Dunaway and Cullen (1991) touch on this issue, showing that conservative parents are more effective than liberal parents in transmitting their crime ideology to their children. But this research is only a beginning effort. We also have little understanding of whether views about crime-related policies remain largely stable across the life course or whether intra-individual change is common. If people's views fluctuate over time, moreover, a life-course perspective would urge us to examine the potential causal influence of the major life transitions that most people experience, such as marriage, joining a church, changing peer groups, and entry into the labor market. A life-course perspective thus offers rich research possibilities by focusing attention on how developmental continuities and changes—factors that affect so much else in people's lives—may also play a role in shaping their views on punishment and corrections.

Sixth, in a recent study using data from the 1996 British Crime Survey, Hough and Roberts (1998, 1999) found that respondents both had limited awareness of sanctions other than imprisonment and underestimated the punitiveness of the sentences actually imposed on offenders. Almost four in five respondents believed that sentences were too lenient to "some degree," while one in two thought that the sanctions were "much too lenient." Even so, when asked to rate a specific case in which the offender—a burglar—was actually given a three-year sentence, the respondents assigned a median prison term of twelve months, a "result that might surprise those who believe that the British public are highly punitive" (Hough and Roberts 1999, p. 20). Further, when given a menu of possible sanctions, including noncustodial penalties, almost half the sample favored a sentence that did not involve imprisonment.

Notably, if the nationality of the sample had not been disclosed, one might have thought that the study had been conducted in the United States: the findings for the British sample are strikingly similar to the views expressed on surveys by U.S. residents. There is a tendency in cross-national research to emphasize how peoples diverge in their views; and, to be sure, understanding how cultural factors differentially shape views toward sanctioning is an important task (see, e.g., Sanders, Hamilton, and Yuasa 1998). Still, the commonality in opinions among citizens of different nations is equally important to investigate. Why do shared views, as well as shared gaps in knowledge, exist? Is this phenomenon a by-product of the broad social force of modernization that constrains thinking into limited categories? Or, in the other extreme, might sociobiology provide the answer, with certain qualities of the brain and adaptive orientations rooted in evolution restricting how humans, regardless of location, think about conduct, like crime, that threatens their safety (Wilson 1998, pp. 226–27)? Further, what does all this say about the role of public opinion in shaping correctional policy cross-nationally? If thinking about crime and punishment falls within a limited range of variation, what then accounts for cross-national differences in penal practices?

Many more topics could be listed that warrant detailed investigation: gender differences in public opinion about punishment and how these might be illuminated by theories emphasizing how men and women hold distinctive views of justice; how broader theories of public opinion might direct research on citizens' views on crime-related policies (Kinder 1998); and how respondents' use of computers to complete surveys might affect their willingness to disclose their opinions, especially on sensitive topics (Turner et al. 1998)—to name but a few issues. But if the roster of topics to study seems virtually unending, in another, albeit limited, way additional future research is unlikely to revise what we now know.

Two decades ago, Sherman and Hawkins (1981, p. 46) commented that "our knowledge of public opinion about breakfast food is far deeper than our knowledge of public opinion about criminal justice." This assessment still may be accurate, but only because marketing researchers know a great deal about breakfast food, not because social science insight into public opinion has not substantially advanced. We hasten to reiterate the need for more research to firm up and flesh out our understanding of what people want done with lawbreakers. Nonetheless, we also want to counter any suspicions that knowledge about public opinion remains shallow. We have now accumulated enough research that the basic parameters of public opinion about punishment and corrections outlined earlier in this section are unlikely to be substantially revised as further research appears (see Roberts 1992; Roberts and Stalans 1997, 1998). In particular, we should have a measure of confidence that members of the public, although punitive in important ways, hold a complex vision of corrections that includes the capacity to temper harsh sentiments and to endorse a range of policies that seek the betterment of offenders. We end this essay with the policy implications of this central finding.

C. Policy Implications

By the mid-1970s, the United States had experienced a dramatic shift in correctional paradigms (Cullen and Gilbert 1982). Prior to this time, there was a notion—admittedly too infrequently realized in practice (Rothman 1980)—that concerted efforts should be made to reform the wayward. Consistent with the thrust of the welfare state, there was a sense that the government should invest resources in offenders with the intent of fixing the defects, psychological and social, that had led them astray. Since this time, however, there has been a steady effort to make punishments longer and life for offenders— whether under community supervision or inside prisons—more painful. The major investment has been in prisons and in the technology of supervision, not in people. Clear (1994) has used the term "penal harm movement" to capture this paradigm shift and the array of policies enacted explicitly to discomfort offenders. Although later in developing and perhaps less strident in its embrace of harming offenders, similar trends appear afoot in other nations, such as Canada (Roberts, Nuffield, and Hann 1999) and Great Britain (Sparks 1996; Hough and Roberts 1999).

Any meaningful policy discussion, at least in the United States, must start by confronting the seeming intractability of this "get tough" or "penal harm" movement. This obligation seems especially required in the case of "public opinion." To be honest, we do not know what precise role public opinion has played in fueling the vitality of this punishment movement, but it is clearly implicated in sustaining it. For much of the past three decades, the idea of a "punitive public" has been used to legitimate virtually every law that has ratcheted up the punishment on offenders (Scheingold 1984; Cullen, Clark, and Wozniak 1985; Beckett 1997). To cite but one of many recent examples, Ditton and Wilson (1999, p. 2) argue that "over the past two decades, sentencing requirements and release policies have become more restrictive, primarily in response to widespread 'get tough on crime' attitudes in the Nation."

These claims likely are not without some merit. Citizens do harbor punitive sentiments and, conversely, do not use their vote to throw get-tough legislators, prosecutors, and judges out of office. Still, claims linking harsh policies to public opinion risk creating a distorted reality that forecloses consideration of a wider range of policy options. The very notion of a punitive public too often looms above policy discussions, prompting the refrain that the "public will never support" a given progressive initiative. It is instructive that surveys reveal that policy makers invariably overestimate rather than underestimate the punitiveness of the public (Roberts 1992; Roberts and Stalans 1997).

Further, in a democratic nation, an underlying legitimacy attaches to the claim that one's position reflects the public's collective will. Those who challenge the public's views—who depict that average citizen as ill-informed or as suffering false consciousness—run the risk of being called an "elitist" or a "so-called expert" who is "out of touch" with the "common man and woman." Advocates of the punishment paradigm often revel in the polling numbers that ostensibly show that the public wants to put offenders to death or behind bars. It is why they argue that the "people know best."

The portrayal of public opinion as exclusively punitive thus serves as a potentially powerful social reality that inhibits efforts to choose a different correctional future. It makes policy makers wary of appearing too liberal on crime-related issues; it places advocates of a progressive correctional paradigm in the position of appearing antidemocratic. Reviews of public opinion, such as ours, we hope, can serve to challenge or "deconstruct" this reality. Our central message—based on a growing body of survey data—is that citizens want their correctional system to be more than a machinery for inflicting harm. Lifetime imprisonment rather than capital punishment, alternatives to incarceration, restorative justice, investing in offenders through rehabilitation, and early prevention programs—all these policies and more the public is willing to consider if they are implemented in a responsible way.

In the end, public opinion is not an intractable barrier to developing a balanced, rather than a punitive, agenda for responding to offenders. We should not claim too much for citizens: there is no evidence that they are clamoring for a reversal of current correctional policy. Yet neither should we claim too little, as is most often the case in popular commentaries about "what the public wants." The ideological space exists for reforms that reflect both progressive sentiments and demonstrable utility. Moving in this direction thus depends not on changing the public will but on mustering the political will to do so.

REFERENCES

Anderson, David C. 1998. *Sensible Justice: Alternatives to Prison.* New York: New Press.

Andrews, D. A., and James Bonta. 1998. *The Psychology of Criminal Conduct,* 2d ed. Cincinnati: Anderson.

Applegate, Brandon K. 1997. "Specifying Public Support for Rehabilitation: A Factorial Survey Approach." Ph.D. dissertation, University of Cincinnati.

Applegate, Brandon K., Francis T. Cullen, and Bonnie S. Fisher. 1997. "Public Support for Correctional Treatment: The Continuing Appeal of the Rehabilitative Ideal." *Prison Journal* 77:237–58.

Applegate, Brandon K., Francis T. Cullen, Bonnie S. Fisher, and Thomas Vander Ven. Forthcoming. "Forgiveness and Fundamentalism: Reconsidering the Relationship between Correctional Attitudes and Religion." *Criminology.*

Applegate, Brandon K., Francis T. Cullen, Bruce G. Link, Pamela J. Richards, and Lonn Lanza-Kaduce. 1996a. "Determinants of Public Punitiveness toward Drunk Driving: A Factorial Survey Approach." *Justice Quarterly* 13: 57–79.

Applegate, Brandon K., Francis T. Cullen, Michael G. Turner, and Jody L. Sundt. 1996*b*. "Assessing Public Support for Three-Strikes-and-You're-Out Laws: Global versus Specific Attitudes." *Crime and Delinquency* 42:517–34.

Barkan, Steven E., and Steven F. Cohn. 1994. "Racial Prejudice and Support for the Death Penalty by Whites." *Journal of Research in Crime and Delinquency* 31:202–9.

Beckett, Katherine. 1997. *Making Crime Pay: Law and Order in Contemporary American Politics*. New York: Oxford University Press.

Bennett, William J., John J. DiIulio, Jr., and John P. Walters. 1996. *Body Count: Moral Poverty . . . and How to Win America's War against Crime and Drugs*. New York: Simon & Schuster.

Berns, Walter. 1979. *For Capital Punishment: Crime and the Morality of the Death Penalty*. New York: Basic Books.

Biemer, Paul P., Robert M. Groves, Lars E. Lyberg, Nancy A. Mathiowetz, and Seymour Sudman, eds. 1991. *Measurement Errors in Surveys*. New York: Wiley.

Bishop, George F., Alfred J. Tuchfarber, and Robert W. Oldendick. 1986. "Opinions on Fictitious Issues: The Pressures to Answer Survey Questions." *Public Opinion Quarterly* 50:240–50.

Blumstein, Alfred, and Jacqueline Cohen. 1973. "A Theory of the Stability of Punishment." *Journal of Criminal Law and Criminology* 64:198–206.

———. 1980. "Sentencing of Convicted Offenders: An Analysis of the Public's View." *Law and Society Review* 14:223–61.

Bohm, Robert M. 1987. "American Death Penalty Attitudes: A Critical Examination of Recent Evidence." *Criminal Justice and Behavior* 14:380–96.

———. 1991. "American Death Penalty Opinion, 1936–1986: A Critical Examination of the Gallup Polls." In *The Death Penalty in America: Current Research*, edited by Robert M. Bohm. Cincinnati: Anderson.

Bohm, Robert M., Louise J. Clark, and Adrian F. Aveni. 1991. "Knowledge and Death Penalty Opinion: A Test of the Marshall Hypotheses." *Journal of Research in Crime and Delinquency* 28:360–87.

Bohm, Robert M., Timothy J. Flanagan, and Philip W. Harris. 1990. "Current Death Penalty Opinion in New York State." *Albany Law Review* 54:819–43.

Borg, Marian J. 1997. "The Southern Subculture of Punitiveness? Regional Variation in Support for Capital Punishment." *Journal of Research in Crime and Delinquency* 34:25–45.

Bowers, William J., Margaret Vandiver, and Patricia H. Dugan. 1994. "A New Look at Public Opinion on Capital Punishment: What Citizens and Legislators Prefer." *American Journal of Criminal Law* 22:77–150.

Braithwaite, John. 1989. *Crime, Shame and Reintegration*. Cambridge: Cambridge University Press.

———. 1998. "Restorative Justice." In *The Handbook of Crime and Punishment*, edited by Michael Tonry. New York: Oxford University Press.

Brenner, Allyson. 1998. "Public Opinion on the Death Penalty." Senior Thesis, Wheeling Jesuit College.

Britt, Chester L. 1998. "Race, Religion, and Support for the Death Penalty: A Research Note." *Justice Quarterly* 15:175–91.

Brown, Michael P., and Preston Elrod. 1995. "Electronic House Arrest: An Examination of Citizen Attitudes." *Crime and Delinquency* 41:332–46.

Clark, John, James Austin, and D. Alan Henry. 1997. *"Three Strikes and You're Out": A Review of State Legislation.* Research in Brief. Washington, D.C.: U.S. Department of Justice, National Institute of Justice.

Clear, Todd R. 1994. *Harm in American Penology: Offenders, Victims, and Their Communities.* Albany, N.Y.: SUNY Press.

Cook, Kimberly J. 1998. "A Passion to Punish: Abortion Opponents Who Favor the Death Penalty." *Justice Quarterly* 15:329–46.

Costanzo, Mark. 1997. *Just Revenge: Costs and Consequences of the Death Penalty.* New York: St. Martin's.

Crouch, Ben M. 1993. "Is Incarceration Really Worse? Analysis of Offenders' Preferences for Prison over Probation." *Justice Quarterly* 10:67–88.

Cullen, Francis T., and Brandon K. Applegate, eds. 1997. *Offender Rehabilitation: Effective Correctional Intervention.* Aldershot: Ashgate.

Cullen, Francis T., Gregory A. Clark, Bruce G. Link, Richard A. Mathers, Jennifer Lee Niedospial, and Michael Sheahan. 1985. "Dissecting White-Collar Crime: Offense Type and Punitiveness." *International Journal of Comparative and Applied Criminal Justice* 9:15–28.

Cullen, Francis T., Gregory A. Clark, and John F. Wozniak. 1985. "Explaining the Get Tough Movement: Can the Public Be Blamed?" *Federal Probation* 49(June):16–24.

Cullen, Francis T., John B. Cullen, and John F. Wozniak. 1988. "Is Rehabilitation Dead? The Myth of the Punitive Public." *Journal of Criminal Justice* 16:303–17.

Cullen, Francis T., and Karen E. Gilbert. 1982. *Reaffirming Rehabilitation.* Cincinnati: Anderson.

Cullen, Francis T., Kathryn M. Golden, and John B. Cullen. 1983. "Is Child Saving Dead? Attitudes toward Juvenile Rehabilitation in Illinois." *Journal of Criminal Justice* 11:1–13.

Cullen, Francis T., Richard A. Mathers, Gregory A. Clark, and John B. Cullen. 1983. "Public Support for Punishing White-Collar Crime: Blaming the Victim Revisited?" *Journal of Criminal Justice* 11:481–93.

Cullen, Francis T., Sandra Evans Skovron, Joseph E. Scott, and Velmer S. Burton, Jr. 1990. "Public Support for Correctional Treatment: The Tenacity of Rehabilitative Ideology." *Criminal Justice and Behavior* 17:6–18.

Cullen, Francis T., John Paul Wright, and Brandon K. Applegate. 1996. "Control in the Community: The Limits of Reform?" In *Choosing Correctional Options That Work: Defining the Demand and Evaluating the Supply,* edited by Alan T. Harland. Thousand Oaks, Calif.: Sage.

Cullen, Francis T., John Paul Wright, Shayna Brown, Melissa M. Moon, Michael B. Blankenship, and Brandon K. Applegate. 1998. "Public Support for Early Intervention Programs: Implications for a Progressive Policy Agenda." *Crime and Delinquency* 44:187–204.

Currie, Elliott. 1998. *Crime and Punishment in America*. New York: Metropolitan Books.

Delli Carpini, Michael X., and Scott Keeter. 1996. *What Americans Know about Politics and Why It Matters*. New Haven, Conn.: Yale University Press.

Dickey, Walter J. 1998. "Forgiveness and Crime: The Possibilities of Restorative Justice." In *Exploring Forgiveness*, edited by Robert D. Enright and Joanna North. Madison: University of Wisconsin Press.

DiIulio, John J., Jr. 1995. "The Coming of the Super-Predators." *Weekly Standard* (November 27), pp. 23–28.

———. 1997. "Are Voters Fools? Crime Public Opinion, and Representative Democracy." *Corrections Management Quarterly* 1(3):1–5.

DiMascio, William M., with the assistance of Marc Mauer, Kathleen DiJulia, and Karen Davidson. 1997. *Seeking Justice: Crime and Punishment in America*. New York: Edna McConnell Clark Foundation.

Ditton, Paula M., and Doris James Wilson. 1999. *Truth in Sentencing in State Prisons*. Washington, D.C.: U.S. Department of Justice, Bureau of Justice Statistics.

Doble, John, Stephen Immerwahr, and Amy Richardson. 1991. *Punishing Criminals: The People of Delaware Consider the Options*. New York: Public Agenda Foundation.

Doble, John, and Josh Klein. 1989. *Punishing Criminals: The Public's View—an Alabama Survey*. New York: Public Agenda Foundation.

Doble Research Associates. 1994. *Crime and Corrections: The Views of the People of Vermont*. Englewood Cliffs, N.J.: Doble Research Associates.

———. 1995*a*. *Crime and Corrections: The Views of the People of North Carolina*. Englewood Cliffs, N.J.: Doble Research Associates.

———. 1995*b*. *Crime and Corrections: The Views of the People of Oklahoma*. Englewood Cliffs, N.J.: Doble Research Associates.

———. 1995*c*. *Crime and Corrections: The Views of the People of Oregon*. Englewood Cliffs, N.J.: Doble Research Associates.

———. 1997. *Crime and Corrections in Iowa: The Views of 451 Participants at a Series of Statewide Forums*. Englewood Cliffs, N.J.: Doble Research Associates.

———. 1998. *Crime and Corrections: The Views of the People of New Hampshire*. Englewood Cliffs, N.J.: Doble Research Associates.

Doob, Anthony N., and Julian V. Roberts. 1984. "Social Psychology, Social Attitudes, and Attitudes toward Sentencing." *Canadian Journal of Behavioral Sciences* 16:269–80.

———. 1988. "Public Punitiveness and Public Knowledge of the Facts: Some Canadian Surveys." In *Public Attitudes to Sentencing*, edited by Nigel Walker and Michael Hough. Aldershot: Gower.

Doob, Anthony N., Jane Sprott, Voula Marinos, and Kimberly N. Varma. 1998. *An Exploration of Ontario Residents' Views of Crime and the Criminal Justice System*. Toronto: University of Toronto, Centre of Criminology.

Duffee, David, and R. Richard Ritti. 1977. "Correctional Policy and Public Values." *Criminology* 14:449–59.

Dunaway, R. Gregory, and Francis T. Cullen. 1991. "Explaining Crime Ideology: An Exploration of the Parental Socialization Perspective." *Crime and Delinquency* 37:536–54.

Durham, Alexis M., III. 1993. "Public Opinion Regarding Sentences for Crime: Does It Exist?" *Journal of Criminal Justice* 21:1–11.

Durham, Alexis M., H. Preston Elrod, and Patrick T. Kinkade. 1996. "Public Support for the Death Penalty: Beyond Gallup." *Justice Quarterly* 13:705–36.

Ehrlich, Isaac. 1975. "The Deterrent Effects of Capital Punishment: A Question of Life and Death." *American Economic Review* 65:397–417.

Ellsworth, Phoebe C., and Lee Ross. 1983. "Public Opinion and Capital Punishment: A Close Examination of the Views of Abolitionists and Retentionists." *Crime and Delinquency* 29:116–69.

Elrod, Preston, and Michael P. Brown. 1996. "Predicting Public Support for Electronic House Arrest: Results from a New York County Survey." *American Behavioral Scientist* 39:461–73.

Evans, T. David, Francis T. Cullen, and Paula J. Dubeck. 1993. "Public Perceptions of Corporate Crime." In *Understanding Corporate Crime*, edited by Michael B. Blankenship. New York: Garland.

Fairbank, Maslin, Maullin & Associates. 1997. *Resources for Youth California Survey*. Santa Monica, Calif.: Fairbank, Maslin, Maullin & Assoc.

Farkas, Steve. 1993. "Pennsylvanians Prefer Alternatives to Prison." *Overcrowded Times* 4(2):1, 13–15.

Farrington, David P. 1994. "Early Developmental Prevention of Juvenile Delinquency." *Criminal Behaviour and Mental Health* 4:209–27.

Feld, Barry C. 1997. "Abolish the Juvenile Court: Youthfulness, Criminal Responsibility, and Sentencing Policy." *Journal of Criminal Law and Criminology* 88:68–136.

———. 1998. "Juvenile and Criminal Justice Systems' Responses to Youth Violence." In *Crime and Justice: A Review of Research*, vol. 24, edited by Michael Tonry. Chicago: University of Chicago Press.

Finkel, Norman J., Stephen T. Maloney, Monique Z. Valbuena, and Jennifer Groscup. 1996. "Recidivism, Proportionalism, and Individualized Punishment." *American Behavioral Scientist* 39:474–87.

Flanagan, Timothy J. 1996a. "Community Corrections in the Public Mind." *Federal Probation* 60(3):3–9.

———. 1996b. "Reform or Punish: Americans' Views of the Correctional System." In *Americans View Crime and Justice: A National Public Survey*, edited by Timothy J. Flanagan and Dennis R. Longmire. Thousand Oaks, Calif.: Sage.

Flanagan, Timothy J., and Susan L. Caulfield. 1984. "Public Opinion and Prison Policy: A Review." *Prison Journal* 64(Fall–Winter):31–46.

Flanagan, Timothy J., and Dennis R. Longmire, eds. 1996. *Americans View Crime and Justice: A National Public Opinion Survey*. Thousand Oaks, Calif.: Sage.

Frank, James, Francis T. Cullen, Lawrence F. Travis III, and John L. Borntrager. 1989. "Sanctioning Corporate Crime: How Do Business Executives and the Public Compare?" *American Journal of Criminal Justice* 13:139–68.

Friedman, Lawrence M. 1985. *Total Justice.* New York: Russell Sage.

Friedrichs, David O. 1989. "Comment—Humanism and the Death Penalty: An Alternative Perspective." *Justice Quarterly* 6:197–209.

Gallup Report. 1982. "Public Backs Wholesale Prison Reform." *Gallup Report* 200(May):3–16.

Gendreau, Paul, Kathleen Clark, and Glenn A. Gray. 1996. "Intensive Surveillance Programs: They Don't Work." *Community Corrections Report* 3(3):1, 14–15.

Gendreau, Paul, Francis T. Cullen, and James Bonta. 1994. "Intensive Rehabilitation Supervision: The Next Generation in Community Corrections?" *Federal Probation* 58(1):72–78.

Gerber, Jurg, and Simone Engelhardt-Greer. 1996. "Just and Painful: Attitudes toward Sentencing Criminals." In *Americans View Crime and Justice: A National Public Opinion Survey,* edited by Timothy J. Flanagan and Dennis R. Longmire. Thousand Oaks, Calif.: Sage.

Grasmick, Harold G., Robert J. Bursik, Jr., and Brenda Sims Blackwell. 1993. "Religious Beliefs and Public Support for the Death Penalty for Juveniles and Adults." *Journal of Crime and Justice* 16:59–86.

Grasmick, Harold G., John K. Cochran, Robert J. Bursik, Jr., and M'Lou Kimpel. 1993. "Religion, Punitive Justice, and Support for the Death Penalty." *Justice Quarterly* 10:289–314.

Grasmick, Harold G., Elizabeth Davenport, Mitchell B. Chamlin, and Robert J. Bursik, Jr. 1992. "Protestant Fundamentalism and the Retributive Doctrine of Punishment." *Criminology* 30:21–45.

Grasmick, Harold G., and Anne L. McGill. 1994. "Religion, Attribution Style, and Punitiveness toward Juvenile Offenders." *Criminology* 32:23–46.

Hadden, Jeffrey K. 1987. "Toward Desacralizing Secularization Theory." *Social Forces* 65:587–611.

Hahn, Paul H. 1998. *Emerging Criminal Justice: Three Pillars for a Proactive Justice System.* Thousand Oaks, Calif.: Sage.

Hamilton, V. Lee, and Steve Rytina. 1980. "Social Consensus on Norms of Justice: Should the Punishment Fit the Crime?" *American Journal of Sociology* 85:1117–44.

Hamm, Mark S. 1989. "Legislator Ideology and Capital Punishment: The Special Case for Indiana Juveniles." *Justice Quarterly* 6:219–32.

Harlow, Robert E., John M. Darley, and Paul H. Robinson. 1995. "The Severity of Intermediate Penal Sanctions: A Psychophysical Scaling Approach for Obtaining Community Perceptions." *Journal of Quantitative Criminology* 11:71–95.

Harris, Louis. 1968. "Changing Public Attitudes toward Crime and Corrections." *Federal Probation* 32(4):9–16.

Harris, Philip W. 1986. "Over-Simplification and Error in Public Opinion Surveys on Capital Punishment." *Justice Quarterly* 3:429–55.

Hood, Roger. 1998. "Capital Punishment." In *The Handbook of Crime and Punishment,* edited by Michael Tonry. New York: Oxford University Press.

Hough, Michael, and Julian V. Roberts. 1998. *Attitudes to Punishment: Findings from the British Crime Survey*. London: Home Office, Research and Statistics Directorate.

———. 1999. "Sentencing Trends in Britain: Public Knowledge and Public Opinion." *Punishment and Society* 1:11–26.

Howell, James C., and J. David Hawkins. 1998. "Prevention of Youth Violence." In *Youth Violence*, edited by Michael Tonry and Mark H. Moore. Vol. 24 of *Crime and Justice: A Review of Research*, edited by Michael Tonry. Chicago: University of Chicago Press.

Howells, Gary N., Kelly A. Flanagan, and Vivian Hagan. 1995. "Does Viewing a Televised Execution Affect Attitudes toward Capital Punishment?" *Criminal Justice and Behavior* 22:411–24.

Hunter, James D. 1991. *Culture Wars: The Struggle to Define America*. New York: Basic Books.

Innes, Christopher A. 1993. "Recent Public Opinion in the United States toward Punishment and Corrections." *Prison Journal* 73:222–36.

Jacobs, Gloria. 1993. *Punishing Criminals: Pennsylvanians Consider the Options*. New York: Public Agenda Foundation.

Jacoby, Joseph E., and Francis T. Cullen. 1998. "The Structure of Punishment Norms: Applying the Rossi-Berk Model." *Journal of Criminal Law and Criminology* 89:245–312.

Jacoby, Joseph E., and Christopher S. Dunn. 1987. "National Survey on Punishment for Criminal Offenses: Executive Summary." Paper presented at the National Conference on Punishment for Criminal Offenses, Ann Arbor, Mich., November 9–10.

Johnson, Byron. 1994. "To Rehabilitate or Punish? Results of a Public Opinion Poll." *American Jails* 8(November–December):41–45

Johnson, Paul. 1994. "Crime: The People Want Revenge." *Wall Street Journal* (January 4), p. A-10.

Kinder, Donald R. 1998. "Opinion and Action in the Realm of Politics." In *The Handbook of Social Psychology*, edited by Daniel T. Gilbert, Susan T. Fiske, and Gardner Lindzey. Vol. 2, 4th ed. Boston: McGraw-Hill.

Lane, Jodi S. 1997. "Can You Make a Horse Drink? The Effects of a Corrections Course on Attitudes toward Criminal Punishment." *Crime and Delinquency* 43:186–202.

Layman, Geoffrey C. 1997. "Religion and Political Behavior in the United States: The Impact of Beliefs, Affiliations, and Commitment from 1980 to 1994." *Public Opinion Quarterly* 61:288–316.

Leiber, Michael J., and Anne C. Woodrick. 1997. "Religious Beliefs, Attributional Styles, and Adherence to Correctional Orientations." *Criminal Justice and Behavior* 24:495–511.

Leiber, Michael J., Anne C. Woodrick, and E. Michele Roudebush. 1995. "Religion, Discriminatory Attitudes, and the Orientations of Juvenile Justice Personnel: A Research Note." *Criminology* 33:431–49.

Levrant, Sharon, Francis T. Cullen, Betsy Fulton, and John F. Wozniak. 1999. "Reconsidering Restorative Justice: The Corruption of Benevolence Revisited?" *Crime and Delinquency* 45:3–27.

Lipsey, Mark W., and David B. Wilson. 1998. "Effective Intervention with

Serious Juvenile Offenders: A Synthesis of Research." In *Serious and Violent Juvenile Offenders: Risk Factors and Successful Interventions,* edited by Rolf Loeber and David P. Farrington. Thousand Oaks, Calif.: Sage.

Longmire, Dennis R. 1996. "Americans' Attitudes about the Ultimate Weapon: Capital Punishment." In *Americans View Crime and Justice: A National Public Opinion Survey,* edited by Timothy J. Flanagan and Dennis R. Longmire. Thousand Oaks, Calif.: Sage.

Maguire, Kathleen, and Ann L. Pastore, eds. 1995. *Sourcebook of Criminal Justice Statistics 1994.* Washington, D.C.: U.S. Department of Justice, Bureau of Justice Statistics.

———. 1997. *Sourcebook of Criminal Justice Statistics, 1996.* Washington, D.C.: U.S. Department of Justice, Bureau of Justice Statistics.

———. 1998. *Sourcebook of Criminal Justice Statistics, 1997.* Washington, D.C.: U.S. Department of Justice, Bureau of Justice Statistics.

McCorkle, Richard C. 1993. "Research Note: Punish and Rehabilitate? Public Attitudes toward Six Common Crimes." *Crime and Delinquency* 39: 240–52.

McGarrell, Edmund F., and Marla Sandys. 1996. "The Misperception of Public Opinion toward Capital Punishment." *American Behavioral Scientist* 39: 500–513.

Menninger, Karl. 1968. *The Crime of Punishment.* New York: Penguin.

Miller, Jerome G. 1991. *Last One over the Wall: The Massachusetts Experiment in Closing Reform Schools.* Columbus: Ohio State University Press.

Mitford, Jessica. 1971. *Kind and Usual Punishment: The Prison Business.* New York: Vintage.

Moon, Melissa M., Jody L. Sundt, John Paul Wright, and Francis T. Cullen. 2000. "Is Child Saving Dead? Public Support for Juvenile Rehabilitation." *Crime and Delinquency* 46:38–60.

Moon, Melissa M., John Paul Wright, Francis T. Cullen, and Jennifer A. Pealer. 1999. "Putting Kids to Death: Specifying Public Support for Juvenile Capital Punishment." Paper presented at the annual meeting of the Academy of Criminal Justice Sciences, Orlando, Fla., March 9–13.

Moore, David W. 1994. "Majority Advocate Death Penalty for Teenage Killers." *Gallup Poll Monthly* 348(September):2–6.

———. 1995. "Americans Firmly Support Death Penalty." *Gallup Poll Monthly* 357(June):23–25.

Morris, Norval, and Michael Tonry. 1990. *Between Prison and Probation: Intermediate Punishments in a Rational Sentencing System.* New York: Oxford University Press.

Muircheartaigh, Colm. 1997. "Measurement Error in Surveys: A Historical Perspective." In *Survey Measurement and Process Quality,* edited by Lars Lyberg, Paul Biemer, Martin Collins, Edith de Leeuw, Cathryn Dippo, Norbert Schwarz, and Dennis Trewin. New York: Wiley.

NAACP Legal Defense and Educational Fund. 1999. *Death Row U.S.A.* Spring issue. New York: NAACP.

Neuman, W. Russell. 1986. *The Paradox of Mass Politics: Knowledge and Opinion in the American Electorate.* Cambridge, Mass.: Harvard University Press.

Newport, Frank, and Lydia Saad. 1997. "Religious Faith Is Widespread but Many Skip Church." *Gallup Poll Monthly* 378(March):20–29.

Page, Benjamin I., and Robert Y. Shapiro. 1992. *The Rational Public: Fifty Years of Trends in Americans' Policy Preferences.* Chicago: University of Chicago Press.

Petersilia, Joan. 1997. "Probation in the United States." In *Crime and Justice: A Review of Research*, vol. 22, edited by Michael Tonry. Chicago: University of Chicago Press.

Petersilia, Joan, and Elizabeth Piper Deschenes. 1994. "What Punishes? Inmates Rank the Severity of Prison vs. Intermediate Sanctions." *Federal Probation* 58(1):3–8.

Petersilia, Joan, and Susan Turner. 1993. "Intensive Probation and Parole." In *Crime and Justice: A Review of Research*, vol. 17, edited by Michael Tonry. Chicago: University of Chicago Press.

Pettinico, George. 1994. "Crime and Punishment: America Changes Its Mind." *Public Perspective* 5(6):29–32.

Piehl, Anne Morrison, and John J. DiIulio, Jr. 1995. "'Does Prison Pay?' Revisited." *Brookings Review* 13(Winter):21–25.

Platt, Anthony M. 1969. *The Child Savers: The Invention of Delinquency.* Chicago: University of Chicago Press.

Rankin, Joseph H. 1979. "Changing Attitudes toward Capital Punishment." *Social Forces* 58:194–211.

Reichel, Philip L., and Angela Kailey Gauthier. 1990. "Boot Camp Corrections: A Public Reaction." In *Issues in Justice: Explaining Policy Issues in the Criminal Justice System*, edited by Roslyn Muraskin. Bristol, Ind.: Wyndham Hall Press.

Resources for Youth. 1998. *Mapping California's Opinion.* San Rafael, Calif.: Resources for Youth.

Rich, Robert F., and Robert J. Sampson. 1990. "Public Perceptions of Criminal Justice Policy: Does Victimization Make a Difference?" *Violence and Victims* 5:109–18.

Roberts, Julian V. 1992. "Public Opinion, Crime, and Criminal Justice." In *Crime and Justice: A Review of Research*, vol. 16, edited by Michael Tonry. Chicago: University of Chicago Press.

———. 1996. "Public Opinion, Criminal Record, and the Sentencing Process." *American Behavioral Scientist* 39:488–99.

Roberts, Julian V., Joan Nuffield, and Robert Hann. 1999. "Parole and the Public: Attitudinal and Behavioral Responses." Unpublished manuscript. Ottawa: University of Ottawa.

Roberts, Julian V., and Loretta J. Stalans. 1997. *Public Opinion, Crime, and Criminal Justice.* Boulder, Colo.: Westview.

———. 1998. "Crime, Criminal Justice, and Public Opinion." In *The Handbook of Crime and Punishment*, edited by Michael Tonry. New York: Oxford University Press.

Ross, E. A. 1907. *Sin and Society: An Analysis of Latter-Day Iniquity.* Gloucester, Mass.: Peter Smith.

Rossi, Peter H., and Richard A. Berk. 1997. *Just Punishments: Federal Guidelines and Public Views Compared.* New York: de Gruyter.

Rossi, Peter H., Richard A. Berk, and Alec Campbell. 1997. "Just Punishments: Guideline Sentences and Normative Consensus." *Journal of Quantitative Criminology* 13:267–90.

Rossi, Peter H., and Steven L. Nock, eds. 1982. *Measuring Social Judgments: The Factorial Survey Approach.* Beverly Hills, Calif.: Sage.

Rothman, David J. 1980. *Conscience and Convenience: The Asylum and Its Alternatives in Progressive America.* Boston: Little, Brown.

Sampson, Robert J., and John H. Laub. 1993. *Crime in the Making: Pathways and Turning Points through Life.* Cambridge, Mass.: Harvard University Press.

Sanders, Joseph, V. Lee Hamilton, and Toshiyuki Yuasa. 1998. "The Institutionalization of Sanctions for Wrongdoing Inside Organizations: Public Judgments in Japan, Russia, and the United States." *Law and Society Review* 32:871–929.

Sandys, Marla, and Edmund F. McGarrell. 1995. "Attitudes toward Capital Punishment: Preferences for the Penalty or Mere Acceptance?" *Journal of Research in Crime and Delinquency* 32:191–213.

———. 1997. "Beyond the Bible Belt: The Influence (or Lack Thereof) of Religion on Attitudes toward the Death Penalty." *Journal of Crime and Justice* 20:179–90.

Scheingold, Stuart A. 1984. *The Politics of Law and Order: Street Crime and Public Policy.* New York: Longman.

———. 1991. *The Politics of Street Crime: Criminal Process and Cultural Obsession.* Philadelphia: Temple University Press.

Schiraldi, Vincent, and Mark Soler. 1998. "The Will of the People? The Public's Opinion of the Violent and Repeat Juvenile Offender Act of 1997." *Crime and Delinquency* 44:590–601.

Schuman, Howard, and Stanley Presser. 1981. *Questions and Answers in Attitude Surveys: Experiment on Question Form, Wording, and Context.* New York: Academic Press.

Schwartz, Ira M. 1992. *Combatting Juvenile Crime: What the Public Really Wants?* Ann Arbor: University of Michigan, Center for the Study of Youth Policy.

Scull, Andrew. 1977. *Decarceration: Community Treatment and the Deviant—a Radical View.* Englewood Cliffs, N.J.: Prentice-Hall.

Senese, Jeffrey D. 1992. "Intensive Supervision Probation and Public Opinion: Perceptions of Community Correctional Policy and Practice." *American Journal of Criminal Justice* 16:33–56.

Sherman, Michael, and Gordon Hawkins. 1981. *Imprisonment in America: Choosing the Future.* Chicago: University of Chicago Press.

Shichor, David, and Dale K. Sechrest, eds. 1996. *Three Strikes and You're Out: Vengeance as Public Policy.* Thousand Oaks, Calif.: Sage.

Shorto, Russell. 1997. "Belief by the Numbers." *New York Times Magazine* (December 7), pp. 60–61.

Sickmund, Melissa, Howard N. Snyder, and Eileen Poe-Yamagata. 1997. *Juvenile Offenders and Victims: 1997 Update on Violence.* Washington, D.C.: U.S. Department of Justice, Office of Juvenile Justice and Delinquency Prevention.

Skovron, Sandra Evans, Joseph E. Scott, and Francis T. Cullen. 1988. "Prison Crowding: Public Attitudes toward Strategies of Population Control." *Journal of Research in Crime and Delinquency* 25:150–69.

———. 1989. "The Death Penalty for Juveniles: An Assessment of Public Support." *Crime and Delinquency* 35:546–61.

Smith, M. Dwayne. 1995 . "The Death Penalty in America." In *Criminology: A Contemporary Handbook*, edited by Joseph F. Sheley. 2d ed. Belmont, Calif.: Wadsworth.

Smith, Tom W. 1998. "Trendlets: B. Crime and Punishment: An Update." *GSS News* 12(August):5.

Sommer, Robert. 1976. *The End of Imprisonment.* New York: Oxford University Press.

Sparks, Richard. 1996. "Penal 'Austerity': The Doctrine of Less Eligibility Reborn?" In *Prisons 2000: An International Perspective on the Current State and Future of Imprisonment*, edited by Roger Matthews and Peter Francis. New York: St. Martin's.

Spelman, William. 1995. "The Severity of Intermediate Sanctions." *Journal of Quantitative Criminology* 32:107–35.

Sprott, Jane B. 1998. "Understanding Public Opposition to a Separate Youth Justice System." *Crime and Delinquency* 44:399–411.

Stalans, Loretta J., and Gary T. Henry. 1994. "Societal Views of Justice for Adolescents Accused of Murder: Inconsistency between Community Sentiment and Automatic Legislative Transfers." *Law and Human Behavior* 18: 675–96.

Steinhart, David. 1988. *California Opinion Poll: Public Attitudes on Youth Crime.* San Francisco: National Council on Crime and Delinquency.

Streib, Victor. 1998. "The Juvenile Death Penalty Today: Death Sentences and Executions for Juvenile Crimes, January 1973–October 1998." http://www.law.onu.edu/faculty/streib/juvdeath.htm.

Sundt, Jody L., Francis T. Cullen, Brandon K. Applegate, and Michael G. Turner. 1998. "The Tenacity of the Rehabilitative Ideal Revisited: Have Attitudes toward Rehabilitation Changed?" *Criminal Justice and Behavior* 25: 426–42.

Sutherland, Edwin H. 1940. "White-Collar Criminality." *American Sociological Review* 5:1–12.

Thomson, Douglas R., and Anthony J. Ragona. 1987. "Popular Moderation versus Governmental Authoritarianism: An Interactionist View of Public Sentiments toward Criminal Sanctions." *Crime and Delinquency* 33:337–57.

Toby, Jackson. 1964. "Is Punishment Necessary?" *Journal of Criminal Law, Criminology, and Police Science* 55:332–37.

Tonry, Michael. 1992. "Mandatory Penalties." In *Crime and Justice: A Review of Research*, vol. 16, edited by Michael Tonry. Chicago: University of Chicago Press.

———. 1995. *Malign Neglect: Race, Crime, and Punishment in America.* New York: Oxford University Press.

———. 1996. *Sentencing Matters.* New York: Oxford University Press.

———. 1998. "Intermediate Sanctions in Sentencing Guidelines." In *Crime and Justice: A Review of Research*, vol. 23, edited by Michael Tonry. Chicago: University of Chicago Press.

Triplett, Ruth. 1996. "The Growing Threat: Gangs and Juvenile Offenders." In *Americans View Crime and Justice: A National Public Opinion Survey*, edited by Timothy J. Flanagan and Dennis R. Longmire. Thousand Oaks, Calif.: Sage.

Turner, C. F., L. Ku, S. M. Rogers, L. D. Lindberg, J. H. Pleck, and F. L. Sonenstein. 1998. "Adolescent Sexual Behavior, Drug Use, and Violence: Increased Reporting with Computer Survey Technology." *Science* 280:867–73.

Turner, Michael G., Francis T. Cullen, Jody L. Sundt, and Brandon K. Applegate. 1997. "Public Tolerance for Community-Based Sanctions." *Prison Journal* 77:6–26.

Turner, Michael G., Jody L. Sundt, Brandon K. Applegate, and Francis T. Cullen. 1995. "'Three Strikes and You're Out' Legislation: A National Assessment." *Federal Probation* 59(3):16–35.

Tyler, Tom R., and Robert J. Boeckmann. 1997. "Three Strikes and You Are Out, but Why? The Psychology of Public Support for Punishing Rule Breakers?" *Law and Society Review* 31:237–65.

Van Ness, Daniel, and Karen Heetderks Strong. 1997. *Restoring Justice*. Cincinnati: Anderson.

Wald, Kenneth D. 1992. *Religion and Politics in the United States*. Washington, D.C.: Congressional Quarterly.

Wall Street Journal. 1994. "Dick Tracy Wins." *Wall Street Journal* (January 26), p. A14.

Walther, Lynne, and John Perry. 1997. "The Vermont Reparative Probation Program." *ICCA Journal on Community Corrections* 13(2):26–34.

Warr, Mark. 1980. "The Accuracy of Public Beliefs about Crime." *Social Forces* 59:470.

———. 1982. "The Accuracy of Public Beliefs about Crime: Further Evidence." *Criminology* 20:185–204.

———. 1994. "Public Perceptions and Reactions to Violent Offending and Victimization." In *Understanding and Preventing Violence: Consequences and Control*, vol. 4, edited by Albert J. Reiss, Jr., and Jeffrey A. Roth. Washington, D.C.: National Academy Press.

———. 1995a. "The Polls—Poll Trends: Public Opinion on Crime and Punishment." *Public Opinion Quarterly* 59:296–310.

———. 1995b. "Public Perceptions of Crime and Punishment." In *Criminology: A Contemporary Handbook*, 2d ed., edited by Joseph F. Sheley. Belmont, Calif.: Wadsworth.

Warr, Mark, Robert F. Meier, and Maynard L. Erickson. 1983. "Norms, Theories of Punishment, and Publicly Preferred Penalties for Crimes." *Sociological Quarterly* 24:75–91.

Warr, Mark, and Mark Stafford. 1984. "Public Goals of Punishment and Support for the Death Penalty." *Journal of Research in Crime and Delinquency* 21:95–111.

Whitehead, John T. 1998. "'Good Ol' Boys' and the Chair: Death Penalty

Attitudes and Policy Makers in Tennessee." *Crime and Delinquency* 44:245–56.

Williams, Frank P., III, Dennis R. Longmire. and David B. Gulick. 1988. "The Public and the Death Penalty: Opinion as an Artifact of Question Type." *Criminal Justice Research Bulletin* 3:1–5.

Wilson, Edward O. 1998. *Consilience: The Unity of Knowledge.* New York: Vintage.

Wilson, James Q. 1975. *Thinking about Crime.* New York: Basic Books.

Young, Robert L. 1991. "Race, Conceptions of Crime and Justice, and Support for the Death Penalty." *Social Psychological Quarterly* 54:67–75.

———. 1992. "Religious Orientation, Race, and Support for the Death Penalty." *Journal for the Scientific Study of Religion* 31:76–87.

Young, Robert L., and Carol Y. Thompson. 1995. "Religious Fundamentalism, Punitiveness, and Firearm Ownership." *Journal of Crime and Justice* 18:81–98.

Zeisel, Hans, and Alec M. Gallup. 1989. "Death Penalty Sentiments in the United States." *Journal of Quantitative Criminology* 5:285–96.

Zimmerman, Sherwood E., David J. Van Alstyne, and Christopher S. Dunn. 1988. "The National Punishment Survey and Public Policy Consequences." *Journal of Research in Crime and Delinquency* 25:120–49.

Donna M. Bishop

Juvenile Offenders in the Adult Criminal Justice System

ABSTRACT

Most state legislatures have instituted punitive reforms in response to rising rates of youth crime, including provisions that transfer an increasing number and range of adolescents to criminal courts for adult prosecution. Proponents assert that juvenile court sanctions and services constitute neither just nor effective responses to savvy juvenile offenders and propose that criminal prosecution will insure more proportionate punishments, provide more effective deterrence, and achieve greater incapacitation. The empirical evidence is too limited to be definitive, but it suggests that most of those assertions are wrong. Expansive transfer policies send many minor and nonthreatening offenders to the adult system, exacerbate racial disparities, and move adolescents with special needs into correctional systems ill prepared to handle them. Transfer results in more severe penalties for some offenders, but there is no evidence that it achieves either general or specific deterrent effects. There is credible evidence that prosecution and punishment in the adult system increase the likelihood of recidivism, offsetting incapacitative gains. Transfer also exposes young people to heightened vulnerability to a host of unfortunate experiences and outcomes.

Transfer of juvenile defendants to criminal courts for adult prosecution has traditionally been justified on the grounds that the juvenile court is ill equipped to handle two classes of offenders. In cases of seri-

Donna M. Bishop is associate professor of criminal justice in the College of Criminal Justice at Northeastern University. This essay is based on an earlier essay prepared with Charles E. Frazier for publication in *The Changing Borders of Juvenile Justice: Transfer of Adolescents to the Criminal Court* (edited by Jeffrey Fagan and Franklin E. Zimring [Chicago: University of Chicago Press, forthcoming]). I am grateful to Charles Frazier for his assistance with the earlier version and to Ruth Peterson and Michael Tonry for their thoughtful comments and suggestions.

ously violent crimes, the public has historically demanded heavy penalties that exceed the authority of the juvenile court (Tanenhaus, forthcoming). While commission of a repugnant act neither transforms a young offender into a fully responsible adult nor makes her a poor candidate for juvenile intervention, such considerations are largely irrelevant. The community will not tolerate mild responses to heinous offenses. Removal to the criminal court makes possible the imposition of harsh punishments believed to be more justly deserved.[1] The other class traditionally targeted for removal consists of chronic offenders who have been afforded all appropriate interventions at the juvenile court's disposal and have not responded to them. The court reasonably concludes that they are so intractable that further efforts to reform them would be futile. As a last resort, they are transferred to criminal courts that are better equipped to incapacitate those who present a continuing threat to the public welfare.

The historical record shows that although judicial waiver was available in nearly all states from the inception of their juvenile courts, in practice it was used very rarely (Flicker 1981; Whitebread and Batey 1981; Tanenhaus, forthcoming). Sparing use of transfer is consistent with foundational principles of the juvenile court, according to which juveniles differ from adults in ways that generally make criminal processing inappropriate and counterproductive. A fundamental tenet is that adolescents are immature (Bernard 1992; Scott and Grisso 1997; Feld 1999). Their lesser capacities for reasoning and moral judgment diminish their culpability and render them undeserving of the full burden of retributive punishments (Zimring 1981, 1991, 1998; Forst and Blomquist 1991; Scott and Grisso 1997). Moreover, from a purely utilitarian perspective, their limited ability to anticipate and weigh long-term consequences makes it unlikely that threats of criminal sanctions will deter them (Teitelbaum 1991).[2] Finally, cultural conceptions of

---

[1] From the beginning, juvenile courts responded to the public outrage generated by heinous offenses by subordinating the interests of youths to demands for penal proportionality (Tanenhaus 1999). Although transfer of these cases was inconsistent with basic precepts of the juvenile court, it was politically expedient. Demands for harsh punishment threatened the legitimacy of the court and its therapeutic mission (Zimring 1981, 1991; Bortner 1986). By relinquishing authority over a few seriously violent offenders, the court placated the public and preserved its rehabilitative commitment to the vast majority of juveniles (see also Sargent and Gordon 1963; Feld 1978).

[2] Not long ago, the Supreme Court of Nevada affirmed this premise when it observed: "It is questionable whether a thirteen-year-old can even imagine or comprehend what it means to be imprisoned for sixty years or more" (Naovarath v. State, 779 P.2d 944 at 947 [Nev. 1989]).

children and adolescents have traditionally emphasized youths' dependency and vulnerability, characteristics that tend to evoke compassionate responses rather than punitive ones.

Another foundational assumption is that teens are more malleable than adults. Adolescence is understood as a transitional period that involves exploration of new roles and behaviors. In this view, youths' bad actions are more often transitory than prophetic. Prudent social policy gives youths "room to reform" (Zimring 1982, 1998) by responding to adolescent missteps in ways that do not interfere with the normal transition to responsible adulthood (Zimring 1982, 1998). From this perspective, transfer is ill advised because it exposes young people to the stigmatizing consequences of a criminal conviction and because it may result in lengthy incarceration that fosters dependency at a critical stage when youths should be moving toward independence.

Malleability also implies that young people are especially susceptible to external influences. It suggests that they are well suited to efforts to shape them in positive ways (Scott and Grisso 1997), making rehabilitative strategies particularly attractive. It also denotes that they need to be shielded from negative influences. The traditional view has been that criminal punishment might do serious harm by exposing youths to the corrupting influence of mature and experienced offenders in adult correctional facilities. Indeed, the perceived evil of mixing impressionable young offenders with adult criminals was a primary force behind the development of a separate juvenile justice system (Fox 1970; Whisenand and McLaughlin 1982). For all these reasons, then, resort to the criminal court has historically been viewed as appropriate only in instances where youths were seen as irredeemable, either on moral grounds or as a matter of fact.

In the past two decades, and for a variety of reasons, legislators and justice officials have become more sanguine about criminal punishment of young offenders (Feld 1999). Rapid increases in juvenile crime in the 1970s led many to question the juvenile court's effectiveness. A series of negative appraisals of juvenile treatment programs (e.g., Lipton, Martinson, and Wilks 1975; Wright and Dixon 1975; Sechrest, White, and Brown 1979) prompted further skepticism. Proponents of rehabilitation countered that negative assessments reflected methodological flaws, weak evaluation research, and poor program implementation rather than the absence of viable treatment methods (e.g., Palmer 1991; Lipsey 1992; Fagan and Forst 1996), but these responses drew little attention. Juvenile justice policy gradually shifted away from the *parens patriae* mission to provide individualized treatment toward schemes in which punishment played an increasing role (Feld 1987, 1988; Torbet et al. 1996).[3] A "get tough" movement was born that gained momentum in the late 1980s, fueled by yet another crime wave. This new surge was marked by sharp increases in gun crimes and homicides, especially among minority youths (Snyder and Sickmund 1995; Cook and Laub 1998). Almost contemporaneously, ideas about adolescent offenders began to shift (Scott and Grisso 1997). Media accounts (e.g., Annin 1996), public officials, and even some academics (Bennett, DiIulio, and Walters 1996) portrayed them as vicious and savvy, challenging the more benign images of the past. Conceptions of juvenile offenders as adult-like, incipient career criminals legitimized a different set of penal responses. For offenders who are by no means "worst cases,"[4] legislators began to demand more in the name of desert than the juvenile court could provide and touted the virtues of criminal punishment for social defense.

The transformation of transfer policy has been quick and dramatic. Between 1992 and 1997, legislatures in forty-four states and the District of Columbia enacted provisions to facilitate the removal of young offenders to criminal court (Torbet et al. 1996; Torbet and Szymanski 1998). To make transfer more expedient, they established offense-based, categorical, and absolute alternatives to individualized, offender-oriented waiver proceedings in the juvenile court (Feld 1987; Dawson, forthcoming). Besides streamlining the transfer process, most states expanded the list of cases eligible for transfer by making modifications in offense, age, and prior record criteria. Others took a far more sweeping approach and lowered the maximum age of the juvenile court's original jurisdiction, thereby transferring entire age categories of young offenders no matter what the offense. As a result, in many states transfer implicates a broad range of offenders who are neither

[3] The shift was manifest in a number of ways. Notions of "just desert," long absent from the lexicon of juvenile jurisprudence, gained popularity. In many states, juvenile justice purposes clauses were rewritten to emphasize sanctions and accountability and to elevate concerns about public safety (Torbet and Szymanski 1998). About one-third of the states followed Washington's lead in implementing determinate sentencing in the juvenile courts, and several established mandatory minimum sentences for designated felonies. Rates of confinement increased markedly. Nearly one-third of the states extended into the adult years the continuing jurisdiction of juvenile courts over youths under supervision (Torbet et al. 1996; Torbet and Szymanski 1998). For a comprehensive discussion and analysis of these changes, see Feld (1999).

[4] For example, in 1999 the Florida legislature authorized the transfer of juveniles as young as fourteen who are charged with a second offense of auto theft (Florida Statutes, Title 47, § 985.227).

particularly serious nor particularly chronic, some of whom are not yet in their teens.

The pace and direction of these reforms are consistent with either of two conclusions. In their zeal for retribution, policy makers fail to comprehend or are willing to ignore the jeopardy into which large numbers of adolescents are placed as a result of criminal processing and punishment. Alternatively, they trust that criminal punishment will ultimately prove beneficial to young offenders and to society—by deterring youths in ways that juvenile justice sanctions cannot and by incapacitating them for longer periods. In either event, we must be concerned about consequences.

The purpose of this essay is to examine the effects of transfer from several vantage points. The ongoing debate about juvenile and criminal court line-drawing must be informed by an appreciation of what is at stake for the system, for young offenders, and for society. Three broad goals define the structure of the inquiry: to identify how transfer practices and trends affect (and are likely to affect) the organization and operation of juvenile and criminal courts and correctional agencies; to review what is known about the effects on young offenders of criminal court processing and exposure to adult correctional environments; and to consider the implications of transfer for crime control.

My overall conclusion is that the recent and substantial expansion of transfer has been ill advised for a number of reasons. It has produced large increases in the number of juvenile offenders prosecuted, convicted, and sentenced to adult sanctions, many of whom are young, nonviolent, and charged with minor crimes. Recent reforms disproportionately affect minority youths, producing racial disparities that are likely to grow if current trends continue. From an organizational standpoint, the expansion of transfer places additional burdens on already overtaxed adult courts and correctional agencies. It also presents significant correctional security and programming issues, new problems of interagency articulation, and the prospect of widening the net of control over lesser offenders who remain in the juvenile system.

Extant studies of the effectiveness of transfer as a crime control policy are too few to be definitive, but they all point toward the same conclusions. There is no evidence that transfer has any general deterrent value: the enactment and implementation of well-publicized transfer legislation does not appear to decrease the incidence of target offenses. Similarly, there is no evidence that transfer has marginal specific deterrent benefits over processing in the juvenile system. The existing research indicates that juveniles prosecuted as adults reoffend more quickly and at rates equal to or higher than comparable youths retained in the juvenile system. When transfer is applied broadly to offenders who are neither particularly serious nor particularly chronic, any short-term incapacitative gains appear to be quickly offset.

Drawing on corrections research, I suggest that the differential effects of juvenile and criminal justice processing may be due in part to negative consequences associated with criminal prosecution and punishment. Qualitative research on the subjective experiences of young offenders in the juvenile and criminal justice systems suggests that criminal court processing frequently engenders a sense of injustice, which undercuts the legitimacy of the criminal sanction. The same research also points to multiple iatrogenic effects of incarceration in the adult system, including exposure to negative shaming, opportunities for criminal socialization, and modeling of violence. Other corrections research corroborates these conclusions and additionally suggests that the adult penal system is limited in its capacity to respond to the needs of adolescent offenders. Differential effects of juvenile and criminal justice processing may also be linked to the stigmatization that follows from a criminal conviction, which reduces offenders' opportunities to obtain legitimate employment and become integrated into conventional social networks. Finally, that youths processed in the juvenile system do better than comparable youths prosecuted as adults may be attributable in part to positive effects of exposure to some juvenile correctional interventions. Recent meta-analyses of correctional program evaluations, as well as qualitative research on youths' subjective reactions to correctional environments, indicate that substantial benefits are associated with behavioral, skills-focused programs that provide intense staff-youth interaction over a period of several months.

While broad transfer policies may serve the goal of retribution, they do so at a considerable price. The same end might be better attained by modestly extending the upper boundary of the juvenile court's continuing jurisdiction. In light of recent credible evidence of the effectiveness of some intensive treatment strategies, it seems that the goals of doing justice and controlling crime may both be advanced by retaining the vast majority of transferred offenders in a juvenile system with extended jurisdiction and an expanded portfolio of carefully selected treatment options.

This essay is organized in five parts. In Section I, I provide an overview of recent transfer reforms and estimate the reach of jurisdictional

shifts, including the number and characteristics of adolescents transferred nationwide and the processing and outcomes of their cases. The
discussion of transfer strategies and reforms is informed by several recent and comprehensive reviews (Torbet et al. 1996; Griffin, Torbet,
and Szymanski 1998; Torbet and Szymanski 1998).[5] Data on national
trends and practices are derived primarily from statistical reporting
programs maintained by the Office of Juvenile Justice and Delinquency
Prevention (OJJDP) and the Bureau of Justice Statistics (BJS). To fill
some gaps in the series data and to illustrate cross-jurisdictional variations in practice, I also discuss selected local, state, and regional quantitative studies.

Section II explores systemic implications of transfer for the administration of justice. I draw inferences from the trends reported in Section
I regarding caseload issues for the criminal justice system and discuss
problems of articulation between the juvenile and criminal justice systems. The discussion of systemic consequences is also informed by surveys of correctional officials and by quantitative research on young offenders' adjustment in adult correctional settings (e.g., Goetting and
Howsen 1986; McShane and Williams 1989; Memory 1989). I also
consider how transfer trends are likely to affect the juvenile justice system. I rely on the single study of how the implementation of transfer
laws affected juvenile court operations in one state (Singer 1996) and
on evaluations of other juvenile reform initiatives (e.g., Klein 1976;
Blomberg 1979) to draw some inferences about potential consequences
for the juvenile system.

Section III reviews the literature on the effectiveness of transfer as
a method of crime control. Two quantitative studies have explored
general deterrent effects associated with the implementation of transfer legislation (Singer and McDowall 1988; Jensen and Metsger 1994).
Another small body of research has assessed the comparative advantages of juvenile versus criminal justice processing in terms of levels of
incapacitation achieved and effects on recidivism (Fagan 1991, 1995,
1996; Bishop et al. 1996; Winner et al. 1997).

In Section IV I consider the impact on young people of processing
and punishment in the adult system. With the juvenile system as a
point of contrast, I take a hard look at criminal court processing and
adult correctional environments, and consider the responses of youths

[5] See Heilbrun et al. (1997), Merlo, Benekos, and Cook (1997), and Redding (1997)
for more detailed review and analysis.

to processing and incarceration in the two systems. This section is informed by objective data on juvenile and adult corrections systems, by research on special problems faced by adolescents in adult correctional settings, and by other corrections research that has uncovered some potentially important links between organizational goals and inmate attitudes and behaviors. I draw especially heavily on the only qualitative studies to have compared the court and correctional experiences of transferred youths with those of adolescents processed in the juvenile system. Forst, Fagan, and Vivona (1989) interviewed violent juvenile offenders in four states in the mid-1980s, half of whom were incarcerated in adult prisons and half of whom were incarcerated in juvenile training schools. My colleagues and I (Bishop et al. 1998) interviewed adolescent offenders in Florida in 1997, including transferred youths in adult prisons and a comparison group of offenders housed in deep-end juvenile justice programs. Research from the vantage point of offenders is limited: the studies are few, the samples are small, and the jurisdictions represented may not be typical. However, when findings of these studies are considered in conjunction with other research reported in this section, conclusions about the differential impacts of criminal and juvenile justice processing seem warranted. In Section V, I consider theoretical frameworks that may be useful in interpreting observed differences in the behavioral trajectories of youths processed in juvenile and criminal courts. The essay concludes with a discussion of policy implications and suggestions for future research.

I. Changes in Transfer Law and Practice

The traditional approach to deciding whether a youth should be treated as a juvenile or prosecuted as an adult has been to vest the juvenile court with authority to waive jurisdiction on a discretionary basis (Feld 1987). Judicial waiver statutes most often set very expansive eligibility criteria,[6] giving judges a great deal of discretion when making waiver decisions. In 1966 the Supreme Court made the judicial waiver process more cumbersome when, in an effort to introduce greater regularity to decision making, it ruled that juveniles are constitutionally entitled to a formal hearing and a determination of their suitability for transfer in accordance with explicit criteria (*Kent v. United States* 383

---

[6] Typical is the Illinois statute, which permits judicial waiver of juveniles age thirteen and older charged with any criminal offense (705 ILCS 405/5-4). For a description of applicable statutes in each state at the end of 1997, see Griffin, Torbet, and Szymanski (1998).

U.S. 541). In response to *Kent,* states most often required the court to determine whether a youth is "amenable to treatment" or "poses a danger to the public" and, in making that determination, to consider eight criteria endorsed in *Kent* related to the offender's background and circumstances, his prior record and past treatment, and the seriousness of his offense. Following the *Kent* decision, the waiver process became protracted and highly adversarial (Dawson, forthcoming), which undoubtedly contributed to the spate of legislation endorsing more expedient transfer methods (Feld, forthcoming; White et al. 1999).

A. Transfer Reforms

Expedited transfer strategies shift the locus of decision making from the judicial to the legislative or executive branches and replace individualized, offender-oriented decision making with categorical approaches that most often focus on the seriousness of the offense (Feld, forthcoming). Legislative exclusion removes certain offenses (or offense/age combinations) from the jurisdiction of the juvenile court. All youths who meet the statutory criteria are automatically tried in criminal court, subject only to a prosecutorial decision to charge one of the enumerated offenses. In 1998, twenty-eight states use legislative exclusion (see table 1), compared to only eleven states two decades earlier (Hamparian et al. 1982).[7]

All of the current exclusion statutes apply to one or more serious violent felonies. In addition, consistent with my observations regarding lowered thresholds of tolerance for juvenile crime, many statutes have been modified to exclude lesser offenses against persons as well as drug, weapons, and property offenses (Griffin, Torbet, and Szymanski 1998). The Illinois experience is instructive. When enacted in 1982, Illinois' exclusion statute applied only to youths fifteen and older charged with first degree murder, aggravated sexual assault, and robbery with a firearm. In 1985, it was amended to include drug and weapons (not simply firearm) offenses that take place in or near schools. In 1990 in an action that clearly had an impact on minorities and the poor, it was modified once again to include drug and weapons (not simply firearm) offenses that take place on or near public housing, as well as gang-related felonies. In 1995, the law was changed yet again

---

[7] Some states exclude only traffic, water craft, and fish and game violations. States that exclude only these minor offenses are not included in these counts.

TABLE 1
Transfer Provisions, Upper Age of Juvenile Court Jurisdiction (1998), and Expansion of Transfer (1992–98)

State	Judicial Waiver			Direct File	Statutory Exclusion	Reverse Waiver	Once an Adult, Always an Adult	Upper Age Jurisdiction	Criteria Expanded since 1992
	Discretionary	Mandatory	Presumptive						
AL	x				x		x	17	x
AK	x		x		x			17	x
AZ	x		x	x	x	x	x	17	x
AR	x			x		x		17	x
CA	x		x				x	17	x
CO	x		x	x		x		17	x
CT		x				x		15	x
DE	x	x			x	x	x	17	x
DC	x		x	x			x	17	x
FL	x		x	x	x		x	17	x
GA	x	x		x	x	x		16	x
HI	x						x	17	x
ID	x				x		x	17	x
IL	x	x	x		x			16	x
IN	x	x			x		x	17	x
IO	x				x	x	x	17	x
KS	x		x				x	17	x
KY	x	x				x		17	x
LA	x	x		x	x			16	x
ME	x						x	17	
MD	x				x	x		17	x
MA		x		x	x			16	x

90

State							Year (15–17)	
MI	x			x			16	
MN	x		x		x		17	x
MS	x		x			x	17	x
MO	x				x		16	x
MT	x		x		x	x	17	
NE	x			x		x	17	x
NV	x				x	x	17	x
NH	x					x	16	
NJ	x		x			x	17	
NM					x	x	17	x
NY					x	x	15	x
NC	x	x				x	15	
ND	x	x					17	x
OH	x		x			x	17	x
OK	x			x	x	x	17	x
OR	x				x	x	17	x
PA	x		x		x	x	17	x
RI	x	x		x	x	x	17	x
SC	x	x			x	x	16	
SD	x					x	17	x
TN	x						17	x
TX	x						16	x
UT	x		x		x	x	17	x
VT	x			x	x	x	17	x
VA	x	x			x	x	17	x
WA	x				x	x	17	
WV	x		x	x	x	x	17	x
WI	x						16	x
WY	x			x	x	x	17	x

SOURCES.—Torbet et al. 1996, figs. 3 and 4; Griffin, Torbet, and Szymanski 1998; and Torbet and Szymanski 1998, tables 2 and 3.

91

to lower the age limit to thirteen for murder and sexual assault (Clarke 1996). Although originally designed to apply to very serious offenders, the statute was expanded incrementally to include felonies of only moderate severity and to encompass youths barely in their teens.

Prosecutorial waiver (or direct file) gives juvenile and criminal courts concurrent jurisdiction over cases meeting certain offense, age, and/or prior record criteria and vests the prosecutor with discretionary authority to select the forum in which youths meeting these criteria will be tried. Only seven states permitted prosecutorial waiver in 1978 (Hamparian et al. 1982), but fifteen did in 1998 (see table 1). Prosecutorial waiver statutes are typically much broader than exclusion statutes and frequently target a wide range of offenses and offenders. In Florida, for example, prosecutors may transfer sixteen- and seventeen-year-olds charged with any felony; sixteen- and seventeen-year-olds charged with any misdemeanor if they have two prior convictions, one of which involved a felony; and fourteen- or fifteen-year-olds charged with any of several enumerated offenses.[8]

In two other streamlined approaches, transfer remains at least nominally a function of the juvenile court. Fourteen states in 1998 provided for mandatory judicial waiver, which requires the juvenile court to waive offenders meeting certain criteria. Most often, mandatory waiver statutes target youths charged with serious felonies against person. Because the juvenile court has no authority to retain jurisdiction over cases where the statutory criteria are met, for all intents and purposes mandatory judicial waiver is equivalent to legislative exclusion. Presumptive judicial waiver, used in fifteen states in 1998, creates a rebuttable presumption in favor of waiver and shifts the burden to the defendant to prove that waiver is not justified. Usually, the defendant must demonstrate that she is amenable to treatment in the juvenile justice system. The criteria that trigger the presumption that waiver is appropriate differ widely across jurisdictions. Some focus on violent offenses, regardless of the age of the offender; others focus on older offenders, regardless of the seriousness of the offense; still others emphasize prior record (Griffin, Torbet, and Szymanski 1998).

[8] The offenses are arson; sexual battery; robbery; kidnapping; aggravated child abuse; aggravated assault; aggravated stalking; murder; manslaughter; unlawful throwing, placing, or discharging of a destructive device or bomb; armed burglary; aggravated battery; lewd or lascivious assault or act in the presence of a child; carrying, displaying, using, threatening, or attempting to use a weapon or firearm during the commission of a felony; grand theft in the first degree; and second-offense auto theft. Waiver is permitted "when in the state attorney's judgment and discretion the public interest requires that adult sanctions be considered or imposed" (Florida Statutes, chap. 985.227 [1] [a]).

Table 1 shows the status of transfer provisions in the fifty states and the District of Columbia as of 1998.[9] It can be seen that only five states continue to rely exclusively on discretionary judicial waiver, and five no longer use it at all. Of those that no longer use discretionary waiver, three rely exclusively on mandatory judicial waiver or legislative exclusion, one uses prosecutorial waiver exclusively, and one uses a combination of legislative exclusion and prosecutorial waiver. Forty-one jurisdictions use discretionary judicial waiver in combination with other strategies. Frequently, three or more strategies are in place (twenty jurisdictions). When more than one strategy is available, they often overlap: cases eligible for discretionary judicial waiver often can be transferred more expeditiously through an alternative method.

The last column of table 1 shows that most states have recently expanded the substantive criteria for transfer (Torbet et al. 1996; Torbet and Szymanski 1998). Between 1992 and 1997, twenty-seven states added crimes to the list of legislatively excluded offenses and seven lowered the age limits on excluded offenses. Eleven expanded prosecutorial waiver provisions to encompass more crimes, a broader age range of offender, or both. Seventeen added crimes eligible for judicial waiver and fourteen lowered the age limits for judicial waiver. In many jurisdictions, transfer can be applied to youths who are not yet in their teens.[10]

In addition, some states have adopted what has been called a "wholesale" approach to transfer (Feld 1999) by simply lowering the maximum age of the juvenile court's original jurisdiction. Table 1 shows that the traditional boundary line dividing the juvenile and criminal courts—the eighteenth birthday—is not applicable in thirteen states. In three states, juvenile offenders become adults at age sixteen, and in ten states at age seventeen (Griffin, Torbet, and Szymanski 1998).[11] Although not usually thought of as "transfers," these juveniles face criminal prosecution, jailing, incarceration in state prison facilities, and all of the other consequences of transfer discussed below.

---

[9] See Griffin, Torbet, and Szymanski (1998) for a more complete description of each method and for the criteria and procedures that apply in each state.

[10] Kansas and Vermont permit transfer of offenders as young as age ten; Colorado, Missouri, and Montana allow transfer at age twelve; and twenty-three states have at least one transfer provision for which no minimum age is specified (Griffin, Torbet, and Szymanski 1998).

[11] Since 1992, three states—New Hampshire, Wisconsin, and Wyoming—lowered the maximum age of original juvenile court jurisdiction (Sickmund, Snyder, and Poe-Yamagata 1997).

Table 1 also shows that twenty-three states had adopted reverse waiver provisions, which allow the criminal courts to return transferred cases to the juvenile system. Most often, cases are eligible for reverse waiver when they come to the criminal courts through mandatory judicial waiver, legislative exclusion, or prosecutorial waiver, that is, in circumstances where the juvenile courts have not had an opportunity to consider youths' suitability for removal from the juvenile system. Reverse waiver hearings frequently employ *Kent* standards and criteria (i.e., the focus is on amenability to treatment and dangerousness). Nineteen states and the District of Columbia in 1998 used one or more transfer methods that circumvent the juvenile courts but have no provision for reverse waiver. In these jurisdictions, transfer decisions made by prosecutors are not subject to any sort of judicial review: they are absolute.

Thirty-one jurisdictions adopted the policy of "once an adult, always an adult" (see table 1). In twenty-six of these, youths who have been transferred to criminal court must be prosecuted as adults for all subsequent offenses. In the other five, the policy applies more restrictively to some categories of offenses or to offenders above a certain age (Griffin, Torbet, and Szymanski 1998).[12] Thirteen of the jurisdictions with unrestricted "once an adult, always an adult" policies do not permit reverse waiver although they provide for mandatory judicial waiver, legislative exclusion, or prosecutorial waiver. In these jurisdictions, initial transfer decisions made categorically and without judicial oversight trigger automatic prosecution as an adult for any subsequent offense.

B. Adolescents in Adult Court

Surprisingly little information is available on the numbers and characteristics of juveniles transferred to criminal court nationwide. There has been only one comprehensive national study of transfer (Hamparian et al. 1982). It involved a long and painstaking effort to collect data on cases transferred by each method from automated and paper files covering over 3,100 counties in 1978. The study is outdated but provides an important basis for historical comparison.

Reliable national estimates of cases waived judicially, including

---

[12] In three states, "once adult/always adult" is limited in its application to subsequent felonies. In one other, it applies only to youths who are at least sixteen, and in yet another it is restricted to youths sixteen or older who are charged with a transferable offense (Griffin, Torbet, and Szymanski 1998).

counts and characteristics of waived offenders, have been published for many years from data routinely collected by juvenile courts and assembled in the National Juvenile Court Data Archive (NJCDA).[13] As long as discretionary judicial waiver remained the vehicle used to transfer almost all cases, the NJCDA data were quite adequate for the purpose of tracking national transfer trends and practices. However, data collection efforts have not kept pace with transfer reforms. The NJCDA data do not distinguish discretionary waivers from mandatory and presumptive ones, nor do they include information on transfers that altogether bypass the juvenile courts. For information on youths transferred through legislative exclusion and prosecutorial waiver, we must look to criminal court and prosecutorial record-keeping systems. Unfortunately, within the population of criminal defendants, prosecutors and court officials traditionally have not viewed a defendant's age as a particularly important variable. In those states where offenders age sixteen or seventeen are legally defined as adults, it is difficult to find counts, descriptors, or processing information for this subset of the criminal population. When state courts do record information on transferred offenders, their record-keeping systems rarely differentiate among offenders transferred via different methods.

In the 1990s several national reporting programs operated by BJS began to gather data from state criminal courts and prosecutor's offices regarding both transferred offenders and offenders under age eighteen who are legally defined as adults.[14] Unlike the NJCDA data, none is a

[13] Data on youths processed in juvenile courts, including those judicially waived to criminal courts, are included in the NJCDA, which is maintained by the National Center for Juvenile Justice (for descriptions of the data, see Sickmund et al. 1998; Stahl 1999). The data are generated from nonprobability samples of cases referred to juvenile courts that cover approximately two-thirds of the youth population at risk. Weighted estimation procedures are used to generate national estimates. Although these procedures cannot completely overcome threats to validity associated with nonprobability samples, the estimates are believed to be reasonably accurate.

[14] National data on offenders under eighteen prosecuted in state criminal courts are compiled in BJS's biannual National Survey of Prosecutors (NSP), State Court Processing Statistics (SCPS), and National Judicial Reporting Program (NJRP) collections. The NSP collects prosecutorial filing data from a nationally representative sample of prosecutors' offices serving courts of general jurisdiction. The data include both felony and misdemeanor cases. (The misdemeanor data are not representative because courts of limited jurisdiction are excluded from the data collection). The SCPS obtains charge, conviction, and sentencing data, for felony cases only, from a sample of courts representing the nations seventy-five most populous counties. Felony cases in these seventy-five counties account for approximately half of these cases nationally (Bureau of Justice Statistics 1999a). The NJRP gathers information on characteristics of convicted felons and the sentences they receive. The data come from court and prosecutorial records in a nationally representative sample of felony courts. The three reporting programs use different but overlapping samples.

census. Each reporting program uses a different sampling technique and sampling frame: some samples are nationally representative while others are not, making comparison across data sets difficult. The unit of count also differs across reporting programs, a problem that is compounded by lack of uniformity across jurisdictions in definitions, reporting methods, transfer mechanisms and, of course, the availability of data. There are also some significant gaps in the data collected by the national reporting programs. They cannot be disaggregated to identify cases transferred through legislative exclusion or prosecutorial waiver, making it impossible to assess national numbers and trends in the use of these strategies or to describe characteristics of youths transferred by them. There are also no data at the national level on reverse waiver. We might try to fill the gaps with data from several states. However, of the fifteen states that employ prosecutorial waiver, only a few maintain good records (General Accounting Office 1995), and, in most states, data on legislative exclusion and reverse waiver are either spotty or nonexistent.

At the corrections level, BJS has several reporting programs that collect sample survey and census data from local jails and state correctional agencies.[15] Although jail record-keeping systems generally include information on inmates' ages, neither the national nor most state reporting systems differentiate between juveniles awaiting criminal prosecution and those sentenced as adults. Prior to 1994, the national jail reporting system also failed to differentiate between youths held for processing in the juvenile versus the adult systems. National record-keeping systems on persons admitted to state prisons and other state correctional programs are generally thought to be quite reliable and include information on offender age as well as other sociodemographic and offense characteristics. However, because corrections reporting programs typically record only age at admission, it is difficult to generate accurate counts of transferred offenders. Time from arrest to conviction for felony defendants averages several months (Brown,

---

[15] Information on juveniles in adult correctional systems nationwide is limited. Counts of juveniles held in jail are included in BJS's Annual Survey of Jails and in the Jail Census. BJS's National Corrections Reporting Program (NCRP) gathers information from state departments of corrections, including data on the age distribution of new admissions and of the general correctional population. These data cover approximately 90 percent of state prison admissions (Beck 1998). In addition to these sources, the National Institute of Corrections and the American Correctional Association occasionally conduct surveys of correctional administrators that include information on inmates under age eighteen.

Langan, and Levin 1999), is frequently much longer for transferred youths, and is highly variable. Consequently, many offenders admitted to the adult corrections system at age eighteen or even nineteen were probably seventeen or younger at the time of their offenses.

For all of these reasons, it is very risky to try to draw any definitive conclusions about the effects of transfer reforms in terms of the numbers and kinds of offenders transferred through various methods and their movement through the justice system. However, mindful of the limitations of the data, I think it is reasonable to offer at least some broadly bounded estimates of the total number of juveniles transferred. For 1996, I estimate that at least 210,000 and as many as 260,000 offenders under eighteen were prosecuted in the nation's criminal courts. Of these, 180,000–220,000 youths were prosecuted as adults in the thirteen states that draw the boundary line separating juvenile from criminal court jurisdiction at an age lower than eighteen.[16] An additional 30,000–40,000 youths were transferred from juvenile court jurisdiction.[17] The NJCDA data for 1996 indicate that approximately 973,000 youths under eighteen were formally processed in the juvenile courts and received dispositions other than waiver (OJJDP 1999). This means that, nationally, 20–25 percent of offenders under age eighteen are treated as adults.

In the remainder of Section I, I present an overview of what is known about national transfer trends, about the nature of transfer cases, and about case processing. As the data permit, I include information on the various subcategories of transfer, about offense and sociodemo-

[16] For this estimate, I am indebted to researchers at the National Center for Juvenile Justice. They report that, in 1996, approximately 218,000 youths under eighteen were prosecuted in criminal courts in the thirteen states where youths age sixteen or seventeen are defined as adults (Snyder and Sickmund 1999). It is based on the assumption that arrested youths age sixteen and seventeen are referred to criminal court at the same rate at which arrested sixteen- and seventeen-year-olds are referred to juvenile court in states that define the upper boundary of the juvenile court's jurisdiction at age eighteen. My bounded estimate includes a considerably lower figure. Research suggests that criminal courts may be more likely than juvenile courts to divert minor cases from processing.

[17] The 1996 NSP surveyed a nationally representative sample of 308 chief prosecutors in courts with jurisdiction over felony cases. Of the 272 respondents who completed the questionnaire, 240 reported proceeding against juveniles transferred to criminal court. Of these, 12 percent were unable to provide any information on the numbers of cases handled, and many were uncertain of the reliability of their estimates. From the data submitted, DeFrances and Steadman (1998) estimated that 26,568 transfer cases were proceeded against in criminal courts. My estimate of 30,000–40,000 cases is based on these data, taking into account the level of nonresponse and adjusted to include a small number of cases initiated in criminal courts of limited jurisdiction, which are not included in the NSP data.

graphic characteristics of transferred offenders, and about youths under eighteen in states where they are legally defined as adults. Where there are state and local studies to supplement the national data, I include these to fill in gaps and to shed light on a number of issues that cannot be addressed with the national data. The presentation is organized around the flow of cases through the justice system, from referral to criminal court, to incarceration in adult correctional facilities.

1. *Waiver from Juvenile to Criminal Court.* Data on judicial waivers for the period 1985–96 are reported in table 2 and indicate that there was a steady increase in the number of cases waived from 1985 to 1994 (from 7,200 to 12,300) that kept pace with increases in cases processed in the juvenile court. Throughout this period, the rate of waiver remained stable at approximately 1.4 percent of all cases petitioned in juvenile court. In 1995 and 1996 the rate of judicial waiver declined. It is likely that the decrease occurred because some cases eligible for judicial waiver were transferred instead by other methods.

Judicial waiver in practice is not highly selective in targeting cases of violence. This can be seen in table 3, which reports offense profiles of cases waived in selected years from 1986 to 1995. Historically, more juveniles were waived for property offenses than for crimes against persons. Since 1993, more person than property crimes have been waived, but person offenses still make up fewer than half of judicial waivers.

Between 1988 and 1994 the rate of waiver for person crimes rose steadily from 1.8 to 2.6 percent of all petitioned cases (see table 2). The rate peaked in 1994 and decreased in both 1995 and 1996. Waiver rates for drug offenses have tended to mimic the temper of the "war on drugs" and, at the beginning of the decade, were nearly twice the rate for violent crimes. Waiver rates for drug offenses peaked at 4 percent of petitioned cases in 1991 and, by 1996, declined to 1.2 percent. Today, person offenses are waived at a higher rate than drug crimes, while property offenses and offenses against public order are waived at the lowest rates (0.8 percent and 0.3 percent, respectively). Although only a very small percentage of property offenses are waived, their incidence is so high that they make up a third of all waivers.

Because judicial waiver typically requires a finding that the offender is not amenable to treatment, it is reasonable to expect that waived offenders might have histories of multiple juvenile program placements. At the national level there is no information on waived youths' arrest or dispositional histories. However, state and local studies suggest that there is considerable variation in the extent to which waived offenders

TABLE 2

Judicial Waivers to Criminal Court, 1985–96

Year	Number of Petitioned Cases	Cases Waived Judicially	Percent Waived	Percent Waived by Offense Type			
				Person	Property	Drug	Public Order
1985	505,400	7,200	1.4	2.5	1.3	1.0	.7
1986	545,500	7,300	1.3	2.2	1.2	1.2	.7
1987	547,400	7,000	1.3	1.9	1.2	1.6	.5
1988	569,800	7,000	1.2	1.8	1.1	1.6	.5
1989	610,600	8,300	1.4	1.9	1.1	2.8	.6
1990	656,400	8,700	1.3	1.9	1.1	2.6	.6
1991	718,100	11,100	1.5	2.4	1.2	4.2	.7
1992	764,000	11,500	1.4	2.4	1.1	2.5	.7
1993	796,600	11,600	1.5	2.6	1.0	2.1	.7
1994	855,200	12,300	1.4	2.6	1.0	1.7	.6
1995	928,200	9,700	1.1	2.1	.8	1.3	.4
1996	983,100	10,000	1.0	1.9	.8	1.2	.3

SOURCES.—Butts et al. 1996; OJJDP 1999.

TABLE 3

Offense Distribution of Judicial Waivers, 1986–95 (%)

Offense	1986	1989	1992	1995
Person	31	28	39	47
Property	54	48	41	34
Drugs	7	16	11	13
Public order	8	7	99	7
Total	100	99	99	101

SOURCES.—Sickmund et al. 1998; OJJDP 1999.
NOTE.—Percentages do not add to 100 due to rounding.

have previously been committed to juvenile programs. Across studies, the percentage of waived youths who have any prior placements ranges from 33 percent to 75 percent, the average being below 50 percent (see, e.g., Heuser 1985; Gragg 1986; Nimick, Szymanski, and Snyder 1986; Houghtalin and Mays 1991; Podkopacz and Feld 1995, 1996; McNulty 1996). Research also indicates that, among waived offenders, offense seriousness is inversely related to prior offending (e.g., Podkopacz and Feld 1996; Bishop et al. 1998). This finding suggests that variation across studies in the proportion of waived youths with prior placements may be attributable to cross-jurisdictional variation in the kinds of offenders selected for transfer.

Youths waived to criminal court are disproportionately older, male, and nonwhite. Most youths waived are sixteen or seventeen years of age, although youths in their early teens account for an increasing proportion of waivers. Those fifteen and under made up 6 percent of the waived population in 1985 (Butts 1997) and 15 percent in 1996 (Stahl 1999). The changing age composition of the waived population is due to declining waiver rates overall among older teens coupled with increasing waiver rates among younger offenders charged with offenses against person[18] (see table 4).

Waiver is applied disproportionately to minority youths. In 1995,

[18] Both these shifts are consistent with a general trend to transfer greater numbers of offenders and to use expedited transfer methods. Most legislative exclusion statutes combine offense criteria with minimum age limits. Typically, very young offenders do not come within their reach unless they are charged with capital crimes or other very serious violent felonies. Judicial waiver is frequently the only means of transferring young offenders charged with lesser felonies against person, while other methods are available for older offenders.

TABLE 4

Percentage of Petitioned Cases Waived Judicially, 1986–95

By Age

Most Serious Offense	1986		1991		1995	
	< 16	16–17	< 16	16–17	< 16	16–17
Person	.4	4.4	.6	4.9	.8	4.1
Property	.1	2.7	.1	2.7	.2	1.6
Drugs	.2	1.9	.5	6.6	.3	1.9
Public order	.1	1.2	.2	1.3	.1	.6
All offenses	.2	2.7	.3	3.2	.3	2.0

By Gender

	1986		1991		1995	
	Male	Female	Male	Female	Male	Female
Person	2.4	.8	2.7	.6	2.5	.3
Property	1.3	.6	1.3	.3	.8	.2
Drugs	1.3	.6	4.3	2.2	1.4	.4
Public order	.8	.2	.8	.0	.4	.1
All offenses	1.5	.5	1.7	.4	1.2	.2

By Race

	1986			1991			1995		
	White	Black	Other	White	Black	Other	White	Black	Other
Person	1.7	2.7	2.4	1.9	2.9	2.2	1.5	2.7	2.7
Property	1.2	2.4	.3	1.1	1.3	.5	.7	1.0	.5
Drugs	.8	2.0	1.7	1.6	5.9	.5	.6	2.1	.5
Public order	.6	.9	.0	.5	1.0	.2	.2	.6	.2
All offenses	1.1	1.7	.7	1.2	2.2	.8	.8	1.6	1.0

Source.—Sickmund et al. 1998, tables 26, 35, and 44.

whites made up approximately 80 percent of the population at risk for delinquency (Sickmund et al. 1998, p. 26) and accounted for 66 percent of the delinquency cases formally disposed by the juvenile courts. However, only 46 percent of those waived were white offenders (Sickmund et al. 1998). Racial disparities in waiver appear to have increased over time. Hamparian et al. (1982) reported that in 1978, 39 percent of waived youths were nonwhite. By 1985, the proportion nonwhite had increased to 44 percent; a decade later, 54 percent of waived offenders were nonwhite (Sickmund et al. 1998). Table 4 shows that blacks are waived at higher rates than whites in all offense categories.

To examine race differences in waiver more closely, table 5 shows race, age, and offense-specific waiver rates for males for the period 1985–95 (OJJDP 1999). It can be seen that for all offense types, all age categories, and all years, black youths were more likely to be waived to criminal court than their white counterparts. Racial disparities are greater among older than among younger offenders. They are greatest for youths charged with person and drug offenses. I noted earlier that rates of waiver for drug offenses rose dramatically during the period 1989–91. Table 5 shows that almost all of that change was due to selective increases in waiver among black offenders. In 1991, black males charged with drug offenses were much more likely to be waived than their white counterparts (among seventeen-year-olds, 13.2 percent vs. 3.7 percent; among sixteen-year-olds, 5.8 percent vs. 1.0 percent). Rates of waiver for drug offenses have declined since 1991 for both black and white offenders and racial disparities are smaller (though still larger than they were in the mid-1980s). In 1995, racial disparities in rates of waiver are most pronounced for older males charged with person crimes.

Almost without exception, state and local studies that have explored issues of race and waiver report disproportionate minority representation in the population of youths for whom prosecutors seek judicial waiver as well as in the population of youths waived by juvenile courts (e.g., Keiter 1973; Eigen 1981; Bortner 1986; Fagan, Forst, and Vivona 1987; Barnes and Franz 1989; Poulos and Orchowsky 1994; Podkopacz and Feld 1995, 1996; Clarke 1996; McNulty 1996). A key question is whether these disparities can be explained by race differences in criminal involvement or whether they reflect racial bias in justice processing. Although few in number, those studies that have addressed this question using multivariate techniques with controls for legally relevant variables (e.g., offense seriousness, number of prior convictions)

TABLE 5

Waiver Rates for Males by Race, Age, and Offense Type, 1987, 1991, 1995

	1987						1991						1995					
	15 and Under		Age 16		Age 17		15 and Under		Age 16		Age 17		15 and Under		Age 16		Age 17	
	Black	White	Black	White	Black	White	Black	White	Black	White	Black	White	Black	White	Black	White	Black	White
Person	.6	.3	3.4	1.5	7.2	5.2	1.0	.4	5.0	3.2	9.4	5.8	1.4	.5	5.5	2.7	7.8	4.6
Property	.2	.1	2.0	.9	5.0	4.5	.3	.1	2.2	1.0	6.1	4.6	.3	.1	2.1	1.2	3.4	2.0
Drug	.2	.0	2.1	.7	4.8	2.4	.8	.1	5.8	1.0	13.2	3.7	.6	.1	2.1	.8	4.8	1.3
Public order	.2	.1	.9	.2	1.9	1.1	.4	.1	1.3	.6	3.0	1.9	.4	.1	1.0	.3	1.5	.6
Total	.3	.1	2.2	.8	5.0	3.8	.5	.2	3.3	1.3	7.7	4.3	.7	.2	2.7	1.3	4.4	2.1

SOURCE.—OJJDP 1999.

most often report little or no evidence of racial bias in judicial waiver decisions (Fagan, Forst, and Vivona 1987 [no race effect in three of four sites; race effect limited to homicide cases in one site]; Barnes and Franz 1989 [small race effect compared to legal variables]; Poulos and Orchowsky 1994 [no race effect]; Podkopacz and Feld 1995, 1996 [no race effect]). However, each of these studies confined the analysis to the waiver decision itself and did not inquire into the effects of race at earlier stages in processing (e.g., the decision to charge, the decision to seek waiver). If race influences earlier processing decisions—and there is a great deal of evidence that it does (see, e.g., Kempf-Leonard, Pope, and Feyerherm 1995; Bishop and Frazier 1996)—selection bias is introduced in analyses of waiver decisions that can minimize or altogether obscure the role that race plays in determining waiver outcomes.

The proportion of males among those waived judicially has remained stable at around 96 percent since 1985 (Butts 1997; Stahl 1999). The very small percentage of females in the waived population is due in large measure to the comparatively low incidence of female offending. Over the period 1985–96, females accounted for approximately 20 percent of all delinquency cases referred to the juvenile court and about 15 percent of delinquency cases petitioned (OJJDP 1999). In addition, as can be seen in table 4, females consistently have been waived at substantially lower rates than males across all offense categories. There has been little research on gender disparities in waiver. Two studies reported that gender had no impact on waiver decisions once the effects of offense seriousness, prior record, and prior commitments were controlled (Barnes and Franz 1989; Poulos and Orchowsky 1994). However, the concerns noted earlier about selection bias apply to these studies as well.

2. *Transfers Prosecuted in Criminal Courts.*   Three recently published reports represent the first efforts to generate national estimates of the number of transfers prosecuted since Hamparian et al.'s (1982) seminal research. Hamparian et al. (1982, p. 99) reported a total of 12,600 transfer cases for 1978: 9,106 (72 percent) via judicial waiver; 2,131 (17 percent) via prosecutorial waiver; and 1,363 (11 percent) via legislative exclusion. These figures provide points of comparison for more recent estimates presented below. (All reasonably credible national estimates of transfers at various points in processing are reported in table 6.)

In 1993, officials of the General Accounting Office (1995) requested data on prosecutorial waivers and excluded cases from all jurisdictions that used these methods. No data on excluded cases could be obtained. Counts of prosecutorial waivers thought to be relatively complete were obtained from only four of the eleven jurisdictions that employed this method at that time. In the other seven, data either were unavailable or could be acquired in at most a few counties. The total number of prosecutorial waivers reported in these very partial data was 9,040.[19]

A recent report generated from data submitted to BJS's State Court Processing Statistics program (SCPS) included estimates of all transferred youths prosecuted for felony offenses in a representative sample of the nation's seventy-five largest counties during a one-month period in each of 1990, 1992, and 1994 (Strom, Smith, and Snyder 1998). From these data, I calculated annualized, national estimates. They indicate that felony prosecutions in transferred cases numbered approximately 12,000 in 1990 and increased to 15,500 in 1994 (see table 6).

A third and more recent estimate comes from BJS's National Survey of Prosecutors (NSP), which in 1996 asked a nationally representative sample of felony prosecutors to report the total number of juveniles transferred by any method (DeFrances and Steadman 1998).[20] Sixty-eight percent of those surveyed were able to provide the information requested. Based on these returns, DeFrances and Steadman estimate that 27,000 transfer cases were prosecuted nationally in criminal courts with felony jurisdiction. (Unlike the SCPS estimate, the NSP estimate includes misdemeanor cases processed in courts of general jurisdiction.)

Several conclusions can be drawn from these national estimates. First, it seems clear that there are major discrepancies across data sources. For example, if we add the number of judicial waivers from the NJCDA data in 1993 to the General Accounting Office's partial count of prosecutorial waivers, it appears that nearly 21,000 cases were transferred. Yet the SCPS estimates for 1992 and 1994—which should also include the balance of prosecutorial waivers and all cases transferred via exclusion—are well shy of this figure.

Second, even assuming there is considerable error in the estimates,

---

[19] The reporting jurisdictions were Arkansas, Florida, Utah, and Vermont. Of these, Florida (7,232 filings) and Arkansas (1,327 filings) accounted for 95 percent of the total filings reported.

[20] The 1994 National Survey of Prosecutors for the first time queried prosecutors about transfers, but the data generated by that survey are believed to be quite unreliable (DeFrances 1999). Respondents were asked to report the number of "transfers" but the term was not defined. The 1996 survey was more explicit in referring to specific transfer methods.

TABLE 6
National Estimates of Juveniles in Adult Courts and Corrections, by Source and Year

	1978	1988	1990	1992	1993	1994	1995	1996	1997
Judicial waiver:									
Hamparian et al. (1982)	9,106	...	...	...	...	...	...	...	...
NJCDA	...	7,000	8,700	11,500	11,600	12,300	9,700	10,000	...
Prosecutorial waiver:									
Hamparian et al. (1982)	2,131	...	...	...	...	...	...	...	...
GAO (1995)	...	...	...	...	9,040	...	...	...	...
Legislative exclusion:									
Hamparian et al. (1982)	1,363	...	...	...	...	...	...	...	...
Total transfers to criminal court:									
Hamparian et al. (1982)	12,600	...	...	...	...	...	...	...	...
Strom, Smith, and Snyder (1998)*	...	...	12,288	11,520	...	15,504	...	...	...
DeFrances and Steadman (1998)	...	...	...	...	...	...	...	27,000	...
Adult by definition, prosecuted:									
Sickmund, Snyder and Poe-Yamagata (1997); Snyder and Sickmund (1999)	...	...	...	...	...	180,000	...	218,000	...
Transfers convicted in criminal court:									
Strom, Smith, and Snyder (1998)	...	...	7,864	7,373	...	9,923	...	...	...
Transfers convicted of felonies in criminal court:									
Strom, Smith, and Snyder (1998)	...	...	7,471	7,004	...	9,427	...	...	...
Brown and Langan (1998)	...	...	...	...	...	12,000	...	...	...
Adult by definition, convicted of felonies:									
Brown and Langan (1998)	...	...	...	...	...	12,000	...	...	...

Total under 18 convicted of felonies:						
Brown and Langan (1998); Brown (1999)	...	...	24,000	...	38,000	...
Transfers convicted of felonies:						
Sentenced to prison:						
Strom, Smith, and Snyder (1998)	3,922	3,677	4,949	...	...	...
Brown and Langan (1998)†	...	...	7,560	...	...	...
Sentenced to jail:						
Strom, Smith, and Snyder (1998)	1,233	1,156	1,555	...	...	...
Brown and Langan (1998)†	...	...	1,920	...	...	...
Adult by definition, convicted of felonies:						
Sentenced to prison:						
Brown and Langan (1998)†	...	...	6,480	...	...	...
Sentenced to jail:						
Brown and Langan (1998)†	...	...	1,320	...	...	...
Total under 18 held in jail as adults (one-day):						
Gilliard and Beck (1998)	...	...	5,100	5,900	...	7,007
Prison admissions of persons under 18:						
BJS (1999b);‡ Perkins (1994)	6,230	5,757	...	...	...	...
Library Information Specialists (1995)	...	6,229	...	7,420	...	...
Total under 18 in prison (one-day):						
Library Information Specialists (1995)	...	...	4,832	...	5,700	...
Levinson and Greene (1999)	...	...	5,309	...	...	7,242

NOTE.—NJCDA = National Juvenile Court Data Archive; GAO = General Accounting Office; BJS = Bureau of Justice Statistics.

* These estimates were derived by annualizing the weighted estimates reported by Strom and Smith (1998) for May of each year, then adjusting for coverage.

† These estimates were derived from figures reported by Brown and Langan (1998), adjusted for rates of conviction and incarceration.

‡ These estimates were adjusted for coverage.

TABLE 7

Sociodemographic Characteristics of Transferred Offenders,
Combined Years, 1990–94

Gender	%	Race	%	Age	%
Male	92	White	31	< 15	8
Female	8	Black	67	15	24
		Other	2	16	27
				17	40

the conclusion is inescapable that there have been substantial increases in transfer over the past two decades. Hamparian et al. (1982) estimated a total of 12,600 in all courts in 1978, compared to the NSP estimate of 27,000 cases in felony courts in 1996.

Third, the available data indicate that prosecutorial waivers have increased dramatically (more than fourfold) since the late 1970s, while judicial waivers have increased hardly at all (9,106 in 1978; 10,000 in 1996). Finally, although the relative magnitude of prosecutorial waivers and excluded cases is unknown, there can be little doubt that the expedited transfer methods in combination have eclipsed judicial waiver in terms of frequency of use.[21]

3. *Characteristics of Youths Transferred.* Information on the offense and sociodemographic characteristics of juvenile felony defendants transferred to criminal court are gathered as part of the State Court Processing Statistics program (Strom, Smith, and Snyder 1998). Data for the combined years 1990–94 are reported in tables 7 and 8. They indicate that 66 percent of transferred offenders were charged with a violent offense, 17 percent were charged with property crimes, while drug and public order offenses made up 14 percent and 3 percent of the total, respectively. A comparison of this profile to that for cases waived judicially during 1992 (see table 3) reveals significant differences between them. While the two data sources are in substantial agreement with respect to the proportions of juveniles charged with drug and public order offenses, the judicial waiver data show a much smaller proportion of violent crimes (39 percent vs. SCPS's 66 percent) and a much larger proportion of property offenses (41 percent

---

[21] In 1993, nearly 12,000 judicial waivers were recorded (see table 5). Surely once we add the balance of prosecutorial waivers to the 9,040 cases known, then add cases transferred by legislative exclusion, the total will exceed the number of judicial waivers.

TABLE 8
Offense Distribution of Transferred Defendants, Combined Years, 1990–94 (%)

	Total	Gender			Race			
		Male	Female	Total	White	Black	Other	Total
Violent	66	92	8	100	25	73	2	100
Murder	11	96	4		25	69	6	
Rape	3	89	11		28	72	0	
Robbery	34	87	13		16	82	3	
Assault	15	97	3		39	61	0	
Property	17	95	5	100	61	31	6	100
Burglary	6	100	0		82	13	4	
Theft	8	95	5		49	42	9	
Drug	14	92	8	100	19	81	0	100
Public order	3	89	11	100	23	77	0	100

SOURCE.—Strom, Smith, and Snyder 1998, tables 1 and 4.

vs. 17 percent). That the judicial waiver data come from juvenile courts nationwide while the court processing data are obtained from a sample of urban counties is not likely to account for these differences. Data on convictions in transfer cases from nationally representative court samples (discussed below) show an offense profile very similar to that obtained from the SCPS data. Nor can criminal court decisions to reverse waive disproportionate numbers of property offenders account for the difference. The SCPS program tracks defendants from point of charging by the prosecutor, prior to any action by the criminal courts. The most likely explanation is that cases transferred via methods other than judicial waiver contain large numbers of offenders charged with person crimes.

There are also substantial differences in the sociodemographic profiles of transferred offenders reported from the two sources. According to the SCPS data for 1990–94, 32 percent of transferred juveniles were under age sixteen, 92 percent were male, and 31 percent were white. The judicial waiver data tell a very different story. For the same time period, they indicate that 13 percent of youths waived were under sixteen, 96 percent were male, and 47 percent were white. While the gender proportions are very similar, the age and race discrepancies across the two data sources are quite substantial. They suggest that prosecutorial waiver and legislative exclusion bring younger defendants into the criminal justice system and exacerbate racial disparities.

Research conducted in two states is consistent with this conclusion. In Florida, where over 90 percent of transfers are made by prosecutorial waiver, it was reported that 20 percent of the nearly six thousand juveniles transferred in 1993 were under sixteen and 55 percent were nonwhite (Bishop et al. 1998). Research on youths transferred by legislative exclusion has been carried out only in New York, where a Juvenile Offender Law was enacted in 1978 that excluded from juvenile court jurisdiction cases involving thirteen- to fifteen-year-olds charged with several serious and violent felonies.[22] (The exclusion statute does not apply to older offenders because New York defines the sixteenth birthday as the upper boundary of juvenile court jurisdiction.) Singer (1996) reported that, over the period 1978–85, 10,000 youths aged thirteen to fifteen were arrested and charged under the statute. Of

---

[22] The offenses excluded are murder and attempts, manslaughter, kidnapping, robbery (armed or with injury), forcible rape, forcible sodomy, aggravated sexual abuse, assault (aggravated battery), arson of an occupied structure or vehicle, and armed burglary.

these 85 percent were minority offenders (16 percent Hispanic, 69 percent black).

In a study conducted in a single urban jurisdiction, Singer (1996) explored the influence of race on prosecutorial decisions to seek indictments of juveniles arrested under the Juvenile Offender Law. Race had no direct effect on decision making after family status, legal, and contextual factors were controlled. However, prosecutors were significantly more likely to seek indictments of youths from single-parent families, and minorities were much more likely to come from single-parent homes. Thus implementation of the law at the formal charging stage exacerbated racial disparities and further disadvantaged minority defendants.

There is other evidence that laws that target violent crimes have the effect of exposing greater proportions of minority offenders—particularly young minority offenders—to criminal prosecution. Data from the Uniform Crime Reports (UCR) indicate that black juveniles are arrested for violent crimes at a rate more than five times greater than whites (Cook and Laub 1998). Statutes that target violent offenses for legislative exclusion or presumptive or mandatory judicial waiver most often have no prior record criteria. Subject only to prosecutorial nullification, young, disproportionately minority offenders will be transferred under these statutes.

The effect of transfer policies aimed at crimes against persons was illustrated dramatically in research conducted by Podkopacz and Feld (1996). They examined judicial waiver practices in Hennepin County, Minnesota, from 1986 to 1992. Over that period, minorities constituted less than 20 percent of the juvenile population but 65 percent of those arrested for Part I violent crimes. During the course of the study, the prosecutor's office changed its waiver policy. Instead of focusing on offenders with lengthy records of arrest and prior placement, it began to concentrate instead on youths charged with crimes of violence. With the shift in focus, the proportion of minority defendants in the waived population increased from 65 percent in 1986 to 88 percent in 1992.

4. *Convictions in Criminal Court.* Information on court outcomes for transferred youths is very limited. Twenty-two states have reverse waiver provisions that permit the criminal courts to return cases to the juvenile system (Torbet et al. 1996). Unfortunately, there are virtually no national data on the extent to which this option is exercised. Two studies that examined reverse waiver at the state level reveal consider-

able variation in practice. Bishop et al. (1998) reported that in Florida less than 10 percent of cases transferred in 1993 and 1995 were returned to the juvenile system. In contrast, Singer (1996) found in New York that 31 percent of the youths charged as adults under the state's exclusion statute were returned to the juvenile court. Singer (1996) also examined the characteristics of cases returned to the juvenile system. Females, younger offenders, those without prior arrests, and those charged with lesser felonies were more likely to have their cases returned.

National data are available on the rate at which transfers prosecuted as adults are convicted in state criminal courts. From the SCPS data for 1990–94, Strom, Smith, and Snyder (1998) report that 64 percent of transferred felony defendants were convicted (59 percent for felonies, 5 percent for misdemeanors). Defendants charged with public order crimes were most likely to be convicted (91 percent), followed by those charged with property offenses (74 percent), drug offenses (70 percent), and violent crimes (59 percent).

The 64 percent conviction rate reported in SCPS for 1990–94 compares unfavorably to the 90 percent conviction rate reported by Hamparian et al. (1982) for cases transferred in 1978. Other more recent state and local studies reported in the criminological literature suggest that conviction rates for transferred offenders are considerably higher than those reported in SCPS (see, e.g., Fagan 1990 [violent offenders in urban courts in four states, 1981–84, 90 percent conviction rate]; Podkopacz and Feld 1996 [Hennepin County Minnesota, 1986–92, 97 percent conviction rate]; Bishop et al. 1998 [Florida, 1993–95, largely nonviolent offenders, 92 percent conviction rate]).

At the time of this writing, there are no published documents from the national reporting programs that indicate whether there are race or gender differences in rates of criminal court conviction among transferred offenders. In his study of transferred offenders in New York, Singer (1996) found that both gender and race had a significant impact on criminal court conviction. After controlling in multivariate models for legal and organizational variables, he found that male defendants were 1.5 times more likely to be convicted than females. The effect of race was found to vary by jurisdiction. In the large urban counties of New York City, race had no effect when other variables were controlled. In the rest of the state, black youths were 1.45 times more likely to be convicted than whites.

Estimates of the total number of transferred offenders convicted of felonies in criminal court for various years are reported in table 6. They come from two sources: the SCPS program (data from the nation's seventy-five largest counties) and BJS's National Judicial Reporting Program (NJRP), which gathers data from a nationally representative sample of 300 felony courts. The estimates for 1994 range from 9,400 (SCPS) to 12,000 cases (NJRP). According to these estimates, transferred offenders accounted for approximately 1.4 percent of all felony convictions.

The SCPS and the NJRP are in substantial agreement with respect to the offense distributions of transferred offenders convicted in state felony courts. The NJRP data are presented in column 1 of table 9. For comparative purposes, the offense profiles of convicted offenders eighteen and over are also reported (col. 2). Examination of the table shows that approximately half of the transfers were convicted of a violent felony crime. Although there are many lesser offenders in the transfer group, the transfers as a group are more serious offenders than

TABLE 9

Offense Profiles of Transferred Youths and Adults Convicted in
Felony Courts, 1994

Most Serious Conviction Offense	Transferred Offenders (%)	Offenders 18 and Over (%)	Under 18 but Adult by Definition (%)
Violent offenses	53	19	28
Murder	7	1	3
Rape	2	2	2
Robbery	28	5	17
Aggravated assault	16	8	5
Other violent	1	3	1
Property offenses	24	31	31
Burglary	15	11	18
Larceny	8	13	12
Fraud	1	7	1
Drug offenses	13	32	24
Possession	3	13	7
Trafficking	10	19	17
Weapons offenses	4	4	8
Other offenses	6	14	9
Total	100	100	100

Source.—Brown and Langan 1998.

adults convicted in felony courts. Fewer than 20 percent of the adult felons were convicted of violent offenses.

5. *Sentencing of Transferred Offenders.* At the time of this writing, national data on sentences received by transferred offenders are available only for the 1994 felony court samples included in the NJRP (Brown and Langan 1998). Table 10 reports information on sentences received by transferred offenders and by offenders eighteen and over, organized by offense type. The left-hand side of the table indicates that transferred youths convicted in criminal court are very likely to be incarcerated. Seventy-nine percent of all transferred youths convicted in 1994 were sentenced to terms of incarceration. Sixteen percent were sentenced to jail. Sixty-three percent were sentenced to prison, many for lengthy terms. The average maximum sentence for transferred offenders sentenced to prison was 9.25 years. The remaining 21 percent were sentenced to probation. In contrast, offenders eighteen and over are slightly less likely to be incarcerated (73 percent) and, when incarcerated, are less likely to be sentenced to prison (46 percent).

Most transferred youths convicted of violent offenses receive sentences far more severe than could be imposed in the vast majority of the nation's juvenile courts. (This is true except in those few states, such as Texas, that permit the juvenile courts to sentence some categories of violent offenders to lengthy terms of incarceration.) Seventy-eight percent are sentenced to prison, with an average maximum term of nearly twelve years. Even assuming generous gain time provisions, most will serve far longer terms than if they had been retained in the juvenile courts and committed to residential programs.[23] Nearly half of those convicted of property, drug, and weapons offenses also receive prison sentences, with average maximum terms of 4.25, 6.67, and 5.5 years, respectively. The rest—a slight majority of youths transferred for property, drug, and weapons offenses—receive jail sentences or are placed on probation, sentences well within the range that may be imposed by juvenile courts. Overall, the results suggest that more than half of transferred offenders who are convicted are sentenced to terms that exceed those they would have received had they remained in the juvenile system.

Data aggregated at the national level obscure considerable variability in practice at the state and county levels. Many studies of state and

---

[23] It is estimated that serious and violent offenders incarcerated in the juvenile justice system remain confined for eight months on average (DeComo et al. 1995).

TABLE 10

Sentences Received by Transferred Offenders Compared to Offenders 18 and Over: Sentence Type and Mean Maximum Sentence Length in Months (Felony Offenses Only)

	Transferred Youths						Offenders 18 and Over					
	% to Prison	Prison Length	% to Jail	Jail Length	% to Probation	Probation Length	% to Prison	Prison Length	% to Jail	Jail Length	% to Probation	Probation Length
All offenses	63	111	16	8	21	51	46	69	27	6	28	36
Violent Offenses	78	139	10	10	12	57	62	115	21	7	17	42
Murder*	97	287	2	10	1	46	95	258	2	7	3	54
Rape	84	200	6	3	10	54	72	149	17	7	11	54
Robbery	75	139	9	10	16	59	77	112	12	9	11	46
Aggravated assault	74	75	16	10	10	52	49	81	28	6	23	38
Other	71	130	14	4	14	…	45	70	32	7	23	42
Property offenses	42	50	23	8	36	45	42	56	27	6	30	38
Burglary	46	52	18	10	36	52	53	67	34	7	24	42
Larceny	36	45	28	6	36	32	38	45	30	6	32	36
Fraud	21	44	49	9	30	14	33	51	30	5	37	38
Drug offenses	45	80	25	7	30	52	43	60	29	6	29	34
Possession	37	66	28	4	35	45	36	48	34	4	30	32
Trafficking	47	83	24	8	29	54	47	66	25	7	28	35
Weapons offenses	49	66	20	9	31	47	44	46	28	5	28	29
Other offenses	67	61	24	7	9	51	37	40	30	6	33	34

Source.—Brown and Langan 1998, derived from tables 6.2, 6.3, 6.5, and 6.6.
Note.—Ellipses indicate that the figure is unknown.
* Includes nonnegligent manslaughter.

local transfer practices and outcomes have been conducted (see Howell 1997). Some report that transferred offenders receive sentences of equal or lesser severity than those imposed by the juvenile courts (see, e.g., Heuser 1985; Sagatun, McCollum, and Edwards 1985; Barnes and Franz 1989; Podkopacz and Feld 1996), while others have concluded that transferred youths are more often incarcerated and receive longer sentences than youths adjudicated in juvenile court (e.g., Rudman et al. 1986; Barnes and Franz 1989; Fagan 1995, 1996; Podkopacz and Feld 1996). The bulk of the evidence suggests that violent youths receive more severe sentences in criminal courts than they would have received in juvenile courts, while young property offenders—who often have lengthy prior records—are treated more leniently by criminal courts. In criminal courts, offense seriousness seems to weigh more heavily than prior record, while in juvenile courts, the reverse is true (Feld 1999).

There are also significant jurisdictional variations both in the kinds of offenders selected for transfer and in sentencing practice. The effects of offense and place are perhaps best illustrated in a seven-state comparison of transfer practices and outcomes conducted by the General Accounting Office (1995). Marked differences were observed across jurisdictions in the offenses for which youths were transferred. For example, 12 percent of the transfers in Vermont involved crimes of violence, compared with nearly 40 percent in Missouri. Property offenders constituted only 21 percent of California's transfer population, compared with 84 percent of Vermont's. There was also considerable variability in conviction rates and rates of incarceration by state and by offense type. At the extreme, Vermont incarcerated fewer than one-third of juveniles convicted in criminal court of a violent, property, or drug crime, while Minnesota incarcerated more than 90 percent of youths in all three offense categories. Pennsylvania incarcerated more than 90 percent of youths convicted of violent and drug offenses, but only 10 percent of those convicted of property crimes. There is much evidence of "justice by geography" in the selection, adjudication, and sentencing of transferred offenders (see also Feld 1991; Bishop, Lanza-Kaduce, and Winner 1996; Lanza-Kaduce, Bishop, and Winner 1997).

There is a paucity of research on the effects of gender and race on the criminal sentencing of transferred offenders net of controls for offense seriousness and other legally relevant variables. In one such analysis, Singer (1996) examined decisions of New York's criminal courts to designate transferred offenders as "youthful offenders." Criminal courts in New York have broad discretion to grant this status, which results in reduced penalties. In a multivariate analysis that included controls for offense seriousness, prior record, and organizational variables, Singer found that older offenders, males, and minority youths were significantly less likely to be accorded this special designation. Moreover, among those convicted as juvenile offenders (the designation that carries higher penalties), gender and race had significant effects on sentencing. Nonwhites were 1.7 times more likely to be incarcerated than whites and males were 1.9 times more likely to be incarcerated than females. However, among those sentenced to incarceration, whites were sentenced to terms five months longer on average than nonwhites. Singer suggested this was because whites were less likely to be charged and convicted as juvenile offenders unless they had committed particularly brutal or violent offenses.

6. *Youths under Eighteen in Criminal Courts in States Where They Are Adults by Definition.* In addition to youths transferred to criminal court, substantial numbers of offenders under eighteen are processed in criminal courts in the eleven jurisdictions where all offenders aged sixteen or seventeen are defined as adults under state law. Recently, Snyder and Sickmund (1999) estimated that 218,000 cases involving these youths were processed in the nation's criminal courts in 1996, up from 180,000 in 1994 (Sickmund, Snyder, and Poe-Yamagata 1997). Unfortunately, information about this subgroup of criminal offenders has not been routinely maintained by prosecutors or state court administrators.

Based on data from the NJRP court samples, Brown and Langan (1998) estimate that 12,000 youths under eighteen were convicted in criminal felony courts in 1994 in states where they were legally defined as adults. It is difficult to reconcile Sickmund, Snyder, and Poe-Yamagata's (1997) estimate of the number of prosecutions in 1994 with Brown and Langan's (1998) estimate of the number of convictions for the same year. Applying a very conservative assumption that 20 percent of the 180,000 estimated prosecutions involved felonies yields 36,000 cases.[24] To arrive at Brown and Langan's (1998) estimated 12,000 convictions implies a conviction rate of only 33 percent.

The profile of conviction offenses for youths aged sixteen and seven-

[24] This estimate of felonies corresponds to the portion of UCR arrests that involve Part I (Index) crimes. It is conservative in that it assumes that all Part II offenses are nonfelonies, and it assumes that nonserious cases are as likely to be prosecuted as serious ones.

teen who are adult by state definition looks fairly similar to the offense profile for those eighteen and over (cf. cols. 2 and 3 in table 9). Compared with those eighteen and over, those under eighteen are more likely to be convicted of a violent crime or a weapons offense, equally likely to be convicted of a property offense, and somewhat less likely to be convicted of a drug offense. Not unexpectedly, offenders under eighteen in states where they are legally defined as adults are a much less serious group of offenders than those under eighteen who are transferred to criminal court. Slightly more than one-quarter of the former are violent offenders, compared to over half of those in the transfer group.

In table 11, data are presented on the sentences received in 1994 by offenders under eighteen in states where they were defined as adults. Nationally, 54 percent were sentenced to prison. They received average maximum sentences of 7.25 years. Eleven percent were sentenced to jail, while 34 percent were placed on probation.

In some states where all youths aged sixteen or seventeen are tried

TABLE 11

Sentences Imposed on Convicted Felons under 18 in States Where They Were Adult by Definition

	% to Prison	Prison Length	% to Jail	Jail Length	% to Probation	Probation Length
All offenses	54	87	11	8	34	44
Violent offenses	73	128	5	15	23	52
Murder*	97	279	1	12	1	60
Rape	85	117	11	12	5	53
Robbery	70	107	4	22	26	55
Aggravated assault	68	102	8	6	24	49
Other	36	124	...	...	64	40
Property offenses	47	67	14	6	39	51
Burglary	65	68	6	11	30	48
Larceny	21	62	29	5	50	54
Fraud	22	57	9	4	70	43
Drug offenses	47	58	9	9	44	37
Possession	31	42	9	5	60	33
Trafficking	54	62	9	10	37	40
Weapons offenses	47	62	25	9	28	38
Other offenses	47	68	16	7	36	36

SOURCE.—Brown and Langan 1998, derived from tables 6.5 and 6.6.
* Includes nonnegligent manslaughter.

as adults, criminal courts may exercise discretion to sentence offenders using the same sentencing scheme that applies to offenders eighteen and over or, alternatively, to apply a special designation that results in mitigated punishments. In New York, criminal courts can recognize convicted youths aged sixteen and seventeen as youthful offenders, resulting in lighter penalties (much the same as when the designation is applied to transferred youths).[25] In the mid-1980s, a study of the application of New York's youthful offender statute to sixteen- and seventeen-year-olds was conducted by Peterson (1988), who was interested in determining whether conviction and sentencing were influenced by offenders' personal characteristics. In a sophisticated multivariate analysis that included controls for a wide variety of legal factors and contextual variables, Peterson found that gender, race, and ethnicity had substantial effects on adjudicatory and sentencing outcomes. Compared to whites, blacks were 12 percent less likely and Hispanics were 10 percent less likely to receive youthful offender status. Females were 12 percent more likely to be designated youthful offenders than males. Race, ethnicity, and gender also affected sentencing decisions, both for those defined as youthful offenders and those sentenced as adults. In both groups, males, blacks, and Hispanics were more often incarcerated, and for lengthier periods.

7. *Sentencing and Confinement of Offenders under Eighteen.* The data on conviction, sentencing, and incarceration of felony offenders discussed in this section include all offenders under eighteen. They are drawn from national corrections reporting programs that do not differentiate between offenders transferred from the juvenile system and those prosecuted in states where sixteen- and seventeen-year-olds are legally defined as adults.

The Bureau of Justice Statistics estimates that a total of 38,000 youths under eighteen were convicted of felonies in 1996. This total was up from 24,000 in 1994, an increase of almost 60 percent. In 1996, offenders under eighteen accounted for 3.8 percent of all felony convictions, compared to 2.8 percent in 1994. Ninety-three percent of those under eighteen convicted of felonies were male and 58 percent were black (Brown 1999). (In the total population of convicted felons, 84 percent were male and 46 percent were black.) Among those under

[25] Youths convicted of very serious offenses—e.g., murder, arson, kidnapping—are not eligible for youthful offender status, while first-time misdemeanants must be treated as youthful offenders. But in all other (the vast majority of) cases, judges have broad discretion in granting this designation.

sixteen—all of whom were transferred—the proportion black was 73 percent, demonstrating once again the disproportionate impact of transfer on young minority offenders.

National Corrections Reporting Program data for 1996 indicate that over 95 percent of youths under eighteen who were sentenced to prison were male, 75 percent were seventeen (at time of admission to prison), and 66 percent were black (Brown 1999). Sixty-one percent of youths under eighteen sentenced to prison were incarcerated for a violent crime, up from 51 percent in 1992 (Perkins 1994). Offenders eighteen and over sentenced to prison in 1996 were much less likely than their juvenile counterparts to have been convicted of a violent crime (28 percent) and racial disparities, though substantial, were not nearly as pronounced among these older offenders (50 percent black; see table 12).

Among offenders under eighteen sentenced to prison, minority youths made up the majority of drug offenders (88 percent), violent offenders (70 percent), and those convicted of public order and "other" crimes (65 percent). Whites accounted for the majority of persons under eighteen sentenced to prison for property crimes (55 percent). The reader may recall from the earlier discussion that youths sentenced to prison for property crimes receive the shortest average maximum sentences (fifty months). Average maximum sentences for "other" offenses are sixty-one months; for drug offenses, eighty months; and for violent crimes, 139 months. As a result, young minority offenders sentenced to prison will serve considerably longer sentences on average than young white offenders.

8. *Youths in Adult Correctional Institutions.* In forty-two states, youths transferred to criminal court may be detained in jail prior to trial (Howell 1997). Jurisdictions that treat all youths aged sixteen or seventeen as adults also permit them to be detained in jail prior to trial. In addition, of course, both sets of youths may be sentenced to jail. The jail data currently available on juvenile offenders are limited to annual one-day counts of youths under eighteen (Gilliard and Beck 1998) and do not differentiate between those held prior to adjudication and those sentenced. The Bureau of Justice Statistics cautions that it is very difficult to gather accurate data on juveniles in jail, especially data that are comparable across jurisdictions. That said, it is estimated that approximately 7,000 juveniles who were being processed as adults were housed in jail at mid-year 1997, compared with 5,100 at mid-year 1994, an increase of 37 percent.[26]

[26] These youths, in 1997, constituted approximately 1.4 percent of the jail population. An additional 2,100 youths were held in jail as juveniles.

TABLE 12

Court Commitments to Prison in 1996 by Age, Race, and Offense

| | Age at Admission (%) | | | | | | | | Total | |
| | Under 18 | | 18–24 | | 25–29 | | 30+ | | | |
Offense	White	Black	White	Black	White	Black	White	Black	Under 18	18 and over
Violent	53	63	30	37	26	27	28	23	61	28
Property	37	16	46	19	36	25	28	30	22	30
Drugs	4	15	17	36	26	40	26	38	11	31
Public order and other	6	6	7	8	12	8	18	9	6	11
Total	100	100	100	100	100	100	100	100	100	100
N*	1,904	3,711	35,783	43,000	22,757	23,250	63,068	56,098		

Race Distribution of New Court Commitments

| | Under 18 | | 18 and Over (%) | |
	Total	White	Total	White
Violent	61	30	28	50
Property	22	55	30	58
Drug	11	12	31	38
Public order	5	35	11	60
Total	99	34†	100	50†

SOURCE.—Bureau of Justice Statistics 1999b.
* Number where offense, age, and race are known.
† Average percent white.

With respect to youths in state prisons, NJRP data indicate that approximately 14,100 offenders who committed offenses while under eighteen were sentenced to prison in 1994 (63 percent of convicted transferred youths and 54 percent of offenders under eighteen convicted in states where they were legally defined as adults). In addition to the sentencing reports, data believed to include approximately 90 percent of all prison admissions are submitted annually to BJS by state corrections officials as part of the National Corrections Reporting Program. Adjusted for coverage, they indicate that 7,420 offenders under eighteen were admitted to state prisons in 1996.[27] This represents an increase of nearly 30 percent over what was reported in 1992. Although offenders under eighteen represent only 2.3 percent of new court commitments to prison, because they receive longer average sentences than older age groups (see table 10) their impact on prison communities will grow as they age. Over time, an increasing proportion of the prison population will consist of offenders who entered during adolescence.

II. Systemic Consequences of Transfer Reform

This section focuses on the known and probable consequences of shifts in transfer practice on the organization and operation of the criminal and juvenile justice systems. Some effects are fairly obvious and predictable (e.g., caseload pressures resulting from increased numbers of young offenders in the adult court system). In addition, there are some less apparent and largely unanticipated consequences—problems of articulation between the juvenile and criminal justice systems and net widening in the juvenile system—that merit consideration. Given the broad scope of this essay, the discussion in this section is limited to an overview of the major systemic effects and issues.

A. Caseload Issues for the Criminal Justice System

The most obvious consequence of recent transfer trends is that the already strained resources of criminal courts and adult corrections agencies are and will be further taxed. Much of the increased pressure is a result of sheer numbers. As Section I showed, there has been a shift from relatively small numbers of transfers in the late 1970s

---

[27] There is a substantial discrepancy in the number under eighteen sentenced to prison compared to the number admitted. Some shrinkage is to be expected for reasons stated earlier. The sentencing data are based on age at arrest. The corrections data are based on age at admission.

(Hamparian et al. 1982) to potentially enormous numbers in the late 1990s.

Criminal prosecutions demand more resources than juvenile ones. They require more hearings, involve more attorney preparation, call on more investigative resources, are more likely to result in jury trials, and take at least twice as long to process as comparable cases in juvenile court. As transfers increase, additional human and financial resources will be required. Absent new resources, if current trends continue the criminal courts will face more congested dockets and greater delays. The system may slow or more pleas may be negotiated at "bargain basement" prices, more prosecutions may be deferred, and more cases may be screened out or returned to the juvenile system to relieve the added burdens on the criminal courts.

The issues raised by the transfer trends relate not only to numbers. They also relate to the composition of the transfer population. That transfer practices increasingly and disproportionately affect minority youths serves to reinforce already serious concerns about unequal justice and the appearance of equal justice.

The composition of the transfer population also poses special challenges for departments of corrections, for which many states are ill prepared (Torbet et al. 1996; see also Orenstein 1996). From a managerial standpoint, young offenders create problems for officials far out of proportion to their numbers in correctional populations. They are more likely to be involved in misconduct while incarcerated (Wolfgang 1961; Johnson 1966; Jensen 1977; Myers and Levy 1978; Goetting and Howsen 1986). They pose far higher risks of suicide (Memory 1989), have more medical and social needs, and will often require special precautions to protect them from harm in jail and prison facilities (McShane and Williams 1989).

A key question is whether corrections officials will recognize and respond to the special needs of young offenders or treat them no differently than older offenders. Although corrections officials are being urged to develop programs for young offenders, Torbet et al. (1996, p. 33) report that this is "a population they neither want nor have the expertise to address." A recent survey of correctional administrators indicated that, in forty states, transferred offenders are placed in the general prison population and, most often, receive no special programs or services (Reddington and Sapp 1997; see also Amnesty International 1998). Transfer trends create the prospect of new and serious issues not only for prison facilities, but for detention centers and jails as well.

Criminal court processing of transfer cases may take a year or more, during which time offenders remain in jail or detention facilities, neither of which have the staffing or programming to meet youths' educational or social service needs over a protracted period.

The influx of young offenders into prisons has resulted in some increases in funding allocations, primarily for new facilities and new beds. However, relatively little attention has been given to the need for new or additional programs (Orenstein 1996; Jepsen 1997) or to the physical limitations of existing facilities given the desirability of age segregation (Library Information Specialists 1995; Jepsen 1997). Corrections experts urge that additional teachers be hired and programming developed to meet young offenders' educational needs. These needs are atypical. Most young inmates have substantial records of school failure, many have learning disabilities (Freasier and White 1983), and traditional educational approaches simply do not work with them. In this population, learning is largely dependent on the development of significant interpersonal relationships between teacher and student (Evans 1978), which requires specialized teacher training and low teacher/student ratios. In addition, corrections experts suggest that, at a minimum, the new wave of juvenile inmates will require staff training or hiring of new staff trained in several areas, including adolescent development, risk factors for aggressive behavior, communication skills, and problem-solving and crisis intervention strategies (Jepsen 1997).

B. Problems of Articulation between the Juvenile and Criminal Systems and Shifts in the Balance of Power

Less anticipated than the consequences associated with caseload pressures are a set of system effects that are not so easily categorized. They involve shifts in the balance of decision-making power from judges to prosecutors, legislatures, and corrections officials, and issues of articulation between the criminal and juvenile justice systems.

Legislative exclusion and prosecutorial waiver have overtaken judicial waiver as the primary vehicles by which transfers are made. Indeed, if current trends continue, judicial waiver may become obsolete. The appeal of prosecutorial waiver lies largely in the fact that it expedites the transfer process by circumventing the juvenile court. To politicians with a "get tough" agenda, who perceive juvenile court judges as "too soft" on crime, prosecutorial waiver is an attractive option. Legislative exclusion has appeal not only because it bypasses the juvenile court but also because it permits legislatures to maintain more control over the transfer process. Legislatures may restrict prosecutorial and judicial discretion and insure greater uniformity and consistency in practice by tying transfer to offense and prior record criteria.

It is now apparent that, despite their surface appeal, streamlined procedures generate new problems for the administration of justice. Because legislative exclusion statutes are inflexible and overinclusive (Zimring 1991; Tonry 1996) they require correctives. These have come in the form of reverse waiver or "transfer back" provisions. As my colleagues and I have argued elsewhere (Bishop, Frazier, and Henretta 1989; Bishop and Frazier 1991), prosecutorial waiver statutes also tend to be too broad. In practice, they frequently require inexperienced assistant prosecutors to make quick decisions based on minimal information. Prosecutorial waiver statutes invite subjective and inconsistent decision making and, thus, have prompted similar counterbalancing measures.

Reverse waiver and "transfer back" options place the burden of correction on the criminal courts. But shifting the locus of decision making from juvenile court judges to criminal court judges makes little sense. Criminal court judges are already overworked and lack special expertise in dealing with young offenders. Moreover, criminal court judges are frequently given little guidance in exercising their discretion to return cases to the juvenile court or to impose juvenile sanctions. Are offense considerations determinative? Should offender needs be considered? Is amenability to treatment an important consideration? If so, is not familiarity with juvenile justice treatment resources essential? To the extent that offender needs, amenability to treatment, and familiarity with juvenile treatment resources matter, such decisions would presumably best be made by the juvenile courts. In a recent survey of criminal court judges in Virginia, 55 percent acknowledged that they knew too little about child development and were insufficiently familiar with community services to handle juvenile cases (Virginia Commission on Youth 1996).

In the sentencing of transferred offenders, other problems of articulation arise. Even with changes in standards of confidentiality of juvenile records and the length of time records are maintained prior to expungement, criminal courts are sometimes faced with articulation difficulties. They often do not have access to, or fail to make use of, juvenile court records when making sentencing decisions (Miller 1997; Sanborn 1998). This explains in part why criminal courts sentence transferred property offenders more leniently than do juvenile courts. Most often, transferred property offenders—unlike a majority of those transferred for violent crimes—are chronic offenders who pose the highest risk of reoffending.[28] If these offenders were incarcerated for significant periods by the criminal courts, substantial incapacitative gains might be realized. Instead, in part because of lack of interagency articulation, the criminal courts sentence most severely those who are least likely to reoffend and sentence most leniently those most likely to reoffend.

Other issues relating to articulation between the juvenile and criminal justice systems arise in the corrections arena. Several states have adopted blended sentencing statutes that permit the criminal courts to impose both juvenile and adult sanctions in sequence (Torbet et al. 1996; Torbet and Szymanski 1998). In many other states, when a juvenile is convicted as an adult and sentenced to a term of incarceration, it is left to corrections officials to decide whether some (or potentially all) of the sentence will be served in a juvenile or an adult facility (Torbet et al. 1996). States that adopt this practice in effect permit "transfer back" to take place at the corrections level. This appears to usurp judicial authority and undermines the court's purpose in sentencing youths as adults. Furthermore, there has been virtually no research on how corrections authorities determine which juveniles will return to the juvenile corrections system or how long they will remain there. Finally, blended sentencing systems raise but do not answer questions about the clash of underlying philosophies and operating principles of the two justice systems. In one sense, blended systems avoid the need to create new facilities and new layers of correctional programming because both the juvenile and the adult systems are available. But in another sense, they create confusion about what philosophy of justice is to be applied.[29]

Other issues arise in the context of pretrial detention. In forty-two

[28] Chronicity is a strong predictor of recidivism, while severity of the current offense is a poor predictor. Ironically, most prosecutorial waiver and legislative exclusion statutes focus on offense seriousness and fail to incorporate prior record criteria (see Griffin, Torbet, and Szymanski 1998).

[29] The organization and operation of the two justice systems are intricately tied to their underlying philosophies. The criminal justice system is rested on a punishment philosophy that assumes individual responsibility, culpability, and accountability. Despite recent and significant changes (Feld 1988; Forst and Blomquist 1992; Fagan 1996), the juvenile justice system still focuses to a greater degree on the malleability of young offenders and the state's responsibility to provide sanctions and programs designed to effect behavioral reform.

states, juveniles are viewed as criminal defendants as soon as criminal charges are filed, which makes them eligible for pretrial detention in jail—where they are commonly housed together with adult offenders—and for release on bail (Coalition for Juvenile Justice 1995). The issue of bail for transferred offenders has not been given much attention. Although systems of bail have long been criticized on the grounds that they discriminate against the poor, at least adults are responsible for their economic circumstances. Bail systems raise additional concerns about fairness when applied to juveniles—especially juveniles under sixteen. Labor laws disallow full-time employment for youths under sixteen. Juveniles under sixteen are also subject to mandatory school attendance laws, which further restrict their ability to become financially independent of their parents. Moreover, bail bondsmen are unlikely to enter into contracts with juveniles. Premising bail for a transferred juvenile on parents' financial resources and on parents' willingness to permit the youth to return home makes release contingent on a youth's status as a dependent minor. It is a strange and awkward irony that youths are held in jail as adults but are essentially dependent children for purposes of bail.

C. Consequences for the Juvenile Justice System

The juvenile justice system is also affected by transfer reforms. Certainly, some portion of older juveniles, juveniles charged with serious offenses, and juveniles having chronic records of offending will be less common in the juvenile justice system. It might also be expected that transfer will result in lighter caseloads for the juvenile system. This leads to the happy prospect of excess resources, which might be redirected to other areas of need within the juvenile justice system or channeled into the criminal justice system.

I am not very hopeful about either the likelihood of smaller caseloads in the juvenile system or the prospect of surplus resources. Courts (and other organizations) tend toward homeostasis. Studies of previous reform initiatives (e.g., diversion and detention; see Klein 1976; Blomberg 1977, 1979; Frazier, Richards, and Potter 1983; Frazier and Cochran 1986) indicate that reforms designed to eliminate segments of the juvenile court's caseload generally fail because of a systemic tendency to widen the net of control. The system adapts to reform initiatives that would reduce its span of control over one portion of the population by increasing the number of persons brought in under other areas over which it has control.

Evidence of this tendency is already apparent. From 1988 to 1994, while rates of referral to juvenile court intake nationally remained stable as a proportion of juvenile arrests, there was an increase in the rate at which referrals to the juvenile justice system were processed formally as well as in the rate of transfer (Sickmund et al. 1998). That is, the system formally handled many less serious cases that previously would have been handled informally or closed without action. In parallel fashion, juvenile courts may respond to rising transfer rates by committing less serious offenders to juvenile correctional facilities. Just as barring status offenders from detention centers and training schools during the 1970s failed to reduce the populations in these facilities, it is unlikely that removal of juvenile offenders to the criminal courts will produce reductions in juvenile institutional populations. In Florida, for example, commitment rates have skyrocketed despite increases in transfers and declines in felony referrals (Frazier, Bishop, and Lanza-Kaduce 1999).[30] Not only is it unlikely that transfer reforms will reduce the size of juvenile court or correctional populations, we must also be concerned about the potentially negative effects of increasing formal control over lesser offenders who remain in the juvenile system.

III. Consequences for Society: Implications of Transfer for Crime Control

Implicit in the strong rhetoric surrounding the criminalization of juvenile offending is a general deterrent purpose to dissuade juveniles from committing crimes through the threat of severe consequences, including lengthy terms of incarceration (Singer and McDowall 1988; Fagan 1995). In addition, the expanded application of transfer to include offenders who are neither particularly serious nor particularly chronic suggests a specific deterrent purpose as well. The general perception seems to be that the "soft" approach of the juvenile court actually contributes to high levels of crime and that getting tough will motivate young offenders to reform. Unfortunately, assessments of the extent to which transfer achieves these dual aims are few and recent. Like so many other reforms, this one did not flow from or build on careful

---

[30] In the past five years, Florida increased its commitments by 85 percent at the same time that transfers increased and felony referrals declined. It is unclear whether transfer and commitment trends are both manifestations of increasingly punitive attitudes toward juvenile offenders or whether commitment rates increased in an effort to fill vacancies in institutional programs that otherwise would have been created as a result of transfer of more juveniles to the adult system.

research. Recent research demonstrates convincingly that if changes in transfer policy had been contingent on scientific evidence of their efficacy, they would have been rejected.

A. General Deterrence

Only two studies to date have evaluated the general deterrent effects of transfer on juvenile crime. Singer and McDowall (1988; see also Singer 1996) conducted a very careful study of the effects of New York's Juvenile Offender Law, which in 1978 lowered the age of criminal court jurisdiction to thirteen for murder and to fourteen for rape, robbery, assault, and violent categories of burglary. Using a time-series design, they examined arrest rates for affected juveniles over a four-year period prior to enactment of the law and for six years following its implementation. Arrest rates for juveniles affected by the law were also compared with those of two control groups, sixteen- to nineteen-year-olds in the same jurisdiction (all of whom were defined as adults under New York law) and thirteen- and fourteen-year-olds in nearby Philadelphia. Singer and McDowall report that the law had little if any measurable impact. It is important to note that the law received significant advance publicity and that it was well implemented. Consequently, the most plausible explanation is that the threat of criminal punishment had no general deterrent effect.

Jensen and Metsger (1994) evaluated the general deterrent effect of an Idaho mandatory transfer statute introduced in 1981. The law required transfer of juveniles as young as fourteen who were charged with one of five very serious crimes: murder, attempted murder, robbery, forcible rape, and mayhem. The researchers examined arrest rates for the five-year period prior to the new law and for five years following its implementation. They also examined rates of arrest in neighboring Montana and Wyoming, states that were demographically and economically similar to Idaho and that used discretionary waiver, as had Idaho prior to the change in the law. Jensen and Metsger (1994) found no evidence of general deterrent effects. Instead, arrests for the target offenses increased in Idaho following the introduction of mandatory transfer, while they decreased in the two comparison states.

B. Specific Deterrence

To assess the impact of transfer on offenders' subsequent behavior, researchers have compared rates of recidivism of transferred youths and those retained in the juvenile system. A critical issue in these comparisons is whether the two groups are equivalent on all risk factors for recidivism other than the jurisdictional forum in which they were processed and sanctioned. Podkopacz and Feld (1995, 1996), for example, compared recidivism rates of youths judicially waived to the criminal court and youths for whom waiver motions were denied. They reported that transferred youths reoffended more often than those retained in juvenile court. But they also showed that waiver decisions were influenced by characteristics of the presenting offense and prior record, which introduce selection bias. The higher rate of recidivism in the transfer group may not mean that transfer has no specific deterrent effect but, instead, may simply mean that juvenile court judges were successful in identifying and transferring the "worst" offenders (Podkopacz and Feld 1995, 1996). Consequently, it is essential that researchers take steps to insure the equivalence of the groups under comparison. The best insurance against selection artifacts is random assignment to juvenile versus criminal processing, but true experimental designs in this context are simply not feasible. Researchers must rely instead on quasi-experimental designs and try to control for variables that are linked to recidivism (Fagan 1996). Two different methodologies have been employed in studies that produced very similar results.

The first study was carried out by Fagan (1991, 1995, 1996), who conducted a natural experiment to evaluate the effects of juvenile versus criminal justice processing. He identified two counties in New York and two in neighboring New Jersey that were part of a single large metropolitan area. All four communities were very similar on socioeconomic, demographic, and crime indicators that constitute risk factors for crime. New York and New Jersey also had very similar statutes for first- and second-degree robbery and first-degree burglary. The key difference was that in New York cases involving fifteen- and sixteen-year-olds charged with these crimes originated in the criminal courts under that state's legislative exclusion statute, while in New Jersey the juvenile courts retained jurisdiction over them. The samples consisted of 400 robbery offenders and 400 burglary offenders charged in 1981–82, who were randomly selected and evenly divided across the two states and four counties.

Fagan's approach provides excellent controls for the environment in which crime is generated and responded to. His selection of comparable statutes also provides a fairly good basis for comparing like crimes in like jurisdictions, varying only the court of original jurisdiction. However, it is possible that the experimental variable (original jurisdiction in juvenile vs. criminal court) could cause the same law to be applied differently. One might expect criminal prosecutors in New York to set a pretty high standard for processing cases they regard as first-degree robberies and burglaries. In contrast, the juvenile courts, with a rehabilitation and early intervention orientation, might select a broader range of offenders, making the pool of cases less serious on average. Another weakness of this study is that juvenile court records were not available for the criminal court cases processed in New York, so there was no way to determine the equivalence of subjects in terms of prior record. However, there is no a priori reason to anticipate cross-jurisdictional variations in prior offending rates or patterns that would confound the comparisons.

Fagan examined postrelease recidivism after a significant portion of the cohorts had completed their sentences and accumulated at least four years of time at risk. Several measures of recidivism were employed, including time to rearrest, prevalence of rearrest, prevalence of reincarceration, and frequency of rearrest adjusted for time at risk. While there were no significant differences in the effects of criminal versus juvenile court processing for burglary offenders, there were substantial differences in recidivism among robbery offenders prosecuted in juvenile versus criminal court.

Among the robbers, transfer was associated with a higher prevalence of rearrest: 76 percent of those processed in criminal court were rearrested, compared with 67 percent of those processed in juvenile court. An even greater effect was observed for the likelihood of reincarceration: 56 percent of the criminal court group were subsequently incarcerated, compared with 41 percent of the juvenile court group. Offenders prosecuted in criminal court also had higher rates of rearrest adjusted for time at risk (2.85 offenses) than those prosecuted in juvenile court (1.67 offenses), and they were rearrested more quickly (457 days compared with 553 days for those processed in juvenile court).

Differences across groups held up for the most part irrespective of the type of sanction imposed by the court. Those who were incarcerated were more likely to reoffend than those who were sentenced to probation, but those sentenced in criminal court to either incarceration or probation fared worse than their counterparts in juvenile court.

Among those who had been incarcerated, those sentenced in criminal court were more likely to be rearrested and to be rearrested more quickly than those sentenced in the juvenile court. Ninety-one percent of those incarcerated by the criminal courts were subsequently rearrested, compared to 73 percent of those incarcerated by the juvenile courts. Those incarcerated by the criminal courts reoffended much more quickly (392 days) than did those incarcerated by the juvenile courts (691 days). Those placed on probation by the criminal court were also more likely to be rearrested and to be arrested more often than those processed in the juvenile court. Eighty-one percent of those sentenced to adult probation were subsequently rearrested, compared to 64 percent of those sentenced to juvenile probation. In each comparison, the robbery offenders handled in the criminal court fared less well.

Subsequent studies conducted by my colleagues and me (Bishop et al. 1996; Winner et al. 1997) reinforce Fagan's findings and conclusions. Our research was conducted in Florida, a state that uses prosecutorial waiver almost exclusively. In the course of other studies of prosecutorial waiver practice in the state, we learned that, although thousands of juveniles are transferred each year, thousands of equally serious or even more serious offenders are not transferred (see, e.g., Frazier 1991). This finding provided the opportunity for a significant policy study similar to Fagan's. Unlike Fagan's research, ours was carried out in a single state. To overcome the problem of selection bias, we used a matching procedure to pair each case transferred to criminal court with an equivalent case retained in the juvenile system. Each pair was matched on seven factors, including the most serious offense charged, the number of counts charged, the number of prior delinquency referrals, the most serious prior offense, age, gender, and race. Using cases processed in 1987, we were able to generate 2,738 transfers who matched with 2,738 juveniles whose cases were retained in the juvenile system.

A weakness of the Florida studies is that the matched-individuals approach does not take into account jurisdictional variations in community context that may be related to both the commission of crime and crime control practices. While all twenty judicial circuits in the state are subject to the same laws, there is considerable variation in crime rates as well as in practices of crime control (Bishop, Lanza-Kaduce, and Winner 1996; Lanza-Kaduce, Bishop, and Winner 1997). The analysis rests on an assumption that transferred youths do not differ systematically from their matches in terms of the community contexts from which they originate. Another weakness is that we have controlled for many, but certainly not all, of the personal offender and offense characteristics that affect the risk of recidivism. It is possible that the two groups differ in terms of factors such as mental health, family background, or neighborhood, which were not controlled. However, we are inclined to believe that there is minimal bias from such sources. In Florida, prosecutors rarely have access to offenders' personal and family background information when they make transfer decisions. Unlike judicial waiver, which occurs only after a hearing where consideration is given to youths' backgrounds and circumstances, in Florida prosecutorial waiver decisions are most often made quickly, based on readily available information regarding the offense, the defendant's age, and prior record (Bishop et al. 1998). These variables were controlled in the matching procedure.

We assessed recidivism over the short and long terms. The short-term analysis followed cases for a maximum of twenty-four months, while the long-term follow-up tracked offenders for up to seven years. The findings of both studies indicated that juveniles transferred to criminal court fared worse than those retained in the juvenile justice system. This was true over every comparison in the short term and over most comparisons in the long-term study.

Several measures of recidivism were employed: rearrest prevalence, incidence of rearrest, severity of the first rearrest offense, and time to failure. Over the short term, 30 percent of the transfers were rearrested, compared with 19 percent of those processed in juvenile court. Transfers were also more likely than those processed in the juvenile system to be arrested for more serious (felony) offenses. The incidence of offending was also higher in the transfer group: transfers had a rearrest rate of 1.9 offenses per person year of exposure, compared with 1.7 for those retained in the juvenile system. The transfers also reoffended more quickly (135 days) than those processed in juvenile court (227 days).

Over the long term, overall differences in rearrest prevalence were no longer significant across the two groups. However, analysis by offense type showed that transfers were more likely to reoffend in five of seven comparisons. Moreover, significant differences in rates of reoffending remained. When we calculated rearrest rates overall and for each of seven classes of offense, rates of rearrest were higher for those who had been transferred across all comparisons. Significant differences in time to failure also remained.

The Florida studies add substantively and substantially to Fagan's research. Not only do they provide a confirmation of the findings in a different jurisdiction, time frame, and sociolegal context using a differ-

ent transfer method, they also add new offenses to the mix. Taken together, and keeping in mind that there is no evidence of any general
deterrent effect of the transfer reforms, they provide a strong case for
more limited use of transfer and more openness to the potential benefits of handling offenders within the juvenile justice system.

IV. Consequences of Transfer for Juvenile Offenders

In order to interpret the findings of the comparative recidivism studies,
it is essential that we develop an understanding of the impact of transfer on young offenders. No consequences of transfer are potentially
more important or less frequently examined than the experiences of
juveniles in the criminal justice system and the meanings they attach
to them. What are the effects on a fifteen-year-old of being tried in
criminal rather than juvenile court? Of being held in jail rather than
juvenile detention? Of serving time in prison rather than a juvenile facility? Of returning to the community with a criminal rather than a
juvenile record? There is an urgent need to address these questions not
only because transfer is more common but also because there are clear
signs that the juvenile justice system is becoming more like the criminal justice system (e.g., explicit endorsement of punishment, adoption
of determinate sentencing, and extended jurisdiction). In addition,
there have been some serious proposals from distinguished scholars to
abolish the juvenile courts and unify the two systems (see, e.g., Ainsworth 1991, 1995; Feld 1993, 1997).

The search for answers takes us in three directions. There are some
objective data about the juvenile and adult corrections systems from
which it is possible to draw limited inferences about possible effects of
transfer on incarcerated offenders. In addition, corrections research
has identified special problems faced by adolescents in adult correctional settings as well as potentially important links between organizational goals and inmate attitudes and behaviors. Finally, and most helpful, are two studies that compared the experiences and reactions of
adolescents processed in the juvenile system and those transferred to
the criminal system. I begin this section with these studies and interject
discussion of the objective data and corrections research as appropriate.

In the early 1980s, Forst, Fagan, and Vivona (1989) interviewed 140
adolescent male offenders in four states, all of whom had been convicted of serious violent crimes. Fifty-nine had been processed in juvenile courts and confined in training schools while the rest had been

transferred and incarcerated in prisons. More recently, my colleagues and I interviewed ninety-five serious and chronic adolescent male offenders in Florida (Bishop et al. 1998). Forty-nine had been transferred to criminal court and either confined in state prisons (N = 46) or placed on probation (N = 3). The balance had been prosecuted in juvenile court and were incarcerated in "maximum risk" juvenile commitment facilities. Both studies inquired into youths' postdisposition experiences in correctional settings, including perceptions of staff, services, and programs. In addition, the Florida study asked youths about their experiences in the juvenile and criminal courts, about perceptions of procedural and substantive justice, and about their experiences in and reactions to preadjudicatory confinement in detention centers and jails.

These studies are valuable because they shed light on the consequences of transfer from the vantage point of offenders. They tune in to the subjective, cognitive, and affective dimensions of the ways processing and incarceration are experienced, dimensions that are not tapped by other research methods. It is also important to acknowledge their limitations. There are only two of these studies, and both employed small samples. The jurisdictions studied may be atypical, and the programs and facilities observed within the study jurisdictions may not be broadly representative of those found either within those jurisdictions or in other parts of the country. Consequently, the studies should be viewed as exploratory. With these caveats in mind, I begin by exploring adolescents' reactions to the "front end" of each system, drawing on the research conducted in Florida.

A. Processing in the Juvenile and Criminal Courts

We (Bishop et al. 1998) were particularly interested in learning what meanings juveniles attached to court hearings, and how they understood or interpreted the actions of the major players involved in the processing and disposition of their cases. From all outward appearances, Florida's juvenile courts take a no-nonsense approach to juvenile crime, which is reflected in high rates of detention, commitment, and transfer to criminal court.[31] Frankly, we anticipated that young offend-

---

[31] Objective indicators of punitiveness abound. For example, the purpose clause of Florida's Juvenile Justice Act identifies protection of public safety as the primary objective. In 1994 the legislature divested the state's major social welfare agency of its authority over juvenile justice operations, and transferred it instead to a new Department of Juvenile Justice, which describes itself as a criminal justice agency (Florida Department of Juvenile Justice 1998). Detention is permitted for purposes of punishment and is mandated for many offenders, including some first-time misdemeanants. Until 1994, juvenile

ers would have negative attitudes toward the juvenile courts and perceive them as highly punitive in orientation. Surprisingly, nearly all of them—including those who had been transferred—described the juvenile courts in favorable terms. In describing their court experiences many commented that judges had interacted with them personally during court proceedings and expressed interest in their problems and concern for their well-being. Most believed that juvenile court judges were motivated to help them. Even those who indicated that the judge's intent was to punish them generally perceived that the punishment was well intended (e.g., "It was for my own good, to teach me a lesson"). Most recognized the purposes of the court as commendable and right. Few regarded either juvenile court processes or outcomes as unfair.

Most transferred offenders described the criminal court in very different terms. Unlike what they had experienced in juvenile court, it appeared to most of them that criminal court judges had little interest in them or their problems. Court proceedings were described as formal and hurried, and many youths reported difficulty understanding legal terminology. Much of what they understood—or thought they understood—about court proceedings came from brief conversations either with their attorneys or with fellow inmates in the jail, more often the latter than the former.

Criminal court processes were perceived as much more complex than juvenile ones, involving gamesmanship and high stakes deal-making. Many youths failed to differentiate the roles and functions of judges, prosecutors, and defense counsel, whom they perceived as one, and as adversarial. Several respondents were especially critical of public defenders, whom they believed feigned advocacy in an effort to manipulate them to accept pleas that were not in their best interests.[32] Often

---

corrections programming had been organized into a four-tier system of "restrictiveness levels." In that year, a fifth tier ("maximum risk") was added and, shortly thereafter, the state's residential commitment capacity increased by nearly 250 percent. From 1993 to 1997, while felony referrals declined, detention populations increased by 34 percent and juvenile commitments increased by 77 percent. Over the same period, an average of over 7,000 cases were transferred to criminal court annually, the highest rate in the nation (Florida Department of Juvenile Justice 1997).

[32] Most respondents drew a distinction between public defenders and "attorneys," the latter designation being reserved for retained counsel. Attorneys were generally held in high regard as advocates. Several youths' families made considerable sacrifice to hire attorneys after observing what they adjudged to be the poor performance of court-appointed public defenders. There were numerous allegations that public defenders did not visit them during many months of pretrial confinement and that they urged them, as one offender put it, to "jump on too much time."

these interpretations were reinforced by family members and fellow jail inmates. Nearly all of the transferred youths eventually pled guilty, but, because they had little basis on which to distinguish a "good deal" from a bad one, they almost always felt dissatisfied with the outcome.

The vast majority of transferred youths reported that the clear purpose of criminal court sentencing was to punish them. Some believed that sentencing decisions were linked to their offenses and were designed to achieve some retributive or deterrent purpose. While these youths frequently complained that their sentences were disproportionate to the gravity of their crimes, they tended nonetheless to grant legitimacy to the idea that offense criteria guided sentencing decisions. However, more respondents believed that sentencing decisions were based not on considerations of what they had done but, rather, on inferences about essential characteristics of their persons, including judgments that they were depraved or irredeemable. Several respondents suggested that judges vilified them and based sentencing decisions on feelings of personal animosity (e.g., "He hated me and wanted to destroy my life"), which they perceived as illegitimate. Not surprisingly, such attributions of hostility provoked feelings of anger and resentment, as well as perceptions of injustice. Attributions of hostility are common among delinquents, especially violent offenders (Dodge et al. 1990; Crick and Dodge 1994). What was unexpected is that these attributions were made frequently in discussions of the criminal courts, but not of the juvenile courts.

B. Preadjudicatory Confinement

There were many similarities in the ways that respondents experienced preadjudicatory confinement in the juvenile and adult systems. Their general comments about juvenile detention centers and jails were much the same. They most often described their purposes as custodial, their staffs as indifferent, and their environments as bleak and (at least initially) threatening. In some critical respects, however, experiences in the two settings differed. For example, after repeated admissions to detention centers, many youths reported having formed significant attachments to at least one line staff member. This was not the case in jails. In addition, preadjudicatory detention stays were generally described as less stressful than stays in jail. In part this was due to the fact that the duration of detention was typically brief in comparison to time spent in jail. Pending the outcome of their criminal cases, the vast majority of transferred youths remained in jail for several months.

Other stressors associated with jail included boredom and anxieties stemming from separation from family and friends, from the unresolved nature of their cases, and from perceived dangers within the jail facilities (see also Gibbs 1982; Adams 1992). Many transferred youths reported difficulty adjusting to being jailed with adult offenders. Several mentioned that jail officials appeared not to differentiate between them and some of the chronic and violent adult offenders with whom they were housed. Most did not perceive themselves as hardened or dangerous criminals and found it disquieting when officials viewed them in these terms. The sense of danger many experienced seemed to be largely a function of the inmate grapevine, which was riddled with stories of older inmates preying on young boys. Several reported that they were fearful of attack by sexual predators and "crazies." Some responded by isolating themselves as much as they could. Others reported that they formed alliances with other inmates for self-protection.

In other research, the strain of confinement in jail has been linked to suicide. Young persons are thought to be especially vulnerable to suicide in jail because they have fewer coping skills to deal with feelings of helplessness, isolation, and fear stemming from the uncertainty of the pretrial period, loss of contact with families, threats of victimization from other inmates, and other stressors associated with incarceration (see, e.g., Liebling 1999). The suicide rate for juveniles in jails is estimated greatly to exceed the rate for the general youth population and to be several times higher than the rate of suicide among youths in juvenile detention centers (Flaherty 1983; Library Information Specialists 1983; Memory 1989). While none of our respondents indicated that they had contemplated suicide while in jail, many reported feeling overwhelmed, confused, and depressed.

C. Characteristics of Juvenile and Adult Correctional Institutions

Many transferred offenders serve sentences in adult correctional facilities. In a majority of states, they are housed with the general adult population (thirty-one states), with youthful offenders up to age twenty-one or twenty-five (seven states), or some combination of the two (five states) (Library Information Specialists 1995). Consequently, it is valuable to consider what we know about adult correctional settings and how they compare with juvenile ones. Unfortunately, while the corrections literature is replete with studies of juvenile and adult institutions, there has been almost no comparative research that spans juvenile and adult correctional settings. Studies of institutions for juveniles have frequently uncovered problems of the same sorts as have been reported in research on adult facilities (e.g., inmate-inmate violence, staff-inmate violence, use of solitary confinement for extended periods, inadequate staffing). While we know little about how pervasive these problems are in either system, there are some dimensions along which we can compare them.

First, the populations in juvenile and adult institutions differ markedly. Obviously, the prison population is older. Nearly half of prison inmates are between the ages of twenty-five and thirty-four (Bureau of Justice Statistics 1997), while more than 70 percent of youths in juvenile facilities are between the ages of fifteen and seventeen (Parent et al. 1994). Corollaries of age in this context include greater size and physical strength, longer criminal histories, and more experience with incarceration (60 percent of prison inmates have previously been incarcerated in an adult jail or prison [Beck et al. 1993]). Adult and juvenile institutions also differ in the types of offenders they house. While 20 percent of youths confined in training schools are there for a violent offense (Parent et al. 1994), nearly 50 percent of prison inmates are violent offenders (Bureau of Justice Statistics 1997). Those incarcerated in juvenile institutions remain confined for much shorter periods, eight months on average (Parent et al. 1994). Prison inmates have average sentences of nine years and, increasingly, they can expect to serve much of that time in confinement. In sum, when juveniles are transferred to criminal court and institutionalized with adults, they are exposed to an older, stronger, more seasoned and more violent group of offenders over an extended period.

Second, there are organizational differences between juvenile and adult institutions. Adult facilities tend to be much larger than juvenile ones. More than 40 percent of adult institutions house more than 500 inmates; nearly 25 percent hold more than 1,000 (Bureau of Justice Statistics 1997). The average daily population in institutions for adults is 700, compared to approximately seventy in juvenile facilities. Even training schools, the largest of the juvenile facilities, have an average population of only 127 (Parent et al. 1994). Overcrowding is a problem in both juvenile and adult institutions. Eleven percent of training schools in 1991 were under consent decrees for overcrowded conditions, as were 17 percent of adult correctional facilities (Parent et al.

1994; Bureau of Justice Statistics 1997). Institutional size and over-crowding have been linked to levels of violence and to other important behavioral and psychological consequences (see, e.g., Adams 1992).

Third, staffing patterns differ markedly in the two systems. Prisons accord a much higher priority to security concerns: two-thirds of all personnel in adult correctional facilities are custody or security staff. Their ratio to inmates is 1:4 (Bureau of Justice Statistics 1997). The most recent census of children in custody showed that only 43 percent of training schools had at least one staff member assigned to custodial or monitoring functions for every eleven residents (the recommended standard). In most, the ratio was higher than that (Parent et al. 1994). Staffing for education is also very different in adult and juvenile facilities. The teacher/inmate ratio in adult institutions is 1:100. A national survey of prison inmates in 1991 indicated that fewer than half received any academic instruction (Beck et al. 1993). In 95 percent of training schools, there is at least one teacher for every fifteen residents. In half these facilities all juveniles are involved in education programs, and in an additional 40 percent of these facilities, more than 75 percent are (Parent et al. 1994). Of 475 incarcerated juveniles included in a recent national survey, most expressed satisfaction that staff did a "very good" job of teaching them something useful (Parent et al. 1994, p. 141).

There are also important differences in the numbers of counseling or treatment staff. In two-thirds of training schools, there is at least one counselor for every ten juveniles; in 85 percent, the ratio is at least 1:25 (Parent et al. 1994). It is difficult to determine the numbers of counseling staff in state prisons. They are included in a very broad category of "professional and technical" personnel—including but not limited to all medical and classification staff—for whom the ratio of staff to inmates is 1:25 (Bureau of Justice Statistics 1997). Whether these differences in programming and staffing patterns are only nominal, or whether they translate into real differences with consequences for quality of life, emotional well-being, behavioral change, or future life chances, is discussed below.

D. *Young Offenders in the Juvenile and Adult Corrections Systems*

A substantial body of research suggests that organizational climates have important consequences for inmate attitudes and behaviors. Inmates behave differently in different settings (Adams 1992). Although inmates' backgrounds and individual characteristics clearly influence their behavior, they may be less predictive of institutional adjustment than the context in which inmates are confined. Some research suggests that inmates adapt in more positive ways to treatment-oriented institutions (Street, Vinter, and Perrow 1966; Feld 1977). Compared to inmates in custody-oriented institutions, those in treatment-oriented institutions reportedly have more favorable perspectives on staff, collaborate more with staff, and are more likely to develop egalitarian relationships with fellow inmates (Feld 1977). They are more receptive to the idea of change, develop greater personal control and problem-solving abilities, and are more optimistic about remaining law abiding following release (Street, Vinter, and Perrow 1966).

1. *Organizational Context.* In correctional settings where custody concerns dominate, inmates tend to perceive institutions as oppressive. Staff and inmates tend to be alienated from each other and to respond to each other based on negative stereotypes, which are thereby reinforced (Street, Vinter, and Perrow 1966). Inmates in custody-oriented institutions also have more incentive to engage in deviant behavior, are more likely to resort to interpersonal violence, and are more resistant to change (Feld 1977; Poole and Regoli 1983). Moreover, there is some evidence that inmates released from custody-oriented programs are more likely to recidivate and, when they do, to commit more serious offenses than those released from treatment-oriented institutions (Feld 1977). While each study just cited involved comparisons across different juvenile institutions, their findings may be applicable in a more general way to differences between juvenile and adult correctional settings. This is not to suggest that some juvenile institutions are not extremely custody oriented, or that some adult institutions are not highly treatment oriented. It is to say, given important differences in philosophy that have traditionally characterized the two systems, that juvenile institutions are likely to place greater emphasis on treatment than are adult institutions.

The findings of our research (Bishop et al. 1998) and Forst, Fagan, and Vivona's (1989) speak directly to this issue. Despite the punitive rhetoric of juvenile justice in Florida in 1997, the juvenile institutions we visited were clearly treatment oriented, as were the institutions observed by Forst, Fagan, and Vivona in the early 1980s. The Florida facilities were organized around a therapeutic model—most often, a cognitive-behavioral one—which provided core principles that governed staff behavior and staff-resident interactions. Residents had a full round of daily activities that included academic classes, social skills training, counseling sessions, and recreational activities. Some youths were also involved in vocational training, substance abuse treatment, and other activities.

Staff in each of the four juvenile programs we visited were expected to model self-discipline, social skills, and strategies for problem solving and impulse control. In the juvenile institutions observed in both studies, even line staff were trained in treatment methodologies and were expected to integrate them into daily activities on a more-or-less ongoing basis (e.g., anger management might well be taught in the midst of a baseball game as well as in evening group sessions designated for that purpose). Significant incentives—salary enhancements and promotions—were linked to therapeutic skills.

Our respondents described most juvenile program staff in very positive terms. The general sense of youths' comments was that most staff cared for them, understood what troubled them, and believed in their potential to become productive and happy adults. Staff were credited with being skilled at modeling and teaching appropriate behaviors, and providing helpful guidance about personal matters.[33] To be sure, some staff in each juvenile institution were described as "nine-to-fivers," individuals with little interest or concern for youths who were simply "working for the money." However, seldom were more than a small fraction of staff characterized in this way.

Similarly, Forst, Fagan, and Vivona (1989) found that, compared to staff in prisons, staff in juvenile facilities were perceived to be more involved in counseling, more concerned about youths' adjustment, more encouraging of their participation in programs, more helpful in assisting them to understand themselves and deal with their problems, and more facilitative of improved relationships with their families. Juvenile program staff were also rated significantly more highly than prison staff in terms of helping youths to set and achieve goals, to improve relationships with peers, to feel better about themselves, and to acquire skills that would be useful on release.

---

[33] The largest of the juvenile facilities we visited housed 150 residents. The smallest held thirty. Although each facility was surrounded by perimeter fencing, some topped with razor wire, inside there did not appear to be a strong focus on security. There were no uniformed staff. Staff-resident contact and interaction were frequent, and most often it appeared positive and supportive. We often observed staff offering youths praise and encouragement. It was not at all unusual to see a staff member put his hand on a boys' shoulder in a gesture of support. Although it appeared that program rules were strictly enforced through the imposition of consequences specified in behavioral contracts (e.g., loss of a weekend pass), the atmosphere was not predominantly one of control.

The prisons we visited, like those observed by Forst, Fagan, and Vivona, were clearly dominated by custody concerns. In part, this was surely a function of the size of the facilities. The eight prisons we visited ranged in capacity from 350 to 1,200. In large institutions, even in settings where the avowed purpose is to treat rather than punish, security concerns tend to become all-consuming. To insure the safety of inmates and staff and to guard against escape, regulations must be enforced governing nearly every aspect of inmate life, and searches, segregation, counts, and restrictions on movement are routine. Quite apart from concerns about safety and prevention of escape, however, the custody-orientation of today's prisons reflects the goal of incapacitation that has gained such favor in policy circles (Spelman 1994; Zimring and Hawkins 1995).

Concerns about order and security were very apparent inside the prisons we observed. The vast majority of the personnel within these institutions were uniformed correctional officers. The correctional officers we observed were highly authoritarian and appeared to be focused exclusively on enforcing rules, maximizing surveillance, and displaying their power. They rarely spoke to inmates except to issue commands. We observed little interaction between correctional staff and inmates that was not formal and impersonal.

Because the prisons were primarily custodial facilities, most of our inmate respondents were not engaged in programs aimed at their personal or social development. Many expressed a desire to participate in rehabilitative programming, but fewer than 10 percent were engaged in any sort of counseling or treatment program.[34] Several attended remedial education classes for part of each day, and some reported that they were learning a trade, usually one related to facility maintenance. Despite these reported activities, it was common for respondents to report that they had a great deal of idle time that they found burdensome. There appeared to be too few work assignments to go around. This is an issue not only in Florida. Across the nation, only one-third of state prison inmates work more than thirty-four hours per week, and a third do not work at all (Bureau of Justice Statistics 1997).

---

[34] Counseling was the responsibility of a few professional staff who met with inmates during segmental time slots. This is not surprising, since treatment often represents an "invasion" in a custody-dominated system. Even at the height of the medical model in the 1960s "those in the custodial ranks tended to view treatment personnel with varying degrees of skepticism, mistrust, or at best, grudging tolerance" (Fox and Stinchcomb 1994, p. 354).

When we asked inmates about prison staff, almost all responded with reference to correctional officers. Although some inmates had contact with teachers and all had occasional appointments with classification officers and medical personnel, their contacts with correctional officers tended to color their thinking about staff in general and, to a considerable degree, about the institution as well. Most respondents believed prison staff viewed them as "convicts," "criminals," or "nobodies" who would never change. Correctional officers were almost uniformly perceived in negative terms, as hostile and derisive. Many respondents reported feeling threatened by correctional staff, both physically and emotionally. Several gave accounts of being humiliated by correctional officers and of being goaded or provoked into conflicts that would result in their being disciplined. (While we had a few similar reports regarding staff in juvenile detention centers, there was no indication that juvenile detainees distrusted staff in general.) Many responded by trying to minimize interactions with staff. Others became confrontational and defiant. They violated rules, accumulated disciplinary reports and, as a consequence, were punished with solitary confinement and loss of gain time.

2. *Criminal Socialization.* The physical setting of the prison provided many more opportunities for private interaction among inmates than was the case in the juvenile facilities. In the juvenile programs, staff participated in activities with small groups of youths throughout the day and, at night, remained in close proximity to them in their dormitories. In the prisons, for much of the day large groups of inmates congregated in the yard while correctional officers watched at a distance from the perimeter. During the evenings, inmates remained in their cells or dormitories supervised by correctional officers separated from them in glass-enclosed control rooms. Youths in prison reported that they spent much of their time talking to more skilled and experienced offenders who taught them new techniques of committing crime and methods of avoiding detection. Strained relations between inmates and staff provided additional incentive to plan unlawful behaviors surreptitiously.

3. *Misconduct and Violence.* One of the most consistent findings in corrections research is that misconduct is most common among young inmates. Indeed, age is the strongest predictor of prison misconduct (see, e.g., Wolfgang 1961; Brown and Spevacek 1971; Ellis, Grasmick, and Gilman 1974; Jensen 1977; Myers and Levy 1978; Mabli et al. 1979; Flanagan 1983, 1996; Goetting and Howsen 1986; McShane and

Williams 1989; Toch and Adams 1989; Craddock 1996). In the only study to explore misconduct among juvenile inmates, McShane and Williams (1989) compared the prison adjustment of serious and violent offenders committed to Texas prisons prior to age seventeen and a matched group of offenders committed between the ages of seventeen and twenty-one. Compared with inmates in their mid-twenties and above, those in the seventeen- to twenty-one-year range have traditionally had the highest levels of misconduct. Yet Williams and McShane found that juvenile offenders were twice as likely as those age seventeen to twenty-one to have disciplinary incidents during the first two years of incarceration, and three times as likely to be placed in administrative segregation for aggressive behavior. Further, because work and good time were linked to good behavior, only half the juvenile inmates had work assignments (compared to more than 80 percent of the young adults) and less than 20 percent earned good time credits at the maximum rate (compared with 40 percent of the young adults).

Prisons are dangerous places where inmate norms frequently support violent behavior (see Toch 1977; Irwin 1980; Lockwood 1980; Bowker 1985). Displays of verbal and physical aggression "prove" one's toughness and masculinity and establish social position in a context in which there are few alternative means of earning status. They are also means by which gangs build cohesion and establish position in the social hierarchy. Because adolescents as a group tend to be highly sensitive to peer pressure, young offenders are especially likely to engage in violent behavior and to develop identities linked to domination and control. In the context of the prison, there is little modeling of constructive ways of building identities, satisfying affiliative needs, developing competencies, or resolving interpersonal problems.

4. *Victimization.* Forst, Fagan, and Vivona (1989) questioned their respondents about victimizations in prisons and training schools. Weapons assaults were reported by one-quarter of training school residents and one-third of juveniles confined in prisons; sexual attacks by 2 percent of training school residents and 9 percent of juveniles in prison; and beatings by staff by 5 percent of training school residents and 10 percent of juveniles in prison. Unlike Forst, Fagan, and Vivona, we (Bishop et al. 1998) did not systematically survey respondents about victimizations. Nevertheless, in describing prison life, about one-quarter of the transferred youths reported that they had either been assaulted or witnessed an act of assault by a fellow inmate, and approximately one-third reported either being assaulted or witnessing an

assault on a fellow inmate by a correctional officer. In addition, many others reported that the danger of violence was far greater in prison than in juvenile facilities.

Other corrections research consistently shows that young inmates who lack the experience to cope with the predatory environment within prisons are at greatest risk for physical and sexual assault (Fuller and Orsagh 1977; Toch 1977; Bowker 1980; Irwin 1980; Wright 1991; Cooley 1993; Gillespie, n.d.). They also feel most vulnerable to physical and sexual predation, which contributes to their exploitation; fear is often interpreted as a sign of weakness. Because of their vulnerability, adolescent inmates are more likely to be placed in protective or "safekeep" custody than are older inmates (McShane and Williams 1989). While this strategy is intended to protect them from harm, protective custody is not without negative consequences. Generally, inmates in protective custody are isolated from others around the clock, do not participate in educational or other programming, and have little recreation.[35]

Fear of victimization has also been linked to psychological well-being, especially among those who are unwilling or unable to retaliate against predators (Toch 1977; McCorkle 1993a, 1993b; Maitland and Sluder 1996). Fearful inmates are frequently anxious and depressed. Thus not only are young inmates more likely to be placed in protective custody because of their vulnerability to attack, but they are also more likely to be placed in specialized units for treatment of mental health problems (McShane and Williams 1989).

5. *Reported Effects.*   In our research, we asked youths about the impact of their experiences in juvenile and adult correctional facilities on their attitudes and behaviors. Nearly all subjects (both the transfers and the nontransfers) had been committed to at least two juvenile pro-

---

[35] Inmates' preferred strategy for coping with threats of victimization (and other difficult situations) is to handle problems themselves (Flanagan 1980; Adams 1992). Reporting to officials is a sign of weakness and violates norms against "snitching" whose breach is likely to be met with violent retaliation. Some inmates respond to threats proactively, trying to prevent victimization through "preemptive self-defense" (Irwin 1980; Lockwood 1980; Johnson 1987; McCorkle 1992). Others adopt avoidance techniques such as staying away from "risky" areas and spending as much time as possible in their cells (Bartollas, Miller, and Dinitz 1976; Lockwood 1980). These responses are age patterned: young inmates are more likely than older ones to employ aggressive responses to threats (McCorkle 1992). Thus the manner in which young inmates tend to respond to threats amplifies problems of disruptiveness, which works to their disadvantage (e.g., loss of gain time, removal from work assignments, greater idle time and boredom) and makes it more difficult for administrators to manage them effectively (Adams 1992; McCorkle 1992).

grams. Although critical of many juvenile programs, the vast majority of youths reported that one or more had been beneficial to them. They were most critical of programs that were impersonal or that were of insufficient duration or intensity to have a real or sustained impact (e.g., community work service, electronic monitoring, standard probation). Youths attributed the greatest benefit to intensive, long-term programs in which they had formed relationships of trust with caring adults, ones who believed in their worth and who encouraged them. While educational and vocational training were seen as important, youths tended to place greater value on programs that taught them how to exercise self-control, those that taught basic interpersonal skills, and those that focused on teaching them values and enhanced self-respect. It is noteworthy that the characteristics of the programs they nominated as most helpful are those that research suggests are most likely to produce reductions in recidivism (Cullen and Gilbert 1982; Garrett 1985; Gendreau and Ross 1987; Andrews et al. 1990; Palmer 1991, 1995; Lipsey 1992; Mulvey, Arthur, and Reppucci 1993; Lipsey and Wilson 1998).[36]

Although the transferred offenders endorsed the juvenile corrections system to the same degree as did those who were still in that system, the vast majority perceived little that was positive in their experience in the adult corrections system. For most, it was at best a test of will and endurance from which they hoped to emerge intact. At worst, it was a painful and denigrating experience that they pointed to as reason or justification for becoming more angry, embittered, cynical, or defeated or more skilled at committing crime.

More than half the respondents who were currently incarcerated in juvenile facilities expressed confidence that they would remain law abiding following release. Most often the optimism they expressed was attributed to shifts in attitudes about themselves and others resulting from relationships with program staff or to new skills they had developed while in the programs. A substantial number of nontransfers (42 percent) were uncertain about their futures, but only 3 percent antici-

[36] The questions whether treatment in general, or specific kinds of treatment, are effective in reducing recidivism have been the subject of considerable controversy. Research reviews have reached widely different conclusions, some showing substantial positive effects, others showing insignificant or even negative effects. Recent meta-analyses, which represent significant improvements over earlier reviews in the comprehensiveness of their coverage of the research literature and in their ability to partition the effects of research methodology from the effects of the treatment itself (see esp. Lipsey 1992; Lipsey and Wilson 1998), have produced encouraging results.

pated that they would commit further crimes. In contrast, only one-third of those in the adult system expected to remain law abiding. Moreover, those who did so attributed change to "time" or maturation, rather than to the development of personal resources or skills that rendered them better able to deal with the outside world.[37] Forty-six percent of those in the adult system were uncertain that they would remain law abiding, and 18 percent expected to reoffend.

E. Postrelease Consequences

Whether or not they are incarcerated, juvenile offenders convicted in criminal court will experience effects of their involvement in the criminal justice system. Criminal conviction carries many consequences that may affect young offenders' lives in a manner that impedes chances for reform long after their sentences have been served. Felony convictions commonly result in a number of civil disabilities, including loss of the right to serve in the military, to vote, to hold public office, and to sit on a jury. Perhaps the most severe consequences of conviction, however, have to do with effects on future employment and conventional associations. In many states, criminal conviction results in loss, suspension, and restriction of professional and occupational licenses as well as disqualification from obtaining some licenses in the future (Kuzma 1996). More important, unlike juvenile delinquency adjudications, criminal convictions must be reported on applications for employment. An adult felony conviction, especially if followed by incarceration, can have a profoundly negative effect on future labor market participation (Freeman 1992; Fagan and Freeman 1999). This effect is all the more serious in light of longitudinal research on criminal career patterns showing that entry into stable employment is a crucial factor in desistance from crime (Sampson and Laub 1993). The informal sanction of being denied employment because of a criminal record presents a formidable barrier to becoming a law-abiding adult. It can be a watershed experience that places a strain on young people to resort to illegal behavior to support themselves and fulfill family responsibilities.

---

[37] Some of these same individuals lamented the fact that they had not previously taken better advantage of programs offered in the juvenile system. This is an interesting group of respondents. Some said the earlier juvenile programs had a positive effect on them, but it was not enough. Others said they had simply not been open to change in the past. Personal maturation and the pain of lengthy incarceration were cited as reasons they were now ready to change.

In addition, as a result of a criminal conviction, offenders who are motivated to remove themselves from the criminogenic influence of former friends and associates may encounter obstacles that make it difficult to become integrated into conventional groups and activities. Development of significant bonds to conventional others has the potential to alter criminal trajectories. For example, research shows the importance of marriage characterized by bonds of affection and commitment in interrupting criminal careers (Sampson and Laub 1993). But the stigma of a criminal conviction limits access to conventional social networks. Ex-offenders may find themselves shunned not only by prospective employers, but by prospective friends and dating partners as well. In our own research (Bishop et al. 1998), a number of respondents recognized these problems. Most transferred youths expressed worry about finding a good job. Several anticipated that they would be turned down by prospective employers for jobs for which they were qualified. Many who expressed a desire to change also clearly recognized the importance of severing ties with past associates and of developing ties with conforming individuals who would support and encourage new behavior patterns. Often they anticipated pressure from the former to continue their criminal activities and feared that the latter would not accept them.

V. Conclusions

Three major findings emerge from studies that compared rates of recidivism among youths transferred to criminal court and youths retained in the juvenile system. First, transfer appears to be counterproductive: transferred youths are more likely to reoffend, and to reoffend more quickly and more often, than those retained in the juvenile system. In addition, Fagan's (1991, 1995, 1996) research suggests that the differential effects of criminal and juvenile justice processing are not dependent on sentence type or sentence length. That is, the mere fact that juveniles have been prosecuted and convicted in criminal rather than in juvenile court increases the likelihood that they will reoffend. Finally, the risk of reoffending is aggravated when a sentence of incarceration is imposed.

These findings lend themselves to several alternative explanations. It may be that processing in the criminal justice system contributes to further offending. Alternatively, and contrary to the sentiment underlying the transfer reforms, processing in the juvenile justice system may be effective in promoting law-abiding behavior, even among serious and violent offenders. Or both explanations may be correct. Based on what we learned from our interviews with young offenders and from related research, an interpretation that is consistent with both of these explanations seems plausible.

Braithwaite's (1989) theory of reintegrative shaming is a promising general theoretical perspective that can inform this discussion (Bishop et al. 1996; Winner et al. 1997). Building on social control theory, Braithwaite argues that children learn prosocial attitudes, values, and behavior through bonding or attachment to others. Children who as teens engage in serious and chronic delinquency have most often failed to develop close attachments to others. For a variety of reasons—some related to their parents, some to the children themselves—they are weakly bonded to their parents, who frequently do a poor job of monitoring and teaching appropriate behaviors (Moffitt 1999). Often the result is that these children are undersocialized and possess traits (e.g., impulsivity, selfishness, aggressiveness) that make it more difficult for them to form positive relationships with others.[38]

Processing in juvenile court is associated with a lower probability of reoffending. One reason this may be so is that juvenile justice officials communicate messages of caring—that is, offers of attachment—to young people whose backgrounds are often replete with alienation from and rejection by conventional adults. Time and again in our interviews with young offenders we were made aware of their sensitivity to signs of interest and concern from judges, detention workers, and juvenile program staff. Where they formed significant attachments, they appeared to be positively affected by them. Although they had behaved unlawfully, and sometimes dangerously and violently, the message they heard most often from juvenile justice officials was one that validated their individual worth and potential. For many youths, such messages had rarely been communicated in the primary spheres of home and school. Braithwaite suggests that these messages are reintegrative. When responses to offenders are disapproving of their lawbreaking behavior but open to forgiveness and restoration, they promote the development of social bonds. Our interviews with juvenile

[38] When children are securely attached to parents, they have the foundation to form significant attachments in other spheres of social life (school, peer groups, religious institutions, etc.). These in turn promote investment of self in conventional lines of activity (Hirschi 1969). Children with secure attachments are motivated to conform to the wishes and expectations of parents, teachers, and other significant others. Consequently, they are more likely to learn and to follow conventional norms.

offenders suggest that even brief positive contacts with conventional adults—say, to judges or detention workers—often have a beneficial effect, at least in the short term. For some youths, these contacts open up the possibility of trusting enough to develop other, more enduring relationships with conventional adults—for example, with a counselor in a long-term commitment program—that may have more lasting effects on attitudes, values, and behaviors. I think it is very significant that young offenders reported to us that most "front end" and even some of the "deep end" juvenile programs they had participated in were insufficient in length and intensity to produce real or lasting change. These observations showed insight into the complexity of their behaviors and their need for sustained support in order to effect behavioral change.

There is a second reason why processing in the juvenile justice system is linked to lower rates of reoffending. A fairly large body of empirical research shows that some programs are quite effective in reducing recidivism, even among serious and violent offenders. Lipsey (1992) conducted a comprehensive meta-analysis that synthesized results of evaluative research on over 400 juvenile treatment programs, subsuming nearly all previous meta-analytic studies. He reported substantial variability in effects across studies that were attributable primarily to the nature of the treatment itself. The most effective programs were structured and focused, and included behavioral (or cognitive-behavioral), skills-oriented (e.g., social skills, anger management), and multimodal approaches. These treatments produced 20–40 percent reductions in recidivism compared to a hypothetical baseline group with a 50 percent recidivism rate. Less structured programs, including individual or group counseling, had no effect on recidivism, while punitive approaches produced negative effects. Program duration and intensity were also important. The greatest reductions in recidivism were associated with interventions that involved frequent client contact over lengthy periods.

More recently, Lipsey and Wilson (1998) updated Lipsey's (1992) data collection and analyzed a subset of research studies on programs for serious juvenile offenders, including those in institutional settings. They reported that the most effective interventions were administered by mental health rather than by juvenile justice personnel. Although this finding is subject to multiple interpretations, it certainly suggests that the organizational climate of institutions matters—more specifically, that institutional settings characterized by a primary commitment to therapeutic intervention are more effective than those that try to deliver treatment in an adjunctive way in otherwise punitive settings where concerns about custody and security dominate. In programs for serious juvenile offenders, the type and amount of treatment also had significant effects. Again, interpersonal skills and behavioral programs, programs of longer duration, and those that had the highest rates of interaction between treatment staff and clients showed the most positive effects. The most effective of the programs for serious offenders produced 30–35 percent reductions in recidivism compared to a baseline group with a 50 percent recidivism rate.

In our research (Bishop et al. 1998), we learned that some of Florida's "deep end" juvenile programs included nearly all the elements of programs identified by Lipsey and Wilson (1998) as most effective. Moreover, these were the programs that the youths themselves identified as most beneficial to them. They were long-term programs (up to thirty-six months) built around a therapeutic model, and characterized by high rates of staff-youth interaction. Staff used techniques such as modeling and social reinforcement and focused on social skills, anger control, and moral education. What is perhaps most significant about both the process and the content of these programs is that they target deficits in socialization that inhibit the formation of social bonds. Many serious and violent offenders have not learned how to handle impulsivity in productive or at least nondestructive ways. Their inability to manage anger is a source of many of the difficulties they have experienced in past relationships and, left unaddressed, will continue to interfere with the development of future attachments. They have social deficits in many other areas as well. Many have not been taught how to make requests, to respond to inappropriate demands or requests without losing "face," to deal with other people's anger, or to work on cooperative tasks. Many have not acquired the cognitive skills to anticipate the consequences of their behavior or to take the perspective of others. Programs that enhance youths' skills in these and other areas facilitate the development of social bonds. In some of the juvenile programs we observed, young offenders were taught the social, emotional, and cognitive skills essential to stable attachments; conventional beliefs were modeled and reinforced; and educational and vocational programs were in place to facilitate commitment to conventional lines of action.

Regardless of whether treatment in the juvenile justice system is beneficial, the criminal justice system may contribute to criminal behavior. Among our interviewees, we found very negative reactions to criminal court processing. Many experienced the court process not so much as a condemnation of their behavior as a condemnation of them. Unlike the juvenile court, the criminal court failed to communicate that young offenders retain some fundamental worth. What transferred offenders generally heard was that they were being punished not only because their behavior was bad but also because they were personifications of their behavior. If another message was intended by the court, it failed to impress the offenders we interviewed.

It is not so much that condemnation and punishment are without value. Rather, it is more that they have value primarily when the person punished grants them legitimacy—that is, accepts the punishment and the agents and agencies administering it as properly motivated (Matza 1964). Far from viewing the criminal court and its officers as legitimate, the juvenile offenders we interviewed saw them more often as duplicitous and manipulative, malevolent in intent, and indifferent to their needs.[39] It was common for them to experience a sense of injustice and, then, to condemn the condemners (Lemert 1951, 1974; Sykes and Matza 1957; Matza 1964), reactions that are inconsistent with compliance to legal norms (Lanza-Kaduce and Radosevich 1987; Tyler 1990).

In the institutional world of the adult prison, youths were more likely to learn social rules and norms that legitimated domination, exploitation, and retaliation. They routinely observed both staff and inmate models who exhibited these behaviors, and they observed these illegitimate norms being reinforced. In addition, youths in prison were exposed to an inmate subculture that taught criminal motivations as well as techniques of committing crime and avoiding detection. Even if the pains of punishment and confinement caused most juveniles to wish to avoid returning to prison, what they learned in prison provided a destructive counterbalance to their positive intentions. Finally, prison staff engaged in negative shaming. The message clearly communicated to the vast majority of offenders was that they were lost causes who could never redeem themselves or return to normal personhood.

---

[39] Some would argue that transfer selects offenders who are more prone to this sort of negativism, those with either serious mental health problems or other personal characteristics conducive to anger and hostility in experiences with authorities. To my knowledge, there has been no research to date addressing this issue. It does not seem likely under prosecutorial waiver systems like Florida's, which transfer offenders with little or no inquiry into their backgrounds.

Perhaps the most harmful effects of transfer to criminal court come in the form of informal sanctions applied in the community. While most youths who engage in delinquency will desist by early adulthood as they move into jobs and marriages that give them a sense of place and purpose, many of those who enter the criminal justice system will carry the stigma of a criminal conviction. The normal transition from risk-taking adolescence to conventional adulthood will be relatively closed to them. Stigmatization and obstruction of conventional opportunities certainly make reoffending more likely.

A. Policy Implications

This essay began by showing that a period of extensive and rapid policy change has produced substantial increases in the number of juvenile offenders, especially minority offenders, prosecuted and convicted in criminal courts and exposed to adult sanctions. Public perceptions to the contrary notwithstanding, many of these offenders are not "extreme cases," that is, youths accused of heinous acts or chronic, hardened criminals who have repeatedly demonstrated their resistance to intervention.

Entry of large numbers of young offenders into the criminal justice system has important systemic consequences. It places additional burdens on already overtaxed courts and corrections systems. For corrections officials, an influx of young offenders presents significant new issues related to institutional security and programming. Whether they will respond by developing age-segregated facilities and programs designed to meet the special needs of a youth population remains to be seen. Further, the expansion of transfer has created new problems of interagency articulation and may precipitate repercussive effects in the juvenile justice system that have not been previously addressed.

Finally, as a crime control policy, transfer tends to be counterproductive. Although the empirical studies on this issue are too few to be definitive, they suggest that transfer is more likely to aggravate recidivism than to diminish it. The factors contributing to this effect are complex and include the sense of injustice young offenders associate with criminal court processing, the multiple criminogenic effects of incarceration in the adult system (e.g., exposure to negative shaming, opportunities for criminal socialization, modeling of violence), and the stigmatization and opportunity blockage that flow from a record of criminal conviction. Compared to the criminal justice system, the juvenile system seems to be more reintegrative in practice and effect.

In short, expansive transfer policies appear to be misguided. Transfer appears to have little deterrent value. Moreover, when applied broadly to offenders who are neither particularly serious nor particularly chronic, any incapacitative gains achieved in the short run appear to be quickly nullified. While broad transfer policies may and likely do serve retributive ends, they do so at a considerable price. The same ends might be better served through modest extensions of the upper boundary of juvenile court jurisdiction. Such a course might avoid the negative effects of criminal processing, conviction, and exposure to adult correctional environments, while possibly even enhancing the prospects of rehabilitation in carefully chosen intensive, long-term juvenile programs. Unless and until future research negates these conclusions, the clear implication is that a policy of retrenchment is in order. Transfer should be reserved for those "extreme cases" to which it has traditionally been applied, where significant retributive and incapacitative benefits can be realized.

B. Future Research

Additional research is needed in nearly every area discussed in this essay. A high priority should be placed on establishing a national reporting program that will permit us to assess the reach of jurisdictional shifts by generating accurate counts and descriptive data on the numbers and kinds of youths transferred to the adult system and their processing through the system. The almost complete absence of information on youths affected by legislative exclusion and reverse waiver stands in the way of a clear understanding of the impact of transfer policies already in place. Lacking even basic information on the numbers and kinds of offenders being removed to the criminal courts and their impact on the court and correctional systems, it is all too easy for legislators to continue to expand transfer criteria incrementally in response to pressures to "get tough" on juvenile crime.

Beyond generating mere descriptive data, further research on the comparative effectiveness of juvenile and criminal processing is needed. This area of inquiry poses formidable obstacles in terms of research design. Experimental designs with random assignment are not practicable. The cross-jurisdictional matched cohorts–matched counties approach should be replicated in other sites, for other age groups, and for other offense types, with careful attention to issues of case equivalence. Concerns about selection bias emanating from differential prosecutorial charging standards in juvenile and criminal courts can only be overcome by gathering data on case characteristics (e.g., weapon use, extent of victim injury) that may influence both prosecutorial decision making and the probability of reoffending. The single-state matched-pairs approach should also be replicated, though it too needs refinement. Geographical variations in crime and justice system responses introduce bias that can be overcome only by selecting smaller, more homogeneous areal units for analysis. Matching also needs to be extended to cover a broader range of variables. Unfortunately, there will be trade-offs from both of these modifications in terms of the numbers of cases available for analysis.

Comparative research on juvenile and criminal court contexts and correctional environments is in its infancy. We need much more research on responses of young people to processing in the juvenile and criminal courts and on their experiences in and reactions to a variety of correctional settings, both community based and residential. Our understanding of the differential effectiveness of alternative treatments can be enhanced significantly by supplementing quantitative research on the objective dimensions of treatment programs with qualitative research into subjective dimensions of the correctional experience. This kind of research can also provide the foundation for recommendations to correctional officials in a number of areas, including staff training, program planning, and strategies to better insure the safety of young inmates.

Longitudinal research that follows youths from juvenile and adult correctional settings into the community would also be extremely valuable. An assessment of the impact of youths' attitudes and orientations toward correctional environments on postrelease recidivism will help us to assess more directly the connection between psychological and behavioral responses to correctional experiences and adjustment in the community. To date, there has been no research comparing the postrelease experiences of young offenders who return to the community following a delinquency adjudication and those who return with a record of criminal conviction. Longitudinal research of this kind should also attend to the obstacles youths encounter following release from correctional settings in their attempts to find employment, complete their educations, and enter into conventional social networks.

REFERENCES

Adams, Kenneth. 1992. "Adjusting to Prison Life." In *Crime and Justice: A Review of Research*, vol. 16, edited by Michael Tonry. Chicago: University of Chicago Press.

Ainsworth, Janet E. 1991. "Re-imagining Childhood and Reconstructing the Legal Order: The Case for Abolishing the Juvenile Court." *North Carolina Law Review* 69:1083–1133.

———. 1995. "Youth Justice in a Unified Court: Response to Critics of Juvenile Court Abolition." *Boston College Law Review* 1995:927–51.

Amnesty International. 1998. *Betraying the Young: Human Rights Violations against Children in the U.S. Justice System.* New York: Amnesty International.

Andrews, Donald A., Ivan Zinger, Robert D. Hoge, James Bonta, Paul Gendreau, and Francis T. Cullen. 1990. "Does Correctional Treatment Work? A Clinically Relevant and Psychologically Informed Meta-Analysis." *Criminology* 28:369–404.

Annin, Peter. 1996. "'Superpredators' Arrive: Should We Cage the New Breed of Vicious Kids?" *Newsweek* (January 22), pp. 56–57.

Barnes, Carole Wolff, and Randal S. Franz. 1989. "Questionably Adult: Determinants and Effects of the Juvenile Waiver Decision." *Justice Quarterly* 6:117–35.

Bartollas, Clemens, Stuart J. Miller, and Simon Dinitz. 1976. *Juvenile Victimization: The Institutional Paradox.* New York: Wiley.

Beck, Allen, Bureau of Justice Statistics. 1998. Telephone conversation with author, October 6.

Beck, Allen, Darrell Gilliard, Lawrence Greenfeld, Caroline Harlow, Thomas Hester, Louis Jankowski, Tracy Snell, James Stephan, and Danielle Morton. 1993. *Survey of State Prison Inmates, 1991.* Washington, D.C.: U.S. Department of Justice, Bureau of Justice Statistics.

Bennett, William J., John J. DiIulio, and John P. Walters. 1996. *Body Count: Moral Poverty and How to Win America's War against Crime and Drugs.* New York: Simon & Schuster.

Bernard, Thomas J. 1992. *The Cycle of Juvenile Justice.* New York: Oxford.

Bishop, Donna M., and Charles E. Frazier. 1991. "Transfer of Juveniles to Criminal Court: A Case Study and Analysis of Prosecutorial Waiver." *Notre Dame Journal of Law, Ethics, and Public Policy* 5:281–302.

———. 1996. "Race Effects in Juvenile Justice Decision-Making: Findings of a Statewide Analysis." *Journal of Criminal Law and Criminology* 86:392–413.

Bishop, Donna M., Charles E. Frazier, and John C. Henretta. 1989. "Prosecutorial Waiver: Case Study of a Questionable Reform." *Crime and Delinquency* 35:179–201.

Bishop, Donna M., Charles E. Frazier, Lonn Lanza-Kaduce, and Henry George White. 1998. *Juvenile Transfers to Criminal Court Study: Phase I Final Report.* Washington, D.C.: U.S. Department of Justice, Office of Juvenile Justice and Delinquency Prevention.

Bishop, Donna M., Charles E. Frazier, Lonn Lanza-Kaduce, and Lawrence Winner. 1996. "The Transfer of Juveniles to Criminal Court: Does It Make a Difference?" *Crime and Delinquency* 42:171–91.

Bishop, Donna M., Lonn Lanza-Kaduce, and Lawrence Winner. 1996. *A Study of Juvenile Case Processing in Florida: Issues of Timeliness and Consistency across Jurisdictions.* Tallahassee, Fla.: Juvenile Justice Advisory Board.

Blomberg, Thomas. 1977. "Diversion and Accelerated Social Control." *Journal of Criminal Law and Criminology* 68:274–82.

———. 1979. "Widening the Net: An Anomaly in the Evaluation of Diversion Programs." In *Handbook on Criminal Justice Evaluation*, edited by Malcolm W. Klein and Katherine S. Teilman. Beverly Hills, Calif.: Sage.

Bortner, M. A. 1986. "Traditional Rhetoric, Organizational Realities: Remand of Juveniles to Adult Court." *Crime and Delinquency* 32:53–73.

Bowker, Lee H. 1980. *Prison Victimization*. New York: Elsevier.

———. 1985. "An Essay on Prison Violence." In *Prison Violence in America*, edited by Michael C. Braswell, S. Dillingham, and Reid H. Montgomery. Cincinnati: Anderson.

Braithwaite, John. 1989. *Crime, Shame and Reintegration*. New York: Cambridge University Press.

Brown, Barry S., and John D. Spevacek. 1971. "Disciplinary Offenders at Two Differing Correctional Institutions." *Correctional Psychiatry and Journal of Social Therapy* 17:48–56.

Brown, Jodi M., Bureau of Justice Statistics. 1999. Telephone conversation with author, June 14.

Brown, Jodi M., and Patrick A. Langan. 1998. *State Court Sentencing of Convicted Felons, 1994*. Washington, D.C.: U.S. Department of Justice, Bureau of Justice Statistics.

Brown, Jodi, Patrick A. Langan, and David J. Levin. 1999. *Felony Sentences in State Courts, 1996*. Washington, D.C.: U.S. Department of Justice, Bureau of Justice Statistics.

Bureau of Justice Statistics. 1997. *Correctional Populations in the United States, 1995*. Washington, D.C.: U.S. Department of Justice, Bureau of Justice Statistics.

———. 1999a. *BJS Court and Sentencing Data Collections*. Washington, D.C.: U.S. Department of Justice, Bureau of Justice Statistics.

———. 1999b. *National Corrections Reporting Program, Spreadsheets*, 1993, 1996. www.ojp.usdoj/gov/bjs.

Butts, Jeffrey. 1997. *Delinquency Cases Waived to Criminal Court, 1985–1994*. Washington, D.C.: U.S. Department of Justice, Office of Juvenile Justice and Delinquency Prevention.

Butts, Jeffrey, Howard N. Snyder, Terrence A. Finnegan, Anne L. Aughenbaugh, and Rowen S. Poole. 1996. *Juvenile Court Statistics 1994*. Washington, D.C.: U.S. Department of Justice, Office of Juvenile Justice and Delinquency Prevention.

Clarke, Elizabeth E. 1996. "A Case for Reinventing Juvenile Transfer: The Record of Transfer of Juvenile Offenders to Criminal Court in Cook County, Ill." *Juvenile and Family Court Journal* 47:3–21.

Coalition for Juvenile Justice. 1995. *No Easy Answers: Juvenile Justice in a Climate of Fear*. Washington, D.C.: Coalition for Juvenile Justice.

Cook, Philip J., and John H. Laub. 1998. "The Unprecedented Epidemic in Youth Violence." In *Youth Violence*, edited by Michael Tonry and Mark H. Moore. Vol. 24 of *Crime and Justice: A Review of Research*, edited by Michael Tonry. Chicago: University of Chicago Press.

Cooley, Dennis. 1993. "Criminal Victimization in Male Federal Prisons." *Canadian Journal of Criminology* 35:479–95.

Craddock, Amy. 1996. "A Comparative Study of Male and Female Prison Misconduct Careers." *Prison Journal* 76:60–81.

Crick, N., and K. Dodge. 1994. "A Review and Reformulation of Social Information-Processing Mechanisms in Children's Social Adjustment." *Psychological Bulletin* 115:74–101.

Cullen, Francis T., and Karen E. Gilbert. 1982. *Reaffirming Rehabilitation*. Cincinnati: Anderson.

Dawson, Robert O. Forthcoming. "Judicial Waiver in Practice and Theory." In *The Changing Borders of Juvenile Justice: Transfer of Adolescents to the Criminal Court*, edited by Jeffrey Fagan and Franklin E. Zimring. Chicago: University of Chicago Press.

DeComo, R., Barry Krisberg, B. Rudenstine, and D. DelRosario. 1995. *Juveniles Taken into Custody Research Program: 1994 Annual Report*. Washington, D.C.: U.S. Department of Justice, Office of Juvenile Justice and Delinquency Prevention.

DeFrances, Carol J. 1999. Personal communication with author, June 29.

DeFrances, Carol J., and Greg W. Steadman. 1998. *Prosecutors in State Courts, 1996*. Washington, D.C.: U.S. Department of Justice, Bureau of Justice Statistics.

Dodge, K., J. Price, J. Bachorowski, and J. Newman. 1990. "Hostile Attributional Biases in Severely Aggressive Delinquents." *Journal of Abnormal Psychology* 99:385–92.

Eigen, Joel Peter. 1981. "The Determinants and Impact of Jurisdictional Transfer in Philadelphia." In *Major Issues in Juvenile Justice Information and Training: Readings in Public Policy*, edited by John C. Hall, Donna M. Hamparian, John C. Pettibone, and Joseph L. White. Columbus, Ohio: Academy for Contemporary Problems.

Ellis, Desmond, Harold Grasmick, and Bernard Gilman. 1974. "Violence in Prison: A Sociological Analysis." *American Journal of Sociology* 80:16–43.

Evans, K. 1978. "Reflections on Education in the Penitentiary." In *Issues in Police and Criminal Psychology*, edited by W. Taylor and Michael Braswell. Washington, D.C.: University Press of America.

Fagan, Jeffrey A. 1990. "Social and Legal Policy Dimensions of Violent Juvenile Crime." *Criminal Justice and Behavior* 17:93–133.

———. 1991. *The Comparative Impacts of Juvenile and Criminal Court Sanctions on Adolescent Felony Offenders*. Final Report, Grant 87-IJ CX 4044, to the National Institute of Justice. Washington, D.C.: U.S. Department of Justice.

———. 1995. "Separating the Men from the Boys: The Comparative Advantage of Juvenile versus Criminal Court Sanctions on Recidivism among Adolescent Felony Offenders." In *Serious, Violent, and Chronic Juvenile Offenders: A Sourcebook*, edited by James C. Howell, Barry Krisberg, J. David Hawkins, and John J. Wilson. Thousand Oaks, Calif.: Sage.

———. 1996. "The Comparative Advantage of Juvenile versus Criminal Court Sanctions on Recidivism among Adolescent Felony Offenders." *Law and Policy* 18:77–112.

Fagan, Jeffrey A., and Martin L. Forst. 1996. "Risks, Fixers and Zeal: Implementing Experimental Treatment for Violent Juvenile Offenders." *Prison Journal* 76:22–60.

Fagan, Jeffrey A., Martin L. Forst, and T. Scott Vivona. 1987. "Racial Determinants of the Judicial Transfer Decision: Prosecuting Violent Youth in Criminal Court." *Crime and Delinquency* 33:259–86.

Fagan, Jeffrey A., and Richard B. Freeman. 1999. "Crime and Work." In *Crime and Justice: A Review of Research*, vol. 25, edited by Michael Tonry. Chicago: University of Chicago Press.

Feld, Barry C. 1977. *Neutralizing Inmate Violence: Juvenile Offenders in Institutions.* Cambridge, Mass.: Ballinger.

———. 1978. "Reference of Juvenile Offenders for Adult Prosecution: The Legislative Alternative to Answering Unanswerable Questions." *Minnesota Law Review* 62:515–618.

———. 1987. "Juvenile Court Meets the Principle of Offense: Legislative Changes in Judicial Waiver Statutes." *Journal of Criminal Law and Criminology* 78:471–533.

———. 1988. "Juvenile Court Meets the Principle of Offense: Punishment, Treatment and the Difference It Makes." *Boston University Law Review* 68: 821–915.

———. 1991. "Justice by Geography: Urban, Suburban, and Rural Variations in Juvenile Justice Administration." *Journal of Criminal Law and Criminology* 82:156–210.

———. 1993. "Juvenile (In)Justice and the Criminal Court Alternative." *Crime and Delinquency* 39:403–24.

———. 1997. "Abolish the Juvenile Court: Youthfulness, Criminal Responsibility, and Sentencing Policy." *Journal of Criminal Law and Criminology* 88: 68–136.

———. 1999. *Bad Kids: Race and the Transformation of the Juvenile Court.* New York: Oxford.

———. Forthcoming. "Legislative Exclusion of Offenses from Juvenile Court Jurisdiction: A History and Critique." In *The Changing Borders of Juvenile Justice: Transfer of Adolescents to the Criminal Court*, edited by Jeffrey Fagan and Franklin E. Zimring. Chicago: University of Chicago Press.

Flaherty, Michael G. 1983. "The National Incidence of Juvenile Suicides in Adult Jails and Juvenile Detention Centers." *Suicide and Life-Threatening Behavior* 13:85–93.

Flanagan, Timothy J. 1980. "The Pains of Long-Term Imprisonment: A Comparison of British and American Perspectives." *British Journal of Criminology* 20:148–56.

———. 1983. "Correlates of Institutional Misconduct among State Prisoners: A Research Note." *Criminology* 21:29–40.

———. 1996. "Discipline." In *Encyclopedia of American Prisons*, edited by Marilyn D. McShane and Frank P. Williams. New York: Garland.

Flicker, Barbara. 1981. "Prosecuting Juveniles as Adults: A Symptom of Crisis in the Juvenile Courts." In *Major Issues in Juvenile Justice Information and*

Training: Readings in Public Policy, edited by John C. Hall, Donna M. Hamparian, John C. Pettibone, and Joseph L. White. Columbus, Ohio: Academy for Contemporary Problems.

Florida Department of Juvenile Justice. 1997. *Profile of Delinquency Cases and Youths Referred.* Tallahassee: Florida Department of Juvenile Justice, Bureau of Data and Research.

———. 1998. Statement of Philosophy. http://www.djj.state.fl.us/challenge.html.

Forst, Martin, and Martha-Elin Blomquist. 1991. "Cracking Down on Juveniles: The Changing Ideology of Youth Corrections." *Notre Dame Journal of Law, Ethics and Public Policy* 5:323–75.

———. 1992. "Punishment, Accountability, and the New Juvenile Justice." *Juvenile and Family Court Journal* 43:1–10.

Forst, Martin, Jeffrey Fagan, and T. Scott Vivona. 1989. "Youth in Prisons and Training Schools: Perceptions and Consequences of the Treatment Custody Dichotomy." *Juvenile and Family Court Journal* 39:1–13.

Fox, Sanford J. 1970. "Juvenile Justice Reform: An Historical Perspective." *Stanford Law Review* 2:1187–1239.

Fox, Vernon B., and Jeanne B. Stinchcomb. 1994. *Introduction to Corrections*, 4th ed. Englewood Cliffs, N.J.: Prentice-Hall.

Frazier, Charles E. 1991. "Deep End Juvenile Placement or Transfer to Adult Court by Direct File?" Report submitted to the Florida Commission on Juvenile Justice, Tallahassee.

Frazier, Charles E., Donna M. Bishop, and Lonn Lanza-Kaduce. 1999. "'Get Tough' Juvenile Justice Reforms: The Florida Experience with Transfer to Criminal Court." *Annals of the American Academy of Political and Social Science* 564:167–84.

Frazier, Charles E., and John C. Cochran. 1986. "Official Intervention, Diversion from the Juvenile Justice System, and the Dynamics of Human Services Work: Effects of a Reform Based on Labeling Theory." *Crime and Delinquency* 32:157–76.

Frazier, Charles E., Pamela Richards, and Roberto Hugh Potter. 1983. "Juvenile Diversion and Net Widening: Toward a Clarification of Assessment Strategies." *Human Organization* 42:115–22.

Freasier, A., and T. White. 1983. "IEP Communicators." *Journal of Correctional Education* 34:27–29.

Freeman, Richard B. 1992. "Crime and the Employment Status of Disadvantaged Youths." In *Urban Labor Markets and Job Opportunity*, edited by G. E. Peterson and W. Vroman. Washington, D.C.: Urban Institute Press.

Fuller, D., and T. Orsagh. 1977. "Violence and Victimization within a State Prison System." *Criminal Justice Review* 2:35–55.

Garrett, Carol J. 1985. "Effects of Residential Treatment on Adjudicated Delinquents: A Meta-Analysis." *Journal of Research in Crime and Delinquency* 22:287–308.

Gendreau, Paul, and Robert Ross. 1987. "Revivification of Rehabilitation: Evidence from the 1980s." *Justice Quarterly* 4:349–409.

General Accounting Office. 1995. *Juvenile Justice: Juveniles Processed in Criminal Court and Case Dispositions.* Washington, D.C.: U.S. Government Printing Office.

Gibbs, Jack. 1982. "The First Cut Is the Deepest: Psychological Breakdown and Survival in the Detention Setting." In *The Pains of Imprisonment,* edited by Robert Johnson and Hans Toch. Beverly Hills, Calif.: Sage.

Gillespie, L. Kay. n.d. "Juveniles in an Adult World: Prison Inmates under the Age of Eighteen." Unpublished Manuscript. Rockville, Md.: National Institute of Justice/National Criminal Justice Reference Service.

Gilliard, Darrell F., and Allen J. Beck. 1998. *Prison and Jail Inmates at Midyear 1997.* Washington, D.C.: U.S. Department of Justice, Bureau of Justice Statistics.

Goetting, Ann, and Roy Michael Howsen. 1986. "Correlates of Prison Misconduct." *Journal of Quantitative Criminology* 2:49–67.

Gragg, Frances. 1986. *Juveniles in Adult Court: A Review of Transfers at the Habitual Serious and Violent Offender Program Sites.* Washington, D.C.: Office of Justice Assistance, Research and Statistics.

Griffin, Patrick, Patricia Torbet, and Linda Szymanski. 1998. *Trying Juveniles as Adults in Criminal Court: An Analysis of State Transfer Provisions.* Washington, D.C.: Office of Justice Programs, Office of Juvenile Justice and Delinquency Prevention.

Hamparian, Donna M., Linda K. Estep, Susan M. Muntean, Ramon R. Priestino, Robert G. Swisher, Paul L. Wallace, and Joseph L. White. 1982. *Youth in Adult Courts: Between Two Worlds.* Major Issues in Juvenile Justice Information and Training. Columbus, Ohio: Academy for Contemporary Problems.

Heilbrun, K., C. Leheny, L. Thomas, and D. Honeycutt. 1997. "A National Survey of U. S. Statutes on Juvenile Transfer: Implications for Policy and Practice." *Behavioral Sciences and the Law* 15:125–49.

Heuser, James P. 1985. *Juveniles Arrested for Serious Felony Crimes in Oregon and "Remanded" to Adult Criminal Courts: A Statistical Study.* Salem: Oregon Department of Justice Crime Analysis Center.

Hirschi, Travis. 1969. *Causes of Delinquency.* Berkeley: University of California Press.

Houghtalin, Marilyn, and G. Larry Mays. 1991. "Criminal Disposition of New Mexico Juveniles Transferred to Adult Court." *Crime and Delinquency* 37:393–407.

Howell, James C. 1997. *Juvenile Justice and Youth Violence.* Thousand Oaks, Calif.: Sage.

Irwin, John. 1980. *Prisons in Turmoil.* Boston: Little, Brown.

Jensen, Eric L., and Linda K. Metsger. 1994. "A Test of the Deterrent Effect of Legislative Waiver on Violent Juvenile Crime." *Crime and Delinquency* 40:96–104.

Jensen, Gary. 1977. "Age and Rule Breaking in Prison: A Test of Sociocultural Interpretations." *Criminology* 14:555–68.

Jepsen, Bradette. 1997. "Supervising Youthful Offenders: Juveniles Sentenced to Adult Facilities Present Supervisory, Staffing Challenges." *Corrections To-day* 59:68–72.

Johnson, Elmer H. 1966. "Pilot Study: Age, Race, and Recidivism as Factors in Prison Infractions." *Canadian Journal of Corrections* 8:268–83.

Johnson, Robert. 1987. *Hard Time: Understanding and Reforming the Prison.* Pacific Grove, Calif.: Brooks/Cole.

Keiter, Robert. 1973. "Criminal or Delinquent: A Study of Juvenile Cases Transferred to the Juvenile Court." *Crime and Delinquency* 19:528–38.

Kempf-Leonard, Kimberly, Carl Pope, and William Feyerherm. 1995. *Minorities in Juvenile Justice.* Thousand Oaks, Calif.: Sage.

Klein, Malcolm W. 1976. "Issues and Realities in Police Diversion Programs." *Crime and Delinquency* 22:421–27.

Kuzma, Susan M. 1996. *Civil Disabilities of Convicted Felons: A State-by-State Survey.* Washington, D.C.: U.S. Department of Justice, Office of the Pardon Attorney.

Lanza-Kaduce, Lonn, Donna M. Bishop, and Lawrence Winner. 1997. *Juvenile Case Processing in Florida: A Comparison of Cross-Jurisdictional Variations in Timing Sequences and Outcomes, 1993–1995.* Tallahassee, Fla.: Juvenile Justice Advisory Board.

Lanza-Kaduce, Lonn, and Marcia J. Radosevich. 1987. "Negative Reactions to Processing and Substance Abuse among Young Incarcerated Males." *Deviant Behavior* 8:137–48.

Lemert, Edwin. 1951. *Social Pathology.* New York: McGraw-Hill.

———. 1974. "Beyond Mead: The Societal Reaction to Deviance." *Social Problems* 21:457–68.

Levinson, Robert B., and John J. Greene. 1999. "Jew Boys on the Cellblock." *Corrections Today* 61:60–63.

Library Information Specialists. 1983. *Suicides in Jails.* Corrections Information Series. Boulder, Colo.: National Institute of Corrections.

———. 1995. *Offenders under 18 in State Adult Correctional Systems: A National Picture.* Special Issues in Corrections, no. 1. Longmont, Colo.: National Institute of Corrections.

Liebling, Alison. 1999. "Prison Suicide and Prisoner Coping." In *Prisons,* edited by Michael Tonry and Joan Petersilia. Vol. 26 of *Crime and Justice: A Review of Research,* edited by Michael Tonry. Chicago: University of Chicago Press.

Lipsey, Mark W. 1992. "Juvenile Delinquency Treatment: A Meta-Analytic Inquiry into the Variability of Effects." In *Meta-Analysis for Explanation,* edited by Thomas D. Cook, Harris Cooper, David S. Cordray, Heidi Hartmann, Larry V. Hedges, Richard J. Light, Thomas A. Louis, and Frederick Mosteller. New York: Russell Sage Foundation.

Lipsey, Mark W., and David B. Wilson. 1998. "Effective Intervention for Serious Juvenile Offenders: A Synthesis of Research." In *Serious and Violent Juvenile Offenders: Risk Factors and Successful Interventions,* edited by Rolf Loeber and David P. Farrington. Thousand Oaks, Calif.: Sage.

Lipton, Douglas, Robert Martinson, and Judith Wilks. 1975. *The Effectiveness* of *Correctional Intervention: A Survey of Treatment Evaluation Studies*. New York: Praeger.

Lockwood, Daniel. 1980. *Prison Sexual Violence*. New York. Elsevier.

Mabli, Jerome, Charles Holley, Judy Patrick, and Justina Walls. 1979. "Age and Prison Violence: Increasing Age Heterogeneity as a Violence-Reducing Strategy in Prisons." *Criminal Justice and Behavior* 6:175–86.

Maitland, Angela S., and Richard D. Sluder. 1996. "Victimization in Prisons: A Study of Factors Related to the General Well-Being of Youthful Inmates." *Federal Probation* 55:24–31.

Matza, David. 1964. *Delinquency and Drift*. New York: Wiley.

McCorkle, Richard C. 1992. "Personal Precautions to Violence in Prison." *Criminal Justice and Behavior* 19:160–74.

———. 1993*a*. "Fear of Victimization and Symptoms of Psychopathology among Prison Inmates." *Journal of Offender Rehabilitation* 9:27–41.

———. 1993*b*. "Living on the Edge: Fear in a Maximum Security Prison." *Journal of Offender Rehabilitation* 20:73–91.

McNulty, Elizabeth W. 1996. "The Transfer of Juvenile Offenders to Adult Court: Panacea or Problem?" *Law and Policy* 18:61–75.

McShane, Marilyn, and Frank P. Williams III. 1989. "The Prison Adjustment of Juvenile Offenders." *Crime and Delinquency* 35:254–69.

Memory, John M. 1989. "Juvenile Suicides in Secure Detention Facilities: Correction of Published Rates." *Death Studies* 13:455–63.

Merlo, A. V., P. J. Benekos, and W. J. Cook. 1997. " 'Getting Tough' with Youth: Legislative Waiver as Crime Control." *Juvenile and Family Court Journal* 48:1–15.

Miller, Neal. 1997. "National Assessment of Criminal Court Use of Defendants' Juvenile Adjudication Records." In *National Conference on Juvenile Justice Records: Appropriate Criminal and Noncriminal Justice Uses: Proceedings of a BJS/SEARCH Conference*. Washington, D.C.: U.S. Department of Justice, Bureau of Justice Statistics.

Moffitt, Terrie E. 1999. "Pathways in the Life Course to Crime." In *Criminological Theory: Past to Present*, edited by Francis T. Cullen and Robert Agnew. Los Angeles: Roxbury.

Mulvey, Edward P., M. W. Arthur, and N. Dickon Reppucci. 1993. "The Prevention and Treatment of Juvenile Delinquency: A Review of the Research." *Clinical Psychology Review* 13:133–67.

Myers, Louis B., and Girard W. Levy. 1978. "Description and Prediction of the Intractable Inmate." *Journal of Research in Crime and Delinquency* 15: 214–28.

Nimick, Ellen H., Linda Szymanski, and Howard N. Snyder. 1986. *Juvenile Court Waiver: A Study of Juvenile Court Cases Transferred to Criminal Court*. Pittsburgh: National Center for Juvenile Justice.

Office of Juvenile Justice and Delinquency Prevention (OJJDP). 1999. *Easy Access to Juvenile Court Statistics, 1987–1996*. Washington, D.C.: U.S. Department of Justice, OJJDP.

Orenstein, Bruce W. 1996. "Juveniles Waived into Adult Institutions." *Corrections Today* 58:60–63.

Palmer, Ted. B. 1991. "The Effectiveness of Intervention: Recent Trends and Current Issues." *Crime and Delinquency* 37:330–46.

———. 1995. "Programmatic and Non-programmatic Aspects of Successful Intervention: New Directions for Research." *Crime and Delinquency* 41:100–131.

Parent, Dale G., Valerie Lieter, Stephen Kennedy, Lisa Livens, Daniel Wentworth, and Sarah Wilcox. 1994. *Conditions of Confinement: Juvenile Detention and Corrections Facilities.* Washington, D.C.: U.S. Department of Justice, OJJDP.

Perkins, Craig. 1994. *National Corrections Reporting Program, 1992.* Washington, D.C.: U.S. Department of Justice, Bureau of Justice Statistics.

Peterson, Ruth D. 1988. "Youthful Offender Designations and Sentencing in the New York Criminal Courts." *Social Problems* 35:111–30.

Podkopacz, Marcy R., and Barry C. Feld. 1995. "Judicial Waiver Policy and Practice: Persistence, Seriousness, and Race." *Law and Inequality* 14:101–207.

———. 1996. "The End of the Line: An Empirical Study of Judicial Waiver." *Journal of Criminal Law and Criminology* 86:449–92.

Poole, Eric D., and Robert M. Regoli. 1983. "Violence in Juvenile Institutions." *Criminology* 21:213–32.

Poulos, Tammy Meredith, and Stan Orchowsky. 1994. "Serious Juvenile Offenders: Predicting the Probability of Transfer to Criminal Court." *Crime and Delinquency* 40:3–17.

Redding, Richard E. 1997. "Juveniles Transferred to Criminal Court: Legal Reform Proposals Based on Social Science Research." *Utah Law Review* 1997:709–63.

Reddington, Frances P., and Allen D. Sapp. 1997. "Juveniles in Adult Prisons: Problems and Prospects." *Journal of Crime and Justice* 20:138–52.

Rudman, Cary, Eliot Hartstone, Jeffrey Fagan, and Melinda Moore. 1986. "Violent Youth in Adult Court: Process and Punishment." *Crime and Delinquency* 32:75–96.

Sagatun, Inger J., Loretta McCollum, and Leonard Edwards. 1985. "The Effect of Transfers from Juvenile to Criminal Court: A Loglinear Analysis." *Crime and Justice* 7:65–92.

Sampson, Robert J., and John H. Laub. 1993. *Crime in the Making.* Cambridge, Mass.: Harvard University Press.

Sanborn, Joseph B. 1998. "Second-Class Justice, First-Class Punishment: The Use of Juvenile Records in Sentencing Adults." *Judicature* 81:206–13.

Sargent, Douglas A., and Donald H. Gordon. 1963. "Waiver of Jurisdiction: An Evaluation of the Process in the Juvenile Court." *Crime and Delinquency* 9:121–28.

Scott, Elizabeth S., and Thomas Grisso. 1997. "The Evolution of Adolescence: A Developmental Perspective on Juvenile Justice Reform." *Journal of Criminal Law and Criminology* 88:137–89.

Sechrest, Lee B., Susan O. White, and Elizabeth D. Brown, eds. 1979. *The Rehabilitation of Criminal Offenders.* Washington, D.C.: National Academy of Sciences.

Sickmund, Melissa, Howard N. Snyder, and Eileen Poe-Yamagata. 1997. *Juvenile Offenders and Victims: 1997 Update on Violence*. Pittsburgh: National Center for Juvenile Justice.

Sickmund, Melissa, Anne L. Stahl, Terrence A. Finnegan, Howard N. Snyder, Rowen S. Poole, and Jeffrey A. Butts. 1998. *Juvenile Court Statistics 1995*. Washington, D.C.: U.S. Department of Justice, OJJDP.

Singer, Simon I. 1996. *Recriminalizing Delinquency: Violent Juvenile Crime and Juvenile Justice Reform*. New York: Cambridge University Press.

Singer, Simon I., and David McDowall. 1988. "Criminalizing Delinquency: The Deterrent Effects of the New York Juvenile Offender Law." *Law and Society Review* 22:521–35.

Snyder, Howard N., and Melissa Sickmund. 1995. *Juvenile Offenders and Victims: A National Report*. Washington, D.C.: U.S. Department of Justice, OJJDP.

———. 1999. *Juvenile Offenders and Victims: 1999 National Report*. Washington, D.C.: U.S. Department of Justice, OJJDP.

Spelman, William. 1994. *Criminal Incapacitation*. New York: Plenum.

Stahl, Anne L. 1999. *Delinquency Cases Waived to Criminal Court, 1987–1996*. Washington, D.C.: U.S. Department of Justice, OJJDP.

Street, David, Robert D. Vinter, and Charles Perrow. 1966. *Organization for Treatment*. New York: Free Press.

Strom, Kevin, Steven K. Smith, and Howard N. Snyder. 1998. *Juvenile Felony Defendants in Criminal Courts*. Washington, D.C.: U.S. Department of Justice, Bureau of Justice Statistics.

Sykes, Gresham, and David Matza. 1957. "Techniques of Neutralization: A Theory of Delinquency." *American Journal of Sociology* 22:664–70.

Tanenhaus, David S. Forthcoming. "The Evolution of Waiver in the Juvenile Court." In *The Changing Borders of Juvenile Justice: Transfer of Adolescents to the Criminal Court*, edited by Jeffrey Fagan and Franklin Zimring. Chicago: University of Chicago Press.

Teitelbaum, Lee. 1991. "Youth Crime and the Choice between Rules and Standards." *Brigham Young University Law Review* 1991:351–402.

Toch, Hans. 1977. *Living in Prison: The Ecology of Survival*. New York: Free Press.

Toch, Hans, and Kenneth Adams. 1989. *Coping: Maladaptation in Prison*. New Brunswick, N.J.: Transaction.

Tonry, Michael. 1996. *Sentencing Matters*. New York: Oxford University Press.

Torbet, Patricia, Richard Gable, Hunter Hurst IV, Imogene Montgomery, Linda Szymanski, and Douglas Thomas. 1996. *State Responses to Serious and Violent Juvenile Crime*. Pittsburgh: National Center for Juvenile Justice.

Torbet, Patricia, and Linda Szymanski. 1998. *State Legislative Responses to Violent Juvenile Crime: 1996–97 Update*. Washington, D.C.: U.S. Department of Justice, OJJDP.

Tyler, Tom R. 1990. *Why People Obey the Law*. New Haven, Conn.: Yale University Press.

Virginia Commission on Youth. 1996. *The Study of Juvenile Justice System Reform*. House Document no. 37. Richmond: General Assembly of Virginia.

Whisenand, Lucia B., and Edward J. McLaughlin. 1982. "Completing the Cycle: Reality and the Juvenile Justice System in New York State." *Albany Law Review* 47:1–47.

White, Henry George, Charles E. Frazier, Lonn Lanza-Kaduce, and Donna M. Bishop. 1999. "A Socio-legal History of Florida's Juvenile Transfer Reforms." *University of Florida Journal of Law and Public Policy* 10:249–76.

Whitebread, Charles H., and Robert Batey. 1981. "The Role of Waiver in the Juvenile Court: Questions in Philosophy and Function." In *Readings in Public Policy*, edited by John C. Hall, Donna M. Hamparian, John C. Pettibone, and Joseph L. White. Major Issues in Juvenile Justice Information and Training. Columbus, Ohio: Academy for Contemporary Problems.

Winner, Lawrence, Lonn Lanza-Kaduce, Donna M. Bishop, and Charles E. Frazier. 1997. "The Transfer of Juveniles to Criminal Court: Reexamining Recidivism over the Long Term." *Crime and Delinquency* 43:548–63.

Wolfgang, Marvin E. 1961. "Quantitative Analysis of Adjustment to the Prison Community." *Journal of Criminal Law, Criminology, and Police Science* 51:587–618.

Wright, Kevin N. 1991. "The Violent and Victimized in the Male Prison." *Journal of Offender Rehabilitation* 16:1–25.

Wright, W., and M. Dixon. 1975. "Community Treatment of Juvenile Delinquency: A Review of Evaluation Studies." *Journal of Research in Crime and Delinquency* 19:35–67.

Zimring, Franklin E. 1981. "Notes toward a Jurisprudence of Waiver." In *Readings in Public Policy*, edited by John C. Hall, Donna M. Hamparian, John C. Pettibone, and Joseph L. White. Major Issues in Juvenile Justice Information and Training. Columbus, Ohio: Academy for Contemporary Problems.

———. 1982. *The Changing Legal World of Adolescence.* New York: Free Press.

———. 1991. "The Treatment of Hard Cases in American Juvenile Justice: In Defense of Discretionary Waiver." *Notre Dame Journal of Law, Ethics and Public Policy* 5:267–80.

———. 1998. "Toward a Jurisprudence of Youth Violence." In *Youth Violence*, edited by Michael Tonry and Mark H. Moore. Vol. 24 of *Crime and Justice: A Review of Research*, edited by Michael Tonry. Chicago: University of Chicago Press.

Zimring, Franklin E., and Gordon Hawkins. 1995. *Incapacitation: Penal Confinement and the Restraint of Crime.* New York: Oxford University Press.

Martha J. Smith and Ronald V. Clarke

Crime and Public Transport

ABSTRACT

Crime in public transport covers a bewildering variety of offenses
committed in forms of transport including trams, buses, subways,
commuter trains, taxis, and jitneys. The targets of crime can be the system
itself (as in vandalism or fare evasion), employees (as in assaults on ticket
collectors), or passengers (as in pickpocketing or overcharging). A
distinction must be made between crimes facilitated by overcrowding
and by lack of supervision. Both are the result of financial constraints,
plaguing all forms of public transport, which result in too little space for
passengers at busy periods and not enough staff to supervise vehicles and
facilities at other times. Many successful measures have been reported
in dealing with specific crimes. More generally, much crime can be
"designed out" of new subway systems and older train and bus stations,
and order maintenance may be an effective transit policing strategy.
Research has been less successful in determining whether transit systems
spread crime from high- to lower-crime areas and whether some transit
systems and forms of transport are much less safe than others are. Little
success in deliberately reducing fear has been achieved. The security
challenges presented by new light rail systems and forms of taxi service
may not differ greatly from those encountered at present.

Crimes cannot be properly explained, nor effectively prevented, without a thorough understanding of the environments in which they occur. Nowhere is this more apparent than in urban public transport.

Martha J. Smith is former research director of the Rutgers University Center for
Crime Prevention Studies. Ronald V. Clarke is a professor in the School of Criminal
Justice at Rutgers. We are grateful to Nancy LaVigne and to anonymous reviewers for
their comments and to Frank Sergi for his assistance. Phyllis Schultze at the NCCD/
Criminal Justice Library at Rutgers was of incalculable help in tracking down fugitive
literature on the topic of this essay.

Here, the settings for crime are sufficiently familiar to us, yet often separate enough from our everyday experience, that we can readily appreciate how they shape and structure crime. Many of us have felt afraid when stranded at some dark, deserted station. We have felt uncomfortable when sitting in a bus or train with rowdy or inebriated youths. We have kept our purses and wallets safe at crowded bus stops or railway platforms. We have sighed with relief when a police officer has entered our subway car late at night. Finally, many of us have yielded to temptation and traveled on a bus or train without paying the fare. In all these ways we have acquired some understanding of the criminal opportunities and inducements presented by the public transport environment. In the same way, we may have grasped how these opportunities and inducements could be reduced: better lighting, improved staffing, more patrolling, more surveillance, and less crowding.

Few of us, however, have much understanding of how the conditions favoring crime on public transport have arisen and why they persist. We have limited knowledge of the mix of forces and constraints—political, geographical, economic, engineering, and others—which have combined to shape and form modern public transport. We do not know how much room there is for planners and engineers to overcome these constraints, or for transit managers to maneuver within them. Finally, we have little detailed understanding of the conditions that favor a particular crime, but not others, and little detailed information about specific interventions that have succeeded or failed.

These topics are addressed in this essay, which provides a comprehensive review of the research on crime and public transport. The framework is provided by situational crime prevention, which emphasizes reducing opportunities for specific categories of crime by increasing the associated risks and difficulties, reducing the rewards, and removing the excuses (Clarke 1995, 1997). Situational crime prevention draws on a variety of "opportunity" theories—such as routine activity theory (Cohen and Felson 1979), the rational choice perspective (Clarke and Cornish 1985), and environmental criminology (Brantingham and Brantingham 1991). These perspectives are very flexible, using concepts that can be adapted to describe traveling behavior and situations. For example, it is possible to look at travelers' decisions using a rational choice approach. Thus it can be assumed that their choices are influenced by the rewards offered by efficient modes of transport (such as speed and dependability), the effort they must expend to reach their destinations (such as the proximity of stations), and the risks involved (including possible crime victimization). While the travel decisions made by offenders may differ from those made by the general public, both groups are operating within the same transport environment.

In fact, this environment is difficult to control. It is open to anyone who pays for entrance and often to those who choose not to pay. It contains a variety of settings and targets configured in predictable patterns. Many of the targets are stationary and unguarded. Potential victims are often crowded together in intimidating conditions or in conditions that make it hard for them to guard their property and for others to see what is happening. On the street, offenders may not know what people will do next, but on public transport the choices for behavior are more limited and, therefore, more predictable.

A crime-specific approach, focusing on offender decision making, allows managers and police to use situational measures precisely tailored to meet these conditions. To a greater extent than many other public environments, public transport is controlled by managers who can manipulate situational controls.[1] For example, limiting entry to those who have paid helps to keep off the system robbers who are short of money, as well as youngsters intent on vandalism. Limiting the time that passengers (offenders or targets) spend on the system puts additional constraints on those searching for victims. Limiting physical contact between passengers (through better crowd control and incentives to travel off-peak) may help prevent indecent assaults involving fondling or rubbing. At the same time, this makes pickpocketing more difficult and should reduce tensions that result in assaults. Increased supervision would deter many offenders anxious to avoid detection and arrest. This can be accomplished through the use of more conductors and station staff, and by the provision of closed-circuit television (CCTV) surveillance.

Use of police and security guards can also, in theory, provide improved surveillance and supervision. Much of the debate about the policing of transit has focused on the question of whether this is more adequately provided by a dedicated force or by the regular metropolitan police. In individual jurisdictions this question seems to turn primarily on local politics and funding. More recently the policing debate has centered on the value of order maintenance strategies. The experi-

---

[1] See Smith (1998) for a discussion of the theoretical links between situational controls, environments, and offender actions.

ence of applying these in the New York City subway has been associated with a fall in crime, though more evidence is needed of their effect. Somewhat clearer evidence of success has been found for comprehensive efforts, such as in the Washington, D.C., Metro, to include crime prevention design as an integral part of new systems and in the renovation of existing facilities, such as the Port Authority Bus Terminal in Manhattan. Together with many smaller successes obtained in dealing with specific crimes on particular systems, these design and management successes speak to the value of opportunity reduction in mass transit.

This essay has been divided into six sections. Section I anchors the discussion in a brief history of public transport and an account of the financial and operational constraints that help to determine crime opportunities. Section II presents incidence and prevention information about the variety of crimes committed. Section III explores three key issues for planners and managers: the measurement of victimization risks, the effect of public transport on the distribution of crime, and the effects of fear on ridership. Section IV examines the scope for "designing out crime" in new and older transit facilities and for "order maintenance" policing on subways. Section V considers future security needs in the context of predicted changes in public transport. Section VI offers some concluding observations on future research needs.

I. Public Transport in an Urban Environment

The design and operation of public transport systems provide an essential context for considering transport crime and security. In this section we review the development of public transport and describe some operational constraints that have implications for crime. We begin with some definitions.

A. Definitions

"Public" transport refers to passenger transport that any member of the public may pay to use (Vuchic 1981). It does not refer to the level of privacy in the vehicle itself, to ownership of the service, or to any financial support it may receive. Most of the forms of public transport discussed here are forms of urban mass transit. "Mass transit" is "a conveyance that operates along fixed routes, with regular stops, on frequent schedules, and with a set rate of fare" (Hood 1996, p. 328, n. 10). It includes subways or metros, buses, trams or streetcars, and trolley buses, as well as other modes of rail rapid transit, such as commuter trains and the newer light rapid transit.

This essay also includes some discussion of public "paratransit." This often operates as a feeder to mass transit and thus affects the traveler's decision to use mass transit with its associated victimization risks. It also presents its own crime opportunities and preventive challenges though little is known about these matters (but see Easteal and Wilson 1991; Groeger 1991; Jammers 1995). Paratransit includes taxis, dial-a-ride, and jitneys operating on public roads (Vuchic 1981). Dial-a-ride operates from a central dispatch office using vans or minibuses with passengers relating their locations and destinations via the telephone (Vuchic 1981). Jitneys run along relatively fixed routes, adjusted in some degree to individual use, and charge a predetermined fee. They operate primarily in developing countries (Vuchic 1981), though they are also found in some U.S. cities, where they may operate without legal authorization (Boyle 1994).

B. Transport and Urban Development

It is clear from its history that public transport is an economically precarious enterprise. It involves a perpetual struggle to match transport "supply"—limited by natural and urban geography, technology, and the availability of capital—with travel "demand"—determined by patterns of housing density and job location and, increasingly, by leisure and shopping needs. Security within the system has tended to be a distant concern, though it has grown in importance in the past forty years. Some of the patterns of urban development linked with transportation are highlighted here to provide a backdrop against which the crime patterns and prevention strategies discussed in the next section can be placed.[2]

Several good histories exist of urban public transport covering the past two centuries. For example, Vuchic (1981) sets out a detailed history of the development of urban public transportation, focused on technological advances (see also Cudahy 1990; Smerk 1992). Other works concentrate on descriptions of developments in one city. Cud-

---

[2] It is beyond the scope of the present discussion to identify crime opportunities presented by the urban landscape resulting from transport developments. For example, areas that are suited to mass transit due to their high-density housing are risky places to own cars if no garage is available. Using British Crime Survey data, Clarke and Mayhew (1998) found that cars are at much less risk of being stolen if they are parked in a garage than if they are not.

ahy (1995), Hood (1996), and Brooks (1997) provide complementary views of the history and development of New York City's subway system, while Cole (1987) includes a discussion of changes in public transport in London, primarily from an economic perspective.

Historically, changes in the source of power, the type of roadway used, and the design of the vehicle have represented interim attempts to solve classic urban transportation problems related primarily to the need to get people to work. Unless there is an affordable means of transporting them to their jobs, workers must live within walking distance of employment. The migration of workers to cities resulted in severely overcrowded living conditions around employment centers. Before the development of public transport in London, for example, workers lived near the factories where they worked and walked there from up to two miles away (Cole 1987). As public transport developed along fixed routes, the cost of travel fell and workers were able to live in less crowded conditions further away from their jobs (Vuchic 1981).

In the latter part of the 1800s, transport operators grappled with two major problems. The first was to find alternative power sources (such as steam and then electricity) in place of horsepower (Vuchic 1981), and the second was to find alternative routes to overcome the difficulties of providing reliable public service along congested city streets (Brooks 1997). The solutions to the second problem—use of underground and overhead systems—radically changed the urban environment. Because elevated and underground trains could travel faster than trams on mixed-use roadways, they carried more passengers. Costs were reasonable and allowed workers to live even further away from central areas of employment.

In the nineteenth and early twentieth centuries, urban land development involved growth out from the central business district, initially concentrated along commuter rail or tramlines to suburban areas (Smerk 1992). High-density housing was built close to stations because workers had to walk to them. This pattern can still be seen in London where high-density residential areas exist near Victorian rail stations (Cole 1987). As additional modes of travel to these stations became available, the housing did not have to be as tightly packed together. While workers tend to live further away from the urban core as the urban area becomes more decentralized, they tend to travel toward the center when they travel to work (Ingram 1998).

Technological changes in transport have tended to carry with them the need for more capital investment. For example, electric-powered trams (or trolleys) required larger capital investments than did horse-powered systems, resulting in the merger of companies that had previously operated monopolies along a single route. This led to increased coordination between routes and integrated fare payment (Smerk 1992). The electricity generated by the tram companies was later also supplied for domestic and commercial use (Cudahy 1990), which helped subsidize the costs of transport.

After World War I, operators began to face competition from vehicles powered by the internal combustion engine that could operate along flexible routes. In the United States, tram companies faced a number of different barriers that prevented them from raising the capital to compete—such as artificially low fare ceilings and the forced divestiture of their associated power companies (see Cudahy 1990). Buses could carry a fairly large number of passengers, reliably and with relatively cheap fuel (Vuchic 1981), and the private automobile also became increasingly affordable (Saltzman 1992). Today, the bus is the most common form of public transport, particularly in developing countries (Armstrong-Wright 1993).

Except for a surge in public transport ridership during World War II and immediately after, transit ridership peaked in the United States in 1926 (with 17.254 billion total passengers) (Cudahy 1990). As Saltzman (1992) explained, federal housing and highway policies in the United States after World War II contributed to the growth of low-density areas around higher-density urban cores. In the United States, funding of public transport was seen as a local issue during this postwar period. Federal funds were available to help fund low-cost mortgages, build low-density housing in areas around urban cores, and construct highways. It was not until 1964 that Congress passed legislation providing funds for mass transportation. By this time, many forms of mass transit had become less viable because of changes in the urban landscape.

This pattern does not exist to the same extent in European cities due primarily to different postwar policies in some countries that tended to favor public transportation over the private car. For example, while operators discontinued using the tram in the United States and Britain and most of France after World War II, in other European countries tram service was usually consolidated into a single company in each city and was city owned (Vuchic 1981). According to Hall (1995), over 40 percent of work journeys and a quarter of all journeys in European cities are still by public transport. Despite similar rates of increase in car ownership in Germany and the United States between 1950 and 1977, for example, transit ridership remained largely unchanged in Germany while it dropped steeply in the United States (Vuchic 1981). One reason for the greater use of public transport in Europe is the more compact nature of these cities. These conditions exist in other parts of the world as well. Gaylord and Galliher (1991) reported that 40 percent of Hong Kong's homes and half its workplaces are located within a ten-minute walk of a metro station. The Hong Kong Metro is part of a second wave of rapid transit systems built since World War II (see Walmsley and Perrett 1992).

Today, government officials often regard public transport as a vital component of environmental and energy policy (see, e.g., Department for the Environment, Transport, and the Regions [DETR] 1998). They believe that without it, congestion and pollution would overtake the cities. They also believe that public transport is essential to the vitality and economic welfare of metropolitan areas. It provides access for rich and poor alike to the city's amenities, and it permits the central core to serve as the economic engine for the metropolis as a whole (Yaro and Hiss 1996). The importance of providing public transport that is secure is also beginning to be recognized by governments (see, e.g., DETR 1998).

It is not clear, however, that taxpayers are willing to subsidize either existing systems or new developments. The system beneficiaries are not always easy to identify (see Glaister 1991). Those who travel on the system may feel that they already contribute as much as they can. Those with other means of travel available may feel that they do not benefit from it and should not have to support it. Those who are dissatisfied with the performance of existing systems may oppose heavy government subsidies, as may those who think systems should operate more efficiently and bear more of their own capital and running costs. For the present discussion, it is sufficient to note that many pressures exist on operators to keep running costs low whether the system is old or new.

C. Public Transport—Constraints and Crime Opportunities

Well-run systems that regulate fare payment, provide adequate staffing, have easy transfers, and supply frequent and regular service are less likely to provide conditions favorable to crime (see Gaylord and Galliher 1991; LaVigne 1996a, 1996b). As noted above, however, the operation of public transport is heavily constrained by funding, which can make it difficult to meet these ideals. Two consequent operational factors with important consequences for crime are overcrowding during peak periods and lack of supervision from staff in vehicles and stations.

1. *Overcrowding and Peak Travel.* Public transportation is a "fleeting good" (White and Senior 1983). Space available must be used or it is gone, along with any revenues. Vehicles must be available when there is a demand, such as during the morning rush hour in large urban areas. Any capital investment designed to improve capacity during the peak period will be surplus for other periods. This is why peak costs are high. To deal with these high peak costs, operators can provide fewer vehicles than would be desirable for the comfort of their passengers, resulting in overcrowding (Cole 1987). Operators can also take vehicles out of service off-peak or attempt to level the peak by offering concessionary fares to try to get travelers to travel at other times (e.g., Murray 1999).

Overcrowding is an important choice-structuring property (Cornish and Clarke 1987) for many crimes, including pickpocketing and sexual assault (touching and rubbing). These opportunities have long been recognized. For example, the conditions on board the horse-drawn tram would not be wholly unfamiliar to modern urban travelers. A drawing from *Harper's Illustrated Weekly* (in 1871) reproduced in Brooks (1997) shows two women about to get on a vehicle containing leering men. Two signs are attached to the tram—one says "Pickpocket's Paradise" while the other, according to Brooks, contains the warning that Dante saw inscribed over the gates of hell: "All Hope Abandon Ye Who Enter Here." In 1912, although women accounted for only about one-quarter of rush-hour passengers on New York's subways, the contemporary press was concerned about the sexual contact that resulted from conditions of overcrowding on the subway (Hood 1996).

2. *Lack of Supervision.* Passengers often receive little oversight from passersby as they travel. In addition, their actions tend to be predictable as they wait in special places or move through corridors, vehicles, and transfer points. This special vulnerability makes oversight by transit employees, police, and other passengers especially important.

At the same time, the high costs of public transport have resulted nearly everywhere in pressure to reduce staff costs. To cut staff (and to speed up peak-hour service), newer rail systems tend to use automatic fare collection and automatic train control (ATC) to regulate operation along portions of track. Stations, trains, and passengers are also deprived of the supervision that is so important in preventing crime. For buses, staff costs are usually the largest operating expense and pressures to cut costs tend to focus on conductors and inspectors (see Cole 1987; Henderson 1992). The ability of these staff to control fare evasion, rowdiness and assault, or vandalism may not enter into the calculation of costs (cf. van Andel 1992).

II. Crime Types and Crime Prevention
This section discusses the crimes occurring on public transport systems and the situational measures that have been taken to reduce opportunities for crime. Clarke's (1997) classification of opportunity-reducing techniques is used throughout. This describes sixteen separate techniques falling under the four general approaches of increasing the perceived effort required for crime, increasing the risks, reducing the rewards, and removing excuses (see definitions in app. A). Reference is also made throughout to Cornish's (1994) notion of "crime scripts"— step-by-step accounts of the procedures used by offenders to complete crimes.

Although situational prevention requires a crime-specific approach to blocking opportunities, this does not preclude researchers and planners from looking across crimes to try to identify conditions related to the commission of several different types of crimes. By looking at these similar opportunity features, it may be possible for managers to identify prevention measures that could be applied to groups of crimes.

As mentioned above, two such conditions for crime on urban public transport are lack of supervision and overcrowded conditions.[3] In this section, where the focus is on blocking opportunities, crime is dis-

---

[3] We have been unable to find any published studies looking specifically at the relationship between changing levels of staff on public transport and crime commission. To explore this issue, we compared the number of operating staff on the London Underground for an eleven-year period (1975 to fiscal year 1984–85) (London Transport Executive 1976–84; London Regional Transport 1985) to reported crime levels on the Underground (1975–85) (see Department of Transport 1986), as a percentage of all crime in the Metropolitan Police Area. We examined three types of crime: robbery, violence against persons, and theft from persons. As expected, robbery and violence against persons varied inversely with level of operating staff for seven and eight out of the ten years, respectively, while theft from persons only did so for five out of the ten years examined. These findings provide some support for the view that robbery and violence offenses are related to lack of supervision while theft from the person is not. However, given the low overall volume of robbery and violence on the system and the lack of information about staff placement, it seems premature to conclude too much from these findings. A more detailed, place-by-place analysis is needed.

cussed in terms of one of these two broad opportunity clusters.[4] This does not mean that crimes discussed under one of the conditions do not also occur under the other. For example, passenger assault, discussed as a crime facilitated by lack of supervision, may also occur in the overcrowded conditions of the rush hour (see Shellow, Romualdi, and Bartel 1974) or busy interchanges (LaVigne 1996a). And some thefts by staff (e.g., pocketing cash proffered in lieu of a ticket), also discussed under the supervision heading, may be easier to carry out in crowded conditions. The difficulty is that categories such as "theft by staff" often encompass a rather broad range of specific crimes, which are not always facilitated by the same environmental conditions. Nevertheless, the broad division between crowded conditions and lack of supervision is useful in organizing the discussion below.

A. Crimes Facilitated by Lack of Supervision

Under the "routine activities" approach of Cohen and Felson (1979), "absence of a capable guardian" is, by definition, a precondition of crime. While costs may prevent the employment of more staff or more police, technology in the form of CCTV or alarms for passenger use can sometimes fill the need for increased "guardianship." Opportunities for crimes facilitated by lack of supervision can also be blocked in other ways. For example, automatic ticketing may remove opportunities for passengers to avoid paying fares and for staff to pocket fare money.

1. *Robbery of Passengers.* Robbery on mass transit is a rare event, even in systems with relatively high numbers of incidents such as New York City (see Smith et al. 1986b; Kenney 1987). Detailed analyses of passenger robbery incidents suggest that most robberies occur in one of the following three situations.

First, offenders prey on passengers in the deserted parts of large subway station complexes (Falanga 1988) or at times when there are few other passengers around (Clarke, Belanger, and Eastman 1996). Pre-

---

[4] The crime categories discussed here follow the definitions for the offenses used in each study. For example, in the study of crime on the New York City subway system conducted by the New York City Criminal Justice Agency, the Transit Police Department classifications of robbery and grand larceny were used (Smith et al. 1986b). Robberies were thefts or attempted thefts where force was used or threatened, while thefts or attempted thefts where the force was only used to snatch the property (rather than directed against the person) were classified as larcenies. The category of "larcenies" used in Levine and Wachs's (1985, 1986a, 1986b; Levine, Wachs, and Shirazi 1986) study of bus crime in west central Los Angeles includes some nonviolent robberies.

vention measures useful against this type of robbery include the use of CCTV (Burrows 1980; Webb and Laycock 1992) and possibly blocking off parts of the station (Shellow, Romualdi, and Bartel 1974; Falanga 1988).

Second, offenders target passengers waiting at isolated rail stations in off-hours periods, particularly at elevated platforms and in high-crime neighborhoods (see studies reviewed in Shellow, Bartel, and Romualdi 1975). Off-hours waiting areas are used to provide waiting passengers with the benefits of surveillance provided by transit employees, such as token clerks or ticket sellers, and other passengers (see Sandler et al. 1979; Levy 1994).

Third, offenders appear to lie in wait for passengers leaving public transport (Barker et al. 1993; Block and Davis 1996). Prevention techniques focusing on target removal or surveillance may be useful against this type of robbery. Tram operators in Hanover and Stuttgart call ahead for taxis to meet passengers in the evening, charging a flat add-on fee (DETR 1998). Special late-hours parking areas may be used at some stations (Saville 1991). Real-time bus or rail systems (see Sec. V) make it easier for someone to meet late-night travelers at transit stops.

A number of studies of the location of crime on subway systems have found that robbery is more likely to occur in the station than on the train (e.g., Chaiken, Lawless, and Stevenson 1974; Shellow, Romualdi, and Bartel 1974; Kenney 1987; Smith et al. 1986b; Clarke, Belanger, and Eastman 1996). The Criminal Justice Agency study of robbery on the New York subway (Smith et al. 1986b) found that although the period from 4:00 to 6:00 P.M. had the largest number of robbery incidents, the periods when passengers were most at risk were those with low passenger volumes—8:00 P.M. until 6:00 A.M.

Sometimes offenders target particular groups using public transport. The timing of robberies on the New York City subway (Chaiken, Lawless, and Stevenson 1974) and the ages of complainants and arrestees (Smith et al. 1986b) suggest that some offenses involve school children, as both offenders and victims. In response, the New York City subway recently designated the last three cars of selected trains as Safe Passage cars patrolled by a police officer (Winfield 1993). In Mexico City, offenders traveling in other cars sometimes rob taxi passengers by following the cab and then stopping it (Krauss 1997). The public is advised only to use cabs from special taxi stands and to avoid traveling alone (forms of target removal).

2. *Robbery of Staff.*   The substantial amounts of money collected for fares can prove tempting to robbers. In the late 1960s and early 1970s, robberies of bus drivers became a serious problem in many cities throughout the United States. The solution has become a classic of crime prevention. It involved the implementation of exact-change fare collection together with on-board safes into which the fares were dropped. Chaiken, Lawless, and Stevenson (1974) found that these changes led to a dramatic fall in the number of bus robberies in New York City in 1969. This finding was replicated in other U.S. cities where exact-fare systems, involving target removal, had been introduced (Gray 1971).

In other measures to prevent robbery, ticket machines on the London Underground have been designed to permit access to them from a secure area behind, thus preventing robberies when they are emptied (Poyner and Warne 1988). A recent measure to prevent this crime in the New York subway involves staggering shifts for token booth clerks so that a police officer can be present when the boxes are emptied (Roane 1997). Initial findings for three months showed no token booth robberies on the line in Queens where this measure was used compared to seventeen token booth robberies in other parts of Queens. Earlier measures involving extensive target hardening were taken in the New York subway to prevent robberies of the clerks in their booths. Subsequently, fire extinguishers were installed in the booths to prevent robbers from setting fire to them as a way of gaining entry as clerks fled (Perez-Pena 1995).

Transit workers with perhaps the greatest risk of robbery are taxicab drivers, who carry cash, travel by themselves around cities with strangers, and do not choose their destinations. The nature of the vehicle and the type of service provided ensure that taxi drivers experience very little protective surveillance from robbery. A variety of situational prevention measures that have been advocated or adopted are classified in table 1 using Cornish's (1994) method of "script" analysis.

Drivers often use informal passenger screening practices, such as refusing to pick up fares at certain locations (McKinley 1990; Cohen 1996). These practices can discriminate against those who live in poorer areas or are from certain racial or age groups, making it difficult for them to use the service. Other measures, such as carrying a weapon or using alarms, electronic locators, or special radio codes (Easteal and Wilson 1991) increase the risks of offender apprehension or injury.

TABLE 1

Methods for Preventing Taxi Robbery

Stages in Crime	Situational Control	Situational Technique
Get a weapon	Gun-control legislation	Controlling facilitators
Decide on destination	. . .	. . .
Hail a cab	Screen by pick-up location	Entry screening
	Screen by appearance	Entry screening
Request isolated desti-		
nation	Refuse to go to destination	Access control
	Radio destination to base	Surveillance by employees
Get to isolated destination	Use electronic locator	Surveillance by employees
Threaten with weapon	Push alarm button	Formal surveillance
	Bulletproof screen	Target hardening
Take money	Require plastic money	Target removal
	Money in safe	Target hardening
Leave the scene	Police surveillance	Formal surveillance
Get away	Use video footage	Surveillance by employees

NOTE.—This table is based on Cornish's (1994) method of "script" analysis.

Measures, such as bulletproof screens (Newman 1998), increase the effort. Locked money boxes have also been suggested, but Easteal and Wilson (1991) have pointed out that these may result in escalation so that the vehicle is stolen as a way of getting to the money in the box. Random checks, decoy units, and intensive enforcement in high-crime areas also increase the risks to offenders (through formal surveillance), although these measures have been subject to constitutional challenges in the United States (Sullivan 1997). Using regular transit system cards (Lefkowitz 1994) or electronic point of sale (EPoS) technology in cabs—"plastic money" (Jammers 1995)—would reduce the amount of cash carried, helping to eliminate the motive for many robberies.

3. *Assaults on Passengers.*   Assaults on passengers tend to occur during the evening rush hour (Shellow, Romualdi, and Bartel 1974) and later at night (Levine and Wachs 1985; Department of Transport 1986). In the first case, overcrowded conditions and alcohol consumption may be to blame, but the late-night occurrence of these incidents also suggests that offenders are targeting victims because of their relative isolation.

Levine and Wachs (1985) conducted a telephone survey of a random sample of residents in west central Los Angeles, asking them about crimes they had experienced while traveling on buses. They found that crimes committed in the back of the bus were more serious, many in-

volving assaults, and that after 7:00 P.M. nearly half of the crimes occurred there. Levine and Wachs suggested several changes to the design of buses to promote surveillance, including the placement of exits
at the back and mirrors for drivers (see also Sturman 1980). Changes
in seating patterns were also suggested as a way of increasing passenger
surveillance (Levine and Wachs 1985), although, as LaVigne (1996a)
noted, some seating arrangements may increase interactions among
passengers and result in more assaults. When safety, information, and
control officers (VICs) began riding on public transportation in three
Dutch cities in the 1980s, passenger assaults and harassment decreased
(van Andel 1992), showing that security personnel or conductors can
also be used to control aggression (see also New York Times 1998;
Whitney 1998).

   LaVigne (1996a) found that the only significant predictor of assaults
at station parking lots in the Washington, D.C., Metro was the absence of an attendant in the evenings. Within the system itself, assault
was the only crime where the rate on the Metro was related to the area
crime rate above ground. LaVigne suggested that this correlation
might be due to a spillover between actions below- and aboveground.

   Tremblay and Tremblay (1998) compared interracial violence in
Montreal subway stations to violence aboveground. Their findings
suggest that interracial violence is more likely to occur in the transit
environment because individuals from different racial groups that
might not otherwise meet are brought together there. Transit nodes,
such as bus stops, may also provide a place where people linger and
are more noticeable than if they had been walking through an area.
One possible example of this principle is provided by the Stephen
Lawrence case that became a cause célèbre in Britain. Stephen Lawrence was one of two black teenagers attacked by a group of white
youths while waiting for a bus in South London in 1993 (British
Broadcasting Corporation 2 [BBC2] 1999). He was stabbed and he
died. The case gained wide public attention not because of its transport
connection but because of the seriousness of the crime, the unpro-
voked and racial nature of the attack, and the police mishandling of the
investigation (Travis 1999). Yet measures such as a real-time display
system for the bus (see Sec. V), an alarm system, or CCTV might have
averted the crime or lessened its severity.

   4. *Persons Pushed under Trains.* Incidents are rare in which passengers are deliberately pushed onto the tracks but they cause much fear
among passengers (Martell and Dietz 1992). It seems that many of the

perpetrators are mentally disturbed (Martell and Dietz 1992) and that the incidents are more likely to occur when few people are present (e.g., Davenport and McGreevy 1999). Martell and Dietz (1992) looked at the rising number of such incidents on the New York City subway system between 1975 and 1991. While some of the incidents involved robbery attempts and groups of youths victimizing homeless or other vulnerable persons, the increased incidence was attributed to the larger number of offenders referred for psychiatric evaluation, most of whom were psychotic and homeless.

Prevention measures that make it difficult to reach the track area or help to prevent serious injury once someone is there, developed to deal with railway suicide, may also help to prevent pushing incidents. Barriers along the edges of platforms are used in some systems, such as Leningrad, Lille, and Singapore (Clarke and Poyner 1994). So-called suicide pits increase the clearance between the train and the track and reduce fatalities (O'Donnell and Farmer 1994).[5] Fitting trains with air bags or other devices to lesson the impact or prevent bodies getting under the wheels of the train could reduce fatalities (Beskow, Thorson, and Ostrom 1994; Clarke and Poyner 1994).

Some of the surveillance measures that have been suggested for preventing suicides might also be effective in preventing pushing incidents. For example, Gaylord and Lester (1994) reported that in the Hong Kong subway staff keep their eyes open for potential suicides who sometimes dress or act very differently from other passengers. O'Donnell and Farmer (1994) suggested that intensified surveillance at Underground stations where suicides have been found to cluster, such as those serving large psychiatric hospitals, might save some lives. Hospital liaison schemes could aid surveillance efforts (Clarke and Poyner 1994).

5. *Assaults on Staff.* Assaults on staff present one of the most difficult problems for public transport systems. Staff are needed to run the operation. Their presence reassures passengers and helps to control crimes directed against them. At the same time, staff are exposed to the risk of personal attack because they are seen as representatives of the system, enforcing its rules, in settings where they may be isolated and vulnerable.

---

[5] "Suicide pits," according to O'Donnell and Farmer (1994), are channels several feet deep that are located between rails at a number of stations on the London Underground. Their original purpose is not known.

Rose (1979) found that assaults on tube and bus staff in London were associated with a remarkably similar set of factors. Fare disputes and drunken and rowdy behavior were most frequently cited as the trigger on both buses and the tube, followed by theft, vagrancy, and loitering (on the tube) and complaints about service problems (on buses). The majority of assaults occurred in the late afternoon and evening, with incidents clustered on particular bus routes and at certain stations. Hargadine (1983) also found that fare disputes were associated with assaults on bus drivers in Seattle.

Preventive schemes for staff assaults have involved a variety of approaches, including training in passenger management (Hargadine 1983), adoption of more easily understandable fare structures (Poyner and Warne 1988), and use of protective screens (a form of target hardening) (Poyner and Warne 1988). Poyner and Warne (1988) evaluated the effects of protective screens on one-person operated buses with an exact-fare system in northeast England. Changes in the fare structure reduced the number of assaults but the installation of the screens had a far greater effect and almost entirely eliminated assaults on drivers in their cabs. The assaults that continued were on inspectors. While additional staff have been found to reduce passenger assaults, the evidence that they also reduce staff assaults is not as encouraging (van Andel 1992). Dutch research does suggest, however, that the presence of other staff on board, whose primary responsibilities are fare collection and peacekeeping, is viewed favorably by drivers and by many passengers (van Andel 1992; Hauber 1993). (See Whitney [1998] for a similar scheme adopted in Strasbourg.) However, some operators are resistant to their use, primarily because of cost (e.g., Murray 1998).

6. *Vandalism.* The most common form of vandalism in public transport systems for the past thirty years has been graffiti applied by markers or spray paint (see New York State Senate Committee on Transportation 1981; Castleman 1982). Graffiti cleaning has been used successfully in a number of different settings, for example, in Philadelphia (Scott 1989), New York City (Sloan-Howitt and Kelling 1992), and the state of Victoria in Australia (Carr and Spring 1993). This cleaning was usually part of a larger effort involving police enforcement, prosecution of offenders, and publicity surrounding the cleanup efforts. It has also been tied in some places to the use of newer, easier-to-clean or harder-to-mark surfaces. Rapid cleaning of graffiti makes it more difficult for offenders to find a good setting for the offense and

it removes the reward of "getting up" (see Sloan-Howitt and Kelling 1992).[6]

Guards and conductors can act as crime target guardians (a form of employee surveillance), watching over transport property as they carry out other tasks (see Wilson and Healy 1986; Carr and Spring 1993). Sturman's (1980) research on the location of damage on different types of buses—with more damage on buses without conductors and in the parts of buses with low supervision—suggested that supervision is effective in reducing vandalism on public transport. The Department of Transport (1986) study of crime on the London Underground found that the areas of stations and trains most affected by graffiti were those most remote from supervision. The study also suggested that the reduction of staff at some stations and the one-person operation of trains might have contributed to the problem. Poyner (1992b) looked at the effects on bus vandalism of installing video cameras. The campaign used extensive publicity, especially aimed at school children (the presumed primary offenders). Reported damage incidents fell both on buses with live cameras as well as on those with dummy cameras, suggesting a diffusion of benefits (Clarke and Weisburd 1994). The Dutch initiative that put young people (VICs) on public transport in three cities in Holland in the 1980s to help control several forms of minor offending showed limited vandalism on vehicles or at times when the VICs were present (van Andel 1992).

Some transport systems suffer little from vandalism or graffiti, including those in Washington, D.C. (LaVigne 1996a, 1996b), Hong Kong (Gaylord and Galliher 1991), and Calcutta (Armstrong-Wright 1993). LaVigne and Gaylord and Galliher attributed the lack of vandalism to the design and management of the systems they studied. For example, LaVigne reported that the Metro has rough-walled surfaces and barriers in front of walls, making graffiti writing difficult, vaulted ceilings and few column supports so that vandals cannot hide while they are damaging, and a maintenance policy of rapidly cleaning off graffiti and repairing damage.

7. Fare Evasion.   Fare evasion involves not paying for a ride or paying too little. The names it has been given—such as "dodging," "beating," and "fiddling"—indicate that it is often considered a game or competition. As Hauber (1993) noted, it is an attractive form of fraud

---

[6] "Getting up" is the term used by graffiti writers to describe the marking or painting of their names on subway trains (Castleman 1982).

for passengers because, even when detected, they often remain anonymous if they pay immediately. From the system perspective, fare evasion depletes revenue and prevents accurate monitoring of passenger flows. A greater concern is that those who intend to rob or commit another crime often enter the system without paying (Levine 1987; Stockdale and Gresham 1998). As Section IV shows, it has been claimed that measures used to prevent fare evasion and other low-level crime on the New York subway may have reduced the incidence of more serious crimes as well (Finder 1991; Eastman and Yuan 1994).

Prevention measures are discussed below in the context of four actions taken by passengers—paying the fare, entering the system, riding in a vehicle, and exiting the system. Systems have developed a series of measures for each step to prevent fare evasion, including entry barriers, ticket inspection, and exit barriers. These measures can vary between systems where speed and ease of operation compete. Because of these differences, methods of fare evasion are likely to vary dramatically between modes and systems.

The simplest type of fare is a "flat" fare that does not vary with distance traveled. This type of fare is in effect a subsidy for longer journeys paid by short-haul passengers (Cole 1987). Distance-based fares may encourage "overriding," where passengers travel further than they should without paying. Complicated fare structures may lead to inadvertent underpayment (DesChamps, Brantingham, and Brantingham 1992). When fare payment is supervised mechanically, as with ticket machines, inadequate designs may provide opportunities for fare evasion as well as theft (for their study of slug use in new ticket machines on the London Underground, see Clarke, Cody, and Natarajan [1994]).

Entry systems include open access, visual display, mechanical trigger, and electronic trigger. Entry barriers are a form of entry screening and are commonly used in rail systems, although they can be used on buses, as in São Paulo (Armstrong-Wright 1993). Entry media for barriers can be coins, tokens, tickets, electronically coded tickets ("smartcards"), passes, or transfers. The New York City subway is moving to the use of an automatic fare collection system across the entire subway and bus network, with the MetroCard as the magnetically encoded payment and entry medium (Winfield 1993). This change follows a period in which a variety of methods were used to evade fares (see Levine 1987; Pitt 1989; Del Castillo and Lindner 1994; Weidner 1996).

London Underground completed its installation of automated ticket machines at sixty-three central London stations in 1989, with exit checking at suburban stations in the system being carried out visually by staff. Clarke (1993) looked at the rates of fare evasion as measured by system-wide ticket checks made by teams of inspectors, and found that it decreased by two-thirds after the automated system was installed. A commuter rail system in southeast England, Connex, found in a pilot study that automatic ticket gates paid for themselves within a year, though it was not clear whether the increase in revenue resulted from less fare evasion or increased ridership due to a perception of improved security (Ewart 1999).[7]

Some modern systems do not use automated entry (see DesChamps, Brantingham, and Brantingham 1992). DesChamps and his colleagues found that fare evasion rates on Vancouver ferries decreased when more staff were placed on duty to check tickets and passes at rush hour. Redesigned monthly passes made it easier for staff to determine whether they were valid.

On-route checking can only be carried out if the system issues some form of ticket. These tickets can be checked for proof of payment, whether the ticket is valid for the time used, the distance traveled, and the person carrying it, and whether it is counterfeit or has been tampered with. The checking can be done by conductors or inspectors who ride one vehicle or by inspectors who enter only some vehicles (see Cosby 1985; Hauber 1993). The presence of previously unemployed young people hired to help deal with fare evasion, vandalism, and aggression in three cities in Holland resulted in less fare evasion (van Dijk and Junger-Tas 1988; van Andel 1992; Hauber 1993).

When passengers exit the system, tickets can be checked electronically or visually by staff who inspect or collect tickets. LaVigne (1996a) suggested that distance-based automated fare cards that are monitored at entry and exit double the risks of apprehension for fare evasion. The Hong Kong metro limits the time passengers can be on the system allowing little time for loitering (Gaylord and Galliher 1991). Essentially this uses fare-checking procedures to prevent other crimes since offenders are given little time to exploit crime opportunities.

8. *Staff Theft of Fares.* Employees can fail to issue tickets and pocket the fare, they can issue tickets for less than the fare paid, use a

---

[7] For a discussion of the difficulties of measuring fare evasion, see Cosby (1985), who suggested a method for measuring fare evasion on buses as a way of determining whether the revenue lost is greater or less than the costs of increased enforcement.

stolen ticket machine, or tamper with the machines (Armstrong-Wright 1993). As Armstrong-Wright noted, it can be hard to distinguish whether fare evasion or pilfering is causing loss of revenue since there can be collusion among passengers, collectors, and inspectors. In sophisticated systems, repeated counting of money at each stage of processing helps to discourage theft while use of marked notes can help identify those who have stolen money (Mauri, Cooney, and Prowe 1984). Where it is difficult for passengers to determine the correct fare and there is little oversight from others, as with taxicabs, overcharging can occur. While meters are designed to standardize fares and prevent overcharging, they are subject to tampering (see Pierre-Pierre 1995).

B. Crimes Related to Overcrowding

Crowding as a precondition for offending has been noted by a number of different researchers in connection with theft (Kabundi and Normandeau 1987) and sexual assault (Beller, Garelik, and Cooper 1980; Kabundi and Normandeau 1987; Hood 1996; Lopez 1996). Overcrowding may facilitate these offenses in several different ways. With stealth thefts, the victim may be unaware that the offense has occurred. With sexual abuse through contact, the victim may be surprised by the nature of the contact and be unsure how to react. Snatch thefts may surprise victims who are focusing on some other feature of their crowded environment. If these victims then react slowly, the offender may be able to use the crowded conditions to escape more easily.

Lopez (1996) has recommended maximum passenger densities for subways in order to limit overcrowding. He recommends that densities should not exceed two persons per square meter in stations, that passenger flows in passageways should not exceed sixty-six people per meter per minute, and that in trains no more than 40–75 percent of seats should be occupied. Research is needed to see whether crime is lower when these standards are met. Crime volumes and passenger densities on systems adopting peak-leveling measures—such as discount off-peak pricing and more flexible scheduling for schools and businesses (Levine and Wachs 1985; Levine, Wachs, and Shirazi 1986; Cole 1987; Murray 1999)—should also be monitored to see if crime prevention benefits are realized.

1. *Thefts from Passengers.* Victims of theft on rail systems most often lose property that is valuable (jewelry) or easily accessible (handbags) (Smith et al. 1996*b*). Offenders operate in crowds where the vic-

tims are distracted or unable to protect their property and tend to use stealth (pickpocketing) or surprise (snatching). In the Montreal subway, most pickpocketing was found to occur between 3:00 and 6:00 P.M. when subway cars were crowded with both students and workers (Kabundi and Normandeau 1987). Women were especially at risk of certain types of theft, such as handbag snatching. On the London Underground, incidents most commonly occurred midmorning and during the evening travel peak with the volume highest on Fridays (Department of Transport 1986). The majority of reported larcenies on the New York City subway were jewelry and bag snatches or bag opener larcenies (Smith et al. 1986*b*). The two-hour time periods when the system had the highest passenger volumes (morning and afternoon peak periods) were also the times when the highest numbers of felony larcenies occurred, with nearly one-fourth occurring between 4:00 and 6:00 P.M. With the exception of the period from midnight to 6:00 A.M. (where half of the larcenies were "lush worker" larcenies involving sleeping or intoxicated victims), the period from 4:00 to 6:00 P.M. was also the period with the highest incident rate, based on hourly turnstile counts. Just over half of all the larcenies occurred on the train. These studies all found that crimes were concentrated at busy areas of the system—including stations in the city center (Kabundi and Normandeau 1987), near shopping areas or tourist attractions (see Department of Transport 1986; Smith et al. 1986*b*), or where subway lines come together at a transfer station (LaVigne 1996*a*).[8]

The study of bus crime in Los Angeles supports the view that overcrowded conditions on public transport provide thieves with an ideal environment for snatch thefts or thefts involving stealth (Levine and Wachs 1985, 1986*a*; Levine, Wachs, and Shirazi 1986). Overall, nearly three-fourths of the reported crimes were larcenies or robberies without injury. The majority of incidents occurred in the afternoon or during the evening rush hours. Ninety percent of crimes on buses and 20 percent of the crime at bus stops occurred when there were twenty or more people present. Levine and his team (Levine and Wachs 1985; Levine, Wachs, and Shirazi 1986) mapped the reported bus stop incidents. Two of the three high-volume crime stops observed during the afternoon and around rush hour showed crowding as a problem.

[8] Brantingham, Brantingham, and Wong (1991) noted that Chic Conwell, the professional thief studied by Sutherland (1937), reported that streetcar stops that were rich areas for thieves, such as those near factories and business centers, were repeatedly targeted.

Crowded conditions do not have to result in large numbers of thefts because design features can help discourage overcrowding at particular spots. For example, escalators have been placed at both ends of subway platforms on the Hong Kong metro so that riders are more likely to fill up the whole platform rather than crowding at one end (Gaylord and Galliher 1991). Levine and his team recommended construction of a clear shelter at crowded bus stops to separate waiting passengers and prevent thieves from approaching unnoticed (Levine and Wachs 1985, 1986a; Levine, Wachs, and Shirazi 1986). Poyner (1983) made a similar recommendation to prevent purse snatching and pickpocketing at bus queues in the crowded center of one large British city.

Surveillance can operate at several points to disrupt thefts from passengers: to discourage the crime, to detect the offender as the crime is carried out, and to assist the victim in pursuit of the offender. Evidence is mixed about its value. Webb and Laycock (1992) found that CCTV installation at the Oxford Circus station on the London Underground had little positive effect. This may have been due to the difficulty both victims and observers experience in detecting stealth crimes. However, the Hong Kong underground system has few thefts. Apart from the time-limited tickets and station designs that discourage passenger bunching mentioned earlier, it also has a high ratio of officers to civilians, and uses CCTV and staff in plainclothes and uniforms (Rao 1985) who can react quickly when crime alarms are triggered (Gaylord and Galliher 1991).

In keeping with the tenets of situational crime prevention, several studies suggest that there is a need to be crime specific when looking for ways to prevent larcenies. For example, Trivizas and Smith (1997) found that offenders carefully targeted the property they took at London railway and underground stations following terrorist bombing incidents. Different rates of theft of luggage and theft from the person, despite police presence at the stations, suggests that surveillance may have to be closely tailored to the precise nature of theft to be effective. Further, the success of CCTV at four stations on the London Underground reported by Burrows (1980) may have been related to the nature of theft at the stations studied. These stations had neither high passenger volumes nor the highest levels of theft (Department of Transport 1986), suggesting that thefts there were not associated with crowded conditions.

2. *Sexual Assaults.*   The types of sexual crimes that are most commonly reported on public transport involve touching or rubbing of vic-

tims and exposure by offenders. More serious crimes such as rape and sodomy are rare—making up less than one twenty-fifth of all reported sex crimes in one eighteen-month period on the New York City subway (Beller, Garelik, and Cooper 1980). For the more common sexual crimes, Beller and her colleagues stressed the importance of the setting of subway cars, with their busy and distracted potential victims and, in the case of touching and rubbing, crowded conditions.

A similar pattern emerges in studies of other transport systems (Department of Transport 1986; Kabundi and Normandeau 1987), despite probable underreporting of crimes, such as in London (Department of Transport 1986) and Tokyo (Lopez 1996). On the crowded metro in Hong Kong, while the number of reported indecent assaults on a woman was very low in the early 1980s (Rao 1985), 112 were reported in 1993, representing 40 percent of the total reported crimes (Lopez 1996). Lopez has proposed that "lady cars" should be used in metros for routes and times with high levels of indecent assault (see also Greater London Council Women's Committee 1987). A similar scheme was used briefly in 1909 on the Hudson and Manhattan Railway, when the last car was reserved for women during rush hours (Hood 1996). It was abandoned because passenger loads were said not to justify the service.

III. Key Security Issues in Transport Planning

Certain crime-related issues continually plague transport planners and managers. Planners must deal regularly with the fears of suburban communities that extending transit systems or introducing new ones will open up these communities to the reach of criminals from distant parts of the city. Managers are regularly called on to defend their systems against the charge of being insecure, especially in the wake of a serious crime. They are also acutely aware that fear of crime can lead to a decline in ridership and thus in revenues collected.

This section deals with these key security concerns, summarizing the existing research. Methodological difficulties allow few firm conclusions. However, it seems that with the possible exception of the central business district and the areas immediately around stations, transit systems do not usually produce more crime in the areas they serve. Nor are the systems themselves always more dangerous than the areas they serve. However, it does appear that the link between fear and reduced ridership constitutes a real threat to the economic viability of transit systems.

A. Victimization Risks on Public Transport

Public transport has a reputation for being crime ridden, but what are the actual risks of victimization? Risks can be calculated of becoming a victim on particular transport systems per 100,000 passengers or per 100,000 passenger miles, but these can only be interpreted in a comparative context.

These comparisons involve questions such as the following: Are people at greater risk of victimization when using public transport than on the street? Are they safer in their cars? Are they safer in some transit systems than others? Are they generally safer on buses than on the subway? Are they safer on the system than when walking to or from the bus stop or the station? Are they safer on the station platform than in the carriage? Are some people safer than others are?

As well as helping them deal with criticism of their systems, answers to these questions can assist transit managers in pinpointing specific security hazards. However, clear answers can be difficult to obtain, as is shown in this section, which looks at findings about victimization risks on different modes of transportation and on different transport systems. We begin by looking at methods of calculating risk.

1. *Calculating Risk.* Calculation of risks requires measures of exposure to risk such as journeys made, time on the system, the length of different trip stages, and passenger densities. These measures of exposure can be difficult to obtain (Boggs 1965; Clarke 1984), and researchers often fall back on measures calculated by system managers for operational purposes. Thus, when studying the New York subway, various researchers have used the number of fee-paying passengers entering the system during some designated period, which are data routinely collected by the Transit Authority (e.g., Smith et al. 1986*a*; Del Castillo 1992; Clarke, Belanger, and Eastman 1996).

Shellow and his colleagues reviewed how crime risks have been calculated in previous studies. They noted that the American Transit Association (ATA) study of U.S. and Canadian transit systems (Thrasher et al. 1973) found that the relative rankings of systems varied depending on how the rates were calculated, such as by crimes per revenue passenger, crimes per vehicle-hour, and crimes per vehicle-mile. In an attempt to standardize risk measurements, the ATA study proposed calculating an exposure index (EI) for violent crime as follows (Shellow, Bartel, and Romualdi 1975, p. 51):

$$EI = \frac{\text{(Annual number of violent transit crimes per 100,000 population)}}{\text{(Average annual number of trips per person)} \times \frac{\text{(Average trip time [15 minutes])}}{\text{(Number of minutes in a year)}}}$$

The advantage of this type of calculation is that it attempts to take into account exposure time on the system, a meaningful opportunity factor related to victimization. New "smartcard" technology should be able to provide systems with detailed information about how long passengers are on a system and where they get on and off.

Another way of examining victimization risk is to compare passengers who are victimized with those who are not (see Levine and Wachs 1986*b*). This type of analysis depends on victim surveys because it needs to take into account the characteristics of those riding public transport who have not been victimized, as well as those who do not report the crime to the police. And police reports do not usually carry enough detailed information about even the reported crimes (but see Benjamin et al. 1994; Boyd and Maier 1995) to inform research. For example, victimization research can identify whether particular groups (e.g., women, the elderly, or the homeless) are being targeted or whether victimization is due to the time of day when passengers are traveling.[9] It can also identify factors associated with victimization, such as whether the crimes were committed en route to or from public transportation. Trip stage could be important since crime prevention measures, such as better designed bus stops or off-hours waiting areas, may be more useful for those waiting to use the system than for those leaving it—or vice versa. For example, Block and Davis (1996) found that robbery incidents in Chicago clustered around rapid transit nodes and were highest in the late-night and early-morning hours, peaking around 11:00 P.M. This indicates that offenders may be targeting passengers as they walk home from rail stations late at night.

This method of looking at risk recognizes that not everyone using

[9] The most cost-effective way of gathering the needed information would be to add a transit crime section to victim studies, such as the British Crime Survey. This would allow researchers to compare transport victimization to other types of victimization suffered by the respondents. Victimization questions are currently included in some of the surveys conducted by transport systems (e.g., Metropolitan Transportation Authority 1994) and are useful for analyses that look at the factors associated with fear of crime and ridership decisions.

public transportation at any one time or place has the same risk of victimization as someone else. Levine and Wachs (1986*b*) found that, even when they controlled for use, women were more likely to report that they had been victims of bus or bus-related crime (much of which involved larcenies and robberies without injury). Among the elderly, however, men were nearly as likely to report victimization as women were. The logistic regression analysis found that frequency of bus use best predicted victimization, followed by whether the victims were elderly women, elderly Hispanics of both sexes, and renters.

One final measure that may prove useful in making transport-related crime volume comparisons within an area is the location quotient of crime (LQC) developed by Brantingham and Brantingham (1993). The LQC gives a comparative measure of the number of crimes in a given area in relation to the total number of crimes in a larger area. According to Brantingham and Brantingham, location quotients are used in regional science to measure the relative activity of an area. The LQC is not dependent on determining an underlying at-risk population for comparison (such as area population or number of available crime targets) and can be adapted to different boundaries. For instance, Robinson (1998) used this measure in her study of crime patterns around nine SkyTrain stations in Vancouver. Because studies of transport systems have sometimes found that the crime rates on the systems reflected the areas they go through (Chaiken, Lawless, and Stevenson 1974; Levine and Wachs 1995, 1986*a*), it seems useful to use the surrounding areas to look for anomalies in this pattern. For example, Clarke, Belanger, and Eastman (1996) found that not all New York City subway stations within high crime precincts had high platform robbery rates, suggesting that stations with low crime should be examined to find out what was different about them. In addition, it has not always been clear which area should be used for comparison since, as Chaiken and his colleagues (1974) pointed out, sometimes stations are close to or adjacent to more than one precinct in an area. Sophisticated crime-mapping techniques and the LQC have the potential to overcome this type of problem.

2. *System Comparisons.* Discussed here are crime-risk comparisons for transit and nontransit, different systems using the same kind of transport, and different kinds of transport (including automobiles). These comparisons must take into account differences in times spent in each place (see Shellow, Bartel, and Romualdi 1975). They also need to take account of demographic comparability, activity patterns, and

places where risks vary (Smith et al. 1986*a*). Despite these difficulties, a number of studies have provided comparisons of transit and non-transit crime risks, though findings have not always been consistent. For example, Shellow and his colleagues (1975) reported that Thrasher et al. (1973) found it was safer off transit systems and that found crime rates on the system were lower (see also Smith et al. 1986*a*). The use of the LQC should provide researchers with a new tool to make this comparison, although looking at specific crimes and settings appears to hold more promise for devising actual crime-preventive strategies.

Comparisons across systems can help to identify particularly safe or dangerous systems and can help to identify the reasons for such differences. For example, the Southeast Michigan Council of Governments (1981) provided comparative crime rates (total crime per 100,000 passengers and total crime per 10,000 revenue-miles) for U.S. and Canadian public transport systems.[10] This type of information is most useful when it is used to provide a background against which more detailed information about each system is compared. For example, while LaVigne (1997) looked at crimes per 1 million riders for subway systems in Washington, D.C., Atlanta, Boston, and Chicago (see fig. 1), she also looked at other comparative crime figures, such as the distributions of crime types with each system (LaVigne 1996*a*). Her analysis established that the Washington, D.C., Metro is an unusually safe system, despite its location in a high-crime city. The cross-system comparisons helped her build the case that the system's intentional crime prevention design together with vigilant policing and good management were responsible for its low-crime rate.

Shellow, Romualdi, and Bartel (1974) looked at the incidence of crime on the bus portion of a big-city transit system compared to the incidence of crime on the city's rail system. Crime incidence was one-third lower on the bus component while the risk (crime/ridership index) for bus travel was one-tenth that for rail travel. The two modes differ in a variety of ways (such as in the level of supervision on the

[10] The U.S. Federal Transit Administration requirement that transit systems receiving operating grants from the federal government report the number of crimes committed there should permit regular comparisons of U.S. operators, using the FBI's Uniform Crime Reports (UCR) system (Boyd and Maier 1995). Despite noting the limitations of the UCR system and the noncomparability of many of the systems, Boyd and Maier suggested that transit systems can use the new requirements for crime data as an opportunity to develop data systems that capture additional incident information for planning and crime analysis.

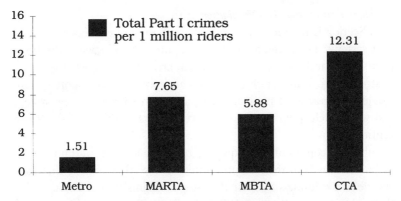

Fig. 1.—Comparison of Part I crimes (per million riders) on four U.S. subway systems—1994. Includes murder, rape, robbery, aggravated assault, burglary, larceny, and arson but excludes auto theft due to the nature of subway crime. The systems included are those in Washington, D.C. (Metro), Atlanta (MARTA), Boston (MBTA), and Chicago (CTA). Source: LaVigne (1997).

system, distances between stops, routes and destinations, and types of passengers) and these differences may also be related to differences in risk. However, later research by Levine and Wachs (1985, 1986*a*, 1986*b*) suggests that much bus-related crime is not reported by the transit system and so the differences found by Shellow and his colleagues may be at least partly due to the underreporting of bus crime.

Shellow and his colleagues (1975, p. 11) have argued that comparisons between public transport and private cars held little promise for public transportation: "Since the probability of being robbed while riding in one's personal automobile may be extraordinarily low, it may well be that no reasonably achievable crime rates on transit systems will ever compare favorably with such alternatives in regard to safety from crime."

While this may be true when the comparisons focus on robbery, it may not be so for other crimes. For example, motorists may be exposed to crime when walking to their cars (Barker et al. 1993; Stockdale and Gresham 1998) or at their destinations. Indeed it is ironic that auto theft is one of the most common offenses associated with public transport (LaVigne 1996*a*). This is because commuter parking lots seem particularly attractive to auto thieves because so many cars are left parked undisturbed for so much of the day (Mancini and Jain 1987; National Roads and Motorists' Association Insurance Limited 1990; Clarke and Mayhew 1998).

B. Mass Transit and the Distribution of Crime

In Section II the focus was on the distribution of crime within transport systems. Here, the focus is on the interaction between the transport system and the surrounding urban area. Knowing whether crime is attracted to transport hubs or spread by various transport systems would help transport planners in deciding on routes for new systems and would help police and local governments in thinking about prevention.

Suburban communities frequently resist the location of train stations or bus terminals in their communities because they believe that these will deliver criminals to their doorsteps (Walmsley and Perrett 1992; Boyd, Maier, and Kenney 1996). In fact, three general patterns of interaction between transport systems and the surrounding area have been identified. First, transport systems often reflect the crime rates and patterns of the areas they serve (though they can be insulated from crime by good design and policing). Second, transport systems seem to attract certain kinds of crime such as pickpocketing or auto theft at commuter lots. Third, offenders sometimes use public transport to commit crime in the central business district but they rarely use it to reach suburban areas beyond their own localities—although the research on transport use is limited.

1. *Transit Crime in Local Context.*   Although crime rates can be compared across systems and cities, the local nature of crime (see Rossmo 1993) suggests that it is often more useful to look at transport crime in terms of patterns of crime within the urban area.

Shellow, Bartel, and Romualdi (1975) reported that a number of studies have found that the distribution of crime within transport systems reflects that of the areas through which they pass, although the correspondence is not perfect (e.g., Chaiken, Lawless, and Stevenson 1974; Shellow, Romualdi, and Bartel 1974). Subsequent researchers have confirmed these patterns with both rail (Department of Transport 1986) and bus systems (Pearlstein and Wachs 1982; Levine and Wachs 1985, 1986a).

It does appear, however, that systems can be insulated from the areas through which they pass. For example, LaVigne (1996a, 1996b) looked at Uniform Crime Reports Part I crime rates, as well as the rates for robbery and assault separately, in the census tracts around stations on the Washington, D.C., Metro. She found no correlation between station crime and aboveground crime for Part I crime or robbery; however, as noted above, there was a correlation between the two areas for assaults. Unlike many older subway systems in the United States and Europe, the Washington, D.C., Metro used uniform design and management features throughout the system that incorporate crime prevention principles complementary to those of situational crime prevention.

While LaVigne found that the Washington, D.C., Metro had less crime than the areas that it went through, crime on the Metro did rise somewhat after the system was extended into poorer neighborhoods of the city in 1991 and 1993 (LaVigne 1996a). She attributed this rise to the large increase in the number of parking lots included in the Metro system as a result of the extensions. Raw incidence figures show that the largest increases were in grand larceny, followed by petty larceny, vandalism, and robbery. The first three of these crimes are frequently associated with car break-ins. Crime in parking areas around stations, in general, accounted for over 60 percent of all Part I crime on the Washington, D.C., Metro system. LaVigne noted that parking facilities did not incorporate the crime-preventive design and management features of the system itself. If the crime increase on the D.C. Metro after 1991 was due to the addition of new parking lots, then these lots need to be better protected from theft and vandalism. Situational measures found successful in other parking facilities—such as the use of full-time attendants (Laycock and Austin 1992), bike patrols (Barclay et al. 1996), CCTV, and pedestrian access control (Poyner 1992a)—might be considered for the Metro.

2. *Transit Systems as Crime Attractors.* Brantingham and Brantingham (1995) distinguish between two kinds of crime hot spots: "crime attractors," which are places where offenders go to commit crime, and "crime generators," which are places where they commit crime having come for some other purpose. That public transport facilities may be crime attractors is of greater concern than that they are crime generators. If a place is a crime attractor, then this implies that there is something about the place that causes offenders to seek out crime opportunities there. One way to gauge whether transport systems attract crime is to compare crime volumes on the system with crime volumes for the city as a whole to see if any crime is disproportionately represented on the system. Using this method, Del Castillo (1992) found a disproportionate incidence for subway robbery and grand larceny in the New York City subway system compared to those aboveground for 1988. A similar comparison in Australia of Queensland railway crimes to all crime in that state showed high proportions

of robbery and motor vehicle theft (Parliamentary Travelsafe Committee 1998).[11]

Robinson's (1998) study of crime around nine stations of the Vancouver SkyTrain found more direct evidence that public transport facilities can attract crime. Specifically, she found that 49 percent of all police calls for service in the city occurred within 750 meters of a SkyTrain station, though this area accounted for only 14 percent of the city. It is possible that the stations may have been built in high-crime locations but some of Robinson's other findings suggest that they were attracting criminals. She found that in most cases crimes tended to cluster within a much tighter range around the stations; and these crimes tended to fit the opportunities presented in these areas—burglary in residential areas and street crimes in business areas.

Transportation facilities can attract or generate specific types of activity that facilitate crime. One of the most noticeable features of large public transportation facilities in the United States in the 1980s was the presence of homeless persons (Schwartz 1988), which was associated in some places, such as New York City, with physical and social incivilities. The response of transit systems in New York has combined outreach for the homeless with station renovation, redesign, and enforcement to control physical and social incivilities. Lovorso (1996) describes the program used successfully at New York City's Pennsylvania Station to deal with the homeless people sleeping in that facility, and Felson et al. (1996) describe similar changes made at the Port Authority Bus Terminal in Manhattan. Kelling and Coles (1996) explain the program developed by the Metropolitan Transportation Authority (MTA) for the subway and describe the organizational and legal obstacles (particularly in relation to begging) met when trying to carry out its plan.

3. *Public Transport and the Journey to Crime.*   Even if transport systems provide opportunities for crime and influence the crime patterns of the areas around them, this does not show that offenders use them in their journey to commit crimes. Much of the evidence about use of public transport in crime is inferential, based on such factors as travel

---

[11] Within-system comparisons across transportation systems can also provide clues about special crime problems encountered by particular systems (see Levy 1994; LaVigne 1996*a*), such as the high percentage of robberies in the New York City subway and the high number of auto thefts for the Washington, D.C., Metro. But caution must be used when comparing across systems because not all systems contain comparable types of property (such as parking facilities) (Boyd and Maier 1995), are open for similar time periods (LaVigne 1996*a*), or serve similar neighborhoods.

distance and direction. For instance, the concentration of thefts in the subway stations near Montreal's busiest streets (Kabundi and Normandeau 1987) suggests that offenders used the subway to get there. However, there is no direct evidence that this was the case.

Use of public transport is unlikely for some crimes, such as residential burglary where it may be necessary to carry away bulky items (Brantingham and Brantingham 1993). For other crimes, like auto theft, walking or taking public transportation are more likely ways of getting to the crime site (Rengert 1997). There is little direct evidence of the use of public transport in crime journeys. One exception is the anecdotal evidence reported by Brantingham, Brantingham, and Wong (1991) that young gang members from central Vancouver used the new SkyTrain to travel to a shopping mall near a SkyTrain station. Another is the study reported by Chaiken, Lawless, and Stevenson (1974) who examined the question of whether the New York City subway system acts to distribute crime from high-crime areas to low-crime areas. They plotted police precincts in New York City according to the distribution of subway robberies per station and the number of surface robberies. They concluded that the subway robberies were distributed away from high-robbery precincts.

Travel toward the central business district is a common pattern for employment (Ingram 1998), so it is not surprising that it has also been a common destination for those leaving their local area to commit crime (see Turner 1969). Wikström (1995) reported that most of the youth crime committed in the city center of Stockholm was committed by youths living outside the center who normally used public transport to get there. The auto thieves in the Rengert and Bost (1987) study of offender patterns in two public housing areas in Charlotte, North Carolina, committed crimes around their homes. But when these offenders left their neighborhoods, they headed toward the city center, providing a bimodal distribution of offense location according to place of residence. Comparisons of borough of residence and borough of crime occurrence of those arrested on the New York City subway suggest that a large portion of crimes were committed by offenders who were using the subway to travel toward or return from Manhattan (see Smith et al. 1986b; Belanger 1997, 1999).

Belanger (1999) found that despite their ability to travel long distances for a single fare, the repeat subway felony offenders in his study committed offenses much closer to home. Three-fifths of the trips were within ten stations of the offenders' home stations. This finding supports other research, not focused on public transport, on offenders' journeys to crime (see Rossmo 1993). Belanger's analysis suggested that in general offenders use time rather than distance as the key factor for determining the range of their offending.

C. Fear of Crime and Ridership

Carr and Spring (1993) have described a "cycle of fear" in which crime on public transport leads to increased fear, which in turn results in a drop in ridership. The drop in ridership means there is less guardianship from other passengers and crime risks increase even more. Fear rises again, with further adverse consequences for ridership, revenues, and security.

Most public transport systems cannot afford to lose passengers, and managers have been acutely aware of the need to address fear as a problem in its own right, associated with but not the same as the problem of crime. Consequently, they have sponsored numerous surveys to help understand and respond to fear among regular travelers. These surveys have sometimes had the additional purpose of finding ways to persuade people to use public transport in off-peak hours. Unfortunately, those with least access to other means of transport, such as the elderly and many women, are also among those most afraid to use it during large parts of the day (see Greater London Council Women's Committee 1985). Some other potential riders prefer to use their cars to commute or for leisure, again, partly because they feel safer doing so (see Gray 1992; Audits and Surveys Worldwide 1996). If members of both groups were more secure and traveled more often on public transport, their travel would help cover the costs of additional personnel in stations and on trains and buses.

Studies providing evidence that fear of crime affects ridership are discussed in this section, as are strategies for dealing with fear. But, first, some methodological considerations for analyzing the problem are set out.

1. *Methodological Considerations.*   Apart from taking fewer trips, fear can lead passengers to shift to other forms of public transport or to private cars. It can also lead some passengers to take additional precautions or cause them to choose other destinations, routes, or travel times. Because there are other reasons for making these same decisions (see Gray 1992), it is not always easy to determine the extent to which fear of crime affects ridership (cf. the reviews in Shellow, Bartel, and Romualdi [1975] with those in Levine and Wachs [1986*b*]).

Owen (1972) pointed out that motorists are encouraged by their financial commitment to generate more trips than the user of mass transit or taxis because once the traveler owns a car, it can be used for the next trip at a very low marginal cost. Thus the user of public transport is likely to weigh more carefully each trip on public transport unless the person has a transit pass. Shellow, Bartel, and Romualdi (1975) suggested analyzing travel decisions by type of trip (e.g., commuting to work in the central business district, off-peak shopping by those without access to transit lines, and daytime travel by central business district workers). They also noted that asking respondents only about fear of crime may lead them to focus excessively on the crime aspects of their travel decision making. It may also fail to distinguish those who would be unlikely to use public transport under any circumstances.

2. *Evidence That Fear of Crime Affects Ridership.*   Shellow, Romualdi, and Bartel (1974) studied crime on a transit system in the United States with both rail rapid transit and bus components. Riders of both bus and rail agreed that both systems were not safe after 9:00 P.M., with 90 percent reporting they used neither system after that time. Almost no respondents reported that they used these forms of public transit after midnight.

Similar findings have been obtained elsewhere. In London, for example, the Department of Transport (1986) study of crime on the Underground found that one-half of their sample of passengers did not use the Underground at night, with one-third of these giving fears about security as the reason. The study of women's travel needs in London (Greater London Council Women's Committee 1985) found that feelings of safety among respondents varied by mode and time of day, with buses ranked as very safe during the day by half of the respondents but by only 9 percent at night or after dark. Walking during the day received a larger percentage of "very safe" ratings (34 percent) than either the Underground or British Rail, but each of these three modes were only considered very safe after dark by 2 percent of the respondents.

In a number of studies, respondents have been asked to compare their feelings of safety in various places on public transport. Shellow, Romualdi, and Bartel's (1974) survey asked about both rail and bus travel and reported that the stairs, ramps, and tunnels of the rail system were rated as least secure, followed by train platforms and the trains themselves. The most secure places, according to respondents, were buses, going from home to rail or bus, and waiting at bus stops. The Department of Transport (1986) study of crime on the Underground found that fears were greater just outside the station than within it and when there were fewer people traveling. Patterson (1985) looked at the concerns about bus use among those attending senior centers in Philadelphia. Most respondents were women, most of whom traveled frequently by bus. However, a quarter of the sample reported that they used buses only sometimes. Fear of crime was just one of the barriers to use (others concerned problems with bus schedules, with bus stops, and with the bus itself). Fear was highest while waiting at the bus stop, followed by walking to and from the stop, and on the bus itself.

In their survey of women's travel patterns in Southampton, England, Lynch and Atkins (1988) found that very few women felt unsafe in the day when using the bus but many felt unsafe at night. Few women reported using trains, expressing concern about being alone in carriages and at stations that were not staffed at night or on the weekends. However, it was not clear from the study how many more women would have used trains as a regular mode of urban travel if they had felt safer.

Brown (1998) explored men and women's experience of traveling to leisure venues in the center of a northern English city during the evenings. Not surprisingly, she found a much larger percentage of women than men felt unsafe at parking lots, waiting at the bus station, and traveling on buses. What is more surprising, however, was that nearly half of the women felt unsafe in taxis, compared to only 4 percent of men.

Much of this research found fear of crime is only one factor among many that affects use of public transport. For example, Austin and Buzawa (1984) found respondents cited lack of security, use of a car, and high fares as common reasons for using the bus less often. Levine and Wachs (1986b) found that having been a victim of a bus crime, witnessing such a crime, and perceiving bus travel as unsafe were all statistically significant predictors of reported intention to use the bus in the future. However, better predictors were access to an automobile and the inconvenience of using buses.

3. *Strategies for Preventing Fear.* Those responsible for security on public transportation systems can be seen as having two principal goals: to make the system as safe as possible by reducing levels of crime and to make passengers feel safer when riding their systems. Several studies have found that fear of crime is related to personal and vicarious experience of crime or to feelings of personal vulnerability (Austin

and Buzawa 1984; Levine and Wachs 1986*b*; Kenney 1987; Del Castillo 1992). It might seem therefore that achieving the first goal would help achieve the second. However, as in other environments, the relationship between actual safety and fear of crime on public transport is not always direct. Levels of reported fear of crime on public transport can be high even when crime rates are low, as in Greensboro, North Carolina (Benjamin et al. 1994; Ingalls, Hartgen, and Owens 1994) or declining, as in New York City in the 1990s (Metropolitan Transportation Authority 1994; Audits and Surveys Worldwide 1996). Benjamin et al. (1994) found that fear of using Greensboro's buses was related to fears about the areas they served, in particular, the downtown area around the central bus depot. These fears were found primarily among nonriders who had little experience with the system.

One response to the finding that fear seems disproportionate to the risks is to publicize the real risks. Benjamin et al. (1994) called for more publicity about the low crime rates on public transport in Greensboro. In New York City, publicity campaigns have been used in recent years to inform the public about greatly reduced levels of crime on the subway (Metropolitan Transportation Authority 1994). Some reductions in expressed concern over crime have resulted, but only a little over half of the respondents in the study by Audits and Surveys Worldwide (1996) said they believed the crime statistics showing a drop in subway crime. This reluctance of New York City residents to believe the figures has some historical basis (see Shellow, Bartel, and Romualdi 1975).[12] And, more recently, the accuracy of transit crime reporting has been questioned (Cooper 1998; Kocieniewski 1998; see also n. 17).

Wilson and Healy (1986) advocated a more sophisticated approach to the use of the media for fear reduction as part of a strategy to combat the problem of graffiti on a train system in Australia. They suggested three sets of measures: discouraging publicity about graffiti, art, and artists; clearly differentiating between vandalism and violent crime incidents occurring on the system; and separately discussing the measures taken to combat vandalism and graffiti and those used against violent crime. These measures serve the dual purpose of reducing offending by making it appear less glamorous and of reassuring riders that graffiti and violence are not the same thing.

[12] Shellow, Bartel, and Romualdi (1975) reported that a chief of the New York City Transit Police resigned "under circumstances where he admitted to 'encouraging the making of false entries concerning the times of commission of crimes in official departmental reports' " (p. 11).

Brantingham, Brantingham, and Wong (1991) claim that fear on public transport is related to the unpredictability and uncontrollability of exposure to potential crime situations. Riders often do not know who will be in a vehicle with them and may be unable to extricate themselves from their surroundings until they reach designated stops. Exiting the vehicle can also expose riders to unknown situations and persons. This lack of personal control is exacerbated by the lack of staff to provide reassurance. Other forms of transport that have little oversight by others, such as minicab services in Britain, have also been found to have high levels of fear among users (see Groeger 1991; Brown 1998).

Some research suggests that the presence of increased staffing or policing and new ways to summon help may reassure the traveling public. These measures have been mentioned by survey respondents as desirable (e.g., Audits and Surveys Worldwide 1996). On the one hand, Lopez (1996) cited research carried out by GVB Amsterdam (1994) showing that following a program to clean up the Amsterdam Metro and increase the amount of formal control, more passengers reported feeling safer, compared to the previous year. On the other hand, Webb and Laycock (1992) reported limited success with initiatives taken by the London Underground to deal with exaggerated fears of crime at quiet, low-crime, suburban stations. The scheme consisted primarily of passenger alarm points monitored by ticket sellers but also included waiting areas, mirrors, and a staffed information point. Off-peak travelers did not seem to feel these stations were any safer three months after the measures were adopted, and the researchers called for more publicity to increase awareness of the changes. Kenney's (1986, 1987) finding that the presence or absence of Guardian Angels in the experimental area of his study did not appear to be related to the respondents' expressed worry about crime is more difficult to interpret. Perhaps, like the measures used in the Webb and Laycock study, the respondents were unaware of the precise level of protection around them.

The importance of knowing that help is at hand, particularly for women traveling at night, is apparent from Brown (1998). Brown's analysis of women's use of town center facilities at night in a medium-sized English town focused on the failure of CCTV coverage to reassure women that an area is safe. She noted that CCTV monitoring can detect only extreme forms of assault while the source of much of the fear is related to the unruly and harassing behavior of men. In addition,

CCTV may even be considered another form of voyeurism. Other research on CCTV has noted that women were skeptical about the level
of monitoring (Trench, Oc, and Tiesdell 1992). Thus, well-placed,
well-publicized call-for-assistance locations, with a quick response
time—along with the presence of staff or police (and carefully monitored CCTV)—seems central to reducing fear among late-night and
female travelers on public transport.

One last approach to fear reduction involves reducing incivilities
since these have been found to increase fear on public transport (Shellow, Bartel, and Romualdi 1975; Austin and Buzawa 1984; Lynch and
Atkins 1988; Del Castillo 1992; Ingalls, Hartgen, and Owens 1994).
This approach is discussed in Section IV when describing the graffiti
cleanup campaign and order maintenance policing on the New York
subway.

IV. "Broken Windows" and Designing Out Crime
The previous discussion and that in Section II showed that public
transport managers and police have adopted a vast range of different
measures to deal with both crime and fear on their systems. This is
only to be expected given the variety of offenses occurring on public
transport, many of which require highly specific interventions. In this
section we focus on the experience of using two broader preventive approaches on transit systems—designing out opportunities for crime
and controlling crime through "order maintenance" policing—both of
which are of much current interest.

Because both approaches depend on an ordered environment, they
are not incompatible and can reinforce each other (LaVigne 1997).
However, they differ importantly in underlying assumptions. Designing out crime assumes that, while some measures may help to control
more than one type of crime, effective design must be carefully tailored
to the highly specific nature of anticipated crimes. Consequently, the
package of design measures selected will vary considerably from one
setting to another depending on the nature of the crimes to be prevented. Order maintenance policing, based on Wilson and Kelling's
(1982) "broken windows" theory, pays less attention to the specific
character of crime. Instead it tends to divide crimes into two main categories: disorder (or "incivilities") and more serious crime. It uses the
metaphor of the unrepaired window to argue that if disorder remains
unchecked, people will become intimidated and will not seek to control
more troublesome antisocial behavior. Soon hardened offenders learn

that even serious crime runs little risk of being sanctioned.[13] The solution to this spiral of decline is to use police to enforce order, what is sometimes called order maintenance policing (Kelling 1985) or, more recently, "zero-tolerance" policing (Dennis 1997).

Some of the best known applications of designing out crime and order maintenance policing are in transit settings. The following review of these transit applications is focused on effectiveness and does not consider their costs or the legal and ethical criticisms made of them.[14]

A. Designing Out Crime

The classic transit example of designing out crime is the Washington, D.C., Metro. The Metro designers incorporated a wide range of crime prevention measures to reduce the opportunities for a variety of crimes. Among the features incorporated were spacious platforms, open escalators and passageways between platforms, use of CCTV with attendants in kiosks near entrances, and lack of vendors and restrooms (see app. B). Because these features were in place from the beginning, their effectiveness is difficult to evaluate. Before-and-after studies cannot be undertaken, and it is difficult to compare the Washington, D.C., Metro with any other subway system in the world. Nevertheless, LaVigne (1996a, 1996b, 1997) used a variety of research methods to make the case that Washington, D.C., Metro's crime rates are lower than those of many other subway systems (in less crime-ridden cities), and also lower than the aboveground crime rates in the

---

[13] There are various descriptions of the broken windows thesis within the original article by Wilson and Kelling (1982), restatements in later writings (e.g., Wilson 1983; Kelling 1991; Wilson and Kelling 1989; Kelling and Coles 1996), and a variety of accounts of the important causal paths set out by other researchers (e.g., Taylor 1987; Matthews 1992). However, all of the accounts by Wilson and Kelling share the following features: disorder decreases informal social control in an area by making the area citizens afraid; disorder leads to crime; and offenders take disorder as a cue that no one in an area cares enough to intervene or call the police. While "disorder" includes both physical and social incivilities, it is the social incivilities that are more closely linked to fear and crime. The solution to this spiral of decline is to use police to enforce order, although area cleanups and problem-oriented and community policing strategies are highlighted in a later discussion (Wilson and Kelling 1989). The deterrence mechanism of order maintenance policing operates through an increased perceived risk of apprehension when offenders pick up cues from the physical and social environment showing that someone cares about the area.

[14] Designing out crime is criticized for infringements of liberty and privacy and for unnecessary regimentation of everyday life (see, e.g., Homel 1997; O'Malley and Sutton 1997; Hughes 1998). Order maintenance policing is criticized for violations of individual liberties (see Kelling and Coles 1996), for producing a high volume of citizen complaints (Greene 1999), and for putting an unacceptable strain on the jails and courts (Krauss 1996).

city. Her findings provide powerful evidence that crime prevention designs (together with good management and policing) can work in unpromising settings. This lesson has not been lost on designers of new subway systems in other parts of the world (Lopez 1996; Myrhe and Rosso 1996).

New subway systems are rarely built and greater potential for designing out crime lies elsewhere—the renovation of existing facilities, particularly train and bus stations. Many of these stations, built in another era, have become hot spots for crime and fear. Some were built as long ago as the nineteenth century and have been changed and renovated many times since then. Major renovations have recently been completed, or soon will be, at some famous railroad stations in the United States, including Grand Central and Pennsylvania Stations in New York City and Union Station in Washington, D.C.

Several different approaches to eliminating crime opportunities in existing stations have been described in the literature, the first of which envisioned complete modification of two busy crime-ridden stations on the subway in Chicago (Falanga 1988). Both stations, similar in design to those on the New York City subway, were soon to be refurbished. Falanga conducted "walk-throughs" of the two stations, questioning transit police and token booth clerks about where crimes occurred, asking them to distinguish between property and personal crimes and between those occurring during rush hours and off-peak. Thefts were reported to occur most often in crowded areas when victims' attention was focused elsewhere. Robbery and vandalism were most common in deserted parts of the station, such as the lower tunnel areas.

Falanga's suggested redesign involved reducing the number of entrances and exits, widening staircases, closing off areas behind staircases and passageways in the lower tunnel areas. During off-peak times the station capacity would be altered by a movable partition. Fare cards would eliminate token booths, and surveillance booths would overlook fare entry points and the platform level.

The security audit of the Newark subway, carried out by Felson and his students (Felson et al. 1990), describes what might be done with a limited budget to renovate existing stations.[15] The researchers made a number of recommendations to increase surveillance by other passengers or passersby, to allow passengers wider lines of sight, and to in-

[15] For other low-cost approaches, see also Project for Public Spaces 1984; Guberman 1994; Felson et al. 1996.

crease their ability to call for help. For example, they suggested that see-through fencing on the periphery should be installed or repaired to prevent access. Multiple entrances should be closed off and the waiting areas moved closer together. Vandal-proof assistance phones should be installed, and development around the station stops should be encouraged to increase surveillance on exiting.

Both Falanga's and Felson's studies were intended to show what might be done to eliminate opportunities for crime. In Newark, no attempt was made to implement Felson's recommendations and no report has been published of the outcome of Falanga's work in Chicago. In fact, little was known about the crime prevention gains achieved in renovations until Felson and another group of his students (Felson et al. 1996) published their evaluation of the massive redevelopment of the Port Authority Bus Terminal in Manhattan. This sprawling, busy facility had become a byword for disorder and crime in the 1980s and early 1990s. It was a refuge for the homeless and a haven for all manner of hustlers and petty criminals who engaged in drug dealing, prostitution, mugging, and a variety of scams perpetrated on hapless commuters and tourists.

Following numerous failures of intensified policing, the management of the facility embarked on a major renovation affecting all parts of the building and its operations. Crime prevention was a vital goal guiding their efforts throughout. To give a flavor of the scope and detail of the changes, table 2 lists those made just to the restrooms, which had become hot spots for drug dealing and prostitution. For example, after the renovation, restrooms were located closer to retailers, attendants were present, corner mirrors were installed, nooks were eliminated, and lighting was improved. The evaluation of the changes made at the terminal showed that crime was greatly reduced in the facility, with little evidence of displacement to the surrounding area (Felson et al. 1996).

The Port Authority Bus Terminal had also become the site of a massive public telephone fraud enterprise involving millions of dollars worth of unauthorized phone use. Bichler and Clarke (1996) explained the reasons for this as follows:

> The large number of pay phones and the fact that they went
> unused for much of the day must have played a part. The terminal
> is well known in the region, is close to centers of poor immigrant
> populations, and is easy to reach via the subway and bus lines. In

TABLE 2

Detailed Characteristics of Restrooms before and after Renovation—
Port Authority Bus Terminal, New York City

Characteristics	Before	After
1. Ceiling panels	Removable	Secure
2. Stall doors	Tall and low	Less so
3. Stall walls	Easy to write on	Graffiti resistant
4. Ventilation	Poor	Good
5. Corner mirrors	Absent	Present
6. Sink size	Six users	One user each
7. Controls[a]	By hand	Automatic
8. Lighting	Poor	Good, secure
9. Tile squares	Small, dark	Large, bright
10. Walls	Angled	Straight
11. Nooks	Present	Absent
12. Entry, retailers	Far	Near
13. Overall size	Small	Large[b]
14. Attendants	Absent	Present

Source.—Felson et al. 1996.

[a] For sinks, toilets, and hand-drying machines.

[b] With steel cutoff to reduce size of restroom during off-hours.

addition, it provides a comfortable environment for the hustlers
who must hang round for long periods of the day because it gives
them shelter from the weather and access to restrooms and fast
food outlets. It also provides them with many entertainment
opportunities, both on-site (a bowling alley and an off-track
betting office) and nearby (with a concentration in 42nd Street
and Times Square of liquor outlets, drug markets and porno movie
theaters). (P. 109)

The bus station redesign, which allowed the removal of some banks of
phones and reduced access to others, along with blocks on the numbers
that could be accessed from the phones, virtually eliminated telephone
fraud in the facility (Bichler and Clarke 1996).

B. Maintaining Order on the New York City Subway

Mass transit was not included in Wilson and Kelling's (1982) description of neighborhood decline and crime, though later writings by
Kelling (1991) and Kelling and Coles (1996) have included the transport environment as one in which the broken windows thesis applies.
In seeking information about its application in mass transit we examine

the drop in crime on the New York City subway in the 1990s and the graffiti cleanup effort in the 1980s.

1. *The Decline in Felonies in the 1990s.*   Felonies began to fall precipitously in the New York City subway in 1991 (Eastman and Yuan 1994; Levy 1994; Lueck 1999). The subway policing practices introduced at that time, involving a crackdown on minor offending (with a focus on fare evasion), have been credited with this turnaround (see, e.g., Transit Policing 1993; Eastman and Yuan 1994).[16] Eastman and Yuan (1994) showed that the numbers of ejections, summonses, and arrests corresponded with lower numbers of reported felonies on the system during this time, particularly in 1992.[17]

In crediting order maintenance with this decline in felonies, Eastman and Yuan speculated that part of its success was the result of picking up offenders for minor offenses (or for weapons possession or outstanding warrants) and removing them from the system before they committed more serious crimes. Another possibility is that when disorderly persons were arrested or ejected from the system this removed potential victims. Neither of these two explanations for the success of the policing strategy depends on offenders believing that police were taking crime seriously (i.e., that they were deterred from crime by believing it had become too risky). In the language of situational prevention (Clarke 1997), removal of offenders is an extreme form of "deflecting offenders" and the ejection or arrest of potential victims could be considered as "target removal." Deflecting offenders and target removal prevent offending by, respectively, increasing the perceived effort of crime and reducing its rewards—not by increasing perceived risk. If these are the primary mechanisms by which order maintenance works, then its success may not necessarily provide support for the broken windows theory.

It must also be noted that the overall decline in the number of subway felony complaints was mirrored by a similar (though less steep)

---

[16] Interestingly, Kelling and Coles (1996) claim that police practices were only one factor among several that brought about the crime reductions. The others were eliminating graffiti, target hardening, and the station managers program—all initiatives that they claim represented the MTA's total commitment to restoring order.

[17] There have been reports in the press of the Transit Police Department failure to include all transit crimes reported to city precincts among transit figures (Cooper 1998), reclassifying crimes such as pickpocketing that might have occurred aboveground (Kocieniewski 1998). However, when individual felony crime totals released by the Transit Police Department are examined, they indicate that there were decreases in all felony crime categories during this period (figures for 1979–92 are reported in DeGeneste and Sullivan 1994). For the purposes of the present discussion, these misreporting problems will not be considered to have changed the overall relative volumes of felonies.

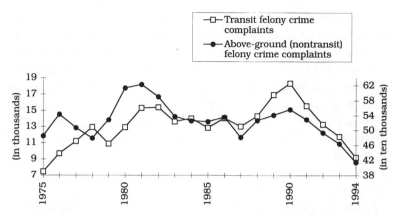

Fig. 2.—New York City aboveground, that is, nontransit (left scale) and transit (right scale) felony crime complaints for 1975–94. The total number of aboveground felony crime complaints was calculated by subtracting the number of felony complaints reported by the Transit Police Department from those reported by the New York City Police Department. Source: New York City Police Department and New York City Transit Police Department.

drop in citywide felony complaints (see fig. 2). A variety of explanations for this wider drop in New York City have been suggested, including demographic changes in the number of teenagers and changes in the drug use patterns from crack to heroin (see Krauss 1995; Greene 1999; Silverman 1999). While these types of explanations do not refute the possibility that policing activity in the subways was at least partially responsible for the crime reductions there, they do suggest that other factors were also at play.

A further complication is that data on the location of subway crimes suggest that in the late 1980s and early 1990s proportionately more crimes occurred on trains than in stations. For instance, the proportion of robberies committed on trains was higher (37 percent) in the early 1990s (Clarke, Belanger, and Eastman 1996) than it had been (31 percent) a little more than ten years earlier (Smith et al. 1986b). A similar change occurring between 1988 and 1992 in the location of crime was reported in a Metropolitan Transportation Authority (1994) victimization survey, which concluded: "This finding might be significant given the shift in patrol assignments away from trains into stations" (p. 39). However, in addition to the posting of more officers on stations, other prevention measures were introduced there from 1982 to 1992, such as off-hours waiting areas and blocking off of little used and isolated passageways (Levy 1994).

To what extent the declines in robbery were due to these physical changes or to intensified policing at stations might be revealed by more detailed analysis of robbery data. A monthly analysis of robbery locations from the late 1970s (when off-hours waiting areas were proposed [Sandler et al. 1979]) through the mid-1990s could help to pinpoint effective prevention measures (see Levy [1994] for a comprehensive list of programs used to tackle subway crime and incivilities from 1982 through 1992). Monthly comparisons with aboveground robberies and other crimes could also help determine the extent to which the decline in subway crime was correlated with or contributed to the wider decline in city crime levels.

2. *The Graffiti Cleanup Effort in the 1980s.* Wilson and Kelling (1982) did not discuss whether getting rid of physical or social incivilities by methods other than order maintenance policing would result in less crime. The broken windows approach, with its emphasis on the signals that potential offenders receive from a disorderly environment, however, suggests that offenders would view a cleanup effort as a sign that those in control of an area cared about what happened there (see Wilson and Kelling 1989). Thus, applying the broken windows perspective to cleanup efforts, one would expect that the cleanup of a widespread physical incivility, like the graffiti problem on the New York City subway, would have resulted in either a drop in crime or a drop in social incivilities or both. Did this happen?

There is no doubt that graffiti writing on the New York City subways was very extensive in the 1970s and early 1980s and that it was exacerbated by the funding problems affecting the subway system. As a result of these funding difficulties, car-cleaning staff fell from 1,021 in fiscal year 1971–72 to 454 in fiscal year 1978–79 (Sandler et al. 1979). The appearance of graffiti at the same time that the city was suffering from financial problems meant that it became associated with other subway problems (Castleman 1982), a sense of lost control, and a fear of crime (e.g., Glazer 1979).

Transit Police Department efforts to control graffiti on the subway involved a complex series of offensives on many fronts that continues today. Castleman (1982) detailed various enforcement efforts carried out during the first decade, such as forming special units to control graffiti, arresting writers, and patrolling yards. Lachmann (1988) reported that some of the enforcement efforts of this period were aimed specifically at breaking up writers' corners, areas where muralists met to exchange ideas and display photographs of their work.

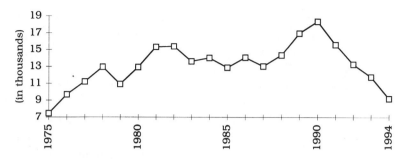

F<small>IG</small>. 3.—New York City transit felony crime complaints for 1975–94. Source: New York City Transit Police Department.

The financial situation changed in 1981 with a massive infusion of capital to the city from the state for infrastructure maintenance and the purchase of new subway cars (see Cohen 1991; Levy 1994). Beginning in 1984, the transit authority used an incremental "chunking" approach to the graffiti problem, cleaning up the system train by train and line by line (Sloan-Howitt and Kelling 1992). Once a line was cleaned up, cars on it had to be cleaned up within two hours or they would be pulled from service. These efforts were supported by a variety of other measures. These included the use of new solvents, police enforcement efforts at the yards and on trains, improved lighting, and the rapid repair of fencing breaches (New York City Transit 1997). By 1989, all cars were virtually graffiti free.[18]

Figures released by the New York City Transit Police Department for 1975–94 (see fig. 3) do not show crime falling on the subway immediately following the graffiti cleanup. Instead, they show that felony crime complaints on the subway were steady from 1983 through 1988. They rose in 1989 and 1990, when they peaked, falling in 1991 and then more steeply in 1992. There is no evidence that the graffiti cleanup led to a reduction in crime on the subway immediately following the success of the program.

Further, incivilities other than graffiti had not disappeared from the New York subway by 1989. Kelling, writing in 1991, described Operation Enforcement, launched in November 1989 to help restore orderli-

---

[18] While graffiti-covered trains disappeared from the system in 1989 (Kelling 1991; Sloan-Howitt and Kelling 1992), over 5,000 minor graffiti hits each week were still being removed by cleaners (New York City Transit 1997) (see also Perez-Pena 1996). This suggests that it is not really accurate to speak of graffiti being eliminated but rather controlled.

ness to the subway, focusing on the presence of vagrants within the system. Since restoring order was the justification provided by Kelling for the new program, at least some social incivilities must have been still present in the system at that time.

With hindsight, it may not be surprising that the graffiti cleanup seems to have had little impact on crime in the New York City subway. Many of the graffiti writers were not serious criminals committing a wide range of crimes. Rather few were arrested or ejected from the system. Despite the removal of graffiti, many other incivilities remained—perhaps allowing these broken windows to continue to have their facilitating effect on more serious crimes.

3. *Conclusions about Order Maintenance in the Subway.* Though a prima facie case exists that order maintenance policing led to a drop in subway crime beginning in 1991, we have noted some questions that remain unanswered. A more detailed analysis of monthly data for subway and citywide crime during the period could help to clarify the picture. At the same time, the mechanisms by which broken windows and order maintenance achieve their effects need to be specified more clearly. The results of the graffiti cleanup suggest that the broken windows thesis needs modifying to accommodate the fact that not all forms of disorder act in the same way to encourage serious crime. Similarly, if order maintenance policing was indeed responsible for the decline in felonies after 1990, this may not have been simply the result of offenders coming to believe that crime was now too risky but also partly the result of ejecting offenders and removing victims.

Understanding whether and how order maintenance policing operates on mass transit systems is important because it is a labor-intensive strategy. This makes it costly and, therefore, more likely to be used where crime levels are high and likely to be modified if crime levels decline. Thus researchers must be prepared to study the effects any changes in enforcement and deployment may have on crime patterns, as well as looking at the costs and benefits of the strategy over time and in comparison to other crime prevention measures.

V. Transportation Trends and Future Security Challenges

Future security challenges are best discussed in the context of likely trends in public transport. Changes have been consistently predicted in rail networks and in the use of buses and taxis in line with four widely held assumptions about future transportation needs. First, some high-density areas in large cities will require new rail transport, with stations located in the central business district and in subcenters around the urban core (Ingram 1998). Second, getting to these rail connections from less densely populated areas will require low-capacity forms of public transport (DETR 1998). Third, more decentralized employment (with or without subcenters) will require more flexible public transport (Ingram 1998). Fourth, smaller cities, with lower density, will require a mix of lower-capacity forms of public transport.

Our discussion below of changes in rail networks and the use of buses and taxis ignores certain other possibilities. For instance, a major technical breakthrough eliminated the pollution caused by automobiles, everyone was able to afford a car, and telecommunication changes eliminated the need for workers and shoppers to move around. While these changes would undoubtedly affect travel needs (see Graham [1997] for a discussion of the possible effects of telecommunication on travel), the basic patterns of decentralization (in industrialized countries) and urbanization (in developing countries) seem likely to continue (see Yaro and Hiss 1996; Ingram 1998).

A. Rail Networks

Light rail transit systems with their faster speeds and high capacity are attracting growing interest around the world. They make use of diverse rights of way and different kinds of vehicles, which makes them easily adaptable for use in various parts of a city (Armstrong-Wright 1993). Their construction can also be more readily undertaken in separate stages than conventional rail systems, which makes them cheaper to build (Henderson 1992). But, according to Armstrong-Wright, they operate best along main traffic corridors—not along secondary or tertiary road networks. This means that passengers must still get to stops (or stations) by foot or in some other way, and they must still wait at the stops for the light rail vehicle to arrive. On the way to or from the stop, or while waiting there for the vehicle, passengers will be vulnerable to theft and robbery of various kinds just as they are now in more conventional systems. However, the risks might be greater because staffing levels on these new systems are designed to be low (see, e.g., Hellewell 1990). If crime does become a problem, the operators of these new systems may need to increase staffing to supervise the system or make greater use of CCTV and other security technology.

Some of the new metro systems, such as those in Washington, D.C., and Hong Kong, were designed with crime prevention in mind and have very low crime rates. However, not all these new systems, especially in developing countries, have utilized crime prevention designs and technology,[19] and not all have very low crime rates (Lopez 1996). This presents a potential problem in terms of the unequal distribution of crime prevention benefits. Armstrong-Wright (1993) has pointed out that the improved service provided by new metro services in developing countries tends to benefit those with higher incomes. If these transit systems also provide crime prevention benefits, then lower income passengers may be doubly disadvantaged by both poorer and less safe service. This may be a general problem requiring research.

B. Buses and Taxis

"Real-time" bus systems, such as that in operation in Ipswich, England, are sophisticated enough to display the arrival times and locations of buses on a map at stops and on special sites on the Internet (Gray 1998). When used as part of larger improvements to bus service, real-time systems may reduce victimization at stops by decreasing waiting times. Passengers may be better able to focus on their surroundings if they know when their bus is due. However, offenders could also use this information to determine whether there is enough time before the bus arrives to commit a crime. This possibility is controlled to some extent by the increased surveillance provided by the newly designed shelters and the anticipated increased ridership.

Rent-by-the-trip public automobile service (PAS) fits into a very limited transport niche between the private car and the taxicab (Henderson 1992). This service can use low-speed, battery-operated cars to shuttle between stands at a city center station and those at various hub destinations for trips of less than one or two miles. For short trips, the PAS might overcome some of the limitations of taxi service—such as driver costs, fuel wastage, and limited service hours (Henderson 1992). The service may provide safer travel for those who can afford to use it instead of taxis. However, the PAS provides two security challenges: theft by drivers and theft or damage while parked ready to be rented. (As Henderson pointed out, the vehicles and stands may be particularly vulnerable to vandalism by those who cannot afford the service—such as the young.) Given the limited utility

---

[19] Some of these newer systems may help prevent crime in other ways, e.g., by reduced overcrowding, lowered waiting times, and faster journeys.

of the system, governments will have little incentive to subsidize its use or its security.

VI. Conclusion

It seems safe to predict that the future security problems of mass transit will be little different from those of the present. Offenders preying on the system, and on staff and passengers, will continue to take advantage of the many criminal opportunities presented by the transit environment. By its very nature this is difficult to secure. It is open to all members of the public, criminal or not. At off-peak times, trains, stations and bus stops tend to lack supervision from staff and tend to be lonely and intimidating. During rush hours, they may be so crowded that passengers have difficulty in protecting their persons or their property. These conditions are often exacerbated by lack of funding, poor administration, bad design, and inadequate policing.

Nevertheless, many successes have been discussed above in making transit less vulnerable to crime. These include the use of crime prevention designs, vigilant maintenance and policing, and situational measures tailored to specific problems of crime. Helping to design and implement these measures in public transport provides criminologists with special opportunities to make a practical contribution to urban safety. They also have an important role in documenting and evaluating the measures.

In addition, their help is needed in exploring some new issues about possible inequities in the delivery of crime prevention benefits on public transport, as well as in continuing to study issues that transport planners and managers have repeatedly confronted in the past. These include questions about ways to reduce travelers' fear of crime (especially of women and the elderly) and ways to reduce community concerns about the effect of new transit routes on the distribution of crime in the city. The former can lead to reduced ridership and the latter can delay the introduction of needed new services. No clear solutions to these problems have yet emerged although numerous studies have been reported. What is needed are long-term programs of study carried out by criminologists knowledgeable about the transport environment who are able to use information about victimization, offender decision making, and the distribution of crime in order to address these problems. Finding the money for this research and developing the necessary expertise, while a challenge for criminologists, governments, and transit providers, should be considered as part of the needed investment in public transport required to keep urban areas productive and desirable places to live in the twenty-first century.

Sixteen Opportunity-Reducing Techniques of Situational Crime Prevention for Use on Urban Public Transport

Increasing the Effort Needed for Crime

1. *Target Hardening.* Target hardening uses physical barriers and impediments—enclosed ticket offices, safes, driver screens, toughened windows, graffiti-resistant surfaces—to obstruct the thief or vandal.

2. *Access Control.* Access control measures are intended to exclude people from vehicles, premises, areas, or facilities, who have no legitimate reason for entering and may be potential offenders.

3. *Deflecting Offenders.* Deflecting offenders refers to measures that are intended to influence the routine activities of potential offenders so as to keep them away from possible crime targets, including passengers, transit employees, and system property.

4. *Controlling Facilitators.* Controlling facilitators includes removing, modifying, or restricting access to objects that can make crime easy, such as removing phone banks in stations and reducing the need for passengers to display cash in crowded areas.

Increasing the Perceived Risks of Crime

5. *Entry/Exit Screening.* Entry screening is intended to increase the likelihood of detecting people not in conformity with entry requirements, such as checking tickets (visually or mechanically) to prevent fare evasion. It is not intended to exclude potential offenders (access control).

6. *Formal Surveillance.* Formal surveillance is provided by local or system police whose main function is to furnish a deterrent threat to potential offenders. This surveillance can be enhanced by closed-circuit television and by passenger and burglar alarms.

7. *Surveillance by Employees.* In addition to their primary duties, some employees are expected to assume some responsibility for monitoring conduct in their workplaces. Conductors, station attendants, and drivers perform a surveillance function by virtue of their position.

8. *Natural Surveillance.* Natural surveillance is designed to promote the kind of supervision exercised by people going about their everyday business whether as travelers or passersby.

Reducing the Anticipated Rewards of Crime

9. *Target Removal.* Cash and other attractive targets for theft can be removed from the reach of offenders. Bus drivers may only accept exact change with no access to the cash received and ticket machines may be built into walls so that they can only be emptied from areas with restricted access.

10. *Identifying Property.* Property, such as system property or tickets with computer chips, can be marked so that its use by thieves is limited.

11. *Reducing Temptation.* The presence of graffiti, damaged objects, or large blank surfaces can act as invitations to crimes such as vandalism by reminding potential offenders of the rewards of these behaviors.

12. *Denying the Benefits.* Benefit denial measures include cleaning graffiti, which denies offenders the gratification of seeing their work displayed.

Removing Excuses for Crime

13. *Rule Setting.* Rule setting is the introduction of new rules or procedures, or the clarification or publicizing of those already in place, that are intended to remove any ambiguity about the conduct or actions allowed on the system.

14. *Stimulating Conscience.* Stimulating conscience involves reminding potential offenders at the point where they may commit a particular offense—such as through signs or public address systems—that the behavior is not allowed.

15. *Controlling Disinhibitors.* Controls on disinhibitors relate to limiting substances that undermine inhibitions and impair judgment since potential offenders using them may be more prone to break the law. Working with area pubs or bars or limiting the use of alcohol on the system itself are two measures.

16. *Facilitating Compliance.* Compliance with rules, regulations, and laws can be made easier with the provision of measures that help passengers conform to requirements. Trash bins help prevent litter and permission-to-ride passes help passengers pay the correct amount when ticket machines have broken down.

APPENDIX B

Design Features to Prevent Crime in the Washington, D.C., Metro[20]

High arched ceilings to provide passengers with a feeling of openness, thus reducing fear.

Spacious, uncrowded platforms to increase the perception of safety.

Long, straight escalators to carry people to and from the street, thus avoiding mezzanines where criminals might lie in wait.

Overhead crossovers between platforms rather than dark frightening tunnels below the tracks.

Restful lighting designed not to cast alarming shadows.

Recessed platform walls and durable easily cleaned surfaces for trains to discourage graffiti and facilitate its removal.

Newspaper recycling and trash bins throughout the stations.

Closed-circuit television cameras (CCTV) at platform ends and station entrances to facilitate surveillance by staff and to make passengers feel safer.

[20] The source for this is LaVigne (1996*a*, 1996*b*).

Two-way radios for all Metro employees to summon assistance or be alerted at any time.

Attendants in kiosks at platform entrances to provide assistance to passengers, to monitor the CCTV screens, and to keep an eye on potential fare evaders.

Intercoms on trains and emergency phones throughout the stations to enable passengers to call for help.

Electronic fare cards that open gates at entrance and exit to discourage fare beating.

No advertisements allowed on platforms since these attract defacement.

No vendors allowed on the system, nor eating or drinking, because of the associated trash.

No restrooms since these facilitate undesirable activities such as prostitution or drug dealing.

REFERENCES

Armstrong-Wright, Alan. 1993. *Public Transport in Third World Cities.* Transport Research Laboratory, Department of Transport. State of the Art Review 10. London: H.M. Stationery Office.

Audits and Surveys Worldwide. 1996. *New York City Transit 1996 Fear and Disorder Survey: Final Report.* New York: Audits and Surveys Worldwide for Metropolitan Transportation Authority.

Austin, Thomas L., and Eve S. Buzawa. 1984. "Citizen Perceptions on Mass Transit Crime and Its Deterrence: A Case Study." *Transportation Quarterly* 38:103–20.

Barclay, Paul, Jennifer Buckley, Paul J. Brantingham, Patricia L. Brantingham, and Terry Whinn-Yates. 1996. "Preventing Auto Theft in Suburban Vancouver: Effects of a Bike Patrol." In *Preventing Mass Transit Crime,* edited by Ronald V. Clarke. Crime Prevention Studies, edited by Ronald V. Clarke, vol. 6. Monsey, N.Y.: Criminal Justice Press.

Barker, Mary, Jane Geraghty, Barry Webb, and Tom Key. 1993. *The Prevention of Street Robbery.* Police Research Group, Crime Prevention Unit Series Paper 44. London: Home Office Police Department.

Belanger, Mathieu. 1997. "Crime Trips on the N.Y.C. Subway." *Transit Policing* 7:11–15.

———. 1999. "Crime Mobility and Public Transport: The Case of the New York City Subway." Ph.D. dissertation, Rutgers—The State University of New Jersey, School of Criminal Justice.

Beller, Anne, Sanford Garelik, and Sydney Cooper. 1980. "Sex Crimes in the Subway." *Criminology* 18:35–52.

Benjamin, Julian M., David T. Hartgen, Tim W. Owens, and Malcolm L. Hardiman. 1994. "Perception and Incidence of Crime on Public Transit in Small Systems in the Southeast." *Transportation Research Record* 1433:195–200.

Beskow, J., J. Thorson, and M. Ostrom. 1994. "National Suicide Prevention Programme and Suicide." *Social Science and Medicine* 38:447–53.

Bichler, Gisela, and Ronald V. Clarke. 1996. "Eliminating Pay Phone Toll Fraud at the Port Authority Bus Terminal in Manhattan." In *Preventing Mass Transit Crime*, edited by Ronald V. Clarke. Crime Prevention Studies, edited by Ronald V. Clarke, vol. 6. Monsey, N.Y.: Criminal Justice Press.

Block, Richard, and Sean Davis. 1996. "The Environs of Rapid Transit Stations: A Focus for Street Crime or Just Another Risky Place?" In *Preventing Mass Transit Crime*, edited by Ronald V. Clarke. Crime Prevention Studies, edited by Ronald V. Clarke, vol. 6. Monsey, N.Y.: Criminal Justice Press.

Boggs, Sarah L. 1965. "Urban Crime Patterns." *American Sociological Review* 30:899–908.

Boyd, Annabelle, and Patricia Maier. 1995. "An Assessment of Transit Crime Data Collection: Looking toward the Future." *Transit Policing* 5:1, 19–24.

Boyd, M. Annabelle, M. Patricia Maier, and Patricia J. Kenney. 1996. *Perspectives on Transit Security in the 1990s: Strategies for Success.* Washington, D.C.: U.S. Department of Transportation.

Boyle, Daniel K. 1994. "Jitney Enforcement Strategies in New York City." *Transportation Research Record* 1433:177–84.

Brantingham, Patricia L., and Paul J. Brantingham. 1991. *Environmental Criminology.* 2d ed. Prospect Heights, Ill.: Waveland.

———. 1993. "Location Quotients and Crime Hot Spots in the City." In *Workshop on Crime Analysis through Computer Mapping, Proceedings: 1993*, edited by Carolyn Rebecca Block and Margaret Dabdoud. Chicago: Illinois Criminal Justice Information Authority.

———. 1995. "Criminality of Place: Crime Generators and Crime Attractors." *European Journal of Criminal Policy and Research* 3:5–26.

Brantingham, Paul J., Patricia L. Brantingham, and Paul S. Wong. 1991. "How Public Transit Feeds Private Crime: Notes on the Vancouver 'Sky-Train' Experience." *Security Journal* 2:91–95.

British Broadcasting Corporation 2 (BBC2). 1999. Report on the Stephen Lawrence Case. *Newsnight.* BBC2, February 12.

Brooks, Michael W. 1997. *Subway City: Riding the Trains, Reading New York.* New Brunswick, N.J.: Rutgers University Press.

Brown, Sheila. 1998. "What's the Problem, Girls? CCTV and the Gendering of Public Space." In *Surveillance, Closed Circuit Television and Social Control*, edited by Clive Norris, Jade Morgan, and Gary Armstrong. Aldershot: Ashgate.

Burrows, J. 1980. "Closed Circuit Television and Crime on the London Underground." In *Designing Out Crime*, edited by R. V. G. Clarke and P. Mayhew. London: H.M. Stationery Office for Home Office Research Unit.

Carr, Kerri, and Geoff Spring. 1993. "Public Transport Safety: A Community Right and a Communal Responsibility." In *Crime Prevention Studies*, vol. 1, edited by Ronald V. Clarke. Monsey, N.Y.: Criminal Justice Press.

Castleman, Craig. 1982. *Getting Up: Subway Graffiti in New York.* Cambridge, Mass.: MIT Press.

Chaiken, Jan M., Michael W. Lawless, and Keith A. Stevenson. 1974. *The Impact of Police Activity on Crime: Robberies on the New York City Subway System.* New York: New York City Rand Institute.

Clarke, Ronald V. 1984. "Opportunity-Based Crime Rates." *British Journal of Criminology* 24:74–83.

———. 1993. "Fare Evasion and Automatic Ticket Collection on the London Underground." In *Crime Prevention Studies*, vol. 1, edited by Ronald V. Clarke. Monsey, N.Y.: Criminal Justice Press.

———. 1995. "Situational Crime Prevention." In *Building a Safer Society: Strategic Approaches to Crime Prevention*, edited by Michael Tonry and David P. Farrington. Vol. 19 of *Crime and Justice: A Review of Research*, edited by Michael Tonry. Chicago: University of Chicago Press.

———, ed. 1997. *Situational Crime Prevention: Successful Case Studies.* 2d ed. Guilderland, N.Y.: Harrow & Heston.

Clarke, Ronald V., Mathieu Belanger, and James A. Eastman. 1996. "Where Angels Fear to Tread: A Test in the New York Subway of the Robbery/Density Hypothesis." In *Preventing Mass Transit Crime*, edited by Ronald V. Clarke. Crime Prevention Studies, edited by Ronald V. Clarke, vol. 6. Monsey, N.Y.: Criminal Justice Press.

Clarke, Ronald V., Ronald P. Cody, and Mangai Natarajan. 1994. "Subway Slugs: Tracking Displacement on the London Underground." *British Journal of Criminology* 34:122–38.

Clarke, Ronald V., and Derek B. Cornish. 1985. "Modeling Offenders' Decisions: A Framework for Research and Policy." In *Crime and Justice: An Annual Review of Research*, vol. 6, edited by Michael Tonry and Norval Morris. Chicago: University of Chicago Press.

Clarke, Ronald V., and Pat Mayhew. 1998. "Preventing Crime in Parking Lots: What We Know and What We Need to Know." In *Reducing Crime through Real Estate Development and Management*, edited by Marcus Felson and Richard B. Peiser. Washington, D.C.: Urban Land Institute.

Clarke, Ronald V., and Barry Poyner. 1994. "Preventing Suicide on the London Underground." *Social Science and Medicine* 38:443–46.

Clarke, Ronald V., and David Weisburd. 1994. "Diffusion of Crime Control Benefits: Observations on the Reverse of Displacement." In *Crime Prevention Studies*, vol. 2, edited by Ronald V. Clarke. Monsey, N.Y.: Criminal Justice Press.

Cohen, James K. 1991. "Structural versus Functional Determinants of New York's Fiscal Policy towards Metropolitan Transportation, 1904–1990." *Social Science History* 15:177–98.

Cohen, Lawrence E., and Marcus Felson. 1979. "Social Change and Crime Rate Trends: A Routine Activity Approach." *American Sociological Review* 44: 588–608.

Cohen, Mark Francis. 1996. "Neighborhood Report: Manhattan Beach/Sheepshead Bay: Fear Changes Cabbies Habits." *New York Times* (March 17), p. 10.

Cole, Stewart. 1987. *Applied Transport Economics.* London: Kogan Page.

Cooper, Michael. 1998. "Police Say Subway Crime Was Undercounted by 20%." *New York Times* (January 8), p. B3.

Cornish, Derek. 1994. "The Procedural Analysis of Offending and Its Relevance for Situational Prevention." In *Crime Prevention Studies*, vol. 3, edited by Ronald V. Clarke. Monsey, N.Y.: Criminal Justice Press.

Cornish, Derek B., and Ronald V. Clarke. 1987. "Understanding Crime Displacement: An Application of Rational Choice Theory." *Criminology* 25: 933–47.

Cosby, Steve. 1985. "A Method for Measuring the Revenue Loss Due to Fraud within a Public Transport Undertaking." *Traffic Engineering and Control* 26:59–61.

Cudahy, Brian J. 1990. *Cash, Tokens, and Transfers: A History of Urban Mass Transit in North America*. New York: Fordham University Press.

———. 1995. *Under the Sidewalks of New York: The Story of the Greatest Subway System in the World*. 2d rev. ed. New York: Fordham University Press.

Davenport, Justin, and Ronan McGreevy. 1999. "Murder by Maniac on the Platform." *Evening Standard* (May 14), p. 1.

DeGeneste, Henry I., and John P. Sullivan. 1994. *Policing Transportation Systems*. Springfield, Ill.: Charles C. Thomas.

Del Castillo, Vincent Richard. 1992. "Fear of Crime in the New York City Subway." Ph.D. dissertation, Fordham University, Department of Sociology.

Del Castillo, Vincent, and Charles Lindner. 1994. "Fare Evasion in New York City Transit System: A Brief Survey of Countermeasures." *Security Journal* 5:217–21.

Dennis, Norman, ed. 1997. *Zero Tolerance: Policing a Free Society*. London: Institute of Economic Affairs.

Department for the Environment, Transport, and the Regions (DETR). 1998. *A New Deal for Transport: Better for Everyone*. The Government's White Paper on the Future of Transport. London: H.M. Stationery Office.

Department of Transport. 1986. *Crime on the London Underground*. London: H. M. Stationery Office.

DesChamps, Scott, Patricia L. Brantingham, and Paul J. Brantingham. 1992. "The British Columbia Transit Fare Evasion Audit." In *Situational Crime Prevention: Successful Case Studies*, edited by Ronald V. Clarke. Albany, N.Y.: Harrow & Heston.

Easteal, Patricia Weiser, and Paul R. Wilson. 1991. *Preventing Crime on Transport: Rail, Buses, Taxis, Planes*. Canberra: Australian Institute of Criminology.

Eastman, James A., and Vivian Yuan. 1994. "Analysis—the Relationship between Misdemeanor Arrests and Reported Felonies on the New York City Subway." *Transit Policing* 4:7–8.

Ewart, David (Connex, Media Relations Manager). 1999. Telephone conversation, September 13.

Falanga, Mark. 1988. "Reducing Crime through Design in the Chicago Subway System." Ph.D. dissertation, University of Michigan, Department of Urban, Technological, and Environmental Planning.

Felson, Marcus, Mathieu E. Belanger, Gisela M. Bichler, Chris D. Bruzinski, Glenna S. Campbell, Cheryl L. Fried, Kathleen C. Grofik, Irene S. Mazur, Amy B. O'Regan, Patricia J. Sweeney, Andrew L. Ullman, and LaQuanda M.

Williams. 1996. "Redesigning Hell: Preventing Crime and Disorder at the Port Authority Bus Terminal." In *Preventing Mass Transit Crime*, edited by Ronald V. Clarke. Crime Prevention Studies, edited by Ronald V. Clarke, vol. 6. Monsey, N.Y.: Criminal Justice Press.

Felson, Marcus, Dory E. Dickman, Denise E. Glenn, Linda M. Kelly, Gregory A. Lambard, Lisa S. Maher, Laura L. Nelson-Greene, Craig S. Ortega, Thomas J. Preiser, A. Rajendran, Trini E. Ross, Lourdes Tous, and James M. Veil. 1990. "Preventing Crime at Newark Subway Stations." *Security Journal* 1:137–42.

Finder, Alan. 1991. "Subway Crime Declines in First Drop since 1987." *New York Times* (November 15), p. B3.

Gaylord, Mark S., and John F. Galliher. 1991. "Riding the Underground Dragon: Crime Control and Public Order on Hong Kong's Mass Transit Railway." *British Journal of Criminology* 31:15–26.

Gaylord, M. S., and D. Lester. 1994. "Suicide in the Hong Kong Subway." *Social Science Medicine* 38:427–30.

Glaister, Stephen, ed. 1991. *Transport Options for London*. Greater London Papers no. 18. London: Greater London Group.

Glazer, Nathan. 1979. "The Subway Graffiti of New York." *New Society* 47: 72–74.

Graham, Stephen. 1997. "Telecommunications and the Future of Cities: Debunking the Myths." *Cities* 14:21–29.

Gray, George E. 1992. "Perceptions of Public Transportation." In *Public Transportation: Planning, Operations and Management*, 2d ed., edited by George E. Gray and Lester A. Hoel. Englewood Cliffs, N.J.: Prentice-Hall.

Gray, Ian (Policy and Network Management, Public Transport Group, Suffolk County Council, Team Leader). 1998. Telephone conversation, February 24.

Gray, Paul. 1971. "Robbery and Assault of Bus Drivers." *Operations Research* 19:257–69.

Greater London Council Women's Committee (GLC). 1985. *Survey Results: The Overall Findings: GLC Survey on Women and Transport*. Women on the Move, vol. 2. London: Greater London Council.

———. 1987. *Implementing the Survey's Findings: Part of the GLC Survey on Women and Transport*. Women on the Move, vol. 10. London: Greater London Council.

Greene, Judith A. 1999. "Zero Tolerance: A Case Study of Police Practices in New York City." *Crime and Delinquency* 45:171–87.

Groeger, John A. 1991. *Relative Risks of Taxi and Minicab Travel: A Summary of the Technical Report of the Research Entitled "Expectations and Experience of Taxi and Minicab Use."* London: Suzy Lampluch Trust.

Guberman, Connie. 1994. "Making Transit Safer for Women." *Transit Policing* 4:9–19.

GVB Amsterdam. 1994. *Eindrapportage Bedrijfsmonitor* (in Dutch). Amsterdam: GVBA.

Hall, Peter. 1995. "A European Perspective on the Spatial Links between

Land Use, Development and Transport." In *Transport and Urban Development*, edited by David Banister. London: E. & F. N. Spon.

Hargadine, E. O. 1983. *Case Studies of Transit Security on Bus Systems*. Washington, D.C.: U.S. Department of Transportation.

Hauber, A. R. 1993. "Fare Evasion in a European Perspective." *Studies on Crime and Crime Prevention* 2:122–41.

Hellewell, D. S. 1990. "Setting Up a New Operator." In *Light Transit Systems*, edited by B. H. North. Proceedings of the Symposium on the Potential of Light Rail Systems in British Cities, organized by the Institution of Civil Engineers, Nottingham. London: Thomas Telford.

Henderson, Clark. 1992. "New Public Transportation Technology." In *Public Transportation: Planning, Operations and Management*, 2d ed., edited by George E. Gray and Lester A. Hoel. Englewood Cliffs, N.J.: Prentice-Hall.

Homel, Ross, ed. 1997. *The Politics and Practice of Situational Crime Prevention*. Crime Prevention Studies, edited by Ronald V. Clarke, vol. 6. Monsey, N.Y.: Criminal Justice Press.

Hood, Clifton. 1996. "Changing Perceptions of Public Space on the New York Rapid Transit System." *Journal of Urban History* 22:308–31.

Hughes, Gordon. 1998. *Understanding Crime Prevention, Social Control, Risk and Late Modernity*. Buckingham: Open University Press.

Ingalls, Gerald L., David T. Hartgen, and Timothy W. Owens. 1994. "Public Fear of Crime and Its Role in Bus Transit Use." *Transportation Research Record* 1433:201–11.

Ingram, Gregory K. 1998. "Patterns of Metropolitan Development: What Have We Learned?" *Urban Studies* 35:1019–35.

Jammers, Victor. 1995. "Commercial Robbery in the Netherlands: Crime Analysis in Practice." *European Journal of Criminal Policy and Research* 3:124–36.

Kabundi, M., and A. Normandeau. 1987. "Crime in the Montreal Subway." *International Criminology and Police Review* 406:24–27.

Kelling, George L. 1985. "Order Maintenance, the Quality of Urban Life, and Police: A Line of Argument." In *Police Leadership in America: Crisis and Opportunity*, edited by W. A. Geller. New York: Praeger.

———. 1991. "Reclaiming the Subway." *City Journal* 1:17–28.

Kelling, George L., and Catherine M. Coles. 1996. *Fixing Broken Windows: Restoring Order and Reducing Crime in Our Communities*. New York: Free Press.

Kenney, Dennis Jay. 1986. "Crime on the Subways: Measuring the Effectiveness of the Guardian Angels." *Justice Quarterly* 3(4):481–96.

———. 1987. *Crime, Fear, and the New York City Subways: The Role of Citizen Action*. New York: Praeger.

Kocieniewski, David. 1998. "Safir Is Said to Seek to Punish a Chief over False Crime Data." *New York Times* (February 28), p. B1.

Krauss, Clifford. 1995. "Mystery of New York, the Suddenly Safer City." *New York Times* (July 23), sec. 4, pp. 1, 4.

———. 1996. "Crackdown Is Intensified in Quality of Life Crimes." *New York Times* (March 6), p. B3.

————. 1997. "Mexico City Journal: South of the Border, a Cab Ride Can Really Cost." *New York Times* (March 31), p. A4.

Lachmann, Richard. 1988. "Graffiti as Career and Ideology." *American Journal of Sociology* 94:229–50.

LaVigne, Nancy G. 1996*a*. "Crime Prevention through the Design and Management of Built Environment: The Case of the D.C. Metro." Ph.D. dissertation, Rutgers—The State University of New Jersey, School of Criminal Justice.

————. 1996*b*. "Safe Transport: Security by Design on the Washington Metro. In *Preventing Mass Transit Crime*, edited by Ronald V. Clarke. Crime Prevention Studies, edited by Ronald V. Clarke, vol. 6. Monsey, N.Y.: Criminal Justice Press.

————. 1997. "Visibility and Vigilance: Metro's Situational Approach to Preventing Subway Crime." In *Research in Brief.* Washington, D.C.: U.S. Department of Justice, National Institute of Justice.

Laycock, Gloria, and Claire Austin. 1992. "Crime Prevention in Parking Facilities." *Security Journal* 3:154–59.

Lefkowitz, Michael C. 1994. "Letter to the Editor: Fare Cards in Cabs?" *New York Times* (April 6), p. A20.

Levine, Ned, and Martin Wachs. 1985. *Factors Affecting the Incidence of Bus Crime in Los Angeles.* Report CA-06-0195. 2 vols. Washington, D.C.: U.S. Department of Transportation Office of Technical Assistance, Urban Mass Transportation Administration.

————. 1986*a*. "Bus Crime in Los Angeles. I: Measuring the Incidence." *Transportation Research* A 20:273–84.

————. 1986*b*. "Bus Crime in Los Angeles. II: Victims and Public Impact." *Transportation Research* A 20:285–93.

Levine, Ned, Martin Wachs, and Elham Shirazi. 1986. "Crime at Bus Stops: A Study of Environmental Factors." *Journal of Architectural and Planning Research* 3:339–61.

Levine, Richard. 1987. "New York City Tries to Match Wits with Transit System Fare-Beaters." *New York Times* (July 19), p. 14, Midwest edition.

Levy, Norman J. 1994. *Crime in New York City's Subways: A Study and Analysis of the Issues with Recommendations to Enhance Safety and the Public's Perception of Safety within the Subway System.* Albany, N.Y.: Senate Transportation Committee, Legislative Commission on Critical Transportation Choices.

London Regional Transport. 1985. *London Transport Report and Accounts, 1984/85.* London: London Regional Transport.

London Transport Executive. 1976–84. *Annual Report and Accounts, 1975–1983.* London: London Transport Executive.

Lopez, Manuel J. J. 1996. *Crime Prevention Guidelines for the Construction and Management of Metro Systems.* The Hague: Result Crime Management.

Loverso, Peter J. 1996. "Policing an Urban Transit Terminal: LIRR Police Efforts at NYC's Penn Station." *Transit Policing* 6:27–30.

Lueck, Thomas J. 1999. "Crime in the Subways Declines Again: Police Report a Significant Drop in the First Four Months of 1999." *New York Times* (May 14), p. B3.

Lynch, G., and S. Atkins. 1988. "The Influence of Personal Security Fears on Women's Travel Patterns." *Transportation* 15:257–77.

Mancini, Alan N., and Rejendra Jain. 1987. "Commuter Parking Lots: Vandalism and Deterrence." *Transportation Quarterly* 41:539–54.

Martell, Daniel A., and Park Elliot Dietz. 1992. "Mentally Disordered Offenders Who Push or Attempt to Push Victims onto Subway Tracks in New York City." *Archives of General Psychiatry* 49:472–75.

Matthews, Roger. 1992. "Replacing 'Broken Windows': Crime, Incivilities and Urban Change." In *Issues in Realist Criminology*, edited by Roger Matthews and Jock Young. London: Sage.

Mauri, Ronald A., Nancy A. Cooney, and Garry J. Prowe. 1984. *Transit Security: A Description of Problems and Countermeasures.* Cambridge, Mass.: U.S. Department of Transportation.

McKinley, James C., Jr. 1990. "Police Say One Man Killed Three Livery Drivers in the Bronx." *New York Times* (April 12), p. B1.

Metropolitan Transportation Authority (MTA). 1994. *New Yorkers' Perceptions of Fear and Disorder in the Subway, 1988 to 1992.* New York: MTA, Department of Policy and Planning.

Murray, Dick. 1998. "We Will Never Put Guards Back on Tube." *Evening Standard* (August 10), p. 15.

————. 1999. "The Early-Bird Rail Fare War: Commuters Are Offered Bargain Train Travel—If They Come to Town by 7 am." *Evening Standard* (May 13), p. 1.

Myhre, Marina L., and Fabien Rosso. 1996. "Designing for Security in Meteor: A Projected New Line Metro in Paris." In *Preventing Mass Transit Crime*, edited by Ronald V. Clarke. Crime Prevention Studies, edited by Ronald V. Clarke, vol. 6. Monsey, N.Y.: Criminal Justice Press.

National Roads and Motorists' Association Insurance. 1990. *Car Theft in New South Wales.* Sydney: National Roads and Motorists' Association Insurance.

Newman, Andy. 1998. "As Passenger Injuries Rise, Changes Are Urged to Taxicab Partitions." *New York Times* (July 20), p. B1.

New York City Transit. 1997. *Clean Car Program.* Brooklyn: New York City Transit.

New York State Senate Committee on Transportation. 1981. *National Conference on Mass Transit Crime and Vandalism: Compendium of Proceedings.* Albany: New York State Senate Committee on Transportation.

New York Times. 1998. " 'Peer Pressure' Bus Patrol Is Called Successful in San Francisco." *New York Times* (February 15), p. 25.

O'Donnell, I., and R. D. T. Farmer. 1994. "The Epidemiology of Suicide on the London Underground." *Social Science and Medicine* 38:409–18.

O'Malley, Pat, and Adam Sutton, eds. 1997. *Crime Prevention in Australia: Issues in Policy and Research.* Leichhardt: Federation Press.

Owen, Wilfred, with the assistance of Inai Bradford. 1972. *The Accessible City.* Washington, D.C.: Brookings Institution.

Parliamentary Travelsafe Committee. 1998. *Brisbane's Citytrain Network: Part II—Passenger Security.* Report no. 24. Brisbane: Legislative Assembly of Queensland.

Patterson, Arthur H. 1985. "Fear of Crime and Other Barriers to Use of Public Transportation by the Elderly." *Journal of Architectural Planning and Research* 2:277–88.

Pearlstein, Adele, and Martin Wachs. 1982. "Crime in Public Transit Systems: An Environmental Design Perspective." *Transportation* 11:277–97.

Perez-Pena, Richard. 1995. "Attackers Set Fire to Token Clerk in Brooklyn Subway Station." *New York Times* (November 27), p. B1.

———. 1996. "Subway Graffiti Creeping Back to Haunt Riders: A Threatened Symbol of the Bad Old Days." *New York Times* (March 21), pp. B1, B4.

Pierre-Pierre, Garry. 1995. "Twist a Dial and Cab Fare Soars, Police Say." *New York Times* (July 19), p. B1.

Pitt, David E. 1989. "Petty Thefts Disable New York Turnstiles a Token at a Time." *New York Times* (August 8), p. A1.

Poyner, Barry. 1983. *Design against Crime: Beyond Defensible Space.* London: Butterworths.

———. 1992a. "Situational Crime Prevention in Two Parking Facilities." In *Situational Crime Prevention: Successful Case Studies,* edited by Ronald V. Clarke. Albany, N.Y.: Harrow & Heston.

———. 1992b. "Video Cameras and Bus Vandalism." In *Situational Crime Prevention: Successful Case Studies,* edited by Ronald V. Clarke. Albany, N.Y.: Harrow & Heston.

Poyner, Barry, and Caroline Warne. 1988. *Preventing Violence to Staff.* The Tavistock Institute of Human Relations report to Health and Safety Executive. London: H.M. Stationery Office.

Project for Public Spaces. 1984. *Times Square Subway Station: Security and Public Use.* New York: Project for Public Spaces.

Rao, Cynthia Kerr. 1985. "When Crime on the Underground Is Good News." *Australian Police Journal* 39:116–18.

Rengert, George F. 1997. "Auto Theft in Central Philadelphia." In *Policing for Prevention: Reducing Crime, Public Intoxication and Injury,* edited by Ross Homel. Crime Prevention Studies, edited by Ronald V. Clarke, vol. 7. Monsey, N.Y.: Criminal Justice Press.

Rengert, G. F., and R. M. Bost. 1987. "The Spillover of Crime from a Housing Project." Paper presented at the annual meeting of the Academy of Criminal Justice Sciences, St. Louis, March.

Roane, Kit R. 1997. "Transit Patrols on 7 Line Cut Night Crimes." *New York Times* (September 1), p. B1.

Robinson, Jennifer B. 1998. "Transit Stations as Crime Generators: A Study of Vancouver." Paper presented at the fiftieth annual meeting of the American Society of Criminology. Washington, D.C., November 11–14.

Rose, J. S. 1979. *A Study of Violence on London Transport.* London: Greater London Council, Director-General's Department, Policy Studies and Intelligence Branch.

Rossmo, Kim. 1993. "Overview: Multivariate Spatial Profiles as a Tool in Crime Investigation." In *Workshop on Crime Analysis through Computer Map-*

ping, Proceedings: 1993, edited by Carolyn Rebecca Block and Margaret Dabdoud. Chicago: Illinois Criminal Justice Information Authority.

Saltzman, Arthur. 1992. "Public Transportation in the Twentieth Century." In *Public Transportation: Planning, Operations and Management*, 2d ed., edited by George E. Gray and Lester A. Hoel. Englewood Cliffs, N.J.: Prentice-Hall.

Sandler, Ross, David Schoenbrod, Eric A. Goldstein, Steven Jurow, and Fred Harris. 1979. *Reducing Crime in the New York City Subway System: Nine Recommendations.* New York: Natural Resources Defense Council, Project on Urban Transportation.

Saville, Gregory J. 1991. "Transdisciplinarity, Environmental Criminology and the Toronto Subway Security Audit." *Security Journal* 2:219–26.

Schwartz, Rita. 1988. *Homeless: The Impact on the Transportation Industry.* 2 vols. New York: Port Authority of New York and New Jersey.

Scott, D. 1989. "Graffiti Wipeout." *FBI Law Enforcement Bulletin* (December), pp. 10–14.

Shellow, R., E. W. Bartel, W. L. Cooley, E. S. Roszner, and J. Pazour. 1973. *Improvement of Mass Transit Security in Chicago: A Report to the City of Chicago Department of Public Works Recommending Specific Security Measures for Demonstration on Chicago Transit Authority Facilities.* Pittsburgh: Carnegie-Mellon University, Transport Research Institute.

Shellow, Robert, Eugene W. Bartel, and James Romualdi. 1975. *Security of Patrons on Urban Public Transportation Systems.* Transportation Research Institute Report, no. 6. Pittsburgh: Carnegie-Mellon University, Transport Research Institute.

Shellow, R., J. P. Romualdi, and E. W. Bartel. 1974. "Crime in Rapid Transit Systems: An Analysis and Recommended Security and Surveillance System." *Transportation Research Record* 487:1–12.

Silverman, Eli B. 1999. *NYPD Battles Crime: Innovative Strategies in Policing.* Boston: Northeastern University Press.

Sloan-Howitt, Maryalice, and George L. Kelling. 1992. "Subway Graffiti in New York City: 'Gettin Up' vs. 'Meanin It and Cleanin It.' " In *Situational Crime Prevention: Successful Case Studies*, edited by Ronald V. Clarke. Albany, N.Y.: Harrow & Heston.

Smerk, George M. 1992. "Public Transportation and the City. In *Public Transportation: Planning, Operations and Management*, 2d ed., edited by George E. Gray and Lester A. Hoel. Englewood Cliffs, N.J.: Prentice-Hall.

Smith, Martha J. 1998. "Regulating Opportunities: Multiple Roles for Civil Remedies in Situational Crime Prevention." In *Civil Remedies and Crime Prevention*, edited by Lorraine Green Mazerolle and Jan Roehl. Crime Prevention Studies, edited by Ronald V. Clarke, vol. 9. Monsey, N.Y.: Criminal Justice Press.

Smith, Martha J., Steven Belenko, Geraldine Staehs, Romualdo Arriola, Robert Shea, Linda Truitt, and Donna Harsch. 1986a. *Transit Crime Study.* Vol. 1, *Summary of Findings and Policy Recommendations.* New York: New York City Criminal Justice Agency.

————. 1986*b*. *Transit Crime Study*. Vol. 2, *Final Report*. New York: New York City Criminal Justice Agency.

Southeast Michigan Council of Governments. 1981. *Crime and Security Measures on Public Transportation Systems: A National Assessment*. Detroit: Southeast Michigan Council of Governments, Public Safety Division.

Stockdale, Janet E., and Peter J. Gresham. 1998. *Tackling Street Robbery: A Comparative Evaluation of Operation Eagle Eye*. Crime Detection and Prevention Series, Paper 87. London: Police Research Group.

Sturman, A. 1980. "Damage on Buses: The Effects of Supervision." In *Designing Out Crime*, edited by R. V. G. Clarke and P. Mayhew. London: H. M. Stationery Office for Home Office Research Unit.

Sullivan, John. 1997. "Judge Limits Police Stops of Taxicabs." *New York Times* (January 4), p. 25.

Sutherland, Edwin. 1937. *The Professional Thief*. Chicago: University of Chicago Press.

Taylor, Ralph B. 1987. "Toward an Environmental Psychology of Disorder: Delinquency, Crime, and Fear of Crime. In *Handbook of Environmental Psychology*, vol. 2, edited by D. Stokols and Irwin Altman. New York: Wiley.

Thrasher, E. J., J. B. Schnell, A. J. Smith, and K. R. Dimsdale. 1973. *Vandalism and Passenger Security: A Study of Crime and Vandalism on Urban Mass Transit Systems in the United States and Canada*. Washington, D.C.: American Transit Association.

Transit Policing. 1993. "New York City Crime Lowest since 1987." *Transit Policing* 3:18.

Travis, Alan. 1999. "Stephen Lawrence's Legacy: Confronting Racist Britain." *Guardian* (February 25), p. 1.

Tremblay, Manon, and Pierre Tremblay. 1998. "Social Structure, Interaction Opportunities, and the Direction of Violent Offenses." *Journal of Research in Crime and Delinquency* 35:295–315.

Trench, Sylvia, Taner Oc, and Steven Tiesdell. 1992. "Safer Cities for Women: Perceived Risks and Planning Measures." *Town Planning Review* 63(3):279–96.

Trivizas, Eugene, and Philip T. Smith. 1997. "The Deterrent Effect of Terrorist Incidents on the Rates of Luggage Theft in Railway and Underground Stations." *British Journal of Criminology* 37:63–74.

Turner, Stanley. 1969. "Delinquency and Distance." In *Delinquency: Selected Studies*, edited by Thorsten Sellin and Marvin E. Wolfgang. New York: Wiley.

van Andel, H. 1992. "Crime Prevention That Works: The Case of Public Transport in the Netherlands." In *Situational Crime Prevention: Successful Case Studies*, edited by Ronald V. Clarke. Albany, N.Y.: Harrow & Heston.

van Dijk, Jan J. M., and Josine Junger-Tas. 1988. "Trends in Crime Prevention in the Netherlands." In *Communities and Crime Reduction*, edited by Tim Hope and Margaret Shaw. London: H. M. Stationery Office for Home Office Research and Planning Unit.

Vuchic, Vukan R. 1981. *Urban Public Transportation: Systems and Technology*. Englewood Cliffs, N.J.: Prentice-Hall.

Walmsley, D. A., and K. E. Perrett. 1992. *The Effects of Rapid Transit on Public Transport and Urban Development.* Transportation Research Laboratory, Department of Transport, State-of-the-Art Review 6. London: H.M. Stationery Office.

Webb, Barry, and Gloria Laycock. 1992. *Reducing Crime on the London Underground.* Crime Prevention Unit Paper 30. London: Home Office.

Weidner, Robert R. 1996. "Target Hardening at a New York City Subway Station: Decreased Fare Evasion—at What Price?" In *Preventing Mass Transit Crime*, edited by Ronald V. Clarke. Crime Prevention Studies, edited by Ronald V. Clarke, vol. 6. Monsey, N.Y.: Criminal Justice Press.

White, H. P., and M. L. Senior. 1983. *Transport Geography.* London: Longman.

Whitney, Craig R. 1998. "To Burden of Poverty in France, Add Racism." *New York Times* (January 16), p. A3.

Wikström, Per-Olof H. 1995. "Preventing City-Center Street Crimes." In *Building a Safer Society: Strategic Approaches to Crime Prevention*, edited by Michael Tonry and David P. Farrington. Vol. 19 of *Crime and Justice: A Review of Research*, edited by Michael Tonry. Chicago: University of Chicago Press.

Wilson, James Q. 1983. *Thinking about Crime.* Rev. ed. New York: Vantage Books.

Wilson, James Q., and George L. Kelling. 1982. "Broken Windows: Police and Neighborhood Safety." *Atlantic Monthly* (March), pp. 29–38.

———. 1989. "Making Neighborhoods Safe." *Atlantic Monthly* (February), pp. 46–52.

Wilson, Paul, and Patricia Healy. 1986. *Graffiti and Vandalism: A Report to the State Rail Authority of New South Wales.* Canberra: Australian Institute of Criminology.

Winfield, David A. 1993. *Security as a Basis for Customer Acceptance—Subway 2000, the New York Concept.* New York: New York City Transit Authority.

Yaro, Robert D., and Tony Hiss. 1996. *A Region at Risk: The Third Regional Plan for the New York–New Jersey–Connecticut Metropolitan Area.* Covelo, Calif.: Island Press.

Leena Kurki

Restorative and Community Justice in the United States

ABSTRACT

Restorative and community justice are becoming increasingly popular.
Although both are conceptually ambiguous and overlapping, they have
distinctive core elements and are separate movements. Restorative justice
is based on values that promote repairing harm, healing, and rebuilding
relations among victims, the offenders, and the communities. Community
justice views crime as a social problem that affects life in communities and
suggests that prevention is an essential part of all criminal justice agencies'
work. Both share goals of community participation, empowerment, and
development. It is unclear whether restorative justice and community
justice initiatives will work and with what effects. The theoretical promise
of community justice has not yet achieved practical success. Although
most participants are satisfied with restorative justice practices, there is
little evidence that intensive emotional experiences have reduced crime,
prevented victimization, or built communities. However, limited results
reflect more the inadequacies of evaluation research to date than the
nonfeasibility of restorative and community justice concepts and goals.

Restorative justice and community justice have evolved from little
known conceptions of justice to terms in wide but divergent use by
criminal justice agencies, victim advocates, grassroots activists, and researchers. There can be no doubt about their popularity, but there is
little agreement about their meaning, content, and relation to each
other.

Some use the terms "restorative justice" and "community justice"

Leena Kurki, senior research associate, University of Minnesota Law School, is grateful to Todd Clear, Roxanne Lieb, Wesley Skogan, and Michael Smith for helpful comments on an earlier draft of this essay.

interchangeably as synonyms to describe any untraditional criminal processes or sanctions that take place in communities instead of in prisons or jails. Hence, for example, they push residential treatment programs, Neighborhood Watch, Weed and Seed, intensive probation, fines, community service, and restitution under the umbrellas of restorative and community justice (e.g., Hahn 1998). All are community-based initiatives that existed long before the recent popularity of restorative and community justice. Others use the concept of restorative justice to encompass many types of victims services, including sex-offender notification laws, victim impact statements in sentencing, and murder victims' families' "rights" to witness executions (e.g., Fattah 1997; Carey 1998; Presser and Gunnison 1999). Some view any kind of crime-related initiatives—residential treatment, community crime prevention, intermediate sanctions, victim services, restorative justice initiatives, and criminal justice agencies' operations—as community justice so long as they are community based or focused (Barajas 1997; Clear and Karp 1998, 1999).

Although conceptions of restorative and community justice are ambiguous and overlapping, each has distinctive core elements. Core restorative justice ideals[1] imply that government should surrender its monopoly over responses to crime to those who are directly affected— the victim, the offender, and the community. The goal is to restore the victim and the community and to rebuild ruptured relationships in a process that allows all three parties to participate (e.g., Zehr 1990; Van Ness and Heetderks Strong 1997; Braithwaite 1998; Bazemore and Walgrave 1999). Community justice is based on the idea that crime is a social problem that corrodes the quality of life in communities, and it redefines the role and operations of criminal justice agencies. Rather than focus solely on punishment, deterrence, or rehabilitation of individual offenders, agencies should broaden their mission to include preventing crime and solving neighborhood conflicts. Operations should be moved to local communities, and citizen involvement should be encouraged (e.g., Barajas 1996; Alpert and Piquero 1998; Trojanowicz et al. 1998; Clear and Karp 1999).

---

[1] This essay discusses restorative justice as a response to crime. Restorative approaches are increasingly used in other than crime-related conflicts, e.g., problems in schools (bullying, truancy), workplaces (labor disputes, sexual harassment), and within families (child welfare, family violence) (e.g., Pennell and Burford 1996; Lowry 1997).

Both approaches share the element of community empowerment and participation. The premise is that communities are strengthened when people have more chances to interact, create personalized relationships, and exercise informal social control. However, restorative justice is based on a set of values that promotes healing, repairing harm, caring, and rebuilding relationships among the victim, the offender, and the community (e.g., Consedine 1995). Thus far, consensus does not exist on values and practices encompassed in community justice theory (see Pranis 1998*b*, pp. 38–39). As a result, most restorative justice initiatives are community focused and based on citizen involvement, but only a few community justice programs incorporate restorative justice values. In addition, restorative justice assigns equally important roles for victims, offenders, and communities in participation and decision making, while conceptions of community justice are typically silent on the roles of victims and offenders.

Theoretical Foundations of Community Justice. Community justice approaches share a fundamental premise: crime is viewed not only as an incident, offender, or case that needs to be processed but also as a social problem that affects life in communities. Instead of focusing on arresting, prosecuting, adjudicating, punishing, or treating offenders after a crime has been committed, criminal justice agencies should find ways to prevent crimes. Community justice suggests that crime prevention—whether building communities through citizen action or providing family, school, or neighborhood-based skills programs or services—is an essential part of criminal justice agencies' work.

However, beyond the fundamental understanding of crime as a social problem, there are several possible theoretical foundations for community justice. And depending on the standpoint, strategies and practices vary significantly. The most often cited foundation is community empowerment and participation. The assumption is that collective participation in crime prevention and neighborhood revitalization efforts reduce crime and fear directly, and increased social interaction and control do so indirectly. As part of community empowerment, criminal justice agencies work together with residents and community groups in solving crime-related problems. Often the goal is to improve relations with communities and to increase public satisfaction with agencies. In practice, there is no shared understanding of the community role. It is difficult to create community participation, and ordinary citizens are seldom included in planning or running programs. Most community policing and prosecution efforts instead use them as "eyes and ears," symbolic supporters, or providers of funds (Buerger 1994).

Another influential foundation is Wilson and Kelling's (1982) theory of broken windows. It argues that minor disorder, if not taken seriously and addressed, will increase crime, fear, and neighborhood deterioration. It has been used to justify zero-tolerance, order maintenance, and heavy street-level enforcement policing; it has also influenced community prosecution and community court initiatives that emphasize attacking nuisance or quality-of-life crimes (see Taylor 1999*b*).

A third foundation is problem solving. As originally proposed by Goldstein (1979) in the context of policing, it was a situational approach to reducing criminal opportunities. In the context of community justice, problem solving has a wider meaning. First, it implies cooperative effort to building partnerships between criminal justice agencies and other governmental agencies and between criminal justice agencies and local communities. Second, it acknowledges that many "crime incidents" result from complex societal conditions and attempts to address some of the underlying social problems (e.g., Trojanowicz et al. 1998). Again, practices vary in real life. Important aspects of community justice are ignored when problem solving is limited to such things as curfew laws, antiloitering laws, antinuisance injunctions, civil code enforcement, street sweeps, or authorization of warrantless or citizen driven searches. A different approach to problem solving might mean, for example, creating preventive programs that focus on prenatal and early development of children and teach parenting and child care skills (e.g., Clayton 1999).

The fourth theoretical foundation for community justice is a simple geographical focus, which does not necessarily incorporate any of the three other core principles. It is based on the idea of location and whether criminal justice agencies are administered, or function, at local levels. For example, "community corrections" often refers to sanctions that are served in the community instead of in prisons or jails. However, agencies may also open neighborhood offices, adapt flexible working hours and service practices, and provide more information to residents.

The foundations of community justice are not new. Similar ideas were proposed by the President's Commission on Law Enforcement and Administration of Justice (1967). The commission recommended that both police and correctional officers should create closer relations to communities, adopt broader roles in addressing local problems, and rely on community resources. The four foundations represent an intellectual continuum in the context of policing: team policing and foot patrols of the 1970s were followed by problem-solving ideas that led to the broken windows theory, the focus of which recently has shifted to the idea that communities themselves must be able to participate in improving the conditions in neighborhoods (see Coles and Kelling 1999, p. 72).

Theoretical Foundations of Restorative Justice. Much of the ambiguity in the relation between restorative and community justice arises because they share the elements of community empowerment and participation. Restorative justice has evolved from predominantly victim-focused mediation to a comprehensive approach that views crime as a rupture in relationships and attempts to restore victims and communities, mend relationships, and build communities. Practices increasingly include face-to-face meetings involving families, friends, other supporters, and local community members (Messmer and Otto 1992; Galaway and Hudson 1996). Advocates identify community development as an essential goal and believe that restorative justice practices can alter existing social structures that cause crime (McCold 1995; Stuart 1996c; Pranis 1998b; Braithwaite 1999).

Because of this community element of restorative justice, community justice proponents tend to regard restorative justice as part of community justice. For example, Bazemore (1997) defines main restorative justice practices—victim-offender mediation, family group conferencing, sentencing circles, and various citizen panels—as new community decision-making models and discusses them under community justice. However, they are based on personal dialogue, communication, and consensus among the victim, the offender, and the community. None of the theoretical foundations of community justice necessarily encourage such face-to-face processes or involvement of victims and offenders. In restorative justice contexts, the victim, the offender, and the community meet to find restorative responses to a crime, to express their opinions and feelings, and to decide appropriate consequences. The process in which the sanctions are determined is often more important than the sanctions, since those are the same as are ordered by the criminal justice system, including restitution, community service, letters of apology, jail visits, anger management, alcohol or narcotic treatment programs, and the like.

The first North American victim-offender mediation program in

Kitchener, Ontario, was established by Mennonite Central Committee workers in 1974. Especially in the United States and Canada, religion and moral theory still provide strong backgrounds for restorative justice (Immarigeon and Daly 1997, 1998). Unlike many other countries, restorative justice initiatives in the United States are typically used as diversion programs for juveniles in minor, nonviolent, and nonsexual crimes. In New Zealand, family group conferences are used for all youth crimes except murder and homicide. In Germany, about 70 percent of both adult and juvenile cases in victim-offender mediation were violent crimes in 1995. Similarly in Austria, 73 percent of adult and 43 percent of juvenile cases were violent crimes in 1996 (Kilchling and Löschnig-Gspandl, forthcoming).

If cases are mediated, there is no doubt about success: in the vast majority of instances, victims, offenders, and other participants are satisfied, an agreement is reached, and a reparation plan is fulfilled by the offenders. The findings are similar in both early and more recent studies of juvenile and adult programs, in evaluations of victim-offender mediation and family group conferencing, and in domestic and international reports. Satisfaction, agreement, and completion rates regularly vary between 75 and 100 percent (e.g., Umbreit 1994; Moore 1995; Fercello and Umbreit 1998; McCold and Wachtel 1998). However, there are legitimate concerns about unequal treatment of indigenous people and minorities (Blagg 1997, 1998; Cunneen 1997) and about young offenders who are more vulnerable and less skilled at representing themselves (Feld 1999). Police officers or other facilitators may dominate discussions (Young and Goold 1999), and young offenders may feel a lack of control or be too intimidated to talk (Maxwell and Morris 1993; Sherman et al. 1998). Critics emphasize the dangers of individualized sentencing by volunteer citizens in a process that does not guarantee any constitutional rights (Ashworth 1993; Roberts and LaPrairie 1996; Levrant et al. 1999).

Although we know that face-to-face meetings are more humane and emotionally intensive than trials dominated by legal professionals (Sherman et al. 1998), there is not yet evidence that the experience yields better results. First, there have been few efforts to estimate traditional effectiveness measures, such as recidivism, crime, and victimization rates, fear of crime, or costs. Practically no evaluation has shown statistically significant reductions in recidivism, mainly because of self-selection effects and low-risk offenders (e.g., McCold and Wachtel 1998). Second, there have been no efforts to estimate restorative justice programs' effects on communities—To what extent are communities involved, social capital and relationships built, citizens empowered, and crimes prevented? Third, there has been little effort to observe whether the critique of lack of constitutional safeguards is warranted. Disparity or disproportionality in reparative agreements has not been examined, nor has the way in which young, minority, inarticulate, or otherwise more vulnerable victims or offenders perform in programs.

Restorative justice programs have been successful in involving volunteers, and many stories describe how participation has changed victims' and offenders' lives. Rigorous evaluations on restorative justice are lacking, though there is little evidence that the traditional criminal justice system performs particularly well or better—many are convinced that it performs worse (e.g., Stuart 1996c; Sherman et al. 1998; Braithwaite 1999). "It is very important for us to recognize that our current criminal justice interventions actually destroy community. So even to get neutral would be a huge step for this system" (Pranis 1998a). No evaluation has shown that restorative justice programs increase recidivism; they just have not been able to show significant decreases.

There are several arguments for a systemwide shift to incorporate restorative values. First, if restorative justice is a better and more humane way to deal with crime, why should it not become the governing principle of the criminal justice system rather than a small-scale response to minor crime? Second, restorative justice is unlikely to have significant or lasting effects if initiatives continue to operate primarily as unorganized and sporadic activities. Third, without a systemwide change, restorative justice programs will be trivialized and criminal justice agencies will remain reluctant to divert offenders to them. Fourth, if crime is seen in both traditional and restorative ways, a double system of punishment may first process offenders through regular criminal trials and then move them to informal restorative programs to agree on a reparative contract. Alternatively, restorative programs may widen formal control over very minor crimes that previously were ignored by the criminal justice system. Fifth, few resources will be saved if restorative solutions only supplement traditional punishments or are used only for minor crimes. Sixth, a systemwide change may improve proportionality, consistency, and equality in restorative practices. There would be more information on principles and practices, funding, and training. Seventh, without official encouragement and support, restorative justice initiatives are likely to be concentrated in middle-class, white neighborhoods or in rural areas. Disadvantaged urban neighborhoods with large proportions of minorities and immigrants—areas disproportionately affected by crime—would be unlikely to benefit.

Community Empowerment. Community empowerment and development is a shared goal of community and restorative justice. Unfortunately, there is little evidence that this type of community crime prevention works: "Much of the effort to alter the structure of communities in order to reduce crime has not been noticeably successful or sustainable" (Hope 1995, p. 23). In addition, success is often achieved when least needed: "Yet the central paradox by a century of research into community crime prevention remains that community responses to crime are easiest to generate in exactly those areas where they are least needed and hardest to establish in those where the need is the greatest" (Crawford 1998, p. 159). Why should we expect that restorative or community justice approaches are more successful in building communities and involving local residents? Thus far, a handful of evaluations on community policing show no great promise as sources of community reconstruction (e.g., Wycoff and Skogan 1993; Grinc 1994; Skogan and Hartnett 1997), and there are no such studies on restorative justice.

Most of the experience with community justice comes from community policing and research focusing on its effects on crime rates, fear of crime, or citizens' attitudes toward police. Most studies have used simple before/after comparisons without control areas (that are not using community policing), and the results are mixed. Community policing may in some cases improve citizens' views of and relations with police and reduce fear of crime, but there is little evidence of effects on crime rates in local neighborhoods (e.g., Cordner 1998; Crawford 1998; Piquero et al. 1998). The theoretical promise has not transferred to practical success: "Unfortunately, the reality looks a little different, at least so far. It has proved difficult to carry out the concept of community policing" (Moore 1999, p. 320).

Critics argue that many community justice efforts are weakening community bonds and social capacity in inner-city neighborhoods as a result of aggressive law enforcement (e.g., Guarino-Ghezzi and Klein 1999). Blacks and other minorities are disproportionately targeted and affected (e.g., Livingston 1997). There are also examples of community justice initiatives that were originated and initially funded by business owners and well-off local residents who were concerned about their economic interests (Boland 1996, 1998*a;* Parent and Snyder 1999). Marginalized youth, beggars, vagrants, drug abusers, and prostitutes are often viewed as causes of disorder rather than its consequences or victims. If they are viewed primarily as causes of neighborhood decline, the question becomes how to remove them from communities, not how to improve social conditions in deprived areas afflicted by high levels of intracommunal crime (Crawford 1998). Experience with community policing has shown that benefits often go to white and better-educated residents of target communities (Skogan 1990).

Research and writing on restorative and community justice is a work in progress rather than a finished product. There are many more new local initiatives than there are people to document them. Practitioners and volunteers of such initiatives have little time to write about them. In this essay, I am mostly limited to published sources. Section I focuses on principles and practices of community justice and discusses separately the four main types of initiatives: community policing, community prosecution, community courts, and community (justice) corrections. Section II examines elements of restorative justice, then describes the main types of projects (victim-offender mediation, family group conferencing, sentencing circles, and citizen panels), and summarizes what is known about their success and effects. Section III examines criticisms of restorative and community justice and suggests some future action. Concluding remarks are presented in Section IV.

I. Community Justice

Rationales for community justice include community empowerment, broken windows theory, problem solving, and a catchment area conception that does not necessarily incorporate any of the others. Goals, methods, and practices of implementation vary depending on the theoretical foundation. The most extensive experiences with community justice arise from community policing, but prosecutors, judges, and correctional officers are increasingly rethinking their missions and operational strategies in order to incorporate community elements.

"Community justice," as I use it here, is understood more narrowly than, for example, Clear and Karp's (1999) conception that encompasses all variants of crime prevention and justice activities that explicitly include the community in their processes. For them, the core elements of community justice are neighborhood-level operations, problem solving, decentralization of authority and accountability, and citizen involvement in the justice process.

A. Theory of Community Justice

A common strand of community justice developments is the notion that criminal justice agencies broaden their view of crime. Instead of thinking of crime solely as an incident or case that needs to be processed efficiently through the regular operations of a criminal justice agency, crime is also viewed as a social problem that affects the quality of life in communities and neighborhoods. Instead of focusing only on offenders and direct victims after a crime has been committed, agencies should also find ways to prevent crimes. Thus crime prevention becomes a legitimate and essential mission for police, prosecutors, courts, and corrections (e.g., Bureau of Justice Assistance 1997).

The President's Commission on Law Enforcement and Administration of Justice (1967) recommended community-oriented changes in the role of police: "Policemen are uniquely situated to observe what is happening in the community. . . . If a park is being badly maintained, if a school playground is locked when it is most needed, if garbage goes uncollected, if a landlord fails to repair or heat his building, perhaps police could make it their business to inform the municipal authorities of these derelictions. . . . The Commission is inclined to think that broadening the role of the police in this fashion would not distract the police from law enforcement. On the contrary, it would contribute to law enforcement by making the police more active and more valued members of the community" (p. 254).

1. *Community Empowerment.* The most cited rationale for community justice is community empowerment and participation. First, it is argued that organizing communities into collective crime prevention projects, such as neighborhood patrols, block-watch groups, and cleaning and beautification projects, directly reduces crime and fear. Second, it is assumed that community participation indirectly reduces crime and fear by generating increased social interaction, which in turn creates a stronger sense of community solidarity, which means more informal social control in the neighborhoods (Hope 1995). Hence, the problem of crime transfers to an opportunity to build networks and increase interaction among local residents.

Many believe that creating positive, caring relationships and strengthening families are the best ways to build communities and prevent crime—and criminal justice agencies should find ways to do this

(Earle 1998). The goal "is to engage as many citizens as possible in building a better community" because "people who share a strong sense of community are far less likely to violate the trust of others" (Maloney and Bryant 1998, p. 2).

The social capital sought is not material improvements (physical capital) or individual skills (human capital), but a social good embodied in the structure of relations among people (Sampson 1999). Social capital is working when you can ask your neighbor to help carry out an old washer and dryer, when your neighbor promises to keep an eye on the house while you are on vacation, or when your neighbor blows snow from your driveway or mows your front lawn without mentioning it. Social capital creates informal social control, which connects residential stability to lower rates of delinquency (Sampson 1999). Informal social control is often described as including block-watch groups, neighborhood patrols, property marking, community meetings, and the like (Skogan 1990; Moore 1999). However, Sampson (1999) sees the promise of informal social control in socializing the youth to community norms and values. Then, informal social control is working when you can comfortably tell your neighbors' kids to quit fighting, to stop harassing your dog, or to pick up the trash they dropped on the sidewalk.

However, efforts to increase social capital, neighborhood self-help, or volunteerism have not been particularly encouraging (Moore 1999). "Indeed, community interventions seem to fall hardest when their major effort is to change individual behaviors by promoting friendships among neighbors" (Sampson 1999, p. 271).

Community empowerment ideas suggest that criminal justice agencies should change the way they interact with the public, learn to listen to ordinary citizens, and work together with local people to prevent crime and solve crime-related problems. Ideally, the role of local neighborhoods and residents should be more than that of a customer or service recipient (e.g., Bazemore 1997). Ordinary community members should have real power and be included in problem-solving and decision-making processes, for example, in defining priorities for local crime prevention strategies or neighborhood revitalization. Moreover, they should be recognized as actors and given shared responsibility of planning and running initiatives.

Experiences with community policing show that there is little shared understanding of the role of communities and that it is extremely difficult to generate citizen participation. Community participation may be reduced to a question of customer service and quality of services (Police Executive Research Forum 1996, p. 5). Buerger (1994) reports that ordinary people are seldom included in planning or decision making; instead, their four most common roles are "eyes and ears of the police" (providing information about crime, criminals, suspicious persons, and places), cheerleader (providing political and symbolic support for community policing), monetary assistant (providing economic support for community policing, e.g., business donations and tax measures), and statement maker (providing public signs of disapproval and intolerance of crime, such as Take Back the Night rallies and Neighborhood Watch signs) (Buerger 1994).

Depending on how seriously the role of local communities and residents is taken, initiatives vary in practice and include newsletters, education and advertising campaigns, citizen surveys, committees or task forces with citizen posts, door-to-door visits in neighborhoods, advisory citizen groups, regular public meetings for citizens, support for existing community groups, and building new community networks.

The goal of community empowerment is to improve relations with communities and to increase public trust and satisfaction with criminal justice agencies, especially among racial and ethnic minorities who are disparately affected in all phases of the system. The President's Commission on Law Enforcement and Administration of Justice suggested similar efforts to improve police relations with communities: "It is a long-range, full-scale effort to acquaint the police and the community with each other's problems and to stimulate action aimed at solving those problems" (1967, p. 258).

Although legitimacy is not regularly mentioned as a major objective for community policing, Skogan and Hartnett (1997) mention the politics of legitimacy as an important factor for its popularity. Riots and violence have frequently been sparked by conflicts between African Americans and the police. Political leaders of all backgrounds want to prevent further violence and curb police abuse—the rhetoric of community policing parallels this political environment (Skogan and Hartnett 1997, p. 9).

2. *Broken Windows.* The theory of broken windows, first articulated by Wilson and Kelling (1982) and developed further by Kelling and Coles (1996; Kelling 1998), is behind many community justice approaches. The broken windows theory assumes that minor disorder, if not taken seriously and attacked, will increase fear of crime, decrease informal social control, and increase crime. Social incivilities (public

urination and drunkenness, drug use, prostitution, loitering teens, and panhandling) and physical incivilities (vacant buildings, empty lots, junk and trash, graffiti, and abandoned cars) contribute to the deterioration of communities. There are variants of the disorder or incivilities thesis, but broken windows especially has influenced policies of community policing (see Taylor 1999*b*).

There is evidence that high levels of disorder are related with high levels of crime. Kelling and Coles (1996) refer to Skogan's (1990) work as a proof of the broken windows theory, since his study of decline and disorder in American neighborhoods showed a relationship among disorder, crime, and deterioration, the consequence of which is a downward spiral of neighborhood decay. However, some have questioned Skogan's study and suggest that his data do not support the findings (e.g., Harcourt 1998) or refer to other studies that do not show links between incivilities and crime (e.g., Greene and Taylor 1988). Others have pointed out that the broken windows theory badly confuses means and ends when community disorder is identified both as the social cause and the effect of crime (e.g., Crawford 1998), not to mention the potential for abuse of power and racial discrimination in implementations (e.g., Livingston 1997).

Skogan's study (1990) can at best support half of the broken windows theory—the downward spiral of neighborhood decline. Nothing suggests that targeting low-level, quality-of-life crimes by police, prosecutors, and courts is the only, the most appropriate, or the best way to stop a downward cycle or produce an upward spiral to neighborhood revitalization. As Skogan himself acknowledged, "One of the 'iron laws' of policy evaluation is that, the more we know about a program, the less confidence we have in it" (Skogan 1990, p. 18). He was also concerned about the consequences of order maintenance policing: constitutionality dangers in street sweeps and roadblocks, virtually unchecked discretion of patrol officers, and abrasive effects on residents of poor, minority neighborhoods.

Recently, there is more reason to doubt whether the main premise—disorder increases fear, crime, and deterioration—is correct after all. Taylor (1999*a*) reports on a study that followed conditions in thirty neighborhoods in Baltimore in 1981, 1982, and 1994. By 1994, physical conditions had worsened significantly, yet there were few changes between 1981 and 1994 in citizens' fear of crime or perception of disorder, amount of crime, or neighborhood decline. Although the research teams expected something else, residents did not report more incivilities, they were no more fearful, increased disorder did not alter or increase crime, and neighborhoods did not experience structural decline (Taylor 1999*b*). The study warned against community policing and prosecution efforts that concentrate heavily on zero-tolerance policies or fixing physical problems—the premise of these methods has been exaggerated, they have been overused, and they have overshadowed other problem-solving and community-oriented strategies.

Nevertheless, zero-tolerance, order maintenance, and heavy street-level enforcement policing continue to be popular. The broken windows theory has influenced community prosecution and community court approaches that emphasize attacking nuisance or quality-of-life crimes. The question remains, whether dispersing, arresting, and punishing homeless, drunk, poor, mentally ill, or loitering people is the right response to the social conditions of poverty, substance abuse, homelessness, and general apathy that are related to crime and deterioration of American inner-city neighborhoods.

3. *Problem Solving.* Another take-off point for community justice is the problem-solving approach Goldstein proposed for policing in 1979. Originally, problem solving was a situational approach aimed at reducing opportunities for crime or increasing risks of apprehension that used both traditional and newer police methods. Examples include identifying patterns of offending, police patrolling in certain places and times, arresting or removing unwanted persons or businesses, improving environmental designs, organizing block watches, and enhancing enforcement of civil code violations. Problem solving was not meant to address root causes of crime (Moore 1992).

Problem solving has a broader meaning in the context of community justice. First, it has developed into a cooperation effort to build partnerships between criminal justice agencies and other governmental agencies and between criminal justice agencies and local communities. Second, it acknowledges that "incidents" are symptoms of more general problems and attempts to address some complex problems that underlie crimes. Equation of symptoms with causes, and targeting symptoms instead of causes, have been called the most serious failure of community-based crime prevention (Buerger 1994), and many newer community justice approaches try to avoid the same mistake.

Experiences with community policing and prosecution show that people worry more about drug dealing, public urination and drunkenness, prostitution, graffiti, junk and trash on streets, abandoned buildings, and other relatively minor things than about serious crimes (e.g.,

Skogan 1990, 1999). The partnership approach acknowledges that the criminal justice system alone cannot handle the social issues and conditions that are associated with quality-of-life disorder. The rhetoric of community justice suggests that criminal justice agencies can help meet basic needs by working with partners—the public and private agencies that provide social services. In contrast with connotations of broken windows theory, some argue that community policing actually explores "new ways to protect and enhance the lives of those who are most vulnerable—juveniles, the elderly, minorities, the poor, the disabled, the homeless" (Trojanowicz et al. 1998, p. ii).

4. *Catchment Area.* A catchment area idea of community justice implies that criminal justice agencies should be administered or function at local levels. "Community corrections," for example, refers to sanctions served in communities instead of in prisons or jails. At minimum, most community justice initiatives have done three things: moved criminal justice operations to decentralized neighborhood locations, adapted flexible working hours and service practices, and provided more information to local residents.

While the theoretical standpoints and their prioritization vary, so do practices. Community justice initiatives come in diverse forms with different goals and routines. While many community policing efforts rely on heavy street-level enforcement, others emphasize better quality of public services, delivery of community-based treatment programs, citizen involvement, or diversionary policing that withholds enforcement as a way to build relationships with communities (e.g., Grinc 1994; Silverman 1995). Goals include reduced crime and victimization, decreased fear of crime, increased citizen involvement, improved neighborhood conditions, and greater citizen satisfaction with criminal justice agencies.

B. Practices of Community Justice

At the beginning of the twenty-first century, community policing approaches are used in the vast majority of urban American police departments. Community prosecution is more recent, less researched, and sporadically implemented. Community courts are gaining support after the positive experience of the Midtown Community Court in New York. Correctional departments also are rethinking their roles and the purpose of community corrections, which has gradually diminished to little more than control and surveillance of offenders while they serve sanctions in the community.

1. *Community Policing.* No matter what the priority of principles or goals, community policing is popular. In a 1994 survey, over 80 percent of U.S. police chiefs said they were implementing or intended to implement some aspects of community policing (McEwen 1994). This is not surprising, since the federal government is generously funding community policing programs and there are economic and political pressures to follow the trend: "The concept is so popular with the public and city councils that scarcely a chief wants his department to be known for failing to climb on this bandwagon" (Skogan and Hartnett 1997, p. vii). The Violent Crime Control and Law Enforcement Act of 1994 authorized $8.8 billion over six years to fund 100,000 community policing officers, to establish community policing institutes, and to promote community policing initiatives. The U.S. Department of Justice Office of Community Oriented Policing Services (COPS) reports that 100,000 officer posts were established by May 1999 (see COPS web page at http://www.usdoj.gov/cops).

There are many reasons why it is difficult to estimate the effects of community policing. Conceptions and principles of community policing are uncertain and prioritized differently; strategies, techniques, and mechanisms of implementation vary; and implementation in practice is often incomplete or partial. Differences between programs are often more significant than similarities, prohibiting direct comparisons (Grinc 1994; Silverman 1995).

Most studies have focused on measuring effects on crime, fear of crime, and citizens' attitudes toward police. Evidence is mixed and most studies have used simple before/after comparisons (lacking control areas) that produce weak results at best. Most inferred that observers agree that community policing may in some cases improve citizens' views of and relations with police and reduce fear of crime but that there is little evidence of effects on crime rates in local neighborhoods (Greene and Taylor 1988; Cordner 1998; Crawford 1998). For example, visible community policing efforts (walking in neighborhoods, talking with people) in Chicago decreased fear of crime and increased satisfaction with police (e.g., Skogan 1999). But many studies have been unable to report positive effects and some researchers say that "there is indeed a cross-country record of failed attempts to implement community policing" (Skogan and Hartnett 1997, p. 12). For example, recent results of community policing in public housing areas in Philadelphia did not show significant differences between the experimental and control groups of residents in perceptions of police, community problems, or fear of crime (Piquero et al. 1998).

Community empowerment, citizen participation, and partnerships with public and private agencies are regularly portrayed as the main features of community policing. For example, the definition of community policing by the Los Angeles police department follows the idea:

> Community Policing is a partnership between the police and the community. It is a partnership in which the police and the community share responsibility for identifying, reducing, eliminating and preventing problems which impact the community. By working together, the police and the community can reduce the fear and incidence of crime and improve the quality of life in the community. In this effort, the community and the police, as partners, identify and prioritize problems of crime and disorder and share responsibility for development and implementation of proactive problem-solving strategies to address identified issues. The strategies used combine the efforts and resources of the police, the community and local government. (Office of the Chief of Police, Management Paper no. 2 on Community Policing, cited in Greene 1998, pp. 139–40)

However, few studies have attempted to measure whether the rhetoric of community empowerment, involvement, and partnership building is achieved in practice, and the results are not particularly encouraging (Skogan 1996). Police attitudes, for example, are an obstacle: many police officers do not want to be labeled as social workers and are suspicious of programs that give power to civilians to set standards for their work or evaluate their performance (Trojanowicz et al. 1998). Typically, the intended role of local citizens is unclear for police officers, and effective partnerships between criminal justice and other agencies are rare.

The Vera Institute of Justice, for example, evaluated drug-focused community policing initiatives (Innovative Neighborhood-Oriented Policing, funded by the Bureau of Justice Assistance) in eight different states (Hayward, Calif.; Houston; Louisville, Ky.; New York; Norfolk, Va.; Portland, Oreg.; Prince George's County, Md.; and Tempe, Ariz.) (Grinc 1994; Sadd and Grinc 1994, 1996). Despite the great differences between the programs, the study found similar problems of implementation. All experienced difficulties in police officers' adoption of the new roles, behaviors, and expectations required by community policing. All had great difficulties in getting local residents involved. All but one (Norfolk) failed to establish adequate partnerships between the police department and other city agencies (Sadd and Grinc 1996).

Interviews with police officers and administrators, residents, and business owners showed that community policing was commonly viewed as an isolated police department phenomenon and that both education of community leaders, groups, and residents and organization of neighborhoods were neglected. As a result, the common obstacles for community involvement were not overcome: frustration with short-lived programs that swiftly come and go, heterogenous and unorganized communities, conflicts among different residential groups, and bad relations between the police and residents in poor, minority communities (Grinc 1994; Sadd and Grinc 1996). The role of local residents in community policing was unclear for many police officers, and mostly administrators understood that citizens were supposed to be partners in problem identification and solving. However, administrators failed effectively to communicate the philosophy, goals, and tactics of community policing to their officers. Although the theory suggests something else, most residents felt they were only used as the eyes and ears of police in reporting incidents in the neighborhoods (Grinc 1994; Sadd and Grinc 1994). Most respondents thought that the original goal of reducing drug demand was not achieved; drug dealing had only been displaced to other locations or different times of day (Sadd and Grinc 1996).

In New York, community policing officers "were not very successful in involving community residents in their problem-solving strategies" (McElroy, Cosgrove, and Sadd 1993, p. 76). If residents participated, it was as members of block watch or tenant patrol groups.

The Madison, Wisconsin, police department began its quality policing effort in the late 1980s. The main ideas were to improve internal workplace conditions by supporting employee participation and creating a healthy working environment and to improve external community conditions by community and problem-solving-oriented policing. A National Institute of Justice evaluation (Wycoff and Skogan 1993), based on panel interviews with department personnel and community residents before and after implementation, showed that internal changes were much more successful than external ones. Only sixteen out of eighty community indicators showed statistically significant improvements in the experimental areas since the implementation of quality policing. And only seventeen out of seventy-one community indicators showed that differences between the experimental areas and other areas in Madison were statistically significant (Wycoff and Skogan 1993).

For example, there were no differences between residents in quality policing neighborhoods and residents in other neighborhoods reporting problems or concerns to police; asking information from police; viewing police as polite, concerned, or helpful; thinking that police are handling neighborhood problems or crime prevention well; or experiencing fear of victimization or incidents of robbery and vandalism. After quality policing began, residents in experimental areas were less likely to say that police paid careful attention to them or were very helpful in self-initiated contacts; they also thought that careless driving and adult and juvenile drug use and dealing had increased. Of course, residents also had positive experiences. They thought that robberies, burglaries, and thefts had decreased, were less likely to see crime as a problem, and were more satisfied with their interactions in police-initiated contacts (Wycoff and Skogan 1993).

Evaluation of the Chicago Alternative Policing Strategy (CAPS), an ambitious and well-implemented community policing initiative, also shows problems in generating community participation (e.g., Skogan and Hartnett 1997; Skogan 1998). The CAPS program started in 1993 in five police districts and was expanded by the end of 1994 to all twenty-five Chicago districts. The most important tool to initiate citizen participation was "beat" meetings, small gatherings of police and residents held each month in schoolrooms, church basements, and park buildings. The study found that they were not working as intended. Police officers specializing in neighborhood relations were dominating meetings and suggesting problem-solving plans that featured traditional enforcement efforts. Collaborations between police and local groups were not particularly successful. Groups representing white and middle-class constituencies were much more likely to use opportunities for involvement than were groups representing lower-class minorities.

Although many community policing initiatives have included occasional public meetings, they are one of the most visible characteristics of the Chicago CAPS. Attendance varied among districts, but overall 10 percent of meetings drew fewer than six residents and 30 percent fewer than ten residents (Skogan and Hartnett 1997). As time passed, residents grew frustrated with meetings: they were run by police, most of the time they lacked clear agendas, and they produced no demonstrable actions or results. Residents brought up problems in the meetings but little was done to solve them: "We want to know what you did about our last meeting's complaints. We come every month and get general information—the same thing every month" (resident, cited in Skogan and Hartnett 1997, p. 127); "You all ask our help and we give it to you and nothing gets done" (another resident, p. 129). Police suggested most of the solutions, and these were typical enforcement-oriented tactics. They promised to increase patrol efforts and arrests and asked residents to be their eyes and ears and call 911. Citizens rarely proposed solutions (7 percent of problems), and there was little talk about the community taking future preventive action (6 percent of cases). Despite sincere and good efforts, such outcomes as empowerment of local citizens, collaboration among police, citizens, and governmental agencies, or resolution of social problems seldom occurred.

The Chicago CAPS study clarifies the difference between descriptive case studies and evaluations. Most literature on community policing, and all literature on community prosecution, community courts, and community (justice) corrections, is based on descriptions of initiatives. For example, claims of community empowerment and participation are often supported by listing various advisory committees or task forces with citizen posts, informative meetings at local neighborhoods, collaborative efforts with existing community groups, and the like. Similarly, the Chicago CAPS could have been portrayed as a success story: beat officers establishing relationships with local residents; residents attending regular, public meetings where they were able to identify and prioritize neighborhood problems, develop strategies to solve them, and participate in multiagency crime prevention and revitalization projects; and new advisory boards with broad community representation advising district commanders about community concerns and proposing and evaluating community projects. All this sounds great, but less was achieved in reality, as Skogan and Hartnett (1997) demonstrate. The point is not so much what kind of structures exist for citizen participation, but whether and how they are used, what happens within them, and what they accomplish. The point is not only that citizens can express their opinions but also to what extent the opinions are taken seriously, whether there are sincere efforts to do something, and how citizens are included in planning and deciding these efforts.

2. *Community Prosecution.* Fundamentals of prosecution have remained basically intact over the past few decades. Changes have fol-

lowed examples in other fields and been fairly modest, mostly related to new information, communication, forensic, and mapping techniques, and changes in sentencing laws that vastly increased prosecutors' discretion. However, community prosecution efforts, though still sporadic and pioneering, may have potential for significant change (Forst 1999).

Most literature on community prosecution is written by a few researchers (Barbara Boland, Catherine Coles, Heike Gramckow, and George Kelling) in the form of descriptive case studies, which typically lack theoretical or critical analysis but, instead, have a promotional tone. Case studies describe developments in Portland, Oregon (Boland 1996, 1998*a*); Manhattan, New York (Boland 1998*b*); Kansas City, Missouri (Jackson County) (Coles and Kelling 1997*a*); Indianapolis (Marion County) (Coles and Kelling 1997*b*); Boston (Suffolk County) (Coles and Kelling 1997*c*); and Austin, Texas (Travis County) (Coles and Kelling 1997*d*).

The picture that emerges is in many ways different from that of community policing. While the theoretical premises for community policing vary in writings and in practice, including empowerment of communities, improvement of poor neighborhoods, and reestablishment of relationships between police and minorities, writings about community prosecution are more homogenous. Two theoretical standpoints are mainly acknowledged: broken windows and problem solving. Both are typically portrayed as a way to promote and improve law enforcement.

The terminology of broken windows is in wide use: "Community prosecution is a local political response to the public safety demands of neighborhoods" (Boland 1998*b*, p. 51); "The major element is according higher priority than previously to quality of life issues and low-level crimes that are especially troublesome to citizens" (Coles and Kelling 1998, p. 45); "The solution of a community problem may be expedited by a swift and harsh prosecution of a minor crime—one that normally would have received scant attention" (Gramckow 1997, p. 14).

Focus groups convened by the American Prosecutors Research Institute to discuss the concept of community prosecution produced the following definition: "Community prosecution focuses on targeted areas and involves a long-term, proactive partnership among the prosecutor's office, law enforcement, the community and public and private organizations, whereby the authority of the prosecutor's office is used to solve problems, improve public safety and enhance the quality of life in the community" (American Prosecutors Research Institute 1995, p. 1).

The idea of problem solving is typically understood narrowly, more in the sense of situational crime prevention than in the sense of improving or changing the social conditions that underlie crimes (Gramckow and Mims 1998). Problem solving is presented as a strategy that targets special areas and crimes and uses both traditional and nontraditional methods. Traditional methods include better cooperation with police, heavy enforcement, street sweeps, and foot patrols. Identifying hot spots, training landlords and property managers, creating citizen-driven search warrants, and pursuing code violations, forfeiture orders, nuisance orders, and restraining orders are described as untraditional methods (Boland 1996; Coles and Kelling 1998, 1999).

The *Community Prosecution Implementation Manual*, prepared by the American Prosecutors Research Institute (1995), gives, for instance, the following examples of problem solving.

Problem: There are persistent problems with violations of city ordinances, such as blocking the sidewalks and preventing access to businesses, intimidating members of the public, creating nuisances and engaging in other violations of law.

Solution: The prosecutor may enforce uniform prosecution of all types of criminal street disorders and provide for the consistent issuance of arrest warrants when those offenders fail to appear in court. With help from the police department, the prosecutor's office may train private security providers on how to identify and report violations, how to develop communication links with police officers and how to educate business owners on networking with the private security providers.

Problem: Prostitutes are soliciting on certain streets in the area.

Solution: In addition to aggressively prosecuting the prostitution arrests, the community prosecutor may support or lead the neighborhood group effort to . . . reroute area streets. . . . Moreover, the community based prosecutor may encourage the vice squad to utilize more police decoy operations in the area or to effect enforcement of the loitering ordinance against prostitutes. The prosecutor also may initiate auto forfeiture proceedings against "Johns" using their vehicles to solicit prostitutes. (American Prosecutors Research Institute 1995, pp. 54–55)

Many community prosecution efforts target drug dealing by closing drug houses, evicting dealers from apartment buildings or hotels, and issuing restraining orders to enter certain areas or housing developments (Coles and Kelling 1997*b*, 1997*c*). For example, community prosecution in Kansas City is built around a countywide authorization to control antidrug efforts based on Community-Backed Anti-Drug Sales Tax (COMBAT) funds (Coles and Kelling 1997*a*, 1998).

Another common target is nuisance crime in business areas. For example, in Portland, a group of business owners viewed intensified law enforcement "crucial" and initially raised the money for a community prosecution project (Boland 1996, p. 3). A partnership was built between the business leaders and governmental agencies since they "became legitimately worried that criminal activity in the District would negate the economic benefits these investments were expected to bring into the city" (Boland 1998*a*, p. 256).

Ironically, while many advocates of community policing suggest that police officers should learn ways to help and listen to ordinary people and to address social conditions that produce crime in poor neighborhoods, many advocates of community prosecution suggest that prosecutors should participate in old-fashioned, hard-core police work. Prosecutors are drawn "into the law enforcement task of street order maintenance, traditionally performed by the police" (Boland 1998*a*, p. 254).

An essential premise of other kinds of community justice initiatives, community empowerment and participation, receives little attention in the community prosecution literature. It is seldom mentioned that prosecutors could generate increased social interaction, create a stronger sense of community solidarity, build relationships among community residents, or establish local networks of people.

Even though community prosecution envisions partnerships with communities, the role of ordinary people is typically limited to giving information and providing extra eyes and ears. Citizen involvement is understood narrowly, including community impact statements in sentencing or court watch groups (Coles and Kelling 1997*d*, 1998). For example, in Manhattan, tenants were trained to observe and report drug activities (Boland 1998*b*); in Portland, "citizen driven search warrants" can be based on ordinary people's observations of suspicious locations and activities (Boland 1998*a*). Three goals for community prosecution were identified in Manhattan: inform the community that the prosecutors' office has resources citizens can use; educate the public how the legal system works; and reach out to the community and work with citizens. However, that citizens bring information about crime to the prosecutors so they can do their part was described as the most important feature (Boland 1998*b*, p. 54).

The broken windows theory has been criticized because it creates a barrier between offenders and communities, and the same problem seems to apply to community prosecution. Marginalized youth, beggars, vagrants, drug abusers, and prostitutes are characterized as authors of disorder; they are the cause of neighborhood change and decline rather than its results or victims (Crawford 1998, p. 133). They are viewed as outsiders against whom the community needs to defend itself. Then, the question becomes how to remove criminals from communities, not how to improve deprived urban areas. However, as Hope has observed, highly victimized neighborhoods often have high rates of offenders among their residents (1995, p. 67).

For example, a project to remove a problem of illegal camping at an intersection of two main railroads in Portland began with major police sweeps and cleanups, followed by citizen patrols and steel bar barriers to close off the space campers used as shelters under a highway. Little passion or interest was shown for the homeless: "No one can say exactly where the campers went (the joking response is Seattle)" (Boland 1998*a*, p. 265). No one seemed to care either.

3. *Community Courts.* Current knowledge of community courts in the United States is mainly based on reports on one local but well-publicized project, New York City's Midtown Community Court, opened in 1993 (Feinblatt and Berman 1997; Midtown Community Court 1997; Feinblatt, Berman, and Sviridoff 1998). Interest in community courts has increased rapidly since then: the Portland Community Court (Oregon) opened in March 1998, and plans for community courts are underway in Atlanta, Austin (Tex.), Baltimore, Denver, Hartford (Conn.), Hempstead (N.Y.), Indianapolis, Memphis (Tenn.), Minneapolis, San Diego, St. Louis, West Palm Beach and Miami (Fla.), and no doubt elsewhere (see Center for Court Innovation web page at http://www.communitycourts.org). Initial funding has been available from Bureau of Justice Assistance community courts grants and the U.S. Justice Department's weed and seed grants.

The philosophy and practices of the Midtown Community Court are based on three community justice standpoints: broken windows theory, community empowerment, and problem solving. The court is located on Manhattan's west side and targets low-level, quality-of-life crimes such as prostitution, drug possession, vandalism, and graffiti. A community advisory committee, consisting of community residents, attorneys in neighborhood law firms, and administrators of local service providers, informs the court about neighborhood conditions and suggests new projects; it also keeps in touch with communities and offenders. A court ombudsman manages relations with local merchants, community groups, and elected officials (Feinblatt, Berman, and Sviridoff 1998).

The court combines punishment with help and is committed to addressing social problems. New partnerships were created, and most service providers are located at the court: the Department of Health, the Board of Education, the Department of Homeless Services, the Human Resources Administration, drug treatment providers, and nurse practitioners. A resource coordinator, stationed in the courtroom, helps match defendants with programs. The court organizes educational classes and job training, maintains mediation services for community-level conflicts, houses a health care area, and provides counseling rooms and space to perform community service. An outreach program sends a counselor from the court on patrol with local police officers—together they walk the streets and bring prostitutes, addicts, homeless, and other needy people voluntarily to the court to receive free services (Midtown Community Court 1997).

Nearly 75 percent of offenders are ordered to perform community work in neighborhoods and nearly 75 percent complete their work without violations. Neighborhood residents are encouraged to participate in shaping community sanctions and in identifying projects for community service. The court handles an average of sixty-five cases per workday, a total of more than 16,000 cases per year. The average time from arrest to arraignment is eighteen hours (Feinblatt, Berman, and Sviridoff 1998).

4. *Community (Justice) Corrections.*   In the majority of conceptions of "community corrections" or "community-based corrections," community is understood as a place; there are seldom suggestions that the community or community residents are in any other way significant as customers, partners, or actors. The two terms generally refer to sanctions served in communities instead of in prisons or jails—probation and parole are the oldest and most common of such sanctions. In the 1980s and 1990s, their use in the United States has increased almost

at the same pace as imprisonment, and there are steadily about three times as many offenders serving criminal sentences in the community as there are prisoners (e.g., Petersilia 1998).

Probation and parole were products of the positivist (sociological) school of criminology, which insisted on individualized treatment and sanctions and argued that government is responsible for and able to reform criminals to productive citizens. Between 1900 and 1925, the number of states with parole rose from a few to over forty, and probation was introduced in every state for juveniles and in over thirty states for adults (Dean-Myrda and Cullen 1998). Broad support for rehabilitation and treatment lasted until the early 1970s; prisons were considered stigmatizing institutions that isolated criminals from communities, and community corrections were portrayed as a solution to the inefficiency and inhumanity of the criminal justice system. Despite the strong belief in rehabilitation and reintegration, community corrections were in former times, as they are today, understaffed and underfunded, and as a consequence, programs often were poorly administered and implemented (Petersilia 1995, 1998). The President's Commission on Law Enforcement and Administration of Justice (1967, p. 399) suggested that improvement in the quality of community treatment should be a major goal for community-based corrections.

The function of community corrections changed rapidly in the political climate of the 1970s, when several reports concluded that most forms of treatment, rehabilitation, or integration programs were ineffective and failing. Community corrections has developed in two major ways since then. First, there are more options, including intensive supervision, day-reporting centers, electronic monitoring, home confinement, and community service. Second, the core function turned from rehabilitation ("social work") to law enforcement ("get-tough approaches"), which focuses on controlling offenders and minimizing their risk to communities (Clear and Braga 1995; Petersilia 1998, 1999). New sanctions may be part of the get-tough policies: they typically increase the control of offenders and are used in addition to other community-based sanctions (probation and parole), not instead of custodial sanctions (prisons or jails) (Tonry 1998).

As Dean-Myrda and Cullen (1998) put it, "Intermediate sanctions . . . would not be used to rehabilitate criminals, the chief goal of traditional community corrections, but rather would be used to supervise offenders closely and to punish them if they dared to depart from the law" (p. 14). Numerous studies point out that in current forms intermediate, community-based sanctions have not fulfilled their ambitions of recidivism reduction but have been most successful in catching offenders for minor technical violations (e.g., Tonry 1998). Some say probation became "prison-in-the-community" when the perspective shifted from rehabilitation and offender reintegration to incapacitation and deterrence (Leaf, Lurigio, and Martin 1998, p. 167).

The President's Commission on Law Enforcement and Administration of Justice (1967) saw a significantly different future for community-based corrections. The vision was to change the role of community corrections, to create closer relationships to the communities, and to mobilize community institutions to help offenders. The commission suggested that "much is to be gained by developing new work styles that reach out to community resources. . . . The officer of the future must be a link between the offender and community institutions; a mediator when there is trouble on the job or in school; an advocate of the offender when bureaucratic policies act irrationally to screen him out; a shaper and developer of new jobs, training, recreation, and other institutional resources" (p. 407). The commission also recommended that community corrections begin to rely on help from volunteer citizens in everyday operations.

In the 1990s, there were signs that the focus of community corrections might start shifting back to rehabilitation and reintegration and take a new turn toward community orientation. Sporadic moves toward community justice emerged in the literature and practices of community corrections. For example, in Chicago the aim was to return probation to its roots by creating a community-based probation center, Project Safeway. The main goals are to strengthen relationships with the community; to offer comprehensive services of treatment, education, skills development, and job placement; and to create permanent, positive changes in offenders' lives through personal, family, and neighborhood interventions. The project staff is required to create support networks throughout the community by visiting service providers, organizations, clubs, businesses, and churches. The project distributes a newsletter and has hosted special events for judges, politicians, business people, neighborhood residents, and offenders. A local advisory council includes neighborhood residents and business owners who identify needs for program development, communicate with the larger community, and recruit community volunteers to work with offenders (Leaf, Lurigio, and Martin 1998).

Deschutes County, Oregon, applies community justice principles throughout its corrections system. The Deschutes County Board of Commissioners passed a Community Justice Resolution in fall 1996. It recognizes "community justice as the central mission and purpose of the county's community corrections effort." The resolution calls for balance among crime prevention, early intervention, and correctional efforts; participation and restoration of victims; community decision making in crime prevention and reduction; and accountability of offenders. The Community Corrections Department was renamed the Department of Community Justice (see Maloney and Bryant 1998).

A lay citizen body, the Commission of Children and Families, has budget authority over the Community Justice Department's budget. The commission set specific budget principles for the department for the first time in fiscal year 1998–99. These included: enhance efforts that demonstrate accountability, responsibility, and skill development of offenders; incorporate findings of research about cost-effective interventions; focus on restoration and define offenders' accountability as fulfillment of obligations to victims and the community; stimulate volunteer involvement and reduce dependence on professional delivery; and manage crime problems in the most cost-effective manner, use reallocated resources to crime prevention, and view prevention investments as first order of business (see Maloney and Bryant 1998).

A community action team uses most of its time and resources for crime prevention in local neighborhoods. It helps establish neighborhood groups, seeks information about the needs of the neighborhoods, and delivers intervention programs (e.g., training for parents, after-school activities for kids, and behavioral change programs for risk groups).

A new community justice center is a facility for juveniles but also houses criminal justice agencies, victim assistant services, other nonprofit organizations, and a public meeting room for community groups. The department, if it uses fewer juvenile beds and money than are allocated by the state of Oregon, may use the savings on crime prevention initiatives. Citizens through the Commission on Children and Families are in charge of using funds.

Deschutes County provides victim-offender mediation in criminal cases and dispute resolution in other conflicts. Merchant accountability boards, consisting of local business owners, adjudicate low-level shoplifting cases. Reparative community service projects are run in cooperation among business owners, neighborhood residents, and community leaders. Offenders have built houses for Habitat for Humanity, cut and distributed firewood for elderly citizens, and built and maintained parks.

Cooperative initiatives between corrections and police are becoming common. They seem to fit under community justice as part of problem-solving efforts to build partnerships between criminal justice agencies. However, the typical goal is limited to enhanced supervision of offenders. Police and correctional officers supervise high-risk offenders jointly and share information in hopes that increased supervision will reduce new crimes and technical violations. Boston's Operation Nightlight is one of the best known police-corrections partnerships (see Clear and Karp 1999; Parent and Snyder 1999).

Community justice is a magic box for criminal justice agencies. Variety and flexibility in theoretical standpoints ensure that there is always something for everyone and that many kinds of things can be done under the community justice heading. Exactly for the same reason, community justice may in practice become a Pandora's box. For example, the domination of broken windows theory has led to practices that primarily increase formal control and law enforcement. Simple techniques such as aggressive arrest policies, street sweeps, and curfew laws are used to fix neighborhood decline and crime. However, it is easier to repair broken windows than to solve complex social problems.

While the theory and practices of community justice are vague, so is evidence of its results. Evaluations on community policing are not particularly encouraging. All we know about community prosecution, community courts, and community (justice) corrections is based on descriptive case studies or promotional literature that lack critical and evaluative aspects.

II. Restorative Justice

Restorative justice has evolved from the first victim-offender reconciliation programs in the early 1970s to a comprehensive approach toward crime. The goal is to create processes and responses that repair harm, heal parties, mend broken relationships, and build communities. Families, friends, supporters, and other community residents are involved in practices that include victim-offender mediation, family group conferencing, sentencing circles, and various types of citizen panels.

A. Principles of Restorative Justice

Despite the recent popularity of restorative justice, its intellectual history and development have received little attention. The first North

American victim-offender reconciliation program (VORP) was established in 1974 in Kitchener, Ontario, and the term "restorative justice" was probably used for the first time by Albert Eglash in a 1977 article (Eglash 1977; Zehr 1990; Van Ness and Heetderks Strong 1997). It is unclear how restorative justice developed from the social context of the 1960s or how it relates to other popular movements. Nevertheless, restorative justice is typically associated with various social movements or theories, for example, informal justice, the restitution movement, the victims' movement, the reconciliation/conferencing movement, and social justice (Van Ness and Heetderks Strong 1997); the civil rights movement, indigenous justice, the women's movement, and penal abolitionism (Immarigeon and Daly 1997, 1998; Bazemore 1998).

Restorative justice developed at the same time as many other grassroots movements that some political analysts call the new American populism (e.g., Boyte and Riessman 1986). The rhetoric of the new populism parallels that of restorative justice. "The essence of populism is ordinary people getting involved with others to collectively control their lives. . . . They are struggling for empowerment. Another feature of populism is its emphasis on traditional values like family, neighborhood, religion, and patriotism. . . . A third leg in the populist ideology is the emphasis on communitarian, cooperative, self-initiated activities emanating at the grass-roots level. This bottom-up participatory approach is rooted in American traditions and has been powerfully reactivated" (Riessman 1986, pp. 54–55). "All of this is expressed in the self-help movement with its anti-expertism, critique of professionalism, and concomitant respect of the average person" (Riessman 1986, p. 57). "The new populism usefully stresses the importance of community, both as an arena of action and as a critical building block in the democratic vision" (Ansara and Miller 1986, p. 147).

Some argue that the roots of restorative justice go back to Arab, Greek, and Roman civilizations and ancient Buddhist, Hindu, Taoist, Confucian, and Christian traditions (e.g., Braithwaite 1999). Many recognize that something akin to restorative justice was the dominant response to crime before centralized and organized state power and church, when victims' and offenders' families and, later, village meetings began to negotiate restitution agreements. Proponents view this history positively as an ideal of individualized and informal justice in which people handle their conflicts without state interference (e.g., Wright 1990; Zehr 1990; Weitekamp 1999).

Another underresearched area is the role of religion in the theory and practice of restorative justice. In North America, many of the most visible early supporters shared religious beliefs and were part of the faith community (Wright 1990; Zehr 1990; Van Ness and Heetderks Strong 1997). The first North American victim-offender reconciliation program was established by the Mennonite Central Committee workers. The Mennonite Central Committee promoted the idea, developed educational material, and trained primarily church-related groups in the late 1970s and early 1980s, and it continues to be a solid supporter of restorative justice (Coates 1990; Umbreit 1995b). For example, Zehr (1990, p. 173) states that "VORP embodies a vision of justice that is inherently biblical and thus provides an arena where the church can implement its vision." The Justice Fellowship (affiliated with Prison Fellowship Ministries) teaches "the Biblical principles of restorative justice" (Justice Fellowship 1999). Immarigeon and Daly (1997, p. 16) state that "the bedrock of restorative justice, in Canada and the U.S. at least, is religious and moral theory."

Many advocates believe in grassroots efforts and spontaneous citizen activity and want to keep restorative justice initiatives separate from the criminal justice system. They fear two things. First, they are afraid that criminal justice agencies will add new programs in order to look progressive and fashionable or to solve a particular crime problem—without fundamentally rethinking their missions (Zehr 1990; Van Ness 1993a; Umbreit and Carey 1995). Some are skeptical whether restorative justice goals and principles can meaningfully be adopted by bureaucratic criminal justice agencies, which tend to value passionless, specialized, professionalized, and routinized operations. Second, they fear that governmental agencies or experts will establish guidelines, standards, and requirements for restorative justice programs, thereby bureaucratizing them (Zehr 1990; Van Ness 1993a), and thus, once again, "steal the conflicts" from ordinary people and communities (Christie 1977). The challenge for government will be to encourage and provide support for the new initiatives without stifling the spontaneity, creativity, and grassroots ties that have been their strengths.

Most restorative justice advocates agree on five basic ideas (see, for definitions, Van Ness and Nolan 1998, apps. 1–3). First, crime consists of more than violation of the criminal law and defiance of the authority of government (Van Ness 1993a). Instead, and second, crime involves disruptions in a three-dimensional relationship among the victim, the offender, and the community (Van Ness and Heetderks Strong 1997; Braithwaite 1998). Third, crime harms the victim and the community, and the primary goals should be to restore the victim and the community, repair harms, and rebuild relationships among the victim, the offender, and the community (Wright 1990; Consedine 1995; Bazemore and Walgrave 1999). Fourth, the victim, the community, and the offender should all participate in determining what happens, and government should surrender its monopoly over responses to crime (Umbreit 1994; Pranis 1997). Fifth, the disposition should be based primarily on the victim's and the community's needs and not solely on the offender's needs or culpability, the dangers he presents, or his criminal history (Zehr 1990).

In short, restorative justice is about relationships—how relationships are harmed by crime and how they can be rebuilt to promote recovery and healing for people affected by crime (Pranis 1998*b*). Restorative justice respects equally victims and offenders, and this is why it cannot be seen as part of the victims rights' movement. The victims' movement has been used to justify more punishment: "Sympathy for crime victims has been increasingly (and successfully) used in recent years to generate a backlash against criminal offenders" (Fattah 1997, p. 263). Victims' and offenders' rights are balanced against each other and many successes of the movement have worked only in one direction: victim impact statements, victims' input in bail and parole decisions, community notification laws, and mandatory arrest policies have increased punishment and control (see Fattah 1997).

It may be true that the essence of restorative justice is more in its processes than in its outcomes. The victim, the community, and the offender are equally important in face-to-face meetings and all must agree on offenders' responsibilities. Outcomes, however, are often similar to those ordered by criminal justice agencies: community service, restitution, apologies, jail visits, alcoholics or narcotics anonymous, anger management, and the like. For example, Marshall (1996, p. 37) defines restorative justice as a process in which all the parties with a stake in an offense come together to resolve collectively how to deal with its aftermath and implications for the future.

The first restorative justice initiatives in the 1970s and 1980s were victim-offender reconciliation programs. They typically lacked community orientation and instead focused on restoring the harmony between victims and offenders. A recent development has been in thinking about the role of local communities and residents (McCold 1995; Bazemore and Griffiths 1997; Bazemore 1998). Community-based ideas emerged in the theory of restorative justice in the 1990s. Advocates began to identify community participation and development as an essential element of restorative justice (Pranis 1998*b*) and argued that a major community need should be considered: mechanisms to address and alter the existing social structures that cause crime (McCold 1995; Stuart 1996*c*; Braithwaite 1999). About the same time, new restorative practices surfaced. First, family members, other relatives, and friends were recognized as important supporters for victims and offenders. Family group conferences include them in the process to work out an agreement between the victim and the offender. Second, local residents can participate in determining responses to crime in sentencing circles and various types of citizen panels.

Empowerment of people and communities was the main ethos of the new populism and its movements, including community mediation. Neighborhood justice centers, community boards, community dispute resolution centers, and other mediation programs that focused on resolving conflicts between local residents emerged in the 1970s and spread rapidly in the 1980s (McGillis 1997). Many saw the individual case and its successful negotiation as a priority, but some clearly envisioned a broader social change—empowerment of participants and community building—as being at least as important a goal. For example, San Francisco community boards were described as a long-term social investment in the health and stability of individuals and communities. Development of neighborhoods and recruitment, organization, and training of volunteers was perhaps more important than delivery of mediation services (Merry and Milner 1993; Bush 1996). It will be interesting to know whether community mediation programs were able to empower citizens and develop communities, since many restorative justice practices now have similar goals.

A 1993 book reports results of a multiyear (1977–84) evaluation of the San Francisco community boards. Until then, no other study had tried to estimate or measure the impact of community mediation on the quality of life of communities (Lowry 1993). During the first six years, the San Francisco program received approximately 365 case referrals per year and trained over a thousand volunteers. However, the empowerment mission did not succeed: contributors to the evaluation were unable to document neighborhood building or improvement effects (DuBow and McEwen 1993). Local residents did not feel more attached to the neighborhood, their confidence in neighborhood improvement did not increase, and they did not fear crime less (Thomson and DuBow 1993). Instead, volunteers built their own internal community, felt a strong sense of belonging, and developed close relationships with each other. They reported that participation in the program was a significant feature in their lives and that the single most satisfying part of the work was the sense of community they felt (Lowry 1993).

In short, the San Francisco community boards were able to build a community of volunteer workers who felt attached to their neighborhoods but were unable to alter the average residents' relationships or commitment to their communities.

B. Practices of Restorative Justice

Evaluations of restorative justice practices tend to focus on completion and satisfaction issues—how often agreements are reached and completed and whether participants are satisfied with the process, the facilitator, the agreement, and each other's behavior. Reductions in fear of victimization are addressed sometimes, reductions in recidivism seldom, and cost savings or reductions in jail or prison use hardly ever. Typically, reports do not discuss potential differences based on demographic characteristics, for example, gender, race, and ethnic origin. Most evaluations focus on victim-offender mediation, although some exist on family-group conferencing. Literature on sentencing circles and citizen panels is descriptive and provides only anecdotal accounts of their success.

1. *Victim-Offender Mediation.* The first U.S. victim-offender mediation program was established in 1978 in Elkhart County, Indiana (Coates 1990). By the 1990s, victim-offender mediation programs had spread to all Western countries, and conservative estimates report at least seven hundred programs in Europe, three hundred in the United States, and twenty-six in Canada (Umbreit and Greenwood 1997). In some countries, they are an official part of the criminal justice system and available for juveniles and adults in all jurisdictions, such as in Austria and Germany (Löschnig-Gspandl and Kilchling 1997). Since 1985, Austrian public prosecutors have referred juveniles to mediation, probation officers coordinated cases, and social workers acted as mediators. If an agreement is reached and completed, the case is dismissed. In 1992, mediation was expanded to adults. By the end of 1997, more than 20,000 juvenile cases and 11,000 adult cases had been resolved by victim-offender mediation. The annual in 1997 was over 2,700 juvenile and 3,400 adult cases. In Germany, an estimated 6,000 juvenile and

3,000 adult cases were mediated in 1996 (Kilchling and Löschnig-Gspandl, forthcoming).

In other countries, victim-offender mediation may be in wide use but is unregulated and operates outside the judicial system, as in Finland, where organizing and training of volunteers is handled primarily by social service offices. Despite the lack of clear legal status, mediation projects existed in 1993 in at least 110 Finnish cities and communities and a total of 5,000 conflicts with 6,300 offenders were mediated (Lappi-Seppälä 1996). The number of offenders who participate in mediation in Finland is significant, which becomes evident when compared to the use of traditional sanctions: for example, 6,754 offenders received an unconditional prison sentence, 2,803 community service, and 13,624 a suspended (conditional) prison sentence in 1995 (Lappi-Seppälä 1998).

A phone survey of 116 victim-offender mediation programs in the United States, conducted by the Center for Restorative Justice and Mediation at the University of Minnesota School of Social Work (Umbreit and Greenwood 1997), reported that most of them are operated by private nonprofit organizations (43 percent community based and 23 percent church based), handle mostly juvenile cases, and function as diversion programs for low-level, first-time, nonviolent crimes. Misdemeanors constituted 67 percent and felonies 33 percent of all referrals. On average, 87 percent of cases resulted in an agreement and 99 percent of agreements were completed. About 35 percent of programs take cases in the beginning of the criminal justice process before offenders are charged, about 30 percent divert cases during the process before a final disposition, and about 30 percent are postadjudication programs. Although private organizations handle most mediation programs, there is a movement toward development of victim-offender mediation programs established and operated (or at least initiated) by correctional departments, police, or prosecutors and used as a condition of probation or dropping charges.

Unlike in the United States, victim-offender mediation is used for more serious crimes in other countries. For example, in Germany, about 70 percent of both adult and juvenile cases mediated in 1995 were violent crimes. Similarly in Austria, 73 percent of adult and 43 percent of juvenile cases were violent crimes in 1996 (Kilchling and Löschnig-Gspandl, forthcoming). In the United States, it is more likely that serious crimes are mediated inside prisons. These meetings are not oriented to a tangible goal, such as an agreement on restitution or community service, and the offender does not gain benefits in early release or parole consideration. Usually the victim wants to meet the offender and to learn more about what happened in order to reach beyond fear and anger and to facilitate healing (Umbreit 1995*a*, pp. 148–54; Flaten 1996; Immarigeon 1996). A Canadian survey found that 89 percent of victims of serious violent crimes wanted to meet the offender in a safe environment and only 11 percent would have refused to meet the offender in any circumstances (cited in Gustafson 1997). Serious violent crimes are usually mediated on a case-by-case basis, but there is growing need for permanent programs. Such programs are offered, for example, by the Correctional Service of Canada in British Columbia and the Yukon Territory and by the Texas Department of Criminal Justice.

Although victims and offenders meet to work out a restitution agreement, reaching an agreement is often seen as secondary to emotional healing and growth. Victims consistently report that the most important element of mediation is to be able to talk with the offender and to express their feelings. Also, offenders report that being able to tell what happened is often more important than the restitution agreement (e.g., Umbreit 1994; Umbreit 1995*b;* Umbreit and Warner Roberts 1996).

Most advocates see the value of restorative justice in the healing that takes place during mediation and in repairing victims' harms. Many believe that developing an offender's empathy for the victim has individual preventive effects and reduces subsequent criminal behavior. However, whether mediation saves money, reduces recidivism, or widens the net of the criminal justice system is secondary for most activists. Some are concerned that restorative justice approaches cannot achieve promises and expectations that are often unrealistic (e.g., Young and Goold 1999). These are among reasons why many evaluations ignore standard measures used in other criminal justice program evaluations (e.g., Umbreit and Bradshaw 1997).

That victims, offenders, volunteers, and communities are satisfied and happy with restorative practices is a legitimate end in itself, but only if there are no unacceptable negative consequences. Harm may be done if offenders going through mediation are more likely to commit new crimes than similarly situated offenders going through the regular criminal process. More harm may be done if mediation is used for minor crimes or in addition to traditional criminal sanctions.

If cases are mediated, there is no question about short-term success:

the vast majority of victims and offenders are satisfied with the process and outcomes, an agreement is reached in practically all cases, and the vast majority of restorative plans are fulfilled by offenders. The results are similar in the earlier and more recent studies, in juvenile and adult programs, and in U.S. and international evaluations. Satisfaction, agreement, and completion rates typically vary between 75 and 100 percent.

However, it is possible that these outcomes are largely the result of selection effects: if control groups are used, they are usually matched comparison groups and only rarely are based on random assignments. Many cases that are initially referred to programs are never mediated because the victim or the offender refused to participate or could not be contacted. For example, 53 percent of victims from six programs in Indiana, Wisconsin, and Oregon refused to meet the offender (Gehm 1990); 40 percent of cases in the Orange County, California, juvenile program were not mediated (Niemeyer and Shichor 1996); 39 percent of referrals in four Canadian programs were not mediated (Umbreit 1995b); and 44 percent of referred crimes against acquaintances in the Brooklyn Dispute Resolution Center were not mediated (Davis, Tichane, and Grayson 1980).

Besides satisfaction, victims are typically asked whether mediation reduced their anxiety and fear of the offender or of crime in general. Davis, Tichane, and Grayson (1980) report that victims in the mediation group were less likely to fear revenge (21 percent) than victims in a random control group (40 percent). They were also less angry at the offenders (23 percent vs. 48 percent). Other studies have found similar results. For example, an evaluation of four Canadian programs found that only 11.2 percent of victims feared revictimization by the same offender, but 53 percent of victims were still upset about the crime after mediation (Umbreit 1995b). Similarly, 16 percent of victims were afraid of further victimization in two English programs (Umbreit and Warner Roberts 1996). In four U.S. juvenile programs, 67 percent of victims were upset about crime before and 49 percent after mediation; 23 percent were afraid of revictimization before and 10 percent after mediation (Umbreit and Coates 1992; Umbreit 1994).

Many suspect that immediate positive experiences of mediation fade away with time and cannot affect future offending. Results of a handful of evaluations are mixed, but the most common conclusion is that mediation has no statistically significant effect on recidivism. Although more research is needed, current evaluations show that mediation neither decreases nor increases recidivism. To my knowledge, there is only one U.S. study based on random sampling: Davis, Tichane, and Grayson's (1980) evaluation of the Brooklyn Dispute Resolution Center. However, this initiative was in many significant ways an atypical mediation program: only crimes against acquaintances were mediated, most of the cases were felonies, and the majority of cases involved immediate family members or lovers with a history of interpersonal problems between them. After cases were approved for mediation, they were randomly assigned to an experimental group, which went through mediation, and a control group, which went through ordinary criminal procedure.

All participants were interviewed after a four-month follow-up period and asked, among other things, about continuing interpersonal problems, calling for police, and new arrests. The main conclusion was that hostility and conflicts between disputants declined, but there was basically no difference between the mediation group and the court group. Police were called to resolve new conflicts in 12 percent of mediation cases and 13 percent of court cases. The share of new arrests (either party of the original conflict) was 4 percent in both groups.

Recidivism studies that used matched control groups include Schneider (1986), Umbreit and Coates (1992, 1993), Roy (1993), Umbreit (1994), Nugent and Paddock (1995), and Niemeyer and Shichor (1996). All programs were for juveniles, but from different parts of the country: Albuquerque, New Mexico, Austin, Texas, Minneapolis/St. Paul, and Oakland, California (Umbreit and Coates 1992, 1993; Umbreit 1994); Elkhart County, Indiana (Roy 1993); Anderson County, Tennessee (Nugent and Paddock 1995); and Orange County, California (Niemeyer and Shichor 1996).

Besides Nugent and Paddock (1995), none of the other studies found that mediation had significantly reduced reoffending. Recidivism rates were around 20–30 percent for both mediation and control groups. However, there was evidence in some studies that mediation may have delayed recidivism. Niemeyer and Shichor (1996) report that a larger proportion of the mediation group was arrested in the second year of the follow-up period than in the first year.

Although evaluations of victim-offender mediation programs are common, we still know little about important questions. For example, recidivism has been measured only in juvenile programs. Whether mediation has more or less effect on adult recidivism has not been investigated. Another neglected area is the effect of demographic characteristics on results. Combined evaluations exist of programs that had very different racial demographics. For example, in Umbreit and Coates's (1992, 1993) analysis, offenders in the first program were 65 percent Hispanic, in the second 25 percent black and 42 percent Hispanic, and in the third 70 percent white. One might expect that race is a significant factor in the satisfaction and success of mediation programs, in the same way it is a significant factor in every phase of the official criminal justice system. However, all U.S. studies have neglected race in the analysis: although reported in descriptions of offender and victim characteristics, it is not carried to the results. The same problem in reporting applies to other demographic characteristics, including gender.

2. *Family Group Conferencing.* There are two main differences between family group conferencing and victim-offender mediation. First, conferencing involves a broader range of people and family members, and supporters tend to take collective responsibility over the offender and fulfillment of his or her agreement. Thus conferencing may be more effective in creating positive community involvement, rebuilding relationships, and preventing future offending. Second, conferencing relies more often on official agencies and police, probation, or social officers often organize and facilitate conferences.

In 1989, New Zealand introduced a new juvenile justice model that shares basic principles with restorative justice (the Children, Young Persons and Their Families Act 1989); the juvenile justice system deals with offenders aged fourteen to seventeen years. The goal was to create a culturally sensitive and appropriate criminal process, incorporating Maori traditions of involving the family and the community in addressing wrongdoing (on Maori and Australian Aboriginal traditions, see Consedine 1995). The reorganized system relies heavily on informal sanctions and one of the main goals was to divert juveniles from courts to avoid criminal records and labeling. It includes four dispositional options: an immediate police warning; "youth aid section" dispositions in which a special police unit may require, for example, an apology to the victim or community service; family group conferencing organized by the department of social welfare; and juvenile court sentencing. Family group conferences operate as diversions at the pretrial stage, but they may also be ordered to produce sentencing recommendations for the youth court (Maxwell and Morris 1993, 1994, 1997; Morris, Maxwell, and Robertson 1993; McElrea 1998).

In the first full year of implementation in 1990, about 60 percent of juvenile offenders received an immediate police warning or went to the youth aid section, about 30 percent to family group conferencing, and about 10 percent to the youth court (Maxwell and Morris 1993). Conferences are facilitated by a youth justice coordinator and ideally include the victim and the offender and their families and supporters, a police officer, a social worker, and the offender's lawyer (the youth advocate), if so requested. At least in the beginning, the practice did not meet the ideal: only 41 percent of victims attended conferences and lawyers were present in 59 percent of court-ordered conferences (Maxwell and Morris 1994). However, most victims would have liked to participate in conferencing, but were unable to do so because they were not invited (37 percent of those who did not attend), the· time was unsuitable (29 percent), or the notice came too late (18 percent). Only 6 percent did not want to meet the offender (Morris, Maxwell, and Robertson 1993).

Fewer juveniles went to the youth court and prisons after the new system took effect. In the 1980s, the number of cases in the youth court varied between 10,300 and nearly 13,000 or from fifty-seven to seventy-two per thousand. In 1990, the figure had dropped to 2,587 cases, or sixteen per thousand (Maxwell and Morris 1993). Juvenile admissions to prisons fell over 60 percent from 173 in 1989 to sixty-four in 1990, and although admissions have since increased slightly (eighty-one in 1996), they still are less than half of the prereform levels (McElrea 1998).

By the mid-1990s, family group conferences were adopted in various forms in every state and territory of Australia. In South Australia, conferencing is used statewide as a component of the juvenile justice system, and it resembles the New Zealand approach (Wundersitz 1994). In Wagga Wagga, New South Wales, conferences were originally part of a police diversion program and were organized and facilitated by police officers, often in uniforms (Moore and O'Connell 1994). In Western Australia, conferences are the main strategy of the youth justice teams, a diversionary step between police cautioning and courts consisting of a youth justice coordinator, police officer, education officer, and Aboriginal community worker (Alder and Wundersitz 1994). In Canberra (Australian Capital Territory), the Australian federal police set up a conferencing program based on the Wagga Wagga model with over one hundred trained police officers, the "Reintegrative Shaming Experiment" (RISE) (e.g., Sherman et al. 1998).

Theoretical frameworks, objectives, bureaucratic positioning, and severity of offenses vary in each of the settings (e.g., Alder and Wundersitz 1994). For example, in New Zealand and Western Australia, cultural sensitivity and involvement of Maori and Aboriginal people in planning and decision making were important concerns. The Wagga Wagga and Canberra conferencing programs rely heavily on Braithwaite's theory of reintegrative shaming (Braithwaite 1989; Braithwaite and Mugford 1994; Moore and O'Connell 1994). The South Australian juvenile justice system was introduced as a way to ensure that young people are held accountable, to increase the severity and range of penalties, to enhance the role of the police, and to make families more responsible for their children's behavior (Wundersitz 1994; Wundersitz and Hetzel 1996). Family group conferencing may be used for severe and repeat crimes in New Zealand, where only murder and manslaughter are statutorily ineligible. The Australian approaches are typically limited to minor crimes, for example, in Western Australia and the Northern Territory, to first-time offenders.

The original Wagga Wagga and later the Canberra police conferencing model have particularly influenced family group conferencing in the United States, Canada, and England (Umbreit and Zehr 1996; Jackson 1998; Dignan 1999). More than 2,000 law enforcement and probation officers and volunteers have been trained in family group conferencing by Real Justice, a nonprofit organization in Pennsylvania.

While family group conferencing is gaining more support in the United States and spreading, an increasing number of critics are pointing out problems of implementation in Australia: suitability of reintegrative shaming as the theoretical background, concentration of power and discretion in the police, ignorance of indigenous traditions and values, and discrimination in practice (Sandor 1994; White 1994; Blagg 1997, 1998; Cunneen 1997). All these aspects are handled differently in the New Zealand approach.

First, conferences in New Zealand are not portrayed as a chance for collective shaming that has a positive and reintegrative purpose in contrast to denigrative and stigmatizing shaming by the retributive criminal justice system (Braithwaite 1989). Rather, conferences are presented as a chance for the victims, offenders, and communities to be empowered and to repair broken relationships (Maxwell and Morris 1993, 1994). When people meet and establish personal connections, they are less likely to disappoint or harm each other. The offender is less likely to break the victim's and community's trust by violating his or her agreement. The concept of reintegrative shaming is problematic for pure practical reasons—there are examples of people who forget the reintegrative part and remember the shaming part.

Second, conferences in New Zealand are organized and facilitated by youth justice coordinators hired by the department of welfare. The most severe critique has been against those Australian approaches that allow police officers to determine which cases go to conferences, to organize and facilitate meetings, and, in some cases, to veto the agreement reached by other participants (e.g., Sandor 1994; Blagg 1997). Such a supplementation and extension of police powers raises questions of neutrality and impartiality in any case, but especially in situations where the Aboriginal people and youth already have suspicious and hostile relations with police (e.g., Cunneen and McDonald 1997). In addition, the New Zealand Children, Young Persons and Their Families Act strictly restricted police powers to stop, question, search, and detain young people. Such limitations were not introduced at the same time as the Australian family group conferences (Blagg 1997, p. 485).

Third, some argue that conferencing in Australia has been "an add-on feature to more punitive changes in juvenile justice legislation" that occurred at the same time penalties were increased for more serious offenses and mandatory and indeterminate sentences created for repeat offenders (Cunneen 1997, p. 296; Yeats 1997). Conferencing was introduced with Aboriginal friendly terms, yet many agree that there was little negotiation with or input by the Aboriginal people. Police are less likely to refer Aboriginal youth to conferences than whites, and they and their parents are less likely to participate. Critics claim that indigenous people have benefited little from conferencing; for example, the incarceration rate for indigenous youth rose by 24 percent between 1993 and 1996, and by 5 percent for the nonindigenous youth (Cunneen 1997).

Responsibility for conferencing in New South Wales, including Wagga Wagga, was transferred to juvenile justice agencies in 1998, and trained community members now facilitate conferences. To modify the exclusive police power to determine referrals to conferences, prosecutors and courts were authorized to initiate conferencing and a presumption in favor of conferencing was extended to a larger number of offenses.

Advocates of restorative justice in the United States have pointed out the potential dangers of adapting the original Wagga Wagga police conferencing model. Among other things, they are concerned that many adults present at conferences, including police and parents, will dominate discussions and decision making, that police officers may fall into authoritarian leadership patterns and conferences become shaming and blaming experiences for kids, and that programs will select easy cases that would not otherwise have gone through the criminal justice system (Umbreit and Zehr 1996). Experiences of restorative police cautioning in England by the Thames Valley police show that police officers often dominated meetings and young offenders contributed little to discussions (police officers' questions and comments accounted for 58–70 percent of the words spoken). In addition, observers concluded that reintegrative shaming of offenders was sometimes too intense: "In our view the emphasis we saw in Aylesbury on 'promoting behavioural change' was sometimes excessive. Most young offenders do not 'need' the strong deterrent messages communicated. . . . Moreover, when harm was exaggerated [by police], or too much remorse expected, the intended additional deterrent effect may have been offset or even outweighed by the sense of unfairness" (Young and Goold 1999, p. 138).

The concept and models of family group conferencing are reasonably new and evolving. Descriptive client satisfaction evaluations exist from New Zealand (Maxwell and Morris 1993), Wagga Wagga, New South Wales (Moore 1995), and Minnesota (Umbreit and Fercello 1997; Fercello and Umbreit 1998). More sophisticated studies with comparison groups include a multiyear project of the Canberra, Australian Capital Territory, police conferencing (Sherman and Barnes 1997; Sherman and Strang 1997a, 1997b; Strang and Sherman 1997; Harris and Burton 1998; Sherman et al. 1998) and the Bethlehem, Pennsylvania, police conferencing (McCold and Wachtel 1998).

The initial evaluation of the New Zealand family group conferencing raised concerns about the satisfaction and involvement of the victims and juveniles: victims participated in 41 percent of meetings; 51 percent of victims who participated were pleased with the process and agreement, one-third felt better after conferencing, one-third felt worse; 34 percent of juveniles felt involved in the conferencing process, and only 9 percent thought they were able to influence outcomes. Yet juveniles and their parents were satisfied with the outcomes (over 80 percent) (Maxwell and Morris 1993).

More recent evaluations of practices elsewhere show very high satisfaction rates for all participants. A study of the Wagga Wagga conferencing reports that victim participation exceeded 90 percent, participants felt involved in the process and satisfied with the outcomes, and an agreement was reached in 95 percent of conferences and completed in 95 percent of cases (Moore 1995). In twelve Minnesota sites, over 90 percent of victims, juveniles, and support persons were satisfied with the facilitator, progress, and outcomes (Fercello and Umbreit 1998).

Evaluation of the Bethlehem, Pennsylvania, Police Family Group Conferencing is the first completed study on conferencing that is based on random assignment and measures recidivism (McCold and Wachtel 1998). The eligibility was limited to first-time juvenile offenders who were arrested for misdemeanor and summary offenses. Since participation in conferencing was voluntary, three different groups of juveniles emerged: those randomly assigned to formal adjudication, those randomly assigned to conferencing who participated, and those randomly assigned to conferencing who refused to participate. Conferences were conducted in only 42 percent of the cases selected for conferencing because offenders or victims refused to participate. Thus the problem of selection bias was not avoided by random sampling.

The Bethlehem study reports that over 90 percent of victims, offenders, and offenders' parents would recommend conferencing to others, would choose conferencing again, found meeting with the other parties helpful, felt they were treated fairly, and thought that the tone of the conference was friendly. Victims felt their opinion was adequately considered (94 percent), and offenders developed a positive attitude toward the victim (80 percent), had a better understanding of how their behavior had affected the victim (94 percent), and found conferencing a more humane response to crime (92 percent) (McCold and Wachtel 1998).

The Bethlehem evaluation followed recidivism for a twelve-month period following the arrest that led to adjudication or conferencing. Like the majority of victim-offender mediation evaluations, it concluded that conferencing had no independent influence on reoffending. The difference in recidivism between the conference group and control groups was more a function of the offender's positive attitude toward conferencing than conferencing itself (McCold and Wachtel 1998). The study reports that typical American police officers were able to conduct conferences in conformity with restorative justice and due process principles if given adequate training and supervision. However, the exposure of few officers to restorative justice principles and community involvement did not change overall police attitudes, organizational culture, or role perceptions in the Bethlehem police department.

The Canberra Reintegrative Shaming Experiment is a large multi-year project that evaluates family group conferencing ("diversionary conferencing") by the Australian federal police. The RISE project is expected to work better than the current criminal justice system in three different ways: conferences treat victims and offenders more fairly than courts, conferences lower recidivism, and conferences cost less money. Data and results concerning fairness of conferencing are available, but data collection concerning recidivism and costs is not yet complete (Sherman et al. 1998).

Data on fairness and client satisfaction were collected by systematic observation (coded indications of stigmatizing and reintegrative shaming, participation in discussions, domination, disapproval, apologies, forgiveness, and so on by trained observants) and interviews with participants. The analysis consists of four different groups of cases: drunk driving (any age), juvenile property crime with an individual victim (under eighteen), juvenile shoplifting from stores (under eighteen), and violent crime (under thirty). Offenders in each group were randomly assigned to conferencing or courts (Sherman et al. 1998). Only brief summaries of some of the results are possible here.

The RISE observations show the fundamental difference between restorative justice and traditional criminal justice approaches: face-to-face meetings in a setting where everyone has equal freedom to talk are more humane and emotionally intensive than structured court sessions dominated by legal professionals. Observations show that any kind of shaming, whether reintegrative or stigmatizing, seldom occurs at courts. In conferences, participants are the main actors. They are the ones who talk, express concerns, and try to find appropriate responses to the crime. Other problems and worries are regularly discussed besides the offense.

The RISE evaluation shows that in general victims and offenders were pleased with conferencing and its outcomes. However, the report failed to address some differences between the four categories of crime. First, victims of violent crime were less satisfied with conferencing than were victims of property crime. For example, 96 percent of property crime victims compared to 73.7 percent of violent crime victims thought that the conference had been fair. None of the property crime victims felt too intimidated to speak, but 15.8 percent of violent crime victims did. While 91.7 percent of property crime victims thought conferences took account of their opinions in the decision, only 63.2 percent of violent crime victims thought so. However, all victims were less angry with the offender after conferences; the percentage of victims being angry fell from 52 to 28 percent in the property crime group and from 63.2 to 36.8 percent in the violent crime group (Sherman et al. 1998).

Second, the predominantly adult drunk drivers were the most satisfied (generally over 90 percent) and juvenile property offenders the least satisfied with conferencing. Only 55.9 of those juveniles thought they had some control over the outcome, 26.5 percent felt too intimidated to speak, and none of the procedural justice measures (Sherman et al. 1998, table 5.18) were statistically significantly higher in the conference group than in the court group. It is also worth noting that about one-third of the violent offenders thought they were pushed around by others with power in conferences and about one-fourth felt they were pushed to do things they did not agree with. Unfortunately, we do not know more about the offenders who felt intimidated or powerless. Although the evaluation gives detailed characteristics of victims and offenders, for example, by gender, ethnic origin, place of birth, marital status, and employment, none of these is reported with the results. While there is widespread concern about the unequal treatment of Aboriginal people in diversion programs, including family group conferencing, it is unclear why this important aspect was ignored.

Second wave interviews with offenders two years after they entered the RISE study did not show significant differences between the conference groups and court groups in life events (e.g., school attendance or graduation, unemployment, homelessness, divorce, or serious troubles with others) (Strang et al. 1999).

3. *Sentencing Circles.* Sentencing circles represent the evolution of restorative justice to include local residents in decision making in order to empower and develop communities. Sentencing circles involve the victim and the offender and their supporters, but also key community members, and are open to everyone in the community. According to Stuart (1996c), the primary objective is to achieve "real differences in the behaviour, attitudes, life style and conditions of all parties, and to make real differences in the well-being of the immediate personal and geographic communities affected by crime" (p. 3).

Circles are typically organized in two different ways. First, individual judges may refer cases to circle sentencing; the agreements reached are then sentencing recommendations for them. Second, the judge, prosecutor, and defense attorney may participate in the sentencing circle; the agreement is then the final sentence. In both cases, a community committee, established by volunteer citizens, makes the final decision of acceptance to the circle, but the criteria for acceptance and details of the circle process vary in each community (see Stuart 1996*a*, 1997).

Sentencing circles have their origin in traditional Native Canadian and American peacemaking and healing processes (see, e.g., Yazzie and Zion 1996; Aboriginal Corrections Policy Unit 1997). Participants sit in a circle and a "talking piece" is passed around. The person with the talking piece explains his or her feelings about the crime and expresses support for the victim and the offender. A successful circle needs lots of preparation and is time consuming—separate healing circles often are held for the offender and the victim before they join in a shared circle. The process is based on peacemaking, negotiation, and consensus and each circle member must agree on the outcomes (e.g., Stuart 1996*b*).

Judge Barry Stuart from the Yukon Territory, Canada, was among the first criminal justice officials who became interested in aboriginal circle processes. The initial sentencing circles were held in the early 1980s, and they have been used regularly in several communities in the Yukon since 1991 (Stuart 1996*a*). Sentencing circles are more than experimental or occasional practices in other Canadian communities, for example, in Saskatchewan, Manitoba, and Quebec (see Green 1997). Sentencing circles are one of several community-oriented approaches underway in Canada. Aboriginal justice initiatives that are based on community volunteerism and attempt to reduce incarceration, enhance community development, increase native direction and control over justice matters, and deal with broad social problems are increasingly challenging the traditional criminal justice system (e.g., Gosse, Youngblood Henderson, and Carter 1994; Clairmont 1996). In 1993, the government received 125 proposals from aboriginal communities for diversion projects, including sentencing circles, healing circles, community justice committees, advisory sentencing boards, elders' sentencing panels, and the like (Clairmont 1996).

In the United States, sentencing circles are used in eight Native American, rural white, suburban, and inner-city black communities in Minnesota (see Kurki 1999). These communities have established community justice committees, which consist of key volunteer citizens, handle organizational and administrative tasks, and usually provide "keepers" for circles.

Sentencing circles differ in many ways from family group conferencing. First, the vast majority of family group conferencing programs are limited to juvenile offenders. Sentencing circles are regularly used for both juvenile and adult offenders. Second, except in New Zealand, eligibility for family group conferencing is typically restricted to minor crimes, often excluding violent and sexual crimes. Similar restrictions apply to sentencing circles in Minnesota, but in Canada they have been used for all kinds of crimes ranging from underage drinking to sexual assault and manslaughter. Thus admission to a circle does not exclude a jail or prison sentence, although punishments usually are community based, such as house arrest, community service, residential treatment, or restrictions in privileges (Stuart 1996a). Third, sentencing circles are more effective in involving the community. While family group conferencing is regularly organized and facilitated by police or other governmental agencies, the responsibility for running circles is solely on the volunteer community members. In addition, sentencing circles involve many more local people in the actual meetings—it is not unheard of to have over sixty people participate in one circle.

When one talks with people who are actively involved in circle processes, something happens. One cannot avoid being affected by their passion, dedication, and sincere belief that what they are doing is good. There are many touching stories of success. However, written descriptions of practices and cases are not equally powerful, not enough to convince most people, and not enough to show that sentencing circles work better than traditional criminal justice approaches. We need more information, and it is time for sentencing circle processes to be evaluated (see also Roberts and LaPrairie 1996).

4. *Reparative Probation and Other Citizen Boards.* Various types of citizen boards or panels are used in the United States and Canada to produce dispositions for minor crimes. Adult citizen panels are adjudicating nonviolent crimes in many U.S. juvenile court jurisdictions (e.g., in Denver, Austin, and Philadelphia); offenders appear before a small panel of fellow community members in several Canadian aboriginal and nonaboriginal communities (Clairmont 1996; Green 1997); local downtown neighborhoods have organized their own citizen conferencing in Minneapolis, and reparative citizen board members and offenders in Vermont agree on a contract that is the only condition of probation (Gorczyk and Perry 1997).

In Vermont, reparative citizen boards heard their first cases in spring 1995. The boards are part of reparative probation in which a judge sentences the offender to probation with a suspended sentence, volunteer board members (five to seven) meet with the offender and the victim, and together they agree on a contract, which the offender agrees to carry out. Fulfillment of the contract is the only condition of probation (Dooley 1996; Gorczyk and Perry 1997; Sinkinson and Broderick 1997; Walther and Perry 1997). The contract is based on five restorative goals: the victim is restored and healed, the community is restored, the offender understands the effects of the crime, the offender learns ways to avoid reoffending, and the community offers reintegration to the offender.

In 1998, forty-four reparative boards handled 1,200 criminal cases, more than one-third of the targeted probation caseload. Currently, over three hundred trained volunteers participate as board members (information provided by the Vermont Department of Corrections). Ten reparative coordinators, hired by the Department of Corrections, are in charge of case management and organization for the boards. The Department of Corrections estimates that around 17 percent of offenders fail to complete their agreements or to show up at follow-up meetings of the boards. These offenders are referred back to courts for sentencing. The goal is to increase the number of boards, volunteers, and case referrals until about 70 percent of targeted probation cases are handled by reparative boards.

Vermont's program is different from most restorative justice initiatives in the United States. It was designed by the Vermont Department of Corrections, it is implemented statewide, it handles adult cases, and it involves a sizable number of citizen volunteers (over three hundred board members). Recently, the department has focused on improving the quality of the process, for example, by revising the training curriculum and beginning systematic observations of board meetings.

The restorative resolutions project in Manitoba, Canada, is a community-based alternative to incarceration and ideally offenders, staff, and victims together develop sentencing recommendations for judges. During the first eighteen months, all sentencing plans suggested community service as a condition of probation (type or amount was not identified), 61 percent required restitution, and 89 percent included some form of personal counseling or therapy. Judges accepted the recommended plans in 81 percent of cases (Richardson, Galaway, and Joubert 1996).

A more recent evaluation covers the restorative resolutions program from its inception to May 9, 1997 (approximately three years and eight months), and includes estimates on recidivism (Bonta, Rooney, and Wallace-Capretta 1998). During this period, the program received 297 referrals, 120 sentencing plans were submitted to the court, and 99 plans (82.5 percent of submitted plans) were accepted. The average sentence was probation of 28.5 months, supplemented with specified requirements of sentencing plans. The evaluation indicates that the project followed restorative justice principles more effectively than regular probation in Manitoba, since sentencing plans were more likely to include restitution (56.4 percent vs. 24.9 percent) and community service (96 percent vs. 13.8 percent). Two major problems existed in implementation, though. First, although the project staff managed to contact 83.9 percent of victims, only 10.3 percent of them (twenty-five) actually met with the offender. However, 78.6 percent of victims provided written impact statements and seventy-nine victims received personal or written apologies. Second, nearly 20 percent of offenders received a custodial sentence before the placement to the project—a net-widening problem witnessed in other diversion programs as well (Bonta, Rooney, and Wallace-Capretta 1998).

In order to examine recidivism, the study used two different measures and three different control groups. The measures were defined as any new conviction with a custodial disposition (conviction) and any new arrests or convictions or violations of supervision (violation). The control groups were matched groups of male prison inmates, female and male probationers, and female and male probationers who had either restitution or community service as a condition of probation. Compared with the inmate group, the male offenders in restorative resolutions had significantly fewer violations (16.7 percent vs. 37 percent) and slightly fewer convictions (6.7 percent vs. 16.7 percent; not statistically significant). They also had significantly fewer supervision violations than probationers in general (16.7 percent vs. 48.6 percent) or probationers with community service or restitution (14.1 percent vs. 56.3 percent). Calculations of phi coefficients showed that the restorative resolutions project can be expected to reduce overall recidivism by 13 percent (the inmate group) to 22 percent (probationers with community service or restitution) (Bonta, Rooney, and Wallace-Capretta 1998). The project will be extended to parole, and the restorative parole project will begin to develop parole release plans for offenders in 1999.

III. Critiques of Restorative and Community Justice

There are three main objections that apply to both restorative and community justice: vagueness of the concept and practices, lack of knowledge of effects and results, and impairment of procedural safeguards.

A. Problems of Restorative Justice

Proponents have not been particularly clear about what kind of practices constitute restorative justice, and the recent popularity of community justice and intermediate and community-based sanctions has contributed to the confusion. Opponents ask how restorative justice practices differ from the rehabilitative idea of individualized sentences, diversionary strategies that are used in juvenile and adult courts, and intermediate sanctions that fall between prison and regular probation (e.g., Feld 1999). In these murky areas, it becomes more and more important to emphasize the principles of restorative justice.

Some proponents have been perhaps too eager to claim that restorative justice efforts can solve complex social problems and prevent crime (e.g., Stuart 1996c; Braithwaite 1999). We know too little to suggest that restorative justice can change behavioral patterns, foster moral growth, empower individuals, create safer communities, and thus remove causes of crime (Roberts and LaPrairie 1996; LaPrairie 1998). Although we know that face-to-face meetings are more humane and emotionally intensive than structured trials dominated by legal professionals (Sherman et al. 1998), there is not yet evidence that the positive experience transfers to better results. Qualitative improvements are difficult to measure. There have been too few efforts to estimate traditional measures, such as recidivism, crime, and victimization rates, and to create new measures to estimate community involvement, empowerment, and crime prevention.

We know that the majority of victims, offenders, and their supporters are pleased and happy with restorative justice practices. However, existing evaluations do not show effects on recidivism or crime rates. Recidivism in restorative justice programs is not significantly lower or higher than recidivism in traditional criminal justice programs, although the restorative resolutions project in Manitoba was able to reduce new violations, arrests, and convictions (Bonta, Rooney, and Wallace-Capretta 1998).

Restorative justice practices do not provide procedural safeguards (Levrant et al. 1999). Offenders may have lawyers present in some programs, but typically the only right is to withdraw from the program and instead choose the regular criminal justice process. There are legitimate concerns about power balances in face-to-face meetings—unequal treatment of indigenous people and minorities and the position of young offenders who are vulnerable and less skilled to defend and represent themselves (Orlando 1992; White 1994; Umbreit and Zehr 1996; Blagg 1997, 1998; Cunneen 1997; Feld 1999). For example, in the RISE project in Canberra, approximately one-third of the young offenders thought they lacked control over the outcome or felt too intimidated to speak (Sherman et al. 1998). In New Zealand, 84 percent of juveniles were pleased with the outcomes of family group conferences, but only 34 percent felt involved and 9 percent thought they were able to decide outcomes (Maxwell and Morris 1993). In the Thames Valley experiment in England, police officers dominated discussions by accounting for 58–70 percent of the words spoken (Young and Goold 1999).

However, there is no evidence that the traditional criminal justice system does a better job, and many are convinced that it does a worse one (e.g., Stuart 1996c; Sherman et al. 1998; Braithwaite 1999). Juveniles are unlikely to feel more powerful or comfortable among legal professionals, and indigenous people and minorities are overrepresented in jails and prisons and underrepresented in diversion programs all over the world.

The most severe critique against restorative justice comes from lawyers and researchers who support just desert or structured sentencing approaches (von Hirsch and Ashworth 1992, 1998, chap. 7; Ashworth 1993; Roberts and LaPrairie 1996; Feld 1999; see also Van Ness 1993b). Just deserts and sentencing guidelines were responses to problems of rehabilitative, indeterminate sentencing, and critics view restorative justice as a step backward to unfair, unequal, individualized sentencing. However, as Tonry (1999) points out, sentencing systems have already fragmented in the United States. Even those states that have sentencing guidelines (about twenty) have abandoned strict proportionality requirements by implementing mandatory minimum, three-strikes, and sexual predator laws. Restorative justice would mean a big step toward uncertain and inconsistent sentences if the baseline were certain and equal sentences. At least in the United States, such a baseline does not exist. All states, the District of Columbia, and the federal government have distinctive sentencing systems. The core elements of American sentencing are plea bargaining and wide discretion of prosecutors to manipulate their charges. Everything is relative. Coming, as I do, from a civil law country that does not use plea bargaining, restricts prosecutors' discretion to a minimum, implements just deserts in sentencing, and has an incarceration rate one-tenth that of the United States, it is hard to see consistent, equal, and proportionate American sentencing.

Critics worry that giving substantial punishment powers to lay volunteers will result in random, unfairly different, and capriciously severe sanctions (Ashworth 1993; Warner 1994; Roberts and LaPrairie 1996; Feld 1999; Levrant et al. 1999). But restorative justice is not punitive by nature, and if participants understand and accept the principles of restorative justice, there need not be extreme consequences. Similarly, there is no reason why restorative justice cannot respect the requirements of proportionality and equality, if they are interpreted as demanding comparable responses for comparable offenses. Then, responses may vary so long as they are meaningfully related to the nature and effects of the crime. Just as rules and guidelines cannot guarantee equal and fair sentencing, lack of rules and guidelines does not necessarily result in unequal and unfair sentencing.

There are several arguments for a systemwide change to incorporate restorative justice values. First, if restorative justice is a more humane and participatory way to deal with crime and does not have inappropriate effects, why should it not become the leading principle of the whole criminal justice system rather than be confined to small-scale activities?

Second, restorative justice is unlikely to have significant or lasting effects on the official criminal justice system if it continues to operate primarily as unorganized and sporadic activities. Even if restorative justice principles could not completely transform the justice system, they may turn criminal justice policy and values in another direction.

Third, if the criminal justice system endorses restorative justice principles, but does not participate in design, implementation, and monitoring of restorative programs, it is not likely to refer other than trivial cases to them. Criminal justice agencies are unlikely to rely on practices whose outcomes they cannot comprehend, influence, predict, or trust. For the same reason, they are often reluctant to divert offenders to these programs.

Fourth, if crime is seen in both traditional and restorative ways—as an offense against the state and as harm to the victim and the community—a double system of punishments may be created. Offenders will first be processed through the traditional system and receive punishment and then move to the informal restorative programs to agree on a reparative contract. As a consequence, offenders will be subjected to greater social control and more sanctions. Alternatively, restorative justice programs may widen control to minor crimes that were previously ignored by the traditional system.

Fifth, it would be unrealistic not to consider costs of restorative justice initiatives in the current climate of exploding correctional costs. Few resources will be saved if restorative solutions only supplement traditional punishments or are used only for minor crimes.

Sixth, a systemwide change will promote comprehensive training on restorative justice principles and provide more information and funding. This will improve consistency, proportionality, and equality in restorative justice practices. Without a systemwide shift, restorative programs will probably continue to handle mostly minor offenses. Then it will not matter much whether one offender receives ten hours of community service and $50 of restitution and another, for an equal crime, receives twenty hours of community service and $100 restitution. However, the more serious the crimes, the more unjust the differences could become, and the greater the need for consistent practices.

Seventh, without official encouragement and support, restorative programs are likely to be concentrated in middle-class, white neighborhoods or rural areas, and volunteers will disproportionately be white, middle-class, and middle-aged or older. If establishment of new practices is left to citizen activists alone, they will probably be concentrated in areas with relatively minor crime problems. Disadvantaged urban neighborhoods with large proportions of minorities and immigrants would be unlikely to benefit.

B. Problems of Community Justice

Conceptions and practices of community justice are even less well-defined than those of restorative justice. Critics of community policing argue that appealing rhetoric of principles is seldom carried out in practices. Political pressures and availability of federal monies to implement community policing have been so influential that few police departments have stepped aside from the popular path. "Who could be against community, cooperation, and crime prevention?" (Klockars 1988, p. 257). However, many claim that most changes have remained lip service: correct terms and rhetoric are used, but business continues as usual (e.g., Bayley 1988).

Even if intentions are sincere, it is still unclear whether community justice can be done and whether it will work (e.g., Greene and Taylor

1988). There is little evidence that the promise of reduced crime and fear, increased satisfaction with agencies, and community empowerment and development can be achieved. However, discouraging results tend to reflect inadequate implementation rather than impossible goals. Comprehensive efforts should tackle a combination of obstacles: agency culture and hierarchical organization, poor understanding of problem solving and the role of communities, neighborhood infrastructures that obstruct civic participation, and bureaucratic boundaries between city, county, and state departments that prohibit true partnerships among them.

The dominant influences of the broken windows theory are doing more harm than good for the community justice movement. Aggressive law enforcement against minor nuisance crime is weakening community bonds and destroying social capacity in urban neighborhoods. It is disproportionately targeting blacks and other minorities and increasing discretionary powers of field officers. The premise that continuing minor disorder increases fear and crime has been challenged (Harcourt 1998; Taylor 1999a), and there is no evidence that targeting quality-of-life crimes is the way to boost neighborhood revitalization. Broken windows theory contributes to the idea that marginalized youth, prostitutes, alcohol and drug addicts, beggars, and vagrants are authors of decline rather than its victims. Many think that the disorder metaphor and intrusions into public space—for example, in the forms of street sweeps and weeding and seeding—have taken on Orwellian tinges and undermine the spirit of community justice (e.g., Trojanowicz et al. 1998, p. 296).

Some community justice efforts have impaired constitutional rights and procedural safeguards. The constitutionality of antiloitering and curfew laws and street sweeps has been questioned (e.g., Livingston 1997). Citizen-driven search warrants and authorization of warrantless searches in special housing projects are new methods to combat drug use and sale (Boland 1996). A broad power of warrantless searches by probation and parole officers may be abused and legal procedures circumvented in police-corrections partnerships (Parent and Snyder 1999).

Then there is the question of who will benefit from community justice programs. If forums for citizen involvement are meetings with business owners, corporate executives, and community leaders or discussions with media and political representatives, average citizens are excluded and there is no true democracy in action (Trojanowicz et al. 1998). Many efforts have been initiated by business owners or well-off local residents who were concerned about economic interests and the effects of unwanted persons in their neighborhoods (e.g., Portland, Oreg., community prosecution, Midtown Community Court, and Minneapolis police-probation partnership). Funding came from business communities to benefit business communities.

Experience with community policing has shown that benefits tend to go to white and middle-class communities. Community policing in Houston favored the interests of whites and homeowners, while African Americans, Hispanics, and renters were excluded (Skogan 1990). In Chicago, neighborhood groups that represented white and middle-class constituencies were much more likely to use opportunities for involvement than groups representing lower-class minorities (Skogan and Hartnett 1997).

Critics in the 1980s raised many questions on community policing that remain unanswered (e.g., Greene and Mastrofski 1988). Besides pure implementation issues, community justice is facing two major challenges. First, how to build communities in ways that expand freedom and promote tolerance. Second, how to overcome structural boundaries of race, class, and culture (see Moore 1999).

IV. Conclusions

Trends in criminal justice and sentencing policies in the United States are often represented by the cliché of a pendulum that swings from social work to law enforcement or from rehabilitation to retribution. The opposing approaches either attempt to change offenders' behavior or to punish them. Restorative and community justice are bringing in new community-based values that do not fit the two-dimensional symbol of a pendulum: restoring victims, creating relationships, and building communities. Both movements are becoming increasingly popular among practitioners and scholars.

So far, restorative and community justice have just touched the surface and may have resulted in more, deeper, and wider control of low-level offenders. Most restorative justice practices are targeting first-time, misdemeanor juvenile offenders. It is questionable whether resources are used wisely when 62 percent of offenses in a family group conferencing program are shoplifting (Fercello and Umbreit 1998). Reitz (2000) identifies "the ongoing experiment in low-level law enforcement" as "the most recent manifestation of the new intolerance toward criminal deviance." So far, few community building effects of restorative or community justice have been reported or measured. It remains to be seen how deep or lasting their effects will be on the criminal justice system.

REFERENCES

Aboriginal Corrections Policy Unit. 1997. *The Four Circles of Hollow Water.* Ottawa: Solicitor General Canada.

Alder, Christine, and Joy Wundersitz. 1994. "New Directions in Juvenile Justice Reform in Australia." In *Family Conferencing and Juvenile Justice: The Way Forward or Misplaced Optimism?* edited by Christine Alder and Joy Wundersitz. Canberra: Australian Institute of Criminology.

Alpert, Geoffry P., and Alex Piquero, eds. 1998. *Community Policing: Contemporary Readings.* Prospect Heights, Ill.: Waveland.

American Prosecutors Research Institute. 1995. *Community Prosecution Implementation Manual.* Alexandria, Va.: American Prosecutors Research Institute.

Ansara, Michael, and S. M. Miller. 1986. "Democratic Populism." In *The New Populism: The Politics of Empowerment,* edited by Harry C. Boyte and Frank Riessman. Philadelphia: Temple University Press.

Ashworth, Andrew. 1993. "Some Doubts about Restorative Justice." *Criminal Law Forum* 4:277–99.

Barajas, Eduardo. 1996. "Moving toward Community Justice." In *Community Justice: Striving for Safe, Secure, and Just Communities.* Washington, D.C.: U.S. Department of Justice, National Institute of Corrections.

———. 1997. "Community Justice: Bad Ways of Promoting a Good Idea." *Perspectives* (Summer), pp. 16–19.

Bayley, David H. 1988. "Community Policing: A Report from the Devil's Advocate." In *Community Policing: Rhetoric or Reality,* edited by Jack R. Greene and Stephen D. Mastrofski. New York: Praeger.

Bazemore, Gordon. 1997. "The 'Community' in Community Justice: Issues, Themes, and Questions for the New Neighborhood Sanctioning Models." *Justice System Journal* 19:193–228.

———. 1998. "Restorative Justice and Earned Redemption: Communities, Victims, and Offender Reintegration." *American Behavioral Scientist* 41:768–813.

Bazemore, Gordon, and Curt Taylor Griffiths. 1997. "Conferences, Circles, Boards, and Mediations: The 'New Wave' of Community Decisionmaking." *Federal Probation* 61(2):25–37.

Bazemore, Gordon, and Lode Walgrave. 1999. "Restorative Juvenile Justice: In Search of Fundamentals and an Outline for Systemic Reform." In *Restorative Juvenile Justice: Repairing the Harm of Youth Crime,* edited by Gordon Bazemore and Lode Walgrave. Monsey, N.Y.: Criminal Justice Press.

Blagg, Harry. 1997. "A Just Measure of Shame? Aboriginal Youth and Conferencing in Australia." *British Journal of Criminology* 37:481–501.

————. 1998. "Restorative Visions and Restorative Justice Practices: Conferencing, Ceremony and Reconciliation in Australia." *Current Issues in Criminal Justice* 10:5–14.

Boland, Barbara. 1996. "How Portland Does It?" Final report submitted to U.S. Department of Justice, National Institute of Justice.

————. 1998a. "Community Prosecution: Portland's Experience." In *Community Justice: An Emerging Field*, edited by David R. Karp. Lanham, Md.: Rowman & Littlefield.

————. 1998b. "The Manhattan Experiment: Community Prosecution." In *Crime and Place: Plenary Papers of the 1997 Conference on Criminal Justice Research and Evaluation.* Washington, D.C.: U.S. Department of Justice, National Institute of Justice.

Bonta, James, Jennifer Rooney, and Suzanne Wallace-Capretta. 1998. *Restorative Justice: An Evaluation of the Restorative Resolutions Project.* Ottawa: Solicitor General Canada.

Boyte, Harry C., and Frank Riessman. 1986. *The New Populism: The Politics of Empowerment.* Philadelphia: Temple University Press.

Braithwaite, John. 1989. *Crime, Shame and Reintegration.* Cambridge: Cambridge University Press.

————. 1998. "Restorative Justice." In *The Handbook of Crime and Punishment*, edited by Michael Tonry. New York: Oxford University Press.

————. 1999. "Restorative Justice: Assessing Optimistic and Pessimistic Accounts." In *Crime and Justice: A Review of Research*, vol. 25, edited by Michael Tonry. Chicago: University of Chicago Press.

Braithwaite, John, and Stephen Mugford. 1994. "Conditions of Successful Reintegration Ceremonies: Dealing with Juvenile Offenders." *British Journal of Criminology* 34:139–71.

Buerger, Michael E. 1994. "A Tale of Two Targets: Limitations of Community Anticrime Actions." *Crime and Delinquency* 40:411–36.

Bureau of Justice Assistance. 1997. *Crime Prevention and Community Policing: A Vital Partnership.* Washington, D.C.: U.S. Department of Justice.

Bush, Robert A. Baruch. 1996. "The Unexplored Possibilities of Community Mediation: A Comment on Merry and Milner." *Law and Social Inquiry* 21:715–36.

Carey, Mark. 1998. "Building Hope through Community Justice." In *Community Justice: Concepts and Strategies.* Lexington, Ky.: American Probation and Parole Association.

Christie, Nils. 1977. "Conflicts as Property." *British Journal of Criminology* 17:1–15.

Clairmont, Donald. 1996. "Alternative Justice Issues for Aboriginal Justice." *Journal of Legal Pluralism and Unofficial Justice* 36:125–57.

Clayton, Susan L. 1999. "Children's Initiatives: Louisiana Corrections Makes Prevention a Priority." *Corrections Today* 6(2):116–19.

Clear, Todd R., and Anthony A. Braga. 1995. "Community Corrections." In *Crime*, edited by James Q. Wilson and Joan Petersilia. San Francisco: Institute for Contemporary Studies.

Clear, Todd R., and David R. Karp. 1998. "The Community Justice Movement." In *Community Justice: An Emerging Field*, edited by David R. Karp. Lanham, Md.: Rowman & Littlefield.

———. 1999. *The Community Justice Ideal: Preventing Crime and Achieving Justice*. Boulder, Colo.: Westview.

Coates, Robert B. 1990. "Victim-Offender Reconciliation Programs in North America: An Assessment." In *Criminal Justice, Restitution, and Reconciliation*, edited by Burt Galaway and Joe Hudson. Monsey, N.Y.: Criminal Justice Press.

Coles, Catherine, and George Kelling. 1997*a*. "Prosecution in the Community: A Study of Emergent Strategies: Jackson County (Kansas City), Missouri Case Study." Unpublished manuscript. Cambridge, Mass.: Harvard University, John F. Kennedy School of Government.

———. 1997*b*. "Prosecution in the Community: A Study of Emergent Strategies: Marion County/Indianapolis, Indiana Case Study." Unpublished manuscript. Cambridge, Mass.: Harvard University, John F. Kennedy School of Government.

———. 1997*c*. "Prosecution in the Community: A Study of Emergent Strategies: Suffolk County (Boston), Massachusetts Case Study." Unpublished manuscript. Cambridge, Mass.: Harvard University, John F. Kennedy School of Government.

———. 1997*d*. "Prosecution in the Community: A Study of Emergent Strategies: Travis County (Austin), Texas Case Study." Unpublished manuscript. Cambridge, Mass.: Harvard University, John F. Kennedy School of Government.

———. 1998. "Prosecution in the Community: A Study of Emergent Strategies: A Cross Site Analysis." Unpublished manuscript. Cambridge, Mass.: Harvard University, John F. Kennedy School of Government.

———. 1999. "Prevention through Community Prosecution." *Public Interest*, no. 136 (Summer), pp. 69–84.

Consedine, Jim. 1995. *Restorative Justice: Healing the Effects of Crime*. Christchurch: Ploughshares.

Cordner, Gary W. 1998. "Community Policing: Elements and Effects." In *Community Policing: Contemporary Readings*, edited by Geoffrey P. Alpert and Alex Piquero. Prospect Heights, Ill.: Waveland.

Crawford, Adam. 1998. *Crime Prevention and Community Safety: Politics, Policies and Practices*. Dorchester, Mass.: Longman.

Cunneen, Chris. 1997. "Community Conferencing and the Fiction of Indigenous Control." *Australian and New Zealand Journal of Criminology* 30:292–311.

Cunneen, Chris, and David McDonald. 1997. *Keeping Aboriginal and Torres Strait Islander People out of Custody: An Evaluation of the Implementation of the Recommendations of the Royal Commission in Aboriginal Deaths in Custody*. Canberra: Aboriginal and Torres Strait Islander Commission.

Davis, Robert C., Martha Tichane, and Deborah Grayson. 1980. *Mediation and Arbitration as Alternatives to Prosecution in Felony Arrest Cases: An Evaluation of the Brooklyn Dispute Resolution Center*. New York: Vera Institute of Justice.

Dean-Myrda, Mark C., and Francis T. Cullen. 1998. "The Panacea Pendulum: An Account of Community as a Response to Crime." In *Community Corrections*, edited by Joan Petersilia. New York: Oxford University Press.

Dignan, James. 1999. "The Crime and Disorder Act and the Prospects for Restorative Justice." *Criminal Law Review* (January):48–60.

Dooley, Michael. 1996. "Restorative Justice in Vermont: A Work in Progress." In *Community Justice: Striving for Safe, Secure, and Just Communities*. Washington, D.C.: U.S. Bureau of Prisons, National Institute of Corrections.

DuBow, Fredric L., and Craig McEwen. 1993. "Community Boards: An Analytic Profile." In *The Possibility of Popular Justice: A Case Study of Community Mediation in the United States*, edited by Sally Engle Merry and Neal Milner. Ann Arbor: University of Michigan Press.

Earle, Ronald. 1998. "Community Justice and Creating of Peace." Paper presented at the Executive Sessions on Sentencing and Corrections, University of Minnesota Law School, Minneapolis, September 10–12.

Eglash, Albert. 1977. "Beyond Restitution: Creative Restitution." In *Restitution in Criminal Justice*, edited by Joe Hudson and Burt Galaway. Lexington, Mass.: D. C. Heath.

Fattah, Ezzat A. 1997. "Toward a Victim Policy Aimed at Healing, Not Suffering." In *Victims of Crime*, edited by Robert C. Davis, Arthur J. Lurigio, and Wesley S. Skogan. 2d ed. Thousand Oaks, Calif.: Sage.

Feinblatt, John, and Greg Berman. 1997. *Responding to the Community: Principles for Planning and Creating a Community Court*. Washington, D.C.: U.S. Department of Justice, Bureau of Justice Assistance.

Feinblatt, John, Greg Berman, and Michele Sviridoff. 1998. "Neighborhood Justice at the Midtown Community Court." In *Crime and Place: Plenary Papers of the 1997 Conference on Criminal Justice Research and Evaluation*. Washington, D.C.: U.S. Department of Justice, National Institute of Justice.

Feld, Barry C. 1999. "Rehabilitation, Retribution, and Restorative Justice: Alternative Conceptions of Juvenile Justice." In *Restorative Juvenile Justice: Repairing the Harm of Youth Crime*, edited by Gordon Bazemore and Lode Walgrave. Monsey, N.Y.: Criminal Justice Press.

Fercello, Claudia, and Mark Umbreit. 1998. *Client Evaluation of Family Group Conferencing in 12 Sites in 1st Judicial District of Minnesota*. St. Paul: University of Minnesota, Center for Restorative Justice and Mediation.

Flaten, Caren L. 1996. "Victim-Offender Mediation: Application with Serious Offenses Committed by Juveniles." In *Restorative Justice: International Perspectives*, edited by Burt Galaway and Joe Hudson. Amsterdam: Kugler.

Forst, Brian. 1999. "Prosecution's Coming of Age." Paper presented at the Committee on Law and Justice of the National Research Council meeting, Washington, D.C., July 15.

Galaway, Burt, and Joe Hudson, eds. 1996. *Restorative Justice: International Perspectives*. Amsterdam: Kugler.

Gehm, John. 1990. "Mediated Victim-Offender Restitution Agreements: An Explanatory Analysis of Factors Related to Victim Participation." In *Crimi-*

nal Justice, Restitution, and Reconciliation, edited by Burt Galaway and Joe Hudson. Monsey, N.Y.: Criminal Justice Press.

Goldstein, Herman. 1979. "Improving Policing: A Problem-Oriented Approach." *Crime and Delinquency* 25:236–58.

Gorczyk, John, and John Perry. 1997. "What the Public Wants: Market Research Finds Support for Restorative Justice." *Corrections Today* 59(7):78–83.

Gosse, Richard, James Youngblood Henderson, and Roger Carter. 1994. *Continuing Poundmaker and Riel's Quest: Presentations Made at a Conference on Aboriginal Peoples and Justice.* Saskatoon, Saskatchewan: Purich.

Gramckow, Heike. 1997. "Community Prosecution in the United States." *European Journal of Criminal Policy and Research* 5(4):9–26.

Gramckow, Heike, and Rhonda Mims. 1998. "Community Prosecution." In *Community Justice: Concepts and Strategies.* Lexington, Ky.: American Probation and Parole Association.

Green, Ross Gordon. 1997. "Aboriginal Community Sentencing and Mediation: Within and without the Circle." *Manitoba Law Journal* 25:77–125.

Greene, Jack R. 1998. "The Road to Community Policing in Los Angeles: A Case Study." In *Community Policing: Contemporary Readings*, edited by Geoffrey P. Alpert and Alex Piquero. Prospect Heights, Ill.: Waveland.

Greene, Jack R., and Stephen D. Mastrofski, eds. 1988. *Community Policing: Rhetoric or Reality.* New York: Praeger.

Greene, Jack R., and Ralph B. Taylor. 1988. "Community-Based Policing and Foot Patrol: Issues of Theory and Evaluation." In *Community Policing: Rhetoric or Reality*, edited by Jack R. Greene and Stephen D. Mastrofski. New York: Praeger.

Grinc, Randolph M. 1994. "'Angels in Marble': Problems in Stimulating Community Involvement in Community Policing." *Crime and Delinquency* 40:437–68.

Guarino-Ghezzi, Susan, and Andrew Klein. 1999. "Protecting Community: The Public Safety Role in a Restorative Juvenile Justice." In *Restorative Juvenile Justice: Repairing the Harm of Youth Crime*, edited by Gordon Bazemore and Lode Walgrave. Monsey, N.Y.: Criminal Justice Press.

Gustafson, Dave. 1997. "Facilitating Communication between Victims and Offenders in Cases of Serious and Violent Crime." *International Community Corrections Association (ICCA) Journal on Community Corrections* 8:44–49.

Hahn, Paul H. 1998. *Emerging Criminal Justice: Three Pillars for a Proactive Justice System.* Thousand Oaks, Calif.: Sage.

Harcourt, Bernard E. 1998. "Reflecting on the Subject: A Critique of the Social Influence Conception of Deterrence, the Broken Windows Theory, and Order-Maintenance Policing New York Style. *Michigan Law Review* 97:291–389.

Harris, Nathan, and Jamie Burton. 1998. "The Reliability of Observed Reintegrative Shaming, Shame, Defiance and Other Key Concepts in Diversionary Conferences." Reintegrative Shaming Experiments (RISE) Working Paper. Canberra: Australian National University.

Hope, Tim. 1995. "Community Crime Prevention." In *Building a Safer Society:*

Strategic Approaches to Crime Prevention, edited by Michael Tonry and David P. Farrington. Vol. 19 of *Crime and Justice: A Review of Research*, edited by Michael Tonry. Chicago: University of Chicago Press.

Immarigeon, Russ. 1996. "Prison-Based Victim-Offender Reconciliation Programs." In *Restorative Justice: International Perspectives*, edited by Burt Galaway and Joe Hudson. Amsterdam: Kugler.

Immarigeon, Russ, and Kathleen Daly. 1997. "Restorative Justice: Origins, Practices, Contexts, and Challenges." *International Community Corrections Association (ICCA) Journal on Community Corrections* 8(2):13–18.

———. 1998. "The Past, Present, and Future of Restorative Justice: Some Critical Reflections." *Contemporary Justice Review* 1:21–45.

Jackson, Shirley E. 1998. "Family Group Conferences in Youth Justice: The Issues for Implementation in England and Wales." *Howard Journal of Criminal Justice* 37:34–51.

Justice Fellowship. 1999. Conference brochure for the National Forum on Restorative Justice, Washington, D.C., February 18–19.

Karp, David R, ed. 1998. *Community Justice: An Emerging Field*. Lanham, Md.: Rowman & Littlefield.

Kelling, George L. 1998. "Crime Control, the Police, and Culture Wars: Broken Windows and Cultural Pluralism." In *Perspectives on Crime and Justice: 1997–1998 Lecture Series*. Washington, D.C.: U.S. Department of Justice, National Institute of Justice.

Kelling, George L., and Catherine M. Coles. 1996. *Fixing Broken Windows: Restoring Order and Reducing Crime in Our Communities*. New York: Free Press.

Kilchling, Michael, and Marianne Löschnig-Gspandl. Forthcoming. "Legal and Practical Perspectives on Victim-Offender Mediation in Austria and Germany." *International Review of Victimology*, vol. 6.

Klockars, Carl B. 1988. "The Rhetoric of Community Policing." In *Community Policing: Rhetoric or Reality*, edited by Jack R. Greene and Stephen D. Mastrofski. New York: Praeger.

Kurki, Leena. 1999. *Incorporating Restorative and Community Justice into American Sentencing and Corrections*. Washington, D.C.: U.S. Department of Justice, National Institute of Justice.

Lappi-Seppälä, Tapio. 1996. "Finland." In *Reparation in Criminal Law: International Perspectives*, edited by Albin Eiser and Susanne Walther. Freiburg: Max Planck Institute for Foreign and International Criminal Law.

———. 1998. *Regulating the Prison Population: Experiences from a Long-Term Policy in Finland*. Helsinki: National Research Institute of Legal Policy.

LaPrairie, Carol. 1995. "Conferencing in Aboriginal Communities in Canada: Finding Middle Ground in Criminal Justice." *Criminal Law Forum* 6:576–99.

———. 1998. "The 'New' Justice: Some Implications for Aboriginal Communities." *Canadian Journal of Criminology* 40:61–79.

Leaf, Robin, Arthur Lurigio, and Nancy Martin. 1998. "Chicago's Project Safeway: Strengthening Probation's Links with the Community." In *Community Corrections*, edited by Joan Petersilia. New York: Oxford University Press.

Levrant, Sharon, Francis T. Cullen, Betsy Fulton, and John F. Wozniak. 1999. "Reconsidering Restorative Justice: The Corruption of Benevolence Revisited?" *Crime and Delinquency* 45:3–27.

Livingston, Debra. 1997. "Police Discretion and the Quality of Life in Public Places: Courts, Communities, and the New Policing." *Columbia Law Review* 97:551–672.

Löschnig-Gspandl, Marianne, and Michael Kilchling. 1997. "Victim/Offender Mediation and Victim Compensation in Austria and Germany—Stocktaking and Perspectives for Future Research." *European Journal of Crime, Criminal Law and Criminal Justice* 5:58–78.

Lowry, Jolene M. 1997. "Family Group Conferences as a Form of Court-Approved Alternative Dispute Resolution in Child Abuse and Neglect Cases." *University of Michigan Journal of Law Reform* 31:57–92.

Lowry, Kem. 1993. "Evaluation of Community-Justice." In *The Possibility of Popular Justice: A Case Study of Community Mediation in the United States*, edited by Sally Engle Merry and Neal Milner. Ann Arbor: University of Michigan Press.

Maloney, Dennis, and Neil Bryant. 1998. "In Pursuit of Community Justice." Paper presented at the Executive Sessions on Sentencing and Corrections, University of Minnesota Law School, Minneapolis, September 10–12.

Marshall, Tony F. 1996. "The Evolution of Restorative Justice in Britain." *European Journal on Criminal Policy and Research* 4:21–43.

Maxwell, Gabrielle, and Allison Morris. 1993. *Family, Victims and Culture: Youth Justice in New Zealand*. Wellington: Victoria University of Wellington, Social Policy Agency and Institute of Criminology.

———. 1994. "The New Zealand Model of Family Group Conferences." In *Family Conferencing and Juvenile Justice: The Way Forward or Misplaced Optimism?* edited by Christine Alder and Joy Wundersitz. Canberra: Australian Institute of Criminology.

———. 1997. "Family Group Conferences and Restorative Justice." *International Community Corrections Association (ICCA) Journal on Community Corrections* 8(2):37–40.

McCold, Paul. 1995. "Restorative Justice: The Role of the Community." Paper presented at the annual conference of the Academy of Criminal Justice Sciences, Boston, March. http://www.realjustice.org/community3.html.

McCold, Paul, and Benjamin Wachtel. 1998. *Restorative Policing Experiment: The Bethlehem Pennsylvania Police Family Group Conferencing Project*. Pipersville, Pa.: Community Service Foundation.

McElrea, Frederick W. M. 1998. "The New Zealand Model of Family Group Conferences." *European Journal on Criminal Policy and Research* 6:527–43.

McElroy, Jerome E., Colleen A. Cosgrove, and Susan Sadd. 1993. *Community Policing: The CPOP in New York*. Newbury Park, Calif.: Sage.

McEwen, T. 1994. *National Assessment Program: 1994 Survey Results*. Washington, D.C.: U.S. Department of Justice, National Institute of Justice.

McGillis, Daniel. 1997. *Community Mediation Programs: Developments and Challenges*. Washington, D.C.: U.S. Department of Justice, National Institute of Justice.

Merry, Sally Engle, and Neal Milner. 1993. *The Possibility of Popular Justice: A Case Study of Community Mediation in the United States*. Ann Arbor: University of Michigan Press.

Messmer, Heinz, and Hans-Uwe Otto. 1992. *Restorative Justice on Trial: Pitfalls and Potentials of Victim-Offender Mediation*. Dordrecht: Kluwer.

Midtown Community Court. 1997. *The Midtown Community Court Experiment: A Progress Report*. New York: Midtown Community Court.

Moore, David. 1995. *A New Approach to Juvenile Justice: An Evaluation of Family Conferencing in Wagga Wagga*. Wagga Wagga: Charles Sturt University.

Moore, David, and Terry O'Connell. 1994. "Family Conferencing in Wagga Wagga: A Communitarian Model of Justice." In *Family Conferencing and Juvenile Justice: The Way Forward or Misplaced Optimism?* edited by Christine Alder and Joy Wundersitz. Canberra: Australian Institute of Criminology.

Moore, Mark. 1992. "Problem-Solving and Community Policing." In *Modern Policing*, edited by Michael Tonry and Norval Morris. Vol. 15 of *Crime and Justice: A Review of Research*, edited by Michael Tonry. Chicago: University of Chicago Press.

———. 1999. "Security and Community Development." In *Urban Problems and Community Development*, edited by Ronald F. Ferguson and William T. Dickens. Washington, D.C.: Brookings Institution Press.

Morris, Allison, Gabrielle Maxwell, and Jeremy Robertson. 1993. "Giving Victims a Voice: A New Zealand Experiment." *Howard Journal of Criminal Justice* 32:304–21.

Niemeyer, Mike, and David Shichor. 1996. "A Preliminary Study of a Large Victim/Offender Reconciliation Program." *Federal Probation* 60:30–34.

Nugent, William R., and Jeffrey B. Paddock. 1995. "The Effect of Victim-Offender Mediation on Severity of Reoffense." *Mediation Quarterly* 12:353–67.

Orlando, Frank. A. 1992. "Mediation Involving Children in the U.S.: Legal and Ethical Conflicts: A Policy Discussion and Research Questions." In *Restorative Justice on Trial: Pitfalls and Potentials of Victim-Offender Mediation*, edited by Heinz Messmer and Hans-Uwe Otto. Dordrecht: Kluwer.

Parent, Dale, and Brad Snyder. 1999. *Police-Corrections Partnerships*. Washington, D.C.: U.S. Department of Justice, National Institute of Justice.

Pennell, Joan, and Gale Burford. 1996. "Attending the Context: Family Group Decision-making in Canada." In *Family Group Conferences: Perspectives on Policy and Practice*, edited by Joe Hudson, Allison Morris, Gabrielle Maxwell, and Burt Galaway. Monsey, N.Y.: Criminal Justice Press.

Petersilia, Joan. 1995. "A Crime Control Rationale for Reinvesting in Community Corrections." *Prison Journal* 75:479–96.

———. 1998. "Probation and Parole." In *The Handbook of Crime and Punishment*, edited by Michael Tonry. New York: Oxford University Press.

———. 1999. "Parole and Prisoner Reentry in the United States." In *Prisons*, edited by Michael Tonry and Joan Petersilia. Vol. 26 of *Crime and Justice: A Review of Research*, edited by Michael Tonry. Chicago: University of Chicago Press.

Piquero, Alex, Jack Greene, James Fyfe, Robert J. Kane, and Patricia Collins. 1998. "Implementing Community Policing in Public Housing Developments in Philadelphia." In *Community Policing: Contemporary Readings*, edited by Geoffrey P. Alpert and Alex Piquero. Prospect Heights, Ill.: Waveland.

Police Executive Research Forum. 1996. *Themes and Variations in Community Policing*. Washington, D.C.: Police Executive Research Forum.

Pranis, Kay. 1997. "Rethinking Community Corrections: Restorative Values and an Expanded Role for the Community." *International Community Corrections Association (ICCA) Journal on Community Corrections* 8(1):36–39, 43.

———. 1998a. Communications at the Executive Sessions on Sentencing and Corrections, University of Minnesota Law School, Minneapolis, May 7–9.

———. 1998b. "Promising Practices in Community Justice: Restorative Justice." In *Community Justice: Concepts and Strategies*. Lexington, Ky.: American Probation and Parole Association.

President's Commission on Law Enforcement and Administration of Justice. 1967. *The Challenge of Crime in a Free Society*. Washington, D.C.: U.S. Government Printing Office.

Presser, Lois, and Elaine Gunnison. 1999. "Strange Bedfellows: Is Sex Offender Notification a Form of Community Justice?" *Crime and Delinquency* 45:299–315.

Reitz, Kevin. 2000. "The Disassembly and Reassembly of U.S. Sentencing Practices." In *Sentencing and Sanctions: The Evolution of Penal Systems in Western Countries*, edited by Michael Tonry and Richard Frase. New York: Oxford University Press (forthcoming).

Richardson, Gord, Burt Galaway, and Michelle Joubert. 1996. "Restorative Resolutions Project: An Alternative to Incarceration." *International Journal of Comparative and Applied Criminal Justice* 20:209–19.

Riessman, Frank. 1986. "The New Populism and the Empowerment Ethos." In *The New Populism: The Politics of Empowerment*, edited by Harry C. Boyte and Frank Riessman. Philadelphia: Temple University Press.

Roberts, Julian V., and Carol LaPrairie. 1996. "Sentencing Circles: Some Unanswered Questions." *Criminal Law Quarterly* 39:69–83.

Roy, Sudipto. 1993. "Two Types of Juvenile Restitution Programs in Two Midwestern Counties: A Comparative Study." *Federal Probation* 57(4):48–53.

Sadd, Susan, and Randolph Grinc. 1994. *Issues in Community Policing: Problems in the Implementation of Eight Innovative Neighborhood-Oriented Policing Projects*. Washington, D.C.: U.S. Department of Justice, National Institute of Justice.

———. 1996. *Implementation Challenges in Community Policing: Innovative Neighborhood-Oriented Policing in Eight Cities*. Washington, D.C.: U.S. Department of Justice, National Institute of Justice.

Sampson, Robert J. 1999. "What 'Community' Supplies." In *Urban Problems and Community Development*, edited by Ronald F. Ferguson and William T. Dickens. Washington, D.C.: Brookings Institution Press.

Sandor, Danny. 1994. "The Thickening Blue Wedge in Juvenile Justice." In

Family Conferencing and Juvenile Justice: The Way Forward or Misplaced Optimism? edited by Christine Adler and Joy Wundersitz. Canberra: Australian Institute of Criminology.

Schneider, A. 1986. "Restitution and Recidivism Rates of Juvenile Offenders: Results From Four Experimental Studies." *Criminology* 24:533-52.

Sherman, Lawrence W., and Geoffrey C. Barnes. 1997. "Restorative Justice and Offenders' Respect for the Law." Reintegrative Shaming Experiments (RISE) Working Paper 3. Canberra: Australian National University.

Sherman, Lawrence W., and Heather Strang. 1997a. "The Right Kind of Shame for Crime Prevention." Reintegrative Shaming Experiments (RISE) Working Paper 1. Canberra: Australian National University.

———. 1997b. "Restorative Justice and Deterring Crime." Reintegrative Shaming Experiments (RISE) Working Paper 4. Canberra: Australian National University.

Sherman, Lawrence W., Heather Strang, Geoffrey C. Barnes, John Braithwaite, Nova Ipken, and Min-Mee The. 1998. *Experiments in Restorative Policing: A Progress Report to the National Police Research Unit on the Canberra Reintegrative Shaming Experiments (RISE).* Canberra: Australian Federal Police and Australian National University.

Silverman, Eli B. 1995. "Community Policing: The Implementation Gap." In *Issues in Community Policing,* edited by Peter C. Kratcoski and Duane Dukes. Cincinnati: Anderson.

Sinkinson, Herbert, and John Broderick. 1997. "Restorative Justice in Vermont—Citizen's Reparative Boards." *Overcrowded Times* 8(4):1, 12–13, 20.

Skogan, Wesley G. 1990. *Disorder and Decline: Crime and the Spiral of Decay in American Neighborhoods.* New York: Free Press.

———. 1996. "The Community's Role in Community Policing." *National Institute of Justice Journal* (August), pp. 31–34.

———. 1998. "Community Policing in Chicago." In *Community Policing: Contemporary Readings,* edited by Geoffrey P. Alpert and Alex Piquero. Prospect Heights, Ill.: Waveland.

———. 1999. "Measuring What Matters: Crime, Disorder, and Fear." In *Measuring What Matters: Proceedings from the Policing Research Institute Meetings,* edited by Robert Langworthy. Washington, D.C.: U.S. Department of Justice, National Institute of Justice.

Skogan, Wesley G., and Susan M. Hartnett. 1997. *Community Policing, Chicago Style.* New York: Oxford University Press.

Strang, Heather, Geoffrey S. Barnes, John Braithwaite, and Lawrence W. Sherman. 1999. *Experiments in Restorative Policing: A Progress Report on the Canberra Reintegrative Shaming Experiments (RISE).* Canberra: Australian Federal Police and Australian National University.

Strang, Heather, and Lawrence W. Sherman. 1997. "The Victim's Perspective." Reintegrative Shaming Experiments (RISE) Working Paper 2. Canberra: Australian National University.

Stuart, Barry. 1996a. "Circle Sentencing in Canada: A Partnership of the Community and the Criminal Justice System." *International Journal of Comparative and Applied Criminal Justice* 20:291–309.

———. 1996*b*. "Circle Sentencing: Turning Swords into Ploughshares." In *Restorative Justice: International Perspectives*, edited by Burt Galaway and Joe Hudson. Amsterdam: Kugler.

———. 1996*c*. *Sentencing Circles . . . Making "Real Differences."* Ottawa: Department of Justice, Canada.

———. 1997. *Building Community Justice Partnerships: Community Peacemaking Circles.* Ottawa: Department of Justice of Canada, Aboriginal Justice Directorate.

Taylor, Ralph B. 1999*a*. *Crime, Grime, Fear, and Decline: A Longitudinal Look.* Washington, D.C.: U.S. Department of Justice, National Institute of Justice.

———. 1999*b*. "The Incivilities Thesis: Theory, Measurement, and Policy." In *Measuring What Matters: Proceedings from the Policing Research Institute Meetings*, edited by Robert H. Langworthy. Washington, D.C.: U.S. Department of Justice, National Institute of Justice.

Thomson, Douglas R., and Fredric DuBow. 1993. "Organizing for Community Mediation: The Legacy of Community Boards of San Francisco as a Social Movement Organization." In *The Possibility of Popular Justice: A Case Study of Community Mediation in the United States*, edited by Sally Engle Merry and Neal Milner. Ann Arbor: University of Michigan Press.

Tonry, Michael. 1998. "Intermediate Sanctions." In *The Handbook of Crime and Punishment*, edited by Michael Tonry. New York: Oxford University Press.

———. 1999. *The Fragmentation of Sentencing and Corrections in America.* Washington, D.C.: U.S. Department of Justice, National Institute of Justice.

Trojanowicz, Robert, Victor E. Kappeler, Larry K. Gaines, and Bonnie Bucqueroux. 1998. *Community Policing: A Contemporary Perspective.* 2d ed. Cincinnati: Anderson.

Umbreit, Mark S. 1994. *Victim Meets the Offender: The Impact of Restorative Justice and Mediation.* Monsey, N.Y.: Criminal Justice Press.

———. 1995*a*. *Mediating Interpersonal Conflicts: A Pathway to Peace.* West Concord, Minn.: CPI.

———. 1995*b*. *Mediation of Criminal Conflict: An Assessment of Programs in Four Canadian Provinces.* St. Paul: University of Minnesota, Center for Restorative Justice and Mediation.

Umbreit, Mark S., and William Bradshaw. 1997. "Victim Experience of Meeting Adult vs. Juvenile Offenders: A Cross-National Comparison." *Federal Probation* 61(4):33–39.

Umbreit, Mark S., and Mark Carey. 1995. "Restorative Justice: Implications for Organizational Change." *Federal Probation* 59(3):47–54.

Umbreit, Mark S., and Robert B. Coates. 1992. *Victim Offender Mediation: An Analysis of Programs in Four States of the U.S.* St. Paul: University of Minnesota, Center for Restorative Justice and Mediation.

———. 1993. "Cross-Site Analysis of Victim-Offender Mediation in Four States." *Crime and Delinquency* 39:565–85.

Umbreit, Mark S., and Claudia Fercello. 1997. *Woodbury Police Department's*

Restorative Justice Community Conferencing Program. St. Paul: University of
Minnesota, Center for Restorative Justice and Mediation.

Umbreit, Mark S., and J. Greenwood 1997. *National Survey of Victim Offender
Mediation Programs in the U.S.* St. Paul: University of Minnesota, Center for
Restorative Justice and Mediation.

Umbreit, Mark S., and Ann Warner Roberts. 1996. *Mediation of Criminal Conflict in England: An Assessment of Services in Coventry and Leeds.* St. Paul: University of Minnesota, Center for Restorative Justice and Mediation.

Umbreit, Mark S., and Howard Zehr. 1996. "Restorative Family Group Conferences: Differing Models and Guidelines for Practice." *Federal Probation*
60(3):24–29.

Van Ness, Daniel. 1993*a*. "New Wine and Old Wineskins: Four Challenges
of Restorative Justice." *Criminal Law Forum* 4:251–76.

———. 1993*b*. "A Reply to Andrew Ashworth." *Criminal Law Forum* 4:
301–6.

Van Ness, Daniel, and Karen Heetderks Strong. 1997. *Restoring Justice.* Cincinnati: Anderson.

Van Ness, Daniel, and Pat Nolan. 1998. "Legislating for Restorative Justice."
Regent University Law Review 10:53–110.

von Hirsch, Andrew, and Andrew Ashworth. 1992. "Not Not Just Deserts: A
Response to Braithwaite and Pettit." *Oxford Journal on Legal Studies* 12:83–
98.

———, eds. 1998. *Principled Sentencing: Readings on Theory and Policy.* Oxford:
Hart.

Walther, Lynne, and John Perry. 1997. "The Vermont Reparative Probation
Program." *International Community Corrections Association (ICCA) Journal on
Community Corrections* 8(2):26–34.

Warner, Kate. 1994. "Family Group Conferences and the Rights of the Offender." In *Family Conferencing and Juvenile Justice: The Way Forward or Misplaced Optimism?* edited by Christine Adler and Joy Wundersitz. Canberra:
Australian Institute of Criminology.

Weitekamp, Elmar G. M. 1999. "The History of Restorative Justice." In *Restorative Juvenile Justice: Repairing the Harm of Youth Crime,* edited by Gordon Bazemore and Lode Walgrave. Monsey, N.Y.: Criminal Justice Press.

White, Rob. 1994. "Shame and Reintegration Strategies: Individuals, State
Power and Social Interests." In *Family Conferencing and Juvenile Justice: The
Way Forward or Misplaced Optimism?* edited by Christine Adler and Joy
Wundersitz. Canberra: Australian Institute of Criminology.

Wilson, James Q., and George L. Kelling. 1982. "Broken Windows: The Police and Neighborhood Safety." *Atlantic Monthly,* March, pp. 29–38.

Wright, Martin. 1990. *Justice for Victims and Offenders: A Restorative Response to
Crime.* Winchester, Mass.: Waterside.

Wundersitz, Joy. 1994. "Family Conferencing and Juvenile Justice Reform in
South Australia." In *Family Conferencing and Juvenile Justice: The Way For-
ward or Misplaced Optimism?* edited by Christine Adler and Joy Wundersitz.
Canberra: Australian Institute of Criminology.

Wundersitz, Joy, and Sue Hetzel. 1996. "Family Conferencing for Young Offenders: The South Australian Experience." In *Family Group Conferences: Perspectives on Policy and Practice*, edited by John Hudson, Allison Morris, Gabrielle Maxwell, and Burt Galaway. Monsey, N.Y.: Criminal Justice Press.

Wycoff, Mary Ann, and Wesley S. Skogan. 1993. *Community Policing in Madison: Quality from the Inside Out*. Washington, D.C.: U.S. Department of Justice, National Institute of Justice.

Yazzie, Robert, and James W. Zion. 1996. "Navajo Restorative Justice: The Law of Equality and Justice." In *Restorative Justice: International Perspectives*, edited by Burt Galaway and Joe Hudson. Monsey, N.Y.: Criminal Justice Press.

Yeats, Mary Ann. 1997. "Three Strikes and Restorative Justice: Dealing with Young Repeat Burglars in Western Australia." *Criminal Law Forum* 8:369–85.

Young, Richard, and Benjamin Goold. 1999. "Restorative Police Cautioning in Aylesbury—from Degrading to Reintegrative Shaming Ceremonies?" *Criminal Law Review* (1999), pp. 126–38.

Zehr, Howard. 1990. *Changing the Lenses*. Scottdale, Pa.: Herald.

Brandon C. Welsh and David P. Farrington

Monetary Costs and Benefits of Crime Prevention Programs

ABSTRACT

Few attempts have been made to calculate the monetary costs and benefits of crime prevention programs. Existing calculations for situational, developmental, and community prevention, and correctional intervention programs give hopeful indications that benefits often exceed costs. However, the noncomparability of methods used in different studies makes it impossible to determine which program or class of programs is the most economically efficient. A "how-to" manual should be developed and followed. A wide range of benefits should be measured, including health, employment, and education benefits, as well as crime reduction. Research is needed on issues such as using average versus marginal costs, using capital versus operating costs, discounting costs and benefits over different time periods, using tangible versus intangible victim costs, and calculating costs and benefits from different perspectives (such as victim, taxpayer, or program participant). Because the value of an economic analysis is limited by the quality of the research design, greater use should be made of high quality research designs combined with benefit-cost analyses. Funding agencies should commission and support benefit-cost evaluations of new and existing prevention programs.

The costs of crime are enormous. It is not easy to convert them into monetary terms, but Miller, Cohen, and Wiersema (1996) estimated that they totaled $450 billion in the United States in 1993. There are tangible costs to victims, such as replacing stolen goods and repairing

Brandon C. Welsh is an assistant professor in the Department of Criminal Justice, University of Massachusetts at Lowell. His work was supported by the Department of Criminology and Criminal Justice, University of Maryland. David P. Farrington is professor of psychological criminology at the Institute of Criminology, Cambridge University. We are grateful to Steve Aos for helpful comments.

damage, and intangible costs such as pain and suffering, costs that are harder to quantify. There are costs to the government or taxpayer for police, courts, prisons, crime prevention activities, and so on. There are also costs to offenders—for example, those associated with being in prison or losing a job.

To the extent that crime prevention programs are successful in reducing crime and offending, they will have benefits. These benefits can be quantified in monetary terms according to the reduction in the monetary costs of crime. In an economic analysis, the monetary costs of a program can be compared with its monetary benefits to determine whether the program is economically efficient (i.e., if the benefits outweigh the costs). We focus on the ratio of benefits to costs, calculated in a benefit-cost (or cost-benefit) analysis. This is somewhat analogous to calculating the monetary return on an investment. Some prevention programs can have monetary benefits not only from reducing the costs of crime, but also from reducing the costs of associated social problems such as unemployment, divorce, educational failure, drug addiction, welfare dependency, and so on.

In this essay, we focus on four principal crime prevention strategies, as articulated in the typology advanced by Tonry and Farrington (1995): situational, developmental, community, and criminal justice prevention. Only twenty-six crime prevention studies meeting the criteria for inclusion were identified: thirteen situational prevention, six developmental prevention, six criminal justice prevention, and one community prevention. For criminal justice prevention, it was possible only to investigate correctional intervention or offender treatment, because of an almost complete absence of benefit-cost studies of law enforcement- and court-based interventions.

The adequacy of an economic analysis of the monetary benefits and costs of a crime prevention program depends crucially on the methodological rigor of the underlying evaluation design. Determining that a program prevented crimes requires an estimate of how many crimes would have been committed in the absence of the program, and a disentangling of program effects on crime from all the other possible influences. Ideally, our review should have been restricted to benefit-cost analyses of programs with high-quality evaluation designs, but the small number of existing analyses militated against this.

We searched criminological, psychological, health, economic, and medical literatures throughout the Western world for published studies on the prevention of crime that had carried out an economic analysis and had either calculated or permitted the calculation of a benefit-cost ratio for the purpose of assessing the program's economic efficiency. Studies that did not perform an economic analysis were included if they presented sufficient cost and benefit data to enable an assessment of economic efficiency. We also contacted leading scholars, researchers, and practitioners working in the fields of crime prevention and welfare economics in an effort to identify unpublished or in-press reports. Studies have been included only if there was a measure of personal crime, in which the primary victim was a person or household, and if they were "real-life" programs—that is, program outcomes were neither assessed using statistical modeling techniques alone nor hypothesized on the basis of case study data, but rather research designs were employed with the capacity to control for threats to internal and external validity, such as experimental and quasi-experimental designs.

The greatest problem that we faced was the noncomparability of many benefit-cost analyses. Researchers have used different methods for calculating costs and benefits (e.g., marginal or average), included different program costs (operating, capital, or both), monetized different program effects (e.g., on crime, employment, education failure, etc.), and aggregated program costs and benefits on different theoretical assumptions. This all made it difficult or impossible for us to determine which program or class of programs was the most economically efficient. Our main recommendation is that a standard how-to manual for carrying out benefit-cost analyses of prevention programs be developed and followed. It will need continuous updating.

We offer several other main conclusions. First, economic analysis is an underused research tool in the study of crime prevention; few programs have been the subject of economic analyses that have rigorously and comprehensively assessed the resources used (costs) and program effects (benefits or disbenefits). Second, evidence from economic analyses often suggests that monetary benefits outweigh costs for three of the four principal crime prevention strategies; for community prevention, there was insufficient evidence to make an assessment. Third, developmental prevention and, to a lesser extent, correctional intervention, provide important monetary benefits beyond crimes reduced, while the benefits of situational prevention appear to be confined largely to crime reduction. Fourth, economic analysis studies need to be both methodologically rigorous and comprehensive in their coverage of costs and benefits. Fifth, the value of an economic analysis is limited by the quality of the research design; greater use of high-quality experimental research designs, particularly randomized experiments, is needed to assess the effects of crime prevention programs and their benefits and costs.

The organization of this essay is as follows. Section I discusses recent developments and key issues in the economic analysis of crime prevention programs, including the main techniques, the methodological framework for conducting economic analyses, and the different measures of economic efficiency. Sections II, III, IV, and V review, respectively, the monetary costs and benefits of situational prevention, developmental prevention, correctional intervention, and community prevention. Each of these sections reviews the theoretical bases of the respective prevention strategies, summarizes (with the exception of Section V) key features of the studies and the main findings pertaining to monetary costs and benefits, and reviews in detail a selected study. Section VI brings together the main conclusions and identifies gaps in knowledge and priorities for research.

I. Economic Analysis of Crime Prevention Programs

Economic analysis is a tool that allows choices to be made between alternative uses of resources or alternative distributions of services (Knapp 1997, p. 11). Many criteria are used in economic analyses. The most common is efficiency, which is the focus throughout this essay. Efficiency is about achieving maximum outcomes from minimum inputs. One measurement of efficiency involves "aggregating all the gains and losses from a program in such a way that the net gain from one program can be compared to that of an alternative" (Barnett and Escobar 1987, p. 389). From this, the most economically efficient program can be identified. What cannot be concluded from an economic analysis, however, is the fairness or equity in the distribution of the services available (e.g., Are those individuals or families most in need of the services receiving them?). This decision, as noted by Barnett and Escobar (1990), must be left to the values of the policy makers.

Discussions of the economic efficiency of crime prevention programs can be very persuasive and have gained wide appeal in political, policy, and, more recently, academic settings. In many ways, the interest in attaching dollar values to crime prevention programs can be seen as an outgrowth of the focus on "what works" in preventing crime. Efficiency, performance measures, and targeting resources (among other terms) have become the common currency of discussions about crime prevention. However, compared to the number of outcome evaluation studies of crime prevention programs, which themselves are relatively few, there is a dearth of economic analysis studies in this area. This is also true in many other prevention and intervention areas, such as child and adolescent mental health (Knapp 1997) and substance abuse (Plotnick 1994; Rajkumar and French 1997).

A. Techniques of Economic Analysis

Benefit-cost (or cost-benefit) analysis and cost-effectiveness analysis are the two most widely used techniques of economic analysis. These terms have technical meanings. Barnett and Escobar (1987, 1990) describe cost-effectiveness analysis as an incomplete benefit-cost analysis. The incompleteness in cost-effectiveness analysis is because no attempt is made to estimate the monetary value of effects produced (benefits or disbenefits), only of program resources used (costs). Benefit-cost analysis, by contrast, monetizes both costs and benefits and compares them. Cost-effectiveness analysis does, however, provide a point of comparison between program inputs or costs and outcomes (e.g., X dollars produced Y crimes prevented), hence permitting an assessment of which program represents the most desirable investment. Another way to think about how benefit-cost and cost-effectiveness analysis differ is that "cost-effectiveness analysis may help one decide among competing program models, but it cannot show that the total effect was worth the cost of the program" (Weinrott, Jones, and Howard 1982, p. 179), unlike benefit-cost analysis.

By way of a simple illustration, a benefit-cost analysis of a Head Start program, for example, would first attempt to monetize all program effects on the children and parents (such as reduced crime) and resources used by the program and then divide total monetary benefits by total monetary costs. This gives a "bottom-line" statistic that shows whether the effects produced by the program exceed the resources spent on the program. A cost-effectiveness analysis of the same program would first need to be compared to one or more alternative prevention programs (e.g., Head Start without a parent training component), taking into account the need for like-with-like comparisons (Knapp and Netten 1997). For each program, all resources used are monetized and one program effect (such as crime) is selected, so that for each program there are total costs (resources used) and total crimes reduced. Using these similar metrics a determination of the most cost-effective program can then be made: the program with the lowest cost per crime reduced is the most cost-effective.

Cost analysis also deserves a brief mention here because of its wide application to crime prevention programs, particularly correctional intervention programs. In economic terms, cost analysis is not an economic analysis technique; there is no quantified relationship between program costs and effects, as in the case of cost-effectiveness and benefit-cost analysis. Similar to cost-effectiveness analysis, cost analysis assigns monetary values to all program inputs or resources used and does not value program outcomes. In the example of the Head Start program, a cost analysis would state the monetary value of the total resources used by the program, but would not assess the absolute or comparative economic efficiency of the program. Having information on program costs could, nonetheless, be useful to funders, and could serve as the basis of a cost-effectiveness analysis once costs are linked with outcomes.[1]

B. Doing an Economic Analysis

An economic analysis is a step-by-step process that follows a standard set of procedures. The six steps are as follows: (i) define the scope of the analysis; (ii) obtain estimates of program effects; (iii) estimate the monetary value of costs and benefits; (iv) calculate present value and assess profitability; (v) describe the distribution of costs and benefits (an assessment of who gains and who loses, e.g., program participants, government/taxpayers, crime victims); and (vi) conduct sensitivity analyses (Barnett 1993, pp. 143–48). It is beyond the scope of this essay to discuss each methodological step, but interested readers should consult the excellent reviews and applications of this methodology in the context of early childhood intervention programs by Barnett (1993, 1996) and Barnett and Escobar (1987, 1990). In the case of benefit-cost analysis, all of the six steps are carried out; for cost-effectiveness analysis, the estimation of the monetary value of benefits in step iii is omitted and step v is consequently omitted.

In practical terms, an economic analysis of the efficiency of a program is an extension of an outcome evaluation, and is only as defensible as the evaluation on which it is based. Weimer and Friedman (1979, p. 264) recommend that, in the context of correctional intervention, benefit-cost analyses be limited to programs that have been evaluated with an "experimental or strong quasi-experimental design." The most convincing method of evaluating crime prevention programs is

---

[1] See Knapp, Robertson, and McIvor (1992) for an excellent cost study of alternative criminal justice sanctions in Scotland.

the randomized experiment (Farrington 1983), which is often referred to as the gold standard. The key feature of randomized experiments is that the experimental and control groups are equated before the experimental intervention on all possible extraneous variables. Hence, any subsequent differences between them must be attributable to the intervention.

The randomized experiment, however, is only the most convincing method of evaluation if a sufficiently large number of units is randomly assigned to ensure that the program group is equivalent to the control group on all possible extraneous variables (within the limits of statistical fluctuation). As a rule of thumb, at least fifty units in each category are needed (Farrington 1997). This number is relatively easy to achieve with individuals but very difficult to achieve with larger units such as areas (see Section V for a discussion of this issue). For larger units such as areas, the best and most feasible design usually involves before-and-after measures in experimental and control areas, together with statistical control of extraneous variables. Nonrandomized experiments and before-after designs without a control group are less convincing methods of evaluating crime prevention programs.

We have used the scientific methods score developed by Sherman et al. (1997), which seems extremely valuable in assessing the methodological quality of intervention studies. This is as follows, with level 1 being the lowest and level 5 the highest:

1. Correlational evidence: low offending correlates with the program.

2. Nonequivalent control group or one-group pre/post design: program group compared with nonequivalent control group; program group measured before-and-after intervention (with no control group).

3. Equivalent control group design: program group compared with comparable control group, including pre/post and experimental-control comparisons.

4. Control of extraneous variables: program group compared with control group, with control of extraneous influences on the outcome (e.g., by matching, prediction scores, or statistical controls).

5. Randomized experiment: units assigned at random to program and control groups.

C. Measures of Economic Efficiency

The benefit-cost ratio is an expression of the ratio of monetary benefits to costs and is, ultimately, a measure of economic efficiency. In this essay, we have used the benefit-cost ratio to measure the economic efficiency of programs rather than net value (benefits minus costs) for three principal reasons: it controls for differences in national currencies; it controls for the different time periods of programs (e.g., the benefit-cost ratio of a program that used 1992 U.S. dollars can reasonably be compared with the benefit-cost ratio of a program that used 1976 British pounds); and it provides a single measurement of the benefits of a program that are gained from a one monetary unit of investment or expenditure. Arguments such as "for every dollar spent, seven dollars were saved in the long run" (Schweinhart, Barnes, and Weikart 1993) have proved to be very powerful. The decision to use the benefit-cost ratio is particularly important because, in many cases, it is a direct measurement of the value the taxpaying public receives for its investment.[2] It could be argued that expressing the value of publicly funded programs in this understandable form is concordant with the movement by governments toward a greater degree of transparency and accountability.

The "public" (government/taxpayer and crime victim) and "society" (government/taxpayer, crime victim, and program participant)[3] are the two perspectives most commonly used in the economic analysis of crime prevention programs. The decision about which perspective to take has important implications for evaluating the program, particularly if it is being funded by public money. That is, if conclusions are to be drawn about the monetary value of a program to the public, the benefits or costs must be those that the public will either receive or incur. More important, the perspective one takes can have important implications for the program's monetary value. For instance, adopting the society perspective for a marginally successful program, hence increasing the number of parties to which benefits may accrue, will likely increase the chances that the program will produce a return rather than a loss on investment. However, if the same program is the subject of a benefit-cost analysis that takes only the government or taxpayer

---

[2] Increasingly, over recent years, private foundations have begun to play a larger role in funding crime prevention programs.

[3] In the context of correctional intervention programs, lost legitimate earnings caused by imprisonment should be weighed against any benefits accrued to program group participants. Cohen (1998, p. 16) estimates the annual "preconviction (legitimate) earnings of convicted felons" at $7,542 in 1997 dollars (see also Cohen, Miller, and Rossman 1994, p. 137). In a similar vein, victimization costs (e.g., pain, suffering, lost quality of life) to imprisoned offenders should be weighed against similar costs avoided (benefits) to crime victims. In their review of the literature on incarcerated offender costs, Cohen, Miller, and Rossman (1994) did not locate any studies that had estimated the victimization costs to offenders in prison.

perspective, the chances of producing a return rather than a loss on investment will likely decrease. In this essay, we have taken the middle-of-the-road approach, by reporting on, as far as possible, the public (government/taxpayer and crime victim) perspective in calculating benefits and costs. For some of the studies reviewed here, it was not possible to disaggregate the published benefits and costs to meet our desired perspective.

D. Other Key Issues in Economic Analysis

Although this is not the place for an exhaustive discussion of technical issues to be addressed in benefit-cost studies, several fundamental issues warrant introduction and brief discussion.

1. *Marginal versus Average Costs.* In the context of program resources used, "marginal costs describe how the total cost of an operation changes as the unit of activity changes by a small amount," while "average costs are derived by simply dividing total costs by total workload in a given period of time" (Aos 1998, p. 13). The main limitation of average costs, as noted by Aos (1998, p. 13), is that "some of those costs . . . are fixed and do not change when workload changes." By using marginal cost estimates for a correctional intervention program in a custodial setting, for example, only the direct costs of an additional inmate (e.g., food, utilities) would be taken into account, while the most expensive prison operating budget item—personnel costs—would be excluded up to the point where the number of additional inmates required additional staff coverage.

In the context of costs to victims of crime, Cohen (1998, p. 8) notes that using marginal cost estimates excludes "such important costs as fear of crime, private security expenditures, and 'averting' behavior such as taking cabs instead of walking or changing one's lifestyle due to the risk of victimization." These costs are excluded because they are not affected by the actions of any one criminal (Cohen 1998, p. 8). It would, however, be important to assess these costs if a prevention program operated on a scale large enough (e.g., citywide) to have a potential impact on them. In the majority of the benefit-cost studies reviewed here, and in almost all of the situational crime prevention studies, average costs were used.

2. *Operating versus Capital Costs.* Program resources used (costs) can be divided into two main categories: operating costs (e.g., staff salaries and benefits, overhead) and capital costs (e.g., constructing facilities). A detailed description of the program and the resources it used

are both needed in calculating operating and capital costs. A related issue to capital costs is the borrowing of money to pay for a program. This often occurs in situational crime prevention programs which undertake large scale capital-intensive projects (e.g., installation of technical hardware, such as closed circuit television cameras). A key question is how best to account for the payments on the capital expenditure and debt charges on the loan in calculating the costs of the program. In assessing the economic efficiency of a program that lasts for only a short period of time, it might be unreasonable to include the total capital expenditure, which might dwarf any benefits accrued over this time period. The Safe Neighbourhoods Unit (1993, p. 145) recommends spreading the payments and the debt charges over the life expectancy of the program, but not beyond the loan repayment period, and using this "period as the basis for estimating a more realistic annual capital costs figure." The majority of the studies reviewed here included both operating and capital costs in their benefit-cost calculations.

3. *Present Value.* Present value is concerned with making all monetary costs and benefits of a program comparable over time. The time value of money is best understood by the following: "A dollar today is worth more than a dollar next year because today's dollar can be invested to yield a dollar plus interest next year" (Barnett and Escobar 1987, p. 390). If a program's costs and benefits are confined to one year then the calculation of present value is unnecessary.

Two separate steps must be carried out to adjust for differences in the value of money over time. First, the effect of inflation is removed by "translating nominal dollars from each year into dollars of equal purchasing power, or *real dollars*" (Barnett 1993, p. 146, emphasis in original). This is achieved by the application of a price index to the nominal monetary units, which more or less cancels out the effect of inflation. Second, the time value of money is taken into account "by calculating the *present value* of real dollars from each year" (Barnett 1993, p. 146, emphasis in original). For this to be achieved, real monetary units from different years must be discounted using an inflation-adjusted discount rate (between 3 percent and 7 percent per annum in the United States) to their "common value at the beginning of a program (or earliest program if two are compared)" (Barnett and Escobar 1987, p. 390).

One of the limitations of not calculating present value is that benefits will be slightly larger than they should be. The reason for this is that the calculation of present value reduces future benefits more than present costs. About half of the studies that had costs and benefits lasting for more than one year calculated present value.

4. *Victimization Costs.* Monetary costs to victims of crime can be divided into two main categories: tangible or out-of-pocket (e.g., property loss, medical expenses, lost wages) and intangible (e.g., lost quality of life, pain, suffering, fear), which may also include the risk of death. To give a sense of the relative magnitude of these categories of crime victim costs, of the $450 billion (in 1993 dollars) estimate of the annual cost of violent (including drunk driving and arson) and property crime to victims in the United States, by Miller, Cohen, and Wiersema (1996), intangible losses to crime victims were more than three times greater than tangible or out-of-pocket losses. By comparison, annual criminal justice (police, courts, and corrections) costs in the United States around the same period of time (which were not included in this estimate) were about $90 billion (Mandel et al. 1993). More relevant perhaps, is the victimization cost for a specific crime, like robbery, which Cohen (1998, p. 16, table 2) estimates as follows: $2,700 in tangible costs and $6,700 in intangible costs (in 1997 dollars). This leaves out the monetary value of the risk of death,[4] which adds $6,200, bringing the total cost to $15,600 for a robbery victim.

The estimation of intangible victimization costs and their use in different contexts, including in benefit-cost analyses of crime prevention programs, has attracted some criticism (see Zimring and Hawkins 1995, chap. 7). This is at least in part because of the large estimates that have been produced for victim costs (see Cohen 1988, 1998; Miller, Cohen, and Rossman 1993; Cohen, Miller, and Rossman 1994; Miller, Cohen, and Wiersema 1996), but especially because of the methodology used. Victim costs of pain, suffering, and lost quality of life are typically estimated on the basis of what a civil court would pay crime victims (jury compensation method) or what the public would willingly pay for additional safety (willingness-to-pay method).[5] Zimring and Hawkins (1995, p. 139) are critical of the jury compensation method, contending that "pain and suffering damages for personal injury in Anglo-American law are notorious for both their arbitrariness

---

[4] This is calculated by multiplying the risk of death for an average robbery by the "value of a statistical life" (Cohen 1998, p. 11). Cohen (1998) uses a value of a statistical life of $3.4 million (in 1997 dollars); see Miller, Cohen, and Wiersema (1996, pp. 21–22) for an overview of the published estimates for the cost of a statistical life.

[5] See Rajkumar and French (1997) for a review of different methods for estimating both tangible and intangible victim costs.

and their inflated size." In defense of the jury compensation method, Cohen (1998, p. 8) notes that "jury awards exhibit identifiable patterns that can be distilled from a large sample of cases through regression analysis that controls for factors such as the involvement of the plaintiff, deep pocket of the defendant, etc." In fact, both methods have been endorsed by various U.S. government agencies (e.g., Consumer Product Safety Commission) and are used in benefit-cost studies (Cohen 1998, p. 8). Only one of the benefit-cost studies reviewed in this essay—the Perry Preschool program of Schweinhart, Barnes, and Weikart (1993; see Sec. III)—included intangible costs to crime victims.

5. *Standard Variables.* The most crucial issue involved in carrying out benefit-cost studies in crime prevention or other areas is deciding which program resources used (costs) and effects produced (benefits) should have dollar figures attached. No prescribed formula exists for what to include (or exclude). Prest and Turvey (1965, p. 683) note that benefit-cost analysis "implies the enumeration and evaluation of all the relevant costs and benefits." Estimating the monetary value of program benefits requires a great deal of ingenuity on the part of the evaluator. Unlike program costs, program benefits are disparate and involve a number of assumptions in order to arrive at reasonable estimates of monetary value. In some ways, estimating the monetary value of the benefits of crime prevention programs is limited (beyond the limits imposed by the quality of the outcome evaluation) only by the ingenuity of the evaluator and the resources available to the evaluator. A standard list of costs and benefits that should be measured, and how they should be monetized, might overcome some of the difficulties that face researchers in conducting benefit-cost analyses of crime prevention programs, and would greatly facilitate comparisons of the benefit-cost findings of different crime prevention programs. It is beyond the scope of this essay to attempt the development of such a comprehensive list of costs and benefits that should be measured in all studies, but it is useful to sketch an outline of what a standard list might comprise.

Key outcome variables that should be measured in crime prevention programs include crime and delinquency, substance abuse, education, employment, health, and family factors. For crime, an assessment of benefits should focus on affected agencies within the criminal justice system (e.g., police, courts, corrections, probation) and crime victims and their families. Tangible and intangible crime-victim costs should be assessed in accordance with a theoretically sound and standardized methodology. Many of the same benefits assessed for crime can also be examined in relation to substance abuse. For education, benefits should be assessed for educational output (e.g., high school completion, enrollment in college or university) and schooling expenses (e.g., remedial classes, support services). Increased wages (tax revenue for governments) and decreased use of welfare services are two of the potential benefits that should be examined in relation to employment. For health, benefits should be assessed for use of public health care (e.g., visits to hospitals or clinics) and mental health. For family issues, benefits should be assessed for childbirths to at-risk women, parental time spent with children, and divorce and separation. This short list of some of the most relevant benefits of crime prevention programs demonstrates the potential scope needed in benefit-cost studies in this area, a scope that will not always be feasible nor affordable. At minimum, benefit-cost studies should measure the most salient benefits and costs.

E. Recent Developments

In recent years, there has been a steady growth of economic evaluation research in the crime prevention area. Benefit-cost studies, which are the focus of this essay, are only one of the many types of approaches that have been used to assess the independent and comparative economic efficiency of different crime prevention programs and policies. Sophisticated mathematical modeling techniques such as simulation models, which attempt to imitate the effects of real-life events through the modeling of behaviors and systems, have helped to overcome some of the shortcomings of past research in this subject area, such as Zedlewski's (1987) application of benefit-cost estimates to a hypothetical example of increased incapacitation (for a critique of this study, see Zimring and Hawkins 1988, 1995). Although this essay is focused on benefit-cost evaluations of "real-life" programs,[6] it is useful to take a look at leading research studies in the broader area of the economic evaluation of crime prevention.

The recent development of high-quality economic evaluation research in the crime prevention area is largely due to the efforts of the RAND Corporation. Their reports have explored the cost implications and crime reduction effectiveness of California's three-strikes law

---

[6] Particularly those employing research designs with the capacity to control for threats to internal and external validity, such as experimental and quasi-experimental designs.

(Greenwood et al. 1994), the cost-effectiveness of early intervention versus incarceration (Greenwood et al. 1996), the cost-effectiveness of mandatory minimum sentences and alternative policies for reducing illicit drug use and crime (Caulkins et al. 1997, 1998), and the monetary costs and benefits of early childhood intervention programs (Karoly et al. 1998). Perhaps the best known of these studies is *Diverting Children from a Life of Crime* (Greenwood et al. 1996). This study assessed the cost-effectiveness of four early intervention programs (home visit/ daycare, parent training, graduation incentives, and supervising delinquents) and California's "three-strikes" law. A mathematical model of "criminal populations in prison and on the street, as affected by criminal career initiation, arrest and sentencing, release, and desistance from criminal activity" was used to compute each program's impact on crime and criminal justice system costs (Greenwood et al. 1996, p. 17). General and offender population data sets for the State of California were used to derive estimates. This study found that graduation incentives was the most cost-effective program, and that only the home visit/daycare program was less effective (i.e., produced fewer serious crimes reduced per million dollars) than the three-strikes law.

The Dutch Ministry of Justice has also carried out some important economic evaluation research in the crime prevention area (van Dijk 1996, 1997). In the early 1990s, it initiated research to assess the cost-effectiveness of four hypothetical crime prevention strategies over time: extrapolating current trends (doing the same), increasing the number of police by 2–3 percent, increasing investment in situational crime prevention by 30 percent, and strengthening "network criminality prevention" to achieve a 10 percent reduction in delinquency and criminal behavior. The basis of the research was a computer-generated simulation model that forecast the expected impact of the different, but comparable, strategies on the workload of the criminal justice system, as measured in monetary terms. The situational prevention scenario was predicted to have the strongest effect on reducing criminal justice spending over time. Network criminality prevention was predicted to be the next most effective strategy in reducing costs, but only in the long term, while the police scenario was found to have the most undesirable impact.

Donohue and Siegelman (1998, p. 31; emphasis in original) investigated "whether the social resources that will be expended a decade or more from now on incarcerating today's youngsters could instead generate roughly comparable levels of crime *prevention* if they were spent today on the most promising social programs." On the basis of a 50 percent increase in the U.S. prison population over a fifteen-year period, assumed from the level in December 1993 and trends at the time, it was estimated that this policy would cost between $5.6 and $8 billion (in 1993 dollars) and result in a 5–15 percent reduction in crime. From the selected prevention programs—targeted early childhood intervention and vocational training for youth—it was found that comparable reductions in crime could be achieved if they were allocated the upper bound amount that would have been spent on prisons.

Most recently, the Washington State Institute for Public Policy initiated a rigorous program of research to "identify interventions that reduce crime *and* lower total costs to taxpayers and crime victims" (Aos, Barnoski, and Lieb 1998, p. 1, emphasis in original). This research adopted a benefit-cost model to assess each program's economic contribution. Of the sixteen crime prevention programs assessed, five were found not to have paid off program costs when only savings to the criminal justice system were included. Of these five, three did not pay off program costs when savings to crime victims were added. Out of eleven juvenile offender programs assessed, ten produced a net gain when criminal justice and crime victim savings were compared to program costs, and many had payback periods (for criminal justice costs avoided) of only one or two years.

These examples show that the economic analysis of crime prevention programs is a quickly expanding field. A review of the topic in ten years time should be able to include many more analyses. Eventually, it may be possible to carry out a meta-analysis in which benefit-cost ratios are related to key features of projects such as the quality of the evaluation design, the costs and benefits measured, and methods of calculating costs and benefits. Because of the current state of knowledge, our essay has to be a ground-clearing exercise rather than a meta-analysis.

II. Situational Crime Prevention

Thirteen situational crime prevention studies meeting the criteria for inclusion were identified. Table 1 summarizes key features of these thirteen studies. One of them—the Kirkholt Burglary Prevention Project (Forrester et al. 1990)—is reviewed in detail below. This project was chosen for review, despite its weak research design, because of its prominence and perceived importance in British crime prevention.

TABLE 1

Summary of Situational Crime Prevention Studies

Study Author, and Location	Crimes Targeted	Context of Intervention	Duration and Primary Technique of Intervention*	Sample Size	Scientific Methods Score	Follow-Up and Results†	Benefits Measured	Benefit-Cost Ratio‡
Cirel et al. (1977), Seattle	Burglary	Home	1 year; natural surveillance (Block Watch)	1,474 homes	3 (before-after, experimental-control)	Immediate outcome: burglary +	Crime victim expenses (person, direct)	.40
Schnelle et al. (1979), Nashville	Armed robbery	Store	6 and 11 months; formal surveillance (silent alarms)	48 stores	2 (before-after)	5 and 15 months: armed robbery 0	Crime victim expenses (private sector, direct)	.36
Laycock (1986) Caerphilly, Wales	Burglary	Home	1 year; identifying property (property marking)	2,234 homes	2 (before-after)	Immediate outcome: burglary +	Criminal justice system (police)	.78
Skilton (1988), South Kilburn Estate, London Borough of Brent	Vandalism	Public housing estate	1 year; employee surveillance (concierges)	305 homes (in two high rises)	3 (before-after, experimental-control)	Immediate outcome vandalism +	Crime victim expenses (public sector, direct), public housing	1.44
van Andel (1989), VICs, The Netherlands	Vandalism, toll fraud, assault	Public transport system	3 and 4 years; formal surveillance (special transport officials)	Metro, tram, and bus in three cities	2 (before-after)	Immediate outcome: vandalism +, toll fraud +, assault +	Crime victim expenses (public sector, direct), toll revenue	.32
Clarke and McGrath (1990), Victoria, Australia	Robbery	Betting shop	1–8 years; target hardening (time-locks, cash limits)	429 betting shops (average)	2 (before-after, some control)	Immediate outcome: robbery +	Crime victim expenses (public sector, direct)	1.71
Forrester et al. (1990), Kirkholt Burglary Prevention Project, Rochdale, England	Burglary	Public housing estate	3 years; target removal (removal of coin meters)	2,280 homes	2 (before-after, some control)	Immediate outcome: burglary +	Crime victim expenses (person, direct), criminal justice system, public housing	5.04

320

Study	Crime type	Setting	Context	Sample size	Methodological quality*	Immediate outcome†	Cost categories	Benefit-cost ratio‡
Poyner (1992), North Shields, England	Vandalism	Public transport system	9 months; employee surveillance (CCTVs)	80 buses	2 (before-after)	Immediate outcome: vandalism +	Crime victim expenses (public sector, direct)	2.35
Davidson and Farr (1994), Mitchellhill Estate, Glasgow	Vandalism, burglary	Public housing estate	15 months; employee surveillance (CCTVs)	5 housing blocks	2 (before-after)	Immediate outcome: vandalism +, burglary +	Crime victim expenses (public sector, direct), rental income	.47
Knight (1994), Possil Park Estate, Glasgow	Vandalism, burglary	Public housing estate	1 year; formal surveillance (security guards)	1,767 homes	2 (before-after)	Immediate outcome: vandalism +, burglary +	Crime victim expenses (person and private sector, direct)	1.31
Ekblom, Law, and Sutton (1996), Safer Cities Programme, England and Wales	Burglary	Home	1–2 years; target hardening (locks, alarms, entry systems)	7,500 households	4 (before-after, experimental control and statistical analyses)	Immediate outcome: burglary +	Crime victim expenses (person, direct), criminal justice system (police)	1.83
Painter and Farrington (1997), Dudley, England	Property and personal crime in general	Residential streets	1 year; natural surveillance (street lighting)	1,200 homes	4 (before-after, experimental-control and statistical analyses)	Immediate outcome: burglary +, theft +, vandalism +, vehicle theft +, personal crime +	Crime victim expenses (person, direct), criminal justice system (police)	4.34
Painter and Farrington (1999b), Stoke-on-Trent, England	Property and personal crime in general	Residential streets and footpaths	1 year; natural surveillance (street lighting)	756 homes	4 (before-after, experimental-control and statistical analyses)	Immediate outcome: burglary +, theft +, vandalism +, vehicle theft +, personal crime +	Crime victim expenses (person, direct), criminal justice system (police)	2.93

* Based on Clarke and Homel's (1997) classification.

† The period of time in which program effects were evaluated after the intervention had ended. '0' = no intervention effects; '+' = desirable intervention effects.

‡ Expressed as a ratio of benefits to costs in monetary units (national currencies).

The detailed review illustrates many key features of situational prevention and of economic analysis.

Situational crime prevention is defined as "a preventive approach that relies, not on improving society or its institutions, but simply on reducing opportunities for crime" (Clarke 1992, p. 3). Reducing opportunities for crime is achieved essentially through some modification or manipulation of the environment. The origins of situational prevention are based in the larger body of opportunity theory, which sees the offender "as heavily influenced by environmental inducements and opportunities and as being highly adaptable to changes in the situation" (Clarke 1995a, p. 57). An elaboration of the theoretical bases and principles of situational prevention is beyond the scope of this essay; however, excellent reviews of these topics are provided by Clarke (1995b, 1997) and Newman, Clarke, and Shoham (1997).

Clarke and Homel (1997) classified situational crime prevention into sixteen techniques divided into four main approaches: increasing perceived effort (target hardening, access control, deflecting offenders, and controlling facilitators); increasing perceived risks (entry/exit screening, formal surveillance, surveillance by employees, and natural surveillance); reducing anticipated rewards (target removal, identifying property, reducing temptation, and denying benefits); and inducing guilt or shame (rule setting, strengthening moral condemnation, controlling disinhibitors, and facilitating compliance).

We have limited our review of the monetary costs and benefits of situational prevention to those programs that have targeted violent or property crimes (e.g., robbery, burglary, vandalism). Excluded are programs that have targeted various forms of fraud, shoplifting, and employee theft. Some of these excluded programs are: business initiatives in the United Kingdom to reduce "bouncing checks," bank passbook fraud, check and credit card fraud, shoplifting, and employee theft (Burrows 1991); the London Underground's attempt to reduce fare evasion (Clarke 1993; Clarke, Cody, and Natarajan 1994); a shoplifting prevention experiment (DiLonardo 1996); and a U.S. prison's attempt to reduce the high costs of illicit telephone use (La Vigne 1994). These programs have been excluded because the primary victim, for the most part, was a business, not a person or a household. The inclusion of four of the thirteen studies where the context of the intervention was a shop or transport system (see table 1) was justified because there was also a measure of personal crime. Three other situational prevention studies that assessed costs and benefits and focused on crimes relevant to this review have also been excluded because two (Field 1993; Hakim et al. 1995) were not real-life programs and the third (Bridgeman 1996) provided incomplete cost and benefit data.

The studies in table 1 have been organized in chronological order. In those cases where a program targeted more than one of the crimes of interest, it was classified under the crime(s) for which cost and benefit data were presented. The studies originated in four different countries: Australia, the Netherlands, the United Kingdom, and the United States. In nine of the thirteen studies, residential areas provided the context for the intervention, while the remaining four took place in commercial premises or in public facilities (e.g., transport systems). The observed length of the intervention (the changed circumstances during which measurements were taken) ranged from six months to eight years. The most common primary intervention technique of the reviewed studies was surveillance by employees (three studies), formal surveillance (three studies), and natural surveillance (three studies). In only one of the projects (Schnelle et al. 1979) was there follow-up (defined as the period of time in which program effects were evaluated after the intervention had ended). Usually, the changed circumstances of the intervention continued to apply during the "after" period; there was no "reversal" design. Three of the thirteen studies used a methodologically sophisticated quasi-experimental evaluation design, comparing experimental and control units before and after, with control of extraneous variables in a regression analysis, and each was assigned a scientific methods score of four. Twelve of the thirteen studies reported a successful crime-reducing effect of the intervention (all except Schnelle et al. 1979).

It is important to draw attention to two important issues not addressed in table 1: displacement and diffusion of benefits.[7] Displacement is often defined as the unintended increase in targeted crimes in other locations following from the introduction of a crime reduction scheme (see Barr and Pease [1990] for a discussion of "benign" effects of displacement). Five different forms of displacement have been identified by Reppetto (1976): temporal (change in time), tactical (change in method), target (change in victim), territorial (change in place), and

---

[7] These issues are not unique to situational crime prevention, but also apply to, at least, community crime prevention and law-enforcement prevention (e.g., tough drug-law enforcement in a city may shift drug dealing to the surrounding county). They are discussed here because of their prominence in the situational crime prevention literature.

functional (change in type of crime). Diffusion of benefits is defined as the unintended decrease in nontargeted crimes following from a crime reduction scheme, or the "complete reverse" of displacement (Clarke and Weisburd 1994). Eight of the studies rigorously investigated the possibility of displacement following the introduction of the prevention measures, and four studies (Forrester et al. 1990; Poyner 1992; Davidson and Farr 1994; Painter and Farrington 1999*b*) considered the possibility of diffusion of benefits.

A. Summary of Economic Analysis Findings

Nine of the thirteen studies carried out some form of economic analysis, while the other four merely provided cost and benefit data. The benefits that were measured by the studies were largely confined to decreases in direct or tangible costs for crime victims[8] and, to a lesser extent, decreased criminal justice system costs. A desirable benefit-cost ratio (greater than 1.0) was calculated in eight of the thirteen studies. In these eight studies the measured economic return on a one monetary unit investment ranged from a low of 1.31 units to a high of 5.04 units (in the Kirkholt project). For the five projects that showed an undesirable benefit-cost ratio, the economic return on a one unit investment ranged from a low of 0.32 units to a high of 0.78 units. Seven of the eight studies published in 1990 or later yielded a desirable benefit-cost ratio, compared with only one of the five earlier studies.

Comparisons of the studies' benefit-cost ratios with both the primary intervention technique employed and the primary crime targeted by the intervention revealed no consistent findings. The three primary intervention techniques used in the majority of studies (nine of thirteen)—employee surveillance, formal surveillance, and natural surveillance—produced a desirable benefit-cost ratio in five of the nine studies. The two studies that employed target hardening as the primary intervention technique (Clarke and McGrath 1990; Ekblom, Law, and Sutton 1996) produced desirable benefit-cost ratios. For those (eleven) studies that targeted a primary type of crime (the studies by Painter and Farrington [1997, 1999*a*] targeted property and personal crimes in general), no clear relationship was found between type of crime and the studies' benefit-cost ratios. In those (four) projects that addressed

---

[8] In table 1, we distinguish between crime victims as a person/household, private sector (e.g., business), or public sector (e.g., government department).

burglary as the primary crime, there were an equal number of desirable and undesirable benefit-cost ratios. For vandalism, three out of the five studies (Skilton 1988; Poyner 1992; Knight 1994) that targeted this crime produced desirable benefit-cost ratios.

From the available evidence, it appears that situational prevention can be an economically efficient strategy for the reduction of crime. No conclusions, however, can be drawn about which situational technique is most economically efficient. Crime-specific reviews of situational prevention provide some conclusive findings about what works most effectively, and this is helpful in thinking about why a program did or did not produce a desirable economic result. For instance, the failure and undesirable benefit-cost ratio of the armed robbery intervention program reported by Schnelle et al. (1979), which involved the use of silent alarms transmitted to police, is not at all surprising. This is because the literature on commercial robbery prevention (see Hunter and Jeffery 1992) suggests that a multilevel combination of situational interventions (e.g., two store clerks and security cameras) is needed to have any effect on this category of crime. On their own, alarms are an ineffective situational measure in the prevention of commercial robberies.

Aside from the limitations that are also evident in reviews of the monetary costs and benefits of developmental prevention (Sec. III) and correctional intervention (Sec. IV), two limitations are specific to the situational prevention studies we reviewed. First, there is almost a complete absence of follow-up of program effects.[9] Follow-up research is needed to establish how long the effects (and benefits) persist after the program ends. This is also important for assessing how the benefit-cost ratio varies over time (see Welsh and Farrington 1998). Second, there are a number of methodological problems associated with the research designs of the studies. Few used experimental-control, before-after designs, which are needed to eliminate threats to internal validity. Ideally, randomized experimental designs should be used by researchers to test the merits of situational crime prevention programs. It is important to note, however, that it is difficult to assess program effects using randomized designs where the units of interest are areas, as opposed to individuals (Farrington 1997).

---

[9] The follow-up period is defined as the time period after the intervention has ended in which program effects are evaluated.

B. The Kirkholt Burglary Prevention Project

High rates of domestic burglary and repeat burglary victimization in the local authority estate of Kirkholt (2,280 dwellings), located in Rochdale, England, prompted a (British) Home Office-sponsored crime prevention scheme involving situational measures[10] (Forrester et al. 1990).

1. *Design and Method.* Kirkholt used a before-after design (with no control estate) to assess the number of domestic burglaries prevented on the estate. Situational measures involved the replacement of electricity and gas prepayment meters (activated by depositing coins much like a parking meter) by other devices in burgled homes (a target removal technique), marking of property, reduction of vulnerable points of entrance through upgrading security (a target hardening technique), and Neighborhood Watch (a natural surveillance technique). The Neighborhood Watch measure resembled the cocoon or microgroup approach used in the Seattle burglary prevention program (Cirel et al. 1977), which involves residents watching nearby homes (e.g., homes behind, in front, at sides, diagonally opposite). Importantly, residents of homes surrounding a previously victimized home were recruited to watch.

The evaluation covered the three-year period of the scheme (March 1987 to February 1990). The preintervention period covered the year prior to the onset of the scheme. In this period (the base year), a total of 526 burglaries were recorded by the police, and it was assumed that burglaries would have continued at this rate in the absence of the program. No follow-up data were collected by the authors, meaning that once the scheme had ended program effects were no longer assessed. The main sources of data included police-recorded burglaries and probation department reports. Territorial displacement was measured in the remainder of the police subdivision to which the Kirkholt estate belonged.

2. *Results.* Over the course of the three years of the scheme, a 74.9 percent reduction in the annual number of burglaries (from 526 to 132 per year) was observed. After the first year alone, burglaries were reduced by 57.6 percent (526 to 223). Compared with the preintervention rate, 1,056 burglaries were prevented in three years (to the extent

---

[10] Community crime prevention measures were also planned as part of the scheme, but were never fully implemented due to, in large part, practical difficulties (Gilling 1994). As a result, the Kirkholt project has secured its place in history as a situational crime prevention scheme (see Pease 1992).

that the reduction could be attributed to the intervention). A substantial (24 percent after three years) reduction in the aggregate number of burglaries in the remainder of the subdivision occurred as well, suggesting that territorial displacement did not occur. A diffusion of benefits might possibly be inferred from this reduction in burglaries in nontargeted areas, although the reduction could also reflect other changing influences over the time period. It is important to note that the comparison of prevented burglaries between Kirkholt and the remainder of the subdivision does not represent an experimental-control evaluation because the larger area was not comparable to the experimental area.

3. *Economic Analysis.* A benefit-cost analysis was carried out.[11] The total cost of the scheme was estimated at just under £300,000 (£298,398). This was made up of Home Office grants, housing department budgets allocated to improvements in safety and security on the estate, and the cost of police and probation staff seconded to the project (Safe Neighbourhoods Unit 1993). The total benefits of the scheme after three years were estimated at a little more than £1.5 million (£1,504,664). Benefits were calculated by estimating the monetary value of the number of burglaries prevented. The method of calculating the number of prevented burglaries involved applying subdivision burglary trends to the 1986 figure (the year prior to the scheme) to establish a baseline and subtracting the actual number of burglaries from that baseline. The prevented burglaries each year were then multiplied by a series of cost items per burglary: average electricity meter losses; average police costs (per undetected burglary); average detection, sentencing, and disposal costs ("assuming a 20 percent detection rate for reported burglaries" [Osborn 1994, p. 68]); average value of property/cash losses; and average housing repair costs (Safe Neighbourhoods Unit 1993, p. 141). Forrester and his colleagues considered that benefits were conservatively estimated since a number of them were not examined or not monetized, including income generated by the reduction in the number of empty properties on the estate, savings in insurance claims, and psychological effects of victimization.

Dividing total benefits by total costs produced a desirable benefit-cost ratio of 5.04. For each £1 that was invested in the Kirkholt scheme, taxpayers and victims of crime gained £5.04 in return (from

---

[11] No base year was reported for the calculation of costs and benefits, so it is unlikely that the effect of inflation was removed or present value was calculated.

prevented burglaries). The benefit-cost calculations were, however, the subject of some criticism. The Safe Neighbourhoods Unit (1993) questioned the estimated total benefits on the basis that the Kirkholt evaluators assumed that criminal justice costs associated with reduced burglaries (police, probation, and courts) were "wholly savable," meaning that a direct reduction in real expenditures was achieved. It was argued that these benefits were unlikely to be realized from such a small-scale project because the same level of resources (e.g., police officers) still had to be maintained. This was essentially an argument about using average as opposed to marginal benefits. Husain (1994, p. 23) argued that "such notional savings should not be ignored, since the aggregate effect of successful initiatives will be to depress such expenditure, even if the gains from individual projects cannot be clearly identified." For example, the project freed up police time that could be directed elsewhere.

Our assessment of Kirkholt's crime reduction and benefit-cost findings are mixed. On the one hand, the evaluation design was relatively weak. A before-after design with no control site makes it difficult to attribute reductions in crime unambiguously to the program. The addition of a control site would have greatly improved the quality of the design, and increased its scientific methods score from level 2 to level 3. On the other hand, despite some shortfalls in methodological rigor (e.g., not calculating net present value), Kirkholt's benefit-cost analysis was relatively robust, which increases confidence in the benefit-cost findings. As noted above, many potential benefits were not measured, suggesting that its benefit-cost ratio may have been an underestimate.

III. Developmental Crime Prevention

Six developmental crime prevention studies meeting the criteria for inclusion were identified. Table 2 summarizes key features of the six studies. The most prominent of these studies and the one with the highest quality benefit-cost analysis—the Perry Preschool program (Schweinhart, Barnes, and Weikart 1993)—is reviewed in detail.

Developmental prevention aims to influence the scientifically identified risk factors or "root causes" of juvenile delinquency and later criminal offending. It is informed generally by motivational or human development theories on criminal behavior, and specifically by longitudinal studies that follow samples of young persons from their early childhood experiences to the peak of their involvement with crime in their teens and twenties (e.g., Farrington 1995). The developmental perspective postulates that criminal offending in adolescence and adulthood is influenced by "behavioral and attitudinal patterns that have been learned during an individual's development" (Tremblay and Craig 1995, p. 151). Detailed reviews of the theoretical bases of developmental prevention have been presented elsewhere (e.g., McCord 1995; Farrington 1996).

Two well-known developmental prevention studies that have measured delinquency and childhood aggression and presented data on the monetary value of the programs—the Syracuse University Family Development Research Project (Lally, Mangione, and Honig 1988) and the Yale Child Welfare Research Program (Seitz, Rosenbaum, and Apfel 1985)—are not included here, because the published data were insufficient to calculate benefit-cost ratios to assess the economic efficiency of the programs. The Syracuse program began prenatally, providing program mothers with a range of educational and health services. Following birth, trained paraprofessionals visited the homes weekly to assist mothers (and other family members) with issues of childrearing, family relations, employment, and community functioning. Children were provided with four and one-half continuous years of enriched child care (fifty weeks a year), commencing with five half-days a week at six to fifteen months and, thereafter, with five full days a week until the age of sixty months. Lally, Mangione, and Honig (1988) did not provide data on the resources used (costs), only on the cost savings to the criminal justice system.

The Yale program also began prenatally. It involved four main interventions administered up to thirty months postpartum. First, professional home visits were provided to assist with short-term (e.g., reducing physical danger) and long-term (e.g., reaching career goals) family problems and link families to community services. Second, pediatric care services were provided to the mother and child, decreasing in intensity from birth to infancy. Children received from thirteen to seventeen examinations. Emphasis was placed on educating parents in observing their child's health. Third, each child attended an enriched day care program which focused on the child's emotional and social development for, on average, 13.2 months. Fourth, regular developmental examinations were carried out with the child, with the parent present, using standardized instruments. Seitz, Rosenbaum, and Apfel (1985) provided information on program resources used and benefits, but this was insufficient to provide a fair assessment of program efficiency.

A third study (Coopers and Lybrand 1994), the only one found in

TABLE 2
Summary of Developmental Crime Prevention Studies

Authors and Locations	Age at Intervention	Risk Factors Manipulated	Context of Intervention	Duration and Type of Intervention	Sample Size	Scientific Methods Score	Follow-up and Results*	Benefits Measured	Benefit-Cost Ratio†
Long, Mallar, and Thornton (1981), Job Corps, United States	18 years (average)	Education, employment	Residential-based center	N.A.; vocational training, education, health care	5,100 youths: T = N.A., C = N.A.	4 (before-after, experimental-control with matching)	18 months (average): police arrests +, substance abuse +, school achievement +, employment +, wages +	Crime victim expenses (direct), criminal justice system, employment earnings, social service use	1.45
Lipsey (1984), Los Angeles County Delinquency Prevention Program	< 15 years (average)	Behavioral problems	Community-based center	10 weeks; family counseling, academic tutoring, employment training	7,637 youths (all in program) youths: T = N.A., C = N.A.	2 (before-after) and 3 (before-after, experimental-control)	Immediate outcome: police arrests +†	Criminal justice system	1.40
Schweinhart, Barnes, and Weikart (1993), Perry Preschool Program, Ypsilanti, Mich.	3–4 years	Cognitive development	Preschool, home	1–2 years; preschool intellectual enrichment, parent education	123 children (72 boys, 51 girls): T = 58, C = 65	5 (randomized experiment-stratified assignment)	9–10 years: delinquency +, school achievement +, cognitive functioning 0 22 years: police arrests +, school achievement +, social service use +, educational achievement +	Crime victim expenses (direct and indirect), criminal justice system, educational output and public school expenses, employment earnings, social service use	9–10 years follow-up: 2.48 14 years follow-up: 3.00 22 years follow-up: 7.16

Hahn (1994), Quantum Opportunities Program, United States	15 years (average)	Education	Community-based agency, home	4 years; education, skill development	250 youths: T = 125, C = 125	5 (randomized experiment)	6 months: police arrests +, school achievement +, social services use +	Educational output, fewer children	3.68
Earle (1995), Hawaii Healthy Start	Prenatal and birth	Parenting, family planning	Home	4 years; parent education, parent support, family planning, community support	2,706 families: T = 1,353, C = 1,353	3 (before-after, experimental-control)	Immediate outcome: child abuse and neglect +	Child protective services	.38
Olds, Eckenode, et al. (1997); Olds, Henderson, et al. (1998); Prenatal/Early Infancy Project, Elmira, N.Y.	Prenatal	Parenting, family planning	Home	2 years; T1 = parent education, parent support, community support, family planning, T2 = T1 minus postnatal home visits, C = 2 conditions not receiving home visits (screening services and free transportation to clinic)	400 mothers: T1 = 116, T2 = 100, C = 184	5 (randomized experiment)	Immediate outcome (T1 vs. C): mothers: child abuse and neglect +, discipline +; children: developmental quotient + 13 years (T1 vs. C): mothers: child abuse and neglect +; higher risk mothers: arrests and convictions +; children: arrests +	Child protective services, employment earnings, public health care, social service use	2 years follow-up: higher risk sample = 1.06, whole sample = .51 13 years follow-up: higher risk sample = 4.06, lower risk sample = .62

NOTE.—T = treatment group; C = control group; N.A. = not available.

* The period of time in which program effects were evaluated after the intervention had ended. "0" = no intervention effects; "+" = desirable intervention effects.

† Expressed as a ratio of benefits to costs in monetary units (national currencies).

‡ Based on earlier studies that employed both before-after (no control group) and before-after, experimental-control designs.

the United Kingdom, has also been excluded because it did not evaluate a real-life program. This study employed a case study design to assess the program costs of a nonrepresentative sample of Youth Service schemes that had as an explicit aim the prevention of crime. The Youth Service is a network of organizations (statutory and voluntary sectors) that provides the majority of the youth work schemes across England and Wales. It is a nonschool program aimed principally at fostering the "planned and social education" of young people.

The studies in table 2 have been organized in chronological order. All were conducted in the United States. At the outset of the intervention, subjects ranged in age from prebirth to eighteen years, with half of the projects commencing prior to the formal school years. The studies manipulated a variety of different risk factors, including parenting, education, cognitive development, and behavioral problems. The duration of the intervention ranged from ten weeks to four years. Two of the studies (Schweinhart, Barnes, and Weikart 1993; Olds et al. 1997) had long follow-up periods to assess outcomes. The methodological rigor of the six studies was very high, with three (Schweinhart, Barnes, and Weikart 1993; Hahn 1994; Olds et al. 1997) employing random assignment to experimental and control conditions. All interventions were successful. Five of the six studies performed a benefit-cost analysis, while the one study that did not (Earle 1995) provided sufficient cost and benefit data to permit an estimation of its economic efficiency.

A. Summary of Economic Analysis Findings

The benefits measured by the six developmental prevention studies were wide-ranging, including reduced crime victim expenses, criminal justice system costs, public health care, and social service use. Five of the six studies yielded a desirable benefit-cost ratio. For these five studies the economic return on a one dollar investment ranged from a low of $1.06 to a high of $7.16 (in the Perry program). The one study that did not show a desirable benefit-cost ratio (Earle 1995) was the one for which we carried out a simple benefit-cost analysis. It is important to note that the Elmira Prenatal/Early Infancy Project of Olds et al. (1997) reported a desirable benefit-cost ratio for the higher risk sample and an undesirable benefit-cost ratio for the whole sample at two years postintervention. A more recent benefit-cost analysis of the Elmira program by RAND (Karoly et al. 1998), which also measured program effects on children's delinquency at age fifteen, found a favorable benefit-cost ratio for the higher risk families, but not for the lower risk families.[12]

A desirable benefit-cost ratio was found for each of the four studies in which the intervention commenced after birth, ranging from 1.40 to 7.16. By comparison, the two studies that began prenatally (Earle 1995; Olds et al. 1997) reported mixed results. The Hawaii Healthy Start and the lower risk sample for Elmira (at the latest follow-up) showed undesirable ratios of 0.38 and 0.62, respectively, while the higher risk sample for Elmira (at the latest follow-up) showed a desirable ratio of 4.06. In the case of Hawaii Healthy Start, limited program effects—only program effects on child abuse and neglect could be monetized—contributed to its poor economic showing.

For three of the four studies in which the intervention began after birth (Long, Mallar, and Thornton 1981; Lipsey 1984; Schweinhart, Barnes, and Weikart 1993), savings from reduced delinquency and later offending, as measured by less involvement with the justice system and fewer victims of crime, accounted for a substantial proportion of the measured benefits. Reduced offending in the Perry program at age twenty-seven accounted for four-fifths (79.6 percent) of the total economic benefits, or $5.70 of $7.16. In the case of the Job Corps program, reduced criminal activity accounted for one-quarter (28.8 percent) of the total benefits, or $0.42 of $1.45. Some of the other benefits produced by these programs included reduced reliance on welfare, increased economic output of the program participants that generated increased tax revenue for the government, and increased educational achievement which, in some cases, meant less use of remedial school services. Overall, developmental prevention appears to be a promising strategy in reducing monetary costs associated with delinquency and later criminal offending and improving the life course development of at-risk children and their families.

B. The Perry Preschool Program

Perry Preschool started in 1962 in Ypsilanti, Michigan. The Perry study is perhaps the best known longitudinal study in the Western world that has rigorously charted the effects of an early childhood intervention program. The principal hypothesis of Perry was that "good preschool programs can help children in poverty make a better start in

---

[12] Karoly et al. (1998) report on analyses of higher (unmarried and low SES) and lower (two-parent or higher SES) risk families, while Olds et al. (1993) report on analyses of higher risk families and the sample as a whole (higher- plus lower-risk families).

their transition from home to community and thereby set more of them on paths to becoming economically self-sufficient, socially responsible adults" (Schweinhart, Barnes, and Weikart 1993, p. 3).

1. *Design and Method.* Prior to the start of the program, 123 children ages three to four years were randomly assigned to either an experimental group that received the preschool program ($n = 58$) or a control group that did not ($n = 65$). The sample consisted of seventy-two boys and fifty-one girls. Families were recruited if they had low socioeconomic status and their children showed low intellectual performance. Some of the characteristics of the sample families at the time of recruitment included: 40 percent unemployed, 49 percent receiving welfare assistance, 47 percent single-parent households, and low high school completion rates (11 percent for men; 21 percent for women).

The main intervention strategy involved high quality, active learning preschool programming administered by professional teachers for two years. Preschool sessions were one-half day long and were provided five days a week for the duration of the thirty-week school year. The educational approach focused on supporting the development of the children's cognitive and social skills through individualized teaching and learning. The children planned what they were going to do, did it, and then reviewed what they had done. Weekly home visits were also carried out by the teachers to provide parents with educational information and to encourage parents to take an active role in their child's early education.

The sample was most recently assessed at the age of twenty-seven years, or twenty-two years postintervention. Data sources included personal interviews, school, police, court, and social service records, and a standardized survey to test general literacy. The sample attrition was exceedingly low at this follow-up stage (only 4.9 percent). Earlier assessments were carried out annually from ages three to eleven, at fourteen to fifteen (hereafter referred to as age fifteen), and at nineteen years.

2. *Results.* At age twenty-seven, compared to the control group, program group participants showed a number of benefits across a range of prosocial functioning indicators. They had fewer police arrests, with the mean number of lifetime arrests being 50 percent lower for program compared to control participants (2.3 vs. 4.6). Also, fewer program participants were chronic offenders (five or more arrests) compared to controls (7 percent vs. 35 percent). Other statistically significant benefits realized by the program compared to the control

group, at age twenty-seven, included: higher monthly earnings (27 percent vs. 7 percent earning $2,000 or more per month); higher percentages of home ownership (36 percent vs. 13 percent) and second-car ownership (30 percent vs. 13 percent); a higher level of schooling completed (71 percent vs. 54 percent completing twelfth grade or higher); and a lower percentage receiving welfare benefits at some time in the previous ten years (59 percent vs. 80 percent) (Schweinhart, Barnes, and Weikart 1993, p. xv).

3. *Economic Analysis.* A comprehensive benefit-cost analysis of the Perry program (Barnett 1993) found that the program's effects translated into substantial savings for both the program group participants and the public. In the benefit-cost analysis, which adjusted all figures to 1992 dollars, the program's measured effects through age twenty-seven and the program's projected effects beyond age twenty-seven were both included. Although the projected effects may be controversial, this combined measure is what is reported throughout the literature, and is used here. Monetary benefits through age twenty-seven accounted for 70.1 percent of total program benefits ($61,972 out of $88,433). Also, we report on program benefits accruing to the public (taxpayers and crime victims); benefits received by individual participants are not included in the benefit-cost calculation.

Total costs of the program were estimated at $12,356 per program group participant. Program costs were derived from two categories: basic operating costs, which included instruction, administration and support staff, overhead, supplies, and psychological screening; and capital costs, which took into account the school district classrooms and other facilities used by the program (Barnett 1993). Total program benefits were estimated at $88,433 per program group participant. The greatest benefits were from savings to the justice system ($12,796) and crime victims ($57,585). Savings to the justice system alone covered program costs.

Participants' arrest and incarceration histories were used to estimate savings to the main components of the criminal justice system: police, prosecutors, court, prison, and probation. Savings to crime victims were estimated in a two-step process. First, participants' arrest histories were linked with national data on the ratio of arrests to crimes committed, which provided an estimate, by age, of the numbers and types of crimes actually committed by program group participants. Second, these crime estimates were then combined with previously developed estimates of crime-specific costs to victims (Cohen 1988,

1992), which produced estimates of costs to victims of crimes committed by program group participants at each age (Barnett 1993, p. 160).
Costs to crime victims were not limited to tangible or out-of-pocket
monetary losses (e.g., lost property, wages, medical expenses), as is
usually the case in such calculations. Also taken into account, where
applicable, were the intangible costs of reduced quality of life, pain,
and suffering, as well as the risk of death.[13]

The other monetary benefits received by the public, expressed per
preschool participant, included: higher educational output and reduced
schooling costs, $6,287; revenue generated from taxes on increased
earnings, $8,847; and reduced reliance on welfare, $2,918. Dividing total benefits per participant ($88,433) by total costs per participant
($12,356) produced a highly desirable benefit-cost ratio of 7.16. In
other words, for every dollar spent on the program, $7.16 was returned
to the public, making the Perry program a very sound investment of
public resources.

Two earlier benefit-cost analyses of the Perry program, when subjects were ages fifteen and nineteen, also showed that the program was
a sound investment of taxpayer dollars. At age fifteen, a benefit-cost
ratio of 2.48 was reported (Weber, Foster, and Weikart 1978;
Schweinhart and Weikart 1980) and at age nineteen, a benefit-cost ratio of 3.00 was reported (Berrueta-Clement et al. 1984). The differences between these two ratios, as well as the age twenty-seven ratio
of 7.16, stem largely from the continued improvements of the program
group compared to the control group and from benefits being calculated cumulatively. Another important reason for the change in benefit-cost findings over time, particularly between the latter two assessments (age nineteen and twenty-seven), has to do with the inclusion of
intangible crime victim costs in the most recent analysis.

The crime reduction estimates and benefit-cost findings in the Perry
project are among the most defensible in the field. Although the sample size was small, the evaluation design was of high quality in controlling for threats to internal and external validity. The low attrition in
the long-term follow-up also strengthens confidence in the findings.
The benefit-cost analysis, performed by Barnett (1993), was methodologically rigorous, not to mention comprehensive in its coverage of
costs and benefits. However, questions can be raised about the inclu-

[13] Information reported by Barnett (1993) did not make it possible to disentangle tangible and intangible costs.

sion of intangible crime victim costs of pain, suffering, reduced quality of life, and risk of death.

IV. Correctional Intervention

Six correctional intervention studies meeting the criteria for inclusion were identified. Table 3 summarizes key features of the six studies. One of these—the New York City Supported Work social experiment (Friedman 1977)—is reviewed in detail, because it had the highest quality research design and benefit-cost analysis.

Correctional intervention attempts to modify offender behavior through some combination of treatment and external controls (Palmer 1992). Treatment, according to Palmer (1992, p. 3), attempts to "affect the individual's future behavior, attitudes toward self, and interactions with others by focusing on such factors and conditions as the individual's adjustment techniques, interests, skills, personal limitations, and/or life circumstances." In this essay, correctional intervention is mainly concerned with offender treatment programs.

Offender treatment programs serve many purposes and, as a result, their effectiveness can be measured using many different outcomes. Three main outcomes can be delineated: to decrease offending behavior in the community; to increase the offender's psychological and social adjustment within the institution (e.g., to reduce suicide and self-harm) (Skett 1995, p. 20); and to improve other life course outcomes, such as education, employment, health, relationships, and social service use.

MacKenzie (1997, p. 1, chap. 9) classified, from a policy perspective, correctional programs focused on reducing reoffending in the community into six categories, which are by no means mutually exclusive: incapacitation, "depriving the offender of the capacity to commit crimes usually through detention in prison or capital punishment"; deterrence, "punishment that is so repugnant that neither the punished offender (specific deterrence) nor others (general deterrence) will commit the crime in the future [because of fear of punishment]" (e.g., shock probation, fines); rehabilitation, "treatment directed toward changing the offender and thereby preventing future criminal behavior of the treated individual" (e.g., cognitive skills training, academic programs); community restraints, "surveillance and supervision of offenders in the community in order to reduce their capacity and/or opportunity for criminal activities" (e.g., intensive supervision probation, house arrest, electronic monitoring); structure, discipline, and chal-

TABLE 3
Summary of Correctional Intervention Studies

Authors and Locations	Age at Intervention	Targeted Offending Behavior	Context of Intervention	Duration and Primary Type of Intervention	Sample Size	Scientific Methods Score	Follow-up and Results*	Benefits Measured	Benefit-Cost Ratio†
Holahan (1974), Project Crossroads, Washington, D.C.	18–25 years	Property offending in general	Community	3 months: pretrial diversion with counseling, job training, and remedial education	307 adults: T = 200, C = 107	3 (before-after, experimental-control)	12 months: police arrests +	Crime victim expenses (direct), criminal justice system, employment earnings	2.36
Friedman (1977), Supported Work Social Experiment, New York City	32 years (average; T only)	N.A.	Community	8 months (average): employment	229 adults: T = 120, C = 109‡	5 (randomized experiment)	16 months (average): police arrests +, social service use +, employment +, health –, education –	Crime victim expenses, criminal justice system, employment earnings, social service use, public goods and services	1.13

Austin (1986), Early Release Program, Illinois	19–40 years (87.9% of sample)	Criminal offending in general	Community	Not applicable: early release	1,557 adults and youths: T = 1,202, C = 355	3 (before after, experimental-control)	2.5 years: police arrests +	Criminal justice system	2.82
Pearson and Harper (1990), New Jersey Intensive Supervision Program	N.A.	Nonviolent offending in general	Community, institution	18 months (average): employment, intensive supervision, incapacitation	686 adults: T = 554, C = 132	3 (before after, experimental-control)	N.A.: convictions +, institution time +	Criminal justice system, community service work, employment earnings	1.48
Prenky and Burgess (1990), Massachusetts	N.A.	Child molestation	Institution (maximum security)	5.1 years (median): rehabilitation§	182 individuals: T = 129 (adults), C = 53	2 (before-after, experimental-control, retrospectively chosen C)	5 and 25 years: victim-involved sexual offenses (15 charges) +	Crime victim expenses (direct), criminal justice system	1.16
Gerstein et al. (1994), California Drug and Alcohol Treatment Assessment	33.3 years (mean)	Criminal offending and substance abuse in general	Community, residential	2.8 months (mean): substance abuse (4 modalities)	3,055 adults	2 (before-after)	15 months (average): criminal activity +, substance abuse +, health +, social service use +, employment −	Crime victim expenses (direct), criminal justice system, employment earnings, public health care	7.14

NOTE.—T = treatment group; C = control group; N.A. = not available.

* The period of time in which program effects were evaluated after the intervention had ended. "0" = no intervention effects; "+" = desirable intervention effects; "−" = undesirable intervention effects.

† Expressed as a ratio of benefits to costs in monetary units (national currencies).

‡ This comprises the remaining sample after two years from the start of the program; no information was provided on the sample at the onset of intervention.

§ No information was provided on the type of rehabilitation used.

lenge, "physically and/or mentally stressful experiences to change the offenders in a positive way or deter them from later crime (specific deterrence)" (e.g., boot camps, wilderness programs); and combining rehabilitation and restraint "to insure that offenders make changes that are associated with a reduction in future criminal behavior" (e.g., drug treatment with urine testing). In the academic literature, correctional intervention is often distinguished from punishment, as in MacKenzie's (1997) classification scheme. We did not locate any studies meeting our criteria for inclusion that focused solely on punishment.

Unlike the other crime prevention strategies covered in this essay, a great deal has been published on the application of economic evaluation techniques to offender treatment. For the most part, however, these studies have consisted of statistical modeling exercises and analyses of hypothetical examples of correctional practices (e.g., Hofler and Witte 1979), and cost and cost-effectiveness analyses. The former have not been included here because they are not real-life programs, while the latter have been excluded because they do not provide an assessment of economic benefits, only of costs (see Sec. I).

The studies in table 3 have been organized in chronological order. All were conducted in the United States. Interventions were targeted on a wide range of offending behaviors. In five of the six studies, the community was the setting for treatment; however, in two of these (Pearson and Harper 1990; Gerstein et al. 1994), treatment was also administered in institutional or residential settings. The base sample size was quite large in some cases, with two of the studies (Austin 1986; Gerstein et al. 1994) having fifteen hundred and three thousand subjects, respectively. Few similarities were evident in the duration and primary type of intervention employed. Postprogram treatment effects were assessed in each of the studies, and the length of follow-up ranged from twelve months to twenty-five years.

Five of the six studies used an experimental evaluation design and one of these (Friedman 1977) employed random assignment to experimental and control conditions. Gerstein et al. (1994) used a before-after design with no control group. Each of the six studies assessed recidivism and, in each case, the first rearrest or reconviction was the measure of recidivism used. Five of the studies carried out an economic analysis. The sixth study (Pearson and Harper 1990) carried out only a cost analysis, but published data that enabled us to calculate monetary benefits and hence a benefit-cost ratio to assess the program's economic efficiency.

A. Summary of Economic Analysis Findings

In addition to costs avoided to the criminal justice system and crime victims, other benefits measured by the six correctional intervention studies covered employment earnings, public health care, and social service use. All of the six studies showed a desirable benefit-cost ratio. For these six studies the economic return on a one-dollar investment ranged from a low of $1.13 to a high of $7.14.

No significant patterns emerge from a comparison between key features of the six studies and their benefit-cost ratios. Some findings are, however, noteworthy. The two studies with the largest sample sizes (Austin 1986; Gerstein et al. 1994) produced the highest benefit-cost ratios: 2.82 and 7.14, respectively. However, the study with the largest sample size (Gerstein et al. 1994) used a comparatively weak evaluation design, relying on before-after measures with no control group. Also, a reduced sample size of unknown magnitude was used to estimate economic benefits. For the study by Austin (1986), which used an experimental-control design, the benefit-cost analysis was based on the treatment group only.

It is noteworthy that four of the six studies (Holahan 1974; Friedman 1977; Pearson and Harper 1990; Gerstein et al. 1994) assessed and quantified in monetary terms outcomes other than recidivism. Education, employment, health, social service use, and illicit substance use were the different kinds of outcomes monetized in these studies. In two of these four studies (Friedman 1977; Pearson and Harper 1990), economic benefits from improvements in these outcomes outweighed benefits from reduced recidivism. Although far from conclusive, this is an important finding because it suggests that correctional intervention programs have the potential to influence other important areas of an offender's life and produce, in some cases, substantial economic benefits for publicly funded services such as health and welfare.

A notable feature of all studies is the omission of indirect or intangible costs to victims of crime (e.g., pain, suffering, reduced quality of life, fear of future victimization) in the benefit-cost calculations. In four of the six studies[14] the monetary costs to crime victims were limited to out-of-pocket expenses, such as property loss and damage and medical expenses. To be fair to the authors, the majority acknowledged the difficulties involved in assessing and quantifying intangible costs to

---

[14] One study (Friedman 1977) did not explain the type of victim costs quantified, while the other (Pearson and Harper 1990) did not assess or quantify victim costs.

crime victims in monetary terms. These difficulties include: the lack of existing estimates of the intangible costs to victims of crime, which first appeared in the published literature in Cohen (1988), and the doubts of many researchers about the validity of these costs and the underlying theory used in their calculation (see Zimring and Hawkins 1995, p. 138).

The importance of assessing and quantifying intangible costs to crime victims in economic analyses is illustrated in Cohen's (1988) re-analysis of Austin's (1986) benefit-cost calculations, where the inclusion of intangible costs to victims of crime had the effect of changing drastically the conclusions of the benefit-cost analysis. By adding a pain and suffering component to Austin's (1986) estimates of the direct costs to crime victims, while maintaining the other costs incurred by the program,[15] Cohen (1988) reported a sixfold increase in total program costs. This resulted in a reversal of the benefit-cost findings, from producing a dividend on public expenditure to an investment loss. Austin's (1986) benefit-cost findings (see table 3) have been retained because in many of the studies reviewed in this essay insufficient data was provided to permit the recalculation of costs and benefits.

Most of the studies had large samples and reasonable follow-up periods. Of the six studies reviewed, four had a high-quality research design: an experimental-control design with before-and-after measures, making it possible to exclude threats to internal validity and ensure that the intervention produced the observed effects. In these four studies (Holahan 1974; Friedman 1977; Austin 1986; Pearson and Harper 1990), a desirable benefit-cost ratio was achieved, ranging from 1.13 to 2.82. The use of before-after measures without a control group in the study by Gerstein et al. (1994) and the use of a nonequivalent (retrospectively selected) control group in the study by Prentky and Burgess (1990) limit the confidence that can be placed in their reported intervention effects and benefit-cost findings. Notwithstanding the methodological limitations of some of the studies reviewed here, the available evidence on the monetary costs and benefits of correctional intervention programs suggests that this approach to reducing reoffending in the community is promising.

---

[15] Costs of the program were made up of criminal justice system reprocessing of recidivists (e.g., arrest, prosecution), parole supervision of early releasees, and direct costs to crime victims (caused by early releasees).

B. The New York City Supported Work Social Experiment

First started in 1972 in New York City and then expanded to other U.S. cities, the Supported Work social experiment was aimed at reintegrating former offenders and drug addicts into the community through the provision of paid employment and after-care (e.g., methadone maintenance for exaddicts). A "reasonable wage, working with peers, and flexible length of time in the program [were] intended to create a low-stress, rehabilitative environment" (Friedman 1977, p. 148). The main goals of the program were to: deliver public services (e.g., work in libraries, painting, newspaper recycling); reduce crime; improve the health and well-being of clients; reduce social service use; and increase unsupported employment (non-wage-controlled jobs in the public and private sectors) after the program.

1. *Design and Method.* A randomized experiment was used to test the effectiveness of the Supported Work program. Eligible candidates were randomly assigned either to the treatment group who received the program (the approximately three hundred employment positions filled in the program's first year) or to the control group who did not. The exact number of individuals in the treatment and control groups at the start of the study was not reported by the author. The criteria for admission to the program included: for exaddicts, enrollment in a drug treatment program for a minimum of three months, eligible to receive federal Supplemental Security Income benefits, and unemployed for at least twelve months in the past two years.

Characteristics of the treatment and control groups, prior to the start of the program, were not provided. Instead, some characteristics were aggregated to give an overall picture of the two groups together. For example, their average numbers of prior arrests and criminal convictions were 8.2 and 4.5, respectively. Some of the characteristics of the treatment group prior to the start of the program included: 92 percent were male, half were single, the average age was thirty-two years, three-fourths had not completed high school, and 80 percent had not been employed in the last six months. The program lasted an average of eight months, and follow-up data were available for an average of sixteen months from the time the program ended. Although the author claimed that a sample retention rate of approximately 90 percent was achieved two years after the start of the program (Friedman 1977, p. 159), information on program effects and economic efficiency is based on only 120 treatment and 109 control group members. Data sources used to evaluate the program included extensive annual and quarterly supplemental interviews with the experimental and control groups, and official documentation, such as police and welfare records.

2. *Results.* The Supported Work program was assessed on six criteria: criminal activity, education, employment, health, participation in drug treatment programs, and social service use. Observed differences between the treatment and control groups were found on all of the outcome variables with the exception of participation in drug treatment programs. At sixteen months follow-up, program effects on the outcomes of criminal activity, employment, and social service use favored the treatment over the control group, while the control group fared better on the outcomes of health and education. For criminal activity, the average treatment group member was arrested 0.05 fewer times per year than the average control group member, an insignificant difference. More substantial, desirable differences were evident for social service use ($1,797 less) and employment earnings ($3,289 more) over the course of a year for the average experimental compared to the average control. For education, the average control was enrolled longer per year in vocational programs (1.97 vs. 0.25 weeks) than the average experimental. The number of weeks of enrollment per year in college and high school equivalency courses was higher for experimentals than controls, but only marginally.

3. *Economic Analysis.* A rigorous benefit-cost analysis was carried out. Costs and benefits (in 1974 dollars) were estimated only for the (average) eight months of the program. Four benefit-cost calculations were presented, each concerned with different recipients of benefits and costs of the Supported Work program. The four perspectives and their central interests were as follows: society (Is society as a whole more efficient with or without the program?); taxpayer or nonprogram participant (How much do taxpayers have to pay to operate the program and how much do they receive from it?); welfare department— a principal funding agency of the program (How much would have been paid out in welfare funds without the program?); and participant (What do participants have to give up to enter the program and what do they get in return?) (Friedman 1977, pp. 163–66). In keeping with our attempt to maintain consistency in the reporting of benefit-cost findings, only the perspective of the taxpayer (including victims) is discussed here. The taxpayer perspective includes the welfare department perspective, by virtue of the welfare department being a publicly funded institution.

The Supported Work program produced a dividend for the taxpaying public. For each dollar the public invested in the program it received $1.13 in return; a desirable benefit-cost ratio of 1.13. Total program costs and benefits, expressed as per treated person per year, were estimated at $6,131 and $6,920, respectively. Total program benefits were derived from: savings in public goods and services, $4,519; reduction in social service or welfare use, $1,797; increased income tax, $311; reduced crime, $293 ($86 in savings to the criminal justice system and $207 in savings to crime victims). No information was provided about how the benefits from reduced crime were calculated.

The Supported Work program's crime reduction and benefit-cost findings engender confidence. It used a randomized experimental design to assess program effects, hence controlling for threats to internal and external validity. Its benefit-cost analysis was rigorous and comprehensive. The main limitations concern missing information on initial sample size, which did not allow us to assess sample attrition, and on how the benefit of crimes reduced was measured.

V. Community Crime Prevention

Remarkably, only one community crime prevention study meeting the criteria for inclusion was identified. Due to this limitation, the layout of this section differs from Sections II, III, and IV. The only community prevention study available—the Participate and Learn Skills Program (Jones and Offord 1989)—is reviewed in detail.

More often than not, community crime prevention is thought to be some combination of situational and developmental crime prevention. Unlike these two crime prevention strategies, there is little agreement in the academic literature on the definition of community prevention and the types of programs that fall within it (Bennett 1996). Hope (1995, p. 21) defines community prevention as "actions intended to change the social conditions that are believed to sustain crime in residential communities." Program mechanisms are the defining feature of this view of community prevention. Hope notes that local social institutions (e.g., families, associations, churches, youth clubs) are usually the medium by which these programs are delivered to tackle crime problems (1995, p. 21).

Hope (1998) identified six general categories of community crime prevention programs, which are by no means mutually exclusive: (i) community organization—establishment of community-based associations to foster desirable socialization and integrate young people into the wider community (e.g., recreational services, after school drop-in centers); (ii) community defense—increasing the perceived risks of offending (e.g., Neighborhood Watch); (iii) order maintenance—tackling physical and personal disorder or petty crimes (e.g., removing graffiti, banning public drinking); (iv) risk-based—targeting scientifically identified risk factors for delinquency and other antisocial behaviors at the individual and community level (e.g., "Communities that Care," Hawkins and Catalano [1992]); (v) community development—"rebuild[ing] the social, physical and economic fabric of neighbourhoods" (e.g., decentralization of housing management and services) (Hope 1998, p. 57); and (vi) structural change: altering macrolevel social and economic policies (e.g., social services, education). Unlike the other five categories, vi is less likely to be driven by local action (Hope 1998). It is important to note that categories ii and iii are more closely associated with situational prevention, and category iv overlaps with both developmental and situational prevention.

Two community prevention studies that have measured crime and presented data on the monetary value of the programs have not been included here, because the published data are insufficient for the calculation of benefit-cost ratios. The first (Dignan, Sorsby, and Hibbert 1996), carried out in the United Kingdom, assessed the monetary costs of mediation and conventional approaches (e.g., U.K. Department of Housing notice to seek possession of property) to dealing with neighbor disputes. This study was excluded for two reasons: first, program effects were based solely on case studies, which provide very little confidence that the interventions produced the observed outcomes, and second, program effects were not valued in monetary terms, hence not allowing an assessment of economic efficiency. The second community prevention study, the Children at Risk program (Harrell et al. 1997), a large scale, multisite program in the United States that employed a randomized experimental design, was not included here because it too only presented monetary costs and did not value benefits (or disbenefits). Although having only one study raises questions about the usefulness of this section, nonetheless we thought it important to try to cover all four principal strategies of crime prevention, including community prevention. Also, if nothing more, this section illustrates the need for future research on the monetary costs and benefits of community crime prevention programs.

A. The Participate and Learn Skills Program

The Participate and Learn Skills (PALS) program was implemented in a public housing complex in Ottawa, Canada, in the early 1980s. It had two main objectives: to advance the participating children toward higher nonschool skill development levels (e.g., skills in sporting and cultural activities) and to integrate children from the public housing community into the larger community (Jones and Offord 1989, p. 739).

1. *Design and Method.*   The study employed an experimental-control group design, with before-after measures to assess the effects of the community-based intervention. One public housing complex served as the no-treatment control group and another received the intervention. The control complex was not exactly equivalent to the experimental complex. The two complexes were the largest in size that were under the management of the city housing authority and had comparable sociodemographic characteristics. On average there were 417 children between the ages of five and fifteen years at the program site and 488 at the control site. Children were distributed evenly by gender and by ages five to fifteen years at both sites. Approximately one-half of families at both sites relied on some form of social assistance for income and the other half were considered "working poor"; and 56 percent of households at both sites were headed by single parent mothers (Jones and Offord 1989, pp. 738–39).

In its first year (1980), the nonschool, skill development program offered forty courses free of charge in twenty-five different skill areas. Sporting activities dominated (e.g., swimming, ice hockey). Other activities included music and art. Age-eligible children were recruited actively through direct contact, notices, and follow-up contacts made with those who did not participate in prior rounds of the program. In the first year, the rate of participation in at least one course among age-eligible children reached 70.8 percent (228 of 322). In the second and third years, the participation rates fell to 60.2 percent and 49 percent, respectively. The authors suggest that the drop in participation was largely due to fewer courses being offered. During the thirty-two months of the program, the number of children living in the experimental complex remained fairly stable.

The effects of PALS were assessed at completion of the program (thirty-two months) and sixteen months later. Data sources included records from PALS (e.g., skill level reached) and the housing authority, family surveys of the program housing site which included standardized tests of the parent/child relationship and children's self-esteem, school teacher ratings, and a number of unobtrusive measures (e.g., housing security records).

2. *Results.*   Children in the program housing site fared better than their control counterparts on a range of measures. The strongest program effect was found for juvenile delinquency. During the thirty-two months of the program, the monthly average of juveniles (in the age-eligible program range) charged by the police was 80 percent less (0.2 vs. 1.0) at the experimental site compared to the control site. This statistically significant effect was diminished somewhat in the sixteen months postintervention: 0.5 juveniles were charged per month at the experimental site compared to 1.1 at the control site. Possibly, the effects of the program were wearing off. Substantial gains were observed in skill acquisition, as measured by the number of levels advanced in an activity, and in integration in the wider community among experimental site children compared with the controls. Spillover effects on participating children included an increase in self-esteem, but no change in behavior at school or home was observed.

3. *Economic Analysis.*   A benefit-cost analysis was carried out. Program costs (operational and research) and immediate benefits for the intervention and follow-up phases were measured, using 1983 Canadian dollars (C$). The calculation of monetary benefits was limited to including only those areas where significant differences were observed between the experimental and control complexes: fewer police charges against juveniles, reduced private security reports, and reduced calls for fire department service. Altogether, benefits were estimated for four affected publicly funded agencies: police, housing authority, community center, and fire department.

Over the course of the forty-eight months, program costs totaled C$258,694 and benefits were estimated at C$659,058. The city housing authority reaped the largest share of the benefits (83.8 percent or C$552,118). These benefits were due to the reduced demand for private security services in the experimental housing complex relative to the control complex. The next largest portion of the total benefits from the program were realized by the city fire department (13.4 percent or C$88,416). Monetary benefits accruing to the youth liaison section of the city police were relatively small (1.8 percent or C$11,758). Dividing the total benefits realized by the four public agencies (C$659,058) by the total cost of the program (C$258,694) produced a desirable benefit-cost ratio of 2.55. In other words, for each dollar the public invested in the skill development program, C\$2.55 were saved.

Our confidence in the outcome and benefit-cost findings of the PALS program is quite high. A high quality experimental-control group design with before-and-after measures was used, and there was a reasonable follow-up period. On Sherman et al.'s (1997) scientific methods score, we rate the study at level 3. A fairly rigorous and comprehensive benefit-cost analysis was carried out.

B. Evaluating Community Crime Prevention Programs

Surprisingly, even the most notable reviews of what works in community crime prevention (Rosenbaum 1986; Hope 1995; Sherman 1997; Catalano et al. 1998) do not include any meaningful discussion about economic costs and benefits. The simplest explanation for this paucity of economic evaluation research is that there are comparatively few well-designed impact evaluations of community crime prevention programs, which are, of course, needed in the first place to conduct an economic analysis.

Knowledge about what works in this area of prevention is hampered by a number of methodological issues (see Hope 1995, 1998; Farrington 1997; Sherman 1997; Catalano et al. 1998) that do not appear to be as critical in the other prevention strategies covered in this essay. Catalano et al. (1998, pp. 278–80) identify three key methodological issues which need to be addressed as part of impact evaluations of community crime prevention programs: (i) mixed units of analysis, (ii) heterogeneity of effect across different populations, and (iii) systematic attrition, accretion, and ecological validity.

Arguably, issues ii and iii are not encountered only in evaluations of community prevention programs; they also face researchers in other areas of crime prevention. Issue i, on the other hand, is more often applicable to community crime prevention programs. Mixed units of analysis occur when the unit of analysis differs from the unit of assignment. For example, if the community is the unit that is assigned to experimental or control conditions, it follows that the community should be the unit of analysis in assessing the impact of the intervention. All too often, however, communities are assigned but individuals are the unit of analysis in evaluating the impact of the intervention. As noted by Biglan and Ary (1985, cited in Catalano et al. 1998, p. 279), "Community, school, or classroom differences are thus confounded with program effects on individuals."

One way of advancing knowledge about community crime prevention without unduly compromising methodological rigor and hence the confidence that can be placed in observed outcomes, is to define communities at the level of census tract, which could, for a large city, produce hundreds of units for assignment and analysis (Sherman 1997, p. 38, chap. 3). However, randomly assigning census tracts to conditions could lead to problems of contamination, since the areas are not clearly distinct. Catalano et al. (1998, p. 279) report on a number of alternatives that can be adopted when resources do not allow for the minimum number of units to be randomly assigned, some of which include, "matching communities prior to randomization on variables related to the outcomes of interest," "randomized block and factorial designs to stratify communities by factors known to affect key outcomes," and "generalized estimating equations to estimate both the individual- and group-level components of variation."

While there are important methodological issues that need to be addressed in evaluating community prevention programs, there is also a need for more experimentation with this form of crime prevention, with a particular emphasis on assessing monetary costs and benefits. Having only one study that has assessed costs and benefits is a major drawback of this review. Although beyond the scope of this essay, it would be desirable, in the absence of knowledge about ongoing studies with plans to assess costs and benefits, to undertake a number of retrospective economic evaluations of well-designed community prevention programs that have measured crime and other outcomes. This could also be helpful in identifying important issues for prospective economic evaluations.

VI. Conclusions, Gaps in Knowledge, and Research Priorities

This essay reviewed research on the monetary costs and benefits of the four principal crime prevention strategies: situational, developmental, community prevention, and criminal justice (correctional) intervention. It was not possible to determine which of the strategies produced the greatest economic return on investment. This was because of the small number of studies identified (and reviewed here), the varied methodological rigor of the program evaluations and economic analyses, and limited or missing information in the studies.

Despite the problems experienced in comparing the economic efficiency of the different crime prevention strategies, some noteworthy points can be made about the relative monetary benefits of the three approaches for which evidence is available (situational prevention, developmental prevention, and correctional intervention). For situational prevention and correctional intervention programs it appears more likely that benefits will exceed costs in the short-term, while for developmental prevention programs there is a greater chance that benefits will not begin to surpass costs until the medium- to long-term. In this sense, the different strategies seem to complement one another. This is perhaps more true for the comparison of situational and developmental prevention, largely because these strategies address crime and offending, respectively, as opposed to correctional intervention's focus on reoffending.

Another conclusion that can be drawn from the benefit-cost findings of the three strategies is that developmental prevention and, to a lesser extent, correctional intervention provide important monetary benefits beyond reduced crime. These can take the form of, for example, increased tax revenues from higher earnings, savings from reduced usage of social services, and savings from less health care utilization. The benefits of situational prevention, on the other hand, appear to be largely confined to reduced crime. However, this may be because only crime was measured in situational evaluations. A wide range of benefits should be measured in all evaluations.

This essay has several important limitations. First, it is necessarily based on a small number of studies: thirteen for situational prevention, six for developmental prevention, six for correctional intervention, and one for community prevention. Second, costs and benefits were not estimated comparably in all studies. Some used a rigorous economic analysis methodology to assess costs and benefits, while others used a less adequate design. Also, benefits tended to be estimated conservatively, while costs were often taken account in full. Third, different perspectives (e.g., the public or society) were used in the economic analyses, so that the parties who were the recipients of the economic benefits or losses were not always comparable. For many of the studies it was not possible to disaggregate the benefit-cost findings to provide a consistent perspective across the studies. As far as possible, we used the perspective of the public (government/taxpayers and crime victims).

In order to learn more about the independent and relative monetary value of the four principal crime prevention strategies, a number of key issues need to be addressed. First, policy makers and researchers should play a greater role in ensuring that prevention programs include, as part of the original research design, provision for an economic analysis, preferably a benefit-cost analysis. Prospective economic analyses have many advantages over retrospective ones. However, it would also be desirable, as part of a program of research, to carry out a number of retrospective economic evaluations of crime prevention programs, particularly for programs shown to be effective in reducing delinquency and crime. Programs could be selected according to criteria which would increase confidence in the benefit-cost findings, including high-quality research designs (preferably randomized experimental designs), large samples, and long-term follow-ups with low sample attrition.

Second, researchers must ensure that economic analyses are not only methodologically rigorous, but also comprehensive: all resources used (costs) and all relevant program effects (benefits) need to be monetized. Research is needed on key issues such as using average versus marginal costs, using capital versus operating costs, and discounting costs and benefits over different time periods. Sensitivity analyses need to be conducted.

Third, there is the need for a standard list of costs and benefits that should be measured in all studies. This is an important issue that we have identified previously (Welsh and Farrington 1998, 1999; Welsh 1999), and one that raises key questions about the inclusion of certain types of costs and benefits, in particular, the intangible costs to crime victims of pain, suffering, and reduced quality of life. In section I, we outlined the key outcome variables that should be measured in crime prevention programs (crime and delinquency, substance abuse, education, employment, health, and family outcomes) and some of the relevant benefits that need to be assessed in those areas. A standard list of costs and benefits would greatly facilitate comparisons of the benefit-cost findings of different crime prevention programs.

Fourth, greater use of experimental research designs, particularly randomized experiments, is needed. For programs based on large units such as communities, experimental-control designs with before-and-after measures are most appropriate and feasible. As an economic analysis is only as strong as the evaluation on which it is based, the stronger the research design of the outcome evaluation, the more confidence that can be placed in the findings of the economic analysis. Fifth, funding bodies must be prepared to finance economic evaluation research. Governmental agencies with responsibility for the prevention of crime should commit a percentage of their research budgets to support economic evaluations of a number of new and existing prevention programs. Also, governmental agencies, foundations, private sector organizations, and other groups that fund crime prevention schemes need to make future funding conditional on a built-in evaluation component that includes an assessment of monetary costs and benefits.

In tandem with recent efforts to elevate the understanding of what works in preventing crime to new scientific heights, through the application of meta-analytic techniques (e.g., Lipsey and Wilson 1998) and methodological rating scales (Sherman et al. 1997), action on these research priorities will go a long way toward improving our ability to say with a greater degree of certainty which approaches are worthy of increased public (and private) investment and which will provide the best economic returns to governments and taxpaying citizens. Answering these questions more adequately will lead to more responsible expenditure on crime prevention and—importantly—to increased public safety.

REFERENCES

Aos, Steve. 1998. "Costs and Benefits: Estimating the 'Bottom Line' for Crime Prevention and Intervention Programs: A Description of the Cost-Benefit Model, Version 2.0." Unpublished manuscript. Olympia: Washington State Institute for Public Policy.

Aos, Steve, Robert Barnoski, and Roxanne Lieb. 1998. "Preventive Programs for Young Offenders Effective and Cost-Effective." *Overcrowded Times* 9(2): 1, 7–11.

Austin, James. 1986. "Using Early Release to Relieve Prison Crowding: A Dilemma in Public Policy." *Crime and Delinquency* 32:404–502.

Barnett, W. Steven. 1993. "Cost-Benefit Analysis." In *Significant Benefits: The High/Scope Perry Preschool Study through Age 27*, by Lawrence J. Schweinhart, Helen V. Barnes, and David P. Weikart. Ypsilanti, Mich.: High/Scope Press.

———. 1996. *Lives in the Balance: Age-27 Benefit-Cost Analysis of the High/Scope Perry Preschool Program.* Ypsilanti, Mich.: High/Scope Press.

Barnett, W. Steven, and Colette M. Escobar. 1987. "The Economics of Early Educational Intervention: A Review." *Review of Educational Research* 57:387–414.

———. 1990. "Economic Costs and Benefits of Early Intervention." In *Handbook of Early Childhood Intervention, edited by Samuel J. Meisels and Jack P. Shonkoff. Cambridge: Cambridge University Press.

Barr, Robert, and Ken Pease. 1990. "Crime Placement, Displacement, and Deflection." In Crime and Justice: A Review of Research, vol. 12, edited by Michael Tonry and Norval Morris. Chicago: University of Chicago Press.

Bennett, Trevor H. 1996. "Community Crime Prevention in Britain." In Kommunale Kriminalprävention: Paradigmenwechsel und Wiederentdeckung alter Weisheiten, edited by Thomas Trenczek and Hartmut Pfeiffer. Bonn: Forum Verlag Godesberg.

Berrueta-Clement, John R., Lawrence J. Schweinhart, W. Steven Barnett, Ann S. Epstein, and David P. Weikart. 1984. Changed Lives: The Effects of the Perry Preschool Program on Youths through Age 19. Ypsilanti, Mich.: High/Scope Press.

Biglan, Anthony, and Dennis Ary. 1985. "Methodological Issues in Research on Smoking Prevention." In Prevention Research: Deterring Drug Abuse among Children and Adolescents, edited by Catherine S. Bell and Robert J. Battjes. National Institute on Drug Abuse research monograph no. 63. Washington, D.C.: U.S. Government Printing Office.

Bridgeman, Cressida. 1996. Crime Risk Management: Making It Work. Crime Detection and Prevention Series Paper no. 70. London: Home Office.

Burrows, John. 1991. Making Crime Prevention Pay: Initiatives from Business. Crime Prevention Unit Paper no. 27. London: Home Office.

Catalano, Richard F., Michael W. Arthur, J. David Hawkins, Lisa Berglund, and Jeffrey J. Olson. 1998. "Comprehensive Community-and School-Based Interventions to Prevent Antisocial Behavior." In Serious and Violent Juvenile Offenders: Risk Factors and Successful Interventions, edited by Rolf Loeber and David P. Farrington. Thousand Oaks, Calif.: Sage.

Caulkins, Jonathan P., C. Peter Rydell, William Schwabe, and James Chiesa. 1997. Mandatory Minimum Drug Sentences: Throwing Away the Key or the Taxpayers' Money? Santa Monica, Calif.: RAND.

———. 1998. "Are Mandatory Minimum Drug Sentences Cost-Effective?" Corrections Management Quarterly 2:62–73.

Cirel, Paul, Patricia Evans, Daniel McGillis, and Debra Whitcomb. 1977. An Exemplary Project: Community Crime Prevention. Washington, D.C.: National Criminal Justice Reference Service.

Clarke, Ronald V. 1992. "Introduction." In Situational Crime Prevention: Successful Case Studies, edited by Ronald V. Clarke. Albany, N.Y.: Harrow & Heston.

———. 1993. "Fare Evasion and Automatic Ticket Collection on the London Underground." In Crime Prevention Studies, vol. 1., edited by Ronald V. Clarke. Monsey, N.Y.: Criminal Justice Press.

———. 1995a. "Opportunity-Reducing Crime Prevention Strategies and the Role of Motivation." In Integrating Crime Prevention Strategies: Propensity and Opportunity, edited by Per-Olof H. Wikström, Ronald V. Clarke, and Joan McCord. Stockholm, Sweden: National Council for Crime Prevention.

———. 1995b. "Situational Crime Prevention." In Building a Safer Society:

Strategic Approaches to Crime Prevention, edited by Michael Tonry and David P. Farrington. Vol. 19 of *Crime and Justice: A Review of Research*, edited by Michael Tonry. Chicago: University of Chicago Press.

Clarke, Ronald V., ed. 1997. *Situational Crime Prevention: Successful Case Studies*, 2d ed. Guilderland, N.Y.: Harrow & Heston.

Clarke, Ronald V., Ronald P. Cody, and Mangai Natarajan. 1994. "Subway Slugs: Tracking Displacement on the London Underground." *British Journal of Criminology* 34:122–38.

Clarke, Ronald V., and Ross Homel. 1997. "A Revised Classification of Situational Crime Prevention Techniques." In *Crime Prevention at a Crossroads*, edited by Steven P. Lab. Cincinnati: Anderson.

Clarke, Ronald V., and Gerry McGrath. 1990. "Cash Reduction and Robbery Prevention in Australian Betting Shops." *Security Journal* 1:160–63.

Clarke, Ronald V., and David Weisburd. 1994. "Diffusion of Crime Control Benefits: Observations on the Reverse of Displacement." In *Crime Prevention Studies*, vol. 2, edited by Ronald V. Clarke. Monsey, N.Y.: Criminal Justice Press.

Cohen, Mark A. 1988. "Pain, Suffering, and Jury Awards: A Study of the Cost of Crime to Victims." *Law and Society Review* 22:537–55.

———. 1992. "A Note on the Cost of Crime to Victims." *Urban Studies* 27: 139–46.

———. 1998. "The Monetary Value of Saving a High-Risk Youth." *Journal of Quantitative Criminology* 14:5–33.

Cohen, Mark A., Ted R. Miller, and Shelli B. Rossman. 1994. "The Costs and Consequences of Violent Behavior in the United States." In *Understanding and Preventing Violence*, vol. 4, *Consequences and Control*, edited by Albert J. Reiss, Jr. and Jeffrey A. Roth. Washington, D.C.: National Academy Press.

Coopers and Lybrand. 1994. *Preventative Strategy for Young People in Trouble*. London: ITV Telethon/The Prince's Trust.

Davidson, Jo, and John Farr. 1994. "Mitchellhill Estate: Estate Based Management (Concierge) Initiative." In *Housing Safe Communities: An Evaluation of Recent Initiatives*, edited by Steve Osborn. London: Safe Neighbourhoods Unit.

Dignan, James, A. Sorsby, and J. Hibbert. 1996. *Neighbour Disputes: Comparing the Cost-Effectiveness of Mediation and Alternative Approaches*. Sheffield: University of Sheffield, Centre for Criminological and Legal Research.

DiLonardo, Robert L. 1996. "Defining and Measuring the Economic Benefit of Electronic Article Surveillance." *Security Journal* 7:3–9.

Donohue, John J., and Peter Siegelman. 1998. "Allocating Resources among Prisons and Social Programs in the Battle against Crime." *Journal of Legal Studies* 27:1–43.

Earle, Ralph B. 1995. "Helping to Prevent Child Abuse—and Future Consequences: Hawaii Healthy Start." *Program Focus*, October. Washington, D.C.: U.S. Department of Justice, National Institute of Justice.

Ekblom, Paul, Ho Law, and Mike Sutton. 1996. *Safer Cities and Domestic Burglary*. Home Office Research Study no. 164. London: Home Office.

Farrington, David P. 1983. "Randomized Experiments on Crime and Justice." In *Crime and Justice: An Annual Review of Research*, vol. 4, edited by Michael Tonry and Norval Morris. Chicago: University of Chicago Press.

———. 1995. "The Development of Offending and Antisocial Behaviour from Childhood: Key Findings from the Cambridge Study in Delinquent Development." *Journal of Child Psychology and Psychiatry* 36:929–64.

———. 1996. "The Explanation and Prevention of Youthful Offending." In *Delinquency and Crime: Current Theories*, edited by J. David Hawkins. Cambridge: Cambridge University Press.

———. 1997. "Evaluating a Community Crime Prevention Program." *Evaluation* 3:157–73.

Field, Simon. 1993. "Crime Prevention and the Costs of Auto Theft: An Economic Analysis." In *Crime Prevention Studies*, vol. 1., edited by Ronald V. Clarke. Monsey, N.Y.: Criminal Justice Press.

Forrester, David, Samantha Frenz, Martin O'Connell, and Ken Pease. 1990. *The Kirkholt Burglary Prevention Project: Phase II*. Crime Prevention Unit Paper no. 23. London: Home Office.

Friedman, Lee S. 1977. "An Interim Evaluation of the Supported Work Experiment." *Policy Analysis* 3:147–70.

Gerstein, Dean R., Robert A. Johnson, Henrick J. Harwood, Douglas Fountain, Natalie Suter, and Kathryn Malloy. 1994. *Evaluating Recovery Services: The California Drug and Alcohol Treatment Assessment (CALDATA)*. Sacramento: State of California, Department of Alcohol and Drug Programs.

Gilling, Daniel. 1994. "Multi-Agency Crime Prevention in Britain: The Problem of Combining Situational and Social Measures." In *Crime Prevention Studies*, vol. 3, edited by Ronald V. Clarke. Monsey, N.Y.: Criminal Justice Press.

Greenwood, Peter W., C. Peter Rydell, Allan F. Abrahamse, Jonathan P. Caulkins, James Chiesa, Karyn E. Model, and Stephen P. Klein. 1994. *Three Strikes and You're Out: Estimated Benefits and Costs of California's New Mandatory-Sentencing Law*. Santa Monica, Calif.: RAND.

Greenwood, Peter W., Karyn E. Model, C. Peter Rydell, and James Chiesa. 1996. *Diverting Children from a Life of Crime: Measuring Costs and Benefits*. Santa Monica, Calif.: RAND.

Hahn, Andrew. 1994. *Evaluation of the Quantum Opportunities Program (QOP): Did the Program Work?* Waltham, Mass.: Brandeis University, Heller Graduate School, Center for Human Resources.

Hakim, Simon, Mary A. Gaffney, George Rengert, and Johannan Shachmurove. 1995. "Costs and Benefits of Alarms to the Community: Burglary Patterns and Security Measures in Tredyffrin Township, Pennsylvania." *Security Journal* 6:197–204.

Harrell, Adele V., Shannon E. Cavanagh, Michele A. Harmon, Christopher S. Koper, and Sanjeev Sridharan. 1997. *Impact of the Children at Risk Program: Comprehensive Final Report*, vol. 1. Washington, D.C.: Urban Institute.

Hawkins, J. David, and Richard F. Catalano. 1992. *Communities That Care*. San Francisco: Jossey-Bass.

Hofler, Richard A., and Ann D. Witte. 1979. "Benefit-Cost Analysis of the

Sentencing Decision: The Case of Homicide." In *The Costs of Crime*, edited by C. M. Gray. Beverly Hills, Calif.: Sage.

Holahan, John. 1974. "Measuring Benefits from Prison Reform." In *Benefit-Cost and Policy Analysis 1973: An Aldine Annual on Forecasting, Decision-Making, and Evaluation*, edited by Robert H. Haveman, Arnold C. Harberger, Laurence E. Lynn, William A. Niskanen, Ralph Turvey, and Richard Zeckhauser. Chicago: Aldine.

Hope, Tim. 1995. "Community Crime Prevention." In *Building a Safer Society: Strategic Approaches to Crime Prevention*, edited by Michael Tonry and David P. Farrington. Vol. 19 of *Crime and Justice: A Review of Research*, edited by Michael Tonry. Chicago: University of Chicago Press.

———. 1998. "Community Crime Prevention." In *Reducing Offending: An Assessment of Research Evidence on Ways of Dealing with Offending Behaviour*, edited by Christopher Nuttall, Peter Goldblatt, and Chris Lewis. Home Office Research Study no. 187. London: Home Office.

Hunter, Ronald D., and C. Ray Jeffery. 1992. "Preventing Convenience Store Robbery through Environmental Design." In *Situational Crime Prevention: Successful Case Studies*, edited by Ronald V. Clarke. Albany, N.Y.: Harrow & Heston.

Husain, Sohail. 1994. *Counting the Cost: A Briefing Paper on Financial Losses Arising from Crime*. Swindon: Crime Concern/The Thames Valley Partnership.

Jones, Marshall B., and David R. Offord. 1989. "Reduction of Antisocial Behaviour in Poor Children by Nonschool Skill-Development." *Journal of Child Psychology and Psychiatry* 30:737–50.

Karoly, Lynn A., Peter W. Greenwood, Susan S. Everingham, Jill Houbé, M. Rebecca Kilburn, C. Peter Rydell, Matthew Sanders, and James Chiesa. 1998. *Investing in Our Children: What We Know and Don't Know about the Costs and Benefits of Early Childhood Interventions*. Santa Monica, Calif.: RAND.

Knapp, Martin. 1997. "Economic Evaluations and Interventions for Children and Adolescents with Mental Health Problems." *Journal of Child Psychology and Psychiatry* 38:3–25.

Knapp, Martin, and Ann Netten. 1997. "The Cost and Cost Effectiveness of Community Penalties: Principles, Tools and Examples." In *Evaluating the Effectiveness of Community Penalties*, edited by George Mair. Aldershot: Avebury.

Knapp, Martin, Eileen Robertson, and Gill McIvor. 1992. "The Comparative Costs of Community Service and Custody in Scotland." *Howard Journal of Criminal Justice* 31:8–30.

Knight, Barry. 1994. "Possil Park Estate: Security Scheme." In *Housing Safe Communities: An Evaluation of Recent Initiatives*, edited by Steve Osborn. London: Safe Neighbourhoods Unit.

La Vigne, Nancy G. 1994. "Rational Choice and Inmate Disputes over Phone Use on Rikers Island." In *Crime Prevention Studies*, vol. 3, edited by Ronald V. Clarke. Monsey, N.Y.: Criminal Justice Press.

Lally, J. Ronald, Peter L. Mangione, and Alice S. Honig. 1988. "The Syracuse

University Family Development Research Program: Long-Range Impact of an Early Intervention with Low-Income Children and Their Families." In *Parent Education as Early Childhood Intervention: Emerging Directions in Theory, Research and Practice*, edited by D. R. Powell. Norwood, N.J.: Ablex.

Laycock, Gloria. 1986. "Property Marking as a Deterrent to Domestic Burglary." In *Situational Crime Prevention: From Theory into Practice*, edited by Kevin Heal and Gloria Laycock. London: H. M. Stationery Office.

Lipsey, Mark W. 1984. "Is Delinquency Prevention a Cost-Effective Strategy? A California Perspective." *Journal of Research in Crime and Delinquency* 21: 279–302.

Lipsey, Mark W., and David B. Wilson. 1998. "Effective Intervention for Serious Juvenile Offenders: A Synthesis of Research." In *Serious and Violent Juvenile Offenders: Risk Factors and Successful Interventions*, edited by Rolf Loeber and David P. Farrington. Thousand Oaks, Calif.: Sage.

Long, David A., Charles D. Mallar, and Craig V. D. Thornton. 1981. "Evaluating the Benefits and Costs of the Job Corps." *Journal of Policy Analysis and Management* 1:55–76.

MacKenzie, Doris L. 1997. "Criminal Justice and Crime Prevention." In *Preventing Crime: What Works, What Doesn't, What's Promising*, by Lawrence W. Sherman, Denise C. Gottfredson, Doris L. MacKenzie, John E. Eck, Peter Reuter, and Shawn D. Bushway. Washington, D.C.: U.S. Department of Justice, National Institute of Justice.

Mandel, Michael J., Paul Magnusson, James E. Ellis, Gail DeGeorge, and Keith L. Alexander. 1993. "The Economics of Crime." *Business Week* (December 13), pp. 72–75, 78–81.

McCord, Joan. 1995. "Motivational Crime Prevention Strategies and the Role of Opportunity." In *Integrating Crime Prevention Strategies: Propensity and Opportunity*, edited by Per-Olof H. Wikström, Ronald V. Clarke, and Joan McCord. Stockholm: National Council for Crime Prevention.

Miller, Ted R., Mark A. Cohen, and Shelli B. Rossman. 1993. "Victim Costs of Violent Crime and Resulting Injuries." *Health Affairs* 12:186–97.

Miller, Ted R., Mark A. Cohen, and Brian Wiersema. 1996. *Victim Costs and Consequences: A New Look*. Washington, D.C.: U.S. Department of Justice, National Institute of Justice.

Newman, Graeme, Ronald V. Clarke, and Schlomo Shoham, eds. 1997. *Rational Choice and Situational Crime Prevention: Theoretical Foundations*. Aldershot: Ashgate.

Olds, David L., John Eckenrode, Charles R. Henderson, Harriet Kitzman, Jane Powers, Robert Cole, Kimberly Sidora, Pamela Morris, Lisa M. Pettitt, and Dennis Luckey. 1997. "Long-Term Effects of Home Visitation on Maternal Life Course and Child Abuse and Neglect: Fifteen-Year Follow-Up of a Randomized Trial." *Journal of the American Medical Association* 278: 637–43.

Olds, David L., Charles R. Henderson, Robert Cole, John Eckenrode, Harriet Kitzman, Dennis Luckey, Lisa M. Pettitt, Kimberly Sidora, Pamela Morris, and Jane Powers. 1998. "Long-Term Effects of Nurse Home Visitation on

Children's Criminal and Antisocial Behavior: 15-Year Follow-Up of a Randomized Controlled Trial." *JAMA* 280:1238–44.

Olds, David L., Charles R. Henderson, Charles Phelps, Harriet Kitzman, and Carole Hanks. 1993. "Effects of Prenatal and Infancy Nurse Home Visitation on Government Spending." *Medical Care* 31:155–74.

Osborn, Steve. 1994. "Kirkholt Estate: Burglary Prevention Scheme." In *Housing Safe Communities: An Evaluation of Recent Initiatives*, edited by Steve Osborn. London: H.M. Stationery Office.

Painter, Kate A., and David P. Farrington. 1997. "The Crime Reducing Effect of Improved Street Lighting: The Dudley Project." In *Situational Crime Prevention: Successful Case Studies*, 2d ed., edited by Ronald V. Clarke. Guilderland, N.Y.: Harrow & Heston.

———. 1999*a*. "Improved Street Lighting: Crime Reducing Effects and Cost-Benefit Analyses." *Security Journal* 12 (forthcoming).

———. 1999*b*. "Street Lighting and Crime: Diffusion of Benefits in the Stoke-on-Trent Project." In *Crime Prevention Studies*, vol. 10, edited by Kate A. Painter and Nick Tilley. Monsey, N.Y.: Criminal Justice Press (forthcoming).

Palmer, Ted. 1992. *The Re-emergence of Correctional Intervention*. Newbury Park, Calif.: Sage.

Pearson, Frank S., and Alice G. Harper. 1990. "Contingent Intermediate Sentences: New Jersey's Intensive Supervision Program." *Crime and Delinquency* 36:75–86.

Pease, Ken. 1992. "Preventing Burglary on a British Public Housing Estate." In *Situational Crime Prevention: Successful Case Studies*, edited by Ronald V. Clarke. Albany, N.Y.: Harrow & Heston.

Plotnick, Robert D. 1994. "Applying Benefit-Cost Analysis to Substance Use Prevention Programs." *International Journal of the Addictions* 29:339–59.

Poyner, Barry. 1992. "Video Cameras and Bus Vandalism." In *Situational Crime Prevention: Successful Case Studies*, edited by Ronald V. Clarke. Albany, N.Y.: Harrow & Heston.

Prentky, Robert, and Ann W. Burgess. 1990. "Rehabilitation of Child Molesters: A Cost-Benefit Analysis." *American Journal of Orthopsychiatry* 60:108–17.

Prest, A. R., and Ralph Turvey. 1965. "Cost-Benefit Analysis: A Survey." *Economic Journal* 75:683–735.

Rajkumar, Andrew S., and Michael T. French. 1997. "Drug Abuse, Crime Costs, and the Economic Benefits of Treatment." *Journal of Quantitative Criminology* 13:291–323.

Reppetto, Thomas A. 1976. "Crime Prevention and the Displacement Phenomenon." *Crime and Delinquency* 22:166–77.

Rosenbaum, Dennis P., ed. 1986. *Community Crime Prevention: Does It Work?* Beverly Hills, Calif.: Sage.

Safe Neighbourhoods Unit. 1993. *Crime Prevention on Council Estates*. London: H. M. Stationery Office.

Schnelle, John F., Robert E. Kirchner, Frank Galbaugh, Michelle Domash,

Adam Carr, and Lynn Larson. 1979. "Program Evaluation Research: An Experimental Cost-Effectiveness Analysis of an Armed Robbery Intervention Program." *Journal of Applied Behavior Analysis* 12:615–23.

Schweinhart, Lawrence J., Helen V. Barnes, and David P. Weikart. 1993. *Significant Benefits: The High/Scope Perry Preschool Study through Age 27.* Ypsilanti, Mich.: High/Scope Press.

Schweinhart, Lawrence J., and David P. Weikart. 1980. *Young Children Grow Up: The Effects of the Perry Preschool Program on Youths through Age 15.* Ypsilanti, Mich.: High/Scope Press.

Seitz, Victoria, Laurie K. Rosenbaum, and Nancy H. Apfel. 1985. "Effects of Family Support Intervention: A Ten-Year Follow-Up." *Child Development* 56:376–91.

Sherman, Lawrence W. 1997. "Communities and Crime Prevention." In *Preventing Crime: What Works, What Doesn't, What's Promising*, by Lawrence W. Sherman, Denise C. Gottfredson, Doris L. MacKenzie, John E. Eck, Peter Reuter, and Shawn D. Bushway. Washington, D.C.: U.S. Department of Justice, National Institute of Justice.

Sherman, Lawrence W., Denise C. Gottfredson, Doris L. MacKenzie, John E. Eck, Peter Reuter, and Shawn D. Bushway. 1997. *Preventing Crime: What Works, What Doesn't, What's Promising.* Washington, D.C.: U.S. Department of Justice, National Institute of Justice.

Skett, Sarah. 1995. "What Works in the Reduction of Offending Behaviour?" *Forensic Update* 42:20–27.

Skilton, Mike. 1988. *A Better Reception: The Development of Concierge Schemes.* London: Estate Action and Department of the Environment.

Tonry, Michael, and David P. Farrington. 1995. "Strategic Approaches to Crime Prevention." In *Building a Safer Society: Strategic Approaches to Crime Prevention*, edited by Michael Tonry and David P. Farrington. Vol. 19 of *Crime and Justice: A Review of Research*, edited by Michael Tonry. Chicago: University of Chicago Press.

Tremblay, Richard E., and Wendy M. Craig. 1995. "Developmental Crime Prevention." In *Building a Safer Society: Strategic Approaches to Crime Prevention*, edited by Michael Tonry and David P. Farrington. Vol. 19 of *Crime and Justice: A Review of Research*, edited by Michael Tonry. Chicago: University of Chicago Press.

van Andel, Henk. 1989. "Crime Prevention that Works: The Care of Public Transport in the Netherlands." *British Journal of Criminology* 29:47–56.

van Dijk, Jan J. M. 1996. "Assessing the Costs and Benefits of Crime Control Strategies." Unpublished manuscript. The Hague: Ministry of Justice.

———. 1997. "Towards a Research-Based Crime Reduction Policy: Crime Prevention as a Cost-Effective Policy Option." *European Journal on Criminal Policy and Research* 5:13–27.

Weber, Carol U., P. W. Foster, and David P. Weikart. 1978. *An Economic Analysis of the Ypsilanti Perry Preschool Project.* Ypsilanti, Mich.: High/Scope Press.

Weimer, David L., and Lee S. Friedman. 1979. "Efficiency Considerations in Criminal Rehabilitation Research: Costs and Consequences." In *The Reha-*

bilitation of Criminal Offenders: Problems and Prospects, edited by Lee Sechrest, Susan O. White, and Elizabeth D. Brown. Washington, D.C.: National Academy of Sciences.

Weinrott, Mark R., Richard R. Jones, and James R. Howard. 1982. "Cost-Effectiveness of Teaching Family Programs for Delinquents: Results of a National Evaluation." *Evaluation Review* 6:173–201.

Welsh, Brandon C. 1999. "Economic Costs and Benefits of Primary Prevention of Delinquency and Later Offending: A Review of the Research." In *Early Prevention of Adult Antisocial Behaviour,* edited by David P. Farrington and Jeremy W. Coid. Cambridge: Cambridge University Press (forthcoming).

Welsh, Brandon C., and David P. Farrington. 1998. "Assessing the Effectiveness and Economic Benefits of an Integrated Developmental and Situational Crime Prevention Programme." *Psychology, Crime, and Law* 4:281–308.

———. 1999. "Value for Money? A Review of the Costs and Benefits of Situational Crime Prevention." *British Journal of Criminology* 39:345–68.

Zedlewski, Edwin W. 1987. "Making Confinement Decisions." *Research in Brief,* July. Washington, D.C.: U.S. Department of Justice, National Institute of Justice.

Zimring, Franklin E., and Gordon Hawkins. 1988. "The New Mathematics of Imprisonment." *Crime and Delinquency* 34:425–36.

———. 1995. *Incapacitation: Penal Confinement and the Restraint of Crime.* New York: Oxford University Press.

Jens Ludwig

Gun Self-Defense and Deterrence

ABSTRACT

Recent research on the prevalence of defensive gun use has prompted growing concern that government efforts to regulate gun ownership and use may be counterproductive. Estimates of defensive gun use from the National Crime Victimization Survey (on the order of 100,000 per year) appear to be too low. However, estimates from one-time telephone surveys (from 1.5 to 2.5 million per year) appear to be too high; even a modest rate of false positives may lead to substantial upward bias. A more promising approach is to examine the net effects of gun policies on rates of crime and injury directly. Evidence for a substantial deterrent effect of permissive concealed gun–carrying laws comes from a recent study by Lott and Mustard. Reanalysis of their data suggests that the estimated "treatment effects" are due in part or whole to unmeasured variables. More recent studies find no evidence of a significant negative effect of these laws on crime, though the available research remains far from definitive.

On the contentious topic of guns in the United States, there are several points on which most observers can agree. First, gun violence is an enormous problem and should be reduced. Since the early 1970s, the United States has averaged nearly 34,000 fatal firearm injuries annually; approximately 40 percent are homicides, 50 percent are suicides,

Jens Ludwig is assistant professor of public policy, Georgetown University and a member of the National Consortium on Violence Research. Thanks to Dan Black, Christina Clark, Philip Cook, Otis Dudley Duncan, Heath Einstein, Gary Kleck, David Hemenway, Arthur Kellermann, Michael Maltz, David McDowall, James Mercy, Daniel Nagin, Mark Rom, Michael Tonry, Jon Vernick, Garen Wintemute, Daniel Webster, Franklin Zimring, and two anonymous referees for helpful comments and assistance. All opinions and any errors are my own.

and the remainder are unintentional shootings.[1] In addition, perhaps another 100,000 people suffer nonfatal gunshot injuries each year (Cook 1985; Annest et al. 1995; Cook et al. 1999).

Second, guns are more lethal than most other instruments of violence. Evidence that the type of weapon used in an attack matters, known as an "instrumentality effect," was first documented by Franklin Zimring (1968). Zimring showed that in most gun assaults the assailant's intent to kill is apparently ambiguous, as suggested in part by the small proportion of cases in which the victim suffers multiple wounds. The case-fatality ratio for assault was also shown to be higher when guns rather than knives are used, even though gun and knife attacks typically have similar circumstances and other characteristics in common. A similar finding for gun and nongun robberies was demonstrated by Philip Cook (1983, 1987, 1991), and most scholars now accept the instrumentality hypothesis, even if there remains some disagreement about the magnitude of the effect (Wright, Rossi, and Daly 1983; Cook 1991; Kleck 1991). As a result, most students of gun violence essentially agree that causing criminals to use knives and other weapons rather than guns will result in fewer lethal injuries.

Whether a similar instrumentality effect holds for suicide is less clear, since highly lethal alternatives to guns are more readily available. While the available case-control research seems to suggest that gun ownership is positively correlated with the risk of suicide (Kleck 1991; Miller and Hemenway 1999; Wintemute et al. 1999), interpretation of this finding is complicated by the possibility of unmeasured differences between those who do and do not own guns that may also affect health outcomes. In any event, the question of whether an instrumentality effect exists for suicide has been less central to debates about gun policies, since most interventions have focused on reducing criminal gun use.

Third, even those who disagree about whether the Second Amendment guarantees the individual's right to own firearms agree that there are some who should not be granted access to guns, a group that includes teenagers, the mentally ill, and those with a history of violent criminal activity. More generally, constitutional scholars Laurence Tribe and Akhil Reed Amar (1999, p. A31) have argued that "the right to bear arms is certainly subject to reasonable regulation in the interest

[1] Unpublished figures from the National Center for Health Statistics' Vital Statistics Program for fatal gunshot injuries from 1972 onward were provided by James Mercy of the Centers for Disease Control and Prevention.

of public safety. . . . As a matter of constitutional logic, to uphold reasonable regulations is not to say that no right exists, or that anything goes."

What remains highly controversial is whether enhanced regulation of gun ownership and use will increase or decrease crime. The reason behind this controversy is that, while guns make criminal violence more lethal, guns may also have the beneficial effect of enabling private citizens to defend themselves against criminal attack. Proponents of more restrictive gun regulations argue that such efforts will do little to reduce defensive gun use since most law-abiding citizens will retain access to guns under most policy proposals and that, in any case, private citizens can substitute other means of self-defense when guns are not available. Opponents argue that additional regulations will reduce gun ownership rates among ordinary citizens but not among criminals and, thus, impede the ability of law-abiding people to defend themselves against better-armed criminal predators and to deter crime. For example, James Q. Wilson (1995, pp. 494–95) has argued that "guns are almost certainly contributors to the lethality of American violence, but there is no politically or legally feasible way to reduce the stock of guns now in private possession to the point that their availability to criminals would be much affected. . . . And even if there were, law-abiding people would lose a means of protecting themselves long before criminals lost a means of attacking them."

Concern that additional gun regulations may be counterproductive has increased in recent years, motivated in large part by a series of influential studies of defensive gun use and the deterrent effects of such uses. Research by criminologist Gary Kleck and his colleagues suggests that guns are used in self-defense by private citizens around 2.5 million times each year, far higher than previous estimates (Kleck 1988, 1991; Kleck and Gertz 1995; Kates and Kleck 1997). Kleck's findings have been invoked in support of arguments that gun regulations, such as waiting periods for handgun purchases and restrictions on gun carrying in public, will increase rather than decrease crime (e.g., see Lott 1999). Supporting evidence of substantial deterrent effects from gun self-defense use comes from the widely publicized research conducted by John Lott and his colleagues (Lott and Mustard 1997; Bronars and Lott 1998; Lott 1998b; Lott and Landes 1999), which suggests that permissive concealed gun-carrying laws reduce crime. Lott's research findings have figured prominently in recent debates about concealed-carry laws in states such as California, Colorado, Kansas, Minnesota, and Missouri. Given the substantial policy attention that has been devoted to both research literatures, this essay assesses what is known about the prevalence and deterrent effects of self-defense gun use.

Estimates for the prevalence of defensive gun use come from three sources, none of which is ideal. First, several studies have used data from vital statistics or police administrative records to estimate the number of legally justified defensive gunshot injuries (Kellermann and Reay 1986; Kleck 1988; Kellermann et al. 1995). This approach excludes those cases where the victim uses a gun in self-defense but does not injure the perpetrator. The second source of data is the National Crime Victimization Survey (NCVS), a national panel survey that provides crime victims with the opportunity to report on defensive actions they may have taken (Kleck 1988; Cook 1991; McDowall and Wiersema 1994; Cook, Ludwig, and Hemenway 1997).[2] The NCVS appears to understate the prevalence of defensive gun use because respondents are never directly asked whether they have used a gun in self-defense and are only provided with an opportunity to report defensive gun use for a subset of all crimes (Smith 1997). The third source of data is one-time telephone surveys that directly ask respondents whether they have used a gun in self-defense (Kleck 1988; Kleck and Gertz 1995; Cook and Ludwig 1996, 1997, 1998). These surveys appear to overstate the prevalence of defensive gun use because of "telescoping" (which occurs when respondents report on events that are outside of the survey-question recall period), self-presentation bias, and other sources of measurement error. Thus relatively little is currently known about the prevalence and incidence of civilian gun use in America.

Even unbiased estimates of the prevalence of defensive gun use, however, may leave many important policy questions unanswered. The benefits that civilian gun uses provide to society are difficult to identify from survey data for several reasons. First, only the gun user is interviewed; whether neutral observers would have classified the gun use as defensive or in society's best interests is often not clear. Second, almost nothing is known about what would have happened to victims had a gun not been available. Equally important, estimates of the frequency of defensive gun uses under the status quo provide no information about how a specific change in gun policy will affect the number of

---

[2] Information about the NCVS is available from the Bureau of Justice Statistics at www.ojp.usdoj.gov/bjs/.

socially desirable and undesirable gun uses, which is ultimately the question of interest for public policy.

A more promising approach for learning about the effects of defensive gun use and deterrence is to measure directly the net effects of gun policies on rates of crime and injury. John Lott and David Mustard (1997) follow this strategy to learn about the deterrent effects of defensive gun use by examining the net effects of permissive concealed-carry laws. These laws may reduce crime and injury rates by increasing the opportunities for private citizens to use guns in self-defense, thereby deterring criminal behavior. Crime may increase if those who carry guns misuse them or if criminals are more likely to arm themselves in response to these laws or become more likely to resort to force. Since both positive and negative effects are plausible, empirical evidence is required to determine which effects dominate.

The challenge for researchers is that the crime rates that states with permissive concealed-carry laws would have experienced had they not enacted this legislation cannot be observed. Lott and Mustard (1997) draw inferences about the effects of concealed-carry laws by comparing crime in states with and without such laws. Their evaluation improves on previous criminological work on the effects of gun policies by using national data and sophisticated statistical methods that help control for unmeasured differences across states that may affect crime levels and suggests that concealed-carry laws substantially reduce violent crime.

While the Lott and Mustard analysis has raised the standard for empirical evaluations of gun policies, evidence from a reanalysis of their data by Dan Black and Daniel Nagin suggests that the effects estimated by Lott and Mustard are due in part or whole to unmeasured variables (Black and Nagin 1998). More recent evaluations that use alternative methods to control for unmeasured variables produce no evidence of a significant crime-reducing effect of permissive concealed-carry laws (Black and Nagin 1998; Ludwig 1998), though the available evidence remains far from definitive.

This essay is organized as follows. Section I provides descriptive information about patterns of gun ownership, acquisition, and violence in the United States as background for the ensuing discussion of defensive and deterrent benefits arising from the civilian gun stock. Section II reviews the research literature on defensive gun use, while Section III discusses in detail the Lott and Mustard estimates and other evaluations of the effects of concealed-carry laws on crime. Section IV discusses directions for future research.

I. A Primer on Guns in America

While there are enough guns in the United States to arm every adult, gun ownership is actually quite concentrated. Estimates from survey and production data suggest that there are around 200 million guns in private circulation in America. The majority (around 135 million) are long guns that are kept primarily for hunting and other recreational purposes, in contrast to the 65 million handguns in circulation, which are primarily kept for self-protection. This enormous gun stock is owned by roughly one-quarter of America's adults, three-quarters of whom have two or more guns (Cook and Ludwig 1996). Those who are most likely to own handguns or long guns are in sociodemographic groups that are, on average, least likely to commit or be victimized by crime: gun ownership rates increase with educational attainment and income, are higher among the middle-aged than the young and in rural areas compared with cities, and are highest in the southern and western regions of the country (Wright, Rossi, and Daly 1983; Kleck 1991; Cook and Ludwig 1996).

Guns also tend to be quite "sedentary" in that most do not change hands very frequently—the average gun was acquired around thirteen years ago by its current owner (Cook and Ludwig 1996). Notwith-standing the 500,000–600,000 guns that are stolen each year (Cook, Molliconi, and Cole 1995; Cook and Ludwig 1996), these statistics suggest that most guns are in the hands of those who are unlikely to misuse them and likely to stay there for some time. The important exception are those guns kept by juveniles and criminals, which change hands quite frequently (Cook, Molliconi, and Cole 1995; Ash et al. 1996).

The number of new guns that enter into circulation each year in the United States (the "flow" of guns across owners) is equal to only around 3 percent of the total civilian gun stock. In 1994, around 7.2 million new guns were sold in the United States, split about evenly between handguns and long guns.[3] In addition, another 1 million used handguns and 1.5 million long guns change hands in off-the-books transactions among private parties who are not federally licensed fire-arms dealers, or "FFLs" (Cook and Ludwig 1996).

The distinction between transactions that do versus those that do not involve an FFL (termed the "primary" and "secondary" markets,

---

[3] Unpublished statistics from the Bureau of Alcohol, Tobacco, and Firearms are re-ported in Cook and Ludwig (1996).

respectively, by Cook, Molliconi, and Cole [1995]) is important because only licensed dealers are required by law to follow state and federal regulations regarding firearm transactions, such as waiting periods and background checks. The 30–40 percent of all gun exchanges that occur in the secondary market are, not surprisingly, responsible for a disproportionately large share of gun assaults. For example, a survey of incarcerated juveniles found that 79 percent had obtained their most recent handguns from a family member, friend, or street connection; only 12 percent had stolen their last handgun; and 7 percent obtained the weapon from a gun or pawn shop (Sheley and Wright 1993).

Much gun violence in America is perpetrated by young men. Around one-sixth of all people arrested for homicide are under the age of eighteen, and nearly two-thirds are under the age of twenty-five (Cook and Laub 1998). A large share of those arrested for gun homicides have had previous contacts with the criminal justice system. For example, a study of all homicide suspects ages twenty-one and under in Boston for the period 1990–94 found that fully 77 percent had been arrested for other crimes prior to committing their homicides (Kennedy, Piehl, and Braga 1996).

Gun policy in the United States has been motivated in large part by the two central facts documented here: crimes are more likely to result in death when guns are used rather than other weapons, and some population subgroups, particularly teens and convicted criminals, are at disproportionately high risk of criminal gun misuse. The first observation has led to policies that attempt to keep guns out of public spaces where there may be altercations; the hope is not necessarily to reduce the number of fights but, rather, to make them less lethal. The second observation has led to prohibitions on primary-market gun sales to teens and convicted criminals and to efforts to stem the flow of guns from primary to secondary markets (such as "one-gun-a-month" laws) and to reduce gun thefts (e.g., by encouraging gun owners to keep their weapons securely locked up). These policies may produce a modest increase in the money or nonmoney price of guns to proscribed groups. The result will be a modest reduction in gun ownership by members of these groups, so long as the decision to keep guns by some group members rests at least in part on the effective price of doing so.

The sparse evidence suggests that at least some members of proscribed groups are somewhat sensitive to the effective price of guns. For example, one incarcerated juvenile in North Carolina reported that "when [people] are short on money they have no choice but to sell [their guns]," while another remarked that he had "traded a .22 for a Super Nintendo and some other guns for a VCR and for my waterbed" (Cook, Molliconi, and Cole 1995). Similarly, in a survey of incarcerated adult felons who committed their crimes without guns, 21 percent reported that the trouble of acquiring a gun was somewhat or very important in their decision not to use a gun, while 17 percent reported "cost" as a somewhat or very important consideration (Wright and Rossi 1994).

The challenge for public policy is that strategies for reducing gun misuse may in principle also impair the ability of citizens to defend themselves against criminal attack, which represents a cost that must be weighed against any beneficial effects from reductions in gun misuse. Whether the benefits of various gun policies outweigh their costs is an empirical question.

II. Defensive Gun Use

The prevalence of defensive gun use in relation to gun crime has figured prominently in debates about gun regulation in recent years. Several empirical questions must be answered in order to draw inferences about gun policies. What number of defensive gun use occurs in the United States each year? What are the benefits of defensive gun use for citizens and for society more generally? How would particular gun policies affect the number of socially desirable and undesirable gun uses?

A. Estimates of Defensive Gun Use

Since both law enforcement and public health agencies collect comprehensive and generally reliable mortality data in the United States, a natural starting point for understanding the relative frequency of defensive gun use versus gun misuse is to compare the number of justifiable shootings with the numbers of homicides, suicides, and unintentional injuries. This approach was employed by Arthur Kellermann and Donald Reay (1986), who analyzed mortality records for King County, Washington, over the period 1978–83. Their analysis found that for every justifiable self-defense homicide with a firearm, there were 1.3 unintentional firearm deaths, 4.6 criminal homicides, and thirty-seven gun suicides.

To many gun control proponents, the Kellermann and Reay findings were decisive: if the number of deaths from gun homicide, suicide, and accidents exceeds the number of justifiable shootings, policies to further regulate access to firearms will save lives. Yet the number of fatally injured perpetrators may understate the public health benefits of defensive gun use if, as seems plausible, some gun owners deter potentially fatal criminal attacks but do not fatally injure the perpetrator (Kleck 1991). Mortality data may thus provide an incomplete picture of the benefits of defensive gun uses.

In a follow-up study, Kellermann and his colleagues overcome many of the limitations of using mortality data by focusing on data from police reports. The advantage of law enforcement over mortality data is that the former will include all cases in which gun owners prevent crimes and call the police. Kellermann found that self-defense gun use was reported to the police in only 1.5 percent of all burglaries of occupied homes in Atlanta during a three-month period in 1994, which is far less than the number of domestic gun homicides, suicides, and unintentional shootings that occur in Atlanta (Kellermann et al. 1995). Yet police data may still undercount the number of injuries that are prevented by self-defense gun use if some gun owners do not report their defensive actions to the police, for example because of uncertainty about the legality of the owner's actions (Kleck and Gertz 1995). More fundamentally, national estimates of defensive gun use cannot be obtained from police reports because the official national compilation of such data—the Federal Bureau of Investigation's (FBI) Uniform Crime Reporting (UCR) system—does not include information on gun self-defense.

Because of the controversy over the interpretation of mortality records and police data, research on defensive gun use has increasingly relied on population surveys. In principle, surveys have the potential to capture defensive gun uses that do not result in the death of the perpetrator and are not reported to police, cases that would be missed by law enforcement and mortality records. The most notable aspect of this survey literature is the considerable divergence in the published estimates, ranging from a low of 65,000 (McDowall and Wiersema 1994) from the National Crime Victimization Survey (NCVS) to 2.5 million (Kleck and Gertz 1995) from smaller one-time telephone surveys.

The NCVS is a nationally representative survey of between 40,000 and 60,000 households conducted by the Census Bureau for the U.S. Bureau of Justice Statistics. The NCVS attempts to interview everyone in sampled households age twelve and older every six months over a three-year period. Respondents are asked whether they had been the victim of a crime within the past six months. For crimes that involved direct contact with the perpetrator, respondents are also asked, "Did

TABLE 1

Estimates for the Prevalence of Defensive Gun Use from the National Crime Victimization Surveys

Study	NCVS Survey Years	Recall Period	Crimes Defended Against	Estimated Annual Defensive Gun Use
Kleck (1988)	1979–85	6 months	Robbery, assault	68,000
Cook (1991)	1979–87	6 months	All violent crimes and burglary	80,000
McDowall and Wiersema (1994)	1987–90	6 months	All violent crimes and burglary	65,000
Cook, Ludwig, and Hemenway (1997)	1992–94	6 months	All violent crimes and burglary	108,000
Rand (1999)	1996–98	6 months	All violent crimes and burglary	72,000

you do anything with the idea of protecting yourself or your property while the incident was going on?" Respondents are also asked, as a follow-up, "Was there anything you did or tried to do about the incident while it was going on?" If the respondent answers in the affirmative to either question, the interviewer asks, "What did you do? Anything else?" (Rand 1999). Studies that use the NCVS to estimate the prevalence of defensive gun use are reviewed in table 1. The most recent published estimate of 108,000 defensive gun uses per year comes from NCVS data for 1994–96 (Cook, Ludwig, and Hemenway 1997), while estimates using data for 1996–98 suggest 72,000 gun uses annually (Rand 1999).

One concern with the NCVS is that respondents are never directly asked whether they have used a gun in self-defense. This is problematic because, as Tom Smith of the National Opinion Research Center notes, "Indirect questions that rely on a respondent volunteering a specific element as part of a broad and unfocused inquiry uniformly lead to undercounts of the particular of interest" (1997, pp. 1462–63). Also omitted are cases where guns are used in defense against crimes that are not asked about in the NCVS survey, including trespassing, vandalism, and malicious mischief. (Whether the use of a gun to prevent such crimes is in society's best interests is a different question, which is discussed below.)

The limitations of the NCVS motivated criminologists to seek other sources of survey data on defensive gun use, sources that asked respondents directly whether they had ever used a gun in self-defense. Kleck (1988) reviewed the findings from a number of local or national surveys that had included such questions (see table 2), which taken together suggest that defensive gun use is far more common than data from the NCVS had indicated. While the surveys reviewed by Kleck had the advantage of asking respondents directly about whether they used a gun in defense, each survey suffered from other limitations. For example, in five of the eight surveys respondents are asked whether they have "ever" used a gun in self-defense, which makes it difficult to calculate an estimate for the annual prevalence or incidence of defensive gun use. In half of the surveys the respondent is asked to report on defensive gun uses by anyone within the household, which may lead to underestimates of defensive gun behaviors since many respondents are apparently unable or unwilling to report on gun ownership (and presumably gun use) by others within the home (Ludwig, Cook, and Smith 1998). Further, these surveys did not include follow-up questions that would enable analysts to determine whether the gun use was against an animal or a person or whether it was a function of the respondent's employment as a police officer or security guard (Kleck and Gertz 1995).

Thus the 1993 survey of 4,977 adults sponsored by Kleck and Gertz (1995) represented a substantial step forward in the measurement of defensive gun use. The Kleck and Gertz survey, which was conducted expressly for the purpose of measuring defensive gun use, intentionally oversampled residents of high gun-owning areas such as the South and West, and also oversampled males within contacted households. Each respondent was asked: "Within the past five years, have you yourself or another member of your household used a gun, even if it was not fired, for self-protection or for the protection of property at home, work, or elsewhere? Please do not include military service, police work, or work as a security guard." Follow-up questions included: "Was this to protect against an animal or a person?" "How many incidents in-

TABLE 2

Estimates for the Prevalence and Incidence of Defensive Gun Use from One-Time Telephone Surveys

Study and Survey	Question Refers To	Recall Period	Annual Number of People Who Use Guns in Self-Defense
Kleck and Gertz (1995):			
DMIa, 1978 (N = 1,500)	Household*	Ever	2.1 million
DMIb, 1978 (N = 1,010)	Household*	Ever	1.1 million
Hart, 1981 (N = 1,228)	Household*	5 years	1.8 million
Mauser, 1990 (N = 343)	Household*	5 years	1.5 million
Gallup, 1991 (N = 1,002)	Respondent†	Ever	.8 million
Gallup, 1993 (N = 1,014)	Respondent	Ever	1.6 million
L.A. Times, 1994 (N = 1,682)	Respondent	Ever	3.6 million
Tarrance, 1994 (N = 1,000)	Respondent/household	5 years	.8 million
1993 NSDS (N = 4,977)	Respondent	1 year	2.5 million
Cook and Ludwig (1998):			
1994 NSPOF (N = 2,568)	Respondent	1 year	1.3 million
Hemenway and Azrael (1997):			
1996 Fact Finders (N = 1,905)	Respondent	5 years	1.5 million

Sources.—For DMIa and DMIb surveys (separate subgroups), both reported in: Decision/Making/Information (1978); for Hart 1981 survey: Hart Research Associates (1981); for Mauser 1990 survey: Mauser (1993); and for Gallup 1991 and 1993 surveys, L.A. Times 1994 survey, and Tarrance 1994 survey, see Kleck and Gertz (1995, p. 182), which reports that these surveys were "taken from a search of the DIALOG Public Opinion online computer database." For all remaining surveys, see the studies in which they are cited.

Note.—Information on survey sample sizes was kindly provided by Gary Kleck (personal communication). All defensive gun use estimates above use the Kleck and Gertz (1995) definition of "legitimate" defensive gun uses, in which respondent is not employed by police, military, or private security, and gun use is against a human. The estimates from Kleck and Gertz (1995) and Cook and Ludwig (1998) only include defensive gun uses by respondents who saw a perpetrator and actually used a gun, are not employed as police or security personnel, and are against people rather than animals. The estimates by Hemenway and Azrael (1997) exclude gun uses against animals and gun uses by people employed as police officers. DMI = Decision/Making/Information; NSDS = National Self-Defense Survey; NSPOF = National Survey of Private Ownership of Firearms.

* Survey question refers to whether anyone in the household has used a gun in self-defense.

† Survey question refers to whether respondent has used a gun in self-defense.

volving defensive uses of guns against persons happened to members of your household in the past five years?" and "Did this incident [any of these incidents] happen in the past twelve months?"

Using the detailed information available from their follow-up questions, Kleck and Gertz (1995) kept only those cases for which the respondent used a gun in a "meaningful way" against a person and for which the respondent identified the type of crime against which the gun was used in defense. Kleck and Gertz also excluded cases where the respondent was employed by the military, police, or private security. The results of the Kleck and Gertz survey, as shown in table 2, suggest 2.1–2.5 million defensive gun uses per year. Not surprisingly, considerable research attention has since been devoted to explaining the discrepancy between estimates from the NCVS and those from the one-time telephone surveys of Kleck and Gertz.

B. Convergence from Discrepancy?

What explains the discrepancy between the estimates from the NCVS and the cross-sectional telephone surveys, and which of these estimates is most relevant for public policy? One concern with the Kleck and Gertz (1995) findings raised by David Hemenway (1997*b*) is whether their survey design actually produced a nationally representative sample of American adults. While the NCVS regularly obtains response rates on the order of 90–95 percent (Bureau of Justice Statistics 1996), the Kleck and Gertz response rate is something less than 61 percent.[4] Kleck and Gertz do report that their survey oversampled telephone numbers in the South and West, as well as men from within contacted households, but the procedures they use to project their responses up to population estimates are not clearly specified, and the weighted sample characteristics diverge somewhat from other published estimates (Hemenway 1997*b*).

As it turns out, sampling error does not appear to explain much of the difference between the NCVS and the Kleck and Gertz survey, since two more recent telephone surveys that used similar defensive gun-use questions to those employed by Kleck and Gertz produced similar results. The National Survey of Private Ownership of Firearms (NSPOF) was conducted in 1994 by Chilton Research Associates for

---

[4] Kleck and Gertz (1995) report that responses were obtained in 61 percent of cases where a person rather than an answering machine answered the phone, which will overstate their response rate since presumably for some proportion of telephone numbers selected into the sampling frame the interviewers could not make contact with a person.

the National Institute of Justice (Cook and Ludwig 1996). The survey instrument was designed by Gary Kleck, Philip Cook, and David Hemenway and uses a sequence of defensive gun-use questions quite similar to those found with the 1993 Kleck and Gertz (1995) survey. Unlike the Kleck and Gertz survey, the NSPOF randomly selects one adult per sampled household, does not oversample telephone numbers from the South and West, and uses standard sample-weighting techniques (Cook and Ludwig 1996). The results support an estimate of 1.3 million defensive gun users each year (table 2), which is within the 95 percent confidence interval of the Kleck and Gertz estimate (Cook and Ludwig 1998). A more recent national survey sponsored by the National Institute of Justice suggests 1.5 million defensive gun uses per year (Hemenway and Azrael 1997, and forthcoming).

The discrepancies between the NCVS and these one-time phone surveys appear to stem instead from different susceptibilities to "false negatives," cases where the respondent has used a gun in self-defense but conceals this from the survey interviewer, and "false positives," where respondents falsely report that they have used a gun in self-defense when they have not. For different reasons, estimates from the NCVS are probably too low, while those obtained from the one-time telephone surveys appear to be too high.

1. *Measurement Errors with the NCVS.*   That NCVS respondents are never directly asked whether they have used a gun in self-defense is likely to cause the NCVS to understate the prevalence of defensive gun use. The NCVS may suffer additional downward bias because some crimes such as trespassing are not included among the victimization questions that are followed by questions about defensive behaviors. Neither source of downward bias is present with the one-time telephone surveys reviewed in table 2, which directly ask all respondents whether they have used a gun in self-defense.

Because the NCVS provides an opportunity to report defensive gun use only to those respondents who report a criminal victimization, the NCVS may also omit cases where the respondent used a gun to prevent a crime before it occurred. The one-time surveys may be less susceptible to this problem because they ask respondents directly about gun self-defense and do not limit defensive gun-use questions to those who have reported a criminal victimization. Evidence to support this hypothesis comes from a study by McDowall, Loftin, and Presser (1999), who sponsored a survey in which half the sample is asked the NCVS sequence and then the sequence of questions from the Kleck and Gertz survey, while the other half is asked these questions in the reverse order. The McDowall survey shows that respondents are much more likely to report defensive gun uses with the Kleck and Gertz questions than with the NCVS questions, regardless of the question order. Similar evidence comes from the 1994 NSPOF survey, in which only one-third of those who reported a defensive gun use also answered yes to questions earlier in the survey about whether the respondent had been the victim of a violent crime (Cook and Ludwig 1998).

Another source of downward bias with the NCVS suggested by Kleck and Gertz (1995) stems from the possibility that respondents may conceal their defensive gun uses from the government personnel who conduct these interviews. Because some respondents may be uncertain about the legality of their defensive gun use, "in the context of a non-anonymous survey conducted by the federal government, a respondent who reports a defensive gun use may believe that he is placing himself in legal jeopardy" (Kleck and Gertz 1995, pp. 155–56). This phenomenon can only contribute to the discrepancy between the NCVS and the one-time telephone surveys if respondents believe that the confidentiality promise made by private polling firms are more credible than those made by the NCVS interviewers. Yet the best available evidence seems to suggest, if anything, that survey respondents believe that interviews by census staff have greater legitimacy than other surveys (Smith 1997).

Forgetting is a source of downward bias with all surveys, though this is probably less of a problem with the NCVS than with the one-time surveys. The reason is that the NCVS asks respondents to report on defensive gun uses only during the past six months. The one-time telephone surveys ask respondents about defensive gun uses over a longer period of time (typically one to five years prior to the survey). Since memory failure is more likely for events that occurred longer ago in the past (Woltman, Bushery, and Carstensen 1984), proportionately more events may be omitted in the one-time surveys than in the NCVS.

Finally, all surveys will suffer from some measurement error (both false positives and false negatives) because a proportion of all respondents to any nationally representative survey may be unreliable reporters. Recent estimates from the U.S. Department of Health and Human Services suggest that 51.3 million American adults suffer from some form of mental or addictive disorder (Bourndon et al. 1994), many of whom are unlikely to provide reliable responses to social science surveys. The possibility of unreliable reporters in the general population does not invalidate the use of social science surveys, but it does suggest that there will be some additional measurement error beyond sampling variability that complicates any effort to estimate very rare events such as defensive gun use. While there is no reason to believe that the proportion of unreliable reporters should be higher in the NCVS than in the one-time telephone surveys, the net effects of unreliable reporters may be greater with the one-time surveys because a larger proportion of the survey sample is asked to report on defensive gun uses (and thus has an opportunity to report unreliably).

2. *Measurement Errors with One-Time Telephone Surveys.* In contrast to the NCVS, the one-time telephone surveys analyzed by Kleck and Gertz (1995), Cook and Ludwig (1996, 1997, 1998), and Hemenway and Azrael (1997, and forthcoming) are more susceptible to upward bias from false positives. One reason is that the NCVS is less prone than the one-time surveys to false positives from "telescoping"—that is, when respondents report events that occurred outside of the survey question's recall period—because the NCVS uses a panel design that interviews respondents in selected housing units every six months for a specified period. With the NCVS, each respondent is reminded of the criminal victimizations (including those involving defensive behavior) that he or she reported during the previous interview and is also reminded that these events should not be reported as part of the current series of questions about victimizations that occurred during the past six months. Since one-time telephone surveys obviously cannot bound respondent reports about defensive gun uses, telescoping is more of an issue than with the NCVS. Comparisons of bounded and unbounded estimates for criminal victimization from NCVS data suggest that the latter are approximately 30–40 percent higher than the former (Woltman, Bushery, and Carstensen 1984). Whether the degree of telescoping for self-reported defensive gun use should be higher or lower than for self-reported criminal victimization is not clear.

Another possible source of false positives comes from "social desirability bias," which stems from the well-known tendency of respondents to present themselves favorably to survey interviewers. Respondents are more likely to report behaviors or attitudes that the survey interviewers may believe to be socially desirable, such as voting or seat belt use, and less likely to report on particulars that may be viewed as socially undesirable (Sudman and Bradburn 1974). If defensive gun use is viewed as a socially desirable behavior, then social desirability bias works in the opposite direction of respondent concerns about the legality of their gun use. No systematic data are available on public attitudes toward defensive gun use. Yet suggestive evidence that at least some groups view gun self-defense as a socially desirable behavior comes from the fact that the National Rifle Association's publication the *American Rifleman* has published abbreviated newspaper accounts of defensive gun use since 1932.[5] Social desirability bias could lead to false positives in the form of exaggerated accounts of events that actually happened or fabricated accounts of events that did not happen.

A final source of false positives comes, as noted above, from the possible presence of unreliable reporters in any nationally representative survey sample. The propensity of respondents to be unreliable reporters or to misreport because of social desirability bias may not be very different in the NCVS than in one-time surveys, though there is no empirical evidence on this point.

Thus the probability that a given respondent reports a false positive (the false-positive rate) will probably be higher in the one-time surveys than the NCVS because of telescoping. Whether the false-positive rate will differ across the two types of surveys because of social desirability or other reasons is less clear.

The false-positive rate can have a substantial effect on estimates from the one-time surveys, since defensive gun use by any measure is a relatively rare event, and thus even a modest false-positive rate may lead to substantial overestimates (Hemenway 1997a, 1997b). Consider, for example, a survey of 5,000 people in which the true prevalence of defensive gun use is 0.5 percent (i.e., half a percent of all adults use a gun in self-defense each year). With the one-time telephone surveys, every respondent is asked whether they have used a gun in self-defense. In this case, since 4,975 respondents have not used a gun in self-defense, the only reporting error available to this group is a false positive. However, only twenty-five respondents have actually used a gun in self-defense and thus can report a false negative. If the false-positive rate equals, say, 2 percent (because of telescoping, social desirability bias, or other reasons), the one-time survey will overstate the prevalence of defensive gun use by a factor of four even if the false-negative rate is 100 percent (i.e., none of those who have actually used a gun in

[5] From the National Rifle Association web page, www.nrahq.org/administration/publications/index.shtml# (November 29, 1997).

self-defense report their gun use to the interviewers). Put differently, because the net bias in a survey is a function of the false-positive and false-negative rates as well as the true prevalence of the event of interest, a modest false-positive rate can produce substantial overestimates even if the false-negative rate is far higher than the rate of false positives.

The NCVS is less susceptible to this algebra of false positives because only those respondents who report a criminal victimization are given the opportunity to report a defensive gun use (Cook and Ludwig 1998). To continue with the example from above, suppose that none of the twenty-five survey participants who have actually used a gun in self-defense reports their use, so that the false-negative rate is once again 100 percent. Suppose also that 10 percent of the 5,000 survey respondents have been the victim of a crime during the survey recall period. In this case, only 500 respondents are provided with the opportunity to report a defensive gun use, so a false-positive rate of 2 percent only leads to a total of ten reports of defensive gun use. Because only crime victims are asked about defensive gun use in the NCVS, a 2 percent false-positive rate leads to an estimate of only 40 percent of the true number of defensive gun users in the sample, while the same false-positive rate leads to an estimated prevalence of gun self-defense that is four times the true figure in one-time surveys when the gun-use questions are administered to everyone in the sample.

3. *One-Time Gun-Use Surveys: Internal and External Comparisons.* The key empirical question with the one-time surveys is whether the false-positive rate is far enough from zero to produce a net upward bias in estimates for defensive gun use. Some indirect evidence of a net upward bias with the one-time telephone surveys comes from comparing the results of the 1994 NSPOF data with related phenomena estimated from other surveys or administrative data. For example, it is difficult to reconcile the NSPOF estimates for defensive gun use with crime victimization statistics estimated from the NCVS (Cook and Ludwig 1998). The defensive gun uses reported in the NSPOF imply that guns were used to defend against 322,000 rapes and 527,000 robberies in 1994. By contrast, estimates from the NCVS suggest that there were a total of 316,000 total rapes (including attempts) and 1.3 million robberies in 1994. The comparison suggests that an implausibly high proportion of crimes were defended against by gun owners, which in turn suggests that estimates for the prevalence of defensive gun use from the one-time NSPOF survey may be in error.

Kleck and Gertz (1995, p. 167) argue that comparisons of estimates for defensive gun uses from the one-time surveys and victimization estimates from the NCVS are not useful because "a large share [of defensive gun uses] are probably outside the scope of incidents that realistically are likely to be reported to either the NCVS or police." In particular, Kleck and Gertz are concerned that the NCVS will not capture cases where the respondent is uncertain about whether the gun use was legal, for example, because the gun was carried or used in a public area (Kleck 1999). This concern can be addressed by focusing on those NSPOF respondents who report a defensive gun use and report that the police found out about the incident, which turns out to be about half of all NSPOF defensive gun-use reporters. The NSPOF thus implies that there were 265,000 attempted rapes and 141,000 attempted robberies in which the victim used a gun in self-defense and reported the incident to the police. By comparison, the FBI's Uniform Crime Reports imply that the total number of rape and robbery attempts reported to the police in 1994 was 102,000 and 619,000, respectively. This comparison provides further support for the hypothesis that the one-time NSPOF survey overestimates the prevalence of defensive gun use, since the number of rape attempts defended against with a gun and reported to the police cannot logically exceed the total number of rape attempts reported to the police.[6]

A third test of external validity comes from comparing the number of criminal perpetrators who are shot by someone using a gun in self-defense, equal to 117,000 in 1994 according to respondents in the NSPOF survey (Cook and Ludwig 1996), with the estimated number of people who are shot and receive medical treatment each year in the emergency department, equal to around 150,000 in 1992–93 (Annest et al. 1995). This comparison lends itself to three possible interpretations. First, most of the people who are admitted to emergency departments in the United States who reportedly have been injured during the course of criminal assaults, suicide attempts, or unintentional shootings may in fact be criminals who are wounded during the course of committing crimes. This seems unlikely. Second, it is possible that most of the criminals who are shot by those using guns in self-defense

---

[6] It is possible that the UCR undercounts the true number of crimes reported to the police nationwide for various reasons. Yet data from the NCVS suggest that a total of 719,000 robberies and 137,000 rapes and attempted rapes were reported to the police in 1994, which also suggest that the NSPOF estimates for defensive gun use are implausible.

do not seek treatment in the emergency department and, thus, are not reflected in the emergency department admission data. Yet 92 percent of incarcerated criminals who have been shot in the past report that they went to the hospital for treatment (May et al., forthcoming). The third and most plausible explanation is that the NSPOF-based estimate for the number of perpetrators wounded during the course of self-defense is too high. The Kleck and Gertz survey similarly reveals implausibly large numbers of wounded assailants and other inconsistencies with external benchmarks (Kleck and Gertz 1995; Hemenway 1997a, 1997b).

The internal consistency of defensive gun-use reports has also been cited as a measuring stick for the veracity of these accounts. Kleck and Gertz (1995, p. 179) argue that the false-positive hypothesis is implausible "since we asked as many as nineteen questions on the topic [of defensive gun use, and as a result misreporting] would entail spontaneously inventing as many as nineteen plausible and internally consistent bits of false information and doing so in a way that gave no hint to experienced interviewers that they were being deceived." While Kleck and Gertz do not report on the details of their internal-consistency checks, there are some indications of internal inconsistencies in about a third of defensive gun-use reports in the 1994 NSPOF data (Cook and Ludwig 1998). For example, in one-fifth of the cases, the respondent indicated that a serious crime (rape, robbery, or attack) was involved but also reported that the perpetrator neither attacked nor issued a threat. These inconsistencies reflect either internal inconsistencies in the accounts of those who report defensive gun uses or coding errors by the interviewers. The latter seems unlikely to explain all of the apparent inconsistencies, given that senior survey staff monitored interviews and response coding for a random tenth of all calls throughout the study and because these inconsistencies arise in such a large proportion of all defensive gun-use cases.

Internal and external comparisons for the NSPOF data thus suggest that at least some of the details reported by respondents about their defensive gun uses are inconsistent with estimates derived from other sources. While estimates for external benchmarks such as the number of criminal victimizations, crimes reported to the police, or patients admitted to emergency departments are certainly subject to some error, these measurement errors would need to be far larger than is currently believed in order for the NSPOF reports to be consistent with these other facts. Similar inconsistencies between the defensive gun-use reports in the Kleck and Gertz survey and other estimates have also been identified (Kleck and Gertz 1995; Hemenway 1997*a*, 1997*b*). These comparisons do not allow us to determine whether respondents are forgetting, exaggerating, or unintentionally distorting details about gun uses that actually happened or whether they are inventing these events altogether.

But whatever the cause, these apparent measurement errors suggest that the available data from one-time telephone surveys cannot be used to support precise estimates for the annual number of gun uses that are in society's best interests. If the gun uses happened as reported but occurred outside of the survey recall period, estimates for the annual prevalence or incidence of defensive gun use will be overstated. If important details about the gun use are intentionally or unintentionally misreported, then analysts have little way of knowing whether the gun use that actually occurred produced a net benefit or cost from society's perspective. And if some of these events were invented outright by the respondents, there is obviously no gun use to produce either a benefit or cost to society.

4. *Narrowing the Range of Estimates.*   Analysts continue to debate whether the NCVS or the phone-survey estimates are more useful for public policy. Smith (1997) narrows the difference between the two sets of estimates by speculating on the magnitude of the biases that appear to afflict these figures. Smith inflates the latest NCVS estimate of 108,000 (Cook, Ludwig, and Hemenway 1997) by 50 percent to account for the fact that the NCVS does not directly ask about defensive gun use and, then, by another 16–42 percent to account for the fact that the NCVS excludes gun uses against trespassing and vandalism. Whether this second adjustment should be made is not clear, since the legality of using a gun to prevent a case of trespassing or vandalism is questionable. In any event, these two adjustments bring the revised NCVS estimate up to between 256,500 and 373,000. Smith also discounts the average of the smallest estimates reported by Kleck and Gertz (1995) and Cook and Ludwig (1996)—1.8 million—to account for telescoping, which yields an upper-bound estimate of 1.3 million.

While Smith's exercise is useful in narrowing the magnitude of the discrepancy, the deeper problem comes from identifying which gun uses are clearly in society's best interests (however that might be defined), and how these uses should be weighed against the annual number of gun misuses.

C. The Benefits of Defensive Gun Use

Estimates of the prevalence of defensive gun use are routinely compared with the number of gun crimes as a measure of the relative costs and benefits of private gun ownership or more or less restrictive gun policies (see, e.g., Kleck 1991; Kleck and Gertz 1995, 1997; and Lott 1999). Yet the policy implications of civilian defensive gun use will depend in large part on the benefits to society that result from these events, which are often difficult to identify from the available data.

One concern is that survey respondents may report a wide variety of behaviors as defensive gun uses, ranging from legitimate cases of self-defense where life and limb are at stake to more ambiguous cases, including those where the victim provokes the attack. Determining where particular gun uses fall on this continuum is frequently not possible from the available data. One problem is, as noted above, that some respondents may intentionally or unintentionally misreport some details of the events. Another problem is that the information that is available about the event is obtained from only one party to the encounter. For example, in around one-quarter of the gun uses reported in the NSPOF, the respondent indicated that the most serious crime involved in the incident was a fight or attack (Cook and Ludwig 1998). Whether a neutral observer would have classified the survey respondent as the victim in these confrontations cannot be determined from the available data. At a minimum, future surveys of gun self-defense should gather more detailed information about the sequence of events that leads up to the gun use in order to learn more about how the respondent contributes to the escalation of the encounter.

Identifying whether a gun use is in society's best interests is further complicated by the possibility that some respondents may use their guns in defense in the expectation that someone may be seriously injured, though the actual outcome of the event is ambiguous. For example, consider a case where a car is stopped downtown at a red light late at night, a young man approaches the car and knocks on the window, the driver retrieves his handgun from the glove compartment in response, and the other party flees. Is this a thwarted criminal assault, or was the other party simply requesting directions or a ride to the nearest gas station for mechanical assistance? Determining whether this should be counted as a legitimate case of self-defense would require information about the other party's intent. Whether a survey of the other party, or the presence of eyewitnesses, could reliably identify what this person was intending to do is by no means obvious, since if the other party was intending to commit a crime, then he will have obvious incentives to misreport his intentions, while eyewitnesses will be in the difficult position of having to forecast the person's future behavior on the basis of the set of events that they observe (which may be incomplete).

Another complicated scenario arises in the case of defensive gun uses by residents who move back and forth between the legal and illegal worlds. Such cases may account for a large number of defensive gun uses, since a large proportion of homicide victims have prior criminal histories (Kennedy, Piehl, and Braga 1996). While population-survey samples are likely to underrepresent members of this group (Cook 1985), there is nevertheless the problem that social science surveys do not record information about illegal activities associated with the defensive gun use or the gun user more generally.

Even if defensive gun uses associated with illegal activities could be identified, should they be counted as a benefit to society? Consider, for example, the case of a drug dealer who uses a gun to ward off a "client" who attempts to attack the dealer and make off with his supply of narcotics. Presumably some readers will object to the idea of counting this as a socially beneficial gun use, since it is associated with an illegal activity (drug selling). But what if a recreational drug user, after consuming narcotics within his home, uses a gun to ward off a burglar? What if an otherwise law-abiding citizen is carrying a concealed handgun in violation of local laws and then uses the weapon in self-defense, in order to prevent a robber from taking his wallet? Does the illegal-activity argument imply that both of these gun uses produce no benefit to society? If gun defenses by some "criminals" are judged to be benefits and others are not, what rules guide these distinctions?

Finally, the notion that a gun use produces some benefit to society implies that the outcome of the event is better in some sense than what would have happened to the respondent had he not used a gun. Yet nothing is known about what would have happened to the survey respondent had a gun not been available. Uncertainty about the counterfactual scenario can be divided into two components: Had the survey respondent not had access to a gun, how would the outcome of the event be affected once a hostile confrontation with the perpetrator was unavoidable? And, how does access to a firearm influence the likelihood that a would-be victim comes into contact with a perpetrator or escalates a confrontation? Because these questions cannot be answered from the available survey data, how many of those who report defensive gun uses would have been victimized had a gun not been available remains unclear.

While there is a large research literature that examines the consequences of victim resistance with a gun once contact with a perpetrator is unavoidable, far too little is known on this point. Even the best available dataset for studying victim resistance, the NCVS, is inadequate for identifying what would have happened to the victim had some alternative defensive strategy been employed. One problem is that the NCVS does not provide detailed data about the sequence of robber and victim behavior, which makes it difficult to determine whether the victim's actions improve the outcome of the event (Cook 1986; Kleck and DeLone 1993). For example, the victim may use force only in response to a robber's attack or may try to resist in response to the robber's threat and provoke an attack. Both cases will be recorded in the NCVS as ones in which both the victim and the robber use force.

More generally, when and how victims choose to resist is almost surely based in part on aspects of the encounter that are not measured by the NCVS. As a result, comparisons of victim outcomes will confound the causal effects of the victim's behavior with the unobserved aspects of the event that contribute both to the victim's decision to resist and to the probability that the resistance will be successful. For example, consider Kleck and DeLone's (1993) state-of-the-art analysis of victim resistance in robberies using NCVS data for 1979–85. Kleck and DeLone use a multivariate regression approach to control for two dozen potentially confounding variables, including the victim's age, whether the victim was employed by the police or otherwise trained in the use of a gun, whether the incident occurred "when it was dark," and whether the incident occurred in a "private location." Now consider the following scenarios:

A thirty-year-old economist, standing 5′9″ and 150 pounds, confronts a physically imposing, determined perpetrator in a dark alley at 11:30 P.M. The perpetrator attacks, the economist resists by yelling and punching the perpetrator but is nevertheless injured as a result of the assault.

A thirty-year-old graduate student who works part time as a bouncer, standing 6′9″ and 350 pounds, confronts a slightly built perpetrator shortly after dusk near a heavily trafficked entrance in a shopping mall parking lot. The perpetrator is nervous, scared, and inebriated. The perpetrator attacks, the bouncer fends off the attacker while retrieving a handgun from the glove compartment of his car, and the perpetrator flees.

Despite the relatively large number of covariates included in the Kleck and DeLone (1993) regression models, their analysis nevertheless treats the two cases described above as observationally equivalent in all respects other than the defensive behavior of the victim and the outcome of the event. Yet presumably most readers will agree that there is some ambiguity about how the presence of a gun contributed to the outcome of the second case.

The literature on victim resistance described above ignores the more general question of victimization avoidance. Studies of victim resistance typically examine the effects of victim behavior conditional on there being a hostile confrontation between the victim and the perpetrator. Yet whether such a confrontation occurs may stem in part from the decisions made by the victim and may be influenced by the availability of a firearm. For example, armed citizens may escalate verbal arguments that otherwise might be defused or ignored or may choose to walk dark streets that would otherwise have been avoided. While the avoidance of certain parts of town at certain parts of the day or night surely imposes some cost on citizens, these costs are very different from those associated with a criminal victimization.

The hypothesis that guns may induce "compensating risks" or "offsetting behavior" is motivated in part by research showing similar effects in other contexts. For example, improvements in automobile safety design have been found to lead to riskier driving (Peltzman 1975; Crandall and Graham 1984; Traynor 1993), the introduction of child-resistant packaging for aspirin leads to more careless storage of aspirin bottles by parents (Viscusi 1984), and the frequency of unsafe sex practices among homosexual men seems to increase when the incidence of sexually transmitted diseases decreases (Philipson and Posner 1993). Some direct support for offsetting behavior in the case of gun use comes from the 1994 NSPOF survey data. In one-third of the defensive gun use cases reported in the NSPOF, the respondent indicates that the encounter occurred "near the respondent's home" and also indicates that, when he first wanted to use his gun for protection, the gun was somewhere in the home (Cook and Ludwig 1998). These figures suggest that one-third of all gun defenders had the option of staying inside and calling the police rather than confronting the perpetrator.

D. Conclusions

Surveys of defensive gun use, as with any survey, will almost surely contain both false positives and false negatives. But because defensive gun use by any measure is a relatively rare event, far more respondents have the opportunity to report a false positive than a false negative in the one-time telephone surveys that ask every respondent about defensive gun use. As a result, a relatively low false-positive rate can lead to substantial overestimates of defensive gun use with these surveys even if the false-negative rate is far higher. Some comparisons of the results from the one-time surveys analyzed by Cook and Ludwig (1996, 1997, 1998) and Kleck and Gertz (1995) with other estimates provide some evidence to suggest the point estimates for the prevalence of defensive gun use suffer from an upward bias. However, since only respondents who have reported a criminal victimization are asked about defensive gun use in the NCVS, the relative influence of false positives is far less than in the one-time surveys. False negatives are thus likely to be more important with the NCVS and may lead to a downward bias in estimates for defensive gun use derived from this data source.

The larger difficulties arise in determining how gun uses contribute to public well-being. In some cases, the information necessary for determining whether the survey respondent is the victim or the aggressor in the gun use is not available. More generally, the consequences of gun use cannot be understood without some understanding of whether gun use is more effective than other means of resistance against criminal attack, about which little is currently known. Access to firearms may also affect the probability that a confrontation occurs, as is suggested by evidence from the NSPOF survey. And surveys of defensive gun use provide no information about perhaps the most important benefit of this behavior—the deterrent effect on criminals.

Determining whether a gun use is in the public's best interest also requires answers to difficult normative questions that cannot be answered by social science. Most people will agree that the use of a gun in self-defense when a serious injury is clearly imminent is uncontroversially beneficial to society, assuming that the victim did not contribute to the confrontation in some way. But what if the gun user initiated the incident by engaging in aggressive driving? What if the other party only threatened to attack, or the gun user inferred that the party might attack? What if a gun is used in response to a nonfatal or avoidable attack? What if the gun is used to prevent trespassing or to protect property rather than life and limb? These are difficult questions to answer, as evidenced by the ambivalence with which the public frequently receives the use of guns by law-enforcement officers during the course of their duties, even in cases where police report that they were concerned for their safety.

Estimates for the number of defensive gun uses that are in society's best interests are frequently used as measures of the potential costs of implementing different gun regulations. But these regulations may also produce benefits that must be weighed against these costs, which include any reductions in fatal and nonfatal injuries that may result. The benefits of gun regulations may also include reductions in the number of hostile or inappropriate gun brandishings, which may exceed both the number of gun crimes reported in the NCVS and the number of defensive gun uses reported in one-time telephone surveys (Hemenway and Azrael 1997, and forthcoming).

Moreover, estimates of the frequency of socially desirable and undesirable gun uses under the status quo provide little information about how the prevalence of these behaviors would change in response to specific public policies. The answer is not obvious for most gun policies. For example, requirements that all handgun sales involve a three- or five-day waiting period may prevent some impulsive suicides but may also prevent some people who are being stalked from obtaining guns for their personal protection. No one knows how waiting periods affect the prevalence of either event, even though it is the change in these behaviors produced by a policy rather than their prevalence under the status quo that is most relevant for evaluating gun policies. In other words, a gun policy that prevents 1,000 crimes and suicide attempts each year and has no effect on defensive gun use or deterrence can arguably be judged to be successful, regardless of whether the number of defensive gun uses is currently 100,000 or 2.5 million. The most promising approach for understanding the implications of defensive gun use and deterrence for public policy is to examine directly the net effects of gun policies on the ultimate outcomes of interest—rates of crime and injury.

III. The Effects of Gun-Carrying Laws on Crime

The burgeoning research literature on the defensive and deterrent value of private gun ownership has motivated substantial scholarly interest in the effects of permissive concealed-gun carrying laws (or, equivalently, "concealed carry laws"), which seek to enhance the ability of citizens to use guns in self-defense. In particular, the influential evaluations conducted by John Lott and his colleagues (Lott and Mustard 1997; Bronars and Lott 1998; Lott 1998*b*; Lott and Landes 1999) have contributed to the growing perception that the deterrent effects of defensive gun use are substantial and that concealed-carry laws produce substantial reductions in violent crime.

A. Permissive Concealed-Carry Laws and Their Potential Effects

Within the past five years, ten states have enacted permissive concealed-gun carrying laws, bringing the total number of states with such laws on the books to thirty-one.[7] These laws require local law enforcement authorities to issue a permit to carry a concealed handgun in public to any adult who meets a minimal set of criteria related to criminal background, mental competence, and, in some states, training in the handling of firearms. (These are also known as "shall-issue" laws because of the requirement that local police issue permits to any qualified adult.) Permissive concealed-carry laws represent a sharp departure from the prior legal regime that had been in place in most of these states, under which local police were given considerable discretion over the issuance of concealed-carry permits ("may-issue"). Since police had typically been quite restrictive in the issuance of concealed-carry permits (McDowall, Loftin, and Wiersema 1995), the more permissive state-level concealed-carry laws have the potential to increase substantially the proportion of adults who are legally licensed to carry a concealed handgun in public areas.

The degree to which the prevalence of gun carrying actually increases in response to these laws remains somewhat unclear. One recent review suggests that in twelve of sixteen permissive concealed-carry states that were studied, fewer than 2 percent of adults had obtained permits to carry concealed handguns (Hill 1997). However, the change in the number of concealed-carry permits issued will be different from the change in the overall prevalence of gun carrying, since many people apparently take guns into public areas in the United States without benefit of a permit. For example, survey data from the 1994 NSPOF suggests that 7.5 percent of American adults carried a firearm on their person or in a motor vehicle at some point during the

[7] The ten states are Alaska, Arkansas, Kentucky, Louisiana, Nevada, North Carolina, Oklahoma, South Carolina, Texas, and Virginia. The total number of states is taken from the National Rifle Association Institute for Legislative Action, Compendium of State Firearm Laws, www.nraila.org, downloaded November 20, 1999.

year (Cook and Ludwig 1996). Because many people who obtain permits have already been carrying guns in public, the change in the prevalence of gun carrying may be smaller than the number of permits issued. For example, 85 percent of those with concealed-carry permits in North Carolina who carry a gun in their car and 34 percent of those who carry on their person did so even before they obtained a permit, and a majority of both groups indicate that the frequency of their gun carrying did not increase with the acquisition of the permit (Robuck-Mangum 1997). Thus the data that are available suggest that permissive concealed-carry laws may have only a modest effect on the overall prevalence of gun carrying.

Assuming that permissive concealed-carry laws increase the prevalence of gun carrying, one consequence may be an increase in the frequency of defensive gun use. The net effects of more gun self-defense on injury rates will depend, in part, on the advantages of using a gun rather than other methods of avoiding criminal victimization and injury and, in part, on the degree to which law-abiding citizens change their risk-avoiding behaviors. Perhaps the most important benefit from an increase in gun carrying may be a general deterrent effect on criminal behavior (Lott and Mustard 1997). Some support for the plausibility of a deterrent effect comes from Wright and Rossi's (1994) interviews of incarcerated felons. Around 80 percent of the respondents agreed with the statement that "a smart criminal always tries to find out if his potential victim is armed," and around two-fifths of those who agreed with this statement also report that at some point in their lives they had decided to not commit a particular crime because they "knew or believed that the victim was carrying a gun" (Wright and Rossi 1994, p. 147). These findings are consistent with evidence that the threat of apprehension and punishment from the criminal justice system has a deterrent effect on criminal behavior (Nagin 1998).

Even if there is little or no change in actual gun carrying from the implementation of a permissive concealed-carry law, crime may decrease if criminals perceive the law to have increased the risks of encountering an armed victim. This could happen if criminals update their perceptions of the prevalence of gun carrying in response to the publicity surrounding the implementation of a permissive concealed-carry law, what Zimring and Hawkins (1997) term an "announcement effect." The possibility that the perceived probability of punishment may diverge from the actual probability, at least in the short run, is suggested by evidence that reductions in drunk driving persist through a "residual deterrent" effect even after local police crackdowns have ended (Sherman 1992).

The most obvious potential cost of permissive concealed-carry laws comes from the possibility that those who obtain concealed-carry permits will misuse their guns. Another potential cost that is frequently ignored in policy debates comes from the possibility of undesirable changes in the behavior of criminals in response to these laws. For example, nearly two-thirds of the incarcerated criminals interviewed by Wright and Rossi (1994) who used guns to commit their crimes reported that the prospect of encountering an armed victim was very or somewhat important in their decision to carry a gun themselves. Since guns are currently used in "only" 21 percent of all robberies, 4 percent of sexual assaults and rapes, and 7 percent of assaults (Rennison 1999), permissive concealed-carry laws may have the negative consequence of increasing the proportion of criminals who carry guns to commit their crimes. Increases in the proportion of crimes committed with a gun may in turn increase the proportion of crimes that result in fatal injuries (Cook 1991). Another possibility is that if the probability of encountering an armed victim increases, criminals may be more likely to use their weapons, whether they be guns, knives, or something else entirely, in order to gain a first-mover advantage.

Because both positive and negative effects are plausible from concealed-carry laws, empirical research is required to determine whether the net effects of these laws are to increase or decrease rates of crime and injury. While the sign of the effect from these laws is ambiguous, the magnitude of the effect is probably modest given that concealed-carry laws may have only nominal effects on the prevalence of gun carrying in public spaces. Moreover, increases in gun carrying appear to be concentrated disproportionately in areas where crime rates are quite low, among people who are already at relatively low risk of victimization. Data from the NCVS suggest that victimizations from violent crime are most frequent among low-income, never-married residents of urban areas (Rennison 1999). Yet in Texas and North Carolina, around three-quarters of those who obtain a concealed-carry permit are over the age of forty, almost all are white, and over half live in rural areas (Hill 1997). Permit holders in North Carolina are more likely to be married or college educated relative to other state residents (Robuck-Mangum 1997). The effects from concealed-carry laws may be limited if the prevalence of gun-carrying changes primarily in areas away from where most crimes occur.

B. *The Evaluation Problem*

The causal effect of an intervention such as a permissive concealed-carry law is defined as the difference between the crime rate that is actually observed in a jurisdiction with a permissive concealed-carry law and the crime rate that the jurisdiction would have experienced had the law not been implemented. The challenge for researchers is that the crime rate under the counterfactual scenario in which the state does not enact the law is not observed. (This is true by definition, since "counterfactual" refers to outcomes that could potentially have occurred in place of the events that were actually observed but did not.)

Researchers in medicine, psychology, and other disciplines frequently try to infer the counterfactual outcomes that a particular treatment group would have experienced by conducting randomized clinical trials, known in social science circles as randomized experiments. Since participants who volunteer for an experiment are randomly assigned into the treatment or control group, the baseline health measures and other characteristics of those in the two groups should be similar. As a result, the health outcomes observed for the controls at the end of the experiment should provide an unbiased estimate of what the health outcomes for the treatment group would have been had they not been given the treatment. The contrast in health outcomes between the treatment and control groups provide an unbiased estimate for the effects of the treatment. Thus the keys to valid inference with randomized clinical trials is that analysts choose who receives the treatment, and because of random assignment the outcomes observed for the control group are good proxies for what would have happened to the treatment group had they not received the treatment.

Of course in some situations experiments are not possible because of ethical, financial, or other practical considerations. In such cases, analysts attempt to draw inferences about the outcomes the treatment group would have had if they had not received the treatment using different statistical procedures. The difficulties of this task can be seen by considering the case of using nonexperimental data to evaluate the effects of doctors' office visits on health outcomes for people with influenza. The problem is that for flu victims who visit a doctor, we do not observe what their health outcomes would have been had they not sought treatment, while for those who do not see a doctor we do not know what their health outcomes would have been had they done so. The goal of statistical analysis is thus to draw inferences about what would have happened to each observational unit under the alternative scenario of treatment (or nontreatment). The two most common methods for doing this are "pre/post" comparisons, where the analyst assumes that the person's health outcomes without the treatment will equal (or can be forecast from) her health status before she seeks treatment, and comparisons of people who do and do not voluntarily seek treatment.

One problem with pre/post comparisons is that if patients tend to visit the doctor only after they are sick, we may mistakenly conclude that visiting the doctor causes the flu (depending on when the pre- and post-health measures are recorded). A related challenge stems from the fact that influenza spells are typically of finite duration; since patients will eventually recover whether or not they seek medical treatment, we may mistakenly conclude that doctor visits "cure" the flu, even if they have no effect. (This alternative hypothesis is expressed by the old saying, "A cold will last seven days if one visits the doctor, and otherwise will last a week.")

Comparing health outcomes of people with the flu who have visited versus those who have not visited the doctor can help control for the fact that flu spells are of finite duration, though such comparisons may still be biased if the reasons that cause some people but not others to visit the doctor are related to health outcomes. For example, patients who seek out the doctor may have more severe cases of the flu than those who do not, which might lead us to conclude that doctors exacerbate the severity of the illness. Alternatively, visits to the doctor may be more likely among patients who care about their health and, thus, may recovery more quickly because of their general fitness or because they initiate supplemental treatment activities on their own (such as extra bed rest or time off from work).

Evaluating the effects of concealed-carry laws involves almost all of the same complications raised in the example above. As with influenza patients, states choose whether and when to implement the treatment (concealed-carry legislation). These decisions may in part be a consequence of the outcome measure of interest, since states may enact concealed-carry laws in response to changes in local crime rates. And as with the flu, increases in crime rates are of finite duration—data for the United States as a whole show that periods of increasing crime are regularly followed by periods in which crime rates decrease (Blumstein 1995; Philipson and Posner 1996), and similar patterns can be observed at the state level as well. States that choose to enact permissive concealed-carry laws may be different from other states in ways that are relevant for the local crime rate (e.g., with respect to demographic or economic characteristics of the local population) or may supplement concealed-carry laws with other anticrime measures that will confound attempts to isolate the effects of the gun-carrying intervention. Thus the evaluation of concealed-carry laws requires the difficult task of disentangling the causal effects of a self-imposed treatment that may be both cause and consequence of the outcome of interest.

C. Pre/Post Comparisons

One of the first systematic scholarly attempts to evaluate the effects of concealed-carry laws was conducted by David McDowall, Colin Loftin, and Brian Wiersema (1995). Their study uses data from 1973 through 1992 for five urban counties in Florida, Mississippi, and Oregon, each of which implemented a permissive concealed-carry law during the sample period (October 1, 1987; July 1, 1990; and January 1, 1990, respectively). The key outcome variables for the evaluation are gun and nongun homicides, as recorded by the vital statistics system of the National Center for Health Statistics, and thus should be fairly reliable measures of the rate of lethal violence in these treatment areas.

McDowall and colleagues (1995) attempt to measure the effects of concealed-carry laws by comparing the crime rate in each county after the area's concealed-carry law has gone into effect with the crime rate that the county would have had if the law had not gone into effect, as predicted from the area's crime rates before the law had gone into effect. Their evaluation approach thus assumes that, had these concealed-carry laws not gone into effect, each county's crime rate would have followed the same historical trend as was observed during the prelaw period. The results of the analysis suggest large increases in gun homicides in four of the five counties that they examine. In three of the four counties where gun homicides increased, the effects are enormous (on the order of 20–75 percent) and statistically significant at the conventional 5 percent level. They find no systematic evidence of changes in nongun homicides in these areas.

The central concern with the evaluation by McDowell, Loftin, and Wiersema (1995) is the possibility that the crime rates in these cities may deviate from their historical trends for a number of reasons other than the implementation of concealed-carry laws. For example, beginning in the mid-1980s the use and distribution of crack cocaine is thought to have increased substantially in American cities. This increase in crack is thought to have contributed to an increase in gun violence, as more young people became involved in the distribution of drugs and began to use guns to enforce the terms of these drug transactions (Blumstein 1995; Blumstein and Cork 1996; Cork 1999). McDowall and colleagues attempt to control for the effects of unexpected changes in crime rates by replicating their analysis in different cities, with the expectation that "if similar outcomes occur in several different places after the laws, historical events become a less plausible explanation of the change" (1995, p. 199). Yet the timing of the concealed-carry laws in Florida, Mississippi, and Oregon coincide almost exactly to periods when crack arrests (and juvenile gun homicides) surged (Cork 1999).[8]

While crack may or may not explain the findings by McDowall and his colleagues, the surge in crack activity around the time of these laws highlights the potential problems of drawing inferences about the effects of concealed-carry laws using only crime data for counties that implemented such laws. Information about crime trends in nearby areas that did not enact permissive concealed-carry laws would help eliminate alternative explanations for the authors' pattern of findings. An example of the advantages of using data for control jurisdictions that did not enact whatever legal intervention is being studied comes from the evaluation of a law enacted in Gainesville, Florida, in the mid-1980s that required convenience stores to employ two clerks per shift to deter robberies (Sherman 1992). Initial evaluations found that convenience-store robberies decreased substantially in Gainesville after these laws were enacted. Yet a reanalysis found similar reductions in convenience store robberies in a nearby county that had not enacted such a law, suggesting that some factor other than the two-clerk requirement was responsible for the change in robberies in both Gainesville and the nearby county.

In sum, it is difficult to draw causal inferences from the McDowall

[8] McDowall, Loftin, and Wiersema (1995) also attempt to control for unexpected changes in each treatment area's crime rate over time by including in their regression models a control for the overall U.S. homicide rate. But this will only partially control for the effects of innovations like crack if, as seems plausible, these innovations have greater effects on crime rates in cities than in suburbs and rural areas, so that the urban areas examined by McDowall, Loftin, and Wiersema experience increases in crime rates relative to the nation as a whole.

et al. findings without information about what happened in similar jurisdictions that did not implement concealed-carry laws during the sample period. This unresolved identification problem, together with their provocative findings that concealed-carry laws may substantially increase rates of gun violence, helped generate considerable demand for additional empirical work on this topic, which the academic research market soon filled.

D. The Lott and Mustard Study

An important step forward came with the study by Lott and Mustard (1997), who provided the first attempt to examine the effects of concealed-carry laws using national data on both treatment and control jurisdictions. Their study also exploits the repeated cross-section nature of the dataset (multiple observations for each state over time) in an attempt to control for difficult to measure differences between treatment and control areas. While the Lott and Mustard study has in many ways set a new standard for the empirical evaluation of concealed-carry legislation (and other anticrime interventions), there nevertheless remains some question about whether their analysis has identified the causal effects of these laws.

Lott and Mustard's (1997) dataset consists of county-level observations for the entire United States for the period 1977–92. The authors analyze the effects of concealed-carry laws on different types of crime (violent and property crime rates, as well as disaggregated crime rates for murder, rape, aggravated assault, robbery, burglary, larceny, and auto theft) because concealed-carry laws are likely to have their greatest effect in deterring crimes that involve contact between the perpetrator and the victim, most of which are violent crimes. The dependent variables in the analysis equal the natural logarithm of the county's crime rate per 100,000 people, which has the advantage of ensuring that the predicted crime rates produced by their linear regression models are nonnegative. In counties with no crimes of a particular type in a given year, Lott and Mustard define the value of the dependent value to equal the logarithm of 0.1 since the log of zero is undefined. The choice of substituting 0.1 for 0 before taking the log of the crime rate for these counties is arbitrary and could in principle have some nontrivial effect on the empirical results. In practice this seems to have little effect on the Lott and Mustard estimates, since Black and Nagin (1998) obtain similar results when they restrict the analytic sample to large counties (with populations of 100,000 or more) where zero crime counts are probably not very common.

The crime rate data come from information that local police departments voluntarily report to the FBI's UCR system. The UCR suffers from a number of well-known sources of measurement error, including nonreporting, incomplete reporting, or underreporting by some jurisdictions for particular years (Biderman and Lynch 1991; Maltz 1999). For these and other reasons, the Lott and Mustard (1997) dataset does not include any crime data for Florida for 1988 (the year after the state's concealed-carry law went into effect) or violent crime figures for a number of other large urban areas for a number of years. Other problems with the UCR data include variation across jurisdictions and time in the definitions that police departments use to classify different crimes and variation in the propensity of victims to report crime to the police (Biderman and Lynch 1991). Because there is little discretion in how police may classify homicides, and because police are made aware of most homicides (Cook and Laub 1998), Lott and Mustard's analysis is probably more reliable for homicide than for other crimes.

Lott and Mustard (1997) draw inferences about the effects of concealed-carry laws by comparing the outcomes of counties having concealed-carry laws with those in counties without such legislation while controlling for state "fixed effects" as well as a number of other sociodemographic and other variables that may differ across states.[9] The use of state fixed effects is designed to control for difficult-to-measure, time-invariant factors that cause some states to have persistently higher crime rates than others and essentially involves comparing the crime-rate trends between treatment and control areas. The intuition behind this approach can be seen by considering the case of Idaho, a state that enacted a permissive concealed-carry law in 1990, and California, a nearby state that did not enact such a law. In 1990, the first year in which Idaho's law was in effect, the homicide rate per 100,000 residents equaled 12.4 in California and 2.5 in Idaho. Part of the difference in homicide rates between California and Idaho may be due to Idaho's permissive concealed-carry law, but presumably part of the homicide disparity is also due to other differences between the

---

[9] While there remains some ambiguity about whether Lott and Mustard (1997) have correctly identified the timing of the concealed-carry laws implemented by different states during the 1977–92 period (Webster et al. 1997), the findings generally appear to be robust to alternative decisions about the timing of these laws (Lott and Mustard 1997).

states. In 1989, the year before Idaho's concealed-carry law went into effect, the homicide rates in California and Idaho equaled 10.9 and 2.9, respectively. The fixed-effects analysis helps overcome the problem that crime rates may be higher in California than Idaho for reasons that have nothing to do with Idaho's gun laws by comparing the changes in the crime rates in the two states over the same period of time. A fixed-effects analysis thus essentially consists of comparing the change in California's homicide rate over this period ($12.4 - 10.9 = 1.5$) with the change observed in Idaho ($2.5 - 2.9 = -0.4$), for an estimated treatment effect of ($-0.4 - 1.5 = -1.9$).

The use of state and year fixed effects in Lott and Mustard's (1997) analysis represents a substantial improvement over previous evaluations, since this procedure has the potential to control for the effects of at least some kinds of unmeasured variables that cause crime rates to differ across counties and states. The critical assumption is that California and Idaho would have had similar trends in homicide rates during this period had Idaho not enacted a concealed-carry law. This assumption will be violated if some criminogenic factors changed more substantially in California than in Idaho around the time of Idaho's concealed-carry law. To control for this possibility, Lott and Mustard include in their fixed-effects regression models a number of variables that measure sociodemographic and policy conditions that may change over time. The control variables thus play a critical role even with the fixed-effects research design, since Lott and Mustard assume that whatever differences in crime trends remain between treatment and control jurisdictions after adjusting for these other variables must reflect the effects of concealed-carry laws. If there are unmeasured factors that would have caused California and Idaho to have different crime trends even if Idaho had not enacted a concealed-carry law, Lott and Mustard's estimates will be biased.

Their controls for sociodemographic and economic variables include population density (people per square mile), per capita income, and the proportion of the county's population that falls into different sex/age/race groups (e.g., the proportion of people who are white females between the ages of thirty and thirty-nine). Since poverty-rate information is not available at the county level, Lott and Mustard try to proxy for the local poverty rate by including measures of county spending on social programs (unemployment insurance, income maintenance, and retirement payments) per county resident. These spending variables are unlikely to be useful proxies for the degree of material deprivation within a county, since per capita social spending could be either positively or negatively correlated with the local poverty rate. To see this, consider a county with 100 residents and per capita expenditures on social programs of $500. This level of social spending is consistent with conditions in both an affluent county in which only one family is eligible for assistance and receives $50,000 in benefits and a destitute county in which all 100 residents live in poverty and receive $500 each. Lott and Mustard (1997, p. 24) also experiment with a measure of local cocaine prices to control for the prevalence of drug market activity but report that using this variable "removes observations during a couple of important years during which changes are occurring in concealed handgun laws."

The decision whether and when to implement a concealed-carry law is ultimately a political one, and the same public concern about crime that contributes to the enactment of a gun-carrying law may also lead to other anticrime measures. Lott and Mustard attempt to control for concurrent changes in the criminal justice system by including in their regression models variables for whether states have sentencing add-ons for crimes committed with deadly weapons and waiting period requirements for handgun purchases.

To proxy for unmeasured differences in the effectiveness of local law enforcement, Lott and Mustard (1997) also include the county's arrest rate (number of arrests divided by number of crimes reported to the police) as a control variable. The problems of using the arrest rate as a right-hand-side control variable are well-known: unmeasured variables that affect the dependent variable (the number of crimes reported to the police) will produce a spurious negative correlation with the arrest rate, since the number of crimes reported to the police serves as the denominator for the arrest rate (Nagin 1978).[10] An upper bound on how much influence the arrest rate has on the results is provided by Lott and Mustard's reanalysis of their regression models using only state and year fixed effects, excluding the arrest rate as well as all of the other control variables. Omitting all of these control variables reduces the magnitude of the concealed-carry effect on violent crime by around 50 percent, though this effect is still close to statistically significant with a t-statistic of 1.66 (Lott and Mustard 1997, p. 19).

[10] For example, suppose that the number of crimes in a county increases for some reason that is not modelled by the regression analysis. As the number of crimes (the dependent variable in the regression) increases, the arrest rate (a right-hand-side variable) will decrease, since the increase in the number of crimes serves to inflate the denominator of the arrest rate.

The estimates for which Lott and Mustard present cost-benefit calculations (which presumably are thus their preferred results) suggest that permissive concealed-carry laws reduce homicides by nearly 8 percent, rapes by 5 percent, and aggravated assaults by 7 percent and increase property crimes by around 3 percent. Each of these estimated effects is statistically significant at the conventional 5 percent threshold. The authors attribute the observed increase in property crimes to decisions by criminals to substitute property for violent crimes, in order to reduce the probability of encountering a potentially armed victim. Using estimates for the costs of crime calculated by Miller, Cohen, and Wiersema (1996), Lott and Mustard (1997) suggest that if states without concealed-carry laws had enacted such laws, the result would have been an improvement in social welfare equal to $5.7 billion in 1992 dollars.

Lott and Mustard conduct sensitivity analysis that is far more extensive than is usually found within criminology, and conclude that their findings are generally robust to changes in their statistical procedures (such as including burglary and robbery rates as explanatory variables to control for unmeasured criminogenic factors in their analysis of other property and violent crimes).

The one exception comes from Lott and Mustard's attempt to estimate a more elaborate "instrumental variables" model, which requires them to identify factors that explain why some states enact concealed-carry laws and others do not. In order for the resultant estimates to be valid, these factors must otherwise be uncorrelated with crime rates. Problems with some of the factors identified by Lott and Mustard have been discussed in Nagin (1978). While standard diagnostic statistics can be easily calculated to test whether these assumptions are met (Hausman 1983; Newey 1985), such statistics are not included in the Lott and Mustard study. Some evidence that the conditions for unbiased estimation are not met comes from the implausibly large magnitude of the resultant estimates: Lott and Mustard's two-stage least squares models suggest that permissive concealed-carry laws reduce homicides by 67 percent and rapes by 65 percent (Black and Nagin 1998). Lott and Mustard do not indicate whether they believe these two-stage estimates to be plausible or whether these estimates should be preferred to the other fixed-effects estimates that are one-tenth as large.

Lott's 1998 book also reports on two extensions to his study with Mustard (Lott 1998b). The first extension, also published as a separate article with Stephen Bronars (Bronars and Lott 1998), examines the possibility that the deterrent effects of concealed-carry laws will cause criminals to relocate their activities to neighboring jurisdictions where the risks of encountering an armed victim are presumably lower. Bronars and Lott test this hypothesis by examining whether crime rates changed in counties located within fifty miles of states that adopted concealed-carry laws, using a slight modification of the fixed-effects regression approach used in Lott and Mustard (1997). Their analysis finds a positive correlation between implementation of a concealed-carry law within a given state and the homicide, robbery, and rape rates in neighboring counties and a negative correlation with rates of aggravated assault.

The second extension by Lott and William Landes (1999) also uses the same fixed-effects model specifications employed by Lott and Mustard (1997), but now focuses on multiple-victim shootings as the dependent variable of interest. Lott and Landes use a Lexis-Nexis search of newspaper accounts for the period 1977–95 to identify the number of "multiple victim shootings" in each state per year, defined as shootings in which two or more people are wounded in a church, business, bar, street, workplace, park, or other public place. They exclude shootings that occurred as part of another crime (such as a robbery or drug deal), as well as shootings associated with gang activity, a serial-killing spree (where the shootings occur over the span of two or more days), or "professional hits." As it turns out, the events that are both recorded in Lexis-Nexis and meet the Lott and Landes criteria turn out to be relatively rare. For example, a number of states (including Delaware, Nevada, and Tennessee) had no multiple-victim shootings according to the Lott and Landes data during the nineteen-year sample period, while Washington, D.C., had a total of two such shootings.

The Lott and Landes (1999) fixed-effects regressions suggest that implementation of a permissive concealed-carry law reduces the rate of murders and injuries in multiple-victim shootings by 0.111 murders/injuries per 100,000 residents. For comparison, the average rate of murders and injuries from multiple-victim shootings per 100,000 people during the 1977–95 period in the Lott and Landes dataset is 0.038 for the nation as a whole, and 0.042 in those states that do not enact concealed-carry laws. Thus the Lott and Landes study suggests that permissive concealed-carry laws have a treatment effect that is equal to around 300 percent of the mean murder and injury rate from multiple-victim shootings in the control states. On the basis of these findings,

Lott has suggested that state policy makers should encourage teachers to carry concealed handguns in schools in order to prevent mass shootings (Lott 1998c).

E. Critiques and Reassessments of Lott and Mustard

The primary concern with the Lott and Mustard (1997) study is whether those authors have isolated the causal effects of concealed-carry laws on crime or whether, instead, their estimates are due in part or whole to other difficult-to-measure factors that cause the treatment and control states to have different crime trends. Evidence on this question comes from a reanalysis of Lott and Mustard's data by Dan Black and Daniel Nagin (1998), who examine the central assumption behind the Lott and Mustard study—that after controlling for the variables included in the multivariate regression models, the treatment and control states would have had similar trends in crime rates had the treatment areas not enacted permissive concealed-carry laws. This assumption cannot be tested directly, since we cannot observe what the crime trend would have been in treatment states had they not enacted their concealed-carry laws. But the assumption can be tested indirectly, by examining whether the treatment and control states have similar crime trends before the treatment states enact their laws. Put differently, Black and Nagin test whether the Lott and Mustard models provide evidence of a "treatment effect" between treatment and control states even before the treatment is implemented. This kind of pretreatment difference would suggest that part or all of the difference in crime trends during the postprogram period are a result of factors that are not captured by Lott and Mustard's model.

Black and Nagin's (1998) reanalysis found that violent crime rates were increasing more rapidly in treatment than in control states before the treatment states enacted concealed-carry laws and that these pre-concealed-carry-law differences are statistically significant.[11] The Black and Nagin findings suggest, perhaps not surprisingly, that treatment states enact permissive concealed-carry laws in response to increases in crime. Because crime rates in the United States are cyclical, with periods of increasing crime regularly followed by periods in which crime decreases (Blumstein 1995; Philipson and Posner 1996), the unmea-

---

[11] While Black and Nagin (1998) focus on the basic Lott and Mustard (1997) fixed-effects specification, similar findings of bias are found with extensions to the basic model, including those that include robbery or burglary rates as additional controls for unmeasured variables. (E-mail from Dan Black to me.)

sured factors that cause crime rates to increase more sharply in treatment than in control states before the concealed-carry laws go into effect may be responsible for part or all of the relative decrease in crime rates in treatment states after the laws are implemented.

The Black and Nagin (1998) findings also raise questions about the interpretation of the results on multiple-victim shootings in Lott and Landes (1999) and crime spillover effects from concealed-carry laws in Bronars and Lott (1998). The multiple-victim shooting study by Lott and Landes uses the same fixed-effects regression models as those used in the Lott and Mustard analysis. Since Black and Nagin provide evidence suggesting that the fixed-effects regression models may be biased when UCR homicide and other crime rates are used as the dependent variables of interest, the same biases will presumably arise when the models are estimated using data for a specific subgroup of homicides (multiple-victim shootings) as the dependent variable of interest. Empirical evidence on this point could be easily obtained by applying the model-specification test employed by Black and Nagin to the multiple-victim-shooting data.

The finding in the Bronars and Lott (1998) paper that crime rates are correlated across counties seems uncontroversial, since whatever policy and sociodemographic factors affect crime rates are likely to be correlated across areas. Less clear is whether the correlation in crime rates between permissive concealed-carry areas and nearby counties necessarily reflects the movement of criminal activity across jurisdictions in response to concealed-carry laws, as Bronars and Lott claim, or instead are correlated for other reasons. Black and Nagin's (1998) findings suggest that part or all of the changes in crime rates observed within the states that enact concealed-carry laws are due to factors that are unmeasured or poorly measured in the Lott and Mustard (1997) study. Correlations in crime rates across jurisdictions may thus be due either to the effects of the concealed-carry laws or, instead, to the effects of the unmeasured variables suggested by Black and Nagin's reanalysis. One way to test these competing hypotheses is to examine the correlation between crime rates in states that pass concealed-carry laws and nearby counties during the period before the concealed-carry laws go into effect. A correlation across areas in crime rates before the concealed-carry laws are implemented would suggest that correlations in crime rates after the laws are enacted are due at least in part to unmeasured variables.

While the Black and Nagin (1998) reanalysis provides some evidence to suggest that unmeasured or poorly measured variables bias the estimates derived by Lott and Mustard (1997), little is currently known about which variables are responsible for this bias. Obvious candidates include poverty, gangs, drug-market activity, and the level and deployment of local police resources, though this list is speculative. A better understanding of the factors that produce bias with the Lott and Mustard study should be a priority for criminological research, since this knowledge would also be useful for attempts to evaluate a broad array of other criminal justice interventions.

One way to control for the unmeasured variables that appear to produce bias with the Lott and Mustard analysis is to model each state's crime trend as some nonlinear function of time. This approach captures the pattern that the crime rate within each state increases and then decreases over time, even if the specific factors that are responsible for these changes are not known or not properly measured. When Black and Nagin model local crime rates as a quadratic function of time (i.e., as a function of the year and the year squared, plus the other control variables included in the Lott and Mustard multivariate model), the only statistically significant effect of concealed-carry laws is to increase the rate of assaults.[12] One obvious limitation of the quadratic function used by Black and Nagin is that this approach imposes some specific assumptions on how the unmeasured variables affect each state's crime trend over time.

In my own study of the effects of permissive concealed-carry laws, I control for the time-varying unobserved variables that appear to bias Lott and Mustard's study and produce a positive (but not statistically significant) estimate for the effects of concealed-carry laws on homicide rates (Ludwig 1998). My study applies a difference-in-difference-in-difference (DDD) model to state-level panel data for 1977–94 that relies on juveniles as a within-state control group to control for time-varying state-specific unobserved variables. I focus on homicide victimization rates obtained from vital statistics records to avoid the measurement problems associated with data on victimization rates for robberies, assaults, and other nonlethal crimes. My study uses state-level rather than county-level data to ensure that there are enough

[12] In Lott's (1998a, p. 230) reply to Black and Nagin (1998), he argues that a "problem with using state-specific quadratic trends . . . [is that] allowing a separate quadratic time trend for each state results in the time trend picking up both the upward path before the law and the downward path thereafter." Yet this is the central advantage of the quadratic time-trend approach, not a limitation.

adult and juvenile victimizations for each observational unit in each year to permit reliable estimation.

The estimation approach exploits the fact that even states with permissive concealed-carry laws require applicants to be eighteen years old (or in some cases twenty-one) in order to obtain a concealed-carry permit. While concealed-carry laws produce some crime-reducing benefit for juveniles—for example, because adults in public spaces may deter crimes against juveniles or because some teens may look older than eighteen or twenty-one—any deterrent benefit from these laws should nonetheless be greater for adults than juveniles (since only adults can obtain permits) and as a result should be revealed by a reduction in the adult victimization rate relative to that for juveniles. So long as unmeasured, time-varying variables affect both adult and juvenile victimization rates, these omitted variables will be controlled for with this empirical approach.

The estimated coefficient for the concealed-carry law variable in my analysis is equal to +0.15 homicide victimizations per 100,000 adults, an effect that is not statistically significant. Alternative ways of defining treatment and control states or pre- and post-treatment periods produce qualitatively similar estimates. While these estimates will be unbiased in the presence of time-varying state-specific unobserved variables that have similar effects on both juveniles and adults, there remains the possibility of bias from unobserved variables that have disproportionate effects on a state's juvenile or adult population (e.g., from changes in a state's juvenile justice system). Nevertheless, the results of my analysis together with the quadratic-trend model of Black and Nagin (1998) suggest that concealed-carry laws are as likely to cause crime to increase as to decrease.

Three other reanalyses of the Lott and Mustard (1997) data have also been conducted, though none examines the central question of whether the Lott and Mustard estimates reflect the causal effects of concealed-carry laws or, instead, the effects of unmeasured variables. Bartley and Cohen (1998) examine whether the Lott and Mustard findings are robust to decisions about which of Lott and Mustard's control variables to include in the multivariate regression specification. Their reanalysis suggests that the estimated effects of concealed-carry laws do not change substantially when different combinations of the available control variables are included in the model, though this exercise is not informative about whether other variables that are not included in the Lott and Mustard dataset cause bias in the estimated effects.

While Lott and Mustard (1997) estimate all of their treatment effects using some variant of a linear ordinary least squares regression, Plassmann and Tideman (1998) reestimate the treatment effects using a maximum-likelihood approach that models county-level crime rates as having a Poisson distribution. The central advantage of the Poisson-regression approach is that the standard errors should be smaller than those obtained from ordinary least squares. The disadvantage is that because the Poisson regression model is more computationally intensive, Plassmann and Tideman must exclude many of the control variables that are included in the Lott and Mustard ordinary least squares models, thereby exacerbating the omitted-variables problem that poses the central challenge to valid inference. Thus while Plassmann and Tideman's estimates suggest even larger crime-reducing effects from concealed-carry laws than those obtained by Lott and Mustard, these findings are likely to be unreliable given Black and Nagin's findings that even the more richly specified regression models estimated by Lott and Mustard are biased.

Finally, Dezhbakhsh and Rubin (1998) use the basic linear-regression approach of Lott and Mustard but allow the effects of concealed-carry laws to vary according to the state's sociodemographic and other characteristics. Their reanalysis produces smaller negative effects of concealed-carry laws on homicide than those obtained by Lott and Mustard and mixed (positive and negative) effects of these laws on other crimes such as rape, robbery, and aggravated assault.

F. Summary

Permissive concealed-carry laws have the potential to reduce crime, by enhancing the ability of citizens to use guns in self-defense and thereby deter crime, or to increase crime, through gun misuse by permitted gun carriers or increased weapon carrying and use by criminals. Since both positive and negative effects are plausible, empirical evidence is required to determine which effects dominate.

The widely publicized study by Lott and Mustard (1997) represents a substantial improvement over previous evaluations of concealed-carry laws along several dimensions. First, previous studies have relied on comparisons of crime rates before and after concealed-carry laws went into effect in jurisdictions that implemented such laws, which may confound the effects of gun-carrying laws with other changes in the environment that affect local crime rates. Lott and Mustard instead use national data and draw inferences about the effects of concealed-carry laws (the "treatment") by comparing crime in treatment and control states, which helps eliminate rival hypotheses that may explain crime patterns in the treatment states. Second, Lott and Mustard use fixed-effects analysis to focus on relative trends in crime rates between treatment and control states, which controls for unmeasured or difficult to measure factors that may cause treatment and control states to have different crime rates year after year for reasons that are unrelated to concealed-carry regulations.

While Lott and Mustard find evidence to suggest that permissive concealed-carry laws produce substantial reductions in violent crime, their estimates rest on the assumption that treatment and control states would have had similar trends in crime rates had the treatment states not implemented their concealed-carry laws. A reanalysis of the Lott and Mustard data by Black and Nagin (1998) finds evidence that treatment and control states had different crime trends even before the treatment states' concealed-carry laws went into effect for reasons that are not captured by the statistical model used by Lott and Mustard. The implication is that the differences in crime trends between treatment and control states following the implementation of concealed-carry laws may be due in part or whole to unmeasured, time-varying factors rather than to the effects of the laws themselves. More recent evaluations have used different methods to control for these time-varying unmeasured variables and find no effects or modest positive effects of permissive concealed-carry laws on crime (Black and Nagin 1998; Ludwig 1998). Because even these recent studies will be unbiased only if some assumptions with the data are met, future research that employs alternative strategies for controlling for unmeasured variables would be a useful addition to this literature.

IV. Gun Research and Public Policy

Recent studies of defensive gun use and deterrence have been influential in scholarly and policy debates about gun policy in the United States. The possibility that civilian defensive gun use is prevalent and has substantial deterrent effects on criminal behavior has raised concerns that additional government regulation of gun ownership and use may increase rather than decrease the rate of serious crime and injuries by impairing the ability of private citizens to defend themselves against criminal attacks.

One research strategy that has been used to evaluate this possibility is to measure the prevalence of defensive gun use directly. To date, reliable estimates for the number of defensive gun uses that occur each year are not available. The best available evidence suggests that the number of defensive gun uses is probably somewhere between 300,000 and 1.3 million per year, though there is considerable variation across reported gun uses in the degree to which the events may contribute to the public interest. The range of socially desirable gun uses could be narrowed further by conducting additional survey research that asked all respondents directly whether they have used a gun in self-defense, employed a panel design to reduce telescoping, and asked detailed follow-up questions that might help identify the nature of the gun use (including how the respondent might have contributed to the escalation of the event) and screen out false positives.

Even with such a survey in hand, identifying the benefits to society from reported gun uses will be difficult since only one party to the encounter is being interviewed and very little is known about alternative courses of action the respondent might have taken had a gun not been available and the consequences of these alternatives. Such surveys in any case provide no information about the deterrent benefits of defensive gun use. Determining whether these gun uses are in society's best interests also require answers to difficult normative questions that have yet to be fully resolved in America, as evidenced by the public's ambivalence about many cases of defensive gun use by law enforcement personnel. More generally, the key question for policy makers is how the number of desirable and undesirable gun uses change in response to changes in public policy, effects that are not implied by estimates for the prevalence of defensive gun use under the status quo. A more promising approach for learning about the consequences of defensive gun use and deterrence is to examine the net effects of gun policies on more ambiguous outcomes such as crime and injury rates.

One research literature that follows this strategy seeks to estimate the net effects of permissive concealed-carry laws, which are intended to enhance the ability of citizens to use guns in self-defense and deter criminal activity. The central challenge in evaluating these laws is that we do not observe what rates of crime and injury would have been in states that enact concealed-carry laws had they not enacted these laws. Simply observing the crime trends in these states before and after the law may be misleading. Increases in crime following implementation of a law do not necessarily imply that the intervention was ineffective, since crime may have increased even more rapidly in the absence of the law. Similarly, reductions in crime rates following enactment of a law do not imply that the law was effective, since crime may have decreased by the same amount or more had the law not gone into effect.

The widely publicized study by Lott and Mustard (1997) attempts to rule out alternative explanations for observed crime changes in states that enact concealed-carry laws by comparing the relative changes in crime rates between states with and without such laws, using multivariate regression analysis to control for other factors that may have changed differentially between treatment and control states. While Lott and Mustard find evidence suggesting that concealed-carry laws substantially reduce violent crime, a reanalysis of their data by Black and Nagin (1998) suggests that this estimated treatment effect is due in part or whole to factors that are not adequately captured by the statistical model used by Lott and Mustard. More recent evaluations that control for unmeasured variables in more sophisticated ways suggest that concealed-carry laws are as likely to cause crime to increase as to decrease, though this evidence is far from definitive.

What are the implications for public policy? Most criminologists agree that the number of fatal injuries in America would be lower by some amount if fewer criminals used guns to commit their crimes (Cook 1991). The research literatures on defensive gun use and deterrence have raised important and useful questions for criminologists and public policy makers about the costs of additional gun regulations in the form of reductions in civilian defensive gun use. Nevertheless, the best available evidence suggests that the crime-reducing benefits of policies such as restricting the number of guns carried in public spaces are not outweighed by the costs of fewer defensive gun uses and a reduction in the deterrent threat to criminals.

Learning more about the net effects of concealed-carry and other gun regulations on rates of crime and injury should be an important priority for criminological research. I conclude with some suggestions for how future research might usefully address these questions. First, Lott and Mustard's (1997) use of national data and fixed-effects analysis sets a new standard for the empirical evaluation of gun policies. Wherever possible, future evaluations should strive to use national data with multiple observations over time for both "treatment" and "control" jurisdictions. Moreover, information about whether the treatment and control states have similar crime trends before the interventions go into effect provides useful information about whether differences in trends around the time of the intervention reflect the causal effects of these laws or, instead, are caused by other factors that have not been properly modeled.[13] Similarity in pretreatment crime trends between treatment and control states provide an objective minimum standard for the reliability of future evaluations of gun policies.

Second, if some groups but not others are affected by a policy, analysts may further control for unmeasured state-specific factors by using the empirical approach outlined in Ludwig (1998). Changes in within-state differences in outcomes over time between affected and unaffected (or less-affected) groups may help identify the causal effects of the interventions of interest.

Third, evaluations of policies to restrict access to firearms should focus on gun suicides as well as homicides. Reductions in gun suicides represent an important effect of gun regulations, and ignoring these effects will produce a misleading picture of the net benefits and costs of a given policy. Moreover, gun suicides may be less susceptible to the unobserved criminogenic factors that may confound the analysis of gun crimes. (This suggestion will be less useful for gun policies such as concealed-carry restrictions that should have little effect on suicides but may hold some promise for evaluations of other interventions.)

Finally, criminologists should search for institutional and other factors that produce variation in gun policies that is independent of local criminogenic and criminal justice conditions; this kind of "exogenous" policy variation forms the basis for "instrumental variables" analysis (see Angrist, Imbens, and Rubin 1996). While the instrumental variables estimates presented in the Lott and Mustard (1997) study appear to be biased, as evidenced by their implausibly large magnitudes, a number of other studies have employed the instrumental variables procedure to good effect. Some examples of exogenous policy variation that have been exploited in previous studies include the timing of local election cycles that affect police hiring (Levitt 1997), which has been used to examine the effect of police resources on crime, and prison overcrowding lawsuits that produce sharp changes in prison populations (Levitt 1996), which have been used to study the effects of incar-

[13] If multivariate regression models are used that include controls for other covariates, analysts should compare the regression-adjusted trends (i.e., the trends in the regression residuals) during the preintervention period. Formal statistical tests for differences in such trends are outlined in Heckman and Hotz (1989) and Black and Nagin (1998).

ceration policies on crime. This kind of instrumental variable analysis holds enormous potential for overcoming many of the empirical problems that arise in evaluating the effects of gun policies, though the strategy to date has been underused within criminology.

REFERENCES

Angrist, Joshua D., Guido W. Imbens, and Donald B. Rubin. 1996. "Identification of Causal Effects Using Instrumental Variables." *Journal of the American Statistical Association* 91:444–55.

Annest, Joseph L., James A. Mercy, Delinda R. Gibson, and George W. Ryan. 1995. "National Estimates of Nonfatal Firearm-Related Injuries: Beyond the Tip of the Iceberg." *Journal of the American Medical Association* 273: 1749–54.

Ash, Peter, Arthur Kellermann, Dawna Fuqua-Whitley, and A. Johnson. 1996. "Gun Acquisition and Use by Juvenile Offenders." *Journal of the American Medical Association* 275:1754–58.

Bartley, William A., and Mark A. Cohen. 1998. "The Effect of Concealed Weapons Laws: An Extreme Bound Analysis." *Economic Inquiry* 36:258–65.

Biderman, A. D., and James P. Lynch. 1991. *Understanding Crime Incidence Statistics: Why the UCR Diverges from the NCS.* New York: Springer.

Black, Dan, and Daniel Nagin. 1998. "Do 'Right to Carry' Laws Reduce Violent Crime?" *Journal of Legal Studies* 27:209–19.

Blumstein, Alfred. 1995. "Youth Gun Violence, Guns, and the Illicit-Drug Industry." *Journal of Criminal Law and Criminology* 86:10–36.

Blumstein, Alfred, and Daniel Cork. 1996. "Linking Gun Availability to Youth Gun Violence." *Law and Contemporary Problems* 59:5–20.

Bourndon, K., D. Rae, W. Narrow, R. Manderscheid, and D. Regier. 1994. "National Prevalence and Treatment of Mental and Addictive Disorders." In *Mental Health, United States, 1994.* Washington, D.C.: U.S. Department of Health and Human Services, Center for Mental Health Services.

Bronars, Stephen G., and John R. Lott. 1998. "Criminal Deterrence, Geographic Spillovers, and the Right to Carry Concealed Handguns." *American Economic Review* 88:475–79.

Bureau of Justice Statistics. 1996. *Criminal Victimization in the United States, 1993.* Washington, D.C.: U.S. Department of Justice, Bureau of Justice Statistics.

Cook, Philip J. 1983. "The Influence of Gun Availability on Violent Crime Patterns." In *Crime and Justice: An Annual Review of Research,* vol. 4, edited by Norval Morris and Michael Tonry. Chicago: University of Chicago Press.

———. 1985. "The Case of the Missing Victims: Gunshot Woundings in the

National Crime Victimization Survey." *Journal of Quantitative Criminology* 1:91–102.

———. 1986. "The Relationship between Victim Resistance and Injury in Noncommercial Robbery." *Journal of Legal Studies* 15:405–16.

———. 1987. "Robbery Violence." *Journal of Criminal Law and Criminology* 78:357–76.

———. 1991. "The Technology of Personal Violence." In *Crime and Justice: A Review of Research*, vol. 14, edited by Michael Tonry. Chicago: University of Chicago Press.

Cook, Philip J., and John H. Laub. 1998. "The Unprecedented Epidemic in Youth Violence." In *Youth Violence*, edited by Mark H. Moore and Michael Tonry. Vol. 24 of *Crime and Justice: A Review of Research*, edited by Michael Tonry. Chicago: University of Chicago Press.

Cook, Philip J., Bruce Lawrence, Jens Ludwig, and Ted R. Miller. 1999. "The Costs of Gunshot Injuries in the United States." *Journal of the American Medical Association* 282:447–54.

Cook, Philip J., and Jens Ludwig. 1996. *Guns in America: Results of a Comprehensive National Survey on Firearms Ownership and Use*. Washington, D.C.: Police Foundation.

———. 1997. *Guns in America: National Survey of Private Ownership and Use of Firearms*. Washington, D.C.: U.S. Department of Justice, National Institute of Justice.

———. 1998. "Defensive Gun Uses: New Evidence from a National Survey." *Journal of Quantitative Criminology* 14:111–31.

Cook, Philip J., Jens Ludwig, and David Hemenway. 1997. "The Gun Debate's New Mythical Number: *How* Many Defensive Uses Per Year?" *Journal of Policy Analysis and Management* 16:463–69.

Cook, Philip J., Stephanie Molliconi, and Thomas B. Cole. 1995. "Regulating Gun Markets." *Journal of Criminal Law and Criminology* 86:59–92.

Cork, Daniel. 1999. "Examining Time-Space Interaction in City-Level Homicide Data: Crack Markets and the Diffusion of Guns among Youth." *Journal of Quantitative Criminology* 15:379–406.

Crandall, Robert W., and John D. Graham. 1984. "Automobile Safety Regulation and Offsetting Behavior: Some New Empirical Estimates." *American Economic Review* 74:328–31.

Decision/Making/Information (DMI). 1978. *Attitudes of the American Electorate toward Gun Control*. Santa Ana, Calif.: DMI.

Dezhbakhsh, Hashem, and Paul H. Rubin. 1998. "Lives Saved or Lives Lost? The Effects of Concealed-Handgun Laws on Crime." *American Economic Review* 88:468–74.

Hart Research Associates. 1981. *Violence in America Survey with Marginal Frequencies: Questionnaire*. Washington, D.C.: Hart Research Associates.

Hausman, Jerry A. 1983. "Specification and Estimation of Simultaneous Equation Models." In *Handbook of Econometrics*, vol. 1, edited by Zvi Griliches and Michael Intriligator. Amsterdam: North-Holland.

Heckman, James J., and V. Joseph Hotz. 1989. "Choosing among Alternative Nonexperimental Methods for Estimating the Impact of Social Programs:

The Case of Manpower Training." *Journal of the American Statistical Association* 84:862–80.

Hemenway, David. 1997*a*. "The Myth of Millions of Self-Defense Gun Uses: A Case Study of Survey Overestimates of Rare Events." *Chance* 10:6–10.

———. 1997*b*. "Survey Research and Self-Defense Gun Use: An Explanation of Extreme Overestimates." *Journal of Criminal Law and Criminology* 87: 1430–45.

Hemenway, David, and Deborah Azrael. 1997. "Gun Use in the United States: Results of a National Survey." Final report submitted to the National Institute of Justice.

———. Forthcoming. "The Relative Frequency of Offensive and Defensive Gun Uses: Results from a National Survey." *Violence and Victims.*

Hill, Jeffrey M. 1997. "The Impact of Liberalized Concealed Weapons Statutes on Rates of Violent Crime." B.A. thesis, Duke University, Sanford Institute of Public Policy.

Kates, Don B., and Gary Kleck. 1997. *The Great American Gun Debate.* San Francisco: Pacific Institute for Public Policy.

Kellermann, Arthur L., and Donald T. Reay. 1986. "Protection or Peril? An Analysis of Firearm-Related Deaths in the Home." *New England Journal of Medicine* 314:1557–60.

Kellermann, Arthur L., Lori Westphal, Laurie Fischer, and Beverly Harvard. 1995. "Weapon Involvement in Home Invasion Crimes." *Journal of the American Medical Association* 273:1759–62.

Kennedy, David M., Anne M. Piehl, and Anthony A. Braga. 1996. "Youth Violence in Boston: Gun Markets, Serious Youth Offenders, and a Use-Reduction Strategy." *Law and Contemporary Problems* 59:147–96.

Kleck, Gary. 1988. "Crime Control through the Private Use of Armed Force." *Social Forces* 35:1–21.

———. 1991. *Point Blank: Guns and Violence in America.* New York: Aldine de Gruyter.

———. 1999. E-mail to author, November 23.

Kleck, Gary, and Miriam A. DeLone. 1993. "Victim Resistance and Offender Weapon Effects in Robbery." *Journal of Quantitative Criminology* 9:55–81.

Kleck, Gary, and Marc Gertz. 1995. "Armed Resistance to Crime: The Prevalence and Nature of Self-Defense with a Gun." *Journal of Criminal Law and Criminology* 86:150–87.

———. 1997. "The Illegitimacy of One-Sided Speculation: Getting the Defensive Gun Use Estimate Down." *Journal of Criminal Law and Criminology* 87:1446–61.

Levitt, Steven D. 1996. "The Effect of Prison Population Size on Crime Rates: Evidence from Prison Overcrowding Litigation." *Quarterly Journal of Economics* 111:319–51.

———. 1997. "Using Electoral Cycles in Police Hiring to Estimate the Effect of Police on Crime." *American Economic Review* 87:270–90.

Lott, John R. 1998*a*. "The Concealed-Handgun Debate." *Journal of Legal Studies* 27:221–43.

————. 1998*b*. *More Guns, Less Crime*. Chicago: University of Chicago Press.

————. 1998*c*. "The Real Lesson of the School Shootings." *Wall Street Journal* (March 27), p. A14.

————. 1999. "Gun Laws Can Be Dangerous, Too." *Wall Street Journal* (May 12), p. A22.

Lott, John R., and William M. Landes. 1999. "Multiple Victim Shootings, Bombings, and Right-to-Carry Concealed Handgun Laws: Contrasting Private and Public Law Enforcement." Working paper. Chicago: University of Chicago Law School.

Lott, John R., and David B. Mustard. 1997. "Crime, Deterrence, and Right-to-Carry Concealed Handguns." *Journal of Legal Studies* 26:1–68.

Ludwig, Jens. 1998. "Concealed-Gun-Carrying Laws and Violent Crime: Evidence from State Panel Data." *International Review of Law and Economics* 18: 239–54.

Ludwig, Jens, Philip J. Cook, and Tom W. Smith. 1998. "The Gender Gap in Reporting Household Gun Ownership." *American Journal of Public Health* 88:1715–18.

Maltz, Michael D. 1999. *Bridging Gaps in Police Crime Data*. Washington, D.C.: U.S. Department of Justice, Bureau of Justice Statistics.

Mauser, Gary A. 1993. "Firearms and Self-Defense: The Canadian Case." Paper presented at the forty-fifth annual meeting of the American Society of Criminology, Phoenix, Ariz., November.

May, John P., David Hemenway, Roger Oen, and Khalid R. Pitts. Forthcoming. "Medical Care Solicitation by Criminals with Gunshot Wound Injuries: A Survey of Washington, DC Jail Detainees." *Journal of Trauma*.

McDowall, David, Colin Loftin, and Stanley Presser. 1999. "Measuring Civilian Defensive Firearm Use: A Methodological Experiment." Working Paper. Albany: State University of New York at Albany.

McDowall, David, Colin Loftin, and Brian Wiersema. 1995. "Easing Concealed Firearms Laws: Effects on Homicide in Three States." *Journal of Criminal Law and Criminology* 86:193–206.

McDowall, David, and Brian Wiersema. 1994. "The Incidence of Defensive Firearm Use by U.S. Crime Victims, 1987 through 1990." *American Journal of Public Health* 84:1982–84.

Miller, Matthew, and David Hemenway. 1999. "The Relationship between Firearms and Suicide: A Review of the Literature." *Aggression and Violent Behavior* 4:59–75.

Miller, Ted R., Mark A. Cohen, and Brian Wiersema. 1996. *Victim Costs and Consequences: A New Look*. Washington, D.C.: U.S. Department of Justice, National Institute of Justice.

Nagin, Daniel S. 1978. "General Deterrence: A Review of the Empirical Literature." In *Deterrence and Incapacitation: Estimating the Effects of Criminal Sanctions on Crime Rates*, edited by Alfred Blumstein, Jacqueline Cohen, and Daniel Nagin. Washington, D.C.: National Academy of Sciences.

————. 1998. "Criminal Deterrence Research at the Outset of the Twenty-First Century." In *Crime and Justice: A Review of Research*, vol. 23, edited by Michael Tonry. Chicago: University of Chicago Press.

Newey, Whitney. 1985. "Generalized Method of Moments Specification Testing." *Journal of Econometrics* 29:229–56.

Peltzman, Sam. 1975. "The Effects of Automobile Safety Regulation." *Journal of Political Economy* 83: 677–725.

Philipson, Tomas J., and Richard A. Posner. 1993. *Private Choices and Public Health: The AIDS Epidemic in an Economic Perspective.* Cambridge, Mass.: Harvard University Press.

———. 1996. "The Economic Epidemiology of Crime." *Journal of Law and Economics* 39:405–33.

Plassmann, Florenz, and T. Nicolaus Tideman. 1998. "Does the Right to Carry Concealed Handguns Deter Countable Crimes? Only a Count Analysis Can Say." Working Paper. Blacksburg: Virginia Polytechnic Institute and State University.

Rand, Michael R. 1999. "Circumstances Surrounding Defensive Use of Guns in Crimes Measured by the National Crime Victimization Survey." Bureau of Justice Statistics Working Paper. Presented at the fifty-first annual meeting of the American Society of Criminology, Toronto, November 17–20.

Rennison, Callie Marie. 1999. *Criminal Victimization, 1998.* Washington, D.C.: U.S. Department of Justice, Bureau of Justice Statistics.

Robuck-Mangum, Gail. 1997. "Concealed Weapon Permit Holders in North Carolina: A Descriptive Study of Handgun-Carrying Behaviors." Master's thesis. Chapel Hill: University of North Carolina—Chapel Hill, School of Public Health.

Sheley, J. F., and James Wright. 1993. *Gun Acquisition and Possession in Selected Juvenile Samples.* Washington, D.C.: U.S. Department of Justice, National Institute of Justice.

Sherman, Lawrence W. 1992. "Attacking Crime: Policing and Crime Control." In *Crime and Justice: A Review of Research,* vol. 15, edited by Michael Tonry. Chicago: University of Chicago Press.

Smith, Tom W. 1997. "A Call for a Truce in the DGU War." *Journal of Criminal Law and Criminology* 87:1462–69.

Sudman, Seymour, and Norman M. Bradburn. 1974. *Response Effects in Surveys: A Review and Synthesis.* Chicago: Aldine.

Traynor, Thomas L. 1993. "The Peltzman Hypothesis Revisited: An Isolated Evaluation of Offsetting Driver Behavior." *Journal of Risk and Uncertainty* 7: 237–47.

Tribe, Laurence H., and Akhil Reed Amar. 1999. "Well-Regulated Militias, and More." *New York Times* (October 28), p. A31.

Viscusi, W. Kip. 1984. "The Lulling Effect: The Impact of Child-Resistant Packaging on Aspirin and Analgesic Ingestions." *American Economic Review* 74:324–27.

Webster, Daniel W., Jon S. Vernick, Jens Ludwig, and Kathleen J. Lester. 1997. "Flawed Gun Policy Research Could Endanger Public Safety." *American Journal of Public Health* 87:918–21.

Wilson, James Q. 1995. "Crime and Public Policy." In *Crime,* edited by James Q. Wilson and Joan Petersilia. San Francisco: Institute for Contemporary Studies Press.

Wintemute, Garen J., Carrie A. Parham, James Jay Beaumont, Mona Wright, and Christiana Drake. 1999. "Mortality among Recent Purchasers of Handguns." *New England Journal of Medicine* 341:1583–89.

Woltman, Henry, John Bushery, and Larry Carstensen. 1984. "Recall Bias and Telescoping in the National Crime Survey." In *The National Crime Survey: Working Papers*, edited by Robert G. Lehnen and Wesley G. Skogan. Washington, D.C.: U.S. Department of Justice, Bureau of Justice Statistics.

Wright, James D., and Peter H. Rossi. 1994. *Armed and Considered Dangerous: A Survey of Felons and Their Firearms*, expanded ed. New York: Aldine de Gruyter.

Wright, James D., Peter H. Rossi, and Kathleen Daly. 1983. *Under the Gun: Weapons, Crime, and Violence in America*. New York: Aldine de Gruyter.

Zimring, Franklin E. 1968. "Is Gun Control Likely to Reduce Violent Killings?" *University of Chicago Law Review* 35:721–37.

Zimring, Franklin E., and Gordon Hawkins. 1997. "Concealed Handguns: The Counterfeit Deterrent." *Responsive Community* 7:46–60.

William Spelman

What Recent Studies Do (and Don't) Tell Us about Imprisonment and Crime

ABSTRACT

Despite three decades of study and a nationwide quasi experiment of unprecedented scale, it is still uncertain how large an effect prisons have on the crime rate. Researchers have learned some things along the way. We no longer use cross-sectional data sets because they make it impossible to separate simultaneous effects; we no longer use national time-series data and ratio variables because they produce inflated estimates. Better methods have improved the validity and narrowed the scope of recent estimates. Most studies show that doubling current U.S. prison capacity would reduce Index Crime rates by 20–40 percent. Nevertheless, some problems persist: simultaneity (just as prison affects crime, so does crime affect prison, and it is difficult to isolate one effect from the other); specification error (especially left-out variables); and difficulties in comparing among states (since different states use their prisons very differently). Perhaps most important, the range of estimates itself falls in an awkward spot. At the low end, further prison construction is probably not cost-effective; at the high end, it very likely is cost-effective. Given our uncertainty, further research as to the cost-effectiveness of alternatives to prison may be a better use of scarce resources.

Over the past twenty years, the fifty American states have engaged in one of the great policy experiments of modern times. In an attempt to reduce intolerably high levels of reported crime, the states doubled their prison capacity, then doubled it again, increasing their costs by

William Spelman is associate professor of public affairs at the Lyndon B. Johnson School of Public Affairs, University of Texas at Austin.

more than $20 billion per year. The states and the federal government have given up a lot to get to this point: that $20 billion could provide day care for every family that cannot afford it, or a college education to every high school graduate, or a living wage job to every unemployed youth. But crime levels have (at last) responded, dropping to their lowest level in years. Thus recent history provides a prima facie case for the effectiveness of prisons.

Not everyone has found this evidence persuasive. Some argue, quite convincingly, that recent crime reductions had nothing to do with the prison buildup. Crime has dropped because the number of poverty-stricken youths has dropped, or because police are more effective, or because of any number of other reasons. This correlation does not necessarily guarantee causation.

Perhaps more important, whether more prisons reduce crime matters less than how much. Crime is not the only problem the American public is grappling with. Policy makers may decide to spend taxpayer dollars on child care, college educations, jobs programs, or (for that matter) childhood immunization, infrastructure for decaying cities, subsidies to tobacco farmers, or B2 stealth bombers. (Occasionally, they even decide that the best use of the money is to give it back to taxpayers.) It is not enough to have a small effect on the crime problem if that means forgoing a big effect on an equally thorny social problem.

And prisons are no longer the only way to fight crime. Policy makers may decide to spend money on other agencies in the criminal justice system (e.g., more judges, better-managed police, or better-trained probation officers); on changes in the physical environment that make it more difficult to commit a crime; on community organizing and education efforts that improve the public's capacity to intervene; on education and jobs programs that reduce would-be offenders' motivations to commit crimes; and on a host of other equally plausible alternatives.

With few exceptions, we have been unable to determine the benefit-cost ratios associated with these policies and programs. Nevertheless, we can be fairly sure that most do more good than harm; a few (childhood immunization is a classic case) may yield benefit-cost ratios as high as 5.0. Thus it is no longer sufficient, if it ever was, to demonstrate that prisons are better than nothing. Instead, they must be better than the next-best use of the money.

"Better than nothing" may be a minimal requirement, but it has taken decades to establish whether even this is true. Sellin (1959) examined the effectiveness of the death penalty by comparing homicide rates over time between pairs of neighboring states, one with a death penalty and one without. Although Sellin's work was crude by today's standards, later studies became increasingly sophisticated as computers and knowledge of statistical methods became more widely available. Gibbs (1968) and Chiricos and Waldo (1970) applied contingency tables to data from a cross section of American states; Kobrin et al. (1972) and Logan (1975) used simple and partial correlations; Bean and Cushing (1971) and Sjoquist (1973) pioneered the use of simple regression. The mold for most future studies was cast in 1973, however, when Ehrlich applied state-of-the-art econometric methods and a plausible economic model to a cross section of American states. A raft of similar studies followed, each using similar methods, models, and data sets.

In 1978, the National Research Council (NRC) published an analysis of this burgeoning literature (Blumstein, Cohen, and Nagin 1978). In several essays (e.g., Klein, Forst, and Filatov 1978; Nagin 1978; Vandaele 1978), researchers reviewed the empirical studies, pointed out the principal objections to the most popular analysis methods, and showed that they provided inaccurate or biased results. Just as important, the NRC report clarified the objectives. Henceforth, empirical researchers focused their efforts on finding one of two figures: elasticity, or η (the percentage change in the crime rate associated with a 1 percent change in the prison population) and marginal effectiveness, or λ (the number of crimes prevented by putting one more offender in prison). Though short of a true benefit-cost ratio, persuasive estimates of η and λ would go a long way toward putting prison policy on a firm empirical footing.

The rate of econometric studies dropped after the NRC report was published. The bar had been raised so high that, for a time, no one could jump it. Recently, however, the sheer expense of maintaining a million-plus prison population has stimulated renewed attempts to use the quasi-experimental data. The new studies rely on new theoretical underpinnings (Devine, Sheley, and Smith 1988); they employ new statistical methods, including the burgeoning array of time-series techniques (Marvell and Moody 1994); they recognize that statistical estimates can be fragile, because crime has many causes (Cappell and Sykes 1991) and because the prison population may be both a cause and an effect of crime (Levitt 1996). Collectively, these studies have succeeded in overcoming many of the objections of previous efforts.

Whether closer to the truth or not, they are certainly more defensible than the studies of the 1960s and 1970s.

In the remainder of this essay, I identify and discuss the problems in data collection and analysis encountered by recent researchers (the data problem—Sec. I; the specification problem—Sec. II; the simultaneity problem—Sec. III; differences among states—Sec. IV). I consider the principal solutions adopted, and the effect on the accuracy of the findings obtained. An attempt is made in the conclusion to triangulate among the available results. As it happens, it is not difficult to put reasonable upper and lower bounds on the most important figures. Recent studies have produced elasticities ranging from 0.16 to 0.31. For a variety of reasons described below, the estimates on the low end of this range are probably a bit low; the highest estimate is not especially precise. Nevertheless, we can be fairly sure that the best estimate is somewhere between 0.20 and 0.40; that is, doubling state prison capacity (from its current value of about 1.1 million) would probably reduce the Index Crime rate by somewhere between 20 and 40 percent.

This is still a wide range, and it falls in an awkward spot. If we could be sure that doubling the prison capacity would reduce crime by less than 20 percent, it is not hard to show that the costs of further prison construction exceed the benefits. If doubling capacity would reduce crime by more than 30 percent, we could be fairly sure that the benefits exceeded the costs, at least in the average state. Within this range, however, the policy implications hinge on controversial dollar estimates, statistical assumptions, and similarly unsatisfying issues.

Nevertheless, the results are sufficiently precise to suggest that most states should take a hard look before committing the money to building more prisons. Some have claimed that prison construction is an easy decision to make. Their claims are almost certainly false. The decision is difficult and will become more difficult unless and until alternative means of dealing with crime become politically realistic and demonstrably cost-effective.

The process of improving our estimates of prison effectiveness will continue indefinitely. The best study of twenty years ago would look hopelessly out of date in an academic journal today. Old problems, now largely solved, have been replaced with new and thornier problems. Nevertheless, estimates could be improved considerably if the best data and methods currently available were used consistently. Therefore, I conclude in Section V with a draft research design for the next, presumably not definitive, study of prison effectiveness.

I. The Data Problem

There are two strands of thought in the prison effectiveness literature, corresponding to two very different methods. Bottom-up researchers try to get inside the black box, combining survey information about criminal offenders, published reports on criminal justice system operations, and complex probability models to simulate the detailed workings of the system (Shinnar and Shinnar 1975; Greenwood 1982). This method is well suited to identifying the incapacitation effects of prison.

In contrast, top-down researchers work around the black box, using empirical data on crime rates, prison populations, and other possible causes of crime to link inputs and outputs (Ehrlich 1973; Devine, Sheley, and Smith 1988). Although these methods cannot in general separate incapacitative effects from deterrent and rehabilitative effects, they are much better suited than the bottom-up methods to identifying the full effects. Although this review focuses on the second group of studies, a word or two on the first group will help to put findings in context.

All simulation studies are based on a mathematical model developed by Avi-Itzhak and Shinnar (1973) and refined by Shinnar and Shinnar (1975). Briefly, this model combines estimates of the typical offender's offense rate per year (sometimes referred to as λ, the Greek letter lambda), probability of arrest, prosecution, and incarceration per crime committed, and average sentence served in jail or prison, to estimate the likelihood that a typical offender will be incarcerated at any given time. When combined with information about the length of the typical criminal career, it is possible to estimate the proportion of that career that the typical offender spends behind bars. This proportion represents the reduction in the crime rate due to incapacitation. By plugging in different probabilities of arrest, prosecution, or incarceration, or different average sentence lengths, an analyst could estimate the effect of prison expansion, improved police and prosecution, or other criminal justice system improvements. The 1978 NRC report compared the simulation approach to the top-down, econometric approach and found the simulation model promising but insufficiently developed to produce accurate estimates (Cohen 1978). For example, Avi-Itzhak and Shinnar's (1973) initial model assumed that individual offense rates, arrest and incarceration probabilities, and criminal career lengths were uncorrelated with one another and did not change over time. No empirical data were available to verify this assumption. Likewise, the model did not distinguish among offenders who committed crimes at different rates and assumed that incapacitating one member of an offending group would eliminate all offenses committed by members of that group. These assumptions seemed patently untrue. Perhaps more important, data on the operations of the criminal justice system, and particularly on offense rates and career lengths among active offenders, were sorely lacking. In fact, Cohen estimated that the elasticity of crime rates with regard to time spent in prison per crime committed (roughly similar to the elasticity at issue here) could range anywhere from −0.05 to −0.70, given available data (Cohen 1978, pp. 219–21). The model and the data on which it was based improved in bits and pieces throughout the 1980s. Greenwood (1982) showed how the model could be adapted to include a variety of offense rates. Reiss (1980) provided critical information on the size and behavior of offending groups. The Rand Corporation conducted a series of studies (Petersilia, Greenwood, and Lavin 1978; Peterson, Braiker, and Polich 1980; Chaiken and Chaiken 1982) that showed that tolerably accurate information on offense rates, arrest and incarceration probabilities, and other critical parameters could be obtained from surveys of incarcerated criminals. These surveys were successfully replicated (Mande and English 1988; DiIulio 1990; Horney and Marshall 1991), providing the knowledge base needed to support policy analysis.

Relying on these and further extensions of the model, DiIulio and Piehl (1991), Spelman (1994), and Piehl and DiIulio (1995) collected data from a variety of populations and compared the benefits and costs of increasing prison capacity. Their estimates of the elasticity of crime range from −0.16 to −0.26. Given the limited precision of any of these estimates, a more reasonable range might be anywhere between −0.10 and −0.30.

Although this is a narrow range, these estimates are less useful than they may appear at first glance. Even when the best data currently available are used, elasticities vary widely depending on estimates of average offense and arrest rates, the number of offenders who participate in committing the typical offense, and the length of the typical criminal "career" (Spelman 1994, pp. 219–21). Even if these uncertainties could be resolved, the simulation approach is inherently limited. It only shows the effect of incapacitation on crimes committed by adults, not juveniles. But juveniles are responsible for committing anywhere from 20 to 30 percent of all Index Crimes, and relatively little is known about juvenile offense rates, arrest probabilities, and desistance from crime. Intensive supervision probation and other community sanctions make it difficult for offenders to commit crimes, in effect partially incapacitating them. Yet no persuasive estimates of these partial incapacitation effects are available. Finally, the simulation approach lends itself to incapacitation effects only; if prisons succeed in deterring or rehabilitating even a few offenders, the simulation elasticities will systematically understate the full effects of imprisonment.

These limitations reduce considerably the utility of the bottom-up studies to policy makers. For better or worse, if we are to factor juvenile crimes, community sanctions, and deterrence into our decision making, we will need to rely on top-down models.

Physical and life scientists use top-down models constantly to make decisions in the fields of engineering, medicine, and the "hard" sciences. But they have a tremendous advantage: they can usually conduct experiments, in effect creating new data as needed. Due in part to politics, in part to the size and complexity of the criminal justice system, prison effectiveness researchers cannot conduct such experiments and must work with whatever data they can find. Unfortunately, this makes it very difficult to make fine-grained judgments. In this section, let us consider how and why this is so.

A. One Data Set

Virtually all empirical studies of prisons and crime rely on one of three data sets: a time-series data set of crime rates and prison populations for the entire United States, sometimes beginning as early as the 1930s (Vandaele 1973; Logan 1975); a cross-sectional data set of the fifty states for one (usually census) year (Gibbs 1968; Ehrlich 1973); and a panel data set that combines cross-sectional data for each state over multiple years (Kobrin et al. 1972; Marvell and Moody 1994). After several years of discussion about the relative benefits of cross-sectional and time-series data sets, the consensus has been that panel data sets combine the best of both, even if they must sacrifice a few states or a few years to maintain consistency and accuracy. Nevertheless, it is important to recognize that virtually all empirical studies are on one subset or another of a single data set with no more than about two thousand cases (fifty states × forty or so persuasive years). Further, there is widespread consensus that these are the best data to consider for solving this problem. Other data are not persuasive.

There are several reasons for this. Consider first the unit of analysis. Panel data sets consist of two components: the cross-sectional component (here, the state) and a time-series component (the year). Alternative cross sections are possible. For example, analysts could consider a cross section of counties within one state (Orsagh 1973), cities within the United States (Sjoquist 1973; Sampson 1986), or, conceivably, neighborhoods within a single city (Sampson, Raudenbush, and Earls 1997). Most studies rely on the state, because major decisions on imprisonment are made at the state level. Thus it is reasonable to expect that punishment rates (and their effect on crime) will be relatively homogeneous within states.

One counterargument is that decisions about prison use (as opposed to decisions about prison capacity) are typically made locally, by county prosecutors. Thus we can expect systematically different levels of punishment and crime (and perhaps of λ and η) among different counties in the same state. Aggregating among counties loses valuable information. The problem is, few states report sentences at the county level. This may be an important opportunity for further research, especially if further studies using statewide panel data are inconclusive.

A second counterargument is that other forces for which it is necessary to control are best measured at the city or county level. For example, arrest rates are determined by the policies and practices of local police; presumably arrest probabilities are homogeneous within local jurisdictions (Kobrin et al. 1972; Orsagh 1973; McPheters and Stronge 1974). Social indicators, such as unemployment rates, and community responses to crime, such as informal social control, both vary considerably among neighborhoods within a city (Taub, Taylor, and Dunham 1984). Attempting to measure these effects over a too-large level of aggregation (such as the city or metropolitan area) reduces variation and sample size, thus increasing the standard error and reducing the statistical significance of the effects observed. If time series for these characteristics can be collected, we may get some purchase out of a hierarchical model (Haitovsky 1986; Bryk and Raudenbush 1992).

The argument for the year is essentially one of convenience and habit: states collect annual crime and prison data already and report them to central sources. It would be difficult to choose a smaller unit of time; a larger unit throws away potentially valuable information.

The length of the time series is limited by several factors. First, crime and prison data are simply not available before 1929, putting an absolute limit on the series length. Second, several changes have been made over the years in the reporting requirements for crime and prison populations. Between 1929 and 1957, cities (and not states) had responsibility for reporting crimes to the FBI. As a result, the data are uneven in quality, and rates are not representative of true statewide rates (Bowker 1981). The uniform crime reporting program changed again in 1973, with the addition of larcenies under $50. This increased crime rates considerably. Some states appear to have reported incomplete prison populations between 1968 and 1970 (Hindelang et al. 1973, p. 346). Prison reporting changed in 1977; states began reporting jurisdictional populations, which included state prisoners in local jails. Although this increased reported incarceration rates somewhat, the effect was probably small because overcrowding only became a problem nationwide in the mid-1970s (Schlesinger 1987). Finally, even if compatible data were available from the 1930s and 1940s, the social systems that produce criminals and criminal opportunities were very different then. Some argue that this is true of the 1950s, too (McGuire and Sheehan 1983, p. 79). Thus a case could be made for restricting the starting point of the prison and crime time series to 1958, 1971, 1973, or 1977. In light of the validity questions involved, it would be difficult to justify earlier points.

Although studies have been conducted outside the United States (e.g., Carr-Hill and Stern 1973; Avio and Clarke 1978), it is uncertain how useful they are. The biggest reason is scale. Although American property crime rates are unexceptional, violent crime rates and imprisonment rates are higher in the United States than almost anywhere else in the developed world. The only places where the scale of imprisonment is even close (South Africa, Russia, and some former Soviet republics) are socially very different from the United States. This obviously does not prove that the social processes that produce criminals (and thus deterrence and incapacitation effects) are different in the United States than in other places, but it certainly suggests that they are. For better or worse, few analysts have relied on data collected outside the United States, and there is little clamor for multinational studies.

Since all empirical studies rely on only one data set, does this mean there is only one, best answer? Probably not. As shown below, different kinds of choices must be made when estimating effects. Analysts who make one kind of choice preclude others. Thus complementary approaches allow for triangulation and bounding. Nevertheless, the fact that they must all rely on the same data set limits the extent to which we can be sure of anyone's results.

B. Not a True Experiment

The recent prison construction boom provides a tremendous opportunity to identify the effects of prison capacity on crime rates. Rarely have the states shifted their policies on a single issue so quickly and dramatically. Nevertheless, this shift falls short of a true experiment, for all the obvious reasons. New prison beds were not randomly assigned among states, and sentences were not randomly assigned among counties, classes of offenders, or individuals. Because the principal independent variable is stochastic (i.e., not manipulated by the experimenter), it may be associated with all the other factors that cause crime. Thus we can never be sure of the effect of prison construction or of any other factor. What appears to be the effect of incarceration may turn out to be the effect of some other, as-yet unmeasured variable (Campbell and Stanley 1966; Mohr 1988, pp. 90–96). This is the problem of model specification.

Two other problems stem from the first. One might be termed the bandwagon effect and is due to the fact that many states increased or decreased prison populations at about the same time. The practical effect of this is to reduce the effective number of independent cases. It is difficult to know whether crime went down in one state because of an increase in imprisonment, or because of changing conditions in a neighboring state, or because of a social trend that crosses state boundaries.

The other problem is due to time spillover effects. Unless the effects of imprisonment (and other variables) are immediate and permanent, there will be some correlation between this year's prison population (or even this year's change in the prison population) and next year's. As with the bandwagon effect, this reduces the effective number of independent cases. Two cases that are highly correlated do not provide as much information as two cases that are statistically independent.

Let us consider each of these problems in turn.

1. *Specification and Bias.* Numerous attempts have been made to make systematic the threats to validity stemming from nonexperimental conditions. The framework developed by Campbell and Stanley (1966) provides some examples.

One simple case is sometimes called divergent external events or local history. This would apply to our problem if the social phenomena that caused crime rates to go up or down were occurring in each state at a different time or in a different way. Thus, even if two states increased or decreased their prison populations at the same time, their crime rates may behave independently.

The converse case, convergent external events, may also be true. Two states may have very similar crime rates over time, even though their prison populations are changing in very different ways, because crime is responding to other phenomena that behave similarly in each state. The solution to both external events problems is exactly the same: identify the phenomena to which crime rates are responding and control for them statistically. If the phenomena cannot be found, the results may be badly biased.

Campbell and Stanley (1966) also identify selection effects—in this case, differences between those states that increase prison capacity and those that do not. For example, state legislatures may be more willing to increase prison capacity in times of fiscal distress, providing jobs and social programs during good economic times. If crime is highest when the economy is at its worst, and if we fail to control for economic effects, it may appear that prison capacity has a large effect on the crime rate, even if it has none at all.

A final example is regression to the mean. Here, the bias is due to the timing of the response to a problem. Suppose the crime rate is high due to a random fluctuation—in essence, bad luck. If this trend is sufficiently alarming to state legislators, it may cause them to begin construction of additional prisons. The crime rate then falls, because the bad luck that caused it to rise now runs out. But we may give the credit, falsely, to our newly increased prison capacity. The underlying problem is that, just as crime may respond to changes in the prison population, so may the prison population respond to changes in crime rates. Only by controlling explicitly for both of these effects can we be sure to eliminate this threat to validity.

These by no means exhaust the threats to validity. Nevertheless, it is important to note that the solution to each threat is the same—explicitly include the variables or relationships that may be responsible for the threat in the model to be estimated. If the variable or relationship is controlled for in the specification, the threat dissolves.

The practical result is that our uncertainty extends well beyond statistical significance. The exact nature of the specification is critical. As Leamer (1983) has demonstrated in an analysis of the death penalty deterrence research, the same data set can yield dramatically different results, depending on which variables are included as explanatory variables. In particular, the effects of punishment on crime (and vice versa) can be badly biased if important explanatory variables are left out.

Leamer offers a formal set of procedures for identifying and reporting such specification "fragility" (Leamer 1983). His procedures have proven controversial and are rarely used, in part because of the complex judgments they require of analysts. Nevertheless, few deny that fragility is a critical problem (McAleer, Pagan, and Volker 1985; Granger and Uhlig 1990). The best solution is almost certainly to experiment with different specifications and report any findings that vary from expectations. More on this in Section II, below.

2. *The Prison Bandwagon.*   Since 1958, each state has responded to its crime problems in a remarkably similar way. Throughout the 1960s, prison populations stagnated nationwide. A trend toward increasing populations began in the early 1970s; by 1975, the vast majority of states were on the prison construction bandwagon. Since 1975, per capita prison populations have increased in every state, by an average of over 300 percent.

There have been a few differences. Some states, such as Texas, increased their prison populations throughout the 1980s and 1990s. Others, including Indiana, Maine, and Montana, increased early in the period, then leveled off; still others, such as Georgia and Iowa, did not begin to increase their prison populations until the late 1980s. Nevertheless, the lowest bivariate correlation among the states during this period was 0.67, and the average correlation was a quite healthy 0.93 — clear evidence of a nationwide movement.

The similarity among states has two important effects. First, it reduces the benefits of a panel data set. The principal argument for a panel is to increase the sample size; each state's experience provides a separate case, and we conduct in effect fifty (quasi) experiments. If each state increases its prison population by a similar amount, the variation among experimental conditions is reduced. If all states simply increased their prison populations in lockstep, we would be replicating a single experiment fifty times. This is clearly less valuable than fifty separate experiments.

Of course, state-level data are readily available, and states differ by enough that it makes sense to consider them separately. Unfortunately, the usual regression techniques are liable to overstate the (effective) sample size. Efficiency increases as the square root of the sample size, so the standard errors for a state panel should be $1/\sqrt{50}$ or about one-seventh as large as the nationwide time-series standard errors. If the crime and prison experiences of many states are similar, however, this reduction in the standard error will overstate the increase in efficiency. If every state responded to the national crime problem in exactly the same way, for example, then interstate variation would be zero, the panel results would be identical to the nationwide time series, and the standard errors should be identical to those of the nationwide time series. In general, the larger the bandwagon effect, the greater the extent to which the regression will understate the standard errors.

3. *Time Spillover Effects.* A similar argument concerns time. Most conditions that create crime change little from year to year. As a result, this year's crime rate is very similar to (very highly correlated with) last year's. As with the bandwagon effect, the larger the correlation, the greater the extent to which we overestimate the effective number of cases. Suppose we have collected forty years of data; if the correlation from year to year were near 1.0, we would have not forty cases, but only one, almost unchanging, data point. If, however, the correlation between this year and the last were zero, the cases would be independent and our standard errors and confidence limits would be unbiased.

It is tempting to control for these slowly changing conditions and move on. Unfortunately, this only begins to solve the problem. One issue is that some independent variables are liable to have delayed but prolonged effects. For example, available evidence suggests that increases in unemployment rates have little short-run effect on crime rates (Chiricos 1987). Some, in fact, argue that unemployment reduces the crime rate by keeping potential victims at home (Cantor and Land 1985). The more important effects may come after unemployment levels return to normal. The social disruption created by the recession, especially in neighborhoods that were marginal to begin with, may linger for years. Similarly, many cite the coming of age of the Baby Boomers in the early 1970s as the biggest, single reason for that decade's increase in crime rates. But this trend took a decade or more to come to fruition. In general, we fool ourselves if we think we have gained much by cutting long-term trends like these into neat, annual segments.

A closely related issue is simple inertia. Prison populations depend ultimately on prison facilities, and most facilities have a useful life of fifty years or more. Even if prison construction ground to a halt, prison populations would only decrease by about one-fiftieth or 2 percent per year. Similarly, correctional payrolls, equipment, and budgets rarely change by more than a few percent from year to year. Even if prison populations had a tremendous effect on crime, the slow speed with which prison populations change means that crime rates could change significantly only over decades, not years.

The practical effect is very similar to that of the bandwagon effect. Annual data appear to be more precise than in fact they are. This results in improperly low standard errors and improperly high values of R^2. Simply put, the data are not telling us as much as we think they are.

Limited evidence suggests that this is true. Cappell and Sykes (1991) estimate that the correlation in crime rates from year to year may be as high as 0.40 or 0.50. Marvell and Moody (1994) estimate a lower but still significant correlation (.20 or so). Ultimately, this means that we would identify "phantom effects" (i.e., improperly reject a null hypothesis even though it is true) roughly three or four times as often as we think we would (Park and Mitchell 1980).

The classic solution for this problem is called generalized least squares and involves estimating the proportion of each year's value that is due to holdover and inertia effects, separating this proportion from the rest, and conducting our analysis on the remainder. A variety of methods are available for identifying the proportion due to holdover and inertia (see, e.g., Judge et al. 1985). If the correlation between successive values is high, a simpler method may work almost as well: measure each variable as the difference between that year's value and the previous year's. Even simple methods are liable to be a big improvement over doing nothing.

C. Fuzzy Variables

Proper variable definition is key to effective analysis. Unfortunately, there are a variety of ways to define many of the variables of interest, and criminological theory provides relatively little guidance as to which are appropriate. Bad choices render our results weak and misleading. Specifically, improper definition of any variable reduces the explanatory power of our regressions (as measured by R^2 and the standard deviation of our residuals); as a result, it reduces our confidence as to the true effects of one variable on another (as measured by the statistical significance of our regression coefficients). Further, improper definitions of independent variables bias regression coefficients in unpredictable ways, making our results misleading in size as well as statistical significance. Although good choices ultimately require better theory, careful examination of the alternatives can help.

1. *Defining Crime.* The simplest definition of the extent of crime in an area is the number reported each year to the police. In the United States, these figures have been compiled since the late 1920s by the FBI and are readily available in any good library. As a result of their simplicity and availability, these Uniform Crime Report (UCR) figures are used far more often than any other estimates. Nevertheless, these data pose theoretical and practical challenges to analysts.

The most obvious problem is that the UCR only measures reported crimes, and most crimes are never reported to the police. The principal alternative—the victimization survey—measures unreported crimes but suffers from its own validity problems. Victims may forget when they were victimized or that they were ever victimized at all. They may lie, making up or concealing crimes. They may never even realize they have been victimized. Due to changes in survey procedures over time, official victimization data may be slow to identify shifts in crimes committed (Steffensmeier and Harer 1991). For these and other reasons, reported crime data appear to be somewhat more reliable than victimization data (Gove, Hughes, and Geerken 1985; Blumstein, Cohen, and Rosenfeld 1991; but see O'Brien 1985; Menard 1992).

The relative validity of crime and victimization data remains a judgment call, but a practical problem is dispositive. Victimization surveys were only developed in the mid-1960s, and a national time series has only existed since the early 1970s. This provides, at most, twenty-five or thirty data points—not much to base a major social policy on. More important, data are only available for the United States as a whole and are not broken down by state or region. As described below, this is a fatal flaw. For all practical purposes, we are stuck with reported crimes.

The nonreporting problem can be solved, at least in part, by using reporting rates obtained from victimization surveys to adjust the raw figures and estimate the total number of crimes committed. The focus on reported crimes creates other, more subtle problems, however. Many classes of crimes are so rarely reported that the UCR index does not even include them: drug dealing, forgery and fraud, embezzling and price-fixing, for example. Many argue that such crimes pose substantial costs to the public. For example, Conklin (1986, p. 74) provides evidence that 65 percent of all financial costs of crime are due to white collar crimes and 17 percent are due to vice and drug crimes. Thus, focusing on crimes likely to be reported gives an incomplete picture of the total crime problem. (For obvious reasons, victimization data fare no better in this respect.)

Reported crimes also give an incomplete picture of the potential effects of imprisonment. By the mid-1990s, half of all prison admissions were for crimes not included in the FBI index—mostly drug offenses (Maguire and Pastore 1995, p. 552). If the deterrent and incapacitative effects of imprisoning these offenders are focused on the crime types for which they were convicted, we will never identify such effects by measuring reported crime.

Even among reported crime types, prison is liable to be more effective against some types than others. For example, some have speculated that crimes committed for monetary gain and other "instrumental" reasons are more easily deterrable than violent crimes, which may be committed for "expressive" reasons (Chambliss 1969). Thus increases in prison population can be expected to reduce property crime rates more than they reduce violent rates. However, an incapacitation strategy oriented toward violent offenses may have the opposite effect. A related problem is that murders and rapes are more costly than burglaries and auto thefts, to victims and to society at large. Because each offender commits a different mix of crime types over time, the benefits of imprisoning each offender will generally be different.

The customary solution is to distinguish between violent and property crimes in the analysis, estimating the effects of prison populations on each. This obviously ignores fine distinctions—not all violent crimes are equally severe or deterrable; some states reserve long sentences for murderers and rapists, while others may sentence robbers to life; virtually all murders are reported to the police, but only a fraction of the assaults; and so on. Nevertheless, even so simple a solution as this may be too complex for available statistical procedures. As shown in Section III, crime and prison may be so closely intertwined that estimating the effect of prison on one crime variable may be the limit of our capacity.

Any time series collected over so long a period is susceptible to problems of comparability over time. The UCR is no exception. For example, in many jurisdictions police have improved their internal procedures for recording reported crimes, especially with the advent of computerization. There is evidence that this is especially true for assaults (Reiss and Roth 1993, pp. 413–14). Victimization survey results suggest that citizen crime-reporting rates have increased as well. Taken together, this suggests that official figures may increase, even as the number of crimes committed goes down. Some have speculated that these effects may be greatest in those states most concerned with the crime problem—and most liable to rely on imprisonment to control it (Donohue and Siegelman 1996, p. 31).

Finally, changing definitions and data collection methods force researchers to make tough technical choices. In 1971, the UCR began to include reported thefts of $50 or less; not surprisingly, this dramatically increased the apparent crime rate. Should researchers adjust the pre-1971 figures for comparability, eliminate all pre-1971 data, or eliminate larceny from the analysis? Before 1958, the FBI collected data directly from cities, rather than from states; thus the pre-1958 series focuses on urban areas. Should researchers adjust the pre-1958 figures for comparability or eliminate pre-1958 data entirely? Cantor and Cohen (1980) and Cantor and Land (1985) suggest a variety of adjustments and corrections, and these have found favor with some analysts (e.g., Cappell and Sykes 1991). Nevertheless, the best fix remains a judgment call.

2. *Defining the Prison Population.*   Like "crime," the commonsense notion of a "prison population" hides some basic assumptions that may affect our results considerably. For example, population figures (the stock of prisoners) provide good estimates of the costs of punishment, but prison admissions per year or prisoners received from court (both flows over time) provide better estimates of the outputs of the criminal justice system and the risks to offenders. Stocks may be more appropriate measures of the incapacitative effects of prison, while flows may measure deterrent effects more effectively.

Another question concerns the technical definition of a prisoner. Overcrowded prison systems sometimes pay local jails to keep state prisoners until room becomes available for them. Thus some jail inmates are part of the state's jurisdictional population but not of the custodial population. In 1977, the National Prisoner Statistics program switched from a custodial to a jurisdictional basis. Although only 2.6 percent of state prisoners were housed in jails in 1977, the figures were much higher in some states. This makes the pre- and post-1977 series of dubious comparability (McGuire and Sheehan 1983; Marvell and Moody 1994).

Regardless of the technical definition, researchers invariably rely on state prison statistics. This fails to cover all prisoners, however. Especially since the advent of federal sentencing guidelines in the mid-1980s, many offenders arrested by state and local police are tried in federal courts where they typically receive stiffer sentences. Because breakdowns of federal prisoners by state are not readily available, relying only on state statistics systematically understates the total increase in punishment over the past decade. Underestimates will be greatest among states that make greatest use of the federal courts.

Even the focus on prisons can be questioned. Convicted felons typically serve their time in prisons, while jails are reserved for misdemeanants and those awaiting trial. Due to plea bargaining, however, many offenders charged with felonies do only jail time. Thus jail and prison populations should probably be combined if our objective is to measure the extent of punishment doled out in a given jurisdiction. Jails are typically funded and controlled by counties, not states, and may be used very differently in different states at different times. However they are used, it is impractical to include jail data in a punishment time series. They are only collected on a statewide basis every five years (Levitt 1996).

Imprisonment is not the only punishment available that may reduce crime rates. Fines, probation terms, and even arrest itself may deter some offenders (Spelman 1995); intensive supervision probation is probably at least partially incapacitative because it reduces the time available to steal and deal. These alternative punishments are rarely counted in crime control studies, but they are likely to be used very differently at different times in different states.

In addition to the usual problems of measurement error, the failure to account for alternatives to imprisonment creates a problem of bias. The full extent of punishment will be understated in states that make greater use of jail and alternatives. If these punishments are mostly used in low-imprisonment states (jail, fines, and probation are substitutes for prison), it is not hard to show that the true effect of punishment on crime will be greater than it appears. If these punishments are mostly used in high-imprisonment states (the alternatives are complements to prison), the true effect will be less. The extent of the under- or overestimate depends, of course, on the deterrent and incapacitative effects of alternatives and on the frequency with which they are used.

Other, more technical problems have also cropped up. As described above, officially reported prison statistics for 1967–71 are widely regarded as underestimates; the 1968 figure is especially suspect (Bowker 1981; McGuire and Sheehan 1983). The annual prison census is taken on December 31 each year, but crime rates are based on the entire calendar year. Thus the average of each year and the previous year will probably give a better estimate of the total number of offenders in prison over the course of a year than will the year-end total (Devine,

Sheley, and Smith 1988, p. 413). As with crime rates, failure to manage the details may have a substantial effect on the final result.

3. *Effects of Measurement Error.* As described above, crime reporting and recording change over time and differ among jurisdictions. Whenever our measurements of a dependent variable are imprecise, we can expect it to affect our results. In general, R^2 will be too low, F statistics will be less significant than otherwise, and the standard errors of the coefficients will be too high. If our measure of sanctions is also in error, this biases our estimate of the effects of sanctions toward zero. Because such effects are conservative—they make our results look less sizable and significant than the "true" values—we often ignore the problem.

Measurement errors do not always lead to conservative results, however. Nagin (1978, pp. 114–17) observes that a common form of plea bargaining is "charge bargaining." Offenders are offered a lesser charge in exchange for a guilty plea. Thus many are arrested and sanctioned for serious crimes (such as aggravated assault and robbery) yet are only convicted of less serious but similar offenses (such as simple assault and larceny). If an increase in crime leads to an increase in charge bargaining, this will appear to reduce the number of criminals who receive sanctions for the most serious offenses. This results in an apparent negative relationship between crime and sanctions, even though the number sanctioned has not been reduced, only the severity of the charges. Nagin uses similar arguments to suggest that measurement errors may lead to a falsely negative relationship between crime and arrests (1978, pp. 112–14).

Moreover, even if the errors in measuring crime are completely random and unrelated to the prison population, there is still a bias if ratio variables are used. For example, in the 1970s it was common to suppose that the crime rate (the number of crimes committed, divided by the population) depended on the imprisonment rate (the number of offenders imprisoned, divided by the number of crimes). That is,

$$C/n = \alpha + \beta(P/C) + e, \tag{1}$$

where C is the number of crimes, n is the population, P is the number of offenders imprisoned, e is a random error term, and α and β are coefficients to be estimated. Now suppose there is no relationship at all between crime and imprisonment rates, and the true value of β is zero. However, during some years, C systematically underestimates the true number of crimes committed. For these cases, our measure of the crime rate (C/n) will be lower than the true value, and our measure of the imprisonment rate (P/C) will be higher than the true value. Because high values of the imprisonment rate will tend to occur at the same time as low values of crime rate, our measure of the relationship between the two variables, β, will be less than zero. We may well conclude that putting a higher percentage of offenders in prison will reduce the crime rate. But the apparent relationship is an illusion, caused only by measurement errors in our crime variable.

If we somehow knew the extent of the errors, we could adjust β to account for it and obtain a rough but unbiased solution (Ehrlich 1973). Although the data we need are not generally available, a quick reality check suggests the importance of the problem. If the variance of the errors in measuring C is about the same as the variance of the independent variable (P/C), it is not hard to show that β as measured must be at least -0.5, even if the true value of β is zero. Even if the variance of the measurement error is only one-fourth the variance of the independent variable, our estimate of β must be at least -0.1.

Clearly, measurement errors can be policy relevant. The safest approach is to avoid using ratio variables. Fortunately, with a little creative algebra we can do this without changing the specification of the model. Perhaps more important, we must recognize that previous research studies that rely on ratio variables are biased, and that the bias can be substantial. Here, the safest approach is to discount the results of all such studies and focus attention on those that are not biased in this way.

Although crime and sanctions will occupy most of our attention, we face similar problems when we attempt to measure such control variables as race and age, welfare spending, inflation, and unemployment. Some of these variables are rough proxies for more appropriate concepts; for example, overall unemployment may be the best available estimate for economic opportunities among young adult males. Other variables, such as the percent of the population in poverty, may be theoretically justifiable but measured in an unreliable way. Whatever the reason, poorly measured control variables have several effects: standard errors are too high, R^2 is too low, coefficients on the control variables are biased toward zero; most important, the coefficients on the sanctions variables may also be biased, depending on size of the measurement errors and extent to which the control variable is correlated to sanctions. If sanctions are positively correlated to, say, unemployment, but unemployment is poorly measured, then our estimate of the effects of sanctions will include some of the effect (whatever it may be) of unemployment. This is hardly an argument against including unemployment in our regression; leaving the variable out entirely would bias the regression even more (McCallum 1972; Wickens 1972). Still, we must recognize that the effects of measurement error will not be confined to the erroneously measured variables.

Nevertheless, the biggest problem with control variables is not measuring them but identifying them all in the first place. It is to this problem—and the more general problem of model specification—that we now turn.

II. The Specification Problem

The association of two variables is one of the most basic forms of analysis, and it has been used for years in efforts to explain changes and differences in crime rates. For example, Sellin (1959) investigated the effectiveness of capital punishment by comparing homicide rates for adjacent states, one with a death penalty on the books, and the other without. Nagel (1977) argued for a moratorium on prison construction, in large part because the correlation between incarceration and crime rates among the fifty states was statistically insignificant and positive. Biles (1979) extended Nagel's analysis to Canada and Australia and found larger and more positive correlations. More recently, a raft of observers have used similar methods to explain reductions in crime. Consider, for example, the wide variety of ad hoc explanations offered for the recent reduction in New York City's crime rate. New York Mayor Rudy Giuliani, for instance, claimed the reduction was due to the New York Police Department's strict enforcement or "quality of life" strategy. By cracking down on smoking on buses and drinking in public, the police presumably stifled burglary and robbery as well (Kocieniewski 1997). John Jay College professor Andrew Karmen credited the "little brother syndrome." "I'm more and more convinced that there's a shift in values among 20-somethings," said Karmen. "Having seen what the crack wars and violence caused to their friends and older brothers, they're more and more willing to give the world of legitimate work a try" (Kocieniewski 1997, p. B4). University of Missouri at St. Louis professor Scott Decker believed crack addicts shifted from burglary to robbery. Burglary took too much planning and yielded goods that must be fenced; robbery was faster and yielded cash. The net result is fewer but more dangerous crimes (Butterfield 1997). San Diego Police Chief Jerry Sanders argued that citizen involvement was the key. "[People] are starting to realize they themselves can do something about [crime], so we have lots of citizens out solving problems on their own." San Diego, like New York, had been focusing on involving the community in crime-fighting activities (Butterfield 1997, p. 26). Finally, the usual suspects reared their ugly heads: the economy was good and unemployment was down; fewer young people were smoking crack cocaine; there were fewer young people, crackheads, or otherwise. All of these explanations derive ultimately from a (perhaps casually observed) association of the variable in question with the prevalence of crime. All appear plausible. None is definitive.

As a glance at any introductory criminology text will confirm, crime is a complex phenomenon, with many varied causes. The increases (and recent decreases) in crime that we are trying to explain are part of a long-term trend, not just short-term fluctuations. Our first task, then, must be to identify and account for as many alternative explanations as possible.

One reason for looking for alternative explanations is to find the right one. But there is an even more important reason: failure to control for some explanations—leaving out critical variables—biases our estimates of the effects of the remaining, included variables. What makes this problem especially ugly is that it is impossible to fix completely and that the bias is often of unknown size and direction. Nevertheless, careful modeling can mitigate the problem.

A. Effects of Omitting Variables

Suppose the crime rate, C, depends on two variables: punishment (P, measured as prison inmates per capita) and the young adult population (Y, the proportion of all persons between sixteen and twenty-four). Suppose further that the true relationship between these variables is

$$C = \alpha + \beta_1 P + \beta_2 Y + \epsilon, \qquad (2)$$

but we fail to measure Y and include it in the equation. Thus the model actually estimated is

$$C = a + bP + e. \qquad (3)$$

Applying a little algebra to the standard formulas for regression coefficients shows that our estimate of b will be systematically different from the true value, β_1. Specifically,

$$b = \beta_1 + \beta_2 \text{ covariance } (Y, P)/\text{variance } (P). \qquad (4)$$

The second term of equation (4) shows the direction and size of the bias in b. The bias depends on three factors.

First, note that the variance of P, the denominator in that second term, may be large or small depending on our data set, but it is certain to be positive. The larger the variance, the smaller the bias. If there is a sufficiently large variation among the cases in the value of P, we get good definition as to its effects and the bias is minimal.

Now consider β_2, the true effect of Y on C. In this case, we can safely guess that $\beta_2 > 0$ and fairly large (more young people means more crime). If it were zero, the second term would drop out and $b = \beta_1$. This makes good sense; if $\beta_2 = 0$, equation (2) reduces to equation (3), and we estimated the right model from the beginning.

Finally, consider covariance (Y, P). This is the hard part. If P and Y are independent, their covariance will be zero, the second term in equation (4) drops out, and there will be no bias in b. In general, then, omitting a variable only affects the results if that variable is correlated with the variables left in the equation. Now suppose P and Y are positively correlated; for whatever reason, large prison populations and many young people tend to happen together. In this case, the second term in equation (4) will be positive and $b > \beta_1$. In effect, P will be taking on some of the explanatory power of its unmeasured correlate, Y; it is in part a proxy for Y. Similarly, if P and Y are negatively correlated, $b < \beta_1$. In this case, P and Y are offsetting one another in practice (since when one is high, the other is low). By failing to measure Y, that offsetting is captured, incorrectly, in our estimate of the effects of P.

In general, all variables that affect the crime rate must be included in our model, else we bias the estimates of the variables we do include. Since everything in the world is related to everything else, in practice the best we can do is minimize the bias, not eliminate it altogether.

Biased coefficients are the most serious of the consequences of leaving out variables. There are others. Standard errors are also biased, thus confidence intervals and hypothesis tests are inaccurate. The R^2 statistic is obviously lower than it would have been had the omitted variables been included. In addition, however, R^2 provides a biased estimate of the proportion of the variance really explained by the included variables. If the coefficients are biased to be too large in absolute value (i.e., if positive coefficients are biased high, negative coefficients are biased low), then R^2 will include not only the effect of the included variables but also some of the effects of the omitted variables. Thus it will be too high, giving the false impression that the included variables are more important than they really are. If the coefficients on the included variables are instead biased toward zero, this means the excluded variables would be offsetting their effects. Thus R^2 will be too small; the included variables are more important than they appear to be. It may be that an important variable appears to have no effect whatever; left-out variables have dampened the included variable's effect to the point that it is no longer distinguishable.

Left-out variable problems are not always obvious. For example, some have argued that an apparently positive relationship between punishment and subsequent crime may be due to anticipation on the part of decision makers. That is, the legislature decides to build more prison beds in anticipation of needing them in the future, when crime rates have risen. If crime does continue to increase, it may appear as though it were caused by the preceding increase in the prison population. In fact, the causal linkage works in the opposite direction (Marvell and Moody 1994, p. 123).

In an important sense, the problem of anticipatory variables is simply another manifestation of the left-out variable problem. What is left out in this case is the source of the expectation. If policy makers believe crime will increase because it always has, past values of crime should be an important predictor of current and future capacity. If the expectation resulted from some other information (extrapolation of trends in crack use or job prospects, for example), this information should be controlled for, too. After controlling for past values of crime, crack use, or whatever, the spurious correlation between current capacity and future crime will very likely be much reduced and perhaps even eliminated.

Clearly, left-out variables are a major cause of concern. Fortunately, most analysts have recognized this and taken it into account.

B. Solving the Left-Out Variable Problem

Conceptually, there are two ways to deal with the left-out variable problem. The simplest way is, of course, not to leave anything out. In an effort to cover the most important bases, previous analysts have controlled for a wide variety of social, economic, and criminal justice system factors in estimating the effectiveness of imprisonment. Unfortunately, crime is so complex that we can never be sure we have identified all the variables. A complementary strategy, to manipulate the variables included so as to reduce the potential for left-out variable errors, is a safe choice even if it does not solve the problem by itself.

Option 1: Include Them All. The appendix shows a (still-incomplete) list of the variables that have been included in one crime equation or another. As shown, the variables group themselves naturally into several categories.

Our primary issue of concern is, of course, punishment. Note there are several ways to characterize punishment, depending on whether we are concerned with the flow of cases through the criminal justice system (rates and probabilities of arrest, conviction, and the like) or the stock of results (prison population). During the 1970s, many analysts included two flow variables: the probability of incarceration, given a crime, and the expected time served in prison, given incarceration. These measure the likelihood and severity of punishment.

As described above, the probability measures all suffer from substantial biases. Since crime is included in both the numerator of the dependent variable and the denominator of the independent variable, and since reported crime is probably only measured with considerable error, the errors skew the estimate of the relationship downward. In part as a result, recent studies have collapsed the punishment measures to a single estimate of the total amount of punishment allotted (usually, prison inmates per capita). Although this is a practical solution to the problem, it is important to recognize that certainty of punishment may have different effects than severity of punishment. As described below, some states have adopted punishment strategies that focus on one or the other. By collapsing our punishment measures, we give up our chance to determine which of these strategies is more effective.

These measures of punishment are all outputs, but it may be that criminal justice system activities have effects of their own. For example, it may be that the presence of patrol officers on the street establishes a deterrent effect, over and above arrests, convictions, traffic stops, and other results of the officers' activities. Thus the number of police officers per capita may be an effective variable (McPheters and Stronge 1974; Levitt 1996). Prisons that provide harsh living conditions may deter more effectively than those that are more pleasant. Thus prison spending per inmate, a rough approximation of amenities and conditions, may predict better than time served alone (Forst 1976).

Demographic characteristics are of obvious interest. Blacks and Hispanics are arrested more frequently than whites for Index Crimes; men are arrested more than women, and an individual's chances of arrest appear to peak in the late teens. Socioeconomic characteristics test the observation that poor, lower-class, poorly educated people commit more crimes than their well-off, middle-class, well-educated counter-parts. Economic distress indicators map opportunities in the legitimate economy, with which criminal opportunities are presumably compet-ing (Ehrlich 1973). Inflation, unemployment, low welfare benefits, and low government expenditures per person all suggest an environment where crime may appear to be a reasonable career choice.

These variables all come from the economic paradigm, but sociolog-ical concepts may be just as important. Due to the South's persistently unique culture, the social processes that produce crime may act differ-ently there than elsewhere (Greenwood and Wadycki 1973). Dense ur-ban settings differ from rural areas. Stable neighborhoods where the neighbors know and look out for one another may have lower crime rates than others (Sampson, Raudenbush, and Earls 1997).

Finally, recent criminological research suggests that much crime may be driven by the opportunities available, rather than by social and economic factors that motivate offenders to find these opportunities. Thus the number and size of consumer goods per household (measur-ing the likelihood of finding easily transportable valuables in a house burglary) or the labor force participation rate (measuring the likeli-hood that someone will be at home during the day) may be effective predictors of crime rates (Cohen and Felson 1979). At one point or another, most of these variables have been shown to be associated with crime rates. A prima facie case can be made for all of them. Why not include them all? There are two reasons. First, available data put more or less stringent limits on our ability to add new variables. Recall that the standard nationwide time series only began in 1958; before this time, reported crime rates were essentially noncomparable. This leaves us with forty or so observations. If all the variables in the appendix were included in a single, monster regression, only 10 degrees of free-dom would remain. The standard errors and confidence intervals asso-ciated with these estimates would be too large to tell us much. Moving to a panel data set would gain us degrees of freedom, but only at the cost of making it impossible to draw any conclusions as to differences among states.

What makes the problem worse is that many of the variables in the appendix are highly correlated with one another. Because (say) income per capita, poverty rate, the percentage of white-collar workers, and years of schooling are all tightly intertwined, it would be difficult to pull their individual effects apart even if thousands of cases were avail-able. Although this is no problem in itself—none of these variables are critical to the enterprise—it may be that some of them are highly correlated with the punishment variables. If so, we will have eliminated the bias in our estimates at the cost of making them uselessly imprecise.

We may be able to keep most of the data but solve our degrees of freedom problem by collapsing highly intercorrelated variables into linear combinations called indexes or factors. Presumably, each factor measures an underlying social force; because none of the individual variables have an effect of their own, but are simply manifestations of that force, we gain clarity and lose nothing by collapsing. For example, we may find that our measures of income, poverty, class, and education are highly intercorrelated. Statistical analysis identifies the most reliable combination of these variables. In further analyses, we rely on the scale, rather than individual variables, reducing the collinearity problem and saving degrees of freedom.

There is substantial evidence that, on some units of analysis at least, many of these variables are highly intercorrelated. Thus a cluster or factor score may be sufficient to capture the underlying social forces. In a study of 343 Chicago neighborhoods, for example, Sampson, Raudenbush, and Earl (1997, p. 920) found that the demographic characteristics collected by the U.S. Census clustered neatly into three factors: concentrated disadvantage (measures of poverty, unemployment, female-headed households, and black population); immigrant concentration (Hispanic and foreign-born populations); and residential stability (low migration rate, high rates of owner occupancy). These factors explained over 70 percent of the variance among neighborhoods in violent crime rates, suggesting that relatively little was lost in the translation.

Through judicious use of factor or cluster analysis, we may be able to reduce the control variables to a manageable number. This leads to the second, more difficult problem. Our theories of crime are not sufficiently well developed that we can exclude many variables in advance. The appendix is not a complete list; other variables are available, and plausible arguments can no doubt be made that the new variables are just as important as any now on the list. If our aim is to exhaust the possibilities, we will never succeed. This leaves us open to the problem of Type I error—we never know what the next variable would do. It also leaves us open to Type II error—any variable that appears plausible and produces a statistically significant coefficient must remain in the regression. A "kitchen sink" regression will very likely produce a few of these.

Again, this is not a problem by itself. Including variables that should be omitted does not, as a rule, affect the results for those variables that belong in the regression. If, however, some of these variables are correlated with our punishment variables—if, for example, they follow the same long-term trend—we may mistakenly assign some of the predictive power of punishment to the inappropriate variables. By the same token, if punishment and crime both follow the same, long-term trend (e.g., they are both increasing over time throughout the period in question), we may easily mistake the effect of punishment with the effects of the trend itself.

At some point we will probably need to round up the usual suspects and throw them into our model—institute, in effect, a massive variable incapacitation program. But this is more likely to yield valid results if we first apply an opportunity reduction approach. Through clever design and a few changes in interpretation, we may be able to reduce our risks and obtain a safer estimate of our parameters.

Option 2: Reduce the Size of the Problem. Randomized experiments work by reducing the sources of variation in the dependent variable to two: the experimental condition and random error. If random error is not sufficient to explain the variation in the dependent variable, then the experiment must be responsible. Because all variables can be specified in advance, there is no possibility of other, unidentified variables confusing the results. In a similar way, two general approaches have been used to reduce the potential for confusion in measuring the crime equation. Both work by reducing the potential explanatory power of unidentified variables.

The first method is easily explained: use panel data rather than pure cross-sectional or pure time-series data; then control for the fixed effects of each state, and the fixed effects of each time period, through use of dummy variables. If the panel includes a broad cross section, the state dummy variables will capture the effects of those variables that differ more or less permanently among the states but do not change much over the period within each state. Thus we would expect that the dummy variables would capture the effects of urbanization, weather, geographical position, and to a lesser extent demographic characteristics such as race and income. If the panel also includes a long time series, the time dummy variables will capture the effects of those variables that affect all states over time. For example, nationwide trends such as the increased availability of consumer electronic goods are liable to be roughly similar in all states.

The dummy variables will not capture all effects, of course; some states have become more urbanized, and small-but-valuable electronics goods are still more broadly distributed in California and New York than in, say, West Virginia. Still, they will reduce the effects of these variables, making it less likely that they can bias the coefficients of the remaining variables.

A second approach to opportunity reduction is driven by the nature of changes in crime rates and prison populations over time. Nation-wide, and to a lesser extent on a state-by-state basis, both crime and punishment are changing slowly but steadily over time. The 1960s through 1980s saw a general trend toward higher reported crime rates; this has been reversed in the 1990s. The 1960s and early 1970s saw stagnation in prison populations, since reversed with a vengeance. Short-term fluctuations in prison (and other variables) may explain subsequent short-term fluctuations in crime rates. But if prison or any other variable has affected the crime rate, it has been in the context of these long-term trends.

The presence of a trend creates a tremendous opportunity for mis-understanding. Briefly stated, any two variables that are trending in the same direction will be highly correlated, whether they affect one an-other or not. This is clearly a left-out variable problem; by definition, the presence of a long-term trend suggests that some social force out-side the system is affecting the behavior of the variables within. If the data are available, the conceptually simplest solution is to measure that force and be done with it. In the absence of good measures of that force (or even a clear idea as to what the force is), we model the trend itself (Granger and Newbold 1974).

It is customary to model the trend—in effect, to work around it—rather than to measure it directly. The usual means of modeling a trend is to difference each time series. That is, each variable is trans-formed so that the value of each case is equal to the difference between the level for that case and the level for the previous case. Thus if C_t represents crime in period t, and C_{t-1} represents crime in the previous period, then

$$\Delta C_t = C_t - C_{t-1}. \tag{5}$$

This is the first difference; the resulting estimates can be differenced again to create second differences, these can be differenced again to create third differences, and so on as needed to eliminate the drift up-ward or downward.

A trend can also be measured outright. Whether it is more appropriate to measure the trend or model it depends on the nature of deviations around the trend. If the effect of each deviation tends to die out over time (technically, the deviations are generated according to a memoryless or short-memory process), the variable is called trend stationary. The usual solution is to treat time as an independent variable, while applying autoregressive and moving average techniques to account for any short-term memory effects in the deviations (Davidson and MacKinnon 1993, pp. 700–702). If the deviations are instead generated according to a long-memory process (i.e., the effect of each deviation is retained indefinitely), the process is termed a random walk, and the trend is referred to as drift. In this case, differencing is appropriate (Engle and Granger 1991, pp. 2–6). As described below, available evidence suggests that crime series are long memory and that differencing is necessary.

The random walk plus drift model makes sense on theoretical grounds, too. For crime, the annual deviation represents the number of active offenders entering the population (and thus, roughly, the number of crimes they commit). A high deviation means a higher-than-average number of offenders entered the population; a low deviation means fewer than expected. The "drift" term, like the slope of a trend line, represents the expected change in the population each year. Because most criminals stay in the criminal population for six or seven years (Shinnar and Shinnar 1975; Blumstein, Cohen, and Hsieh 1982), we can reasonably expect that deviation to affect the population and the crime rate for the foreseeable future. The model applies even more clearly to the prison population. Although most prisoners cycle through within a year or two, most prison beds last fifty years or more. Given that the average American prison runs 14–25 percent over rated capacity (Greenfeld, Beck, and Gilliard 1996), it is fairly clear that resource constraints drive prison populations far more than individual sentences. Simply put, if we overbuild our prison system, we are stuck filling needless beds for the next fifty years or so.

There are two practical benefits of differencing. First, it reduces the scope for spurious effects. Variables that are associated with crime rates only because they are both caused by the same long-term social forces are less likely to improve our predictions of crime rates. Variables that are real causes but are also correlated with long-term forces will continue to improve our predictions but only by an amount consistent with their real contribution. Second, differencing eliminates one class of predictor variables that, while hardly spurious, are relatively unimportant for our purposes—the long-term social forces themselves.

In effect, modeling the trend is like changing the focus of a camera. Differencing focuses our attention on short-term, annual changes; it shifts our attention away from long-term trends that may take decades. In the raw, untransformed series, the most effective predictors would be those that can explain why crime rates tripled from 1960 to 1980; in the differenced series, the most effective predictors would explain why the crime rate dropped 5 percent in 1972, then increased by 17 percent only two years later. All the data are still there in the background, and long-run forces may still be important predictors. But they will no longer dominate the prediction as they would otherwise have done.

In addition to shifting the focus to the short run, differencing solves some technical problems. A trending variable is, by definition, nonstationary. That is, the expected value of the variable changes over time. Even if the variance around that expected value is constant, the trend means that, over time, the variance of the entire time series will continue to increase without limit. This renders our confidence intervals and hypothesis tests invalid (Davidson and MacKinnon 1993, pp. 669–73). By making the variable stationary, differencing alleviates this problem.

It may also help to solve the related problem of heteroskedasticity—systematic differences in variance for different cases. The problem here is that the variance around our expected value sometimes depends on the value itself. Suppose, for example, that crime rates fluctuate from year to year by as much as 5 percent. Clearly that 5 percent will be a larger number in the early 1980s (when crime was high) than in the late 1950s (when it was still low). This also affects our standard errors; in the context of our problem, heteroskedasticity would cause us to underestimate our standard errors, thus underestimating the spread of our confidence intervals and overstating the significance of hypothesis tests (Kmenta 1972). By taking the logarithm of the series before differencing it, we may ensure that the variance is about the same throughout the length of the time series.

Finally, differencing (or log differencing) ensures that the correlations between this year's crime rate (C_t) and all previous crime rates (the C_{t-k}'s) are not affected by the trend. This makes it easier to compare among the correlations and identify autoregressive effects, as described below.

Cantor and Land (1985) and Devine, Sheley, and Smith (1988) have examined the nationwide crime time series to determine whether differencing is necessary, and if so how it affects the results. Based on time-series graphs, they make a strong case that first-differencing is needed to eliminate trend effects; second- and higher-order differencing is unnecessary; but differencing of logs is needed to make the variance stationary (Devine, Sheley, and Smith 1988, pp. 411–12). Although formal tests exist to determine the appropriateness of differencing, they have not been applied to crime and prison data.[1] Despite the graphical evidence, this would be a prudent act before the field advances much further.

Differencing solves a variety of technical problems but at the cost of distracting us from any long-term effects. Some have speculated that crime and punishment (and potentially other variables) achieve an equilibrium in the long run (Blumstein and Cohen 1973; Marvell and Moody 1994). We can model this equilibrium, while retaining the practical benefits of the short-run differencing model, if a cointegrated model fits the available data (Engle and Granger 1987). A full description of cointegration is beyond the scope of this essay, and it is unclear whether crime rates and prison populations in fact behave as required for this model to be useful (see Marvell and Moody 1994, for a partial test). The key issue for our purposes is that we may be able simultaneously to estimate both the long-run and short-run effects of punishment on crime. In the meantime, use of log-differencing and a focus on short-run effects, combined with dummy variables to represent individual years and states in a panel data set, will reduce the opportunity for left-out variables to bias our results.

III. The Simultaneity Problem

Simply put, the simultaneity problem is this: If prison affects crime, and at the same time crime affects prison, how can we separate the two effects? If we cannot separate them, our results are uninterpretable. Of

---

[1] Marvell and Moody (1994) conduct one such test, the unit-root test, on a linear combination of panel crime and prison data. They find that the combination need not be differenced, but this can occur even if both series are nonstationary and must be differenced (Engle and Granger 1987).

all the statistical issues, this has proved by far the thorniest. Unlike most issues, there is as yet no clear consensus as to the best solution.

One reason this is a hard problem is that the relationships probably work in opposite directions. Theories of incapacitation and deterrence suggest that more prisons reduce crime (i.e., that the relationship between the two variables is negative); at the same time, judges and state legislatures can be expected to respond to increases in crime with increased prison populations (a positive relationship). Unless the two effects can be separated, any attempt to estimate either relationship alone is bound to bring in the effects of the other—thus averaging the two. The net effect may be positive, negative, or zero, depending on which is larger. Whatever the result, it will not generally be useful, or even meaningful.

This problem has been recognized for at least the last twenty-five years, and many attempts have been made to solve it (e.g., Carr-Hill and Stern 1973; Ehrlich 1973). None have been entirely successful. Criminal justice theory and data have thus far proven insufficient to come up with a satisfactory solution to the problem. Moreover, because the exact method used to identify the relationship between crime and punishment can have a big effect on the results, differences in identification are the biggest reason for differences among current estimates.

A. Crime and Punishment Equations

The simplest case of simultaneity leads to a set of equations that predict the values of crime and punishment. Given information on social and environmental factors that cause crime and punishment, these equations provide the expected values of the crime rate and the prison population.

For simplicity, let us consider two equations, one each for crime and prison population. If we wish our specification to include other sanctions, such as the risk of arrest or conviction, it is straightforward to extend the model to include them. Schematically, we can think of the crime equation as

$$C = \alpha_c + \beta_C P + \delta_C X + \epsilon_C, \tag{6}$$

where C denotes the crime rate, P the prison population per capita, X is a vector of control variables, such as unemployment rates and the proportion of the population that is in a high-risk age category, and ϵ_C is a random error term. We expect that β_C, the coefficient on P, will be negative. That is, all else equal, an increase in punishment should create incapacitative and deterrence effects that reduce the crime rate. Although this equation has been written in linear form, the best functional form may of course be considerably more complex.

The punishment equation is similar:

$$P = \alpha_P + \beta_P C + \delta_P X + \epsilon_P, \tag{7}$$

where again C and P are crime and punishment, X is a vector of control variables and ϵ_P is a random error term. In this equation, we expect that β_P will be positive. An increase in crime will create pressures on the prison system to run above capacity, and also on the public to increase capacity to deal with the growing problem. A reduction in crime will ease the pressure on both fronts. Because capacity may create its own demand (if we build it, they will come), the curve may be more responsive for increases than for decreases. Nevertheless, the level of punishment should respond to both increases and decreases in crime rates.

Since crime and punishment affect one another over time, they will not generally be in equilibrium. That is, if the value of C is too high (somehow defined), it will create pressure on P to increase, which will tend to reduce the value of C, which will reduce the pressure on P, and so on. This sorting out of effects and countereffects may take so long that we never see the equilibrium values. But, if we know equations (6) and (7), the so-called structural equations, we can identify the one value each of C and P that will not cause the other to respond. To find these equilibrium values, we solve the two equations simultaneously and find the reduced-form equations

$$C = a_C + d_C X + e_C$$

and

$$P = a_P + d_P X + e_P. \tag{8}$$

Note that P no longer appears in the crime equation and vice versa.

A graphical explanation is given in figure 1. The negative-sloping crime equation and the positive-sloping punishment equation meet at point A. At this short-run equilibrium, C_0 crimes will be committed and P_0 offenders will be imprisoned. The graph is similar to the supply and demand graphs of basic microeconomics, and the interpretation is similar, too. The crime equation corresponds to the demand for incarceration, and the punishment equation is the supply of it. The market will clear at point A.

The crime and punishment equations describe only those effects

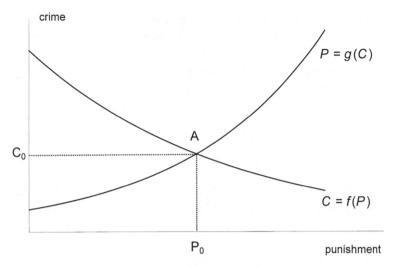

FIG. 1.—Equilibrium in the market for incarceration. Source: all figures are based on my calculations.

that are internal to the system, or endogenous. That is, they show how each variable responds to changes in the other. Other, so-called exogenous, effects are due to changes outside this two-variable system. For example, the Baby Boomers may finally have grown out of their high-crime years, leading to a reduction in the crime rate; the courts may impose restrictions on the prison system to solve an overcrowding problem. These exogenous effects—changes in the X variables in equations (6) and (7)—shift the crime and punishment curves, while keeping their basic downward- and upward-sloping shape.

Thus, for example, the Baby Boomers' coming of age will have several effects. It will shift the crime curve downward, from CC_0 to CC_1; this will cause the intersection of crime and punishment to move from point A to point B; at point B, society will enjoy both a lower crime rate, C_1, and a lower prison population, P_1. The last effect is not obvious at first glance and deserves some explanation. The lower crime rate is due to a reduction in the number of motivated offenders; many former offenders will have "aged out" of the criminal population. The lower prison population is the flip side of the prison system's response to increasing crime rates. During periods of high pressure, prisons will run over capacity to keep up with demand; when the pressure abates, however, prisons return to capacity and the number of prisoners declines.

Conceptually, then, we must separate the effect of crime on punishment from the effect of punishment on crime. Clearly, it will not be enough simply to estimate the two equations separately. As figure 2 shows, both curves are probably changing constantly, shifting outward and inward as social, economic, and political factors affect the number and motivation of offenders, prison capacities and the motivation of the criminal justice system to use them, and so on. Such results may tell us something useful about the effects of exogenous variables on C and P, but they do not necessarily tell us anything about the endogenous effects. Any number of possible relationships between crime and punishment could account for these results. If we were naively to run a regression without doing anything further, we may well find (incorrectly) that there is no relationship between crime and punishment at all.

This problem can be avoided entirely if it can be shown that crime and punishment do not affect one another simultaneously. For example, if punishment affected crime immediately, but crime only affected punishment one or more years into the future, then the current value of C would not appear in the punishment equation at all. Empirical methods that clarify the direction and timing of these causal links have been applied to the crime and punishment problem over the past ten years.

B. Avoiding the Problem: Clarifying Causality

The principal argument for using time-series data in any statistical problem is that it allows us to test not just for association, but for causality. This cannot be "causality" in the dictionary sense, of course. A mere statistical manipulation cannot, by itself, test the real processes by which one event "causes" another. But we can determine whether the sequence of events is consistent with such causal relationships or not. Because the method commonly used for testing this sequence of events was developed by Granger (1969), causality in the statistical sense is sometimes called "Granger causality." The method, naturally enough, is called the Granger test.

The Granger test is based on the commonsense observation that if X causes Y, then X must happen first. If previous values of X are helpful in predicting Y, but previous values of Y are not helpful in predicting X, we can be sure the causal chain works in only one direction. If true, this would eliminate the need for simultaneous equations, saving us no end of trouble.

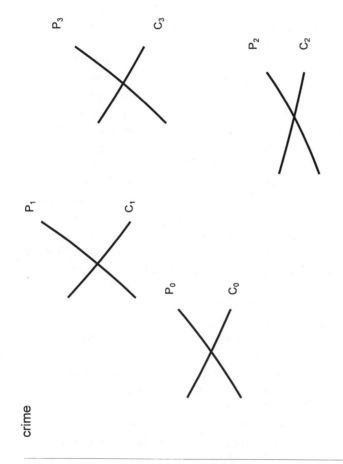

crime

punishment

P_3

C_3

P_2

C_2

P_1

C_1

P_0

C_0

FIG. 2.—Equilibrium conditions are shifting constantly

In this context, the Granger test might work as follows. First, regress crime on past or "lag" values of punishment, current values, and future or "lead" values. Now examine the coefficients on the lag and lead variables. If punishment causes crime (but not the other way around), then the lag and current coefficients should be significant, but not the lead coefficients. If crime causes punishment (and not the reverse), the opposite should be true: current and future values of punishment should be associated with crime rates, not past values. If each causes the other, significant coefficients should be found for past, current, and future values. Rather than examine each coefficient separately, it is customary to conduct an F-test of all past coefficients and another of all future coefficients and make a blanket decision (Bishop 1979).

Because the Granger test is explicitly a test of causality, it is critical that exogenous variables be somehow controlled for. As usual, more complex solutions probably provide better results. For example, Maddala (1988) recommends "prewhitening" each series by conducting the standard Box-Jenkins identification procedure and explicitly accounting for integration, autoregression, and moving average effects. The most important exogenous variables can be controlled for, as well. Nevertheless, most analysts appear to have concluded that simple controls are sufficient to identify the direction of causality correctly. As described above, a bare minimum set of controls includes differencing both variables (to eliminate linear trends) and controlling for the lagged dependent variable (to reduce autoregressive effects). If the level of one or both variables is increasing over time (as it generally is for both crime and prison population), log differences will help to stabilize the variance and ensure that significance tests are unbiased. Although this is not a perfect solution, it is probably sufficient to clarify the general direction of causality.

Several researchers have conducted a Granger test (or something very much like one) as the first step toward estimating a system of simultaneous equations. Their results are summarized in table 1. Although similar methods and data sets were used in each study, the differences may well have affected the final results. To see why, let us consider these findings in more detail.

Bowker (1981) conducted what amounts to a quick and dirty Granger test on the nationwide time series for 1941–78. No attempt was made to control for exogenous variables or long-term trends, either explicitly, through differencing, or through use of lagged dependent variables. The series are in raw (unlogged) form, very likely creat-

TABLE 1

Summary of Granter Test Results

	Bowker 1	Bowker 2	McGuire	Cappell	Marvell
Data used:					
Cross section	National	National	National	National	State panel
Time period	1941–57	1958–78	1960–79	1933–85	1971–89
Controls used:					
ARMA	...	...	yes	yes	yes
Differencing	...	...	yes	yes	yes
Logs	...	...	yes	...	yes
n lags tested:	3	3	2	5	2
Max effect of:					
P on C	+.43*	−.47*	−.540	−.435*	−.080*
C on P	−.57*	+.25	+.080*	+.259*	+.068
Simultaneous	−.08*	+.13*	...	−.187*	...

SOURCES.—Bowker 1981; McGuire and Sheehan 1983; Cappell and Sykes 1991; Marvell and Moody 1994.

* $p < .05$.

ing a serious problem of heteroskedasticity. In addition, only zero-order cross-correlations were calculated. That is, Bowker considered the correlation of C_t and $P_t − 3$, C_t and $P_t − 2$, and so on. Because each correlation was calculated separately, none of them take the others into account. Thus none of the correlations are independent of any of the others, making inference difficult.

The results are inconsistent, at best. For the later and more persuasive part of the series (1958–78), the correlations behaved more or less as expected. Prison populations were negatively associated with subsequent crime rates; crime rates were positively associated with subsequent prison populations. The effects were quite large and, despite the short length of the series, statistically significant. So this appears to confirm the hypothesis of simultaneity.

This confirmation is exceptionally fragile, however, as suggested by the results from the early part of the series (1941–57). During this period, the direction of the relationships appears to be reversed. More prisons led to more crime, not less; in response to higher crime rates, the states appeared to reduce prison populations. As Bowker explains, "The confusion in the lag correlations may be explained if it can be shown that imprisonment and crime respond simultaneously to shifts in differing but overlapping sets of causal variables. . . . Statistically significant correlations between imprisonment and crime are likely to

TABLE 2

Controls Improve Interpretability of Granger Test Results

Incarceration Rate	Crime Rate	Controls Used			
		None	Differences	Log Differences	Lagged Dependent Variable
$t - 3$	t	+.43	−.32	−.30	−.28
$t - 2$	t	+.23	−.07	−.10	−.13
$t - 1$	t	−.06	+.09	+.02	−.03
t	t	−.08	+.37	+.35	+.24
t	$t - 1$	−.52	+.45	+.48	+.29
t	$t - 2$	−.57	+.12	+.17	−.22
t	$t - 3$	−.44	−.08	−.07	−.22

SOURCES.—Bureau of Justice Statistics 1982; Federal Bureau of Investigation (various years); my calculations.

be spurious" (Bowker 1981, pp. 210–11). Unless the exogenous variables can be controlled for, then, these results are basically worthless.[2]

Table 2 shows what happens as each of the usual controls is applied to these otherwise-anomalous data. Differencing both variables changes the direction of the relationships. Now more crime leads to more prison, and more prison leads to less crime, as ˜expected. Taking logs has little effect on the direction and size of each correlation, although it improves our confidence that statistical significance tests apply. Controlling for autoregressive effects shifts all correlations downward, suggesting that they were all biased high before. The correlations obtained after using all controls (the right-most column in table 2) are both very different from the original correlations (the left-most column) and quite consistent with expectations. It is uncertain whether these controls are sufficient to guarantee unbiased results, but we can be sure that failure to use these controls will guarantee bias. Fortunately, other analysts who have applied a Granger test have used most of these controls.

[2] The most important exogenous variable affecting Bowker's (1981) results is World War II, which caused a sharp drop in both prison populations and crime rates as former offenders joined the war effort. After 1945, both crime and prison population increase steadily until 1957. The importance of this long-term trend is suggested by the correlation between the number (not rate) of reported crimes and prison inmates: +.714. The correlation between the rates is close to zero primarily because the denominator of both rates—the population—increased even faster than the number of crimes and prisoners after the war. Virtually all of the population increase was due to an increased birth rate, and the crime and incarceration rates per adult increased steadily throughout the period.

McGuire and Sheehan (1983) make essentially the same corrections to the 1960–79 data as were made above to the 1941–57 data. To test the importance of differences, logs, and lags, they estimate correlations in a variety of ways. The results are similar no matter how they whiten the two series. Crime rates have a positive effect on subsequent punishment, but punishment has a negative effect on subsequent crime. Despite small sample sizes, most results are significant at the .10 level.

Cappell and Sykes (1991) extended the results to include six different crime types, using the full Box-Jenkins tool kit to "prewhiten" the nationwide data from 1933–85. None of the results are as noteworthy as the general pattern. Of thirty correlations between prison and subsequent crime (six crime types × five lags), twenty-two were negative and three were statistically significant. Of thirty correlations between crime and subsequent prison, twenty-five were positive and two statistically significant. Of six correlations between simultaneous prison and crime, five were negative, two were significant, but all were fairly weak. As mentioned above, the correlations for each lag term are not independent, so a significance test of the pattern would be inappropriate. Still, especially in the context of the other studies, the findings are clear. For the nation as a whole, crime and punishment are both cause and effect. There is no way to avoid the simultaneity problem without biasing the results.

Although this does not resolve the issue for panel data, it creates a strong presumption favoring similar results. If a Granger test of panel data shows no long-term trends and short-term carryover effects, it is at least reasonable to ask why. At least two explanations are possible. First, it may be that the nationwide results simply do not apply to the panel. For example, these results may be driven by unmeasured exogenous variables that, through sheer chance, are highly correlated with nationwide changes in crime rates or prison populations. Since the coincidence is unlikely to be repeated in all fifty states, a panel study may produce different results. Second, the panel results may be wrong. State data may be less reliable than nationwide figures for which anomalies will come out in the wash; this would bias all panel correlations toward zero. Differences among states in timing and size of effects may make the panel results more difficult to interpret than the national results.

Let us consider each of these explanations in light of Marvell and Moody's (1994) analysis of 1971–89 state panel data. Like Cappell and Sykes, they prewhitened each series by taking first differences; in addi-

TABLE 3

Improved Granger Analysis Is Still Inconclusive

	Coefficient	Standard Error	90% Confidence Interval	
			Minimum	Maximum
Effects on P_t:				
C_{t-1}	+.068	.061	−.032	+.168
C_{t-2}	+.057	.059	−.041	+.155
Effects on C_t:				
P_{t-1}	−.080	.019	−.049	−.111
P_{t-2}	+.016	.018	−.014	.046

SOURCE.—Marvell and Moody 1994, p. 129.

tion, Marvell and Moody (1994) controlled for the lagged dependent variable, examined all lags simultaneously, and (through perhaps an excess of caution) dealt with heteroskedasticity by both weighting cases and taking logs. They found that prison had a negative and significant effect on the next year's crime rate; this effect did not extend beyond one year but persisted in the face of unweighted cases, linear differences, no differences, and up to four lag terms. Further, crime had a positive but generally insignificant effect on subsequent prison. The effect of a one-year lag was statistically significant when the differences were not logged, the cases not weighted, and three lags were used (but not two or four). Marvell and Moody (1994) explain this as the result of outliers (reduced in importance in the logged difference version) and a few, small states (reduced in importance when cases are weighted). They conclude that, because the logged, weighted version is more accurate, the effect of crime on punishment is sufficiently trivial that a simultaneous equations approach is unnecessary (Marvell and Moody 1994, pp. 129–30).[3]

A closer look at this conclusion reveals that it is dangerous. Marvell and Moody base their claim on the statistical significance of four principal coefficients. The coefficients, their standard errors, and 90 percent confidence intervals are shown in table 3. Of these results, only the coefficient on P_{t-1} is statistically significant; the standard error is sufficiently small that we also can be fairly sure as to its value. The coefficients on C_{t-1} and C_{t-2} are not statistically discernible from zero;

[3] An analysis of the effects of seven different crime types on the prison population presents a consistent picture. Of fourteen coefficients of C_{t-1} and C_{t-2} on P_t, thirteen are positive. $\chi^2 = 10.286$, $p = .001$.

however, they may conceivably be two or three times as large in absolute value as the P_{t-1} coefficient.

Just because we cannot be certain (with 95 percent confidence) that an effect is nonzero does not mean that we can be certain it is irrelevant for policy. On the contrary, in this case it is entirely possible that crime has a larger effect on punishment than punishment does on crime. Perhaps more important, even a modest relationship between crime and subsequent punishment may be policy relevant. Suppose the crime and punishment equations are as given in (6) and (7), above. Suppose further that ordinary least squares (OLS) is used to estimate the crime equation,

$$C = a + bP + cX + e,\tag{9}$$

where b is an estimate of β, the true coefficient of P on C. Then it is not (too) difficult to show that, under fairly general conditions,

$$b = \beta_C + (1 - \beta_C\beta_P)\,[\beta_P/(\beta_P^2 + \rho)],\tag{10}$$

where β_P is the (true) effect of crime on punishment and

$$\rho = \text{variance }(\epsilon_C)/\text{variance }(\epsilon_P),\tag{11}$$

the ratio of the error variance of the crime equation to that of the punishment equation.[4] Note, incidentally, that this ensures that any ordinary least squares estimate of β_C will be an overestimate: $\beta_C < 0$, but $\beta_P > 0$ and ρ must be greater than zero (since variances are always positive); thus both the first term and the second term of the estimation error are positive, and $b > \beta$.

Now suppose that $\beta_C = -0.3$, $\beta_P = +0.1$, and $\rho = 2.0$.[5] Then from equation (10),

$$b = -0.3 + (1 - -0.03)[.10/(2.01)]$$
$$= -0.249,$$

---

[4] The critical assumptions are that C_t and P_t are stationary variables (thus have a finite variance as the sample size approaches infinity) and that covariance $(\epsilon_{Ct}, \epsilon_{Pt}) = 0$ (i.e., that the random errors in the two equations for any given time, t, are uncorrelated). The first assumption is reasonable if C and P are differenced, extremely unreasonable if not. The second assumption is reasonable if the crime and punishment equations both account for autoregressive effects, unreasonable if not. Marvell and Moody (1994), from whom the data used in the text were taken, differenced their variables and accounted for autoregressive effects.

[5] If one is willing to assume that crime and punishment will both be about equally difficult to predict, a rough-cut estimate of ρ can be obtained by estimating the ratio of the variance of prewhitened crime rates to prewhitened punishment rates. For the nationwide data, the ratio is approximately 2.33.

or about −0.5. An elasticity of −0.3 produces a benefit-cost ratio of about 1.15, barely sufficient to justify further prison construction in the average state (Levitt 1996). An elasticity of −0.25 would produce a benefit-cost ratio less than 1.0, and the cost-effectiveness of building another prison bed is questionable, at best. Thus failing to estimate even a minimal relationship between crime and subsequent punishment may bias the effect of punishment on subsequent crime by enough to change the policy implications.

The most reasonable conclusion is that analysts should by all means estimate both the crime and the punishment equation. This is in large part because the United States has built prison beds to very roughly that point where they are no longer cost-effective; small changes can determine whether the benefit-cost ratio is in fact greater than or less than one. Biased coefficients—especially when the biases are of known direction and predictable size—are the primary concern here. Even a very rough estimate will help us to identify β_C, β_P, and ρ, and thus potential, unmeasured bias.

C. Solving the Problem: Identification

All evidence suggests that the simultaneity problem cannot be avoided without biasing the results and rendering the policy implications suspect. Thus we have no choice but to find some way to separate the crime and punishment equations.

Exogenous variables are the key. If we knew there were some variables that affected the punishment rate but not the crime rate, we could be sure that changes in these variables would shift the punishment curve inward or outward but not shift the crime curve at all. Thus changes in these variables would trace out values along a single example of the crime curve, allowing us to estimate the slope of this curve (fig. 3). Similarly, if there were some variables that we knew affected the crime rate but not the punishment rate, any changes in these variables would trace out values along the punishment curve. More generally, the key to being able to estimate or identify an equation in a simultaneous system is to find one or more variables that we can exclude from it, but include in other equations in the system.

The effectiveness of these variables, called instrumental variables or simply instruments, depends on two factors. First, the variables must be good predictors for the equation in which they are included. Consider figure 3: if we are to trace out the crime equation by including a variable in the punishment equation, that variable will be most useful

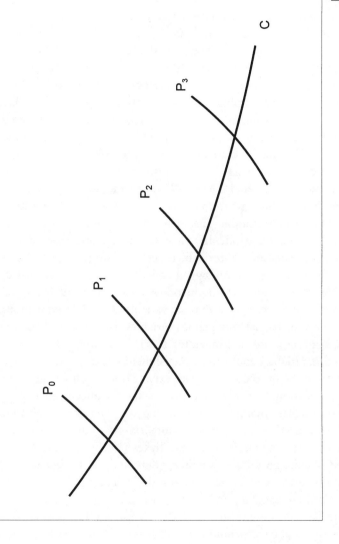

crime

punishment

FIG. 3.—Identification requires changes in omitted variables

if it shifts the punishment equation in and out considerably. If the shift is small, there will be much uncertainty as to the proper slope of the crime equation. All else equal, the more instruments, the better, since they will shift punishment in and out by a wider margin and further narrow our uncertainty as to the crime equation.

The second factor is even more important. Even mildly effective predictors of punishment will help us trace out the crime curve, if not very well. It is imperative, however, that we are correct in excluding them from the crime equation. If an instrument is excluded from an equation but should really have been included, this means that it is really affecting both variables. As our inappropriate instrument changes, we are not really using one curve to trace out the other but are changing both concurrently. This leaves us with the uninterpretable mess of figure 2 and results in biased estimates of the βs.

The practical problem is finding instruments that are even theoretically correct. Fisher and Nagin (1978) provide several examples of inappropriate instruments from the early literature. To demonstrate the difficulties, let us examine one. Avio and Clarke (1978) used the following instruments to identify their crime equation: population density, total population, motor vehicle registration per capita lagged one period, police expenditures lagged one period, and crimes against persons lagged one period. As in the other studies of the 1970s, the instruments are all either socioeconomic variables (density, population, cars per person) or lagged endogenous variables (last year's police expenditures, last year's violent crime rate). It is hard to understand how socioeconomic variables could affect punishment but not crime; in fact, it is not at all difficult to come up with explanations for how and why density, population, and cars per person should affect the crime rate. These variables, then, should be included in the crime equation and cannot be used as instruments. More recent studies rely on similar variables; for example, Cappell and Sykes (1991) used the proportion of the population on active military duty and the proportion of state prisoners discharged. Again, it is not difficult to think of a direct link between these variables and crime rates.

The lagged endogenous variables fail for another reason. Because this year's police expenditures and crime rate are almost certainly highly correlated with last year's, excluding the lagged values from the crime equation (but including them elsewhere) is not really excluding these variables at all. Due to the high correlation, the effect of changes in these variables is liable to linger from year to year. As described above, procedures exist for taking this year-to-year or serial correlation into account in a time-series or panel data set (Kennedy 1992, pp. 119–24). But if this correlation is not somehow accounted for (as it cannot be in a cross-sectional data set), the lagged endogenous variables should not be used as instruments.

If socioeconomic variables and lagged endogenous variables are both problematic, what is left? Possibly nothing. As Fisher and Nagin (1978, pp. 396–97) conclude, after an exhaustive search, "Our conclusions with regard to the feasibility of identification, while not wholly negative, are certainly soberly cautious. In particular, it appears very doubtful that work using only aggregate cross-sectional data can ever succeed in identifying and consistently estimating the deterrent effect of punishment on crime. . . . Analysis using aggregate non-experimental data must have a time-series component in the data (i.e., pure time-series or a time-series, cross-section), and the estimation procedures must account for the possibility of serial correlation." It is no coincidence that all of the recent empirical studies of incapacitation and deterrence use time-series or panel designs. Even so, the lagged endogenous variables with which we are left are only useful as instruments if we succeed in solving the serial correlation problem.

Note, incidentally, that it is not much easier to find appropriate instruments for the punishment equation. This is because many of the same socioeconomic characteristics that affect the crime rate may also affect the scale of punishment. For example, Cappell and Sykes (1991) could find no better instrument for the punishment equation than the previous year's unemployment rates, even though the current year's unemployment rates were included in the equation, previous research had established a clear link between unemployment and subsequent prison populations (e.g., Greenberg 1977; Yeager 1979), and the correlation between previous year's unemployment and current prison population was positive, as expected (Cappell and Sykes 1991, p. 174). The rest of their analysis is quite persuasive, suggesting that the authors tried, and failed, to find a better instrument.

If appropriate instruments can be identified, a variety of methods can be used to estimate the equations themselves. Levitt (1996) used a simple method called instrumental variable estimation to estimate the crime equation; such a method is appropriate if only one of the equations in a multiple-equation system must be measured. If both the crime and punishment equations are important, a straightforward extension of instrumental variable estimation, called two-stage least squares, can be used (Cappell and Sykes 1991). Other methods, including three-stage least squares and maximum likelihood approaches, may provide somewhat more precise results if the necessary assumptions can be met (Kennedy 1992).

Nevertheless, the most complex methods are no better than available data. If we cannot honestly exclude any variables from the crime equation, we will be unable to identify the effect of punishment on crime at all. If the variables we can exclude are not competent predictors of punishment, we may not be able to narrow the range of possible effects by enough to matter. Such problems provide the clearest challenges to any analysis of the effects of imprisonment on crime.

IV. Differences among States

Without exception, studies of the effectiveness of prison, even those relying on state panel data, have produced estimates that approximate a national average. This simplifies the analysis considerably; as detailed above, the basic estimation issues are sufficiently detailed that simplicity is an important virtue. Nevertheless, prison construction and use decisions are not made at the national level but at the state level. If states differ in their use of imprisonment, our policy implications are incomplete.

The simplest differences are those of scale. Some states imprison a much greater percentage of their citizens than do others. This means that the policy implications may well differ among states. Even if it is appropriate to build more prisons nationwide, for example, it may not be appropriate for the most punitive states to do so. By the same token, even if the average effects of a prison increase are insufficient to produce cost-beneficial crime reductions, it may still be cost-effective for the least punitive states to increase capacity.

A subtler set of differences surround the use of prisons. Some states focus scarce prison resources on the most violent offenders; others incarcerate many offenders convicted only of drug and property crimes. Some states have implemented policies to focus special attention on repeat offenders ("three strikes, you're out" laws) or on especially frequent offenders (selective incapacitation). Some states give long sentences to a few (focusing presumably on desert and incapacitation at the expense of deterrence), while others give shorter sentences to many offenders (maximizing deterrence at the expense of incapacitation). It is very likely that some of these options yield better results than others.

If these differences can be sorted out, empirical research could be far more helpful than simply justifying a build/not build decision.

A. Cost-Effectiveness and the Scale of Imprisonment

When analyzing crime and punishment data the most convenient result is often the elasticity. This is especially true if the regression equation has a constant elasticity functional form. That is, if we are willing to believe that the proper relationship between crime and punishment is a simple power function,

$$C = \alpha P^\beta Z^\delta \epsilon, \qquad (12)$$

it is not hard to show that the elasticity of crime with respect to punishment is β, for all values of C and P. By taking logs of both sides, the constant elasticity form reduces to

$$\log C = \log \alpha + \beta \log P + \delta \log Z + \log \epsilon, \qquad (13)$$

the standard linear form. For obvious reasons, this is sometimes called the "log-log" functional form. It can be shown that the log-log is the only form that provides a constant elasticity (Dougherty 1992, p. 124).

In addition to providing an elasticity and associated confidence interval that can be read right off the computer printout, the constant elasticity form provides other benefits. It allows for diminishing marginal returns, which is appropriate in this context. If the scale of the dependent variable varies considerably over time or among states, as crime rates certainly do, the logarithm is liable to have fewer outliers than the raw values. This makes estimates of β and its confidence interval more reliable (Dougherty 1992, pp. 213–14). For many years, the constant elasticity form was the preferred form for mapping economic production functions (Cobb and Douglas 1928; Samuelson 1979). Although economists have largely abandoned it for less restrictive functional forms (Christensen, Jorgenson, and Lau 1971; Diewert 1971), it remains in wide use elsewhere in the social sciences.

Convenient though it may be, if our concern is cost-effectiveness, the elasticity is only an interim calculation. We must next convert the elasticity to λ_M, the offense rate (lambda) of the marginal offender—the last offender through the door before the prison system runs out of room. By costing out the social damage done by the marginal offender per year, and comparing it to the costs of preventing this damage by incarcerating or deterring this offender, we can determine whether it is cost-effective to build the next prison bed.

It is easy to calculate λ_M. The elasticity, β, is defined as the proportionate change in reported crime rate associated with a 1 percent change in prison population. That is,

$$\beta = (\Delta C/C)/(\Delta P/P), \qquad (14)$$

where C and P refer to reported crime rate and prisoners per capita, as usual. Multiplying both sides by C/P yields

$$\beta C/P = \Delta C/\Delta P, \qquad (15)$$

where the right-hand side is now the change in the crimes per capita divided by the change in prisons per capita. The per capita terms cancel, so the right-hand side represents the change in the number of reported crimes divided by the change in the number of prisoners. Since we are interested in the effect of just one more prisoner, we set $\Delta P = 1$. Since we are interested in all crimes, both reported and not, we can divide both sides by r, the average reporting rate, to get the total number of crimes committed by the marginal prisoner—λ_M. That is,

$$\Delta C/r = (\beta/r) \times (C/P) = \lambda_M. \qquad (16)$$

The effect of scale is now clear. If β were in fact the same for all states, then states with high crime rates and low incarceration rates (i.e., high values of C/P) would have high values of λ_M, while low-crime/high-incarceration states would have low values. This is reasonable enough on its face; states that incarcerate many of its citizens are digging deeper into the pool of offenders than states that only incarcerate a few, and the marginal offender is less likely to be frequent and dangerous.

Nevertheless, it is still likely that elasticities will vary from state to state and over time. In particular, we can expect that elasticities will respond to increases in the prison population. Consider, for example, what is known about incapacitation. I estimated a national average production function for incapacitation, under the (admittedly questionable) assumption that deterrence effects were negligible (Spelman 1994). Because the most frequent offenders are most likely to be incarcerated, due to ordinary operation of the criminal justice system, this function strongly resembles the Lorenz curve of offense rates among offenders. The single best-fitting function is shown as the solid curve in figure 4. Note that the elasticity increases as the scale of punishment (here measured in terms of the percentage of active offenders behind bars) increases. That is, the larger a state's jail and prison system is, the higher the predicted elasticity.

Underlying these variations in elasticity is the assumption that the number of active offenders and the frequency with which each commits crime are both fixed in the short run. Thus if all imprisoned offenders were released simultaneously, the crime rate would only increase by the (fixed) offense rates of these individuals. This apparent reduction in future punishment neither would entice new individuals to begin committing crime nor would it persuade established offenders to commit crimes more often (at least not right away). Similarly, if prison capacities were somehow increased to include all active offenders, no new offenders would arise to take their place and the crime rate would drop to zero. Thus the incapacitation function has "corners," exhibiting elasticities that are very high (in the southeast corner of fig. 4) and very low (in the northwest corner).

These differences in elasticity are substantial, even near the center of the function. For a jail and prison system operating at the national average, the pure incapacitation model predicts that about 8.5 percent of active offenders would be incarcerated at any given time, reducing the crime rate by about 20 percent (Spelman 1994, pp. 217–18); the elasticity is −0.16. If this state were to double its jail and prison capacity, incarcerating 17 percent of active offenders, the elasticity would be −0.35. However, if the same state were to cut its jail and prison capacity in half, the elasticity would decrease to −0.08.

Such changes are well within the relevant range. Consider first nationwide changes over time. The average state doubled its prison population between 1975 and 1985 and doubled its population again between 1985 and 1995. These increases were partly in response to increases in the offending population, so the percent of active offenders living in jails and prisons did not double twice. But it very likely doubled once, and the incapacitation production function suggests that a doubling in the prison population roughly corresponds to a doubling in the elasticity.

Differences among states are likely to have the same effect. A rough estimate of the percentage of all active offenders who are in jails and prisons is given by the ratio of the jail and prison population to the number of Index Crimes reported each year. Lenient states (at least so far as imprisonment is concerned) will tend to have lower ratios,

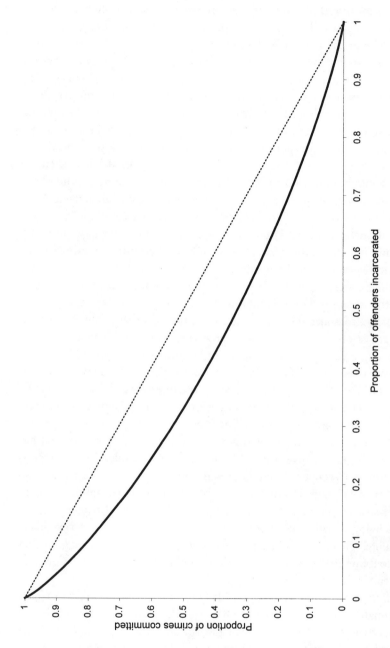

Proportion of offenders incarcerated

Proportion of crimes committed

Fig. 4.—Most reasonable estimate of the incapacitation curve

tougher states higher ratios.[6] The national average is 0.03 inmates per reported crime. The most lenient states (Hawaii and Minnesota) eke out about 0.015 inmates per crime, about half the national average. The toughest states (District of Columbia, Kentucky, and Virginia) rack up 0.05–0.06, about twice the national average. All else equal, we can expect the District of Columbia to put about four times as many of its active offenders in jail or prison than Minnesota; thus the crime elasticity for the District of Columbia should be very roughly four times that of Minnesota. We may reasonably conclude that the assumption of a constant elasticity among states does not bear out, either.

We do not know enough about how deterrence works to predict the functional form of the deterrence production function, and there is no a priori reason to believe it should not display a constant elasticity. Nevertheless, incapacitation will dominate in the short term and play a large role in defining the long-term elasticity. It certainly seems prudent to adopt a form that allows elasticities to vary, both over time and among states.

The simplest way to allow the elasticity to vary builds on the constant elasticity model. It is not hard to show that the elasticity is equal to

$$(\Delta C/C)/(\Delta P/P) = dC^*/dP^*, \tag{17}$$

where $C^* = \log C$ and $P^* = \log P$. In the case of the constant elasticity model, this derivative is identical to the coefficient on P^*—a constant. Now suppose we add an interaction term to the equation. For example,

$$C^* = \alpha + \beta P^* + \gamma P^{*2}. \tag{18}$$

The elasticity is again the derivative; for this somewhat more complicated function,

$$\eta = \beta + 2\gamma P^* = \beta + 2\gamma \log P. \tag{19}$$

If $\gamma > 0$, the elasticity will increase as the log of the incarceration rate. Because the elasticity would be a decreasing function for $\gamma < 0$, this model would be appropriate for both the crime and punishment equa-

---

[6] The ratios will obviously be affected by the length of typical jail or prison sentences; states that mete out many long sentences will probably incarcerate a fair number of older offenders who would not return to crime were they let back on the street. Still, each state's ratio should be roughly proportionate to the percentage of active offenders it puts behind bars.

tions. And elasticity need not depend on the logarithm of P; in practice, a variety of functional forms could be considered simply by trying out several interaction terms.

As it happens, equation (18) fits the incapacitation function much better than the constant elasticity form. For this test case, $R^2 = 0.52$ for the log-log form, but $R^2 = 0.93$ for the interaction equation. More important for our purposes, the elasticity of the incapacitation function had a zero correlation with the constant, log-log elasticity (by definition), but a correlation of 0.93 with the interaction-based elasticity. If it is true that the short-run effects of punishment on crime are mostly incapacitative, the interaction form would appear to be a much better form for identifying these effects accurately.

Does any of this matter? The incapacitation analysis does not take deterrence into account; deterrence could exacerbate or alleviate any differences created by incapacitation effects. Without year-by-year and state-by-state estimates, it is difficult to tell whether any of this is borne out in reality. Nevertheless, it only makes sense that prison expansion should have different effects in Minnesota than in the District of Columbia. We will never know for sure unless we look.

B. Variation in the Use of Prisons

Scale may not be the only, or even the most, important difference among the states. The crime-control effectiveness of each prison bed may also depend on who the state puts in it and for how long.

The simplest distinction is between deterrent and incapacitative strategies. Theory and evidence from cognitive psychology suggest that punishment deters best when it is fast and certain and that the severity of the punishment is relatively unimportant. One explanation for this is diminishing marginal returns: a two-year prison term is worse, but not twice as bad, as a one-year prison term (Kahneman and Tversky 1979). A complementary explanation is based on people's tendency to discount the future: just as next year's dollar is worth less than this year's, so does next year's prison sentence hurt less than this year's (Cook 1980). These expectations were confirmed by the early deterrence literature. As Blumstein, Cohen, and Nagin (1978, p. 22) pointed out, "With few exceptions, the evidence indicates that crime rates are negatively associated with the risks of apprehension, conviction, and imprisonment. The results on the association between crime rate and time served in prison are more equivocal; several analyses have found such an association, but many others have not." Further, the marginal effects of the probability of arrest and incarceration were almost always greater than the marginal effects of the length of the prison sentence (see, e.g., Sjoquist 1973; Vandaele 1973). Thus a state intending to maximize the deterrent effect of prison would probably choose to give relatively short sentences to many offenders, maximizing the probability that each individual would receive some punishment.

An opposite policy can be expected to obtain the maximum incapacitative effect. Since incapacitation works by putting criminals where they cannot get at the rest of us, and since most crimes are committed by a relatively small proportion of offenders, it makes sense to focus scarce prison resources on a few, especially frequent and violent offenders (Greenwood 1982; Zimring and Hawkins 1995). Although statistical means of sorting sheep from goats are not especially accurate, they are considerably more accurate than chance (Gottfredson and Gottfredson 1986). Perhaps more important, much the same effect can be obtained by increasing the sentences for previously convicted offenders (Moore et al. 1984).

States differ considerably in the strategies they pursue. Figure 5 plots the approximate incarceration rate (i.e., the proportion of Index Crimes resulting in incarceration of the offender) against the prison sentence actually served by the median offender. Some states, such as Hawaii, New York, Massachusetts, and Wisconsin, incarcerate a small proportion of their offenders but hold them for long terms—a de facto incapacitation strategy. Other states, such as Alabama, Georgia, Mississippi, and North Carolina, incarcerate more offenders for shorter terms—a deterrence strategy. If one of these strategies is more effective than the other, this should be reflected in each state's elasticity and marginal offense rate. Thus we may exploit differences among states to draw conclusions about the relative effectiveness of each strategy.

Figure 5 captures the variation at one point in time, but each state's strategy is always evolving. For example, the biggest determinant of prison population growth in the 1970s and early 1980s was an increase in imprisonment rates. Increases in reported crime and arrest rates, in drug arrest and imprisonment rates, and in the at-risk population were relatively unimportant; the median sentence actually decreased slightly over the period (Langan 1991; Bogess and Bound 1993). Thus most states were moving toward a deterrence strategy. More recent evidence suggests a shift to incapacitation. By the 1990s, reported crime rates, arrest rates, and incarceration rates for most violent and property crimes were stable or in decline; yet the number of violent and prop-

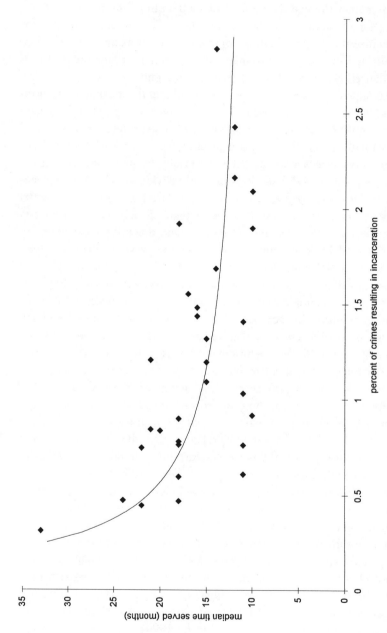

Fig. 5.—Different states pursue different sentencing strategies: incarceration rate by time served, 1981

erty offenders in prison continued to increase due to large increases in time served (Cohen and Canela-Cacho 1994; Blumstein and Beck 1999). This sets up a nifty natural experiment: if the deterrence strategy is more effective, elasticities nationwide should have increased during the 1970s and early 1980s and declined in the 1990s; if the incapacitation strategy is more effective, the opposite should be true. Again, we may use these differences between states and over time to draw conclusions about effectiveness.

States can also choose to pursue another general strategy: to focus on particular types of crime. Nationally, the most obvious such focus has been on drug offenses. Only 1 percent of state prison commitments were for drug offenses in the 1930s, and as late as the mid-1960s the figure was only 4 percent. Since then, the percentage has skyrocketed to 16 percent in the mid-1980s and to 31 percent in the mid-1990s (Langan 1991; Maguire and Pastore 1995). State time-series data on inmate charges are not readily available, but the last published study provides ample clues that at one time they differed considerably (National Criminal Justice Information and Statistics Service 1976).

As figure 6 shows, some states (Massachusetts, Illinois) reserved prisons for violent offenders; over 70 percent of inmates of these states had been convicted of violent crimes. In other states (Washington, Iowa, Vermont, the Dakotas), fewer than 40 percent of all inmates were doing time for violent crimes. These data were collected in 1973, before the war on drugs. Even so, some states were already incarcerating a high percentage of drug offenders. In Connecticut and Indiana, over 30 percent of all inmates were imprisoned for crimes other than violent and property offenses (mostly drug crimes but also including weapons and vice offenses). In Illinois, Minnesota, and South Dakota, the percentage was 6 percent or less.

A state may reasonably decide to mix strategies, using deterrence to deal with some crime problems while using incapacitation on others. For example, it can be argued that deterrence is a more effective strategy for reducing property and drug crimes than violent crimes, because burglars and drug dealers weigh the benefits and costs of their actions more carefully than wife beaters and rapists before choosing a level of criminal activity. (Similar reasoning suggests that incapacitation may be more effective at reducing violent crime rates.) Such theories are speculative; even if they are correct, they may not be borne out in practice. Many offenders commit some combination of violent, property, and drug crimes; the most frequent and dangerous criminals commit

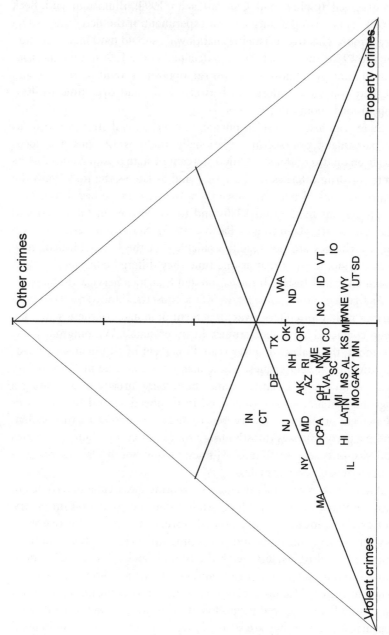

FIG. 6.—States focus prison resources on different crime types

them all (Petersilia, Greenwood, and Lavin 1978; Chaiken and Chaiken 1982). Because many imprisoned drug dealers are also armed robbers and burglars, it is conceivable that the best way to reduce the violent and property crime rates is to increase the sanctions for dealing. (After all, Al Capone was imprisoned for tax evasion.) If, however, most drug dealers are not also violent and property criminals, those states that imprison many drug criminals may be particularly ineffective.

The point is that estimates of the effects of punishment on crime will be more policy relevant if we can get inside the black box and measure differences in the use of prisons. The simplest approach involves adding variables to both the left and right sides of the crime equation. Unfortunately, this is easier said than done.

Suppose we wished to measure the relative success of deterrence and incapacitation strategies. In theory, it is straightforward to separate our punishment variable, P, into two parts: the risks of imprisonment (call it R) and the expected sentence length (S). High coefficients on R and low coefficients on S would suggest that the current trend toward narrowly distributed, relatively long sentences is inappropriate, for example. Unfortunately, this approach fails for the same reason it failed the deterrence researchers of the 1970s. Measurement errors in the number of reported crimes bias the coefficients on R (but not S) to be negative, even in the absence of deterrent effects. In general, there is no way to measure the coefficient on R consistently without knowing the size and shape of these measurement errors.

Another way to get into the black box is to estimate different crime equations for different crime types. For example, Marvell and Moody (1994) and Levitt (1996) both estimated the effect of prison populations separately on homicide, rape, assault, robbery, burglary, larceny, and auto theft. Both used the same independent variable in each equation (P), however, making no attempt to disaggregate prison use and obtain a more policy-relevant result. One reason is that it is difficult to identify the equations in the face of simultaneity. All crime types must affect all sanctions, since an increase in one crime type will require the system to shift resources from the others. Further, all sanctions must affect all crime types, since an increase in punishment for one type of crime may well cause displacement to other crimes that are now less risky. If the number of equations in the system is given by $2k$, where k is the number of crime types, then each equation can only be identified by excluding from it $2k - 1$ variables (one for each of the remaining equations). If we assume that each crime type does not influence the $k - 1$ others,[7] the number of additional restrictions necessary to identify the equations will be equal to $2k - 1 - (k - 1) = k$ (Nagin 1978).

So far, so good. Now the hard part: it is hard to find demographic characteristics that affect prison populations but not crime rates; this leaves aggregate measures of criminal justice inputs, such as gross expenditures and the proportion of prison beds actually in use; there are only two or three of these variables (Fisher and Nagin 1978; Levitt 1996). Thus it is practically impossible to estimate a system with four or more crime types.

As if this were not gloomy enough, note that this assumes only one sanction (the level of imprisonment) is provided for each crime type. The difficulties are compounded if we were to disaggregate the sanction into risks and sentence lengths. Even if we could solve the measurement error problem, we would still need to find $2k$ variables that affected sanction levels but not crime. Hence even a system with two crime types may be beyond our capacity.

Although the identification problem appears nearly insoluble, a simple if prosaic alternative may help advance our understanding. The interaction specification described above allows for varying elasticities due to changes in scale. If elasticities also vary due to differences among states and over time, and if these differences are relatively persistent (in the case of states) and far-reaching (in the case of time), then we may be able to capture much of the variation through a variation of the fixed effects model. Briefly, we include dummy variables to represent changes in the intercept associated with each state and time. This will not by itself capture variations in elasticity, since the formula for elasticity does not include the intercept term. In addition to the intercept term, then, one or two interaction terms must be added to the model: one represents the interaction of the dummy with $\log P$ (and will show up as an intercept in the equation for elasticity); the other represents the interaction of the dummy with $(\log P)^2$ (and will show up as the slope in the elasticity equation). Thus the final specification would be

---

[7] Many offenders commit crimes of several types, and this is especially true of the most frequent and dangerous (Chaiken and Chaiken 1982). Thus many exogenous forces, including changes in prison policy, that affect one crime rate will very likely affect the others. As a result, this assumption is considerably more tenuous than usual. At the same time, it may be practically necessary if the crime equations are to be identified and measured without bias.

$$\log C_{it} = \alpha_{00} + \alpha_{0t}D_{0t} + \alpha_{i0}D_{i0} + \beta_{00}\log P + \beta_{0t}D_{0t}\log P$$
$$+ \beta_{i0}D_{i0}\log P + \gamma_{00}\log P^2 + \gamma_{0t}D_{0t}\log P^2 \qquad (20)$$
$$+ \gamma_{i0}D_{i0}\log P^2 + \delta X,$$

where the D terms are dummy variables associated with each state i and time t, X is a vector of exogenous variables, and δ is a vector of coefficients. The usual series of F-tests would be used to determine whether the interaction terms significantly improve the fit. In the event that one or both sets of interaction terms did, it would be easy to pick out those combinations of state and time where prison expansion was most (and least) effective. Then one could examine the nature of prison use in that state at that time and draw tentative (if biased) conclusions as to effectiveness.

This indirect method of strategy testing is considerably less satisfying than, say, comparing the size of the coefficient on the risks of imprisonment to that on the sentence length. More generally, it is probably impossible to separate incapacitation and deterrent effects using aggregate data. Nevertheless, it eliminates an important source of bias in the crime equation, and that is clearly better than doing nothing. If we allow for differences among states and over time in our crime equation, we must allow for them in our punishment equation as well. Certainly there are good reasons to believe the government response to changes in crime rates should differ among states and over time. One reason is politics. Politically conservative states put more people in prison than politically liberal states (Nagel 1977, pp. 161–63); it is reasonable to expect that conservative states may respond more quickly and severely to an increase in crime rates than liberal states. Another reason is economics. Prisons are a good like any other; it is reasonable to expect that a state will "consume" more of it in good times than in bad; rich states can afford to buy more prisons than poor states.

A third source of differences among states emerges from the strategic choices described above. For example, a wave of property crime may pass over a prison system that focuses virtually all its attention on violent crimes; it will have a large effect on a state that imprisons a large share of its burglars and auto thieves. Similarly, we can expect that states will respond differently to nationwide phenomena such as the Baby Boomers' entry into crime-prone ages in the late 1960s. States that focus on incapacitation may receive little pressure for a few years; it took the boomers a few years to rack up records long enough and violent enough to merit a long prison stay. States that imprison many offenders for short terms may have seen the pressure more or less immediately.

Finally, sentence practices may be inherently more flexible in some states than in others. Indeterminate sentencing statutes and parole and early release guidelines give judges and prison officials broad discretion to fit their sentencing practices to current capacity. States with strict sentencing guidelines may have little choice but to respond, one for one, to any change in the crime rate. The details of the punishment equation are primarily of academic, rather than practical, interest. Nevertheless, there is an important practical reason for considering these differences in the punishment equation. Failure to do so will bias our estimates of the crime equation. For example, suppose an increase in crime leads to an especially large and rapid increase in punishment in the politically conservative southeastern states. If we look for differences among states in the crime equation, but not in the punishment equation, this effect will appear, erroneously, in the crime equation. We may thus mistakenly conclude that an increase in punishment leads to an especially large and rapid increase in crime in the Southeast. We may even tentatively go on to speculate on the counterproductive effects of punitive scale and deterrence strategies, when in fact criminals respond exactly the same way in Mississippi and Alabama as they do everywhere else.

As with the crime equation, the simplest way to incorporate such differences into our punishment equation is to allow the elasticity of punishment response to vary among states and over time. Interactions of state and time dummy variables with the elasticity parameter may be sufficient to capture most of the effect. As with the crime equation, more complex functions may be needed to capture the full effect.

V. Conclusions

The past twenty years have seen considerable improvement in our ability to estimate the effects of prison on crime. Let us conclude by drawing what policy implications we can from the best available estimates, then by considering fruitful avenues for future work.

A. Best Available Estimates

Table 4 summarizes the results of four empirical studies of the relationship between prisons and crime developed over the past decade. Together, these four studies deal with many of the problems associated with earlier estimates. They rely on better data, use more appropriate specifications, and deal with the simultaneity of effects more effectively than the studies of the 1960s and 1970s. They are the best available estimates.

As detailed above, the estimates were derived using similar methods on almost identical data sets. All studies used some form of time series; the most recent used a panel of states. Most studies used several independent variables and the same dependent variable. There is general agreement that the dependent variable should be logged and differenced, that at least some specification search is necessary, that a variety of control variables is needed, and that simultaneity must be taken into account.

Given the similarities among the studies, it should not be surprising that (with one exception) the results are remarkably consistent. A 1 percent increase in prison population (or, in one case, prison commitments per year) would reduce the aggregate Index Crime rate by between 0.16 and 0.31 percent. Although elasticities for violent crime tend to be somewhat less than for property crime, the differences among studies are much greater than the differences among crime types within each study. None of the differences among the elasticities in columns 2–4 approach statistical significance.

The study summarized in column 1 (Devine, Sheley, and Smith 1988) produced results that are deviant by an order of magnitude, and one is tempted to reject them out of hand. It relies on fewer data points and uses fewer controls than the others. Most important, the instruments used to identify the crime and prison equations are not reported. Given the difficulties involved in finding any theoretically valid instruments, it seems most likely that the deviant results were due to bad instrument selection.

It surely would be imprudent to rely on Devine, Sheley, and Smith's (1988) results. Nevertheless, it is clear that some specification is capable of producing such deviant results. Given our uncertainty as to the best specification, it would be equally imprudent to ignore them entirely. The Devine, Sheley, and Smith study (1988) should be kept in mind as a cautionary tale, to remind us that we may be entirely wrong.

Despite their similarities, the three remaining studies reflect a variety of definitions of "best," and all contribute to our understanding.

The strength of the study conducted by Cappell and Sykes (1991) is its extensive search for control variables. Nevertheless, the use of national aggregate data contributes to the specification problem, and the simultaneous equations are not well instrumented. Note, for example,

TABLE 4
Summary of Recent Prison Effectiveness Analyses

	Devine (1988)	Cappell (1991)	Marvell (1994)	Levitt (1996)
Data:				
Cross section	Nationwide	Nationwide	49 states	50 states
Time series	1948–85	1933–85	1971–89	1971–93
n of cases	38	54	748	1,063
Dependent variable	3 Index Crimes	Index total	7 Index Crimes	7 Index Crimes
Independent variable	P pop (t)	P com $(t, t-1)$	P pop (t)	P pop $(t-1)$
Model specification:				
Differenced	Yes	Yes	Yes	Yes
Logs	Yes	No	Yes	Yes
Short run (SR)/long run	SR	SR	Both	SR
Specification search	Some	Yes	No	Some
Control variables:				
Lagged dependent variable	...	$C(t-1)$	$C(t-1)$	...
Criminal justice ops	...	P pop $(t-3)$	...	Police/capita
Demographics	Young men	Young	Age	Age; black

Socioeconomic	...	...	...	Income
Economic distress	Unem; welfare; inflation	Unem (t, t − 1)	...	Unem
Cultural	...	...	...	Metro
Opportunity	LF participation	...	...	...
Panel	...	State, time	State, time	State, time
Simultaneity:				
Method	2SLS	2SLS/3SLS	OLS	IV
C instruments	Not reported	P discharge rate; military active duty	None	Litigation status
P instruments	Not reported	P commit (t − 1); Unem (t − 1)	None	None
Results:				
Average elasticity	−2.2	−.26	−.16	−.31
Violent crimes	−1.25 to −4.44	...	+.05 to −.17	−.02 to −.74
Property Crimes	−1.11 to −2.87	...	−.11 to −.23	−.03 to −.50

Sources.—Devine, Sheley, and Smith (1988); Cappell and Sykes (1991); Marvell and Moody (1994); Levitt (1996).

Note.—P pop = prison population; P com = prison commitments; C = crime rate; unem = unemployment rate; LF participation = labor force participation; 2SLS = two-stage least squares; 3SLS = three-stage least squares; OLS = ordinary least squares; IV = instrumental variables; P discharge rate = prison discharge rate.

that Cappell and Sykes (1991) obtained virtually identical results from their two-stage least squares analysis as their ordinary least squares analysis.

Marvell and Moody (1994) were the first to rely on panel data and used an innovative specification that promised to separate short-run from long-run effects. Nevertheless, they did not report the results of their long-run model, included few traditional controls, and did not account for simultaneity at all. As they and others suggest, the effect of crime rates on prison populations is probably relatively small, so the bias is probably not great. But we can be fairly sure the result is biased, and it would be prudent to expect that the nationwide elasticity is somewhat higher than they report.

Levitt (1996) had the benefit of following Marvell and Moody (1994) and was able to improve on their estimates in several, small ways. He extends the data set a few years and a few states, conducts at least a limited specification search, and uses a theoretically appropriate instrument to identify the crime equation. Levitt's (1996) results demonstrate the importance of dealing with simultaneity. He obtains a much higher elasticity from his instrumental variables model than from his ordinary least squares model. The chosen instrument is not especially highly correlated with the prison population, however, and this is reflected in the wide confidence interval associated with all of Levitt's (1996) elasticities. In short, Levitt's best guess is somewhat higher than Cappell and Sykes's (1991) and Marvell and Moody's and is probably a bit closer to the truth; but by no means does it contradict these previous estimates.

Policy makers looking for a single, best estimate are in error. We will never know enough about the relationship between prisons and crime to reduce our knowledge to a single point. Still, the recent studies suggest that our best guess as to the nationwide elasticity should be in the neighborhood of -0.30. Any figure between -0.20 and -0.40 can be defended, and we should not be too surprised to find that the result is anywhere between -0.10 and -0.50. Because theory is too weak to allow us to distinguish among different crime types, and because the empirical estimates are not statistically significantly different from one another, the most prudent course would be to assume the elasticity for each crime type is about the same, on average.

What, then, can we say about the cost-effectiveness of further prison construction? As a back-of-the-envelope analysis suggests, not much. Recall from equation (16) that the marginal offense rate $\lambda_M = (\beta/r) \times$

(C/P), where β is our estimate of the elasticity, r is the rate at which crimes are reported to the police, C is the number of reported crimes, and P is the number of offenders in prison. In the mid-1990s, about 14 million crimes were reported to the police (C). Accounting for non-reporting on a crime type–by–crime type basis yields about 42 million total offenses committed. Approximately 1 million offenders were incarcerated in state and federal prisons (P). Thus, averaged over the entire nation in the mid-1990s, $\lambda_M \approx 42\ \beta$. Analysis of jury awards in civil suits suggest that the monetary and quality-of-life costs of the average crime sum to about $3,600 (Cohen 1988; Miller, Cohen, and Rossman 1993). Thus putting one additional offender in prison will provide social benefits $= -\ \$3,600\ \lambda_M = -\ \$151,200 \times \beta$. (The negative sign is needed since λ_M and β are both less than zero.) Further, the social costs of imprisonment are (very roughly) $40,000 per year (Spelman 1994; Donohue and Siegelman 1996). Thus the benefits of incarcerating our marginal offender will exceed the costs if $-151,200\ \beta > 40,000$, or if $\beta < -0.265$. If $\beta > -0.265$, the costs exceed the benefits and additional prison expansion is not cost-effective.

The ultimate futility of our analysis is at last revealed. We can be nearly certain the elasticity lies somewhere between -0.1 and -0.5, and we can be fairly sure it lies between -0.2 and -0.4, but we have no idea at all whether it is greater than or less than -0.265.

In a nutshell, then, what the studies of the past ten years tell us is that crime responds to prison capacity and that continued expansion of prisons nationwide will reduce the crime rate. What the studies do not tell us is whether the reduction is large enough to warrant continued expansion.

B. Toward Better Estimates

There are only so many ways to manipulate a single data set, and even the most far-reaching of these manipulations have limited effects on the final results. Practically speaking, then, our estimates will not improve substantially until we find more data to analyze. One reasonable approach may be to collect information for a smaller unit of analysis—a panel of counties, for example. Such a data set would bring several benefits—it would provide the first really new test of prison effects in two decades; it would increase the number of cases and the variance in crime and prison rates, improving the efficiency of all our estimates; and it would provide more accurate estimates of economic distress and opportunity effects, arguably the most important controls in any deterrence study. A smaller unit of aggregation (city or neighborhood) may be even better so long as we recognize that differences in prison rates among small units may not be policy relevant.

We should also take seriously the obvious alternative—multinational comparisons. Certainly it is easy to justify taking a hard look at Canada, Australia, or Great Britain. The language is the same, the legal systems almost identical, the data readily available. Such comparisons would be especially appropriate if we believed that incapacitation were the primary mechanism by which prisons control crime, since we can reasonably expect sentencing and thus resource allocation among convicted offenders to be roughly similar among these countries. To the extent that deterrence, and not incapacitation, is the driving force, then economics becomes more important than criminal justice system operations. Other industrialized countries may be just as persuasive in this respect as those governed by English common law. Finally, though former Communist and developing countries may be less persuasive still, they may provide better resolution of some side issues. For example, to determine the extent to which the production function flattens out as the prison population increases, it would be necessary to find another national time series with the same, tremendous temporal variation as the United States.

A second step would be to reduce the scope of the left-out variable problem. The best response to this problem is fairly clear: researchers should collect a panel data set, estimate fixed effects to control much of the problem, then add variables that capture theoretically appropriate constructs including availability of jobs, population in crime-prone ages, and so on. Some form of extreme bounds analysis would help to demonstrate the fragility of the final estimates. Although cointegration concepts may prove helpful in explaining the behavior of this new, improved data set, there is no a priori reason for believing they should apply to the crime-punishment problem.

The most persuasive estimate would use solid instruments to control for simultaneity. Unfortunately, good instruments have proven scarce. A prima facie case can be made for excluding from the crime equation criminal justice expenditures and prison vacancy rates (Fisher and Nagin 1978) and the presence of a court order to deal with an overcrowding problem (Levitt 1996). It remains to be seen whether these three variables are sufficient to estimate the effects of punishment on crime with the precision needed to support policy implications. It is also unclear which variables, if any, can be plausibly excluded from the punishment equation. Until better instruments surface, critics will be justified in viewing all estimates with suspicion.

Persuasive estimates would take seriously the functional form of the crime-punishment relationship. At a minimum, they would account for diminishing marginal returns and differences over time and among states in the use of prisons. This would provide state-by-state policy implications; it may even show when it is time for each state to stop building. Such an analysis could yield results very different from any developed thus far.

Finally, it is critical that we stop considering prison expansion decisions in a vacuum. Even if we could be certain that prison construction was cost-effective, it may still be true that some other program or policy was more cost-effective. Certainly many primary prevention programs at least appear to be worth their salt: family intervention, Head Start, self-paced education, and job apprenticeship programs are all examples. Many secondary prevention programs, including environmental design initiatives, community organizing, victim training, and even some offender rehabilitation programs, have shown tremendous promise when applied to the offenders, victims, and environments they fit best. It is easily conceivable that initiatives such as these will yield benefit-cost ratios much greater than the 1.50 to 2.00 that is the best we can expect from continued prison expansion.

Of a dullard, Samuel Johnson once proclaimed, "That fellow seems to me to possess but one idea, and that is a wrong one" (Boswell 1976, 1:393). The criminal justice community possesses many ideas. If we are to serve the public well, we must stop pretending otherwise.

APPENDIX

Variables Included in Crime Equations

Punishment
    Probability of arrest, conviction
    Probability of incarceration
    Expected time served in jail and prison
    Total prison population

Criminal Justice Operations
    Police presence
    Prison expenditures

Demographic Characteristics
  Racial composition
  Age structure
  Sex structure
  Household composition

Sociodemographic Characteristics
  Income
  Class structure
  Poverty and income disparity
  Property values and taxes

Economic Distress and Opportunity Costs
  Inflation
  Employment opportunities
  Welfare payments
  Government expenditures per capita

Cultural Characteristics
  Region
  Average temperature
  Total population
  Density and urbanism
  Social cohesion
  Informal social control
  Migration rate

Criminal Opportunities
  Consumer goods per household
  Labor force participation rate
  Active duty in military

REFERENCES

Avi-Itzhak, Benjamin, and Reuel Shinnar. 1973. "Quantitative Models in Crime Control." *Journal of Criminal Justice* 1:185–217.
Avio, Kenneth L., and C. Scott Clarke. 1978. "The Supply of Property Offences in Ontario: Evidence on the Deterrent Effect of Punishment." *Canadian Journal of Economics* 11:1–19.
Bean, Frank D., and Robert G. Cushing. 1971. "Criminal Homicide, Punishment, and Deterrence: Methodological and Substantive Reconsiderations." *Social Science Quarterly* 52:277–89.

Biles, David. 1979. "Crime and the Use of Prisons." *Federal Probation* 43:39–43.

Bishop, Robert V. 1979. "The Construction and Use of Causality Tests." *Agricultural Economics Research* 31:1–6.

Blumstein, Alfred, and Allen J. Beck. 1999. "Population Growth in U.S. Prisons, 1980–1996." In *Prisons*, edited by Michael Tonry and Joan Petersilia. Vol. 26 of *Crime and Justice: A Review of Research*, edited by Michael Tonry. Chicago: University of Chicago Press.

Blumstein, Alfred, and Jacqueline Cohen. 1973. "A Theory of the Stability of Punishment." *Journal of Criminal Law and Criminology* 64:198–207.

Blumstein, Alfred, Jacqueline Cohen, and Paul Hsieh. 1982. "The Duration of Adult Criminal Careers." Final report from the School of Urban and Public Affairs, Carnegie-Mellon University, Pittsburgh, to the National Institute of Justice, Washington, D.C.

Blumstein, Alfred, Jacqueline Cohen, and Daniel Nagin, eds. 1978. *Deterrence and Incapacitation: Estimating the Effects of Criminal Sanctions on Crime Rates.* Washington, D.C.: National Academy Press.

Blumstein, Alfred, Jacqueline Cohen, and Richard Rosenfeld. 1991. "Trend and Deviation in Crime Rates: A Comparison of UCR and NCS Data for Burglary and Robbery." *Criminology* 29:237–63.

Bogess, Scott, and John Bound. 1993. "Did Criminal Activity Increase during the 1980s? Comparisons across Data Sources." NBER Working Paper no. 4431. Cambridge, Mass.: National Bureau of Economic Research.

Boswell, James. 1976. *The Life of Samuel Johnson.* New York: Dutton.

Bowker, Lee H. 1981. "Crime and the Use of Prisons in the United States: A Time Series Analysis." *Crime and Delinquency* 27:206–12.

Bryk, Anthony S., and Stephen W. Raudenbush. 1992. *Hierarchical Linear Models: Applications and Data Analysis Methods.* Newbury Park, Calif.: Sage.

Bureau of Justice Statistics. 1982. *Prisoners, 1925–81.* Washington, D.C.: U.S. Department of Justice, Bureau of Justice Statistics.

Butterfield, Fox. 1997. "Property Crimes Steadily Decline, Led by Burglary." *New York Times* (October 12), p. 1.

Campbell, Donald T., and Julian C. Stanley. 1966. *Experimental and Quasi-Experimental Designs for Research.* Boston: Houghton-Mifflin.

Cantor, David, and Lawrence Cohen. 1980. "Comparing Measures of the Homicide Trends: Methodological and Substantive Differences in the Vital Statistics and Uniform Crime Report Time Series, 1933–75." *Social Science Review* 9:121–45.

Cantor, David, and Kenneth C. Land. 1985. "Unemployment and Crime Rates in the Post–World War II United States: A Theoretical and Empirical Analysis." *American Sociological Review* 50:317–32.

Cappell, Charles L., and Gresham Sykes. 1991. "Prison Commitments, Crime, and Unemployment: A Theoretical and Empirical Specification for the United States, 1933–1985." *Journal of Quantitative Criminology* 7:155–99.

Carr-Hill, Roy A., and Nick H. Stern. 1973. "An Econometric Model of the Supply and Control of Recorded Offences in England and Wales." *Journal of Public Economics* 2:289–318.

Chaiken, Jan M., and Marcia R. Chaiken. 1982. *Varieties of Criminal Behavior.* Santa Monica, Calif.: Rand.

Chambliss, William J., ed. 1969. *Crime and the Legal Process.* New York: McGraw-Hill.

Chiricos, Theodore. 1987. "Rates of Crime and Unemployment: An Analysis of Aggregate Research Evidence." *Social Problems* 34:187–212.

Chiricos, Theodore G., and Gordon P. Waldo. 1970. "Punishment and Crime: An Examination of Some Empirical Evidence." *Social Problems* 18: 200–217.

Christensen, Laurits, Dale W. Jorgenson, and Lawrence J. Lau. 1971. "Conjugate Duality and the Transcendental Logarithmic Production Function." *Econometrica* 39:255–56.

Cobb, Charles, and Paul H. Douglas. 1928. "A Theory of Production." *American Economic Review* 18(suppl.):139–65.

Cohen, Jacqueline. 1978. "The Incapacitative Effect of Imprisonment: A Critical Review of the Literature." In *Deterrence and Incapacitation: Estimating the Effects of Criminal Sanctions on Crime Rates*, edited by Alfred Blumstein, Jacqueline Cohen, and Daniel Nagin. Washington, D.C.: National Academy of Sciences.

Cohen, Jacqueline, and Jose A. Canela-Cacho. 1994. "Incarceration and Violent Crime: 1965–88." In *Understanding and Preventing Violence*, vol. 4, *Consequences and Control*, edited by Albert J. Reiss, Jr., and Jeffrey A. Roth. Washington, D.C.: National Academy Press.

Cohen, Lawrence E., and Marcus Felson. 1979. "Social Change and Crime Rate Trends: A Routine Activity Approach." *American Sociological Review* 44: 588–607.

Cohen, Mark. 1988. "Pain, Suffering, and Jury Awards: A Study of the Cost of Crime to Victims." *Law and Society Review* 22:537–55.

Conklin, John E. 1986. *Criminology.* New York: Macmillan.

Cook, Philip J. 1980. "Research in Criminal Deterrence: Laying the Groundwork for the Second Decade." In *Crime and Justice: An Annual Review of Research*, vol. 2, edited by Norval Morris and Michael Tonry. Chicago: University of Chicago Press.

Davidson, Russell, and James G. MacKinnon. 1993. *Estimation and Inference in Econometrics.* New York: Oxford University Press.

Devine, Joel A., Joseph F. Sheley, and M. Dwayne Smith. 1988. "Macroeconomic and Social-Control Policy Influences on Crime Rate Changes, 1948–85." *American Sociological Review* 53:407–20.

Diewert, W. Erwin. 1971. "An Application of the Shepard Duality Theorem: A Generalized Linear Production Function." *Journal of Political Economy* 79: 482–507.

DiIulio, John J., Jr. 1990. *Crime and Punishment in Wisconsin.* Wisconsin Policy Research Institute report, vol. 3, no. 7. Milwaukee: Wisconsin Policy Research Institute.

DiIulio, John J., Jr., and Anne Morrison Piehl. 1991. "Does Prison Pay?" *Brookings Review* (Fall), pp. 28–35.

Donohue, John, and Peter Siegelman. 1996. "Is the United States at the

Optimal Rate of Crime?" Chicago: American Bar Foundation. Mimeographed.

Dougherty, Christopher. 1992. *Introduction to Econometrics*. New York: Oxford University Press.

Ehrlich, Isaac. 1973. "Participation in Illegitimate Activities: A Theoretical and Empirical Investigation." *Journal of Political Economy* 81:521–65.

Engle, R. F., and C. W. J. Granger. 1987. "Co-Integration and Error Correction: Representation, Estimating, and Testing." *Econometrica* 55:251–76.

———, eds. 1991. *Long-Run Economic Relationships: Readings in Cointegration*. New York: Oxford University Press.

Federal Bureau of Investigation. Various years. *Crime in the United States: Uniform Crime Reports*. Washington, D.C.: U.S. Government Printing Office.

Fisher, Franklin M., and Daniel Nagin. 1978. "On the Feasibility of Identifying the Crime Function in a Simultaneous Model of Crime Rates and Sanction Levels." In *Deterrence and Incapacitation: Estimating the Effects of Criminal Sanctions on Crime Rates*, edited by Alfred Blumstein, Jacqueline Cohen, and Daniel Nagin. Washington, D.C.: National Academy of Sciences.

Forst, Brian. 1976. "Participation in Illegitimate Activities: Further Empirical Findings." *Policy Analysis* 2:477–92.

Gibbs, Jack P. 1968. "Crime, Punishment, and Deterrence." *Southwestern Social Science Quarterly* 48:515–30.

Gottfredson, Stephen D., and Don M. Gottfredson. 1986. "Accuracy of Prediction Models." In *Criminal Careers and 'Career Criminals'*, vol. 2, edited by Alfred Blumstein, Jacqueline Cohen, Jeffrey A. Roth, and Christy A. Visher. Washington, D.C.: National Academy Press.

Gove, Walter R., Michael Hughes, and Michael Geerken. 1985. "Are Uniform Crime Reports a Valid Indicator of the Index Crimes? An Affirmative Answer with Minor Qualifications." *Criminology* 23:451–501.

Granger, C. W. J. 1969. "Investigating Causal Relations by Econometric Models and Cross-Spectral Methods." *Econometrica* 37:424–38.

Granger, C. W. J., and P. Newbold. 1974. "Spurious Regressions in Econometrics." *Journal of Econometrics* 26:1045–66.

Granger, C. W. J., and Harold F. Uhlig. 1990. "Reasonable Extreme-Bounds Analysis." *Journal of Econometrics* 44:159–70.

Greenberg, David F. 1977. "The Dynamics of Oscillatory Punishment Processes." *Journal of Criminal Law and Criminology* 68:643–51.

Greenfeld, Lawrence W., Allen Beck, and Darrell Gilliard. 1996. "Prisons: Population Trends and Key Issues for Management." *Criminal Justice Review* 21:4–20.

Greenwood, Michael J., and Walter J. Wadycki. 1973. "Crime Rates and Public Expenditures for Police Protection: Their Interaction." *Review of Social Economy* 31:138–51.

Greenwood, Peter W. 1982. *Selective Incapacitation*. Santa Monica, Calif.: Rand.

Haitovsky, Yoel. 1986. "The Linear Hierarchical Model and Its Applications in Econometric Analysis." In *Bayesian Inference and Decision Techniques: Es-*

says in Honor of Bruno de Finetti, edited by Prem K. Goel and Arnold Zellner. Amsterdam: North-Holland.

Hindelang, Michael J., Christopher S. Dunn, L. Paul Sutton, and Alison L. Aumick. 1973. *Sourcebook of Criminal Justice Statistics, 1973.* Washington, D.C.: U.S. Department of Justice, Bureau of Justice Statistics.

Horney, Julie, and Ineke Marshall. 1991. "Measuring Lambda through Self-Reports." *Criminology* 29:401–25.

Judge, George G., William E. Griffiths, Carter R. Hill, Helmut Lütkepohl, and Tsoung-Chao Lee. 1985. *The Theory and Practice of Econometrics.* New York: Wiley.

Kahneman, Daniel, and Amos Tversky. 1979. "Prospect Theory: An Analysis of Decision under Risk." *Econometrica* 47:263–91.

Kennedy, Peter. 1992. *A Guide to Econometrics.* Cambridge, Mass.: MIT Press.

Klein, Lawrence R., Brian Forst, and Victor Filatov. 1978. "The Deterrent Effect of Capital Punishment: An Assessment of the Estimates." In *Deterrence and Incapacitation: Estimating the Effects of Criminal Sanctions on Crime Rates*, edited by Alfred Blumstein, Jacqueline Cohen, and Daniel Nagin. Washington, D.C.: National Academy of Sciences.

Kmenta, Jan. 1972. *Elements of Econometrics.* New York: Macmillan.

Kobrin, S., E. W. Hansen, S. G. Lubeck, and R. Yeaman. 1972. *The Deterrent Effectiveness of Criminal Justice Sanction Strategies: Summary Report.* Washington, D.C.: National Institute of Law Enforcement and Criminal Justice, U.S. Department of Justice.

Kocieniewski, David. 1997. "Mayor Gets Credit for Safer City, but Wider Trends Play a Role." *New York Times* (October 28), p. B4.

Langan, Patrick A. 1991. "America's Soaring Prison Population." *Science* 251: 1568–73.

Leamer, Edward E. 1983. "Let's Take the Con Out of Econometrics." *American Economic Review* 23:31–43.

Levitt, Steven D. 1996. "The Effect of Prison Population Size on Crime Rates: Evidence from Prison Overcrowding Litigation." *Quarterly Journal of Economics* 111:319–51.

Logan, Charles H. 1975. "Arrest Rates and Deterrence." *Social Science Quarterly* 56:376–89.

Maddala, G. S. 1988. *Introduction to Econometrics.* New York: Macmillan.

Maguire, Kathleen, and Ann L. Pastore, eds. 1995. *Sourcebook of Criminal Justice Statistics, 1994.* Washington, D.C.: U.S. Government Printing Office.

Mande, Mary J., and Kim English. 1988. *Individual Crime Rates of Colorado Prisoners: Final Report, 1988.* Denver: Colorado Division of Criminal Justice, Research Unit.

Marvell, Thomas B., and Carlisle E. Moody, Jr. 1994. "Prison Population Growth and Crime Reduction." *Journal of Quantitative Criminology* 10:109–40.

McAleer, Michael, Adrian R. Pagan, and Paul A. Volker. 1985. "What Will Take the Con out of Econometrics?" *American Economic Review* 75:293–307.

McCallum, B. T. 1972. "Relative Asymptotic Bias from Errors of Omission and Measurement." *Econometrica* 40:757–58.

McGuire, William J., and Richard G. Sheehan. 1983. "Relationships between Crime Rates and Incarceration Rates: Further Analysis." *Journal of Research in Crime and Delinquency* 20:73–85.

McPheters, Lee R., and William B. Stronge. 1974. "Law Enforcement Expenditures and Urban Crime." *National Tax Journal* 27:633–44.

Menard, Scott. 1992. "Residual Gains, Reliability, and the UCR-NCS Relationship: A Comment on Blumstein, Cohen, and Rosenfeld." *Criminology* 30:105–13.

Miller, Ted, Mark Cohen, and Shelli Rossman. 1993. "Victim Costs of Violent Crime and Resulting Injuries." *Health Affairs* 12:186–97.

Mohr, Lawrence D. 1988. *Impact Analysis for Program Evaluation.* Chicago: Dorsey.

Moore, Mark H., Susan R. Estrich, Daniel McGillis, and William Spelman. 1984. *Dangerous Offenders: The Elusive Target of Justice.* Cambridge, Mass.: Harvard University Press.

Nagel, William G. 1977. "On Behalf of a Moratorium on Prison Construction." *Crime and Delinquency* 23:154–72.

Nagin, Daniel. 1978. "General Deterrence: A Review of the Empirical Evidence." In *Deterrence and Incapacitation: Estimating the Effects of Criminal Sanctions on Crime Rates,* edited by Alfred Blumstein, Jacqueline Cohen, and Daniel Nagin. Washington, D.C.: National Academy of Sciences.

National Criminal Justice Information and Statistics Service. 1976. *Prisoners in State and Federal Institutions on December 31, 1974.* Washington, D.C.: U.S. Government Printing Office.

O'Brien, Robert. 1985. *Crime and Victimization Data.* Beverly Hills, Calif.: Sage.

Orsagh, Thomas. 1973. "Crime, Sanctions, and Scientific Explanation." *Journal of Criminal Law and Criminology* 64:354–61.

Park, Rolla Edward, and Bridger M. Mitchell. 1980. "Estimating the Autocorrelated Error Model with Trended Data." *Journal of Econometrics* 13:185–201.

Petersilia, Joan, Peter W. Greenwood, and Marvin Lavin. 1978. *Criminal Careers of Habitual Felons.* Santa Monica, Calif.: Rand.

Peterson, Mark A., Harriet B. Braiker, and Suzanne M. Polich. 1980. *Doing Crime: A Survey of California Prison Inmates.* Santa Monica, Calif.: Rand.

Piehl, Anne Morrison, and John J. DiIulio, Jr. 1995. "Does Prison Pay? Revisited." *Brookings Review* (Winter), pp. 21–25.

Reiss, Albert J., Jr. 1980. "Understanding Changes in Crime Rates." In *Indicators of Crime and Criminal Justice: Quantitative Studies,* edited by Stephen E. Fienberg and Albert J. Reiss, Jr. Washington, D.C.: U.S. Government Printing Office.

Reiss, Albert J., Jr., and J. A. Roth, eds. 1993. *Understanding and Preventing Violence.* Washington, D.C.: National Academy Press.

Sampson, Robert. 1986. "Crime in Cities: The Effects of Formal and Informal Social Control." In *Communities and Crime,* edited by Albert J. Reiss, Jr., and Michael Tonry. Vol. 8 of *Crime and Justice: A Review of Research*, edited by Michael Tonry and Norval Morris. Chicago: University of Chicago Press.

Sampson, Robert J., Stephen W. Raudenbush, and Felton Earls. 1997. "Neighborhoods and Violent Crime: A Multilevel Study of Collective Efficacy." *Science* 277:918–24.

Samuelson, Paul A. 1979. "Paul Douglas' Measurement of Production Functions and Marginal Productivities." *Journal of Political Economy* 87:923–39.

Schlesinger, Steven R. 1987. "Prison Crowding in the United States: The Data." *Criminal Justice Research Bulletin* 3:1–3.

Sellin, Thorsten. 1959. *The Death Penalty*. Philadelphia: American Law Institute.

Shinnar, Shlomo, and Reuel Shinnar. 1975. "The Effects of the Criminal Justice System on the Control of Crime: A Quantitative Approach." *Law and Society Review* 9:581–611.

Sjoquist, David Lawrence. 1973. "Property Crime and Economic Behavior: Some Empirical Results." *American Economic Review* 63:439–46.

Spelman, William. 1994. *Criminal Incapacitation*. New York: Plenum.

———. 1995. "The Severity of Intermediate Sanctions." *Journal of Research in Crime and Delinquency* 32:107–35.

Steffensmeier, Darrell, and Miles D. Harer. 1991. "Did Crime Rise or Fall during the Reagan Presidency? The Effects of an 'Aging' U.S. Population on the Nation's Crime Rate." *Journal of Research in Crime and Delinquency* 28:330–59.

Taub, Richard D., D. Garth Taylor, and Jan D. Dunham. 1984. *Paths of Neighborhood Change: Race and Crime in Urban America*. Chicago: University of Chicago Press.

Vandaele, Walter. 1973. "The Economics of Crime: An Econometric Investigation of Auto Theft in the United States." In *Proceedings: Papers Presented at the 114th Annual Meeting of the American Statistical Association*, edited by the American Statistical Association, Business and Economic Statistics Section. Washington, D.C.: American Statistical Association.

———. 1978. "Participation in Illegitimate Activities: Ehrlich Revisited." In *Deterrence and Incapacitation: Estimating the Effects of Criminal Sanctions on Crime Rates*, edited by Alfred Blumstein, Jacqueline Cohen, and Daniel Nagin. Washington, D.C.: National Academy of Sciences.

Wickens, Michael R. 1972. "A Note on the Use of Proxy Variables." *Econometrica* 40:759–61.

Yeager, Matthew G. 1979. "Unemployment and Imprisonment." *Journal of Criminal Law and Criminology* 70:586–88.

Zimring, Franklin E., and Gordon Hawkins. 1995. *Incapacitation: Penal Confinement and the Restraint of Crime*. New York: Oxford.